Prentice Hall Advanced Reference Series

Physical and Life Sciences

Ecology and Evolution of Livebearing Fishes (Poeciliidae)

Edited by

GARY K. MEFFE

University of Georgia's
Savannah River Ecology Laboratory
Aiken, South Carolina

and

FRANKLIN F. SNELSON, JR.

Department of Biological Sciences
University of Central Florida
Orlando, Florida

Prentice Hall, Englewood Cliffs, New Jersey 07632

Library of Congress Cataloging-in-Publication Data

Ecology and evolution of livebearing fishes (Poeciliidae)/edited by
 Gary K. Meffe and Franklin F. Snelson, Jr.
  p. cm.
  Bibliography: p.
  Includes index.
  ISBN 0-13-222720-7
   1. Poeciliidae—Ecology. 2. Poeciliidae—Evolution. I. Meffe,
 Gary K. II. Snelson, Franklin F.
 QL638.P73E26 1989
 587'.5—dc19   89–3734
                                                      CIP

Editorial/production supervision
  and interior design: **Nancy Havas Farrell**
Cover design: **Lundgren Graphics, Ltd.**
Manufacturing buyer: **Mary Ann Gloriande**

© 1989 by Prentice-Hall, Inc.
A Division of Simon & Schuster
Englewood Cliffs, New Jersey 07632

Printed in the United States of America

10 9 8 7 6 5 4 3 2 1

ISBN 0-13-222720-7

Prentice-Hall International (UK) Limited, *London*
Prentice-Hall of Australia Pty. Limited, *Sydney*
Prentice-Hall Canada Inc., *Toronto*
Prentice-Hall Hispanoamericana, S.A., *Mexico*
Prentice-Hall of India Private Limited, *New Delhi*
Prentice-Hall of Japan, Inc., *Tokyo*
Simon & Schuster Asia Pte. Ltd. *Singapore*
Editora Prentice-Hall do Brasil, Ltda., *Rio de Janeiro*

Dedicated to the late Donn E. Rosen
and
the many other pioneers of poeciliid biology.

Contents

Foreword

Poeciliids are a medium sized (ca. 200 species) family of fishes that are of great interest for a high diversity of biological fields of research ranging from sex determination and genetics of melanomas to vicariance biogeography. They have contributed significantly to our understanding of transmission genetics (they were a major genetic organism before *Drosophila*), sex linkage, sex determination, evolution of sex chromosomes, unisexuality, the ecological consequences of sexuality/asexuality, evolution of life-history parameters, evolution of cryptic coloration and of sexually-selected traits, and biogeography. They have also proven useful in ethology, parasitology (as hosts), physiology, pharmacology, and pollution monitoring, and have been widely employed (uselessly, see Chapters 17, 18) in mosquito control.

As the reader will see, poeciliids also have tremendous potential to significantly increase our understanding of the evolution of viviparity, internal fertilization, and superfetation (Chapters 3, 7), genetics and evolution of the physiological and molecular mechanisms of growth and maturity (Chapters 4, 9), evolution of courtship (Chapter 6), morphological change in evolution (Chapters 1, 3, 6, 9, 11) as well as the subjects mentioned in the preceding paragraph. There are two potentially productive lines of research only implied in this book, the study of radiations (adaptive or otherwise), and the evolution of sex and sex chromosomes.

The distribution of numbers of species per genus is quite uneven (Chapter 1): there are two very large genera (*Poecilia* with 43 species, *Gambusia* 45), two large (*Xiphophorus* 16, *Poeciliopsis* 19) and two medium (9 and 8) genera, and 14 genera with 4 or fewer species. The patterns of species per subgenus in the larger genera are similar. This is what one would expect if the family and larger genera reflect a recent or current period of adaptive radiation or rapid morphological divergence. This is supported by the extreme (and fascinating) heterogeneity in breeding systems, behavior, sex determination, and other aspects of biology. Since most of the taxonomic and biological diversity is in Mexico, Central America, and the West Indies, this may reflect the recency of invasion by the family there, as well as its complex biogeography. In any case this offers great potential for studying all aspects of diversification in morphology, physiology, genetics, and behavior.

The extreme variation in sex determination in the family is in some ways more reminiscent of plants than animals; we find everything from heterogametic males to heterogametic females, including three-factor as well as the usual two-factor sexual systems, and various degrees of monomorphism and polymorphism in sex determining factors within and among populations (Chapters 4, 9). Some of these are correlated or linked with color pattern and life history genes. Most color pattern genes are sex-linked and often sex-limited. The *P* gene system in *Xiphophorus* (Chapter 9) is especially interesting in that it is a Mendelian factor that affects life history parameters and is sex-linked, but it also is affected by autosomal modifiers, as is sex determination itself. Quantitative genetics of life history traits shows that males usually have a higher additive genetic variance (and hence higher heritability) than females, while females generally have a higher non-additive genetic variance (Chapter 10). All of these observations suggest an active process of the evolution of sex determination as well as sex chromosomes, which would be a splendid testing ground for the growing theoretical literature on the evolution of sex-determining mechanisms (Bull 1983). Both the differentiation in sex-determining mechanisms and the simple inheritance of life history related genes could even give rise to speciation if different populations randomly fix different life history and/or sex-determination alleles (Chapter 9).

Poeciliids are superb organisms for cellular, organismal, population and evolutionary biology because they are easy to study in the field and laboratory, their habitats are restricted enough so that field experiments can be done, and they are easy to breed for genetic studies. Yet one of the most frustrating things about working with poeciliids is the incredibly scattered literature; this book is exactly what is needed. It is a concise summary of most of what is known about all poeciliids, a summary of what sorts of things are unknown and not only worth further study but also practical to study, and a large literature list. The bibliography does not pretend to be complete, but it is the best possible entry into the literature on poeciliids. These chapters provide extensive data on many species, making the book valuable for comparative studies both within the family and with other families of fishes and other organisms. This book should be extremely interesting and useful to anyone interested in poeciliids, fish evolution, and many basic evolutionary problems that are independent of the particular organisms that illustrate them.

John A. Endler
Department of Biological Sciences, University of California,
Santa Barbara, CA 93106

Preface

In 1963, Donn E. Rosen and Reeve M. Bailey produced their now classic monograph on systematics and zoogeography of the family Poeciliidae. They listed some 138 species and presented species-specific information emphasizing morphology, distribution, and taxonomy, based on their own extensive research and on volumes of published work dating back to as early as 1801. In the 25 years since that milestone, hundreds of scientific papers dealing with poeciliids have been produced, yet there has never been a synthetic overview of the biology of the family. This book is intended to fill that void.

Poeciliids are one of the most popular families of fishes used in scientific research. They lend themselves to studies in a wide variety of disciplines, including reproduction and development, Mendelian and population genetics, teratology, behavioral ecology, and evolutionary studies. They are widely (and, in our view, incorrectly) used in biological pest control and themselves may be pests. They are easy to handle, and adapt well to laboratory conditions. Yet, until now, one could not go to a single reference source to learn about current trends in ecological or evolutionary research on the family.

Poeciliids exhibit two unusual adaptations that make them inherently interesting to biologists. First, in contrast to the vast majority of fishes, poeciliid reproduction typically involves live birth (viviparity) rather than egg-laying (oviparity). The physiological and anatomical adaptations associated with live birth permit experimental studies not feasible with most other fishes. Second, some poeciliids have evolved even more specialized reproductive modes involving various degrees of unisexuality. In the most extreme form, females use male sperm only to activate embryonic development, without including paternal genetic material in the zygote.

The result is true clonal inheritance, with offspring genetically identical to the mother and to one another. Both of these topics are at the core of our fascination with these small fishes and have received a great deal of attention from biologists.

Our objectives in developing a text on this intriguing group of organisms were: 1) to collect and organize into one volume the widely scattered literature on ecology and evolution of livebearers; we feel this will be particularly valuable to students entering the field and hope our efforts will quickly put much of the research on these fishes into perspective for new poeciliid biologists; 2) to critically review the evolutionary and ecological research that has been conducted on the group, with the hope that such a review will stimulate new and rigorous approaches in coming decades; 3) to synthesize the major research areas in order to create an overall perspective of poeciliid evolution and ecology; and 4) to clearly outline gaps in our knowledge of the family and illuminate the most fruitful areas for further research. Our primary audience is the student or professional ichthyologist or aquatic ecologist, but the book should also be of interest to evolutionary ecologists, geneticists, and serious aquarists as well.

There was never any question that we would develop a multi-authored volume rather than attempt to write the book ourselves. The expertise and broad perspectives represented in a collaborative effort are compelling arguments for such an approach and well worth the potential price of uneven style, content, and coverage; we hope that judicious editing has minimized these potential problems. We carefully developed a conceptual outline and recruited authors based on the expertise and research concentrations currently available throughout the scientific community. Most of our authors have conducted poeciliid research for much of their careers; other, younger researchers were included because their work in particular cut new ground. Several additional scientists were invited to participate but declined because of other commitments.

The book organization is a biased presentation of poeciliid biology based on areas of concentrated knowledge. We start with five chapters that present an overview of the basic biology of the family: systematics, ecology, reproduction, genetics, and unisexuality. Section Two includes six chapters that concentrate on behavioral, evolutionary, environmental, and genetic features of reproduction, the most heavily researched aspect of the family. Section Three presents evolutionary genetics and ecology in four chapters, addressing population-level questions in both bisexual and unisexual species. The three chapters in Section Four speak to the critical topics of conversation and introductions of poeciliids, contrasting critically endangered species with those causing ecological disaster through misguided transplantation. Finally, the single chapter in Section Five illustrates that the group is far from being thoroughly understood and points to numerous gaps in our knowledge that will provide research questions for decades to come.

There are several major topics within poeciliid biology that we saw as outside the scope of this book and which we chose not to cover. These include mosquito control by poeciliids, biomedical uses of the group, and rearing techniques and methods related to the aquarium trade and aquaculture. Each of these topics could readily fill their own volume, and we encourage their separate development.

We mention here our resolution of a few semantic issues that developed during production of the book. First, we use the term "livebearers" as the accepted common name for the family Poeciliidae, even though there are many other families of fishes that exhibit viviparity. Second, for convenience, we and most of our authors have adhered to the traditional concept of the family Poeciliidae as outlined by Rosen and Bailey (1963) as opposed to the more inclusive concept of Parenti (1981; Chapter 1) based on cladistic analysis. Parenti's family Poeciliidae includes certain groups of Old and New World egg-layers, and her subfamily Poeciliinae is equivalent to Rosen and Bailey's family Poeciliidae. Third, we feel that recent electrophoretic data, combined with karyological and as-yet unpublished morphological evidence, clearly supports the separation of *Gambusis affinis* and *G. holbrooki* at the species level (Wooten et al. 1988; Smith et al., Chapter 13). However, neither we nor most of our authors have distinguished literature references to these two species, since published information on both forms has typically appeared under the name *affinis*. Finally, we freely substitute common names for scientific names where there is a generally accepted substitute. A list of widely accepted common names appears in Appendix 2.

G. K. Meffe
F. F. Snelson, Jr.
Aiken, South Carolina
October 1988

Acknowledgments

Undoubtedly, this project would not have been possible without the cooperation and support of two important groups. First, the University of Georgia's Savannah River Ecology Laboratory has provided extraordinary support with facilities, funding, and, that most precious commodity, time. In particular, we thank Laboratory Director Michael H. Smith, Division Head J. Whitfield Gibbons, and Research Manager William D. McCort for a system that made logistics a nonproblem. Second, our families understood, encouraged, and indulged our preoccupation with this work for nearly three years. To Nancy Meffe and Earline Snelson we offer our affectionate gratitude and promise an honest effort to make up for all the time spent in the office.

The following colleagues provided critical reviews of chapters, and greatly improved many of them: Robert A. Angus, James W. Atz, Reeve M. Bailey, Michael A. Bell, Tim M. Berra, Donald G. Buth, Robert C. Cashner, James P. Collins, Justin D. Congdon, Walter R. Courtenay, Jr., Anthony A. Echelle, David C. Heins, Clark Hubbs, James E. Johnson, Klaus D. Kallman, Paul L. Leberg, Wendell L. Minckley, James M. Novak, Lynne R. Parenti, Alex E. Peden, Edwin P. Pister, David N. Reznick, Michael J. Ryan, C. Richard Robbins, Stephen C. Stearns, Brian K. Sullivan, Joseph Travis, Joel C. Trexler, Bruce J. Turner, Thomas Uzzell, Edward O. Wiley, James D. Williams, John P. Wourms, and Edmund J. Zimmerer. Important habitat photographs were provided by Richard Franz, David W. Greenfield and William B. Montgomery. Richard A. Seigel's experience and advice was invaluable in getting the project started. We thank Joe Travis for suggesting the book title "Deep Insights in Shallow Waters: Dead Reckoning on the Livebearers." We elected to reserve that epithet for the video version.

We thank Oak Ridge Associated Universities for travel support (Participation #S-3305) for F. F. Snelson, and the University of Central Florida for his release time and secretarial support. G. K. Meffe was supported by contract DE-AC09-76SROO-819 between the US Department of Energy and the University of Georgia.

Finally, we thank all participating authors for teaching us so much about poeciliid biology.

List of Contributors

ROBERT A. ANGUS

Department of Biology, University of Alabama at Birmingham, University Station, Birmingham, AL 35294

ANGELA H. ARTHINGTON

School of Australian Environmental Studies, Griffith University, Nathan, Queensland, 4111, Australia

JOSEPH S. BALSANO

Division of Science, University of Wisconsin-Parkside, Box 2000, Kenosha, WI 53141

GEORGE D. CONSTANTZ

Pine Cabin Run Ecology Laboratory, High View, WV 26808

WALTER R. COURTENAY, JR.

Department of Biological Sciences, Florida Atlantic University, Boca Raton, FL 33432

ALICE F. ECHELLE

Department of Zoology, Oklahoma State University, Stillwater, OK 74078

ANTHONY A. ECHELLE

Department of Zoology, Oklahoma State University, Stillwater, OK 74078

JAMES A. FARR

Department of Biological Science, Florida State University, Tallahassee, FL 32303

J. DAVID HERNANDEZ

Department of Zoology, University of Georgia, Athens, GA 30602

CLARK HUBBS

Department of Zoology, University of Texas, Austin, TX 78712

JAMES E. JOHNSON

US Fish & Wildlife Service, Endangered Species Office, P.O. Box 1306, Albuquerque, NM 87103

KLAUS D. KALLMAN

Genetics Laboratory of the Zoological Society, New York Aquarium, Brooklyn, NY 11224

LANCE N. LLOYD

River Murray Laboratory, Department of Zoology, University of Adelaide, GPO Box 498, South Australia, 5001, Australia

GARY K. MEFFE

University of Georgia's Savannah River Ecology Laboratory, Drawer E, Aiken, SC 29801

DONALD B. MILES

Department of Zoological and Biomedical Sciences, Ohio University, Athens, OH 45701

PAUL J. MONACO

Department of Biophysics, Quillen-Dishner College of Medicine, East Tennessee State University, Johnson City, TN 37601

LYNNE R. PARENTI

Department of Ichthyology, California Academy of Sciences, Golden Gate Park, San Francisco, CA 94118

ELLEN M. RASCH

Department of Biophysics, Quillen-Dishner College of Medicine, East Tennessee State University, Johnson City, TN 37601

MARY RAUCHENBERGER

Smithsonian Institution, National Museum of Natural History, Division of Fishes, Washington, DC 20560

DAVID N. REZNICK

Department of Biology, University of California, Riverside, CA 92521

RUSSELL A. SCHENCK

Department of Biology (Zoology), Rutgers College, Nelson Biological Laboratories, Piscataway, NJ 08854

R. JACK SCHULTZ

Biological Sciences Group, University of Connecticut, Storrs, CT 06268

KIM T. SCRIBNER

University of Georgia's Savannah River Ecology Laboratory, Drawer E, Aiken, SC 29801

MICHAEL H. SMITH

University of Georgia's Savannah River Ecology Laboratory, Drawer E, Aiken, SC 29801

FRANKLIN F. SNELSON, JR.

Department of Biological Sciences, University of Central Florida, Orlando, FL 32816

JOSEPH TRAVIS

Department of Biological Science, Florida State University, Tallahassee, FL 32306

JOEL C. TREXLER

Department of Biology, P.O. Box 12560, Eckerd College, St. Petersburg, FL 33733

ROBERT C. VRIJENHOEK

Center for Theoretical and Applied Genetics, Cook College—Rutgers University, P.O. Box 231, New Brunswick, NJ 08903

JEFFERY D. WETHERINGTON

Clinical Development Department, Organon Inc., 375 Mt. Pleasant Ave., West Orange, NJ 07052

DAVID M. WILDRICK

Department of Medical Oncology, M.D. Anderson Hospital and Tumor Institute, Houston, TX 77030

MICHAEL C. WOOTEN

Department of Zoology and Wildlife, Auburn University, Auburn, AL 36849

Section I.

Overview of the Family

Poeciliids encompass nearly 200 species of small fishes, most less than 5 cm long, from tropical and subtropical latitudes of the New World. With a geographic concentration in Central and South America and a popular base in the aquarist industry, they are recognizable to most biologists and even many laypersons. Their unique reproductive biology has engendered unusual interest among biologists throughout the world.

In this section we present an overview of the basic biology of the family, thereby setting the stage for more detailed and specialized chapters in the sections that follow. This overview should be most helpful to the novice seeking an introduction to the family. For the reader interested only in learning about the basic biology of poeciliids and the range of their application in biological research, this may be the only section they need to consult.

In Chapter 1, Parenti and Rauchenberger present the systematic framework for the chapters to follow. Their proposed classification, based on cladistic analysis, reduces the family Poeciliidae, as traditionally used, to the subfamily Poeciliinae, and expands the family boundaries to include certain egg-laying groups presumed to be related to the livebearers. As mentioned in the Preface, this revolutionary hypothesis does not alter the classical way we view livebearers, nor does it alter relationships within the group. The remaining chapters refer to poeciliids in the traditional sense. Parenti and Rauchenberger's classification only goes to the generic level. In Appendix 1, Rauschenberger presents a list of all currently recognized species, updating the listing of Rosen and Bailey (1963).

Meffe and Snelson (Chapter 2) present an ecological review of poeciliids and show that the group exploits numerous habitats, from barren desert arroyos to productive marshes and swamps. Species also run the gamut from narrow, restricted distributions in specialized habitats to broad occurrence in diverse environments. Many species have wide physiological tolerances that enable success under a variety of natural and artificial conditions. The ecology of most poeciliids, however, remains unknown.

Constantz reviews the anatomy and physiology of poeciliid reproduction in Chapter 3, illustrating the wide diversity of structural and physiological adaptations in both sexes. His detailed presentation of female reproductive cycles and fertilization are useful background to later chapters that deal with ecological or evolutionary aspects of reproduction. He concludes by predicting a testable correlation between the anatomy of male genitalia and the type of female reproductive cycle.

Classical genetic studies on the family are reviewed by Angus in Chapter 4. Perhaps no other area of poeciliid biology has been as thoroughly researched as Mendelian genetics, largely because of the abundance of phenotypic markers with a simple genetic basis in some species. Studies dating to the early part of this century deal with the genetics of sex determination, pigmentation, and other traits. More recent research has explored topics such as gene mapping and histocompatibility systems.

This section concludes with a review of unisexuality in poeciliids by Schultz (Chapter 5). One of the original workers in the field, he presents a personal and historical account of the discovery of unisexual fishes and subsequent efforts to probe details of their evolution and ecology. He goes on to discuss laboratory synthesis of unisexual "species," cytological aspects of unisexual reproduction, and clonal diversity in nature.

Chapter 1

Systematic Overview of the Poeciliines

LYNNE R. PARENTI
MARY RAUCHENBERGER

INTRODUCTION

In 1963, Donn E. Rosen and Reeve M. Bailey published a systematic monograph
on the family Poeciliidae (=subfamily Poeciliinae of Parenti 1981 and this chapter),
order Cyprinodontiformes. Their volume did not include a key to the genera or
species, nor did it present definitions of, or relationships among, subgroups using
solely what today we would call synapomorphic characters. Nonetheless, demand
for the exhaustive systematic information contained in that *Bulletin of the American
Museum of Natural History* became so high, it was reprinted in 1973. Rosen and
Bailey's (1963) monograph still stands today, over 25 years later, as the most
comprehensive compilation of systematic and biogeographic data on poeciliid fishes,
one of the more well-studied groups of vertebrates.

Since 1963, numerous descriptions of new species, generic synopses, and
reviews of tribal groups (see Classification of the Poeciliines, following) have
been published. Yet, little attention has been paid to relationships among tribes.
For example, mosquitofishes of the tribe Gambusiini have been the subject of
continuous, focused study, yet their relationship to other poeciliine subgroups
remains obscure (Miller 1975; Rauchenberger 1988).

The written classification of poeciliines by Rosen and Bailey (1963; modified
here in Table 1–1) implied phylogenetic relationships among the tribes. However,
Rosen (1979), in his detailed, well-corroborated, phylogenetic hypotheses and
historical biogeographic analyses of the genera *Xiphophorus* and *Heterandria*,
criticized his earlier, pre-Hennigian (Hennig 1966) definitions of taxa as ambiguous.

Our aim is to summarize the systematic work on poeciliine fishes since

1963. We have not tried to compile a bibliography of poeciliine systematics, but, rather, summarize the major advances and point out promising areas of future research. Application of the cladistic methodology to systematic studies of poeciliines has led to explicit, testable hypotheses of the relationships of the group to other cyprinodontiform fishes (Parenti 1981), and also prompted developments in the theory and methodology of historical biogeography (Rosen 1976, 1978, 1979). The characteristics of poeciliines that have made them the focus of numerous systematic studies—unique reproductive morphology, small size, and ease of collection and maintenance in aquaria—ensure that interest in poeciliine systematics will remain high, and the popularity of the monograph of Rosen and Bailey (1963) will endure.

RELATIONSHIPS OF THE POECILIINES

Rosen and Bailey (1963) discussed relationships of their Poeciliidae (the Poeciliinae of this paper) to other cyprinodontiform and atherinomorph (sensu Rosen and Parenti 1981) fishes, but came to no firm conclusions regarding their sister-group relationships. They considered morphological modifications of poeciliines for embryo-retention to be most like those of the New World tropical cuatro ojos, *Anableps*, and gonopodial modifications most like those of the diminutive Indian ricefish, *Horaichthys*, two atherinomorphs that exhibit internal fertilization via a prominent gonopodium. On the other hand, Rosen and Bailey (1963) observed that in characters such as skull osteology, poeciliines resemble none of the atherinomorphs with modifications for internal fertilization, and are more like some oviparous killifishes. Miller (1979) also proposed a close relationship between poeciliines and *Anableps* because both have the first three anal-fin rays unbranched and retain embryos in ovarian follicles until their birth. A close relationship between *Anableps* and poeciliines is also implied, in a key, by Rosen (1973).

Parenti (1981) reviewed relationships among all cyprinodontiform fishes, traditionally classified in five families, the oviparous Cyprinodontidae, and the "viviparous" Poeciliidae, Goodeidae, Anablepidae, and Jenynsiidae. Cyprinodontiforms are readily defined as monophyletic by numerous derived characters (Parenti 1981; Rosen and Parenti 1981): (1) a symmetrical caudal fin; (2) first pleural rib on second, rather than third, vertebra; (3) an alveolar arm of the premaxilla; (4) a prolonged developmental period; and, (5) a lowset pectoral girdle with a scale-like postcleithrum.

A prolonged developmental period characterizes both oviparous and viviparous species. Parenti (1981) concluded that the division of cyprinodontiforms into oviparous and viviparous groups was artificial (see also Foster 1967), and that poeciliines were not most closely related to any other viviparous cyprinodontiform family, but were, instead, members of a monophyletic group that included the fluviphylacines (the monotypic Amazonian *Fluviphylax*) and the aplocheilichthyines (the tropical African and Madagascan lampeyes or procatopines and *Pantanodon*). These three groups—poeciliines, fluviphylacines, and aplocheilichthyines—share at least five derived characters (Parenti 1981): (1) pectoral fins set high on the side of the body owing to radials placed in a dorsal position on the scapulocoracoid; (2) ventral hypohyal forms a bony cap over the anterior facet of the anterior ceratohyal; (3) pleural ribs present on the hemal arches; (4) thoracic or subthoracic pelvic fins which, possibly through differential growth, migrate or are inferred to migrate anteriorly during ontogeny; and (5) supraorbital pores modified such that neuromasts are found embedded in fleshy grooves.

The proposal that poeciliines are closely related to oviparous, rather than viviparous, cyprinodontiforms is open to further test. Most important about such a hypothesis is that in future phylogenetic studies of poeciliines, the lampeyes, *Pantanodon*, and *Fluviphylax* may provide more logical outgroup comparisons than cyprinodontiforms such as the viviparous goodeids or anablepids. The anablepids (sensu Parenti 1981) are a useful outgroup for determining polarity of gonopodial structures, although any atherinomorph with an anal fin modified for sperm transfer could theoretically provide data for outgroup comparison.

DEFINITION OF THE POECILIINES

The lengthy definition of the poeciliines by Rosen and Bailey (1963), although thorough, does not distinguish between primitive and derived states, and contains many characters found generally within cyprinodontiform fishes. Nonetheless, this compilation remains useful because it includes variation of characters within poeciliines, such as parietals present or absent and posttemporal simple or forked.

Poeciliines are readily defined as monophyletic in a cladistic sense (Hennig 1966), in particular by uniquely derived characters of the gonopodium and gonopodial suspensorium and other reproductive anatomical modifications for viviparity (see Rosen and Bailey 1963; Chambers 1987; and Constantz, Chapter 3).

All poeciliines exhibit internal fertilization (Wourms 1981) but one species (*Tomeurus gracilis*) is oviparous (females lay fertilized eggs) or facultatively viviparous (Breder and Rosen 1966). Degree of dependency on yolk stores has led to a division between ovoviviparous and viviparous poeciliines (Thibault and Schultz 1978). However, if viviparity is defined simply as bearing live young (Wourms 1981), then all poeciliines may be considered viviparous. Thus, viviparity distinguishes poeciliines from their hypothesized closest relatives.

Additional derived characters of poeciliines are (Parenti 1981): (1) expansion of the fourth epibranchial to become the main support of the dorsal portion of the gill arches; (2) exoccipital condyles absent; and (3) neural arches of the first vertebra open, not meeting to form a neural spine. An additional character given by Parenti, modified (swollen or elongate) pelvic fin rays in males, is found only in *Poecilia* and *Xiphophorus*, and, therefore, probably is not derived for the entire subfamily.

CLASSIFICATION OF THE POECILIINES

We list each currently recognized genus (including subgenera), give an estimate of the number of species in each, briefly describe the distribution, and provide citations to important systematic works since 1963. Detailed generic synonymies may be found in Rosen and Bailey (1963). Additional systematic and ecological data are summarized in Meyer et al. (1985a). Currently recognized species in each genus are listed in Appendix 1.

Suggestions have been made to recognize as distinct genera or subgenera, taxa that Rosen and Bailey (1963) considered in synonymy (e.g., Miller 1974; Rivas 1978; Radda and Meyer 1981). Some of these we incorporate into the classification (Table 1–1 and following). However, this compilation is in no way meant to substitute for a needed comprehensive systematic revision and historical biogeographic analysis of poeciliine fishes. The classification is not phylogenetic; if converted into a cladogram, this classification would not represent well-corroborated relationships among subgroups.

Only one new genus (*Scolichthys* Rosen 1967, in his new tribe Scolichthyini) and one new subgenus (*Odontolimia* Rivas 1980, as a subgenus of *Limia*) have been named since 1963. In addition to listing the Scolichthyini, we propose a change in the higher level classification, recognizing *Xenodexia* in its own tribe, the Xenodexiini Hubbs, rather than its own subfamily, the Xenodexiinae Hubbs. In this way, two supertribes, Tomeurini, containing only the oviparous or facultatively viviparous *Tomeurus*, and Poeciliini, containing all other (ovoviviparous or viviparous) poeciliines, reflect the dichotomy in reproductive mode. The distinctness of *Xenodexia* is recognized by its classification in a separate tribe.

Parenti (1981) classified the poeciliines and their hypothesized close relatives, *Fluviphylax* and the aplocheilichthyines, in the family Poeciliidae. We believe that the only logical approach to classification is to place members of a monophyletic group in the same higher taxon, and, further, that the rank of such a taxon is arbitrary. Thus, our subfamily Poeciliinae is equivalent to the family Poeciliidae of Rosen and Bailey (1963), Greenwood et al. (1966), and the other chapters in this volume. This change in classification is not meant to confuse, but rather to alert other biologists, primarily nonsystematists, that the former classification, in which *Fluviphylax* and the aplocheilichthyines were in the family Cyprinodontidae, does not summarize phylogenetic relationships.

Subfamily Poeciliinae (=Family Poeciliidae of Rosen and Bailey 1963)
I. Supertribe Tomeurini
    (1) Genus *Tomeurus* Eigenmann 1909 (type species *Tomeurus gracilis* Eigenmann). A single species occurring in northeastern South America (Rosen and Bailey 1963:38, map 2).
II. Supertribe Poeciliini
    A. Tribe Poeciliini
        (2) Genus *Alfaro* Meek 1912 (type species *Alfaro acutiventralis* Meek). Two

TABLE 1-1. Classification of the Poeciliine Fishes

Subfamily Poeciliinae (= Family Poeciliidae of Rosen and Bailey 1963)
  Supertribe Tomeurini
    Genus *Tomeurus* Eigenmann 1909
  Supertribe Poeciliini
    Tribe Poeciliini
      Genus *Alfaro* Meek 1912
      Genus *Poecilia* Bloch and Schneider 1801
        Subgenus *Poecilia* Bloch and Schneider 1801
        Subgenus *Lebistes* de Filippi 1862
        Subgenus *Pamphorichthys* Regan 1913
        Sugenus *Limia* Poey 1855
        Subgenus *Odontolimia* Rivas 1980
      Genus *Priapella* Regan 1913
      Genus *Xiphophorus* Heckel 1848
    Tribe Cnesterodontini
      Genus *Phallotorynus* Henn 1916
      Genus *Phalloceros* Eigenmann 1907
      Genus *Phalloptychus* Eigenmann 1907
      Genus *Cnesterodon* Garman 1895
    Tribe Scolichthyini
      Genus *Scolichthys* Rosen 1967
    Tribe Gambusiini
      Genus *Brachyrhaphis* Regan 1913
      Genus *Gambusia* Poey 1855
        Subgenus *Gambusia* Poey 1855
        Subgenus *Heterophallina* Hubbs 1926
        Subgenus *Arthrophallus* Hubbs 1926
      Genus *Belonesox* Kner 1860
    Tribe Girardinini
      Genus *Girardinus* Poey 1855
      Genus *Quintana* Hubbs 1934
      Genus *Carlhubbsia* Whitley 1951
    Tribe Heterandriini
      Genus *Priapichthys* Regan 1913
      Genus *Neoheterandria* Henn 1916
      Genus *Heterandria* Agassiz 1853
        Subgenus *Heterandria* Agassiz 1853
        Subgenus *Pseudoxiphophorus* Bleeker 1859
      Genus *Poeciliopsis* Regan 1913
        Subgenus *Poeciliopsis* Regan 1913
        Subgenus *Aulophallus* Hubbs 1926
      Genus *Phallichthys* Hubbs 1924
    Tribe Xenodexiini
      Genus *Xenodexia* Hubbs 1950

species, in Atlantic coastal drainages from southern Guatemala to western Panama (Rosen and Bailey 1963).

(3) Genus *Poecilia* Bloch and Schneider 1801 (type species *Poecilia vivipara* Bloch and Schneider). Approximately 43 species widely distributed throughout southeastern United States, Mexico, and Central America, the West Indies, and

north, north-central and southern South America south to the Río de la Plata, northern Argentina (Rosen and Bailey 1963; Rivas and Fink 1970; Schultz and Miller 1971; Menzel and Darnell 1973a; Miller 1975, 1983; Rivas 1978, 1980; Chambers 1987).

Subgenus *Poecilia* Bloch and Schneider 1801.

Subgenus *Lebistes* de Filippi 1862 (type species *Lebistes poeciloides* de Filippi).

Subgenus *Pamphorichthys* Regan 1913 (type species *Heterandria minor* Garman).

Subgenus *Limia* Poey 1855 (type species *Limia cubensis* Poey). Treated as a genus by Rivas (1978, 1980) and Chambers (1987).

Subgenus *Odontolimia* Rivas 1980 (type species *Limia grossidens* Rivas).

(4) Genus *Priapella* Regan 1913 (type species *Gambusia bonita* Meek). Three species from southeastern Mexico (Rosen and Bailey 1963).

(5) Genus *Xiphophorus* Heckel 1848 (type species *Xiphophorus helleri* Heckel). Approximately 16 species from Atlantic drainages from the Río Grande basin south to Honduras (Rosen and Bailey 1963; Rosen and Kallman 1969; Rosen 1979; Meyer and Schartl 1980; Radda 1980; Meyer and Wischnath 1981).

B. Tribe Cnesterodontini

(6) Genus *Phallotorynus* Henn 1916 (type species *Phallotorynus fasciolatus* Henn). Three species from Argentina, Paraguay and southeastern Brazil (Rosen and Bailey 1963; Oliveros 1983).

(7) Genus *Phalloceros* Eigenmann 1907 (type species *Girardinus caudimaculatus* Hensel). A single species from southeastern South America (Rosen and Bailey 1963).

(8) Genus *Phalloptychus* Eigenmann 1907 (type species *Girardinus januarius* Hensel). Two species from southeastern South America (Rosen and Bailey 1963).

(9) Genus *Cnesterodon* Garman 1895 (type species *Poecilia decemmaculata* Jenyns). Two species from southeastern South America (Rosen and Bailey 1963).

C. Tribe Scolichthyini

(10) Genus *Scolichthys* Rosen 1967 (type species *Scolichthys greenwayi* Rosen). Two species from the Río Chajmayic and tributaries to the Río Chixoy, Guatemala (Rosen 1967).

D. Tribe Gambusiini

(11) Genus *Brachyrhaphis* Regan 1913 (type species *Gambusia rhabdophora* Regan). Eight species from Pacific drainages in southern Mexico, and Atlantic and Pacific drainages of Costa Rica and central and western Panama (Rosen and Bailey 1963; Bussing 1967).

(12) Genus *Gambusia* Poey 1855 (type species *Gambusia punctata* Poey). Approximately 45 species widely distributed in inland, Gulf, and Atlantic coastal drainages from northeastern United States southward through Mexico and Central America to Colombia, and the Greater Antilles east to Hispaniola and the Bahamas (Rosen and Bailey 1963; Minckley 1963; Hubbs and Peden 1969; Rivas 1969, 1971; Miller and Minckley 1970; Campos and Hubbs 1971; Fink 1971a, 1971b;

Peden 1973a; Miller 1975; Greenfield et al. 1982, 1984; Greenfield 1983, 1985; and Wildrick et al. 1985). Rauchenberger (1988) recognizes three subgenera:
Subgenus *Gambusia* Poey 1855.
Subgenus *Heterophallina* Hubbs 1926 (type species *Gambusia regani* Hubbs).
Subgenus *Arthrophallus* Hubbs 1926 (type species *Heterandria patruelis* Baird and Girard, a subjective synonym of *Heterandria affinis* Baird and Girard).
   (13) Genus *Belonesox* Kner 1860 (type species *Belonesox belizanus* Kner). A single species reported to have two subspecies from southern Mexico to northeastern Costa Rica on the Atlantic slope (Rosen and Bailey 1963).
   E. Tribe Girardinini
   (14) Genus *Girardinus* Poey 1855 (type species *Girardinus metallicus* Poey). Eight species from throughout Cuba (Rosen and Bailey 1963; Barus et al. 1981b; Barus and Libosvarsky 1986).
   (15) Genus *Quintana* Hubbs 1934 (type species *Quintana atrizona* Hubbs). One species from western Cuba (Rosen and Bailey 1963).
   (16) Genus *Carlhubbsia* Whitley 1951 (type species *Allophallus kidderi* Hubbs). Two species distributed throughout the lowlands of the base of the Yucatan Peninsula, Atlantic drainage of Mexico, Belize, and Guatemala (Rosen and Bailey 1963).
   F. Tribe Heterandriini
   (17) Genus *Priapichthys* Regan 1913 (type species *Gambusia annectens* Regan). Eight species distributed in both Atlantic and Pacific drainages of Costa Rica, Pacific slope of Panama, Colombia and south to Guayas, Ecuador (Rosen and Bailey 1963; Radda 1987).
   (18) Genus *Neoheterandria* Henn 1916 (type species *Neoheterandria elegans* Henn). Four species from the Atlantic slope of Nicaragua and Costa Rica, Atlantic and Pacific slopes of central Panama, Pacific slope of eastern Panama, and Atlantic drainages of Colombia (Rosen and Bailey 1963; Radda and Meyer 1981).
   (19) Genus *Heterandria* Agassiz 1853 (type species *Heterandria formosa* Agassiz). Nine species in Atlantic and Gulf coastal drainages from southeastern United States to Nicaragua and a single Pacific drainage in Guatemala (Rosen and Bailey 1963; Miller 1974; Rosen 1979).
   Subgenus *Heterandria* Agassiz 1853.
   Subgenus *Pseudoxiphophorus* Bleeker 1859 (type species *Xiphophorus bimaculatus* Heckel).
   (20) Genus *Poeciliopsis* Regan 1913 (type species *Poecilia presidionis* Jordan and Culver in Jordan). Approximately 19 species in Pacific drainages from southwestern United States to Colombia, and Atlantic drainages of southeastern Mexico, Guatemala, and Honduras (Rosen and Bailey 1963; Bussing 1967; Miller 1975; Meyer and Vogel 1981; Meyer et al. 1985a, 1985b).
   Subgenus *Poeciliopsis* Regan 1913.
   Subgenus *Aulophallus* Hubbs 1926 (type species *Poecilia elongata* Günther).

(21) Genus *Phallichthys* Hubbs 1924 (type species *Poeciliopsis isthmensis* Regan). Four species in Atlantic drainages from Belize and northern Guatemala to Costa Rica and western Panama (Rosen and Bailey 1963; Bussing 1963, 1979). Introduced on Pacific slope in Costa Rica (Bussing 1979).

G. Tribe Xenodexiini

(22) Genus *Xenodexia* Hubbs 1950 (type species *Xenodexia ctenolepis* Hubbs). One species in Río Salba, Río Chixoy, and Río Xalbal, Guatemala (Rosen and Bailey 1963; Rosen 1967).

HISTORICAL BIOGEOGRAPHY OF THE POECILIINES

The natural distribution of poeciliines is fresh, brackish, and salt waters of the New World temperate and tropical zones (see Rosen 1973). Poeciliines range from northeastern United States, south to the Río de la Plata drainage, northern Argentina (Rosen and Bailey 1963). The greatest taxonomic diversity of poeciliines is found within Mexico, Central America, and the West Indies (see Classification of the Poeciliines, preceding).

The hypothesized close relationship of poeciliines to the Amazonian *Fluviphylax* and the tropical African and Madagascan lampeyes and *Pantanodon* implies a widespread, transatlantic ancestral distribution that was most likely disrupted by the opening of the Atlantic Ocean (Parenti 1981). Of perhaps greater interest is the usefulness of taxonomic relationships among poeciliine taxa in unraveling the intricate historical biogeographic relationships among plants and animals in Central America and the West Indies. In the genus *Gambusia*, three species groups have both Antillean and mainland members. The mainland member in each is the sister taxon to the rest of the group (Rauchenberger 1988); that is, within each species group, Antillean members form a monophyletic assemblage. Relationships within the Antillean clades give clues to relationships of the Greater Antilles themselves. Both the subgenus *Limia* of the genus *Poecilia*, with just Antillean species on Cuba, Hispaniola, Cayman, and Jamaica, and the tribe Girardinini, with the genera *Quintana* and *Girardinus* confined to Cuba and the genus *Carlhubbsia* in Central America, have the potential to add to our knowledge of Caribbean biogeography once their phylogenetic relationships have been analyzed.

Historical biogeographic analyses of the Mexican and Central American genera *Xiphophorus* and *Heterandria* by Rosen (1979) have figured prominently in development of the theory and methodology of vicariance and cladistic biogeography (Humphries and Parenti 1986). Similar studies are possible for other regions in which the distribution of several poeciliine genera overlap, such as the Río Panuco basin of eastern Mexico with endemic species of *Xiphophorus*, *Gambusia*, and *Poecilia*.

Between the Isthmus of Tehuantepec and the Panama Canal, poeciliines are diverse and abundant; taxa in up to six genera are sympatric in some localities.

Cladistic relationships among these poeciliine taxa are expected to reveal informative biogeographic patterns.

The distribution of poeciliines in South America is comparatively poorly known. Members of the subgenus *Pamphorichthys* in the genus *Poecilia*, and the genera *Cnesterodon, Phalloceros, Phalloptychus*, and *Phallotorynus* are distributed well to the east of the Colombian and Ecuadorian Andes; details of their distribution are not well understood but they are primarily coastal and in the lower courses of large rivers. Species of the genus *Priapichthys* are found in lower Central America and northwestern Colombia and Ecuador. Analyses of biogeographic patterns based on detailed phylogenetic studies of South American freshwater fishes are few in number, but increasing (Weitzman and Weitzman 1982; Parenti 1984). Phylogenetic relationships among groups of poeciliines are expected to add greatly to our understanding of the historical biogeographic patterns within South America.

SUMMARY AND FUTURE RESEARCH

The poeciliine fishes comprise over 190 species (see Appendix 1), currently classified in 22 genera and 12 subgenera. Poeciliines are a well-defined, monophyletic group of oviparous, ovoviviparous, and viviparous killifishes, distinguished from all other cyprinodontiforms by derived osteological and myological characters of the gonopodium and gonopodial suspensorium, gill arches, the skull, and neural arches.

Poeciliines are distributed in fresh, brackish, and salt waters from northeastern United States, south to the Rio de la Plata drainage in northern Argentina, with the greatest taxonomic diversification in Central America, Mexico, and the West Indies. They are hypothesized to be most closely related to the Amazonian *Fluviphylax* and the tropical African and Madagascan aplocheilichthyines. The ancestral, transatlantic distribution of these three groups is inferred to have been disrupted by the opening of the Atlantic Ocean.

Despite the intense study of certain species groups, a well-corroborated phylogenetic analysis of the subfamily as a whole is lacking. Detailed developmental (e.g., Weisel 1967), and comparative chromosomal (e.g., Campos and Hubbs 1971; Wildrick et al. 1985), osteological (e.g., Parenti 1981; Chambers 1987; Rauchenberger 1988), and reproductive anatomical surveys (e.g., Thibault and Schultz 1978; Constantz, Chapter 3), are needed. The gonopodium and gonopodial suspensorium will continue to be a source of data for phylogenetic analysis; however, other systems should be investigated as well. A study of the comparative osteology and myology of the gill arches is the type of review we would expect to provide data on which additional hypotheses of relationship could be formulated. Continued historical biogeographic analyses of poeciliines in Central America and throughout the Caribbean require such well-corroborated, phylogenetic systematic studies.

ACKNOWLEDGMENTS

Preparation of this chapter was supported in part by National Science Foundation grant BSR 87–00351 to L. R. Parenti. We benefited from access to the Genera of Fishes database being compiled by William N. Eschmeyer at the California Academy of Sciences. Two reviewers provided comments that greatly improved the presentation of ideas.

Chapter 2

An Ecological Overview of Poeciliid Fishes

GARY K. MEFFE
FRANKLIN F. SNELSON, JR.

INTRODUCTION

Our understanding of the basic ecology and natural history of poeciliid fishes is surprisingly poor. Part of this ignorance stems from the historical use of poeciliids as laboratory models for genetic, physiological, or medical studies, wherein investigators were not primarily interested in poeciliids in natural settings. More recently, use of these fish in evolutionary and life history research, in the context of natural environments, has begun to close gaps in ecological knowledge of the family. However, a great deal remains to be learned.

Only a small proportion of the nearly 200 poeciliid species (Rauchenberger, Appendix 1) has been studied in an ecological context. The mosquitofishes (*Gambusia affinis* and *G. holbrooki*) are the best known members of the family, due to widespread stocking as mosquito control agents (Courtenay and Meffe, Chapter 17) and resultant studies of diet, habitat, and environmental tolerances. Ecological data exist for other species of *Gambusia*, as well as for some species of *Poecilia*, *Xiphophorus*, *Poeciliopsis*, *Heterandria*, and *Belonesox*. The vast majority of the family, however, is virtually unknown with regard to basic natural history. Because other facets of poeciliid biology are so well understood, an excellent opportunity exists for a synthesis of ecology with genetics, physiology, life history evolution, and development. With a comparative approach across species and genera, insights gained from this family could make significant contributions to a more comprehensive understanding of basic ecological and evolutionary processes.

We herein review ecological aspects of the Poeciliidae. This is undoubtedly a biased perception of the family, because most information is based on a few genera and species. Lack of ecological understanding of the group is illustrated by the combination of several important topics into this single chapter. There are, for example, too few data to justify separate treatments of trophic, physiological, and community ecology. Thus, pertinent information on poeciliids is spotty and uneven across taxa and disciplines, and only a general treatment is given here.

HABITAT USE

Macro-scale Habitat Use

Poeciliids live in a broad array of habitats, occupying temperate to tropical zones, desert to mesic regions, rivers, lakes, springs, fresh and brackish marshes, seacoasts, and saline mangrove swamps (Figures 2–1, 2–2, and 2–3). Within deserts alone, poeciliids span a wide habitat range, including rocky and fluctuating arroyos, constant and chemically harsh springs, small to large rivers, productive ciénegas, and a variety of man-made environments. The diversity of habitats used by the family and individual species indicates that poeciliids are a tolerant and highly adaptive group.

There are two major factors resulting in broad habitat use by poeciliids. First, they are excellent colonizers, and a single gravid female can found a new population. Consequently, poeciliids often occupy "fringe" habitats—geologically unstable and ecologically harsh environments supporting few other fishes. This is particularly evident in arid regions, where poeciliids are one of the few, or the only, species in thermal springs or stream headwaters. In mesic coastal plains they may also be the only fish to colonize isolated springs or shallow freshwater to brackish ponds and bays.

The second factor in their ecological success is high thermal and salinity tolerances (discussed in detail following), resulting in the ability to survive short-term dispersal under harsh conditions and to maintain populations in suboptimal habitats. For example, *G. affinis* can survive in salinities from fresh to full-strength sea water, and lives from semitropical Texas and Mexico to temperate Illinois and Indiana, where it over-winters below ice (Krumholz 1944). *Poeciliopsis monacha* lives in barren, rocky mountain streams in Mexico characterized by low productivity and warm, poorly oxygenated waters in summer (Vrijenhoek 1979b).

Of course, not all poeciliids are so catholic in their habitat use, and many are confined to a few or single localities. This is exemplified by several *Gambusia* species in the Chihuahuan desert of Texas and Mexico that are springhead endemics (Hubbs and Springer 1957; Minckley 1984).

Micro-scale Habitat Use

Poeciliids typically inhabit small, shallow bodies of water (springs, marshes, and ponds), or shallow, marginal areas of larger bodies (rivers and lakes). Even in marine systems, they occupy margins such as mangrove roots or shallow bays

Figure 2–1. Springs and Spring-fed Poeciliid Habitats. a) Gemini Springs, Volusia Co., FL. *Gambusia holbrooki* and *Poecilia latipinna*. (FFS); b) Spring-fed laguna in Cuatro Ciénegas basin, Coahuila, Mexico. *Gambusia longispinis* and *G. marshi*. (GKM); c) Spring-fed tributary of Río Bacu, Dominican Republic. *Poecilia (Limia) zonata*. (R. Franz); d) Monkey Spring, Santa Cruz Co., AZ. *Poeciliopsis o. occidentalis.* (GKM); e) Spring on shore of Lago Enriquillo, Dominican Republic. *Gambusia hispaniolae.* (R. Franz).

(Krumholz 1963). These areas are typically slow-water habitats, often partially or heavily vegetated, or with other cover. A notable exception is *Gambusia puncticulata monticola*, described by Rivas (1971) as being ". . . collected in rapids over gravel bottom and around boulders, at an elevation of 1,250 feet, 198 km upstream from the sea." Rivas (1982) indicated that *Poecilia hispaniolana* also occurs in fast current.

Several factors may result in the use of shallow, marginal microhabitats. First, predation by larger fish may restrict poeciliids to shallow refugia. Haskins et al. (1961) found that smaller guppies (*Poecilia reticulata*) were more likely to stay in shallow stream margins, whereas larger individuals stayed in more central areas; they related this to predation. Seghers (1974a, 1974b) and Liley and Seghers (1975) demonstrated that guppies select shallow water in the presence of predaceous fishes, and deeper water when aerial predators are abundant. In a laboratory study, Noltie and Johansen (1986) documented that guppies prefer shallow water, but this varied depending on past experience, and sex and age of other fish present. Goodyear (1973) discovered that mosquitofish use the sun to orient toward shore and away from predators in deeper water.

The substrate over which a fish orients may also dictate shoreline orientation. Two species of *Gambusia* in Belize appear to have different substrate/cover preferences. *Gambusia sexradiata* prefers heavy cover of emergent vegetation and a substrate of rich organic material; the sympatric *G. puncticulata yucatana* is found primarily over a clay-mud substrate with no vegetation (Greenfield et al. 1983a). Female reproductive condition may also affect substrate use and shoreline orientation. Maglio and Rosen (1969) indicated that female *G. affinis* near parturition moved into shallow, sandy regions of their pond. Endler (1980, 1982) demonstrated that fish predation impacts the intensity and type of color patterns in guppies and *Phalloceros caudimaculatus*. Background coloration, and hence shoreline orientation, affected color pattern in both species through predation on less cryptic individuals.

A third factor in the use of shallow water may be oxygen availability. Gulping air at the surface is apparently an adaptive response to hypoxic conditions in guppies (Kramer and Mehegan 1981; Weber and Kramer 1983). Juveniles with surface access under experimental low oxygen conditions grew faster and had lower mortalities than those without such access. Mosquitofish initiate surface respiration at a partial pressure of O_2 between 20 and 65 torr (12.5% to 40.8% saturation at 25°C and 1 atm pressure) and it is obligatory below 20 torr at 20°C (Cech et al. 1985).

Finally, temperature is important in the selection of shallow microhabitats. During cold weather, poeciliids crowd along shorelines on sunny days; insolation warms these areas more quickly than deep water. In a New York pond, Maglio and Rosen (1969) found that mosquitofish sought the maximum available temperature up to 33°C, resulting in diurnal movements relative to the shoreline. Conversely, in artificially high temperatures, shallows may offer a refuge from deeper, lethal water, through evaporative cooling of a smaller water volume. In a South Carolina

Figure 2–2. Lotic Poeciliid Habitats. a) Río Macal, Mountain Pine Ridge, Belize. *Heterandria bimaculata*, *Poecilia* n. sp., and *Xiphophorus helleri*. (D. W. Greenfield); b) Riv. de Cavaillon, Tiburon Peninsula, Haiti. *Poecilia (Limia) tridens*. (R. Franz); c) Río Choix, Sinaloa, Mexico. *Poeciliopsis latidens* and *P. lucida*. (GKM); d) Arroyo de Jaguari, Sonora, Mexico. *Poeciliopsis monacha*, *P. lucida*, *P. monacha-lucida*, and *P. 2 monacha-lucida*. (GKM); e) Tributary of Río Yuna, Dominican Republic. *Poecilia dominicensis*. (R. Franz); f) Río Frio, Mountain Pine Ridge, Belize. *Heterandria bimaculata*, *Poecilia* n. sp., *Xiphophorus helleri*. Note extensive deforestation adjacent to the stream. (D. W. Greenfield).

nuclear reactor cooling reservoir, we repeatedly observe an abundance of mosquito-fish in shallows, adjacent to deeper, lethal areas.

Other microhabitat preferences have been observed in poeciliids. In southwestern springs, native Sonoran topminnows (*Poeciliopsis occidentalis*) routinely use springheads with high dissolved CO_2 and low pH. Introduced mosquitofish are usually rare or absent from immediate outflows, but swarm in large numbers downstream where conditions moderate (Minckley et al. 1977; Meffe 1983). The same relationship occurs with mosquitofish and *Gambusia heterochir* (Hubbs 1971) and *G. geiseri* (Hubbs and Springer 1957) in Texas.

Microhabitats of sympatric *Gambusia* tend to be distinct, and there are few places where two species co-occur. However, in one canal in Mexico four gambusiins markedly partitioned the habitat, with *G. aurata* close inshore, *G. affinis* in quiet water near vegetation, *G. vittata* adjacent to the main current, and *G. regani* in the current channel (Miller and Minckley 1970).

In a complex of unisexual-bisexual fishes of the genus *Poecilia*, bisexual females were more prevalent in headwaters, whereas unisexual frequencies increased downstream, although both types preferred shaded areas and a gravel substrate (Balsano et al. 1981). Lanza (1983) reported that five members of a unisexual-bisexual species complex of *Poeciliopsis* changed microhabitat use depending on the presence of other species in an artificial stream. Even more subtle microhabitat partitioning occurs in other *Poeciliopsis*. Two distinct clones of *Poeciliopsis* 2 *monacha-lucida* specialize on different feeding microhabitats (Vrijenhoek 1978; Wetherington et al. Chapter 14) and therefore coexist in an unproductive desert arroyo. Other ecological specializations on limited spatial and trophic resources allow coexistence of a number of combinations of these fish "species" and their sexual ancestors (Vrijenhoek 1984a; Schenck and Vrijenhoek 1986; Wetherington et al. Chapter 14).

TROPHIC ECOLOGY

Poeciliids as Consumers

As in habitat use, poeciliids exploit diverse foods. Trophic types range from piscivorous pike killifish, *Belonesox belizanus* (Miley 1978; Turner and Snelson 1984), to omnivorous mosquitofishes (Hess and Tarzwell 1942; Greenfield et al. 1983a, 1983b) to the herbivorous sailfin molly, *Poecilia latipinna* (Harrington and Harrington 1961, 1982; Wetzel 1971). Most poeciliids are omnivores, however, and eat mixtures of terrestrial and aquatic invertebrates, detritus, algae, and vascular plants (Sokolov and Chvaliova 1936; Hess and Tarzwell 1942; Hunt 1953; Harrington and Harrington 1961; Reimer 1970; Schoenherr 1974; Dussault and Kramer 1981).

Poeciliid diets are commonly reflected by morphology: tooth and gut structure are often indicators of diet preference (Al-Hussaini 1949; Barrington 1957; Lagler

Figure 2–3. Lentic and Disturbed Poeciliid Habitats. a) Lake Harney, Seminole Co., FL. *Gambusia holbrooki*, *Heterandria formosa*, and *Poecilia latipinna*. (FFS); b) Long Key, Monroe Co., FL (saline). *Gambusia rhizophorae*. (FFS); c) Mangrove cay near ST. John's College, Belize (saline). *Belonesox belizanus*, *Gambusia yucatana*, and *Poecilia orri*. (D. W. Greenfield); d) Mosquito control impoundment, Cape Canaveral, Brevard Co., FL. *Gambusia holbrooki* and *Poecilia latipinna*. Habitat fluctuates between extreme low (pictured) and high water. (FFS); e) Pond C, Savannah River Plant, Aiken Co., SC. *Gambusia holbrooki*. A thermally impacted nuclear cooling reservoir. (GKM); f) San Vincente Hot Springs, near Santa Elena, Ecuador. *Priapichthys festae*. This is the only known locality for the species. Note the impact of development (a hot bath facility) on the spring habitat; fish exist mostly in the outflow canal (W. B. Montgomery).

et al. 1977). Strong, conical teeth and short guts are typical of predators such as *G. affinis* or *B. belizanus* (Meffe et al. 1983; Turner and Snelson 1984), whereas omnivores/detritivores such as *Poeciliopsis* spp. have longer guts and weaker, spatulate teeth (Vrijenhoek and Schultz 1974; Schoenherr 1981). Cephalic sensory canals also correlate with diet, dentition, and feeding behavior (Rosen and Mendelson 1960). Open canals with exposed neuromasts occur in surface feeders with strong teeth; bottom feeders with movable teeth tend to have covered sensory canals. Open canals presumably aid in detection of moving prey near the surface.

Species-specific food choice may range from narrow and selective to broad and opportunistic. The diet of pike killifish is virtually restricted to fish. In southern Florida 99% of its diet was fish (Miley 1978). In its native Central American habitat adults ate only fish (primarily other poeciliids), but juveniles included a small percentage of insects in their diet (Anderson 1980). In the laboratory, pike killifish readily ate mosquitofish, least killifish (*Heterandria formosa*), and sailfin mollies (Meffe, Snelson, pers. observ.). It accepted only fish, even when offered tadpoles, insects, or small frogs (Turner and Snelson 1984). The few other poeciliids studied, however, exhibit broad food choice, often taking the most abundant item. For example, both *G. affinis* and *P. latipinna* in a Florida salt marsh drastically changed diet when invertebrate prey declined after impoundment (Harrington and Harrington 1982). Mosquitofish switched from a predominantly insect diet to one largely of algae and plant detritus. Sailfin mollies shifted from mostly vascular plants to almost exclusively algae and detritus. Dietary flexibility is also demonstrated by large differences in trophic selection among different populations within a species (e.g., compare Sokolov and Chvaliova 1936; Hess and Tarzwell 1942; Walters and Legner 1980), or within the same population over time (Hunt 1953; Reimer 1970).

Poeciliids have been used in several experimental studies of predation and foraging dynamics. Gerking and Plantz (1980) found that *P. occidentalis* preferentially selected larger prey than was available at random. Wurtsbaugh et al. (1980) found the same pattern in mosquitofish, but Bence and Murdoch (1986) did not; they reported that mosquitofish actively chose small prey, which were more profitable because of lower energetic costs of capture. Predatory efficiencies of mosquitofish on mosquito larvae declined in smaller water volumes (Reddy and Pandian 1973). Grubb (1972) found that eggs from anurans breeding in temporary ponds were preferentially selected by mosquitofish over those from species breeding in permanent systems.

A number of researchers have focused on mosquitofish impacts on prey communities. In a California rice field experiment, Farley and Younce (1977a) documented declines in notonectid, odonate, hydrophilid, chironomid, corixid, and ephemerellid insect populations in the presence of mosquitofish. The desert pupfish (*Cyprinodon macularius*) and mosquitofish both reduced invertebrates in experimental earthen ponds, but pupfish were less damaging to other fishes (Walters and Legner 1980). In experimental pools, mosquitofish reduced crustaceans, insects, and rotifers, which in turn had positive effects on phytoplankton populations and changed physico-chemical parameters (Hurlbert et al. 1972). Hurlbert and Mulla (1981) documented elimination of *Daphnia pulex* and *Ceriodaphnia* sp. and large changes in other zooplankter populations. The mosquitofish obviously has major impacts on community and ecosystem structure through its predatory habit (Courtenay and Meffe, Chapter 17).

We add one final point relative to food studies in poeciliids. In laboratory experimentation, investigators often evaluate food quantity, but neglect food quality as a variable. Two examples are instructive. Reddy and Shakuntala (1979) found that adult female *G. affinis* and *P. reticulata* grew poorly on a diet of mosquito larvae but grew quickly on tubifex worms; the difference in the guppy was almost tenfold. Both species appear to "prefer" worms to larvae and consumed three to four times more worms, by weight, per day. The conversion efficiency was also higher for worms than for larvae, dramatically so for the guppy. Wurtsbaugh and Cech (1983) compared growth rates of juvenile mosquitofish fed to satiation with brine shrimp nauplii and tubifex worms. After 25 days, mean weight of nauplii-fed fish was 22% greater than that of worm-fed fish. Food quality can thus be a relevant factor in experimental studies of poeciliid feeding.

Cannibalism in Poeciliids

A particularly intriguing and poorly understood aspect of the diet of some poeciliids is cannibalism. Several species cannibalize in nature, including *G. affinis* (Seale 1917; Krumholz 1948; Walters and Legner 1980; Harrington and Harrington 1982), *B. belizanus* (Belshe 1961; Miley 1978; Turner and Snelson 1984), and *P. monacha* (Thibault 1974a, 1974b). Several others cannibalize in the laboratory, including *P. reticulata* (Shoemaker 1944), *P. occidentalis* (Meffe 1984a) and *Poecilia latipinna*, *H. formosa*, and *Xiphophorus variatus* (Meffe, pers. observ.). Laboratory observation cannot be extrapolated to natural situations but serves to demonstrate the capability of a species, including some that are typically herbivorous, to cannibalize.

Although little is known about the evolution and maintenance of cannibalism in poeciliids (or other organisms), we do know that it has a genetic basis in at least one species (Thibault 1974a, 1974b) and may limit population size (Moore and McKay 1971). It may also benefit the cannibal as a particularly good nutritive source, allowing enhanced growth and reproduction (Meffe and Crump 1987).

Poeciliids as Prey

Many poeciliids are routinely eaten by predatory fishes, snakes, birds, and invertebrates. *Gambusia affinis*, *H. formosa*, and *P. latipinna* were the top three prey items for four species of water snakes (genus *Nerodia*) in Louisiana bayous, constituting 66% of their diets (Mushinsky and Hebrard 1977). These same poeciliids were also documented as *Nerodia* prey by Kofron (1978). A variety of wading birds feed on poeciliids (especially mosquitofish) in shallows, and the snowy egret

(*Leucophoyx thula*) uses a bill-vibrating behavior to attract mosquitofish (Kushlan 1973). Mosquitofish may even be susceptible as prey for spiders (Suhr and Davis 1974; Williams 1979).

Several predaceous fishes also feed on poeciliids. In particular, mosquitofish are common foods for black basses (*Micropterus* spp.), and gars (*Lepisosteus* spp.) are known to eat mosquitofish, least killifish, and sailfin mollies (Hunt 1953).

The impact of predation on the evolution of morphological and life history characters of poeciliids has been well documented. Endler (1980) studied color patterns in male guppies exposed to different predation intensities. Color spot size in the field and laboratory closely matched background gravel size in the presence of predators, principally the cichlid *Crenicichla alta*. Color spots were larger (due to sexual selection) in the absence of predation. Reznick and Endler (1982) then documented that female life histories also are affected by predation intensity. Guppies exposed to dangerous predators had higher reproductive invest-ments, reproduced sooner, and had larger broods than fish from low predation areas; Reznick (1982b) demonstrated a genetic basis for these differences. Endler (1982) conducted a parallel study of fish predation on *Phalloceros caudimaculatus*. Results were concordant with those in the guppy studies: predation favored less conspicuous fishes, with smaller and duller spots.

Krumholz (1963) studied two populations of *Gambusia manni* in the Bahamas; one was free of fish predation and the other was exposed to a variety of predaceous fishes. Those in the latter situation matured earlier and had larger clutches. Schoen-herr (1977) simulated predation on a small, isolated population of *P. occidentalis* by removing approximately 600 individuals monthly for 18 months. During the second year of study, average brood size in this environmentally constant springhead had increased significantly, presumably the result of his "predation." Poeciliids may thus respond to high predation rates with increased reproductive effort.

Another quantitative study of predation on poeciliids involved mosquitofish as prey for herons in France (Britton and Moser 1982). Heron predation was heavy in marshes but light in ditches. Large female mosquitofish were preferred as food; consequently, sex ratios in marshes were biased toward males, whereas ratios in ditches were close to unity. Evidently, population parameters of poeciliids, as well as morphological and life history characteristics, may be affected by preda-tion.

PHYSIOLOGICAL ECOLOGY

Salinity Tolerance

Based on zoogeographical patterns, Rosen and Bailey (1963) argued that the family Poeciliidae is broadly euryhaline. Of course, many species are confined to inland and montane areas and exclusively occupy freshwater habitats. We are not aware that salinity tolerance of any inland species has been evaluated in detail.

Rosen and Bailey present limited evidence that two such species (*Girardinus uninotatus* and *Quintana atrizona*) may retain the ability to survive elevated salinities, although there also is anecdotal evidence that some freshwater forms (e.g., *Gambusia nobilis*) may have low tolerance (Hubbs and Springer 1957).

Other poeciliids occupy coastal or lowland situations, with some occurring across a broad salinity range. The "record holder" in this regard is *Poecilia sphenops*, a species characteristic of brackish water, but occurring naturally from 0 to 135 ppt (Kristensen 1969; Feltkamp and Kristensen 1970). Other species with a broad salinity range include *P. reticulata* (Haskins et al. 1961), *P. latipinna* (Hubbs 1964; Trexler 1986), and *B. belizanus* (Belshe 1961; Anderson 1980; Turner and Snelson 1984).

Gambusia spp. exhibit an especially broad salinity distribution. Some species occur only in isolated springs (e.g., *G. gaigei* and *G. alvarezi*, Hubbs and Springer 1957) or other exclusively freshwater habitats (e.g., *G. longispinis*, Minckley 1969a; *G. marshi*, Meffe 1985a). Others are confined to high salinities (e.g., 30 ppt for *G. xanthosoma*, Greenfield 1983; 28 to 40 ppt for *G. manni*, Krumholz 1963), or occur across a broad salinity range (e.g., *G. yucatana*, Carter 1981; *G. nicaraguensis*, Greenfield et al. 1982).

Most experimental work on salinity tolerance has involved species of *Gambusia*. Carter (1981) examined preference and tolerance of four populations of three *Gambusia* species that occur across a range of salinities in Belize. All four had the ability to adjust to gradual salinity change regardless of origin or acclimation, but there were differences in toleration of abrupt salinity changes.

Freshwater *G. affinis* have high survival rates when transferred directly from fresh water to up to 50% sea water. Mortality increases abruptly above 50% and virtually no fish survive direct transfer from fresh to full sea water for more than 24 hours (Salibian 1977; Al-Daham and Bhatti 1977). There are other indications (e.g., life history and growth rate differences) that *G. affinis*, although broadly euryhaline, is best adapted to fresh water (Stearns and Sage 1980; Zimmerer 1983).

Salinity tolerance or preference has been examined in only a few other species, including *B. belizanus* (Belshe 1961), *P. reticulata* (Gibson and Hirst 1955; Zimmerer 1983), *P. sphenops* (Feltkamp and Kristensen 1970), and *P. latipinna* (Gunter 1950; Large 1985; Trexler 1986). In general, all four tolerate a wide salinity range but select salinities near those typically occupied in nature.

Temperature Tolerance

Poeciliids occur across a broad thermal range. Unfortunately, the thermal biology of only a few species has been examined in detail, the best studied being the mosquitofish. This species has attracted special interest because it occurs across a broad temperature range, from northern, ice-covered lakes and ponds (Krumholz 1948; Otto 1973) to constant-temperature hot springs (Otto 1973; Winkler 1975) and thermally elevated lakes in which mosquitofish may periodically occur in water 42 to 44°C (Ferens and Murphy 1974; Bennett and Goodyear 1978).

In general, thermal tolerance and preference are determined by a combination of acclimation temperature and genetic adaptation (Hart 1952; Otto 1973). The thermal tolerance domain shows little difference between cold, warm, and "normal" adapted populations (Brett 1956; Otto 1973). Otto (1973) reported a lower lethal temperature of 0.5°C for cold acclimated-cold adapted fish and an upper incipient lethal temperature of 38°C for warm acclimated-warm adapted fish. Thermal tolerance boundaries differed by about 2.5°C between cold and warm-adapted fish, with shifts being in the direction predicted by presumed genetic adaptation.

Results of other authors vary depending on methodology used, source of fish, and acclimation procedures. Smoak (1959) found that mosquitofish from thermally elevated environments did not withstand higher temperature any better than did fish from ambient habitats, if the latter were briefly acclimated to higher temperatures. In contrast, Hagen (1964) reported that survival was correlated with habitat temperature. Arkansas mosquitofish in a thermal gradient preferred 28 to 29°C, but fish selecting different temperatures varied little in their upper lethal temperature (Bacon et al. 1968). *Gambusia affinis* from Arizona preferred 31°C in both the field and laboratory, regardless of whether the source population had experienced acclimation above, below, or at that temperature (Winkler 1979).

Acclimation history is important to the critical thermal maximum (CTM) of mosquitofish (Otto 1974). Short-term heat tolerance was greatly increased in fishes subjected to an acclimation cycle that included brief exposure near or above the upper lethal temperature. Since mosquitofish appear to select a cycling acclimation regime in the field (Winkler 1975), most laboratory thermal studies in this species are probably oversimplified.

Ferens and Murphy (1974) and Bennett and Goodyear (1978) found few meaningful differences in sex ratio, size structure, size at maturity, or size-fecundity relationships between mosquitofish in thermally elevated and ambient environments. Only two consistent differences were found: (1) females from thermal habitats reproduced year-round whereas ambient fish reproduced only in summer, and (2) the percentage of reproductively active females increased with increasing water temperature.

The thermal biology of other poeciliids has been examined, but none in the detail of *G. affinis*. *Gambusia gaigei*, whose native habitat is warm springs, was better able to survive elevated temperatures than was *Gambusia geiseri*, whose native habitat is cool springs (Hagen 1964). Gelbach et al. (1978) reported that the CTM for *G. nobilis* was 38 to 39°C and that the preferred temperature was 21 to 25°C in the morning and 26 to 30°C in the afternoon. The guppy has an incipient upper lethal temperature of about 32°C (Gibson 1954), but males prefer a significantly cooler temperature (24.5°C) than do females (28.2°C) or juveniles (28.2°C) (Johansen and Cross 1980). However, sexual differences in guppy thermal tolerance are not clear-cut. Tsukuda (1960) reported no significant difference in heat or cold tolerance of males and females, and Gibson (1954) found that the sexes were similar at most lethal test temperatures. In the preferred temperature range of 20 to 30°C, the rate and intensity of male guppy courtship behaviors exhibit little variation with temperature after acclimation (Laudien and Schlieker 1981).

Temperature can affect other aspects of poeciliid biology. Aho et al. (1976) reported higher densities of a parasitic brain trematode in mosquitofish from thermally elevated habitats, but lower densities of a body cavity trematode. Temperature influences penetrance and expressivity of a mutation for melanism in *P. latipinna*, with greater expression in cooler water (Angus 1983). In unisexual-bisexual species complexes of the genus *Poeciliopsis*, the hybrid unisexuals are heterotic for temperature tolerance with respect to the bisexual parental forms (Bulger and Schultz 1979, 1982).

Photoperiod Responses

Photoperiod and temperature are often the two most important environmental parameters influencing fish reproductive cycles. Several studies have evaluated their relative effects on reproduction in poeciliids, producing mixed results. Colson (1969) found that *H. formosa* ceased reproduction during winter in ambient environments and constant-temperature (21°C) springs in northern Florida, and hypothesized that photoperiod played the dominant role in initiation and termination of reproduction. This was confirmed by laboratory experiments; there was no reproduction at a 8L:16D photoperiod, regardless of temperature.

Temperature is more important than photoperiod in regulating reproductive periodicity and intensity in the guppy (Bowden 1970). In fact, guppy reproduction is quite insensitive to photoperiods ranging from continuous light to continuous darkness. Bowden (1970) noted that interbrood interval (the rate of embryonic development) in the guppy is not significantly influenced by photoperiod treatments. This is not surprising because guppies naturally live at 10°N latitude, where there is little seasonal variation in photoperiod. However, this contrasts with results for *Poeciliopsis gracilis* and *Poecilia sphenops* (below).

Near Tampa Bay, Florida, reproduction in the sailfin molly ended abruptly in mid-September and commenced in January (Grier 1973). Laboratory studies indicated that ovary development ceased at a critical daily photoperiod between 12 and 14 hours, regardless of temperature. This coincides with the observation that field reproduction ceases at or near the autumnal equinox, even though temperatures satisfactory for reproduction (20 to 22°C) extended beyond that time. Photoperiod effects on initiation of reproduction are less clear. Grier (1973) found that field reproduction began when day lengths were less than the critical 12 to 14-hour photoperiod, and concluded that a complex combination of temperature and photoperiod influenced initiation of reproduction.

Field reproduction of the sailfin molly near Cape Canaveral, Florida also terminates sharply in mid-September to early October, even in constant-temperature (21 to 23°C) springs (Large 1985). In contrast to Grier's results, spring reproduction in east-central Florida normally does not begin until March or April (Wetherington 1982, Large 1985, Snelson, unpublished). However, there are unexplained exceptions. In one ambient study area, reproduction continued at a significant level throughout the winter (Smith 1988), and significant reproduction began in February in a constant-temperature spring (Large 1985).

The role of photoperiod in controlling reproduction in mosquitofishes is also unclear. Medlen (1951) concluded that temperature was of primary significance in controlling *G. affinis* reproduction, with photoperiod playing only a minor role. However, we feel that his work was seriously flawed and thus invalid (see Snelson and Meffe, Chapter 19). Several authors have noted that *G. affinis* ceases winter field reproduction in constant temperature springs warm enough to support reproduction (Brown and Fox 1966; Davis 1978), implicating a strong photoperiod response. Milton and Arthington (1983a) felt that photoperiod was more important than temperature in mosquitofish reproduction in Australia. Yet, Bennett and Goodyear (1978) and Meffe (unpubl. data) found that mosquitofish in a South Carolina thermal pond reproduce year-round. *Gambusia geiseri*, a species presumed to have evolved in constant-temperature (20 to 23°C) springs, reproduces throughout winter in Texas (Davis 1978). Likewise, *P. occidentalis* reproduces throughout the year in a constant-temperature (28°C) spring but ceases reproduction in winter in variable temperature habitats (Schoenherr 1977).

In equatorial environments, where annual photoperiod and temperatures are more constant, significant reproduction may occur year-round (e.g., Turner 1938). However, small photoperiod differences may have a subtle effect even in the tropics. For example, Burns (1985) examined reproduction of *Poeciliopsis gracilis* and *Poecilia sphenops* at photoperiods representing the extremes experienced in El Salvador (11.3 and 12.9 hours of light); in longer photoperiods females had higher fecundities and males had higher gonadosomatic indices. It is obvious that interaction of photoperiod and temperature in the control of poeciliid reproduction is not well understood at this time, and a fuller understanding awaits rigorous and controlled experimentation.

Energetics

Feeding efficiency and energetics have been extensively studied in *G. affinis*. Shakuntala and Reddy (1977) maintained mosquitofish on restricted or ad lib rations of tubifex worms. Fish on the restricted diet grew slowly, food intake (food consumed per weight of fish per day) varied between 64.7 and 79.5 mg/g/day over the 30-day experiment, and conversion efficiency varied between 7 and 8%. Fish on the ad lib diet grew quickly and took in more food, especially at smaller sizes, but consumption declined sharply with increasing fish size; conversion efficiencies were between 13 and 14%.

Shakuntala and Reddy (1979) subsequently showed that temperature and salinity interacted to control food intake in mosquitofish. Consumption increased and conversion efficiency decreased with temperature at each of five salinity levels from 0 to 7 ppt. Maximum growth rate was at 25°C and 5 ppt; maximum conversion efficiency was at 20°C and 3 ppt.

Wurtsbaugh and Cech (1983) investigated the effects of temperature and ration on growth patterns in mosquitofish. On an unlimited tubifex diet, consumption rates increased from 10 to 35°C treatments. Growth rate and conversion efficiency increased from 10 to 30°C, and then declined at 35°C. On a reduced ration, the temperature of peak growth was reduced from 30 to 25°C.

Cech et al. (1985) evaluated respiratory metabolic rates of mosquitofish at various temperatures and dissolved oxygen tensions. Rates generally increased with temperature but were significantly depressed at 30 and 35°C under severe hypoxia. At 20°C the mosquitofish metabolic rate (0.09 mg O_2/hr) is about 30% lower than that of a guppy but is generally in line with other fish of the same size. Based on the fish's metabolic rate and energy content of various sized mosquito larvae, Cech et al. (1980) calculated the food demands of mosquitofish. A 0.5 g fish under normoxic conditions would eat about 80 "small" larvae per day at 10°C and about 475 per day at 35°C.

Little is known about metabolism and energy demands of other poeciliids. The guppy has a higher growth rate and conversion efficiency than the mosquitofish on diets varying from 100% mosquito larvae to 100% tubifex worms (Reddy and Shakuntala 1979). Since the guppy also has a higher metabolic rate (Cech et al. 1985), this result probably could have been anticipated. Most other published information on energetics in poeciliids relates to the costs of reproduction and viviparity (see Reznick and Miles, Chapter 7).

POPULATION DYNAMICS

Although several authors have evaluated relative abundance of poeciliids in different habitats (e.g., Snelson 1980; Meffe 1984b; Hughes 1985a; Botsford et al. 1987), we are not aware of research that attempts reasonable estimates of population size or density. Reasons for this void are obvious. First, poeciliids are small and difficult to mark or tag by conventional means (Heugel et al. 1977). Although some mass-marking techniques have been developed for poeciliids (Vondracek et al. 1980), they have not been applied in any significant way to basic ecological questions. Haskins et al. (1961) used genetically controlled pigmentation markers to investigate movements, gene flow, and local population structure in the guppy, but this technique can only be used in highly polymorphic species or in conjunction with electrophoretic analysis (Echelle et al., Chapter 12). Secondly, poeciliid populations tend to be large and, in many cases, temporally variable, making it necessary to tag many individuals to reasonably estimate population parameters. Both the practical difficulty of tagging and the necessity of marking large numbers of animals render mark-recapture methods for estimating population size difficult to employ. Finally, many poeciliids occupy highly variable, even temporally ephemeral, habitats. For example, small streams occupied by species of *Poeciliopsis* vary from stagnant disconnected pools to flooded torrents, often over short periods of time (Thibault 1974a; Meffe 1984b). Tropical and subtropical marshes that are home to many poeciliids undergo dramatic fluctuations in depth and extent of water coverage during annual or even daily hydrologic cycles (Kushlan 1980). The resultant concentration/dilution effects greatly complicate density or even relative abundance estimates and may confound or mask many basic ecological processes.

The best-studied case of population dynamics in a poeciliid involves mosquitofish stocked into California rice fields for mosquito control. In general, mosquitofish populations increase during the rice-growing season, but timing and rate of increase vary. In many instances, populations do not reach carrying capacity, and final population sizes may differ among fields by more than an order of magnitude (Reed and Bryant 1975; Norland and Bowman 1976; Farley and Younce 1977a). Botsford et al. (1987) attributed some variability to ecological conditions (rice plant height) at the time of stocking, and some to synchronized parturition resulting in pulses of recruitment. Rather than a smooth population increase, growth curves exhibited at least two well-defined peaks, with an intervening period of stability or decline. In most cases, the second peak was approximately the same magnitude as the first, suggesting that a carrying capacity had been reached. Factors responsible for declining populations were not identified but assumed to be predation or habitat (food) limitation.

Because similar studies have not been conducted in natural populations, such experiments are the only available models of poeciliid population dynamics. Circumstantial evidence suggests that most populations are temporally variable, growing and declining erratically during the year under the influence of both biotic and abiotic "regulatory" agents (Schoenherr 1977; Meffe, Snelson, pers. observ.). Such populations probably never reach a plateau or steady-state before they are reduced by seasonal or unpredictable abiotic events.

Abiotic factors may play a dominant role in controlling many poeciliid populations, but this is poorly documented. Although heavy mortality has been associated with periods of environmental stress, such as cold temperatures (Krumholz 1948; Hughes 1985), low-water conditions (Kushlan 1980; Wetherington 1982), or floods (Collins et al. 1981; Meffe 1984b), it is obvious that extensive opportunities exist to explore the role of abiotic limitations in poeciliid population dynamics.

Predation can affect both the evolution and phenotypic variability of morphological, behavioral, and life history traits in poeciliids (Snelson, Chapter 8). This is illustrated in the excellent series of articles by Haskins, Seghers, Endler, and Reznick (all discussed previously) demonstrating the impact of predation on evolution and ecology of the guppy. However, none of these studies makes it clear that predation is a dominant influence in limiting or controlling population size. Predation by introduced mosquitofish on native Sonoran topminnows (*Poeciliopsis occidentalis*) in the American southwest is an exception. In this case, predation is so severe that it has eliminated the topminnow in many habitats (Meffe 1985b; Courtenay and Meffe, Chapter 17).

Breder and Coates (1932) were first to suggest that laboratory guppy populations were self-regulating, stabilizing at nine individuals per tank regardless of original stocking density. This seminal work was followed by many others on the subject (Shoemaker 1944; Silliman 1948, 1968; Rose 1959; Warren 1973a, 1973b, 1973c; Yamagishi 1976a, 1976b; Dahlgren 1979), producing varied results and explanations. Some studies confirmed long-term population stability (Silliman 1948, 1968; Warren 1973a) whereas other populations cycled (Shoemaker 1944) or gradually declined over long periods (Yamagishi 1976a).

Factors now considered important in "regulating" laboratory populations at high densities are depressed reproduction due to increased aggression or reduced courtship (Warren 1973b, 1973c), reduced fecundity (Dahlgren 1979), cannibalism (Shoemaker 1944; Rose 1959; Yamagishi 1976a, 1976b; Meffe 1984a), and the buildup of unknown metabolites or pheromones (Warren 1973b). Relevance of these laboratory results to regulation of natural populations remains unknown.

COMMUNITY ECOLOGY

Poeciliids have rarely attracted the specific or even incidental attention of community ecologists. Most information on poeciliids as part of larger communities derives from faunal studies or species lists. From these data and our simple observations, only a few general comments can be made.

Within native environments, poeciliids range from members of extremely simple to complex communities. In desert arroyos or springs, one poeciliid species (*Poeciliopsis* spp. or *Gambusia* spp.) may constitute the entire fish "community" (Peden 1973a; Vrijenhoek 1979b; Meffe et al. 1983), or be present with only a few other species (Hubbs 1957). In contrast, poeciliids in many lotic and lentic habitats in southeastern United States (e.g., Hunt 1953; Harrington and Harrington 1961) and many areas in Central and South America (e.g., Zaret and Rand 1971) are members of diverse communities composed of many families.

Where introduced, poeciliids often become more abundant than within their native ranges, in some cases eliminating resident species. Community changes from poeciliid introductions are especially evident in the American southwest, where *G. affinis* is prevalent and often dominates new habitats (Meffe 1985b; Courtenay and Meffe, Chapter 17). Success of introduced poeciliids is often high in depauperate habitats, particularly those with few predaceous fishes, or in habitats disturbed by man (Courtenay and Meffe, Chapter 17).

Meffe (1984b) studied effects of flash flooding on community structure in simple, two-species poeciliid communities in Arizona. The native *P. occidentalis* was being replaced through much of its native range by predation from introduced mosquitofish (Meffe 1985b). In a natural, spring-seep ecosystem, replacement was slowed or stopped by periodic flooding that removed a disproportionate number of mosquitofish due to their inappropriate behavioral responses to high flow. In stabilized habitats free of natural floods, mosquitofish typically extirpate the native species.

SUMMARY AND FUTURE RESEARCH

Ecologically, the family Poeciliidae is broadly based. They occur in a variety of habitats, eat many different foods, and are broadly tolerant of environmental conditions in general. These traits also characterize some individual species, whereas others are narrow in habitat use, food choice, or physiological tolerances. However, basic ecology of most poeciliids is unknown.

Considering the economic importance of poeciliids (aquarium trade, biological control, conservation), and the vast amount of literature accumulated, the gaps in our understanding of their ecologies are striking. Most of what is known is based on a few species, notably *Gambusia affinis*, *G. holbrooki*, and *Poecilia reticulata*; furthermore, much of that information is based on "tank ecology." Few species have been extensively studied in the field, and the majority of such studies have been conducted in the United States, at the northern periphery of the familial range.

While we do not dispute the importance of laboratory experimental studies in unraveling complex ecological questions, we are impressed that there remains a great need for basic natural history research, especially on Central and South American and Caribbean species. The genus *Xiphophorus* is a telling example: the genetics of this genus is probably as well known as any comparable-sized group of teleost fishes, but basic aspects of ecology and natural history are often undocumented. We need more information about how and where diverse poeciliid species live before we can hope to make synthetic statements about the ecology of the family.

We also need to promote a fruitful interchange between field and laboratory studies. For example, population self-regulation in the guppy was identified and has been extensively studied in the laboratory. Is it an artifact of the laboratory setting or does the phenomenon have relevance in natural populations? Is cannibalism largely a laboratory artifact or is it important to the trophic and reproductive ecology of some species in the wild? Flow of ideas in the reverse direction is also needed. Field studies have repeatedly shown that many poeciliids are successful, even dominant, in stressful habitats that are at best marginal for most other fishes. What are the adaptations that allow poeciliids to thrive in such habitats? We are intrigued that the mosquitofish seems to have a daily cycle of temperature tolerance. How widespread might this and similar phenomena be? Laboratory investigations into the physiology and behavior of species that range across a diversity of habitats would potentially be fruitful. Here again, we note that what little is known is based on only a few species, and we have no idea whether or not they are typical of the family as a whole.

The livebearing habit has evolved in many other groups of fishes (Wourms 1981), but none has been as successful as the Poeciliidae. The related family Goodeidae, for example, also exhibits specialized viviparity, but has fewer than one-fifth the number of species and is zoogeographically restricted to the Mexican plateau. This suggests that the success of poeciliids, whether defined in terms of diversity, zoogeographic range, or ecological adaptability, is attributable to something more than their mode of reproduction. Additional ecological studies are necessary to clearly define what those generalized adaptations might be.

Finally, the role of poeciliids in communities is virtually unknown and worthy of pursuit. Much can be learned from poeciliids about energy flow (as both predators and prey), competitive and niche relationships, and physiological ecology as related to community concepts.

ACKNOWLEDGMENTS

F. F. Snelson thanks S. T. Clark and Barbara Erwin for their assistance in securing and cataloging library materials. Travel support for his work at the Savannah River Ecology Laboratory was provided by SREL and the Oak Ridge Associated Universities.

Chapter 3

Reproductive Biology of Poeciliid Fishes

GEORGE D. CONSTANTZ

INTRODUCTION

Fishes of the family Poeciliidae display a fascinating suite of reproductive adaptations, setting them apart from most other fishes. Males wield a bony intromittent organ (a modified anal fin called the gonopodium), which is armed with hooks and claws and controlled by a complex set of bones and muscles that functions to impregnate the female. Females store and possibly nourish live sperm within their reproductive tracts for several months. Fertilization and development occur within ovarian follicles; birth thus coincides with ovulation. Poeciliids display a huge diversity in the extent of maternal-fetal nutrient transfer, from virtually none in species with large eggs to complete nutrient provisioning by the mother in species with tiny ova. In some species, a female may carry broods of many different ages (superfetation). All but one species deliver precocious neonates. In this chapter, I summarize current knowledge concerning the form and function of poeciliid reproduction.

MALE REPRODUCTIVE SYSTEM

Testis and Duct

The genital tract of male poeciliids includes a single duct, equivalent to the vas deferens, connecting the central lumen of the testis with a genital papilla. The paired testes are fused into a single, median, tubular organ attached to the

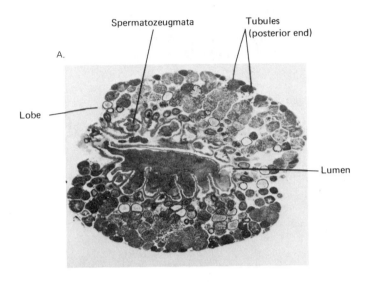

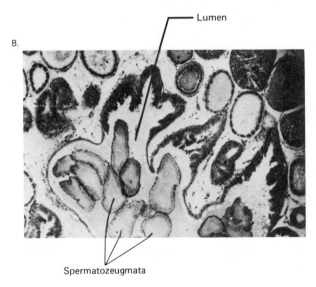

Figure 3–1.   a) Frontal section through testis of the guppy (20X); b) spermatozeugmata in lumen of the guppy's testis duct (1,000X) (photographs by Dr. R. Billard).

dorsal body wall (Kuntz 1913; Rosen and Bailey 1963; Harrington 1974; Billard 1986) (Figure 3–1a). Tubules radiate from the large central lumen (Hoar 1969; Grier 1981; Billard 1986); their blind end, or apex, is apposed against the testicular capsule and contains isolated spermatogonia (Grier 1980). Spermatogonia progress down the tubules toward the center of the testis and join with Sertoli cells to form cysts (Harrington 1974), which eventually become spermatozeugmata, or unencapsulated sperm bundles (Philippi 1908) (Figure 3–1b).

Sperm Production

Spermatogenesis, or gamete formation, depends on long-term environmental variations such as daylength and temperature; spermiation, the detachment of sperm from Sertoli cells, is influenced by short-term variations in environmental factors such as temperature and the appearance of ripe females. In temperate zones, poeciliid testes undergo winter quiescence (Grier 1981), but in tropical areas spermatogenesis continues throughout the year (Colson 1969; Billard 1986).

Within an active testis, nests of spermatogonia proliferate from resting germ cells near the apex of the tubules (Hoar 1969; Billard 1986). Below the apex, the number of Sertoli cells surrounding the cyst increases. Cysts undergo various stages of maturation (e.g., mitotic proliferation of spermatogonia, reduction division of spermatocytes) as they move toward sperm ducts (De Vlaming 1974). By the time spermatogenesis is complete, cysts are near the efferent duct system and spermiation begins. After spermiation, Sertoli cells hypertrophy, transform into efferent duct cells, and assume a secretory function. In addition to contributing to formation of spermatozeugmata and synthesizing steroid hormones, Sertoli cells may phagocytize residual bodies cast off by developing spermatids and nourish germ cells via micropinocytosis (Vaupel 1929; Hoar 1969; Grier 1981; Billard 1986).

Spermatozeugmata and Sperm Cells

Spermatozeugmata, the sperm bundles, are 0.1 to 0.2 mm in diameter (Kuntz 1913) and contain 4,000 to 5,500 sperm cells (Kallman 1975). Sperm heads are embedded in the outer gelatinous matrix of spermatozeugmata, and tails extend into the lumen (Philippi 1908; Rosen and Bailey 1963) (Figure 3–2). This pattern, set at the Sertoli cell stage, is maintained by a sticky, gelatinous secretion acquired in the efferent ducts (Philippi 1908; Kadow 1954; Hoar 1969).

Poeciliid sperm have a greatly elongated nucleus, lance-shaped head (Figure 3–3), highly specialized midpiece with plentiful glycogen stores (Grier 1981; Billard 1986), and a long flagellate tail (Kuntz 1913). Compared to other fishes, poeciliid sperm exhibit lengthy motility (one to two hours, Billard 1986) due to the plentiful glycogen stores (Gardiner 1978); they are not temporally constrained by a cortical egg reaction.

Gonopodium and Suspensorium

The anal fin is sexually dimorphic in all poeciliids. In immature males and adult females, the fin has about nine rays held together by crossing strands of connective tissue. The male's intromittent organ, or gonopodium, is formed when

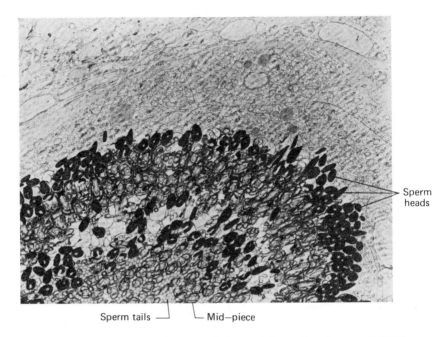

Figure 3–2. Edge of spermatozeugmata in the vas deferens of a male guppy (7,000X) (photograph by Dr. R. Billard).

anal fin rays 3, 4, and 5 elongate and thicken. All three consist of bilaterally paired, non-fused, opposing bony segments (Figure 3–4), between which run blood vessels, nerves, and connective tissue (Rosen and Gordon 1953). Ray 3 becomes the thickest and primary supporting element.

The distal tip of the gonopodium contains bones of species-specific shape

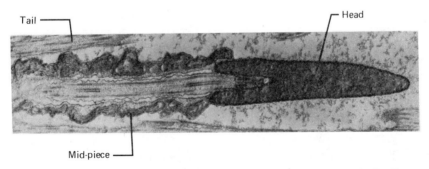

Figure 3–3. Head and midpiece of a guppy sperm (30,000X) (photograph by Dr. R. Billard).

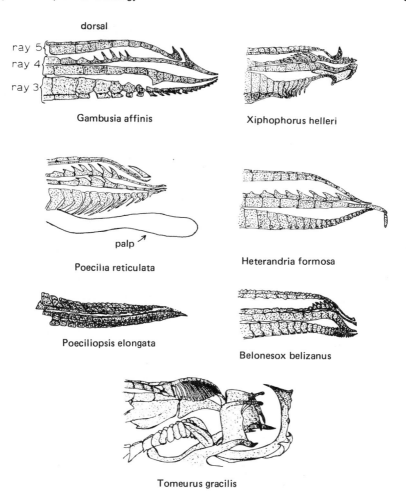

Figure 3–4.   Distal portions of resting gonopodia of representative poeciliids (modified from Rosen and Bailey 1963).

(Meek and Hildebrand 1916). For example, the distal portion of the anal fin rays in *Gambusia* spp. are directed posteriorly, usually with at least one retrorse spine or hook (Figure 3–4). In *Priapichthys* spp., the distal portion is directed anteriorly, with or without antrorse hooks. In *Poeciliopsis* spp., the tip is comparatively plain, with a minute hook, directed anteriorly and to the left. *Tomeurus gracilis* has the most bizarre gonopodial tip, featuring a combination of structures resembling sickles, grappling hooks, and ice tongs (Rosen and Bailey 1963).

In some taxa, mainly those with short gonopodia, development yields a bilaterally symmetrical gonopodium that, when erected, can form a trough on either side of the body (Rosen and Bailey 1963; Chambers 1987). In such taxa (e.g., *Xiphophorus, Gambusia, Poecilia*) the numbers of right and left erections are similar. In other species, anal fin rays grow asymmetrically and form a permanent groove. About 40% of the genera with long gonopodia (e.g., *Poeciliopsis, Phallichthys, Carlhubbsia, Xenodexia*) are asymmetrical (Chambers 1987). Within species, permanent folding (and thereby mating) occurs on either the right or left side (Rosen and Bailey 1963). Asymmetry has evolved independently at least five times in the family. In *Quintana atrizona*, where a few segments are twisted to the left, 90% of erections are sinistral (Rosen and Tucker 1961).

Gonopodial asymmetry has been most studied in *Poeciliopsis* (Hubbs and Miller 1954; Schultz 1963; Chambers 1987). The gonopodium of *Poeciliopsis latidens*, for example, is long, slender, and inserted far forward. Viewed anteriorly, the main rod is gently curved toward its right side. The permanent trough, defined as the concave posterior edge of ray 5, is consistently on the left.

Some highly specialized muscles, bones, and ligaments allow the male to laterally rotate and aim the gonopodium at various angles. This gonopodial suspensorium consists of three kinds of bones (Rosen and Gordon 1953; Rosen and Tucker 1961; Schultz 1963; Lodi 1979) (Figure 3–5). The (1) gonapophyses, modified hemal spines, are greatly enlarged, inclined forward, and commonly possess paired posterior outgrowths, called uncini, to which connective tissues attach. Embedded in the ligament connecting the vertebral column with the (2) gonactinosts, the ligastyle is a relict of the first hemal spine that has no articulation with surrounding bony elements. The gonactinosts, modified interhemal spines, are associated ventrally with gonopodial rays through a series of pivotal subspherical ossicles called (3) baseosts. Because rays 4 and 5 are mechanically supported by ray 3, the ray 3 baseost acts as the center of gonopodial movement during swinging. The gonapophyses, gonactinosts, and baseosts are held firmly together by a tough network of ligaments and fibrous connective tissue.

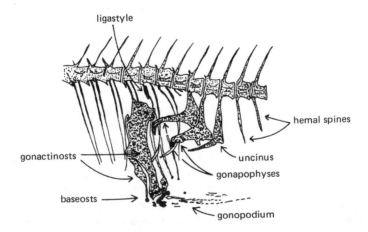

Figure 3–5. Gonopodial suspensorium of *Poeciliopsis catemaco* (drawn from photograph provided by Dr. Robert R. Miller).

Movements of the gonopodium are effected by a series of large, specialized muscles (Rosen and Tucker 1961). Gonactinosts 1, 2 through 4, and 5 through 9 are fitted with erector analis minor (a small erector), erector analis major (a large erector), and depressor analis muscles, respectively. Other muscles function to modify the orientation of erectors, facilitate lateral rotation, or act as tensors to steady the fin (Rosen and Bailey 1963). The most conspicuous muscles insert on the base of ray 3 (Rosen and Gordon 1953).

The gonopodial hood, or palp, is a solid, highly vascularized outgrowth of the integument over the anterior margin of ray 3 (Chambers 1987) (Figure 3–4). Depending on the species, it varies from balloon-like and projecting beyond the tip, to minute and knob-like. On the basis of hood development, Chambers (1987) sorted poeciliids into two groups. Genera with short gonopodia (<34% of standard length [SL], e.g., *Alfaro, Poecilia, Priapella, Belonesox, Xiphophorus*) have a fairly anterior gonopodial base and well-developed hood. Taxa with long gonopodia (50 to 75% SL, e.g., *Poeciliopsis, Phallichthys, Cnesterodon, Heterandria*) have gonopodia inserted even further forward and have either a thin, minute hood or none at all (Hubbs and Miller 1954).

FEMALE REPRODUCTIVE SYSTEM

Ovary and Duct

The paired ovaries of female poeciliids are fused into a single, large, sac-like organ that is moderately vascularized and dorsally suspended in the body cavity (Amoroso 1960; Rosen and Bailey 1963; Monaco et al. 1978; Wourms 1981). When distended with eggs and embryos, the ovary occupies most of the peritoneal cavity.

The ovary consists of few tissues. It is enclosed in an external sac formed by peritoneal folds (Wourms 1981) and lined internally by a loose, richly vascularized germinal epithelium with ovarian follicles and supporting connective tissue (Amoroso 1960). The convoluted lining almost occludes the ovarian cavity (Hoar 1969).

The ovary's muscular wall, elastic connective tissue, and folded inner surface extend posteriorly through a short gonoduct (Philippi 1908; Monaco et al. 1978; Wourms 1981). The gonoduct exits through a urogenital aperture that may be located on a fleshy papilla just posterior to the anus (Kadow 1954; Amoroso 1960) (Figure 3–6).

Egg and Follicle

During early vitellogenesis, oocyte diameter increases and follicles deposit yolk within each oocyte (Amoroso 1960). During late vitellogenesis, yolk vesicles fuse into large, central yolk platelets (Scrimshaw 1944a). The mature ovum is

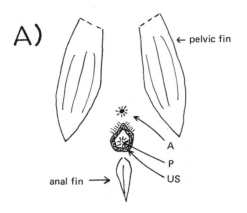

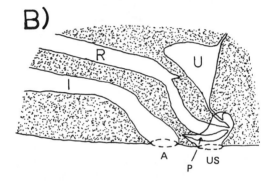

Figure 3–6. Stylized diagram of reproductive system of female mosquitofish. a) ventral view of external genitalia; b) medial view showing relationship among digestive, reproductive, and excretory systems. A = anus, P = urogenital papilla, I = intestine, R = reproductive system (= gonoduct), US = urogenital sinus, U = urinary system (modified from drawings provided by Dr. Alex E. Peden).

spherical, translucent golden-yellow, contains peripheral fat globules, and is covered by a thin vitelline membrane (Kuntz 1913; Constantz, pers. observ.). Ova range from 0.40 to 2.56 mm in diameter (Scrimshaw 1946; Billard 1986; Snelson et al. 1986b), depending on species. All but one poeciliid have unchorionated eggs, that is, without hard egg membranes (Rugh 1962; Balon 1975). The exception, *Tomeurus gracilis*, produces a chorionated egg with adhesive filaments that resembles those of oviparous atheriniformes (Rosen and Bailey 1963); they are shed shortly after internal fertilization.

Each oogonium becomes surrounded by a single layer of small epithelial cells that form an ovarian follicle (Hoar 1969; Monaco et al. 1978). The embryos of all poeciliids except *T. gracilis* develop within these follicles. As the follicle grows, its epithelial cells increase in size and number to form a glandular granulosa, from which the maturing ovum is separated by an extracellular envelope, the zona pellucida (Ryder 1885). Yolk proteins from the liver pass into the blood, traverse the granulosa layer, and enter the developing egg (J. P. Wourms, pers. comm.).

Female Genitalia

The female genitalia consist of the papilla, sinus, and urogenital opening (Figure 3–6). In *Gambusia* spp., where they are best-studied, female genitalia are highly variable. In the species group that includes *G. affinis*, females have a reproductive opening on the end of a large papilla within an open urogenital sinus (Peden 1972b). The group that includes *G. atrora* has a reproductive opening terminating more directly on the exterior surface, with papillae and sinuses weakly formed or absent. A third group, which includes *G. heterochir*, has urogenital openings displaced anteriorly by underlying tissue, causing the sinus to extend posteriorly from the urogenital opening. *Gambusia vittata*, the most distant congener, has the most distinct female genitalia of all gambusiines: a flap of transparent tissue extends anteriorly and covers the urogenital opening.

A small pigmented spot dorsal to the anus occurs in many female poeciliids (Medlen 1951). This spot enlarges at sexual maturity, is largest shortly before birth, and recedes but is never completely lost after parturition. In gambusiines, the anal spot seems to provide a cue for gonopodial orientation during the male's thrust (Peden 1973b).

Ovarian Cycles

Female poeciliids undergo regular cycles of egg production (Breder and Coates 1932; Jaski 1939; Rosenthal 1952; Clark et al. 1954; Kadow 1954; Siciliano 1972; Stacey 1981). Turner (1937) proposed two basic types of ovarian cycles. In one, birth occurs before the younger ova are fertilized, and these females carry embryos at a single stage of development. In the other, younger ova are fertilized before birth of the older brood; these females carry two or more broods at different stages, a condition called superfetation.

Using more specific criteria, Turner (1937) distinguished three types of reproduction without superfetation (the *Gambusia*, *Lebistes*, and *Quintana atrizona* types with seven-, two-, and one-day parturition-to-fertilization intervals, respectively) and two types involving superfetation (the *Poeciliopsis* and *Heterandria formosa* types with two and up to nine overlapping broods, respectively). The *Gambusia* type is also characteristic of *Poecilia sphenops*, *P. latipinna* and *Heterandria bimaculata*, while the *Lebistes* type also applies to *Xiphophorus*. The *Poeciliopsis* type is characteristic of many, if not all, congeners, while the *Heterandria formosa* type fits *Priapella bonita* and *Phalloptychus januarius*. Increasing degree of superfetation is correlated with smaller broods, shorter interbrood intervals, and smaller eggs (Turner 1937; Reznick and Miles, Chapter 7).

The interval between broods ranges from 1 to 10 days in superfetators, up to 23 to 75 days in single-brooded taxa. Variation in length of the yolk-loading period may explain the inter- as well as much of the intraspecific variation in interbrood intervals (Snelson et al. 1986b).

After parturition, females yolk the next brood (assuming a simple ovarian cycle) and secrete steroid hormones (Liley 1966; Lambert 1970; Liley and Wishlow 1974; Stacey 1981). They are more sexually receptive for a brief period after parturition than at other phases of their cycle (Rosenthal 1952; Liley 1966; Parzefall 1973; Crow and Liley 1979; Brett and Grosse 1982; Farr, Chapter 6). Thus, a female is most sexually receptive when yolked eggs are available for fertilization (Kadow 1954; Monaco et al. 1978).

What coordinates these activities? Unlike most fishes, in which postovulatory sexual behavior is stimulated by prostaglandin synthesized in response to ovulated oocytes, poeciliid females seem to be stimulated by estrogen, which becomes more concentrated in the blood as follicles mature (Stacey 1981; Liley and Stacey 1983).

In some poeciliids, old females may go through a period of sterile senility (Krumholz 1963; Constantz 1976; Woodhead 1979). Such females appear emaciated, have sunken areas anterior and posterior to the dorsal fin, have no fat around the viscera, and contain fatty ovarian tissue without oocytes or yolked eggs.

In temperate and subtropical areas, reproductive output by females declines or ends in the fall and winter (Krumholz 1948; Rosen and Bailey 1963; Constantz 1979; Burns 1985). Females in constant-temperature springs may reproduce all year long, but still show cycling of offspring number (Constantz 1979; Burns 1985). In subtropical Florida, decreasing daylength in autumn stops reproduction by *Heterandria formosa* (least killifish), while increasing daylength and high temperatures initiate it in spring (Colson 1969). Lam (1983) reported that long photoperiods stimulate gonadal development in *Gambusia affinis* only if combined with warm temperatures. However, elevated temperature alone results in mosquitofish reproduction through winter in South Carolina, although at much reduced brood sizes (G. K. Meffe, pers. comm.). Thus, in temperate zones, daylength and temperature interact in incompletely understood ways to control female reproduction.

The situation for tropical poeciliids is even less clear. For example, *Brachyrhaphis episcopi* exhibits no seasonal variation in brood size (Turner 1938). On the other hand, when *Poeciliopsis gracilis* and *Poecilia sphenops* were subjected to the shortest (11.3 hours) and longest (12.9 hours) daylengths of their native El Salvador, females had higher gonadosomatic indices at the long photoperiod (Burns 1985). In addition to photoperiod and temperature, environmental control of gonad development in tropical poeciliids may involve dissolved oxygen concentration, changing water level, acoustic stimulation by rain, conductivity, food supply, and population density (Rose 1959; Lam 1983).

COPULATION AND INSEMINATION

Female poeciliids release chemicals that stimulate male sexual behavior (Amouriq 1964, 1965; Gandolfi 1969; Parzefall 1970; Thiessen and Sturdivant 1977; Crow and Liley 1979; Brett and Grosse 1982; Farr and Travis 1986). The chemical, probably estrogen (Amouriq 1967), acts as a releaser of male sexual motor patterns, and is probably perceived via taste (Parzefall 1973). The female's urogenital aperture is the likely site of secretion, which would explain why males typically nip the female's genital region. The oviduct is open for a brief period before and after parturition (Weishaupt 1925; Peters and Mader 1964; Parzefall 1973), the time of maximum male interest.

Is the chemical released by females a sexual pheromone? That is, does the female signal, or is the chemical merely a leaking metabolite? I lean toward the former and have suggested (Constantz 1984) that a function of the chemical is to incite scramble competition among males, thereby intensifying sexual selection (see also Farr, Chapter 6).

At rest, the gonopodium points caudally with ray 3 below rays 4 and 5 (Figure 3–4). During the forward and lateral movement associated with copulation, slippage of rays past one another and straining of connective fibers produces a temporary channel, through which spermatozeugmata presumably pass.

Poeciliids with gonopodia that reach to or beyond the eye (e.g., *Poeciliopsis*, *Heterandria*, *Girardinus*) may visually monitor gonopodial position, possibly by sighting along the tip. In these taxa, aiming is unaided by other body parts and there is only momentary genital contact, usually with an uncooperative female (Chambers 1987).

Species with short gonopodia (e.g., *Poecilia*, *Xiphophorus*, *Gambusia*) have their gonopodia too far behind and below the eye for visual aim. Such species have structures for positioning (hood, sensory spines) and stabilizing (pectoral and pelvic fins) their gonopodia, and undergo prolonged (one to four seconds) copulation, often with a cooperative female (Rosen and Tucker 1961; Rosen and Bailey 1963).

In *Gambusia*, the gonopodium is brought underneath the notched pectoral fin (Rosen and Tucker 1961; Peden 1972b). The outer halves of pectoral fin rays 2 or 3 through 5 are thickened and face downward when the fin is extended. An elbow on gonopodial ray 4 projects upward and contacts, possibly locking with, the pectoral fin. In *Xenodexia*, only the right pectoral fin has a fleshy modification that supports the gonopodium. In *Poecilia* and *Xiphophorus*, the erect gonopodium rests against the underside of a raised pelvic fin (Rosen and Tucker 1961).

Based on its extensive innervation and lack of musculature, Chambers (1987) suggested that the hood is a sensory structure, tactile in function, that assists, but is not essential, in copulation. When hoods of male guppies are removed, insemination still occurs (Clark and Aronson 1951), but its frequency decreases (Kadow 1954). Species that naturally lack the hood may use innervated spines on the ventral surface of ray 3 for aiming the gonopodium (Rosen and Gordon 1953).

Little is known about specific details of insemination. Rosen and Tucker (1961) suggested that males transfer sperm in two ways. Sperm may be (1) deposited externally on or near the female's genital papilla, or (2) inserted directly into the genital opening.

Exterior depositors include *Phalloceros caudimaculatus* (Philippi 1908), *Heterandria* spp. (Rosen and Tucker 1961), and the Gila topminnow (Constantz, pers. observ.). *Heterandria* females have a large foliate genital pad for trapping spermatophores. In these taxa, genital contact is momentary.

Internal copulators include *Gambusia* spp. (Peden 1972b), *Xiphophorus* spp. (Rosen and Tucker 1961), and the guppy (Stepanek 1928; Rosen and Gordon 1953). Once spermatozeugmata are within the female's system, fluid from her gonoduct reduces viscosity of the gelatinous coat binding the sperm cells (Chambers 1987), causing spermatozeugmata to break up within 10 to 15 minutes (Philippi 1908; Collier 1936; Kadow 1954).

In xiphophoriines, the distal serrae or the claw grips the female (Rosen and Gordon 1953; Chambers 1987; Figure 3–4). *Xiphophorus* species with large holdfasts (e.g., *X. helleri*) have longer copulatory contact than species (e.g., *X. maculatus*) with small hooks (Clark et al. 1954). Removal of one holdfast from the swordtail's gonopodium reduces insemination efficiency, and removal of both prevents it (Rosen and Gordon 1953). *Priapella* spp. and the Gambusiini employ ventral hooks and dorsal claws, respectively (Rosen and Gordon 1953).

Xenodexia ctenolepis is unusual because males have a pectoral fin clasper and a long tubular gonopodium. Hubbs (1950) conjectured that the gonopodium is held securely by the main hook of the clasper.

Copulation is obvious in species with large gonopodial hooks because males seem to have their gonopodia caught in the female, and then twist vigorously to free themselves. Observations suggest that at separation, the hooks or claws injure the female's genitalia. Histological preparations of female guppies sacrificed immediately after copulation showed blood clots within the urogenital sinus (Kadow 1954). Clark et al. (1954) reported that some female swordtails bleed from their genital opening following gonopodial withdrawal. Constantz (1984) suggested that a function of some terminal gonopodial structures is to traumatize female genitalia, which may enforce post-copulatory chastity of females and minimize sperm replacement.

Mechanical stimulation of the innervated gonopodial spines may stimulate discharge of spermatozeugmata (Rosen and Gordon 1953; Kadow 1954). Such spines occur in every poeciliid group. This suggestion implies that spermatozeugmata are held within the male's body until copulation is achieved. However, I suspect that external depositors may constantly carry sperm on the gonopodial tip.

The success of ejaculation, at least in some internal copulators, is indicated by a series of spasmodic contractions by the male (Kadow 1954). Bowden (1969) suggested that "jerking" may serve to rearm the gonopodium with spermatozeugmata. How spermatozeugmata are transported to the gonopodial tip, though, is unknown.

INTERACTIONS OF MATERNAL AND PATERNAL GENOMES

Sperm Storage and Fertilization

Female poeciliids store sperm in folds lining the ovary and gonoduct (Winge 1922b; Dulzetto 1928; Stepanek 1928; Purser 1938; Kallman 1975). Sperm may persist there for up to eight broods or eight months (Van Oordt 1928; Winge 1937; Vallowe 1953; Kadow 1954; Turner and Snelson 1984).

Several reports suggest that females nourish the sperm they carry (Hoar 1969). Turner (1937) stated that corpora lutea of *Xiphophorus* spp. produce a copious secretion that nourishes sperm. Guppy sperm may be supported by ovarian sugars (Gardiner 1978). Alternately, sperm may be consumed by ovarian cells. Philippi (1908) claimed that excess sperm are grabbed by epithelial pseudopodia in the dorsal wall of the *Girardinus* ovary. Philippi's report has not been confirmed, but if true, would help explain last-male sperm precedence.

New sperm fertilize most offspring in the next brood (Schmidt 1920; Constantz 1984). Last-male sperm precedence is magnified if the last male mates during the female's fertile period (Rosenthal 1952; Hildeman and Wagner 1954; Farr and Travis 1986). Mixed broods are most readily obtained when two males are with the female at the same time (Winge 1937).

How do sperm survive within the immunologically hostile female reproductive tract? Hogarth and Sursham (1972) established via immunocompatibility tests that guppy sperm are antigenic and that the ovarian storage site is not alymphatic. Thus, there is nothing unique about these two tissues. By eliminating remaining hypotheses, they proposed that the ovary may be a favorable site for sperm survival because estradiol impedes allograft rejection.

Fertilization occurs within ovarian follices (Ryder 1882; Philippi 1908; Kuntz 1913; Liley and Stacey 1983). When the ovarian epithelium contacts the follicular wall, sperm penetrate cells of the weakened follicle (Turner 1947; Amoroso 1960). Fertilization occurs over a period of one to five days and, in a simple ovarian cycle, one to eight days after parturition (Dildine 1936; Hopper 1943; Tavolga 1949; Stolk 1951; Kallman 1975).

Gestation

Gestation ranges from roughly 20 to 30 days, depending on species and temperature (Krumholz 1948, 1963; Haskins et al. 1961; Schultz 1961; Kallman 1975). Embryos remain in the follicle until immediately before parturition (Scrimshaw 1944a; Amoroso 1960; Hoar 1969; Wourms 1981).

Differentiation of playtfish embryos is rapid (Hopper 1943): the embryo is almost completely formed four to five days after fertilization and the remainder of gestation is concerned with further growth of existing organs. Embryonic stages are illustrated by Tavolga and Rugh (1947), Tavolga (1949), and Rugh (1962).

Histocompatibility antigens are present on cells of swordtail embryos (Hogarth

1972a) even though the mother is immunologically competent (Hogarth 1972b). How does the poeciliid fetus avoid immunological rejection? Because transplanted embryos with intact fertilization membranes develop normally, while those without fertilization membranes do not, Hogarth (1973) concluded that this non-cellular membrane, almost entirely of egg and therefore maternal origin, provides a barrier against immune rejection.

Poeciliid "folklore" holds that females resorb embryos. For example, in *Poeciliopsis* sp., 25 of 37 wild females contained degenerating ova (Rugh 1962) that presumably were being resorbed. However, there have been no firm demonstrations of embryo resorption, and Meffe and Vrijenhoek (1981) showed that starvation does not cause resorption in three species (*Poeciliopsis monacha, P. prolifica*, guppy). Although starving females of these three species stop further vitellogenesis, they carry embroys to term.

VIVIPARITY AND SUPERFETATION

Degrees of Maternal Contribution

I recognize two types of livebearing in the Poeciliidae. Lecithotrophy is the process in which embryos are nourished by yolk deposited prior to fertilization (Wourms 1981), and subsumes the terms ovoviviparity (Turner 1947; Amoroso 1960) and obligate lecithotrophic livebearing (Balon 1981). Matrotrophy is the process in which embryos are nourished by matter transferred from the mother (Wourms 1981), and subsumes the terms viviparity (Turner 1947; Amoroso 1960) and viviparous trophodermy (Balon 1981). Between these extremes lies a continuum. One poeciliid, *Tomeurus gracilis*, lies outside the continuum because it combines internal fertilization with external embryonic development. Lecithotrophy seems the primitive condition (Wourms 1981) because it involves retention of yolked eggs without elaboration of specialized membranes for fetal-maternal transfer.

Needham (1931) proposed that the real energetic coefficient, which represents the relative cost in weight to develop embryonic tissues, is about 0.66. Thus, if embryo weight does not change through development, the mother presumably contributed about 34% of the embryo's post-fertilization weight (Scrimshaw 1945). With this reference point in mind, let us consider the lecithotrophy-matrotrophy continuum.

At the lecithotrophic end are species such as *Poecilia latipinna* (Amoroso 1960), *Poecilia formosa* (Monaco et al. 1983), *Xiphophorus helleri* (Amoroso 1960), *Gambusia affinis* (Reznick 1981; Meffe 1986b), *Poeciliopsis monacha* (Wourms 1981), and *Poecilia reticulata* (Trinkaus and Drake 1952). They all produce eggs about 2 mm in diameter that require little post-fertilization contribution from the female. For example, embryos of the latter two species undergo a net loss of 38 and 25% dry weight, respectively, during development (Wourms 1981).

At the other end of the continuum, specialized matrotrophes such as *Heterandria formosa* and several species of *Poeciliopsis* produce small eggs (0.4 to 0.8 mm in diameter) with meager yolk stores, whose embryos receive maternal nutrients (Fraser and Renton 1940; Scrimshaw 1944a, 1944b; Wourms 1981). Embryos of *H. formosa* grow from 0.017 mg at fertilization to 0.85 mg at parturition; those of *Poeciliopsis elongata* grow from 0.02 to 12.5 mg. Lying near the middle of the continuum, *Poeciliopsis occidentalis* could be classified as an unspecialized matrotrophe: the number of calories per embryo increases from 12.6 to 16.4 during gestation, an increase of 31.6% (Constantz 1980). Reznick and Miles (Chapter 7) discuss the adaptive significance of variation in degree of maternal input.

Maternal and Fetal Membranes

In lecithotrophes and unspecialized matrotrophes, the placental barrier consists of a chorion, which is the outer wall of the greatly expanded pericardial sac, and an amnion, the pericardial sac's inner wall (Turner 1939, 1940a; Amoroso 1960; Hoar 1969; Wourms 1981). As the embryo grows, follicular capillaries, which deliver nutrients, increase in size and number. In all, the placental barrier consists of six to seven layers (Wourms et al. 1988).

In addition to the preceding structures, matrotrophes have more specialized modifications. The entire surface of these embryos is covered by absorptive cells that contain microvilli and vesicles (Wourms et al. 1988). During gestation, their follicular walls become thin, heavily vascularized, closely applied to the embryo, and develop elongate vascular villi (Scrimshaw 1944a; Turner 1947; Wourms 1981). Such villi are numerous opposite the belly sac. The pericardial sac ruptures over the forehead, leaving a strap of somatopleure called the "neck strap", which gradually shrinks and disappears as development proceeds (Scrimshaw 1944a). This complex of follicular wall with villi, follicular space, and adjacent vessels of the portal system covering the belly sac is called the follicular placenta (Wourms et al. 1988).

Parturition

Ovulation immediately precedes birth (Amoroso 1960; Kallman 1975). Contraction of the muscular ovarian walls starts the birth process; embryos themselves do not rupture the follicle (Wourms et al. 1988). The embryo then moves into the ovarian cavity, down the gonoduct, and out into the environment.

In mosquitofish, a sudden drop in temperature stimulates delivery of young (Ishii 1963). Most guppy fry emerge head first (Rosenthal 1951). At birth, the yolk sac may be completely absorbed (Kuntz 1913) or fry may contain some of its vestiges (Rosenthal 1951; Amoroso 1960; Kallman 1975).

Superfetation

Superfetation is the situation in which two or more broods at different stages of development occur in the same female (Turner 1940b; Scrimshaw 1944b; Wourms 1981); least killifish may carry up to nine broods simultaneously (Turner 1947). Although Turner (1947) claimed that regular superfetation is unique to poeciliids, it also occurs in European hares (Bourliere 1954). In the Poeciliidae, regular superfetation has probably evolved several times independently (Reznick and Miles, Chapter 7).

How does a superfetating female supply the needs of offspring at different developmental stages? As the younger brood is yolked, female Gila topminnows allocate little to the older brood (Constantz 1980). Then, when the younger brood begins embryogeny, nutrients are again shunted to the older brood. This suggests that superfetating females allocate yolk to eggs, or nutrients to older embryos, but cannot simultaneously do both.

In general, poeciliids with the highest degree of viviparity show well-developed superfetation (Scrimshaw 1944b; Rosen and Bailey 1963). Conversely, regular superfetation has not evolved in poeciliids in which the fertilized egg contains sufficient nourishment to sustain embryogenesis. These observations led Thibault and Schultz (1978) to propose two groups of poeciliids: (1) generalized species with a single brood and lecithotrophy, and (2) specialized species with superfetation and matrotrophy. Reznick and Miles (Chapter 7) discuss this apparent correlation more fully.

SUMMARY AND FUTURE RESEARCH

Highly specialized reproductive systems set poeciliids apart from other teleosts. Among families with internal fertilization, the poeciliid gonopodium is more specialized than the modified anal fin of the Goodeidae, but it is not the large penis with permanent tube seen in the Jenynsiidae and Anablepidae. The poeciliid gonopodial suspensorium is highly modified, especially the enlarged hemal arches that support the anal fin. For steadying and aiming the gonopodium, some poeciliids employ pectoral and pelvic fins with notched and curved rays. Hooks and claws at the gonopodial tip of some species prolong coupling and tear the female's genitalia.

Female poeciliids store live sperm within their ovary and gonoduct. After intrafollicular development, females give birth to competent fry. Among vertebrates, follicular gestation has arisen independently only in the atheriniform families Poeciliidae and Anablepidae, and in two perciform families (Wourms et al. 1988). Among the 20,000 species of teleosts, only 510 species in 122 genera, 13 families, and 2 orders (Atheriniformes, Perciformes) give birth to living young (Wourms 1981).

Within the nearly 200 species of Poeciliidae, all but one (*Tomeurus gracilis*) are livebearing. The poeciliid brand of livebearing may be unique because of its breadth, from primitive lecithotrophy to specialized matrotrophy. Among teleosts, superfetation is unique to the Poeciliidae.

We still have much to learn about reproductive adaptations of poeciliid fishes. For example:

(1) How are spermatozeugmata transported to the gonopodial tip—via cilia, centrifugal force?

(2) Specifically, how are spermatozeugmata transferred to the female? Are they held until needed at the gonopodial tip or ejaculated upon contact with the female?

(3) What specific molecules released by females stimulate male sexual behavior?

(4) What molecules, and in what proportions, move between mother and embryo?

(5) What regulates the amount of nutrients and energy transferred to each embryo?

(6) How does the reproductive physiology of the oviparous *Tomeurus gracilis* differ from other poeciliids?

(7) What stimulates parturition?

I end this chapter with a bit of conjecture. If females of a particular poeciliid species are single-brooded, fertile only briefly, and cooperate during copulation, it would benefit copulating males to render females chaste for the duration of their fertile period. Thus, in species with *Gambusia* and *Lebistes* types of ovarian cycles, males should have hooks and claws. It is consistent that all *Xiphophorus*, *Belonesox*, and all *Gambusia* species except *G. vittata* have gonopodial claws and hooks. Alternately, if a female is often fertile because of superfetation, she may constantly incite pursuit by males and thus be evasive. If so, males of these species need gonopodia that function as long-distance dabbers. In these taxa, males may inseminate by sticking spermatozeugmata onto the exterior of the female's genitalia more often than by insertion. Thus, long gonopodia and a deemphasis on holdfast structures should prevail in these species. The absence of large claws and hooks in all *Priapichthys*, *Phalloptychus*, and *Poeciliopsis* species, *Heterandria formosa*, and *Priapella bonita* is consistent with this hypothesis.

How does the inconsistency of *G. vittata* relate to the pattern? *Gambusia vittata* is an interesting exception to the *Gambusia* pattern because it exhibits both superfetation and a lack of hooks and claws; thus, this exception is actually consistent with the hypothesis.

This hypothesis should be tested more rigorously. My prediction is straightforward: poeciliid species should feature either short, hooked gonopodia and single broods, or long, plain gonopodia and superfetation.

ACKNOWLEDGMENTS

R. Billard (Museum National d'Histoire Naturelle, Paris), Robert R. Miller (University of Michigan), and Alex E. Peden (Royal British Columbia Museum, Victoria), provided photographic materials. The critiques of David Reznick and John Wourms greatly improved the manuscript. Nancy Ailes and Jean Coleman helped with the drawings. Thanks to all.

Chapter 4

A Genetic Overview of Poeciliid Fishes

ROBERT A. ANGUS

INTRODUCTION

Certain poeciliid fishes have been maintained in laboratories as closed aquarium stocks since the early 1900s. This is nearly as long as the age of laboratory stocks of the more well-known organisms of genetic study, *Drosophila* and the laboratory mouse. As a result of research in numerous laboratories throughout the world over many years, a vast literature exists on the genetics of various poeciliids. This research has contributed to our knowledge of genetics of such diverse topics as pigment cells and melanoma, sex determination and evolution of sex-determining mechanisms, gene regulation, conservation of linkage groups through evolution, controls of endocrine function, behavior, and morphological variation. A comprehensive review of that literature would require a volume of its own. Fortunately, numerous reviews have been published on various subsets of the literature. The purpose of this chapter is to introduce the reader to some of the more thoroughly investigated topics of poeciliid genetics, to cite the important papers and reviews that will be of interest for in-depth library research, to summarize the important findings of the studies, and to discuss recent developments in the field.

KARYOLOGY

The average nuclear DNA content of many teleosts is only about 20% that of mammals (Ohno and Atkin 1966). As a result, fish chromosomes present a challenge for karyological research. Most of the chromosomes are small (2 microns long or less) acrocentrics that lack distinctive individual morphologies (Prehn and Rasch 1969). Thus, detailed karyotypic analyses and comparisons are not possible. In general, the most that can be accomplished is to enumerate chromosomes and look for dimorphic sex chromosomes.

The karyotype with 48 chromosomes is most frequent among poeciliids (Kirpichnikov 1981). A survey of the literature by Cimino (1974) indicated that 2n = 48 is characteristic of *Poeciliopsis* (five sexual species and four diploid unisexual populations surveyed) as well as *Xiphophorus helleri* and *X. maculatus*. In contrast, all *Poecilia* spp. included in his survey (six species and one diploid unisexual form) had 2n = 46. In both *Poeciliopsis* and *Poecilia*, triploid unisexual forms have evolved (3n = 72 and 3n = 69, respectively). Black and Howell (1979) noted that *Gambusia affinis affinis* and *G. a. holbrooki* both have 2n = 48, but differ in sex chromosomes (discussed in the following section).

SEX DETERMINATION

Studies with poeciliid fishes have significantly contributed to understanding vertebrate sex determination. Although the literature on this topic is extensive, studies have concentrated on relatively few species. Kallman (1984) noted that "of the more than 130 known species of poeciliid fishes (Rosen and Bailey 1963), the sex-determining mechanism of hardly more than a dozen species has been investigated." Thus, although sex-determining mechanisms are well characterized for a few species, we lack broad knowledge of poeciliid sex determination.

Many fishes (including many poeciliids) lack cytologically distinguishable sex chromosomes. This fact, along with the relatively common occurrence of sex reversal, has led to the conclusion that fishes in general have somewhat primitive sex determining mechanisms (e.g., Chen 1967; Mittwoch 1973; Kirpichnikov 1981). Many groups of fishes have genuine hermaphrodites, either synchronous or sequential. The genetic mechanisms that stipulate hermaphroditism are not understood. Poeciliid fishes normally have separate sexes, and individuals normally remain the same sex throughout life. The occasional literature accounts of spontaneous sex reversal seem to be in error (see Kallman 1984 for a critical discussion). Older, reproductively senile, poeciliid females (and some young ones as well) tend to develop male-limited phenotypic traits (arrhenoidy), such as an elongated anal fin, but they do not become functional males (Kallman 1984). Functional sex reversal has been artificially induced in poeciliids by administration of steroid hormones (Snelson, Chapter 8). Only one case of functional hermaphroditism has been reported in poeciliids, involving a self-fertilizing strain of the guppy (Spurway 1957).

Environmental factors such as temperature and pH can also be important in poeciliid sex determination. Few studies have been done to specifically identify these influences, but they have demonstrated significant environmental effects, at least in some species (Snelson, Chapter 8).

The Guppy, *Poecilia reticulata*

Guppies do not have cytologically distinguishable sex chromosomes (Winge 1923). However, the existence of an XX, XY mechanism has been confirmed by other information, such as inheritance patterns of sex-linked genes. Highly polymorphic sex-linked color genes exist and have been well characterized (see "Genetics of Pigments" section). Winge (1922a, 1927), studying sex-linked pigmentation genes, demonstrated that sex chromosomes retain a rather extensive region of homology where crossing over may occur. Also, unlike mammals, the Y chromosome of guppies has not become so specialized that it has lost other essential genes. YY guppy males are viable and fertile (Winge and Ditlevsen 1938; Haskins et al. 1970).

Sex-determining factors are also located on the autosomes of guppies. As a result, atypical sex determination (e.g., XX males and XY females) occasionally occurs. According to Winge (1930), XX males are produced when autosomal male-determining factors overwhelm female-determining factors on the X chromosomes. By breeding atypical XX males to close relatives, Winge (1934) was able to produce and maintain a strain of guppies that lacked normal XY males entirely. Nayudu (1979), using stocks obtained from commercial breeders, obtained XX males comprising one-fourth of the total progeny of an XY male and an XX female. One such XX male, when mated to a normal XX female, produced all-female progeny. In the case of XY females, X-linked female-determining factors combine with autosomal female-determining factors to overwhelm the influence of the Y chromosome. When an atypical XY female is mated to a normal XY male, viable YY male progeny may be produced (as long as they are not homozygous for Y-linked pigment genes [see following]). The YY males are fertile and, if mated to normal XX females, all-male XY progeny will be produced (Winge and Ditlevsen 1938).

Most cases of atypical sex determination have been observed in laboratory stocks. This may primarily reflect easier detection in these genetically characterized populations. Atypical sex determination apparently does occur outside of the laboratory. For example, Haskins et al. (1961) reported an XX male from a natural population in the Paria River of Trinidad. The frequency of atypical sex determination in nature is unknown.

The tendency to produce individuals with atypical sex seems to be a genetically determined trait. Some laboratory guppy strains produce atypical XY females much more often than do others. According to Schröder (1983), there seem to exist "weak" and "strong" Y chromosomes with regard to either the possible number of male determining factors or their biochemical strength. The weak Y chromosomes are susceptible to being overruled by female-determining autosomal genes, producing exceptional (or atypical) XY females. Kallman (1984), on the other hand, does not attribute atypical sex determination to differences between weak and strong Y chromosomes. He explains it as resulting from the interaction between autosomal genes and a sex-determining locus (*M*), present on the gonosomes.

Farr (1981) reported sex ratios of long-established laboratory strains of guppies as skewed toward females. The magnitude of the imbalance is positively correlated with the amount of time the strain has been maintained. Deficiency of males is not a result of pre- or postnatal mortality. Farr (1981) hypothesized that Y-bearing sperm may tend to become increasingly ineffective or inviable in laboratory strains through time. Any non-recombining genetic material is subject to the accumulation of deleterious genes by a process known as Muller's ratchet (Muller 1964). The portion of the Y chromosome containing most of the male-determining factors does not recombine with the X chromosome and thus shares the same susceptibilities as the genomes of asexual organisms regarding accumulation of deleterious mutations.

Part of the Y chromosome does retain the capacity to recombine with the X, presumably in a region of shared homology. Crossing over between sex chromosomes was first reported by Winge (1923). In fact, some sex-linked genes can pass between the X and Y chromosomes quite frequently by recombination. For example, the recombination frequency between the sex-linked genes Ds and Cp is about 10% (Dzwillo 1959). Nayudu (1979) was able to map certain sex-linked genes in the guppy, based on recombination analysis (see "Gene Maps" section).

The Platys and Swordtails, Genus *Xiphophorus*

The chromosomal and genetic mechanisms of sex determination in *Xiphophorus* were recently reviewed by Kallman (1984). A brief summary of the topic is presented here.

Xiphophorus maculatus (the platyfish) is unusual in having three sex chromosomes: W, X, and Y. Females may have WY, WX, or XX genotypes; males are either XY or YY. The WW (female) sex chromosome makeup has not been found in natural populations but is viable and has been produced in the laboratory (Kallman 1984).

In most of the river systems of southeastern Guatemala and Belize, where *X. maculatus* is native, extensive sampling has revealed that all three sex chromosomes occur in the same populations. The exceptions are the ríos Jamapa and Papaloapan, in Veracruz, where W has not been found (Kallman 1973). The presence of three sex chromosomes in the same population results in some matings that produce unequal sex ratios (Kallman 1965, 1973). Six different kinds of matings can occur between the three female genotypes and the two male genotypes. Of these, four produce an equal sex ratio, one produces three females for every male, and the other produces all-male progeny.

Crossing over occurs between sex chromosomes of *X. maculatus*. However, the frequency is only 0.2 to 0.3% (Bellamy and Queal 1951; Kallman 1965). Recombination data indicate that the sex-determining gene(s) is(are) located proximally, near the chromosome centromere (Anders et al. 1973; Kallman 1975).

Cases of atypical sex determination have been observed in *X. maculatus*, although the overall incidence is low (0.85%, Kallman 1984). Atypical sex determination in platyfish is genetically influenced (as in guppies), and is concentrated in a few pedigrees (Kallman 1965, 1968, 1970a).

The swordtail (*Xiphophorus helleri*) has a history of widely varying sex ratios in laboratory populations. Reports in the earlier literature might be unreliable because most of the fish were not *X. helleri*, but hybrids between *X. helleri* and *X. maculatus* backcrossed to *X. helleri* (Gordon 1937a, 1938; see Kallman 1984). One could question whether the sex ratio fluctuation was simply an effect of gene imbalance in the hybrids. This is not the case, however, because widely fluctuating sex ratios are characteristic of the species. Peters (1964) reported a stock of *X. h. helleri* that produced significantly more males than females (459 males : 164 females). She also noted that, in a Honduran stock of *X. h. guentheri*, frequencies of males produced in various crosses ranged from 18 to 70%. Male size and age at sexual maturity was also correlated with the sex ratio of their progeny. Small, early-maturing males sired significantly more male offspring; large, late-maturing males sired significantly more females. Kallman (1984) suggested that the correlation between male size and sex ratio may be a spurious one resulting from laboratory inbreeding. He provides additional data that sex ratios in many, though not all, laboratory stocks of *X. helleri* frequently deviate significantly from unity. No such correlation exists in the related *X. cortezi* (Zander 1965).

Peters (1964), following Kosswig (1964), concluded that sex determination in *X. helleri* has a polyfactorial basis. Kallman (1984) was unwilling to concur. He did agree that widely fluctuating sex ratios implied that "significant genetic differences with respect to sex determination must exist among the various stocks of *X. helleri*." However, he noted that sex ratios deviating significantly from unity cannot automatically be attributed to a polyfactorial system of sex-determining genes. For example, certain crosses in *X. maculatus* illustrate situations where significantly skewed sex ratios can be produced in a species with well-defined sex chromosomes.

Kallman (1984) concluded that the sex chromosomes of the different *Xiphophorus* spp. are homologous with one another and, presumably, represent derivatives of sex-determining chromosomes in ancestral *Xiphophorus*. In all species, sporadic cases of atypical sex determination occur. This phenomenon has a genetic basis and is caused by interaction between a sex-determining locus (M), present on all sex chromosomes but with different controlling elements on each type, and autosomal modifier genes that determine whether or not the M locus is transcribed. Thus, in Kallman's model, the control elements on the sex chromosomes are the true sex-determining genes, because they represent the only consistent genetic difference between males and females.

The Mollies, *Poecilia latipinna*, *P. sphenops*, and *P. velifera*

Little work has been done on the genetics of sex determination in mollies. Schröder (1964) hybridized various domestic stocks of mollies and, based on sex ratios in hybrid progeny, concluded that *P. velifera* and *P. latipinna* have XX,

XY sex determining mechanisms. *P. sphenops*, on the other hand, apparently had both male (XX, XY) and female (WZ, ZZ) heterogamy. No sex-linked traits, which might provide useful information regarding the chromosomal basis of sex determination, have been found in the mollies.

The Mosquitofishes, Genus *Gambusia*

Black and Howell (1979) identified a large heteromorphic sex chromosome pair in female western mosquitofish, *Gambusia affinis affinis*, indicative of a WZ-ZZ sex determining mechanism. They noted, however, that female eastern mosquitofish, *G. a. holbrooki*, lacked the WZ chromosome pair. Recently, Angus (unpubl. data) produced evidence, based on sex-linked inheritance of melanistic spotting in a strain of eastern mosquitofish, that *G. a. holbrooki* has an XX-XY sex chromosome system. In one of two stocks studied, the melanism trait showed a pattern of almost complete holandric inheritance. Holandric inheritance, in which the trait is expressed only in males and is inherited by all sons of a male with the trait, is compatible with an XX-XY sex determining system, but not WZ-ZZ. It thus appears that the eastern and western mosquitofish, although closely related (traditionally considered to be subspecies but recently argued to be distinct at the species level [Wooten et al. 1988; Smith et al., Chapter 13]), do not share the same chromosomal sex determining mechanism.

GENETICS OF PIGMENTATION

Some poeciliid fishes, notably the guppy (*Poecilia reticulata*) and various platyfishes (genus *Xiphophorus*), are popular as aquarium fishes, primarily because they display a phenomenal diversity of genetically determined pigment patterns. The patterns are usually displayed only by males, and the genes responsible are often sex-linked. Abundant evidence indicates that, in general, conspicuous pigmentation may be advantageous in males, both for agonistic and courtship behavior (Farr 1976; Endler 1980, 1983). The literature on inheritance of pigmentation patterns in poeciliid fishes is vast and extends back more than 70 years. A number of reviews already exist on the topic (Goodrich 1929; Gordon and Gordon 1957; Dzwillo 1959; Atz 1962; Kosswig 1965; Kallman and Atz 1966; Schröder 1974, 1976; Kallman 1975; Yamamoto 1975; Kirpichnikov 1981). Thus, only a general summary will be presented here.

Poeciliid pigmentation results from the combined effect of a variety of different pigment cells distributed in the dermis and epidermis: melanophores (black), xanthophores (yellow), erythrophores (red), and iridophores (reflecting) (Fujii 1969). All are derived from a common embryonic stem cell of neural crest origin (Bagnara et al. 1979). This is thought to be accomplished by differentiation of a primordial organelle into any of the specific pigment-synthesizing organelles characteristic of the various pigment cells.

Micromelanophores are small melanin-containing pigment cells that tend to occur on the edges of scale pockets and, since the scales are arranged in a series of offset overlapping rows, form a network pattern. Micromelanophores tend to visually blend together to influence overall pigmentation. Macromelanophores, in contrast, are much larger (up to 500 microns in diameter), highly pigmented cells, easily seen individually. Aggregations of macromelanophores on various regions of the body are the basis for a number of inherited melanistic spotting patterns.

The Guppy, *Poecilia reticulata*

Male guppies typically display diverse, bright, and colorful pigment patterns; females tend to be unspectacular, usually an olivaceous grey. Pigment polymorphism is a natural phenomenon that occurs in wild populations as well as in domestic stocks (Haskins and Haskins 1951, 1954; Haskins et al. 1961; Endler 1980, 1983). In fact, the diversity of color patterns is so great that, in natural populations in Trinidad and northeastern Venezuela, no two males are identical (Endler 1983). Breeding studies reveal that most of the genes responsible for pigmentation patterns are located on the X or Y chromosomes. As early as 1919, Schmidt (1919) established that many guppy color genes are carried on the Y chromosome and are thus holandrically inherited. Winge (1922a, 1927) determined that, whereas some color genes are always on the Y chromosome, others may be X- or Y-linked as a result of crossing over.

Mutations affecting each of the pigment cell types (melanophores, erythrophores, xanthophores, and guanophores) have been described (Schröder 1969). Kirpichnikov (1981) lists 17 pigmentation traits that always show Y-linked (holandric) inheritance, 16 traits that may be on the X or Y chromosome but which are male sex-limited (most strongly or exclusively expressed in males), and 5 autosomally inherited traits, one of which is male sex-limited. The male sex-limited traits require androgenic hormone for expression. Older female guppies that have become reproductively senile may express pigmentation genes that are normally male-limited (Kirpichnikov 1981). This apparently results from the hormone environment becoming more masculine after the piscine equivalent of menopause. It is possible to induce the expression of male-limited traits in females by administering androgenic hormones (Hildemann 1954; Dzwillo 1962, 1966; Haskins et al. 1970). This makes it possible to identify the female's genotype for genes affecting traits that are normally male-limited.

With one exception (Natali and Natali 1931) all of the exclusively Y-linked traits appear to represent multiple allelic variation at a single gene locus. Any particular Y chromosome will carry the gene for only a single Y-linked color pattern (Kirpichnikov 1981). All of the sex-linked color pattern genes, both those exclusively Y-linked, and those found on both X and Y, act as dominants. When two or more are present in a single male, their effects are additive. Almost all of the sex-linked pigmentation traits are completely male sex-limited in expression (Haskins et al. 1970).

It appears that many, if not all, guppy Y chromosomes carry recessive lethal genes. For example, YY males homozygous for the *Ma* (maculatus), *Ar* (Armatus), or *Pa* (Pauper) Y-linked genes are inviable (Winge and Ditlevsen 1938; Haskins et al. 1970). Each of these genes, in addition to influencing pigmentation, may also function as a distinct recessive lethal. This is supported by the fact that YY males heterozygous for any of these genes are viable. Another possibility is that these genes are closely linked to recessive lethal genes and that each is linked to a different allele. This is supported by Haskins et al.'s (1970) collection of a single $Y_{Ma}\ Y_{Ma}$ male that was both viable and fertile. The authors speculated that the pigment gene and its associated lethal had been separated by recombination in one of the Y chromosomes present in this exceptional male. Thus, although he was homozygous for the *Ma* allele, he was not homozygous for the (usually) closely linked lethal gene. Allelic diversity of pigmentation genes is probably adaptively advantageous in natural guppy populations. This is the most likely reason that such diversity of pigment phenotypes has evolved. In this case, the presence of tightly linked lethal genes serves to promote heterozygosity and to reduce the probability of random loss of alleles due to inbreeding in small populations.

The Platyfish, *Xiphophorus maculatus*

Along with the guppy, the platyfish is one of the genetically best-characterized poeciliid fishes, with genetic studies ongoing since the early 1900s. Kallman and Atz (1966) and Kallman (1975) summarize much of that work.

Platyfish are highly polymorphic for numerous genetically determined pigment patterns, many of which are sex-linked. More than 130 pigmentation types have been identified in nature (Gordon and Gordon 1957; Kallman and Atz 1966; Kallman 1975). Although the number of possible phenotypes is large, the number of major genes controlling this variability is relatively small; phenotypic diversity is due to segregation of numerous alleles at each locus.

Gordon (1948) recognized five macromelanophore patterns in *X. maculatus* from natural populations. He considered them to comprise a multiple allelic series: *Sp* (spot sided), *Sd* (spotted dorsal), *Sr* (stripe sided), *N* (nigra), and *Sb* (black bottom). Patterns are controlled by dominant sex-linked genes tightly linked to the sex-determining locus (<1% recombination). According to Kallman (1975), the genetic basis for these patterns is more complicated than originally thought. The patterns seem to be controlled by a number of closely linked genes, each of which can exist in several allelic states. In many cases, identical macromelanophore patterns have been shown to have a different genetic basis in different river systems (Kallman 1975). This implies that the patterns have an adaptive significance, because they apparently evolved independently more than once.

Genes that control the pterin (red) and carotenoid (yellow) patterns in *X. maculatus* are closely linked to the macromelanophore loci. Originally, only four patterns were known: *Dr* (red dorsal fin), *Ar* (red anal fin), *Rt* (ruby throat), and *R* (red body, or rubra) (Gordon 1927, 1946; Öktay 1964). However, recent collections from wild populations have identified at least 18 red or yellow patterns, and presumably many more remain to be discovered (Kallman 1975; Borowsky and Kallman 1976). All red patterns are more strongly expressed in males than in females, due to the influence of androgenic hormones (Valenti 1972). The extent of difference in expression between sexes is variable, however. In some populations the patterns are entirely male-limited; at the other extreme, the patterns are expressed almost equally in the sexes (Valenti and Kallman 1973). Yellow patterns show equal expression in both sexes. Genes controlling both the red and yellow patterns are located between the sex-determining locus and the macromelanophore locus (Gordon 1927, 1937b, 1950; Öktay 1964; Kallman and Schreibman 1971). The existence of sex chromosomes carrying two red or yellow alleles implies the existence of several gene loci, but the number and linkage order have not been determined (Kallman 1975).

Kallman and Brunetti (1983) identified two autosomal loci that control the presence or absence of micromelanophores and xanthophores in scale epidermis. *St* - *R* - fish had wild-type coloration. The *St* - *r r* genotype produced "gray" fish which lacked xanthophores, but had a normal micromelanophore pattern. Fish of the genotype *st st R* - were uniformly gold. They had many more xanthophores than normal, but almost no micromelanophores. The double recessive fish, *st st r r*, had a whitish "ghost" appearance due to the absence of both melanophores and xanthophores in the integument. The *St* locus had only a minor effect on expression of the sex-linked macromelanophore patterns. Similarly, the *R* locus had no effect on expression of the sex-linked xanthophore and xantho-erythrophore patterns. The authors concluded that several main embryonic lineages of pigment cells exist in *X. maculatus* and that the *St* and *R* loci act on only one of those lines. They felt that the *St* locus of *X. maculatus* is homologous to the *B* locus of *Poecilia reticulata*, and the *R* locus may be homologous to the *R* locus of *Poecilia reticulata* and the *Gr* locus of *Poeciliopsis viriosa*.

Eight alleles are known at the autosomal tailspot locus (Gordon and Gordon 1957; Kallman 1975). They appear to represent a pseudoallelic series, because some chromosomes possess the factors for two patterns (Kallman and Atz 1966; Kallman 1975). The tailspot alleles are codominant to each other, and the wild type (unspotted) is the universal recessive. Frequencies of tailspot alleles differ significantly among wild populations (Kallman 1975). Two modifier genes have been discovered that specifically interact with two tailspot alleles, but not with others, to produce new patterns (Gordon 1956). Three other species of *Xiphophorus* are polymorphic at the same tailspot locus (*X. variatus*, *X. xiphidium*, and *X. milleri*); some alleles are shared by more than one species (Kallman 1975). Three species (*X. montezumae*, *X. cortezi*, and *X. nigrensis*) share a polymorphism at the autosomal caudal blot locus that is not homologous to the tailspot locus of the preceding species.

The Swordtail, *Xiphophorus helleri*

The sex-determining mechanism of *X. helleri* is unknown; sex is usually considered to be determined by segregation of autosomal polygenes (but see Kallman [1968, 1984] for a different view). This is consistent with the fact that all pigmentation genes known in the swordtail show autosomal inheritance patterns. *X. alvarezi*, a swordtail closely related to *X. helleri*, has sex-linked pigmentation traits that affect color of the male sword. Inheritance patterns of these traits imply the existence of a WY-YY sex determining mechanism (Kallman and Bao 1987).

In several populations of *X. h. guentheri* and *X. h. strigatus*, a small proportion of fish exhibit macromelanophore spotting (Rosen 1960). One such pattern was described by Atz (1962), originally called *Sp* but later (Kallman and Atz 1966) as *Db* for dabbed, referring to the irregular size and distribution of spots. It is inherited as an autosomal dominant with 100% penetrance and is homozygous in the Bx swordtail strain. Another strain (Hx), of independent origin from the Bx strain, also carries a dominant autosomal gene for melanistic spotting. However, the spotting pattern is different from that of Bx and is apparently due to a different gene (Kallman and Atz 1966).

A number of color patterns exist in domestic swordtail stocks that are not found in wild populations. These stocks are of hybrid origin and the pigment genes were derived from some species other than *X. helleri*. The orange or orange-red coloration with numerous black spots in the "Montezuma swordtail" appears to be due to introgression of the platyfish genes striped (*Sr*) and red dorsal (*Dr*) (Gordon 1943, 1948). At least two other genes for color patterns of unknown origin have been recorded in domesticated stocks: seminigra (*Sn*), which causes black pigmentation on the lower half of the body, and rubescens (*Rb*), which causes red coloration over much of the body (Breider 1938; Kosswig 1939). Kosswig (1961) and Öktay (1964) concluded that *Rb* was a *X. maculatus* gene introgressed into domestic swordtails.

Xiphophorus variatus

Borowsky (1984) recently reviewed the genetics of pigment variation in *Xiphophorus variatus* from an evolutionary perspective. He noted that *X. variatus* rivals *X. maculatus* in degree of polymorphism. There are six known tailspot patterns and nine sex-linked macromelanophore patterns in *X. variatus*. Borowsky concentrated his review on the tailspot polymorphism and presented evidence that the genetic variability reflects the action of different selection pressures in a variable environment. He also presented evidence that the presence of different pigmentation patterns was correlated with different morphological and physiological characteristics upon which selection could act.

The Gordon-Kosswig Melanoma System

In certain hybrids of the genus *Xiphophorus*, melanomas develop spontaneously and predictably. This phenomenon has been studied since the 1920s (e.g., Bellamy 1924; Haüssler 1928; Kosswig 1929; Gordon 1931, 1951a, 1951b) and, in honor of early researchers, is known as the Gordon-Kosswig melanoma system in platyfishes. These pigment tumors constitute one of the best examples that some neoplasms are under strict genetic control (Kallman 1975). For an excellent, detailed explanation and review of the system, see Vielkind and Vielkind (1982).

A typical hybrid cross involves a strain of platyfish, *X. maculatus*, carrying a gene for a macromelanophore pattern, such as *Sd* (spotted dorsal) or *Sp* (spot-sided), crossed with a laboratory stock of the swordtail, *X. helleri*, which does not develop macromelanophores. The F_1 progeny develop macromelanophores on the dorsal fin (*Sd*) or flank (*Sp*), depending on the genes contributed by *X. maculatus*. The degree of melanophore development in the F_1 progeny is significantly greater than in the platyfish parent. If the F_1s are backcrossed to swordtails, one quarter of the progeny develop benign melanomas, one quarter have malignant melanomas, and one half develop no melanoma. Melanomas occur in hybrids between different geographical populations of platyfish, *X. maculatus*, as well as in platyfish-swordtail hybrids (Gordon 1957). It appears that each of the different platyfish populations has evolved its own balanced system of modifying genes to inhibit overproduction and abnormal growth of macromelanophores. The process of segregation in hybrids, by placing chromosomes against novel genetic backgrounds, serves to unbalance the system.

A genetic model of melanoma in *Xiphophorus* (see Vielkind and Vielkind 1982; Anders et al. 1984a, 1984b) reflects the fact that malignancy is not a simple gene defect but, rather, a failure of multiple interacting structural and regulatory genes. Anders et al. (1974, 1980) argued that macromelanophores are neoplastically transformed pigment cells. The transformation is encoded by a gene, called *Tu* (for tumor), located near the end of the X chromosome of *X. maculatus* (Anders et al. 1984b). This same gene apparently is also responsible for a variety of carcinogen-induced neurogenic, epithelial, and mesenchymal neoplasms (Anders and Anders 1978; Schwab et al. 1978). According to the model, an *X. maculatus* with a macromelanophore pattern, such as spot-sided, carries a *Tu* gene that causes the production of macromelanophores. The fish does not develop melanoma because of the effects of other regulator genes, some of which are located on the X chromosome (linked regulators), whereas others are located on other chromosomes (nonlinked).

A nonlinked regulator gene, called R_{Diff}, or simply *Diff* (Vielkind 1976), prevents melanoma by influencing terminal differentiation of the macromelanophores. Its effects are dosage dependent; a single dose suppresses formation of malignant melanoma and a double dose completely suppresses melanoma formation

(Anders et al. 1980). This gene segregates nonrandomly with one or more esterase-encoding gene loci (Ahuja et al. 1980). Morizot and Siciliano (1983b) determined that a factor (probably *Diff*) that controlled development of inherited melanomas was linked to a group of three linked protein-encoding loci, including two esterase loci, designated as linkage group V.

Studies by Kallman (1970b) and Kallman and Schreibman (1971) provided evidence for linked genes that regulate the expression of macromelanophores. Expression may be increased after crossing-over occurs between the sex chromosomes, and the enhanced expression is stably inherited. They attributed the phenomenon to separation of the macromelanophore allele from a closely linked regulating element. Anders et al. (1973) studied the effects of radiation-induced mutations on macromelanophore expression; mutants showed Mendelian inheritance of altered macromelanophore patterns. Mutation only affected expression of the macromelanophore gene on the same chromosome (i.e., *cis* configuration). The authors suggested that different macromelanophore alleles represent gene complexes, each consisting of a macromelanophore gene and a pattern-specific linked regulator.

Kallman (1975) pointed out some phenomena not easily explained in context of the current *Xiphophorus* melanoma model. For example, according to the model, modifier genes reduce or restrict pigmentation; thus, enhancement after hybridization results from loss of control. This is inconsistent with the fact that a number of pigment genes of the Jamapa population of *X. maculatus* do not develop melanoma after hybridization, but instead often show reduced expression. Recombination between linked pigmentation genes also has produced some perplexing results (Kallman and Schreibman 1971). Hereditary changes at the *Sd* locus of Jamapa produced a new, exaggerated spotted-dorsal phenotype and linkage of *Sd* and *Sr*, apparently as a result of recombination. Surprisingly, the interaction of *Sd*, in combination with a *X. couchianus* gene pool, went in opposite directions, depending on the allele to which it was linked. When linked to an Sr^+ allele, it went to zero penetrance in the hybrid. The same *Sd* allele, linked to an *Sr* allele, produced melanosis and melanoma in the hybrid.

The Sailfin Mollies, *Poecilia latipinna* and *Poecilia sphenops*

Schröder (1964) studied inheritance of melanistic spotting (due to macromelanophores scattered over the body) in domestic molly stocks. Varying intensities of melanism in *P. sphenops* were explained by the action of two independently assorting gene pairs, *N* and *M*. If three or four of these dominant alleles were present (*NN MM*, *NN Mm*, or *Nn MM*), then totally black progeny were obtained. If only two alleles were inherited (*NN mm*, *nn MM*, or *Nn Mm*), the fish were strongly spotted. A single allele produced weak spotting, and the wild-type genotype (*nn mm*) produced no spotting. In contrast, melanism in the sailfin molly, *P. latipinna*, was inherited as an autosomal single-gene trait. Based on the progeny ratio of a single mating, Schröder (1964) concluded that the gene responsible for melanistic spotting in *P. latipinna* is homologous to the *M* gene in *P. sphenops*. The substantial variation in degree of melanistic spotting between different sailfins with the same *M* genotype was ascribed to the action of modifiers (Schröder 1964).

Angus (1983) studied inheritance of melanistic spotting in a strain of *P. latipinna* from Key Largo, Florida. Melanistic spotting was inherited as an autosomal single-gene trait, *M*, and expression was highly temperature sensitive. Penetrance and expressivity of *M* were maximal when fish were raised at 22° C, at which *M* was dominant in heterozygotes, with 100% penetrance. It showed much reduced penetrance and expressivity at 28° C, almost always acting as a recessive in heterozygotes; spotting was induced within six weeks by transferring fish to cool conditions.

Mosquitofishes, genus *Gambusia*

Wild populations of the eastern mosquitofish, *Gambusia affinis holbrooki*, contain rare males with a melanistic color pattern due to dermal macromelanophores scattered over the body (Regan 1961; Martin 1977). Virtually all melanistic fish in wild populations are males. However, Snelson et al. (1986a) reported a single melanistic female from a population in central Florida; she produced a melanistic female progeny in the laboratory. The degree of melanism is highly variable among individuals, which led Regan (1961) to speculate that the melanistic phenotype may be modified by environmental factors, particularly temperature.

Early attempts to determine inheritance of melanistic spotting in mosquitofish were not successful (Regan 1961; Martin 1984), probably because the progeny were not raised under controlled temperatures. Recently Angus (unpubl. data) determined that, in one of two stocks studied, melanistic spotting showed nearly complete holandric inheritance characteristic of a Y-linked trait. The melanism allele was temperature sensitive, with maximal penetrance and expressivity at a relatively cool 22° C. Penetrance and expressivity were much reduced under warmer conditions.

With reference to the melanoma model developed in *Xiphophorus*, the macromelanophore-inducing genes in sailfin mollies and mosquitofish appear to represent the equivalent of the *Tu* gene, but without any linked modifier controlling body location of the macromelanophore pattern. Macromelanophores in mollies and mosquitofish are randomly distributed over the body and the pattern is different in every individual. Another difference is strong temperature-dependent expression of the macromelanophore-inducing gene. With mollies or mosquitofish, it is possible to raise fish to adulthood with the macromelanophore-inducing gene unexpressed and then, by lowering temperature, to induce development of macromelanophores. This demonstrates that some cells in adult fish retain the ability to become macromelanophores; the process is not restricted to immature embryonic cells.

The Genus *Poeciliopsis*

Unlike the previous genera, *Poeciliopsis* is not known for extraordinary pigment polymorphism. Nevertheless, the genetic bases of a few pigment variants have been reported.

Moore (1974) reported on a piebald mutation in *P. lucida*, designated as transparent (*tr*). The *tr* allele causes a patchy absence of iridophores and noncontractible melanophores lining the coelom, and has no visible effect on contractible melanophores. The allele was probably segregating in a natural population; it was observed in second- and third-generation progeny descended from a wild-caught female.

Vrijenhoek (1976) described an autosomal recessive gene, gray (*gr*), affecting the distribution of yellow xanthophores on the scales and fins of *P. viriosa*. The gene was discovered in a laboratory population after six generations of inbreeding and, thus, was considered likely to exist as a natural polymorphism. Males homozygous for the mutant allele were unable to display the normal brassy display coloration typical of the species.

MENDELIAN INHERITANCE OF OTHER TRAITS

Although classical genetic studies with poeciliid fishes have tended to concentrate on the impressively polymorphic pigmentary systems, other hereditary variants do occur and have occasionally been characterized.

The Guppy, *Poecilia reticulata*

In the guppy, a number of the X- and Y-linked alleles affecting pigmentation also produce elongation of fin rays, especially of the caudal fin (e.g., Lineatus, Doppelschwert). These are male sex-limited traits and are the causes of overdeveloped fins in commercial guppy stocks. A number of autosomal mutations also affect various morphological traits such as vertebral column (e.g., hunch-back, curvatus, Palla), eyes (coecus), and fins (elongated, Kalymma). These genes are expressed in both sexes and show Mendelian inheritance (see Kirpichnikov 1981).

Several quantitative genetic studies have focused on inheritance of fin ray number in guppies. Schmidt (1919) and Svärdson (1945) demonstrated that fin ray numbers in guppies respond to selection. Tave (1984), analyzing Schmidt's (1919) data, found "large" heritabilities for dorsal fin ray number; five of six estimates were significantly different from zero. Heritabilities of the same magnitude were observed by Beardmore and Shami (1976) for caudal ray number.

Schröder (1965) investigated inheritance of dorsal fin ray numbers in *Poecilia* hybrids (*Poecilia reticulata, P. sphenops,* and *P. velifera*). He concluded that the number of dorsal fin rays was determined by independently recombining polygenes. He indicated that the number of genes that determine fin ray number are relatively few (10 to 20).

Platyfish, Genus *Xiphophorus*

The so-called "Simpson" form of *X. helleri* expresses elongated dorsal fin rays in both sexes. Schröder (1966) determined that the trait was inherited as an autosomal dominant gene, *Da*. Heterozygote matings did not produce any *Da Da* homozygotes. Schröder explained this as an incompatibility mechanism preventing the joining of two *Da*-carrying gametes. Schröder also stated that females heterozygous for the Simpson factor produced an excess of eggs with the wild-type allele and a deficiency of eggs with the *Da* allele, apparently because of a directed reduction division.

Poeciliopsis

Schultz (1963) reported a recessive mutation (stubby) in laboratory stocks of *P. prolifica*. The mutant phenotype was characterized by regions of vertebral fusions that shorten the vertebral column. This changed the relative position of various parts of the skeleton and produced an increased number of internal skeletal gonopodial supports in males. As a result, males, although fertile, were unable to copulate.

Segregation Studies with Isozymes

Most populations of plants and animals maintain considerable levels of protein polymorphism. It has been popular over the past 20 years to survey that variation to provide data on genetic variability within and between natural populations (see Echelle et al., Chapter 12). Leslie and Vrijenhoek (1977) noted that, in most surveys, a polymorphism was assumed to have a genetic basis if the diploid genotypic frequencies fit Hardy-Weinberg expectations. This is, at best, a weak test. Leslie and Vrijenhoek (1977) went on to document the genetic bases of seven polymorphic proteins in *Poeciliopsis monacha*. Morizot and Siciliano (1983a) agreed, noting that "it is important to assess critically the segregation of allozyme phenotypes and thus of presumed genotypes under a codominant inheritance model, particularly in interspecific crosses." In their review, which included 40 protein-encoding loci in various *Xiphophorus* species, they concluded that, in general, the biochemical loci segregate in backcrosses and intercrosses in excellent agreement with the Mendelian expectations. Morizot and Siciliano (1983a) also noticed no large-scale heterotic effects or excessive homozygosity in interspecific *Xiphophorus* hybrids. It thus appeared that no chromosomal incompatibilities existed that could produce segregation distortion and make it impossible to assess linkage relationships between loci using interspecific hybrids.

GENE MAPS

An important part of thorough genetic study of any related group of organisms is mapping identified genes. Knowledge of the chromosomal location of various genes is useful in evaluating possible gene homology between species and in assessing linkage group conservation during evolution. Although the amount of gene mapping in poeciliid fishes is not extensive, a number of pigmentation and protein-encoding genes have been mapped.

Guppies have numerous sex chromosome-linked genes that affect pigmentation. Many of these lie on a region where the X and Y chromosomes share homology and can cross over. It has thus been possible to map a number of genes by recombination analysis (Winge 1934; Winge and Ditlevsen 1938; summarized by Kirpichnikov 1981). The map includes the portion of the Y chromosome that does not recombine with the X, followed by the pigmentation genes *Co*, *Ti*, *Lu*, *Vi*, and *El* (in that order). More recently, Nayudu (1979) mapped the loci *N-II*, *Fl*, and *Cp* in that order, but did not relate them to the genes mapped by Winge and Ditlevsen (1938).

Most gene mapping in poeciliid fishes has involved electrophoretically surveyed loci. Morizot and Siciliano (1983a) reviewed their extensive and ongoing work on linkage relationships of protein-encoding loci in the genus *Xiphophorus*. Of approximately 100 loci characterized in *Xiphophorus* spp., electrophoretic variants had been identified at 64. Of the 64, 40 had been assessed to some degree for segregation and linkage relationships. Morizot and Siciliano (1983a) noted substantial divergence at structural genes between *Xiphophorus* species. It is not unusual for two species to differ in allozymes at 20 enzyme loci. Fortunately for recombination analysis, the capability of producing fertile interspecific hybrids has been maintained, permitting analysis of segregation in backcrosses of F_1 hybrids between various species. Morizot and Siciliano (1983a) thus described six independent linkage groups in *Xiphophorus* and another two provisionally independent groups. They found no cases of nonhomology between species studied and concluded that many, if not most, gene arrangements are homologous within the genus.

The other poeciliid genus with significant investigation of linkage relationships is *Poeciliopsis*. Leslie (1982) examined inheritance patterns for 17 loci encoding enzymatic and nonenzymatic proteins. With one exception, which was probably due to chance, alleles at all loci segregated in a Mendelian fashion. Backcrosses utilizing *monacha/viriosa* hybrids identified one five-point linkage group and six independently assorting loci. Backcrosses utilizing *lucida/occidentalis* hybrids identified two two-point groups and five independently assorting loci.

Of the 17 loci studied, 12 are probably homologous to loci studied in *Xiphophorus* (Morizot and Siciliano 1983a). Of the five-point linkage group, three loci are also linked in *Xiphophorus*. Additionally, recombination frequencies between these genes are similar in the two species. Among the 35 pairs of probably homologous loci tested in both *Poeciliopsis* and *Xiphophorus*, no conclusive disagreements were observed. For a comparison of poeciliid linkage groups with those of other fishes and other vertebrates, see Morizot and Siciliano (1983a). Certain linkage groups appear to have long-term stability throughout the evolution of vertebrates. As noted by Morizot and Siciliano (1983a), such instances of highly conserved linkage relationships may imply functional significance on a structural or regulatory level.

GENETICS OF THE HISTOCOMPATIBILITY SYSTEM

Kallman (1960, 1964a, 1975) has used inbred *X. maculatus* strains to study the genetics of tissue transplantation. He used fin grafts, which are known to survive only if all or almost all of the donor's histocompatibility alleles are also present in the host. Kallman's experiments used a principle that has been useful in histocompatibility studies in mammals. A certain percentage of the progeny of F_2 and backcross generations will share one complete set of all histocompatibility factors of one or the other parental strain. The percentage will depend on the number of factors that exist. Using this method, Kallman (1964a) estimated the total number of histocompatibility loci in *X. maculatus* at 10 to 15. By comparing the antigenicity of different grafts, Kallman (1960) was able to demonstrate a dosage effect. In general, the more histocompatibility alleles differing between donor and host, the more rapid the graft rejection. Survival time of allografts also depended on tissue type. Heart tissue was more resistant to allograft rejection than were fins.

With the knowledge that the histocompatibility system in fish is as complex as that in mammals has come application of that system for other purposes. Tissue grafting has been used to demonstrate a high degree of inbreeding in natural populations of sexually reproducing fishes (Kallman 1964b) and to confirm a high homozygosity level in laboratory stocks that have been inbred for many years (Angus and Schultz 1979). Grafting studies have been useful in demonstrating clonal reproduction in various natural unisexual populations (Moore 1977b; Angus and Schultz 1979; Dawley et al. 1987) and in identifying clonal diversity in these populations (Moore and Eisenbrey 1979; Angus and Schultz 1979; Angus 1980; Schultz, Chapter 5; Balsano et al., Chapter 15).

SUMMARY AND FUTURE RESEARCH

Some poeciliid fishes have cytologically distinguishable sex chromosomes, but others lack them. Even where they are distinguishable, the sex chromosomes are in a rather primitive state of differentiation and seem to be of relatively recent evolutionary origin. Sex-determining factors are located not only on the sex chromosomes, but also on autosomes. Situations in which autosomal sex-determining factors "overrule" factors on the sex chromosomes to produce atypical sex determination (e.g., XX males or XY females) are fairly common. The sex chromosomes retain relatively large regions of homology, and crossing over between them is not unusual. In fact, traditional recombination analysis has been employed to map genes on the sex chromosomes. At present, the sex-determining mechanisms of relatively few poeciliid fishes are known. It would benefit our understanding of sex determination in fish, and vertebrates in general, if breadth of knowledge on this topic were increased by studying more species. The interaction effects between genetic sex-determining mechanisms and environmental factors have been little studied, and more needs to be done in this area. Kallman (1984) proposed a model of sex determination, mainly derived from work with *Xiphophorus*. Studies of sex determination in other species will help test Kallman's model and determine its generality.

Some poeciliids, especially guppies and platyfishes, display a phenomenal diversity of genetically determined pigment patterns and have been the subject of extensive investigations. Most patterns are sex chromosome-linked and more strongly or exclusively displayed by males. Those present in wild populations probably evolved for sexual display functions and are maintained by sexual selection. Polymorphism for pigment alleles seems to be maintained by a series of linked recessive lethals that prevent homozygosity. Hybrids in the genus *Xiphophorus* have been extremely useful as a model for studying gene interaction involved in the regulation of melanoma. In certain hybrids, melanomas develop spontaneously and predictably. Even today, these fish provide one of the best examples that some neoplasias are under strict genetic control. Further studies with these fish will continue to add to our understanding of the genetic factors involved in malignant transformation. Studies with other poeciliids will be useful for comparative purposes and will permit us to address several questions. For example, what factors make certain *Xiphophorus* hybrids so susceptible to melanoma? What is different about other related fish, which also express macromelanophores, but do not have such a tendency to develop melanoma?

Gene mapping with poeciliids has been done with pigmentation genes (sex chromosomes) and protein-determining genes that can be surveyed electrophoretically. A number of linkage groups have been identified and comparisons made between species. Present data indicate that some linkage associations have been highly conserved throughout vertebrate evolution. Such conservation of linkage groups implies the presence of functional or regulatory interdependence. Expansion of the data base by mapping more loci in more species may well identify other functionally interrelated gene groups.

Poeciliid fishes have functional immune systems; acceptance or rejection of tissue grafts is controlled by a genetically complex histocompatibility system. Studies with fish have provided information on the evolution of the immune system in vertebrates. Tissue grafting studies with fish have also helped detect presence or lack of recombination in suspected asexual forms and levels of genetic variability in unisexual complexes.

ACKNOWLEDGMENTS

I thank Kathy Angus, James W. Atz, Paul Blanchard, Klaus Kallman, and an anonymous reviewer for helpful editorial suggestions. James Atz kindly made available an extensive bibliography on fish genetics that he has accumulated over many years.

Chapter 5

Origins and Relationships of Unisexual Poeciliids

R. JACK SCHULTZ

INTRODUCTION: DISCOVERY OF THE FIRST ALL-FEMALE VERTEBRATE

More than half a century has passed since the discovery (Hubbs and Hubbs 1932) of the first all-female fish, *Poecilia formosa*; yet most people, including many biologists, are surprised to learn that animals as advanced as vertebrates dare depart so drastically from traditional reproduction.

The existence of poeciliid populations comprised mostly of females was not the conspicuous key to discovering the first all-female fish, commonly called the Amazon molly (after a legendary race of female warriors). Rather, it was a product of Carl Hubbs's combined interest in hybridization and cyprinodont systematics that drew his attention to hybrids between "species so distinct that they were long placed in different genera" (Hubbs and Hubbs 1932). The two species, *Poecilia mexicana* and *Poecilia latipinna*, at that time were known as *Mollienesia sphenops* and *M. latipinna*. Initially, *P. formosa* itself was regarded as a distinct species, an error that is understandable because both male and female *formosa*-like hybrids occur at localities where *sphenops* and *latipinna* coexist (e.g., in the Río Papaloapan). When *formosa* lives only with *latipinna* (as in Texas) or only with *sphenops* (inland in Tamaulipis, Mexico), F_1 hybrids are not found. Regardless of the species with which *formosa* lives and the geographic distance between populations, *formosa* females studied by Hubbs looked alike and were morphologically intermediate to *sphenops* and *latipinna*.

Crosses in the laboratory between *sphenops* and *latipinna* resulted in offspring of both sexes, thus accounting for the presence of male and female *formosa*-like offspring where the parental species coexist. Although the Hubbses were able to synthesize a morph comparable to *formosa*, in 12 years of experimentation (Hubbs 1955) they were not able to produce the all-female "species"[1] itself. The F_1 progeny, as well as backcrosses in either direction, resulted in both sexes and normal segregation of quantitatively inherited traits. For example, the dorsal fin of *latipinna* is long, with 13 to 15 rays; that of *sphenops* originates farther back and has fewer rays, usually 9 in the subspecies used. Although the F_1 offspring, like *formosa*, had 10 to 12 dorsal rays, backcross progeny in either direction were intermediate between the F_1 and the high- or low-rayed P_1 used. Matings of *formosa* to either phenotype or to other species, even as distantly related as *Gambusia affinis*, did not alter the *formosa* appearance of progeny in the paternal direction. Because unmated Amazon mollies did not reproduce, the Hubbses believed parthenogenesis could be ruled out but that "gynogenesis" was the proper term (Hubbs and Hubbs 1932) for this mechanism wherein "development is initiated by sperm which for some reason is prevented from taking part in heredity." Hubbs (pers. comm.) believed that successful synthesis of *formosa* depended on combining *sphenops* and *latipinna* from the proper river system.

From the 12 years of experimentation with *P. formosa*, none of the data produced by the Hubbses, nor the details of the crosses, has been published. Dr. Carl Hubbs offered the preserved material to several young fish geneticists, but they always had their own backlog of material to analyze. Although Carl Hubbs died in 1981 at the age of 84 and Laura Hubbs died in 1988 at 95, the specimens from their experiments are still available at the Scripps Institution of Oceanography at La Jolla, California.

The discovery (Miller and Schultz 1959) of the second unisexual fish, also a poeciliid (genus *Poeciliopsis*), came 27 years later in the same laboratory at the University of Michigan where *P. formosa* was unmasked. As with *formosa*, discovery of unisexuality in *Poeciliopsis* was through inquiry into morphological differences and taxonomic relationships rather than the perception of an all-female "species." At the time, Robert R. Miller was attempting to delimit about a half-dozen undescribed species of *Poeciliopsis* from northwestern Mexico. In populations of two tentative species, *P.* "F" (later referred to as *P. occidentalis*) and *P.* "C" (later described as *P. lucida*, Miller 1960), two kinds of females were noted, those that had dentition like the male and those that had an "aberrant dentition," which referred to both the pattern and number of teeth. When pregnant females from nature were brought into the lab, those with "normal" dentition produced male and female offspring at ratios of approximately 1:1, whereas those with the "aberrant" dentition gave birth to only female offspring. Miller designated these two all female-producing fishes as *P.* C_x and *P.* F_x, subsets of the tentative species with which they were found. Miller's initial reaction was that, like *Poecilia formosa*,

---

[1] The quotation marks are mine to indicate that I do not consider this or any of the known unisexual fishes to be full species. Unisexual hybrids, whether they reproduce by gynogenesis, parthenogenesis, or hybridogenesis, should not be considered full species until it is demonstrated that they have evolved adaptations distinct from parental biotypes and have assumed evolutionary directions that are different and independent of them.

they probably reproduced gynogenetically. This view was soon set aside, however, by mating experiments demonstrating that offspring from $P.$ C_x and $P.$ F_x, although consistently female, inherit paternal traits (Miller and Schultz 1959). A spot at the base of the dorsal fin of $P.$ *occidentalis* and $P.$ F_x is absent in $P.$ *lucida* and $P.$ C_x. When host males were switched, so that a clear fin C_x was mated to a spot fin *occidentalis* male, all offspring were spot-finned females; but when a spot fin F_x was mated to a clear fin *lucida* male, all progeny were clear-finned females. The sperm clearly does more than just stimulate development of the eggs, as in *formosa*. True fertilization occurs in what reveals itself to be a completely different form of unisexual reproduction called "hybridogenesis," which at that time (Schultz 1969) had not been previously demonstrated in any other animal.

Discovery of all-female biotypes raises eight major questions. 1) How did unisexuality arise? 2) What sex-determining mechanism causes all female births? 3) How are those mechanisms perpetuated through subsequent generations? 4) What is the long-term survival potential of unisexual biotypes? 5) Are unisexuals monoclonal or polyclonal and genetically variable? 6) Do they have an evolutionary role? 7) How shall we name them? and 8) Are these isolated novelties characteristic of poeciliids or is the phenomenon widespread? This chapter deals with some of these questions; later chapters on unisexuality develop more fully those areas treated lightly here.

THE ORIGIN OF UNISEXUALITY IN *POECILIOPSIS*

From the beginning of their work (Hubbs and Hubbs 1932) with *Poecilia formosa*, the Hubbses recognized that hybridization was a component of the all-female "species." Miller immediately assumed that the unisexual *Poeciliopsis* biotypes were also of hybrid origin. In retrospect, although this assumption proved to be true, it originally had no basis whatsoever. Even though $P.$ *occidentalis* clearly provided a strong morphological contribution to F_x, the only other species of *Poeciliopsis* known at that time to live within the range of *occidentalis* was $P.$ *prolifica*, a very different species with no morphological representation in F_x. The similarity of $P.$ *occidentalis* and $P.$ *lucida*, and the facility with which males effectively fertilize either unisexual biotype, suggested that they may have been the hybrid parents. Although the two species are not sympatric, they live in adjacent river systems and are tolerant enough of salinity to migrate from the mouth of one river to the next.

Poeciliopsis occidentalis is the northernmost species of the genus, ranging from southern Arizona south to the Río Mayo; F_x occurs with it in all five of the northern river systems in Mexico (Figure 5–1). *Poeciliopsis lucida* and C_x are in the next three rivers to the south, the ríos Fuerte, Sinaloa, and Mocorito, where they overlap in distribution with five other species of *Poeciliopsis*: *latidens, viriosa, monacha, prolifica,* and *presidionis*. Our initial experiments consisted of a mindless attempt to cross every biotype of *Poeciliopsis* with each other, including some six to eight species of *Poeciliopsis* that live well to the south of the unisexuals.

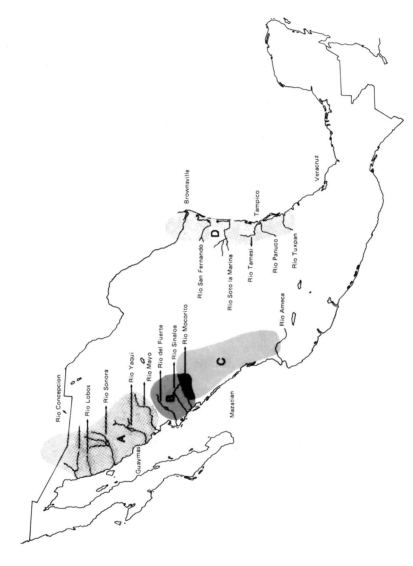

Figure 5–1. Range of unisexual-bisexual populations of *Poecilia* and *Poeciliopsis*. (a) *Poeciliopsis occidentalis* and *P. monacha-occidentalis*; (b) *P. lucida* and *P. monacha-lucida*; (c) *P. viriosa*; (d) *Poecilia formosa*. (Not illustrated is a single upstream locality in the Río Mayo where *P. monacha* has been collected.)

All this was in the hope that an all-female species would spring forth, or that from crosses involving unisexuals a clue to their origin would emerge. This shotgun approach produced three important pieces of information: one bearing on the origin of unisexuality, one on the sex-determining mechanism, and one on the inheritance of unisexuality.

Matings between the all-female forms and males of *P. lucida, occidentalis*, or *infans*, which are closely related species, result in only female progeny. Some strains of unisexuals in our lab date back to 1961 and represent 60 generations of all-female reproduction. This consistent unisexuality was broken, however, when C_x stocks from the Río Fuerte were mated to *P. latidens*, a species distinct from the other paternal contributors: only male progeny were produced (Schultz 1973a, 1973b). *Poeciliopsis latidens* has conspicuous bars and spots on its sides that in F_1 males are expressed as a row of spots along the midline. Remarkable, however, was the expression in the F_1 of a dark, wedge-shaped mark on the lower side above the base of the gonopodium (Figure 5–2), a trait not found in either parent. This mark, which is characteristic of males of *P. monacha* and *P. viriosa*, provided the critical clue to the identity of the unknown female parent of the presumed hybrid, *monacha* or *viriosa*. Matings of C_x to *monacha* or to *viriosa* resulted in offspring of both sexes. The "aberrant dentition" now became understandable; behind the large outer teeth of both *monacha* and *viriosa* are numerous tiny inner teeth that have three cusps, whereas *lucida* and *occidentalis* have two modest rows of unicuspid teeth. The unisexual's inner teeth

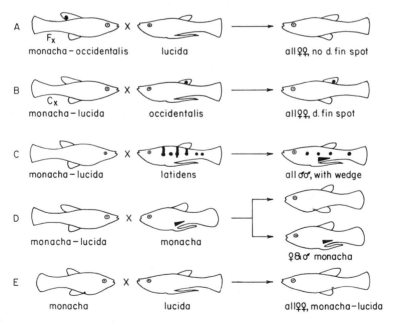

Figure 5–2. Series of matings that led to the discovery of hybridogenesis and the identification of parental species that gave rise to unisexuality in *Poeciliopsis*.

are tricuspid but intermediate in number. In the midst of a *lucida* or *occidentalis* sample, these teeth are striking in appearance.

The few known *P. monacha* localities are small populations confined to headwaters of river systems inhabited by unisexuals, whereas the unisexuals and their sexual host species are found throughout these drainages. At some localities, the ranges of *monacha* and *lucida* overlap, offering the potential for continual hybridization. The major part of the range of *viriosa* is south of the unisexual territory, but spotty populations occur, one in the Río Mocorito near the village of La Huerte and one in the Río Sinaloa at the village of El Sauce, but none in the Río Fuerte.

Matings of $C_x \times$ *monacha* and $C_x \times$ *viriosa*, which produced offspring of both sexes, helped to determine that *monacha* was the originator of unisexuality in *Poeciliopsis*. The critical information revealed was that $C_x \times$ *monacha* progeny could not be distinguished from *monacha*, but $C_x \times$ *viriosa* progeny were not quite identical to *viriosa*; some *monacha* traits were evident. Results of these early matings were later published along with results from additional studies by Vrijenhoek and Schultz (1974). Ten years after the original announcement (Miller and Schultz 1959) of unsexuality in *Poeciliopsis*, identity of the Fuerte unisexual was established to be a hybrid between *P. monacha* and *P. lucida* and was named *Poeciliopsis monacha-lucida* (Schultz 1969).

The question of how this hybrid maintains its F_1 phenotype through successive generations had been answered several years earlier (Schultz 1961, 1966) when it was determined that all paternal traits expressed in the progeny of unisexuals were erased by a single backcross to *lucida*. This was dramatically demonstrated by the fact that *monacha-lucida* can be hybridized, not only with species closely related to *lucida*, such as *occidentalis* and *infans*, but with distantly related species of *Poeciliopsis* such as *latidens*, *fasciata*, and *catemaco* (which live 1,500 miles away in southern Mexico). Thus, the inheritance of many conspicuous characters was tested. In matings back to *lucida*, restoration of the *monacha-lucida* phenotype was always complete, with no evidence of segregation or crossing over between maternal and paternal genomes (Schultz 1961, 1966; Vrijenhoek et al. 1978). Furthermore, successive backcrosses to some of these species did not alter the F_1 phenotype. For example, in the cross of Río Mocorito *monacha-lucida* × *latidens*, the *lucida* genome is replaced and *monacha-latidens* is formed; backcrossing to *latidens* does not increase the genes of *latidens* in the backcross progeny, but only replaces the existing *latidens* genome with another *latidens* genome (Schultz 1966).

The conclusion drawn from such patterns of inheritance was that the *monacha* genome is inherited as a block of genes held together in and out of various hybrid combinations. The paternal genome, although contributing to the phenotype of each generation, does not survive meiosis; only *monacha* genes are transmitted to the eggs of the next generation. This mechanism, called "hybridogenesis" (Schultz 1969), is a clonal form of inheritance, but because only half of the genotype is inherited clonally, Kallman (pers. comm.) suggested that "hemiclonal" inheritance is the appropriate term.

Continuation of the all-female nature of *monacha-lucida* is assured by complete linkage of the *monacha* genome. As long as the father is *lucida*, *occidentalis*, or *infans*, the female-determining genes of *monacha* are strong enough to override the male-determining genes of the paternal contribution. From the numerous hybrid crosses made early in these studies, progeny sex ratios ranged from all-male to all-female, with varying degrees of skewness in between. This suggested that different strengths exist among them so that, in closely related species such as *occidentalis* and *lucida*, deviations from 1 : 1 ratios exist but are not as pronounced as among widely different species. When females of *occidentalis* are mated to males of *lucida* the ratio favors females, whereas in the reciprocal mating, the weaker sex-determining mechanism of *lucida* results in mostly males (Schultz 1961). Although the female sex-determination of *monacha* prevails when *occidentalis* or *infans* is substituted for the paternal genome of Río Fuerte *monacha-lucida*, when *latidens* or *fasciata* is the father the femaleness of *monacha* is overwhelmed and all offspring are males. This provides a test of the hypothesis that the maternal genome of *monacha-lucida* is *monacha*. If *monahca-lucida* × *latidens* produces all male *monacha-latidens*, then *monacha* × *latidens* directly should also produce all male *monacha-latidens*, which in fact is what happens (Schultz 1973b). A diagrammatic summary of the important crosses involved in establishing the parental identity of the unisexual hybrids and working out the mechanism of hybridogenesis is provided in Figure 5–2.

Thus far, discussion of unisexuality in *Poeciliopsis* has focused mainly on *P. monacha-lucida* and its associates in the Río Fuerte. The unisexual originally called F_x, which resides in rivers north of the Fuerte, still needs to be defined. From the spot fin inheritance studies it was apparent that F_x × *lucida* could not be distinguished from C_x (now *monacha-lucida*) and that C_x × *occidentalis* was indistinguishable from F_x. Thus, it turns out that the "mysterious maternal genome" is also from *P. monacha*; it is the same maternal genome in both unisexuals, and *P. F_x* is really *P. monacha-occidentalis* (Schultz 1969). For several years it was assumed that the Río Fuerte was the northern limit of *P. monacha* (Miller 1960) and that unisexuality in *Poeciliopsis* originated there with a *monacha* × *lucida* cross. *Poeciliopsis monacha-occidentalis* was considered to be a second-order hybrid formed after migrants of *monacha-lucida* adopted *occidentalis* as a new sexual host species. Subsequently, a small population of *P. monacha* was discovered by W.S. Moore in a tributary of the Río Mayo, making it likely that *monacha-lucida* and *monacha-occidentalis* have had independent origins (Schultz 1977).

SYNTHESIS OF AN ALL-FEMALE "SPECIES" OF *POECILIOPSIS*

The ultimate proof that unisexual "species" are of hybrid origin and the verification of their parentage is the laboratory synthesis of one of them via the hypothesized pathway. Early in hybridization studies, Miller and I on several occasions attempted, without success, to cross *monacha* and *lucida*. After discovering the wedge-shaped mark above the gonopodium of the offspring of $C_x \times$ *latidens*, and after completing a qualitative and quantitative evaluation of the dentition of all phenotypes involved (Schultz 1966, 1969), the successful crossing of *monacha* × *lucida* became so important that attempts to implement it were vigorously renewed. This was after the colony had been moved to The University of Connecticut where the fish, which are kept in greenhouses, receive better light and the stocks are more vigorous.

Between 1957 and 1973 more than 67 matings of *monacha* × *lucida* were attempted; in five of these progeny were produced that reached adulthood (Schultz 1973a). The cross does not go easily, however, because *P. monacha* has large eggs (2.2 mm) and large embryos, whereas *P. lucida* has small eggs (1.4 mm) and small embryos. The hybrid embryo is intermediate in size, but it is on a large *monacha* egg and reaches full development with a surplus of yolk, which presents three potential hazards: 1) the heart, which is still exposed on the surface of the yolk, may be damaged at birth; 2) the yolk sac may rupture; or 3) the abdominal wall may close before the yolk is absorbed and leave the heart outside. The eggs and embryos of *monacha-lucida* are both medium-sized, so subsequent generations do not have a problem.

Two of the strains synthesized prior to 1970 are still maintained in the laboratory with males of *P. lucida*; they are in their eighteenth generation and continue to produce all female offspring indistinguishable from wild *monacha-lucida*. When they are mated to *latidens*, like wild *monacha-lucida*, they produce all males; if mated back to *monacha*, the full *monacha* phenotype is restored.

For experimental purposes it is sometimes important to initiate new hemiclones of *monacha-lucida*, both in my laboratory and that of Robert Vrijenhoek (Whetherington et al., Chapter 14). The egg-size embryo-size problem can be circumvented by first crossing *monacha* with *occidentalis*, making a *monacha-occidentalis* female, which is then mated to a male *lucida*. Embryos of *occidentalis* are a little larger than *lucida* and have fewer developmental problems on large *monacha* eggs. The *monacha-occidentalis* egg is 1.8 mm and closer to the proper size for a *monacha-lucida* embryo, so the second step of the process, the *monacha-occidentalis* × *lucida* cross encounters no difficulty.

Synthesis of *monacha-lucida* and *monacha-occidentalis* in the laboratory demonstrates that the formation of unisexual species does not involve a long process of mutation and selection, that the F_1 generation is immediately all-female, and that all-femaleness is consistently perpetuated. What triggers hybrodogenesis is not clear, but apparently it is associated with the bringing together of substantially different hereditary material. Atypical meiosis is not induced by hybridization within groups of similar species of *Poeciliopsis*. For example, the species within the following groups are easily crossed with each other and normal segregation occurs in the F_1 progeny: 1) *monacha* and *viriosa*, 2) *latidens*, *fasciata*, and a related undescribed species, and 3) *occidentalis*, *lucida*, and *infans*. Most of the species crosses between groups have been attempted; either they fail, especially between groups 2 and 3, or segregation is abnormal, as in group 1 matings to groups 2 and 3 (Schultz 1961, 1977, and unpubl. data). Meiotic processes among unisexual fishes are discussed later.

Discussion thus far has involved mainly fishes from the Río Fuerte among which results from hybridization experiments are readily interpretable, except for one. Living with *monacha-lucida* is a diploid unisexual with spots along the lateral line, which is abundant at most localities. Once the role of *monacha* was established in unisexual *Poeciliopsis*, it became apparent on the basis of its morphology that this spotted hybrid is a *monacha-latidens*. Either it was formed when *monacha-lucida* mated with *latidens* or when pure *monacha* mated with *latidens*, forming a third highly successful diploid unisexual "species." Although in the laboratory we have made one or the other of these crosses with *latidens* more than 50 times and reared to maturity over 600 offspring, all of them have been males (Schultz 1973b, and unpubl. data). Yet, of the thousands of specimens representing this biotype in preserved collections at the University of Michigan Museum of Zoology (UMMZ), all are females. We have raised 29 generations of wild *monacha-latidens* in the laboratory by mating it to *P. latidens*, as well as offspring from eight different females; all progeny developed into females. Apparently, a rare *monacha* genome, never tested by us in the laboratory, initiated the wild populations of *monacha-latidens*. All specimens of this biotype from the Río Fuerte had identical *monacha* genomes at 22 electrophoretically examined loci (R.C. Vrijenhoek, pers. comm.), suggesting that a single hemiclone originated from a single hybridization event.

A spotted hybrid form in the Río Mocorito also appears to be of a *monacha-latidens* genotype, even though *monacha* has not been found in any of the many collections (UMMZ) taken throughout the river systems. The likely origin is from matings of *monacha-lucida* × *latidens* in which the *lucida* genome is replaced with *latidens*. That this cross occurs in nature is supported by the birth of a mixed brood of young in the laboratory from a wild-caught *monacha-lucida* (Schultz 1966). Most of her progeny were *monacha-lucida*, but one was a *monacha-latidens*. Laboratory crosses (Schultz 1966) between Mocorito *monacha-lucida* and *latidens*, unlike those from the Río Fuerte resulting in all males, produced either all female offspring (from four pairs) or both sexes (from two pairs).

Analysis of Mocorito *monacha-lucida* biotypes indicates that a few *viriosa* genes have introgressed into the *monacha* genome and that this fish really is a trihybrid (Vrijenhoek and Schultz 1974). Incorporation of variable amounts of *viriosa* may account for production of all female offspring by some hemiclones of *monacha-lucida* × *latidens* and both sexes from others. After these studies were completed, I discovered in preserved collections individuals of *latidens* with dentition patterns that resembled *P. viriosa* enough to suggest introgression. Some males used in the *monacha-lucida* × *latidens* laboratory crosses may have had a few *viriosa* genes that influenced sex ratios. An extensive electrophoretic analysis of these Mocorito fishes is called for.

Only a few laboratory matings were carried out with *Poeciliopsis* from the

Río Sinaloa, but since a small tributary of this river near El Sauce has *monacha-latidens*, *monacha-lucida*, *lucida*, *viriosa*, and *latidens* coexisting, it too could offer valuable research material for studying the variation and genetics of *monacha-latidens*.

SYNTHESIS OF *POECILIA FORMOSA*

Early attempts by the Hubbses to synthesize *Poecilia formosa* in the laboratory apparently were with biotypes from unlikely localities. In one experiment the short fin molly of the *sphenops*-type (which was mated to *Poecilia latipinna*) was either from the Río Papagallo on the Pacific slope or it was an F_1 hybrid between the Pacific slope form and an Atlantic coast form (Turner 1982). Other crosses apparently also were made strictly with Atlantic coast forms but were drawn from localities south of the range of *P. formosa* (J.S. Balsano, pers. comm.). Since these experiments, several species and subspecies of *P. sphenops* and *P. latipinna* have become recognized (Schultz and Miller 1971; Menzel and Darnell 1973a; R.R. Miller, pers. comm.), making it unclear which crosses the Hubbses made except for the fact that both sexes were produced among F_1, F_2, and backcross progeny (Hubbs 1955) and no all-female "species" emerged.

Following the Hubbses, several laboratory syntheses were attempted by Darnell and Balsano, then at Marquette University (J.S. Balsano, pers. comm.). When these failed, attention turned to cytological and electrophoretic techniques for determining the origin and affinities of *P. formosa* (Prehn and Rasch 1969; Balsano and Rasch 1974; Turner 1982). Electrophoresis, especially, showed great promise for identifying allozyme patterns that, when put together, could replicate the specific heterozygous loci characterizing the all-female "species." The most recent analysis (Turner 1982) identified *P. mexicana* populations from the ríos Tamesi, Tigre, and San Rafael as "prime candidates" to be combined with *P. latipinna* for the synthesis of *P. formosa*. Matings of *P. mexicana* from the lower Tamesi drainage (Tampico, Mexico) × *P. latipinna* resulted in F_1 hybrids that looked like *P. formosa*, but were bisexual and reproduced sexually (Abramoff et al. 1968; J.S. Balsano, pers. comm.). Similar results were obtained from matings involving the southern subspecies of *P. mexicana*, which was implicated as a parental species based on muscle protein analysis (Monaco et al. 1982). See Balsano et al. (Chapter 15) for further discussion of the putative parental species of *P. formosa*.

POLYPLOIDY

Poeciliids provided the first examples of triploid fish that reproduce as natural populations. During the late 1950s and early 1960s, when the genetics of unisexual *Poeciliopsis* was first being investigated (Miller and Schultz 1959; Schultz 1961), females from the ríos Sinaloa, Mocorito, and Fuerte, were identified from *P.*

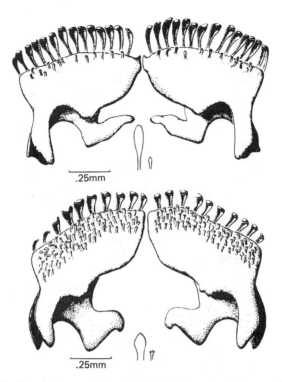

Figure 5–3. Dentary bones of *Poeciliopsis lucida* (upper) and *P. monacha* (lower). (Reprinted with permission from Schultz 1969 [Univ. of Chicago Press]).

lucida collections as having "the aberrant dentition." They consistently produced all female progeny which, when test mated with males of other species, expressed some paternal traits (all but one strain, collected in 1961 from the Río Fuerte). Progeny from this one strain were phenotypically identical to their mothers whether they were mated to clear fin males of *lucida*, spot fin males of *occidentalis*, or *latidens* males with body spots and bars (Schultz 1967). Reproduction by this all-female strain exhibited all of the symptoms of gynogenesis (like *P. formosa*). Chromosome counts on *P. occidentalis*, *P. lucida* and the hybridogenetic unisexual strains associated with them, as well as on other gonochoristic species of *Poeciliopsis*, were 2n = 48 (Schultz 1961), but this apparent gynogenetic strain proved to be 3n = 72. Shortly after this discovery, another previously undiagnosed unisexual form living in the headwaters of the Río Fuerte with *P. monacha* was also established to be 3n = 72 (Schultz 1969). The chromosome numbers coupled with a detailed morphological analysis, particularly comparison of the jaw shapes, tooth shapes, and tooth numbers (Figures 5–3 and 5–4), revealed a five-member hybrid complex. The hybridogenetic 2n *P. monacha-lucida* hybrid apparently provided a stepping-stone to formation of the two triploids, wherein addition of a second *lucida* genome has resulted in *P. monacha-2 lucida* and addition of a *monacha* genome in *P. 2*

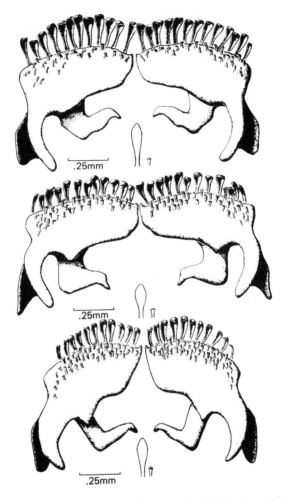

Figure 5–4. Dentary bones of *Poeciliopsis monacha-2 lucida* (upper), *P. monacha-lucida* (middle), and *P. 2 monacha-lucida* (lower). (Reprinted with permission from Schultz 1969 [Univ. of Chicago Press]).

monacha-lucida. The triploids produce 3n eggs that are stimulated to develop by sperm from males of *P. lucida*, the sexual host species of *P. monacha-2 lucida*, or by males of *P. monacha*, the host species of *P. 2 monacha-lucida*. All three unisexual biotypes are highly successful, and at most localities their combined number exceeds that of their host species (Schultz 1977). Unisexuals vary in proportional abundance depending on locality and habitat (Vrijenhoek 1978; Wetherington et al., Chapter 14).

   Inheritance of paternal traits in progeny of *P. formosa* drew attention to the possibility of polyploidy in this all-female ''species.'' Stocks of *P. formosa* maintained in the Genetics Laboratory of the New York Aquarium by matings to *P. vittata* or to a black molly line of *P. sphenops* produced offspring that, for the most part, were identical to their mothers. However, about 1% of them had traits of both parents. For example, some offspring from black fathers had irregular black blotches scattered over their bodies (Kallman 1964c). To determine if an extra set of chromosomes was being added to some of the diploid eggs, the nuclear volumes and relative DNA levels of *P. formosa* and *P. mexicana* were compared (Rasch et al. 1965). The *P. formosa* offspring with paternal traits had half again as much DNA as either parental biotype or nonblotched *formosa*, strongly suggesting that they were indeed triploids. Prior to the cytophotometric determinations of DNA levels, Drewry (1964) had tentatively established chromosome numbers of 2n = 46 for *P. formosa*, *P. latipinna*, and *P. sphenops*. Chromosome counts later made (Schultz and Kallman 1968) on four normally pigmented females, two of which were litter mates of a black blotched "formosa" and two from another clone, were clearly 2n = 46; but the blotched apparent *formosa* × *sphenops* hybrid was 3n = 69.

Subsequent to these laboratory determinations, wild populations of triploids were discovered living in the same communities as diploid *P. formosa* (Strommen et al. 1975b). Two distinct triploid forms have been identified (Rasch et al. 1978; Monaco et al. 1984; Balsano et al., Chapter 15) which, on the basis of their morphology and allozyme patterns, might be called *Poecilia* 2 *mexicana-latipinna* and *P. mexicana-2 latipinna*. The former occurs in the Río Soto la Marina drainage of northeastern Mexico with diploid *P. formosa* and *P. mexicana*; the latter is in the Río Grande drainage of southeastern Texas with *P. formosa* and *P. latipinna*. Monaco et al. (1984) consider it premature to adopt the *Poeciliopsis* system of nomenclature for this group because they believe two subspecies of *P. mexicana* may have contributed genes to the original *P. formosa*, and that these subspecies, *P. m. mexicana* and *P. m. limantouri*, might later prove to be full species. If so, naming these biotypes in terms of the genome dose contributed by the parents would involve three names: *mexicana*, *limantouri*, and *latipinna*. This would be further complicated if *P. formosa* is really an intergrade or a hybrid between *mexicana* and *limantouri* × *latipinna*, as electrophoretic analyses suggest (Turner 1982; Balsano et al., Chapter 15).

CYTOLOGICAL ASPECTS OF UNISEXUALITY

Perpetuation of all-femaleness in unisexual fishes is accomplished by the modification of meiosis or premeiosis. These mechanisms are difficult to study because the maturation period is brief. In viviparous fishes they are entirely concealed from view, unless revealed by dissection at the critical period or manipulated in culture. In *Poeciliopsis monacha-lucida*, hybridogenesis involves the formation of a unipolar spindle before vitellogenesis (Cimino 1972a). The maternal chromosomes, which are aligned on the metaphase plate, are drawn to the pole of a daughter nucleus. The paternal chromosomes are not attached to spindle fibers but remain scattered in the cytoplasm and are eventually lost. Meiosis presumably proceeds through a bipolar equational division, resulting in a haploid polar body and a haploid ovum. What triggers the process is unclear, but based on the range of hybrid matings made early in the *Poeciliopsis* studies (Schultz 1961, 1966, 1973a, 1973b), crosses between closely related species do not lead to abnormal meiosis; it is initiated only in crosses between distinctly different forms. Cimino (1972a) proposed that the paternal half-spindle fails to form properly because the spindle organizers on the paternal chromosomes are incompatible with the ooplasm.

Triploid forms of *Poeciliopsis*, *P. monacha-2 lucida* and *P. 2 monacha-lucida*, undergo a process of endoduplication prior to meiosis during which the somatic chromosome number is elevated from 3n to 6n (Cimino 1972b). This is followed by the formation of "pseudobivalents" and two meiotic divisions. Recombination does not occur, so the 3n eggs produced are identical to each other and to the mother. This mechanism is similar to that described for gynogenetic triploid salamanders *Ambystoma jeffersonianum* (MacGregor and Uzzell 1964), and triploid lizards, *Cnemidophorous uniparens* (Cuellar 1971). Diploid and triploid members of the *Poecilia formosa* complex, although gynogenetic, do not have endoduplication, but instead are propogated by apomixis (Monaco et al. 1984; Balsano et al., Chapter 15). In this form of asexual reproduction, the first meiotic division is replaced by a mitotic division; bivalents are not formed, and there is no reduction in chromosome number. It has not been established if a second division occurs, but if it does, it too is probably mitotic (E.M. Rasch, pers. comm.). In any event, the eggs of *P. formosa* are diploid and those of *P. 2 mexicana-latipinna* are triploid.

CLONAL DIVERSITY

Reproduction in unisexual poeciliids by either hybridogenesis or gynogenesis excludes recombination; genotypes are faithfully replicated from one generation to the next in a clonal or hemiclonal manner. Theoretical biologists over the years have argued that, when multiple clones arise, eventually only one will survive (e.g., Holsinger and Ellstrand 1984). This is based on the assumption that among several closely related genotypes, one will prove superior and will competitively exclude the others, or that fluctuations in population size will eliminate all but one. The fact is, however, most poeciliid communities of unisexual biotypes consist of multiple clones (Kallman 1962a; Schultz 1967; Angus 1980; Angus and Schultz 1979; Wetherington et al., Chapter 14; Balsano et al., Chapter 15).

Identification of clones has been by three methods: tissue graft analysis, mating experiments, and biochemical techniques. Tissue graft analysis was first used for this purpose by Kallman (1962a) who identified eight different clones of *Poecilia formosa* in the northern part of its range. The technique involves the insertion of a small piece of tissue from one individual beneath the skin of another.

If the genes of the donor tissue are different from those of the host, a histocompatability reaction develops and the tissue is rejected in 7 to 10 days.

Since members of the same clone are genetically identical, all grafts are accepted, vascular connections are established, and the tissue grows or at least remains alive and healthy. A variety of tissues are used as donor material: fins, hearts, spleens, scales, and so forth. For populations made up of many clones, multiple scale grafts make it possible to carry out the large number of tests required (Angus and Schultz 1979; Angus 1980) to evaluate clonal variation. With this method, a dark scale is removed from the back of the donor and inserted between the belly scales; the silvery-white background makes it possible to detect the melanin of an accepted scale three weeks later. Up to six scales have been implanted in each side of the belly without overloading the immune system of the recipient or causing an interaction between grafts.

The tissue graft technique is easily employed for identification of clones among parthenogenetic or gynogenetic animals, but in hybridogenetic forms, where every individual has a different paternal genome, the test cannot be used without a genetic manipulation described later.

The presence of more than one hemiclone of *Poeciliopsis monacha-lucida* was first detected from crosses of the unisexuals with *P. latidens* (Schultz 1966, 1967). From different females tested, three classes of hybrid progeny resulted: 1) fully viable males and females, 2) all males that began to mature at a small size but died just prior to maturity, and 3) all males, medium to large size and fully viable.

Shortly after these determinations were made, the use of electrophoresis emerged as a tool for detecting genetic differences among both clonal and hemiclonal biotypes. The number of hemiclones of *P. monacha-lucida* in the Río Fuerte was estimated by this method to be no fewer than eight (Vrijenhoek et al. 1978) and *P. monacha-occidentalis* from the Río Mayo a minimum of four (Vrijenhoek et al. 1977). Although 22 loci were examined in these studies, many alleles were shared by both parental biotypes, thus reducing the number useful for detecting different *monacha* genomes, the clonally inherited portion. By this time, inbred, homozygous strains of *P. lucida* had been developed, making it possible to use the more sensitive tissue graft method. When wild-type *P. monacha-lucida* or *P. monacha-occidentalis* females are mated to males of an inbred, homozygous strain, all progeny inherit their mothers' wild-type *monacha* genomes and receive identical paternal genomes. Grafts among these progeny either result in acceptance, indicating membership in the same hemiclone, or rejection and, hence, affiliation with a different hemiclone.

When the same strains of *monacha-lucida* from the Río Fuerte, which had been separated into eight hemiclones by electrophoresis, were tested by tissue graft analysis, up to six histocompatability hemiclones were found under the same electrophoretic phenotype; yet some electrophoretic phenotypes were represented by a single histocompatability phenotype. From collecting sites in four different tributaries of the Fuerte, 20 hemiclones of *monacha-lucida* were identified (Figure

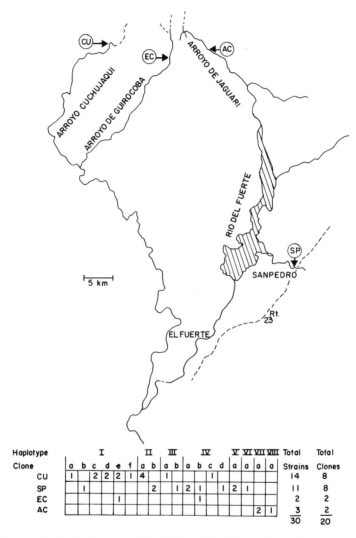

Figure 5–5. Collection sites and distribution of hemiclones of *Poeciliopsis monacha-lucida* from the Río Fuerte in northwest Mexico. Roman numerals designate the *monacha* genomes or haplotypes identified by electrophoresis, lowercase letters indicate histocompatible strains, each founded by a single wild female, comprising each clone. Collection sites are abbreviated as follows: Arroyo Cuchujaqui, CU; Arroyo de Guirocoba at El Cajón, EC; Arroyo de Jaguari at Agua Caliente, AC; and Río San Pedro, SP. (Modified from Angus and Schultz, 1979).

5–5), but since the sample size consisted of only 30 wild strains, this is clearly a gross underestimate of the clonal variation present (Angus and Schultz 1979).

In a similar study (Angus 1980), 33 strains of *P. monacha-occidentalis* from the Río Mayo comprised 4 electrophoretic phenotypes (Vrijenhoek et al. 1977) but 20 histocompatability hemiclones (Angus 1980). This again is a gross underestimate of clonal variation, but both determinations abundantly illustrate the point that this form of unisexual "species" has by no means settled on a single optimum phenotype.

Transition of diploid hemiclones to triploid clones is not a common event in *Poeciliopsis*. It has not occurred in the laboratory, and only two clones each of *P. monacha-2 lucida* and *P. 2 monacha-lucida* have been identified in the Río Fuerte. The *monacha-2 lucida* clones can be separated by differences in the pigment pattern in the genital region (Schultz 1977), but the second two can be distinguished only by electrophoresis (Vrijenhoek 1978) or tissue graft analysis (Moore and Eisenbrey 1979).

In the *Poecilia formosa* complex, where studies of relative abundance were carried out in populations sustained by males of *P. mexicana* (Balsano et al., Chapter 15), the *2 mexicana-latipinna* triploid form outnumbered the *mexicana-latipinna* (or *formosa*) diploid. *Poecilia mexicana-2 latipinna*, which occurs where *P. latipinna* is the host species, is rare and greatly outnumbered by *formosa*.

The numbers of clones or hemiclones found in a unisexual community is determined by such factors as repeated syntheses or recruitment (Angus and Schultz 1979), availability of a niche (Schultz 1971, 1973a, 1982; Vrijenhoek 1978; Schultz and Fielding 1989), population bottlenecks caused mainly by fluctuating water levels, and the capacity to acquire sperm (Keegan-Rogers 1984; Keegan-Rogers and Schultz 1988). Mechanisms for coexistence of multiple clones are complex and interrelated, but in understanding how these closely related genotypes are sustained, the more general issue of the role of variation in populations can be better understood. Chapters by Wetherington et al. (Chapter 14) and Balsano et al. (Chapter 15) address these questions in some detail.

SUMMARY AND FUTURE RESEARCH

Two genera of poeciliid fishes have naturally occurring, highly successful biotypes that produce only female offspring. Unisexual clones of *Poecilia* (the Amazon molly) are found in northeastern Mexico and southern Texas, and all-female forms of *Poeciliopsis* are from northwestern Mexico. Both genera include diploid (2n) and triploid (3n) unisexuals, all of which have arisen through hybridization. In *Poecilia* there are three all-female biotypes, which are named here in terms of their most probable hybrid origin and genome dosage: *Poecilia latipinna-mexicana* (2n) (also known as *P. formosa*), *P. latipinna-2 mexicana* (3n), and *P. 2 latipinna-mexicana* (3n). *Poeciliopsis* has six unisexuals, *Poeciliopsis monacha-lucida* (2n), *P. monacha-occidentalis* (2n), *P. monacha-latidens* (2n), *P. monacha-2 lucida*

(3n), *P. 2 monacha-lucida* (3n), and *P. monacha-viriosa-lucida* (3n). In the last *Poeciliopsis* biotype listed, which is a trihybrid triploid, the proportion of *monacha* to *viriosa* is not established. The system of nomenclature used for these hybrid unisexuals was devised for the purpose of communication and does not infer species status.

All unisexual forms depend on males from one of the bisexual parental species for sperm to initiate the next generation. In 2n and 3n all-female *Poecilia* and in 3n *Poeciliopsis*, the sperm only stimulates the 2n or 3n egg to develop (gynogenesis); inheritance is completely clonal. Diploid unisexual *Poeciliopsis*, however, produce haploid eggs that contain only maternal genes originally from *P. monacha*. Reproduction, after fertilization by males of *P. lucida*, *P. occidentalis*, or *P. latidens*, is by hybridogenesis. During meiosis the maternal (*monacha*) chromosomes align unpaired on the metaphase plate where they attach to a unipolar spindle; they are then drawn to the single pole where they become the sole contributor to the egg nucleus. Since the paternal chromosomes do not pair with the maternal chromosomes and are not attached to spindle fibers, no segregation or crossing-over occurs. The maternal genes are transmitted as a single linkage unit, and inheritance is actually hemiclonal.

A major unresolved question regarding unisexual vertebrates is whether they have an evolutionary destiny or simply constitute a temporary by-product of an inefficient system of reproductive isolation. It has yet to be established that unisexuals undergo adaptive change and are capable of long-term survival. The success of a clone may depend completely on original fortuitous gene combinations and the existence of open niches rather than on evolution subsequent to a hybrid origin (see Wetherington et al., Chapter 14). The most important role unisexual hybrids may play in evolution is to serve as an intermediate step in the formation of sexually reproducing polyploids. Tetraploid fishes such as the Salmonidae and Catostomidae may owe their origin to a hybridization-polyploidy pathway in which a fourth genome is added to a unisexual triploid. The even ploidy value may enable a return to normal meiosis and sexual reproduction and provide freedom from the sexual host species.

Hemiclonal and clonal fishes are becoming increasingly important as models for the study of adaptive variation in natural populations. By holding the genetics constant, the influence of heredity versus environment on life history traits can be assessed. In biomedical research, clonal fishes offer an alternative to inbred, genetically deficient rodents for evaluating the risk of toxicants and carcinogens (Schultz and Schultz 1988). Since many of these substances are water-borne, the development of fish models as sentinels of our water supplies is imperative.

ACKNOWLEDGMENTS

I owe my lifetime of scientific research to Robert Rush Miller who introduced me to *Poeciliopsis* in 1956 and then graciously turned over to me the experimental aspects of the unisexual studies. I am also indebted to a series of stimulating graduate students who opened the doors on diverse areas and developed skills too numerous and complex for one person to be able to deploy in this multifaceted area: Bradley Bowen, Francis McKay, Michael Cimino, William Moore, Robert Vrijenhoek, Roger Thibault, Robert Angus, Janet Lanza, Arthur Bulger, Valerie Keegan-Rogers, Robert Dawley, Katheryn Goddard, and Eileen Fielding. I am grateful to Ellie DeCarli who over much of this span of time typed my manuscripts, including the present one.

I thank the Mexican government for allowing me to collect fish in their country and the National Science Foundation for supporting my research.

Reproduction and the Evolution of Life History Traits

There is little doubt that the scientific allure of poeciliid fishes results largely from the radical departure of their reproductive mode from that typical of most fishes. Behavioral, anatomical, and physiological features of the livebearing process range from simple to complex. However, one feature, retention of young within the ovarian follicle until "hatching," is a common denominator of all but one species. All offspring come "packaged" within the mother, facilitating studies of energetics, size/fertility relationships, genetic and environmental influences on life history traits, and numerous other topics of interest to ecologists and evolutionists.

Reproduction must begin with access to a mate and fertilization, and Farr reviews poeciliid courtship patterns and sexual selection in Chapter 6. He emphasizes the role of male aggression and female choice in molding sexual selection and attempts to explain the wide range of variation in the family with respect to sexual dimorphism and courtship patterns.

Reznick and Miles (Chapter 7) review a basic dichotomy in poeciliid reproduction, the presence or absence of superfetation, the simultaneous provisioning of more than one brood. They conclude that the trait has evolved separately at least four times within the family and that it is usually correlated with other life history features. Their analysis of covariation of life history traits illustrates an approach that holds a great deal of promise for further understanding of life history evolution.

The remaining chapters in this section deal with various proximate factors important in shaping poeciliid life histories. Snelson (Chapter 8) discusses environmental and social factors influencing life history traits such as sex ratios, size, and growth. He indicates that both genetic and environmental factors, including social conditions, interact in complex ways to control important life history traits. We are only beginning to understand these interactions in a few specific cases.

Summarizing more than 25 years of ongoing research, Kallman (Chapter 9) focuses on genetic control of size at maturity in the genus *Xiphophorus*. Through meticulous study in his and other laboratories, single gene loci on sex chromosomes have been identified as controllers of size at, and time to, maturity. Modifying loci on autosomal chromosomes can influence these traits, as can, to some extent, environmental conditions. This system provides opportunities to study the actual sites and mechanisms of gene action, with potential applications far beyond the field of poeciliid biology.

In Chapter 10, Travis lays a conceptual and theoretical framework for the analysis of life history evolution through ecological genetics. By concentrating on experimental, quantitative methods to separate phenotypic variation into its genetic and environmental components, his research with the sailfin molly is breaking new ground. He finds, in general, that male traits tend to be more genetically based, whereas female traits are more subject to environmental influences.

In the final chapter of this section, Trexler reviews phenotypic plasticity and its influence on poeciliid life histories (Chapter 11). Plasticity may be an adaptive response to stressful environments and is one source of geographic variation. Laboratory studies indicate that phenotypic plasticity in poeciliid life history traits is pervasive and that genetic variation in plasticity is present both within and among populations.

Chapter 6

Sexual Selection and Secondary Sexual Differentiation in Poeciliids: Determinants of Male Mating Success and the Evolution of Female Choice

JAMES A. FARR

INTRODUCTION

Courtship, the heterosexual communication system leading up to mating (Morris 1956), has several functions. The traditional view of courtship functions concerns the basic mechanics of mating; courtship allows the temporal and spatial coordination of mating, facilitates species recognition, appeases aggressive or predatory tendencies, and promotes mutual sexual arousal (Tinbergen 1951; Keenleyside 1979). A more recent view is that courtship may also allow individuals to assess the quality of a potential mate. Courtship exchanges information by which an individual can choose a mate that will maximize fitness of its offspring (Maynard Smith 1956, 1978; Trivers 1972; Partridge 1980). It is with this latter aspect of courtship, assessment of mate quality, that this review is concerned.

A fundamental problem in studying the role of courtship in assessing mate quality is that those male traits preferred by females usually do not obviously correlate with any aspect of male fitness. Fisher (1958) was the first to explain how such males traits as conspicuous coloration, plumage, and so forth could evolve through sexual selection, and his runaway process has been treated mathematically by several authors (O'Donald 1962, 1967, 1980; Lande 1980a; Kirkpatrick 1982, 1986; Andersson 1986) and discussed further by Maynard Smith (1978). The essentials of the argument are that a male trait is initially correlated with some aspect of fitness, that female preferences for the fitness indicator evolve, and that males subsequently exploit female preferences by exaggerating the preferred trait. Although the trait is no longer an indicator of viability, females that mate with less conspicuous males produce sons less attractive to females. Basically, then, Fisher assumed an initial coupling of a male trait with viability, followed by a subsequent decoupling.

Two recent theoretical papers by Lande (1980) and Kirkpatrick (1982) take an alternative approach to the evolution of extreme secondary sexual differentiation. In their models, female preferences can arise randomly for traits not associated with fitness and still become fixed in a population. Female choice drives the evolution of male traits in both Fisher's model and those of Lande and Kirkpatrick, but they differ in whether the male trait was ever fitness-related. More recent papers by Heisler (1984), Andersson (1986), and Kirkpatrick (1986) delve further into models of female choice for male traits not associated with fitness. Kodric-Brown and Brown (1984), in another treatment of sexual selection that differs from Fisher, argue that conspicuous male traits might continue to be associated with fitness. This review, while not settling the issue of whether female choice is for extreme male traits once associated with fitness, will at least describe a system in which the original fitness relationships of male secondary sexual characteristics might be inferred.

It is often difficult to separate mate quality assessment from other courtship functions, simply because most species require the mechanical aspects for mating to occur. The livebearing teleost family Poeciliidae offers an exception, however. Rosen and Tucker (1961) pointed out that many poeciliid species exhibit no courtship, while in others, stereotyped male courtship displays and female acceptance postures precede copulation. Fertilization in the family is internal, and the male's anal fin is modified into a copulatory organ, the gonopodium (Philippi 1908; Constantz, Chapter 3). In those species with no courtship, the male simply orients behind a female, brings the gonopodium to a forward position, and swims forward, attempting to insert the gonopodial tip into the female's gonopore. This behavior, termed gonopodial thrusting, has no signal function, and there are no countersignals directed from the female toward the male. Hence, gonopodial thrusting cannot be considered a form of display.

That courtship is lacking in many, perhaps most, poeciliids is ample evidence that the mechanical functions of courtship do not apply to the group; courtship is obviously not necessary for mating to occur. Poeciliids typically live in groups, so bringing the sexes together in space is not a problem. Females have an ovarian cycle of approximately 30 days and can store sperm for several months (Philippi 1908; Van Oordt 1928; Turner 1937; Vallowe 1953; Baerends et al. 1955; Peters 1964; Liley 1966; Carlson 1969; Colson 1969; Siciliano 1972; Parzefall 1973; Peden 1973b; Kallman 1975), so insemination and fertilization can be widely separated in time; a temporal coordination of the shedding of gametes is not necessary. Finally, species recognition appears to be either unnecessary (because of ecological separation of species) or accomplished by the males (Haskins and Haskins 1949; Clark et al. 1954; Hubbs and Delco 1960, 1962; Liley 1966; McKay 1971; Zeiske 1971; Keegan-Rogers 1984; Woodhead and Armstrong 1985), although naturally occurring hybrids have been found between both displaying and non-displaying species (Hubbs 1955; Hubbs and Hubbs 1932; Hubbs 1957, 1959, 1971;

Abramoff et al. 1968; Darnell and Abramoff 1968; Prehn and Rasch 1969; Schultz 1969, 1977; Rosen 1979; Meyer 1983b).

I contend that courtship in the Poeciliidae has evolved only because of its sexually selected function, that it exchanges information whereby both sexes, but particularly females, can choose genetically superior mates. The presence of courtship is thus indicative of female choice, although I show that female choice can be exercised without courtship. This review summarizes what is known concerning sexual behavior and secondary sexual differentiation in the family and thereby points out the diversity of determinants of male reproductive success within the family. I elaborate on the different manifestations of intermale competition in the Poeciliidae and outline the different evolutionary options available to females regarding acceptance or modification of the results of intermale competition. In so doing I construct testable hypotheses concerning the ecological conditions under which the different forms of intermale competition and various female choice options should occur. Thus, I not only provide a summary of existing and previously unpublished data, but hope also to furnish a framework for future poeciliid research.

DEFINITIONS

Before I review the family, it is necessary to discuss the terms and concepts associated with poeciliid behavior and morphology. All poeciliid species are sexually dimorphic. In the following discussion I refer only to secondary sexual differences. If I say a species is sexually monomorphic, I do not mean to imply that the primary sexual differences are lacking. Also, many poeciliids exhibit sexual differences in size. I do not include size differences between sexes in my discussion. Much of the size difference in most poeciliids is because male growth after sexual maturity is negligible, whereas females continue to grow, although at a slower rate than prior to reaching maturity (Turner 1941; Schultz 1961; Farr 1980a; Snelson 1982, 1984; Hughes 1986; Snelson, Chapter 8).

Dimorphism and polymorphism may be morphological, pigmentary, or a combination. Morphological differences may involve fin size or shape, gross changes in body proportions, or inherited size differences within one or both sexes. Pigmentary polymorphisms may be exhibited by both sexes or only males, and they are generally obvious. However, determination of whether a species is sexually dichromatic is more subjective. Sexual coloration differences range from nonexistent to slight to great. In many species there are only differences in intensity of otherwise sexually identical coloration, while in others, one sex, usually males, may exhibit one or more conspicuous color patches on the fins and body not seen in the opposite sex. I will describe, if known, the degree of sexual dichromatism.

To my knowledge, all poeciliid courtship displays are visual and involve a combination of stereotyped swimming motions and fin postures. Most or all species that exhibit courtship also exhibit frequent gonopodial thrusting. Thus, strictly defined, a gonopodial thrust is any copulation attempt that occurs without prior display or, in species that exhibit courtship, without female acceptance of a display. I emphasize again that gonopodial thrusting has no premating communication function and is not to be considered under the heading of courtship.

There is a critical distinction between female choice and female cooperation. A female can cooperate without exercising choice merely by remaining motionless and accepting gonopodial thrusts of any male. This facilitates mating but does not directly influence which male(s) will mate with her. Alternatively, female choice involves both cooperation and direct influence on which of many competing males will sire her offspring. Female choice must also be distinguished from female mechanisms that facilitate or strengthen intermale competition (Cox and LeBoeuf 1977).

Most of our information on poeciliid behavior comes from laboratory observations, an obvious weakness. I will note where observations are from natural populations and emphasize the problem in the sections on aggressive behavior. I am confident that qualitative assessments of the presence or absence of courtship behavior are not affected by the laboratory environment. It is, of course, prudent to remember that one cannot conclude that a behavior pattern never occurs in a species, but only that there is no evidence that it occurs.

SOCIAL BEHAVIOR AND SECONDARY SEXUAL DIFFERENCES IN THE POECILIIDAE

The following review follows the classification scheme of Parenti and Rauchenberger (Chapter 1), except where otherwise noted. Their subfamily Poeciliinae is equivalent to the family Poeciliidae of Rosen and Bailey (1963). There is one monotypic supertribe, the Tomeurini, with the remaining species being grouped in the supertribe Poeciliini. The latter is divided into seven tribes.

Supertribe Tomeurini

The single species in this group, *Tomeurus gracilis*, exhibits internal fertilization like other poeciliids, but the fertilized eggs are usually attached to the substrate at some time prior to hatching (Gordon 1955; Breder and Rosen 1966). No courtship display occurs in this species, and there is no sexual dichromatism or male color polymorphism (Rosen and Tucker 1961). Gordon (1955) reported that females typically avoid males, and that insemination occurs in dim light when the female's guard is down. The description of insemination suggested no cooperation on the part of the female—the gonopodial thrust of the male is fairly violent and apparently occurs opportunistically when the female is less evasive.

Supertribe Poeciliini

Tribe Xenodexiini

Little is known about *Xenodexia ctenolepis*, the only member of this tribe. Hubbs (1950) described coloration of the two sexes as being essentially similar, although males might be slightly more brightly colored than females. Peden (1972a) reported that males use only gonopodial thrusting.

Tribe Cnesterodontini

This tribe consists of eight species in four genera. Descriptions by Henn (1916) indicate that male *Cnesterodon decemmaculatus* are slightly brighter in coloration than females, but that other species exhibit no intraspecific color variation. Philippi (1908) and Jacobs (1969) also reported that *C. decemmaculatus* males are slightly brighter than females. Jacobs (1969) indicated slight color differences between sexes in *Phalloptychus januarius* and *Phalloceros caudimaculatus*, and the latter species shows subspecific color differences. Endler (1982) found that geographic variation in size and number of spots in *Phalloceros caudimaculatus* was correlated with predation intensity. In all cases where sexual coloration differences exist in the Cnesterodontini, they are minimal.

Philippi (1908) reported that *Cnesterodon decemmaculatus* and *Phalloceros caudimaculatus* exhibit only gonopodial thrusting. Rosen and Tucker (1961) observed *P. caudimaculatus* and *Phallotorynus jucundus* and also reported lack of courtship display. No data on aggressive behavior are known from the group. A tentative summary of the tribe is that there are no major intersexual differences in coloration, and that males lack a courtship display.

Tribe Scolichthyini

The two species of this tribe are endemic to Guatemala and are closely related to the Cnesterodontini (Rosen 1967). *Scolichthys greenwayi* males exhibit variation in pigmentation associated with adult size. Those that mature at smaller sizes retain vertical bars on the side of the body characteristic of juveniles, whereas larger males have a midlateral dusky stripe and resemble females. *Scolichthys iota* has no marked pigment variation. No data on sexual behavior are available.

Tribe Girardinini

Of the eight species of *Girardinus*, Jacobs (1969) reported that male *G. denticulatus*, *G. falcatus*, and *G. metallicus* are more intensely pigmented than females. My observations do not support this for *G. metallicus* (Farr 1980a), but Rivas (1958) described sexual differences in *G. denticulatus* and indicated that subspecific forms differ in coloration. In both species of *Carlhubbsia*, males are slightly more intensely pigmented than females (Hubbs 1936; Rosen and Bailey

1959). Finally, there are no sexual pigmentation differences in *Quintana atrizona* (Hubbs 1934).

Rosen and Tucker (1961) reported only gonopodial thrusting in *Quintana atrizona* and *Girardinus falcatus*, and my observations of *G. metallicus* (Farr 1980a) and of *Carlhubbsia stuarti* and *C. kidderi* (pers. observ. in the Haus des Meeres, Vienna, Austria) revealed frequent gonopodial thrusting and no courtship display. There is a high level of intermale aggression in *Girardinus metallicus*, and it probably serves to interfere with the mating attempts of other males (Farr 1980a). Mating in *G. metallicus* is probably determined entirely by males, as no female cooperation was observed.

In summarizing the tribe Girardinini, some species exhibit slight sexual differences in coloration, no polymorphisms exist, and males exhibit only gonopodial thrusting.

Tribe Heterandriini

Priapichthys annectens and *P. chocoensis* exhibit no sexual coloration differences (Jacobs 1969), although there is subspecific color variation in *P. annectens* (Hubbs 1924). Male *P. panamensis* and *P. dariensis* are slightly more intensely pigmented than females (Jacobs 1969). Jacobs (1969) described the bright coloration of male *P. nigroventralis* but mentioned nothing of female coloration, although Henn (1916) alluded to sexual differences. Finally, Rosen and Bailey (1963) reported that male *P. caliensis* are much more vividly colored than are females, and Socolof (in Rosen and Bailey 1963) found differences among males in gonopodial pigmentation. There are no published reports of social behavior in the genus, but my unpublished observations of *P. annectens* revealed that males use only gonopodial thrusting.

Neoheterandria tridentiger is the only one of four species in its genus for which there are adequate data on coloration and social behavior (McPhail 1978). No courtship display is exhibited by this species; all inseminations are the result of gonopodial thrusting. There is frequent aggressive activity among males and from females to males in the field. Males have a prominent black spot on the side of the body, and laboratory experiments showed that it serves as an appeasement signal reducing aggression from females.

Rosen (1979) recognized nine species of *Heterandria*, all of which are sexually monochromatic (Miller 1974; Rosen 1979), although coloration in *H. bimaculata* varies geographically (Hubbs 1926, 1936; Jacobs 1969). *Heterandria formosa* and *H. bimaculata* males use only gonopodial thrusting (Seal 1911; Rosen and Tucker 1961), and no information exists regarding sexual behavior of the remaining species. Intermale aggression in natural populations of *H. formosa* is frequent, although there is no evidence of either territoriality or permanent dominance relationships (Farr, pers. observ.).

Of the 17 known species of *Poeciliopsis*, 5 are included in the *Leptorhaphis* species group (Miller 1960); 3 of these, *P. monacha*, *P. lucida*, and *P. occidentalis*, have been treated extensively in the literature (McKay 1971; Moore and McKay

1971; Constantz 1975). There is a strong aggressive organization in these species. Males establish definite dominance hierarchies, and dominant males exhibit a dark black coloration. Subordinate males resemble females but are able to assume the dark color within 15 minutes if they attain a dominant position in the hierarchy. Dominant males apparently defend territories. McKay (1971) and Moore and McKay (1971) stated that male sexual behavior consists only of gonopodial thrusting, and field observations showed that subordinate male *P. monacha* and *P. lucida* are prevented from approaching females as often as dominant males. The ability of dominant males to interfere with the copulation attempts of other males decreases with increased population density.

Constantz (1975) reported that dominant territorial male *P. occidentalis* were much larger than subordinate males, and that they sometimes exhibited what he interpreted as a courtship display. This display was observed relatively infrequently, and it appeared that gonopodial thrusting was the most common form of copulation attempt in laboratory and natural populations. There were strong behavioral differences between territorial and nonterritorial males, the most notable being the quality of gonopodial thrusting. Territorial males often interrupted copulation attempts of subordinates, and as a result, nonterritorial males used more rapid, fleeting thrusts. In addition, females tended to flee from the approaches of the light-colored nonterritorial males, and thus there appears to be a form of female choice in this species. It is unknown whether size differences between dominant and subordinate males are socially or genetically determined.

Hubbs (1926) noted that some male *P. infans* are black, and Miller (1960) used the presence of dark-colored "nuptial males" to separate the *Leptorhaphis* species from the remaining 12 *Poeciliopsis* species. It is therefore probable that the preceding social organization is typical of this species group.

The remaining *Poeciliopsis* spp. are less well known. With the exception of *P. latidens*, in which males are slightly more brightly pigmented than females (Hubbs and Miller 1954), there are no sexual coloration differences (Heckel 1848; Henn 1916; Hubbs 1926; Bussing 1966; Miller 1975). *Poeciliopsis latidens* males exhibit only gonopodial thrusting (Rosen and Tucker 1961), and females apparently cooperate during mating (Rosen and Gordon 1953). Otherwise, nothing of the sexual behavior of this group is known.

There are slight color differences between sexes in *Phallichthys amates* and *P. fairweatheri* (Henn 1916; Rosen and Bailey 1959), but not in *P. tico* (Bussing 1963). Gonopodial thrusting is the only mode of insemination in *P. amates* (Rosen and Tucker 1961; Farr, pers. observ.), and Rosen and Gordon (1953) reported that females cooperate during mating.

The tribe Heterandriini can be summarized as follows. With the possible exception of *Poeciliopsis occidentalis*, no courtship display is known; even in the one exception it is apparent that gonopodial thrusting is the primary mode of insemination. Generally, males are highly aggressive, and in some *Poeciliopsis* species dominant males change coloration and are able to reduce either the quantity or quality of sexual behavior of less aggressive males. Intraspecific coloration differences are rare, and most that do exist appear to be related to aggressive behavior.

Tribe Gambusiini

Hubbs (1926) reported that breeding male *Brachyrahaphis terrabensis* are more brightly pigmented than females, and that nonbreeding (immature?) males are intermediate in coloration. Bussing (1966) indicated that *B. holdrigei* males are brighter than females. Jacobs (1969) described eight species of *Brachyrahaphis* (all but *B. holdrigei*) and indicated that only *B. episcopi* has slight coloration differences between sexes and that the remaining species are sexually monochromatic. My observations on *B. episcopi* in Panama revealed no sexual coloration differences. Dressler (1971) reported a local polymorphism in *B. episcopi*. The two morphs are cryptic on different bottom types, but there are no differences between the sexes within each habitat. Dominant male *B. parismina* and *B. cascajalensis* in aquaria are pale with dark margins on the unpaired fins, while subordinate males are dark with a darker lateral stripe (Farr, pers. observ.).

There are no published reports on social behavior in *Brachyrahaphis.Brachyrhaphis episcopi*, *B. parismina*, and *B. cascajalensis* performed frequent gonopodial thrusting in the laboratory (Farr, pers. observ.). Additionally, *B. cascajalensis* exhibited what appeared to be a courtship display when a female was introduced to three males previously isolated from females for 24 hours. The males exhibited a linear dominance relationship, and the dominant male dropped his gonopodium to a vertical position and arched his body toward the female. When I removed the dominant male, the second male began the same movements, and when I removed him, the third male exhibited identical behavior. No female response was observed, and attempts to elicit similar behavior from *B. episcopi* and *B. parismina* failed.

There are over 40 species of *Gambusia*, one of which, *G. aestiputius*, is known only from males Minckley 1962; (Rosen and Bailey 1963; Rivas 1969; Hubbs and Peden 1969; Miller and Minckley 1970; Peden 1973a; Miller 1975). There is little intraspecific color variation in the genus (Hubbs 1926; Myers 1935; Hubbs and Springer 1957; Minckley 1962; Jacobs 1969; Rivas 1969; Miller and Minckley 1970). *Gambusia atrora* and *G. manni* males have more brilliantly pigmented unpaired fins than do females (Rosen and Bailey 1963; Krumholz 1963; Sohn 1977a). *Gambusia marshi* has two color phases, each peculiar to a different habitat type (Minckley 1962). Some male *G. affinis* have varying degrees of melanism (Regan 1961). Usually only a small proportion of males are melanistic, and the significance of the coloration is unknown, although Martin (1977) reported that melanistic males are more aggressive and sexually more active than normal males at higher laboratory population densities. There is one spotted population of *G. senilis* that differs from all others, and three color variants occur at very low frequency in one population of *G. gaigei* (= *G. hurtadoi*) (Hubbs and Springer 1957). Finally, females of some species exhibit black pigmentation around the genital opening, and one or both sexes of some species exhibit a black suborbital bar. The significance of both characteristics will be discussed below.

Gonopodial thrusting has been reported as the only means of insemination in *G. affinis*, *G. nobilis*, *G. geiseri*, *G. vittata*, *G. gaigei* (= *G. hurtadoi*), *G. heterochir*, and *G. manni* (Seal 1911; Warburton et al. 1957; McAllister 1958; Hubbs and Delco 1960, 1962; Krumholz 1963; Carlson 1969; Itzkowitz 1971; Peden 1972a; Martin 1975, 1977). Rosen and Tucker (1961) observed *G. manni*, *G. heterochir*, and *G. affinis* and reported that the *Gambusia* spp. exhibit both gonopodial thrusting and a courtship display, but no further details were provided. Peden (1972a) observed what he called lateral and frontal courtship displays in *G. affinis*, *G. heterochir*, *G. atrora*, *G. aurata*, *G. geiseri*, and *G. gaigei* but concluded that displays were rare relative to gonopodial thrusts and that most or all copulations resulted from thrusting in the absence of display. No female response or cooperation has ever been observed in the genus, and McAllister (1958) concluded that because *G. gaigei* males orient and thrust from behind the female (outside her visual range), there is probably no female choice of males. Martin (1975) suggested that orientation behind females in *G. affinis* reduces aggression toward males, and Martin (1977) indicated there is no evidence for female receptivity or choice in the genus.

Females of the following species have dark pigmentation around the genital opening: *G. affinis*, *G. manni*, *G. heterochir*, *G. georgei*, *G. amistadensis*, *G. nobilis*, *G. atrora*, *G. alvarezi*, *G. gaigei*, *G. krumholzi*, *G. caymanensis*, *G. panuco*, *G. marshi*, *G. regani*, and *G. nicaraguensis* (Regan 1913; Hubbs 1926, 1927; Hubbs and Springer 1957; Carlson 1969; Peden 1973a). Only some individuals of *G. aurata* have such pigmentation (Peden 1973b), and it apparently is absent in *G. senilis* and *G. vittata* (Hubbs 1926; Hubbs and Springer 1957). Carlson (1969) hypothesized that such pigmentation provides a visual target for males in their copulation attempts, and Carlson (1969) and Peden (1973b) demonstrated that pigmentation intensity in *G. affinis*, *G. georgei*, *G. amistadensis*, and *G. heterochir* cycles in connection with the ovarian cycle; anal pigmentation is more intense when the female is carrying ripe, unfertilized eggs, and gonopodial thrusting increases with anal spot pigmentation intensity (Carlson 1969). Peden (1973a) performed additional experiments demonstrating the orientation function of the anal spot. Hubbs (1927) suggested that the anal spot of *G. manni* cycles.

There is frequent agonistic interaction in *Gambusia* spp.; in some species, more aggressive individuals are colored differently than less aggressive individuals. George (1960) reported that *G. affinis* males are territorial, and Caldwell and Caldwell (1962) reported monarchistic dominance hierarchies. Itzkowitz (1971) and Martin (1975), however, compared aggressive behavior in laboratory and natural populations and found no evidence of either dominance hierarchies or territoriality in nature, and aggression was much less intense in natural populations. McAllister (1958) reported that dominant male *G. gaigei* are more intensely pigmented than subordinate males in laboratory populations. Dominant *G. heterochir* males are lighter in coloration and have greater access to females (Warburton et al. 1957). Dominant male *G. georgei* and dominant individuals of both sexes in *G. amistadensis* have more intense pigmentation than less aggressive individuals, and they exhibit a dark subocular bar (Hubbs and Peden 1969; Peden 1973a). Miller (1975) reported that some male *G. eurystoma* were brighter than females.

A subocular bar has been observed in several species, sometimes only in males, and may have a function in agonistic interactions, as previously indicated. Most descriptions are from preserved specimens, so it is unknown whether all or only some individuals of one or both sexes have the marking in life. *Gambusia beebei, G. vittata, G. geiseri, G. senilis, G. regani, G. pseudopunctata, G. atrora, G. marshi*, and *G. panuco* apparently lack the bar entirely (Regan 1913; Hubbs 1926; Myers 1935; Hubbs and Springer 1957; Rosen and Bailey 1963; Rivas 1969). It is present only in males of *G. punctata* and *G. rhizophorae* (Rivas 1969) and present in both sexes in *G. nicaraguensis, G. luma, G. sexradiata, G. eurystoma, G. myersi, G. nobilis, G. senilis, G. gaigei, G. alvarezi*, and *G. manni* (Hubbs 1927; Hubbs and Springer 1957; Rosen and Bailey 1963; Bussing 1966; Rivas 1969; Miller 1975). In *G. manni*, the bar is more intense in some males than in others (Hubbs 1927).

In summary, the genus *Gambusia* is typified by a lack of sexual coloration differences, and by gonopodial thrusting as the primary means of inseminating females. Females of some species exhibit visual cues indicating fertility. Intermale aggression is frequent, and there is probably a high degree of aggressive interference among males in competition for females, but structured dominance relationships, as in some *Poeciliopsis* spp., probably never occur in nature. More aggressive animals sometimes change color, but not as prominently as in *Poeciliopsis*.

The third genus in the Gambusiini contains only one species, *Belonesox belizanus*, in which the sexes are identical in coloration. Rosen and Tucker (1961) reported that males exhibit a courtship display, and I confirmed this with several laboratory populations. The display is atypical for poeciliids, in that it is only observed immediately following birth of a brood (Farr, pers. observ.). The male positions himself in front of the female and begins a slow undulating motion with his entire body. This display continues for several minutes without pause, and I have observed some males to continue the motion for more than 90 minutes. Gonopodial thrusting is virtually nonexistent, and I never observed agonistic behavior by either sex at any population density.

With the exception of a few species of *Gambusia*, the tribe Gambusiini generally consists of species in which the sexes exhibit similar markings and coloration. A courtship display is certainly present in *Belonesox belizanus* and perhaps in *Brachyrhaphis cascajalensis*. Although some investigators have included some species of *Gambusia* among those with a courtship display, it is apparent from the more detailed investigations that gonopodial thrusting is the most common and most important means of insemination. It is interesting that *B. cascajalensis* is considered by Rosen and Bailey (1963) to be similar to the ancestral form that gave rise to the genera *Gambusia* and *Belonesox*, and that *Belonesox* today more closely resembles *Brachyrhaphis* than does *Gambusia*. If *B. cascajalensis* does, in fact, utilize a courtship display as its primary means of insemination, perhaps one can use phylogenetic relationships to explain the occasional occurrence of what appears to be a display in *Gambusia*. That is, the display of *Gambusia* may be a relict behavior that is no longer selectively advantageous, but that persists at a frequency sufficiently low as not to be selectively disadvantageous.

Tribe Poeciliini

Because of the complexity of the tribe Poeciliini, particularly the genus *Poecilia*, the following description utilizes the subgeneric and species group classifications of Parenti and Rauchenberger (Chapter 1), Rosen and Bailey (1963), and Hubbs (1933).

The genus *Alfaro* consists of two species, neither of which exhibits color differentiation (Rosen 1952). *Alfaro cultratus* has no courtship display (Rosen and Tucker 1961); gonopodial thrusting is frequent in the field and laboratory, and courtship display is not seen even following parturition (Farr, pers. observ.).

The subgenus *Poecilia* of the genus *Poecilia* can be divided into high-fin and low-fin species (Hubbs 1933). The former includes *P. latipinna*, *P. petenensis*, and *P. velifera*, all of which are characterized by a sexual dimorphism in which males possess a greatly enlarged dorsal fin (Regan 1913; Hubbs 1933; Parzefall 1969). Jacobs (1969) stated that *P. petenesis* males are also slightly different in coloration from females, and Snelson (1985) reported that large male *P. latipinna* have coloration different from females.

In addition to the strong sexual dimorphism in dorsal fin size, there is also high male size variation in *P. latipinna* and *P. velifera*. Baird (1968, 1974) and Simanek (1978) noted differences in male size and development in natural populations; large males are typically more brightly pigmented with large dorsal fins and are aggressively dominant over smaller males. Small males, however, are sexually mature and actively pursue females. Although Baird (1968, 1974), Simanek (1978a), and Luckner (1979) discussed size variation in *P. latipinna* as though there were distinct size classes, the variation is continuous and often unimodal and log-normally distributed (Snelson 1985; Farr et al. 1986). Parzefall (1969) reported that, within broods of *P. velifera*, there is great variation in length at maturity and relative height of the dorsal fin in males. Size variation in *P. latipinna* males has a significant genetic component. Travis et al. (1989b) have found that male size is determined by several (at least four) alleles linked to the Y-chromosome. Further experiments (Farr and Travis, 1989) failed to demonstrate ontogenetic social factors that affect male size at maturity.

All high-fin species of *Poecilia* (*Poecilia*) exhibit a courtship display in which the dorsal fin is erected and presented to the female; females respond by remaining stationary, folding the median fins, and sometimes twisting the abdomen to accept a copulation (Parzefall 1969). Luckner (1979) found that the propensity of male *P. latipinna* to exhibit courtship behavior was positively correlated with size; gonopodial thrusting rate decreased with size.

Courtship display rate in *P. latipinna* is positively allometrically related to male size; the converse is true for gonopodial thrusting rate (Farr et al. 1986). Furthermore, relative male size within populations determines rates of sexual behavior patterns. Thus, a 35 mm male in populations with large average male size would rely primarily on gonopodial thrusting; a male of the same size in a population with smaller average male size would exhibit high frequencies of courtship display.

Farr and Travis (1986) found that sexual behavior of male sailfin mollies is elevated immediately after a female gives birth and is directed more toward virgins than nonvirgins. They concluded that males are capable of recognizing females in the fertile portion of their ovarian cycle.

If one excludes the gynogenetic all-female *Poecilia formosa* (Hubbs and Hubbs 1932) and considers *P. sphenops* as a single species (but see Schultz and Miller 1971; Miller 1983), there are nine low-fin species of *Poecilia (Poecilia)* (Rosen and Bailey 1963; Miller 1975), none of which has a striking sexual dimorphism in fin morphology. There are at most only slight sexual coloration differences in all but the recently described *P. chica* and *P. catemaconis* (Hubbs 1924; Myers 1935; Trewavas 1948; Haskins and Haskins 1949, 1950; Rivas and Myers 1950; Liley 1966; Miller 1975). In *P. catemaconis*, males have bluish-black dorsal and caudal fins rimmed in bright orange; females lack this pigmentation (Miller 1975). In *P. chica*, males are more intensely pigmented than females, and dominant males become very dark, much like the *Leptorhaphis* species group of the genus *Poeciliopsis* previously described (Miller 1975). Miller (1975) also reported extensive variation in male size in this species.

Brett and Grosse (1982) reported that *P. chica* males use only gonopodial thrusting and are able to recognize females with fertilizable ova. Water from tanks with virgins or with females that had just delivered (and therefore had new ripe ova) elicited male sexual behavior and intermale aggression. Water that held gravid females did not.

Poecilia vivipara and *P. sphenops* lack a courtship display (Liley 1966; Parzefall 1969, 1979), although *P. vivipara* females cooperate during copulation (Liley 1966). Balsano et al. (1985) reported that *P. mexicana* females cooperate with males, but it was unclear whether males have a courtship display. There are no published data on sexual behavior of the remaining species. Reproductive success of male *P. sphenops* in some natural populations seems to be determined to a great extent by agonistic interactions. Parzefall (1979) reported that large dominant males exhibit a strikingly different pigmentation than subordinate males, and that they successfully prevent smaller males from all but fleeting approaches to females.

The subgenus *Lebistes* of the genus *Poecilia* includes those species with the greatest degree of sexual dichromatism and polymorphism in the family (Rosen and Bailey 1963). *Poecilia amazonica*, *P. picta*, and *P. branneri* have strong sexual dichromatism (Regan 1913; Haskins and Haskins 1949; Jacobs 1969); the latter also exhibits a marked sexual dimorphism in dorsal fin size and shape (Henn 1916; Mayer 1948). Male *P. parae* are trimorphic in secondary sexual coloration (Rosen and Bailey 1963; Liley 1966), and earlier taxonomic literature regarded the three male morphs as distinct species (Eigenmann 1909; Regan 1913; Hubbs 1926). *Poecilia reticulata* exhibits an elaborate polymorphism in male secondary sexual coloration with a vast number of different color patterns (Regan 1906, 1913; Winge and Ditlevsen 1947; Haskins et al. 1961; Endler 1978). *Poecilia scalpridens* was placed only provisionally in the subgenus *Lebistes* by Rosen and Bailey (1963) and apparently possesses no sexual differences in coloration or secondary sexual morphology (Jacobs 1969).

Poecilia parae, P. picta, P. branneri, and *P. reticulata* all exhibit a courtship display as the primary means of inseminating females, although all, to some degree, can inseminate through gonopodial thrusting in the absence of display and female cooperation (Mayer 1948; Liley 1966; Farr 1975, 1980b). Aggression among males is almost nonexistent in natural populations of *P. reticulata* (Farr 1975), despite reports that dominance relationships exist in some laboratory populations (Gandolfi 1971; Ballin 1973; Gorlick 1976). Farr (1980b) found experimental evidence that intermale aggression actually reduces male reproductive success in this species. Rates of courtship display and gonopodial thrusting vary geographically and are correlated with predation pressure (Farr 1975). Analysis of several inbred strains and wild stocks revealed strong linkage of these quantitative characters to the Y-chromosome (Farr 1983; Farr and Peters 1984).

Houde (1987) demonstrated that female guppies from one drainage in Trinidad prefer males with the most orange coloration. Endler (1978, 1980, 1983) showed that reduction or elimination of predation pressure results in increased conspicuousness of male coloration in guppy populations. He thus provided circumstantial evidence that female preferences result in more intense secondary sexual coloration, although Houde's (1987) work is the first experimental confirmation of female choice for more intense coloration in this species.

The subgenus *Pamphorichthys* of the genus *Poecilia* is almost unknown with respect to sexual behavior and coloration differences. *Poecilia minor* and *P. hollandi* are sexually monomorphic (Henn 1916; Jacobs 1969). *Poecilia hasemani* is known only from four females (Rosen and Bailey 1963), and the strongly dichromatic *P. heterandria* (Jacobs 1969) is only provisionally placed in the subgenus. In many ways it resembles the subgenus *Lebistes* (Rosen and Bailey 1963). There are no published reports of sexual behavior of any species in this group.

The following account of *Poecilia (Limia)* is based primarily on my own work with the group (Farr 1984). There is strong disagreement about how many species exist, so my synonymies may not be entirely correct. Two species, *Poecilia vittata* and *P. dominicensis,* exhibit virtually no secondary sexual differentiation (Regan 1913; Trewavas 1948; Jacobs 1969; Farr 1984). *Poecilia zonata* (= *P. nicholsi*) males have a darkened dorsal fin and caudal peduncle when aggressively dominant over other males; subordinate males are identical in coloration to females. Jacobs (1969) reported that only one male in an aquarium is dark, and if removed, another male assumes the dark pigmentation. My own observations (Farr 1984) of 20 to 30 individuals in large aquaria revealed that many, but not all, males are simultaneously darkly colored. Thus, *P. zonata* is similar to the *Leptorhaphis* group of the genus *Poeciliopsis* and to *Poecilia* (*Poecilia*) *chica* with respect to facultative male coloration associated with aggressive superiority.

Poecilia perugiae (= *P. melanonotata*) males are much more intensely pigmented than are females (Myers 1935; Farr 1984). The dorsal fin is blacker, and the caudal fin is yellowish and rimmed in black; males have a bejeweled appearance in good light. In *P. melanogaster* (= *P. caudofasciata*?), males have a black caudal peduncle and dorsal fin and a yellowish caudal fin rimmed in black. Females lack these markings but possess a large bluish-black pigmented area about the gonopore (Myers 1935; Jacobs 1969; Farr 1984). The female's abdominal pigmentation does not appear until sexual maturity (Farr 1984); to my knowledge this is the only example of a major pigmentary characteristic in female poeciliids that is different from both juvenile and male patterns. *Poecilia nigrofasciata* males are more intensely pigmented (Farr 1984) and deeper bodied (Regan 1913) than females. Older males become even more deep-bodied and assume a humpbacked appearance (Regan 1913; Jacobs 1969).

Only gonopodial thrusting is found in *P. vittata*, *P. dominicensis*, and *P. zonata*. Male *P. perugiae*, *P. melanogaster*, and *P. nigrofasciata* (those species with secondary sexual differentiation) have well-defined courtship displays (Farr 1984). In *P. melanogaster*, virtually no gonopodial thrusting is observed; any attempt by a male to contact physically an unreceptive female results in the female swimming away so rapidly, with the male in pursuit, that it is impossible to follow the action without slow-motion cinematography (Farr 1984). Females respond to male displays by remaining motionless in the water, tilting head-down at a 45° angle, and accepting the copulation.

Priapella bonita and *P. intermedia* have no coloration differences (Jacobs 1969), and nothing could be found concerning the markings and coloration of *P. compressa*. There are no published data on the sexual behavior or social organization of *Priapella*.

The genus *Xiphophorus* is the most complex group of poeciliids with regard to pigmentation and social behavior. Prior to 1979, eight species were recognized, some of which were divided into well-defined subspecies (Rosen 1960; Miller and Minckley 1963; Rosen and Kallman 1969), and Rosen (1960) recognized three distinct species groups. However, Rosen (1979) concluded that subspecies are not valid taxonomic units, so he combined several groups and elevated all to specific status. The result was a reduction in the number of distinct taxonomic entities from 17 to 15. Rosen (1979) also eliminated the designation of species groups. I use Rosen's (1979) scheme, but refer to pre-1979 designations were appropriate.

Xiphophorus helleri, *X. signum*, *X. alvarezi*, and *X. clemenciae* are characterized by a remarkable sexual dimorphism in which the lower rays of the males' caudal fin are elongated to form a pigmented sword-like projection (Heckel 1848; Regan 1907b; Alvarez 1959; Rosen 1960; Rosen and Kallman 1969). Neither *X. clemenciae*, *X. alvarezi*, nor *X. signum* are polymorphic for additional pigment patterns. In a few populations of *X. helleri* (formerly subspecies *X. h. strigatus* and *X. h. guentheri*), a few individuals exhibit a melanophore pattern, and there is some color variation among populations in *X. h. strigatus* (Rosen 1960; Rosen and Kallman 1969). Zander (1979) reported that males in one population of *X. helleri* (pre-1979 subspecies *X. h. helleri*) are dimorphic for size and coloration (note that the subspecific determination of Zander's population is mine, based on a comparison of the collecting site with the distributional data listed by Rosen [1960]). Otherwise, *X. helleri* has no additional pigment variation.

Xiphophorus helleri males exhibit a courtship display characterized by an alternating forward and backward swimming motion in front of a female (Clark et al. 1954; Franck 1964). Rosen (1960) suggested that such a movement might accentuate the sword, or vice versa. *Xiphophorus clemanciae* males have a similar display (Farr, pers. observ.). Kosswig (in Franck 1964) reported that intermale aggression, though frequent in aquaria, is not very intense in nature. Dominance relationships among male *X. helleri* exist only in small, isolated pools.

Both sexes of *X. milleri* are polymorphic for three micro- and two macromelanophore patterns, although more than half of the individuals in any population lack all patterns (Rosen 1960). A low proportion of males also have a black gonopodium (Rosen and Kallman 1969; Kallman and Borowsky 1972). Male *X. montezumae* and *X. cortezi* possess a pigmented sword (Rosen 1960). In two populations of *X. montezumae* the sword is relatively short; at a third locality it is much longer (Rosen and Kallman 1969). Both species are polymorphic for melanophore patterns. Both sexes of *X. cortezi* are polymorphic for three macro- and one micromelanophore pattern, and the pattern frequencies vary among populations (Rosen 1960; Kallman 1971). *Xiphophorus montezumae* is polymorphic for macromelanophore patterns and has at least two sex-linked alleles that determine size at maturity (Kallman 1983).

Male *X. pygmaeus* possess a very short sword that lacks the black pigmentation characteristic of other sword-bearing forms, and they are generally more intensely pigmented than females (Hubbs and Gordon 1943). Hubbs and Gordon (1943) and Rosen (1960) reported two male color morphs. *Xiphophorus nigrensis* males possess longer swords than *X. pygmaeus* (Rosen 1960). They are at least dimorphic for Y-linked coloration (Zander 1968) and occur in three distinct size classes determined by Y-linked genes and an autosomal modifier (Kallman 1976, 1984). Male *X. pygmaeus* are all of the small type (Kallman et al. 1973).

Franck (1964) described the courtship display of *X. cortezi* and later (Franck 1968) reported courtship behavior in *X. montezumae* and *X. milleri*. Farr (pers. observ.) observed courtship, female responses, and copulation in *X. milleri*. Franck (1964) reported a high gonopodial thrusting rate and very little courtship in *X. pygmaeus*. Ryan and Wagner (1987) revealed that larger male *X. nigrensis* exhibit courtship behavior, whereas smaller males primarily use gonopodial thrusting. Females apparently cooperate during mating and exercise an active choice of large males.

Xiphophorus couchianus and *X. gordoni* are neither sexually dimorphic nor polymorphic, with the exception that male *X. couchianus* very rarely exhibit a black gonopodium (Gordon 1943; Rosen 1960; Rosen and Kallman 1969; Miller and Minckley 1963). Breeding male *X. gordoni* are more intensely pigmented than females (Miller and Minckley 1963). *Xiphophorus evelynae* males have orange-yellow pigmentation on the dorsal fins, and in one population the male dorsal fin is enlarged. A single macromelanophore pattern is present in some individuals of each sex (Rosen 1960). Male *X. xiphidium* exhibit a minute sword (Rosen 1960), and populations are polymorphic for two macromelanophore patterns (Kallman and Atz 1966). Gordon (1943) reported that melanophore pattern frequencies vary among populations.

Xiphophorus variatus is polymorphic for at least four macro- and six micromelanophore patterns (Kallman and Atz 1966) and for several yellow and red pigment patterns (Borowsky 1973a). The red and yellow patterns are expressed more intensely in males, particularly in larger individuals (Borowsky 1973a). Considerable variation in male size is attributable to social inhibition of growth rate and size at maturity in both laboratory and natural populations (Borowsky 1973a, 1973b, 1978a, 1987b). There are also at least two Y-linked alleles that determine adult male size in this species (Borowsky 1987a). In natural populations, most aggression is among the most brightly pigmented males; these fish do not often attack less brightly pigmented males, which in turn ignore each other (Borowsky 1973a). *Xiphophorus variatus*, *X. couchianus*, and *X. gordoni* have a courtship display (Franck 1964, 1968).

Xiphophorus maculatus was described by Gordon (1943) as perhaps the most polymorphic vertebrate in North America. Kallman and Atz (1966) reported at least seven sex-linked macromelanophore patterns in this species, although two are known only from laboratory stocks and one was found in only a single male from a natural population. There are also at least eight autosomally-linked micromelanophore tail-spot patterns (Kallman and Atz 1966; Kallman 1975), and Gordon reported in 1943 that there were already 137 known patterns and combinations involving black spots alone. There are at least 18 yellow and red patterns in this species (Kallman 1975). Yellow patterns are expressed equally in both sexes, but red patterns are more intense in males. Some patterns are restricted to males (Kallman 1975). In addition to the great amount of pigmentation polymorphism, there are also five sex-linked alleles that determine size and age at maturity in both sexes and influence brood size (Kallman et al. 1973; Kallman and Borkoski 1978).

There is apparently no courtship in *X. maculatus*. Franck (1964) described a stereotyped approach behavior and copulation attempts but concluded that there is no visual signal from male to female. The approach behavior of *X. maculatus* males occurs outside the female's visual field. Franck (1968) concluded that this behavior is a rudiment of a courtship display that has been secondarily lost and that the behavior patterns are functionless. Wickler (1957) stated that copulations are only possible if the female is motionless, and he described how females tilt their abdomens to accept a male. Franck (1964) reported that two virgin females swam backwards to males.

DISCUSSION

In polygynous or promiscuous species in which females invest more in offspring production than do males, there is greater variance in the mating success of males than of females (Darwin 1871; Bateman 1948; Trivers 1972; Sutherland 1985; Hubbell and Johnson 1987). Most poeciliid females produce a limited number of large yolky eggs that are retained in the ovary for approximately 30 days after fertilization before live, self-sufficient young are born (Constantz, Chapter 3). Although most species are strictly oviparous, some (particularly those in the tribe Heterandriini) produce small unyolked eggs, form a pseudoplacenta, and supply some degree of nourishment to offspring during embryogenesis (Turner 1937, 1940a, 1940b; Scrimshaw 1944b, 1945; Thibault and Schultz 1978; Trexler 1985). Because males contribute only gametes, they can increase their fitness by mating with many females, but the number of offspring a female can produce per unit time is basically fixed. A female poeciliid can increase her fitness by mating with males that will produce genetically superior offspring (if there is heritable fitness variation). There are thus two components to male mating success in poeciliids: the degree to which males are able to inseminate many females to the exclusion of other males (intrasexual competition), and the degree to which females exert a direct influence on the mating success of males (female choice).

The following discussion concerns first the various manifestations of intermale competition in poeciliid fishes, and second the various options available to females with regard to accepting or modifying the results of intermale competition. I also outline hypotheses for various evolutionary schemes that might account for variation among species in how male mating success is determined. I attempt not to repeat literature citations for the behavior and pigmentation of different species, for which the reader can refer to the preceding discussion.

The Manifestations of Intermale Competition

Because female poeciliids can store sperm, an insemination at any time can contribute to a brood. Sperm competition and sperm precedence can alter the probability that an insemination at different stages of the ovarian cycle will result in fertilization (see following), but the basic reproductive biology of females favors males that are continuously sexually active and that are more active than other males. The latter can be accomplished through suppression of sexual activity of competitor males by aggression and through an increase in sexual behavior beyond that of rival males.

The second process has resulted in extreme rates of gonopodial thrusting and/or courtship display observed in most poeciliids. Guppies, *Poecilia reticulata*, exhibit up to 13 displays and three gonopodial thrusts per male per five minutes in natural populations (Farr 1975). *Gambusia affinis* males thrust approximately 30 times per 60 minutes (Itzkowitz 1971; Martin 1975), and *Girardinus metallicus* exhibit up to one thrust per minute in laboratory populations (Farr 1980a). Male *Poecilia (Limia) melanogaster* spend over 26 minutes per hour in courtship activity (Farr 1984). Male *Poecilia latipinna* will exhibit up to three courtship displays per minute in a 30-minute period (Travis and Woodward, in press). Obviously not all displays or thrusts can contribute to a brood even if they all resulted in sperm transfer. A single brood of as many as 100 young is rare, but even with such a high number, only three inseminations per female per day could result in offspring if every insemination fertilized only a single egg.

It seems clear that males with higher gonopodial thrusting rates will inseminate more females than those with lower rates, so selection should favor higher rates. Males with higher courtship display rates will encounter greater numbers of receptive females, so selection should also maximize display rates. Farr (1980b) demonstrated experimentally that male *Poecilia reticulata* with the highest display rates were reproductively more successful because of a higher probability of encountering a receptive female and greater preference by females. Thus, in both thrusting and displaying species there has been intense selection to maximize sexual activity.

The upper level of displaying or gonopodial thrusting is determined both by physiological limitations and by external influences such as predation. Displays in particular are very conspicuous, and Farr (1975) observed that courtship in *P. reticulata* was greatly reduced where predators had easy access to males. Male *Belonesox belizanus* court females only immediately after birth of a brood; *B. belizanus* is a large (relative to other poeciliids) "sit-and-wait" piscivore, and a high level of sexual activity would probably frighten away potential prey.

Most poeciliid species with a courtship display also exhibit gonopodial thrusting. Farr (1980b) concluded from an analysis of determinants of reproductive success in *P. reticulata* that once a species evolves a courtship display, no individuals can depend entirely on gonopodial thrusting for maximum reproductive success. For *P. reticulata*, *X. maculatus*, and *G. affinis*, the only species for which data are available, newer sperm are more viable than older stored sperm (Van Oordt 1928; Winge 1937; Vallowe 1953; Hildemann and Wagner 1954; Robbins et al. 1987), so males that mate when fertilizable ova are present will sire the majority of a female's brood. Because female poeciliids generally accept displays only as virgins or during the fertile portion of their ovarian cycle (Kadow 1954; Franck 1964; Liley 1966, 1968; Farr, pers. observ.), sperm from a chosen male should outcompete that from earlier matings, including those from previous gonopodial thrusts.

A male should not rely only on displaying, however. A male that only displays will be less successful than those who both display and thrust. Gonopodial thrusting does increase a male's reproductive success by contributing to a small fraction of a female's brood (Farr 1980b).

A final consideration of the rate of gonopodial thrusting and courtship concerns two aspects of phenotypic plasticity: Do males alter courtship display rates in response to those of other males, and is the ratio of number of displays to number of gonopodial thrusts constant? Farr (1976, 1980b) and Farr and Herrnkind (1974) demonstrated for *P. reticulata* that males affected courtship display rates of other males. A single male with females displays at a much lower rate than when a competitor male is present. Males in monomorphic populations display at lower rates than those in polymorphic populations, and males with relatively inactive competitors display at lower rates than those with highly active competitors. If females compare the display rates of several males and choose the most active, a male need only be visibly more active than competitors and need not necessarily display at his maximum potential. A male with no competitors has virtually a 100% chance of mating with all females and can safely display at a low rate. It is unknown whether such social facilitation of male sexual behavior exists in other species, although Travis and Woodward (in press) demonstrated that when intermediate-sized male sailfin mollies are placed with large males in experimental situations, they exhibit quantitative sexual behavior patterns similar to those of small males, whereas their behavior is intermediate when large males are removed.

Liley (1966) and Farr (1980c) examined phenotypic plasticity in the relationship between displaying and thrusting in *P. reticulata*. Males were presented either to receptive or unreceptive females, with the following results. Courtship display rate did not change, but gonopodial thrusting occurred more often when females were unreceptive, and displays were typically of lower intensity. The results were explained as follows. Males must exhibit a high display rate. Lower intensity displays probe a female's receptivity. If a female is receptive, a male should switch to high-intensity display, because females respond only to such displays (Farr 1977). If a female is unreceptive, a male should attempt to inseminate her by gonopodial thrusting and/or change females. Display rate remains high regardless of female receptivity, but the gonopodial thrusting rate increases with a decrease in the probability of success through display. This phenomenon has not been investigated in other poeciliids, although Farr and Travis (1986) reported for the sailfin molly that gonopodial thrusting levels remained high for much longer after a female gave birth than did levels of male courtship.

The second method of increased insemination success is to decrease the quantity or quality of sexual activity of other males through aggression. One must distinguish between long-term and short-term effects of aggression in poeciliids. The first involves total domination of some males by others with concomitant reduction in sexual activity of subordinate males. Short-term aggression involves direct interference with the copulation attempts of rival males but does not result in significant reduction of a competitor's sexual activity.

Total domination of competitor males requires low population densities and asymmetries in factors that result in winning an aggressive contest (e.g., size differences, motivational factors). Population density determines the number of potential intermale contacts, hence the potential number of fights, and asymmetries determine the length of fights before a winner is determined. Both are important, because a dominant male must suppress copulation attempts or courtship displays of competitors and still have sufficient time for his own sexual activity.

The number of intermale contacts, thus potential fights, increases exponentially with linear increases in population size. As population size increases, aggressive males must spend more time fighting and less time pursuing females. Also, attacks on nonaggressive males decrease because aggressive males spend more time fighting each other; nonaggressive males are thus free to spend more time in sexual activity. Clearly, at high population sizes it is impossible for aggressive males to be successful because of severe reductions in sexual activity relative to nonaggressive males. Aggressive behavior cannot be maximized to the complete exclusion of sexual behavior. Only in species that typically occur in low population densities is it possible for aggressive males to dominate to the point that sexual behavior is greater in dominant males.

The relationship between population size and the efficiency of aggressive organization was pointed out previously for several species, including *Poeciliopsis monacha*, *P. lucida*, *Gambusia affinis*, and *Xiphophorus helleri*. A knowledge of natural population sizes is therefore essential in interpreting aggression in the laboratory. Several reports of aggressive organization, for example, territoriality in *Xiphophorus* spp. (Heuts 1968; Zayan 1975), or monarchistic dominance hierarchies in *Gambusia affinis* (Caldwell and Caldwell 1962) or *Poecilia reticulata* (Gandolfi 1971; Gorlick 1976), probably have little relevance in nature, simply because population sizes are rarely, if ever, small enough to allow such behavior. However, *Poeciliopsis* spp. occurs naturally in low to high densities, depending on the season, and dominance or territoriality can be beneficial to males able to reduce sexual attempts of subordinates.

There are not yet sufficient data to determine the number of poeciliid species in which male reproductive success is determined primarily by a social structure based on aggression. To date, only the *Leptorhaphis* species group of *Poeciliopsis*, *Poecilia chica*, and one population of *Poecilia sphenops* can be included in this group as confirmed by observations in the field (McKay 1971; Moore and McKay 1971; Constantz 1975; Miller 1975; Parzefall 1979). All of these are characterized by the ability of dominant males to assume a coloration strikingly different from that of females or subordinate males. Because *Poecilia* (*Limia*) *zonata* also exhibits an extreme color change associated with dominance in laboratory populations, I would suspect that it, too, has a social structure based on aggression in natural populations. Although males of other species can alter coloration intensity in aggressive situations (e.g., *Gambusia* spp., *Brachyrhaphis* spp., and other species of *Poecilia* [*Limia*]), none does so as completely and strikingly as the species listed above, and none is known to have structured dominance relationships in nature.

Although in most species conditions do not allow permanent dominance relationships, aggression can still play an important role in determining mating success. All poeciliid females studied have a well-defined ovarian cycle; shortly after parturition, new ova are ready to be fertilized. Because females typically do not synchronize their reproductive cycles, there is high among-female variance in fertility. To reduce sperm competition, males should spend more time attempting to inseminate females with new fertilizable ova. The longer the period until fertilization, the higher the probability that successful insemination will be nullified by a subsequent one. Thus, fertile females should be more attractive to males, and if recognizable, males should attempt to inseminate these few females and exclude other males. Aggressive interactions that drive competitors from fertile females could have a large payoff.

The best examples in which female fertility is recognizable are in several species of the genus *Gambusia*, and in *Poecilia chica* and *P. latipinna*. Carlson (1969) and Peden (1973b) demonstrated that the intensity of gonopore pigmentation varies with the ovarian cycle in several species of *Gambusia*, and that males increase gonopodial thrusting toward fertile females. *Gambusia affinis* males tend to be more aggressive in the presence of females (Itzkowitz 1971). However, it has not been demonstrated that aggression increases in the presence of fertile females, nor have choice experiments demonstrated male preferences for fertile females. Crow and Liley (1979) showed that male guppies prefer water that has contained fertile females, thus suggesting males can recognize ''better'' females through a chemical factor. However, aggressive competition among male guppies is virtually nonexistent (Farr 1975, 1980b).

In a study of the sailfin molly, Farr and Travis (1986) observed elevation in male sexual behavior toward fertile females, but did not examine populations with more than one male. It is thus unknown how fertility advertisement affects male aggressiveness in this species. Baird (1968, 1974) observed frequent intermale aggression in natural populations. The functional significance of aggression in species that do not form permanent dominance hierarchies obviously needs more experimental work.

A variation on the preferred-female theme can be found in the relationship between gonochoristic species of *Poeciliopsis* and all-female ''species'' that sexually parasitize them (McKay 1971; Moore and McKay 1971; Keegan-Rogers 1984). Males establish permanent dominance relationships, and dominant males mate with conspecific females. Subordinate males prefer conspecific females if given a choice but are prevented from mating with them by the dominant males. Subordinate males then mate with unisexual females who need sperm for parthenogenetic development of their ova (gynogenesis) or for an actual fertilization with subsequent shedding of the paternal genome during meiosis (hybridogenesis) (see Schultz, Chapter 5). Males learn to avoid the common clones or hemiclones of the all-female forms, thus conferring a reproductive advantage to rare clones in the sexually parasitic forms (Keegan-Rogers 1984).

Size appears to be the most significant phenotypic character that determines the outcome of fights in poeciliids (Braddock 1945; Baird 1968; Parzefall 1969, 1979; McKay 1971; Borowsky 1973a, 1973b, 1978b; Constantz 1975; Sohn 1977b; Woodhead and Armstrong 1984). Size variation can have both an environmental and a genetic component. The genetics of size variation in poeciliids is discussed in detail by Kallman (1984; Chapter 9).

Environmentally-induced size variation can arise through the action of physical properties such as temperature (Liley and Seghers 1975, for *Poecilia reticulata* and Borowsky 1984, for *Xiphophorus variatus*), through juvenile competition for limited food resources, or directly through agonistic interaction among juveniles. Three species have been investigated with regard to the effects of social interactions on growth rate and size and age at maturity. Aggressive interactions among juvenile *Girardinus metallicus* result in slower growth with delayed maturation and larger size at maturity of subordinate individuals (Farr 1980a). Size and aggressiveness are not correlated in this species, but smaller males tend to be sexually more active and are more able to resist aggression from others. I proposed a model to explain the impaired behavioral capabilities of larger males based on known endocrinological effects of stress and aggression (Farr 1980a).

Borowsky (1973a, 1973b, 1978a, 1987b) studied the effects of dominance relationships among maturing male *Xiphophorus variatus*. The effects are much like those described in *Girardinus*. Dominant males grow faster, mature earlier, and are smaller as adults. Subordinate immature males eventually surpass the dominants in size, become more intensely pigmented, and eventually become dominant as adults. Because this species has a courtship display (Franck 1964), females probably prefer the larger, more intensely pigmented males. The advantage to being dominant as a juvenile apparently lies in the earlier age of maturation. Dominant males then mature at the earliest age when they can be larger than or as large as the other mature males in the population. Early age at maturity is an important life history trait in species that inhabit unpredictable environments (Cole 1954; Lewontin 1965; Gadgil and Bossert 1970; Stearns 1976), although this result does not hold for seasonal breeders. Sohn (1977b) showed that interactions among juveniles, in addition to genetic influences, can affect size at maturity in *Xiphophorus maculatus*.

Caution must be exercised in interpreting laboratory evidence of environmentally or socially induced size variation in poeciliids. It is easy to create an artificial situation that results in intense competition among immature fish but that may not be applicable to nature. Borowsky (1978a) provided field data supporting his experimental work with *X. variatus*. Field data on *Poeciliopsis* spp. show variation in adult male size. These species inhabit very harsh environments that could result in intense competition for resources during at least the dry season (Vrijenhoek et al. 1977; Thibault and Schultz 1978; Vrijenhoek 1978).

The main conclusion to be drawn from our knowledge of aggression in poeciliids is that we know too little. It is relatively easy to create a laboratory situation in which any species can be observed to be aggressive, but many more data, especially from the field, are necessary before we can adequately judge the extent to which intermale aggression influences mating success. The three primary questions to be answered for each species are: 1) is population density ever sufficiently low to allow permanent dominance relationships or territoriality?; 2) do conditions exist that allow environmental or social factors to induce asymmetries in size, motivation, or other factors that can determine a quick decision in a fight?; and 3) is there anything worth fighting for? Specifically, can males recognize better females, or must they divide their time more or less evenly among all females whose fertility is not recognizable?

Female Options

Competition among males, either by aggression or through different levels of sexual behavior, produces a nonuniform distribution of probabilities that any particular male will inseminate a female. Because of differential competitive abilities, some males will have greater access to females. Females have three options with respect to their influence on which males will sire their offspring. They can do nothing and merely accept the distribution of males available as the result of intermale competition, they can strengthen intermale competition, thereby further limiting the number of males available, or they can exercise a direct influence on male mating success by actively choosing from among available males.

The lack of direct influence by females on male mating success appears to be the most common, and probably the primitive, condition in poeciliids. Female choice, the direct influence on male mating success, is limited primarily to those species with a courtship display—the high-fin *Poecilia* (*Poecilia*) spp., *Poecilia* (*Lebistes*) spp., some *Poecilia* (*Limia*) spp., all but one *Xiphophorus* spp. in the tribe Poeciliini, and *Belonesox belizanus* and perhaps *Brachyrhaphis cascajalensis* in the tribe Gambusiini. In one species without a courtship display, *Poeciliopsis occidentalis* in the tribe Heterandriini, females exercise choice by staying in the vicinity of dark territorial males and by avoiding or fleeing from others. There appears to be no female choice in the monotypic supertribe Tomeurini, or in the tribes Xenodexiini, Cnesterodontini, and Girardinini, in most species in the tribes Heterandriini and Gambusiini, and in perhaps half the species in the Poeciliini.

Evidence that lack of female choice, or use of gonopodial thrusting as the only method of insemination, is a primitive trait comes from the monotypic family Horaichthyidae, native to India. *Horaichthys setnai*, described in detail by Kulkarni (1940), is a likely intermediate between the cyprinodontid medakas of the genus *Oryzias* and the Poeciliidae, and it resembles in many respects the peculiar poeciliid *Tomeurus gracilis* (Rosen and Bailey 1963). *Horaichthys setnai* has internal fertilization, but the fertilized eggs are shed and attached to aquatic algae and vascular plants. Kulkarni (1940) observed the mating behavior of *Horaichthys* and reported that males not only exhibit gonopodial thrusting and no courtship display, but also that mating appeared opportunistic, with no female cooperation. Gordon (1955) reported almost identical behavior in *Tomeurus gracilis*. The high proportion of poeciliids using only gonopodial thrusting and the lack of courtship in the primitive *Tomeurus* and in a presumed intermediate between the cyprinodonts and the poeciliids suggest that gonopodial thrusting is the primitive state and that courtship and female choice evolved later in some species.

There are two main questions, then, to be asked concerning the evolution of female sexual behavior in the Poeciliidae. First, under what conditions should females not merely accept the results of intermale competition but either intensify competition or exercise a direct choice of males? Second, if they do exercise choice, what are the criteria? Answers to these questions bear directly on theoretical concerns of the evolution of extreme male secondary sexual characteristics.

Female Intensification of Intermale Competition

Fertility advertisement can serve to focus intermale competition around only those few females in a population most likely to be carrying fertilizable ova. Recognition of fertilizable females can translate into intensification of intermale competition, through either elevated levels of sexual behavior or agonistic interactions.

Although few species have been examined with regard to fertility advertisement, preliminary data suggest that the phenomenon is not universal among the Poeciliidae. An estimate of the number of "advertising" species is impossible at this time, and data on the effects of fertility advertisement on male behavior in natural populations are virtually nonexistent. Any discussion of selective advantages gained by females through advertising fertility can therefore only be speculative.

There are two questions to be asked about the evolution of female mechanisms that intensify intermale competition. What are the ecological conditions that would favor the evolution of fertility advertisement? Does the decreased subset of males available to females as a result of intensified competition differ from that available as a result of a direct active choice of males, and, if so, in what manner?

Cox and Le Boeuf (1977), in their discussion of female mechanisms that intensify intermale competition, pointed out that such behavior should evolve in species in which characters indicative of fitness are correlated with aggressive superiority. They particularly mentioned male size and age, the latter especially when there is a positive correlation between size and age. I propose that there are two situations in which fertility advertisement is favored in poeciliids. The first is similar to that envisioned by Cox and Le Boeuf (1977) and occurs in species that use only gonopodial thrusting (e.g., some *Gambusia* spp.). The second occurs in species with a courtship display.

I suggest that fertility advertisement in species lacking a courtship display increases the probability that females mate with males with traits conferring aggressive superiority. The situation should be similar to cases where mating success is determined primarily by long-term dominance relationships or territoriality (e.g., the *Leptorhaphis* group of the genus *Poeciliopsis*), except that population densities are too high for a stable social structure based on aggression to exist. One would expect variation in male size or other factors influencing the outcome of agonistic interactions. If population sizes are large and a few males cannot dominate the remaining males, females can still increase the probability that larger or aggressively superior males sire their offspring by advertising fertility. The concentration of males around these females allows superior males to prevent others from approaching.

There is no difference in male reproductive success between species with long-term dominance relationships or territoriality and nondisplaying species with female fertility advertisement. In both types, male reproductive success is ultimately determined by aggressive interactions. The ability of males successfully to inseminate females is determined by phenotypic differences in factors influencing agonistic interactions. However, in species with populations small enough that a stable social structure based on male aggressive interactions is possible, one does not need to presume genetic variation underlying aggressive superiority. The system is controlled by males, and variation conferring aggressive superiority can be environmental or genetic. However, in species such as *Poeciliopsis occidentalis*, in which female choice minimizes the ability of nonterritorial males to be reproductively successful, one can assume that a female's offspring benefit from her behavior. One would thus expect a genetic basis for male aggressive superiority at least in species with female choice of territorial or dominant males.

If there is a selective advantage to females that "advertise", one must also assume that differences among males in ability to compete aggressively for females has a genetic component. A female would gain nothing by advertising fertility if variation in male competitive ability were solely environmental. It is important to note, however, that selection might not have acted on females by favoring those that advertise. It is entirely possible that chemical or visual cues indicating fertility are incidental by-products of the normal ovarian cycle. If this is the case, selection would work only on males to recognize fertile females. There could be genetic variation among males in the ability to recognize females, but there would not have to be genetic variation in traits determining the outcome of aggressive competition for females.

Because of the many species of *Gambusia*, the likelihood that not all advertise fertility, and the diversity of habitats in which they are found, a comparative study of this genus is the most promising avenue for examination of these issues. It must first be conclusively ascertained that females of some *Gambusia* species advertise fertility and that others do not. If both types exist, then the following predictions should hold:

1. Male mating success in "advertising" species should be determined primarily by aggression around fertile females, whereas other factors, particularly gonopodial thrusting rate, would be most important in "nonadvertising" species.

2. The differences must have at least a partial genetic basis. Females, by mating with aggressively superior males, must be gaining a competitive advantage for their offspring. Otherwise, there is no advantage to advertising one's fertility.

Fertility advertisement in nondisplaying species would thus allow aggressively superior males access to females in species whose population sizes are high enough to preclude stable dominance relationships or territoriality. Regardless of whether fertility advertisement arose as a direct product of selection or is merely a by-product of ovarian physiology, the result is high reproductive success conferred on aggressively superior males. With no fertility advertisement and no stable social structure based on aggression, male reproductive success is determined by factors such as high gonopodial thrusting rate. Thus, fertility advertisement in nondisplaying species does not merely reduce the subset of males available to females, but can actually cause a different subset of males, those with an aggressive advantage, to have greater access.

Fertility advertisement appears to have been documented in only two species with male courtship—the guppy (*P. reticulata*) and the sailfin molly (*P. latipinna*).

What advantage can be gained by females of these and other species by advertising fertility when they already have the ability to survey displaying males and exercise choice? The answer must be different from the advantages gained by females of species lacking courtship, for aggressive superiority should not be important to either guppies or sailfin mollies. Aggression among male guppies in natural populations is virtually nonexistent (Farr 1975); large sailfin molly males would have an advantage simply because their size and propensity to display (Farr et al. 1986) render them more attractive to females.

I suggest two possible advantages to fertility advertisement in displaying species, both of which arise from the peculiar biology of these species. First, it allows females to assess more accurately male traits that are negatively frequency-dependent in their benefit to females. In guppies, for example, where males are polymorphic for secondary sexual color patterns, fertility advertisement could cause males to be concentrated around a female with fertilizable ova and thus allow her to choose males on the basis of color pattern rarity. Female guppies have been shown to prefer males exhibiting rare color patterns (Farr 1977, 1980b). Farr (1980b) also demonstrated that male mating success in guppies is determined to a great extent by relative courtship display rates. A concentration of males would allow assessment of relative display rates and, because of social facilitation, would tend to force males to display at their maximum rates.

The second advantage could result from the successful invasion of a male morph able to circumvent female choice mechanisms. For example, in sailfin mollies female choice should favor large males. Yet small males persist in natural populations over all seasons of many years (Farr et al. 1986) and are a distinct genetic morph and not merely younger versions of larger males (Snelson 1982; J. Travis, pers. comm.). One possible scenario for the evolution of male size variation is that originally all males were large, and smaller males arose secondarily. Because they mature earlier and can successfully inseminate at any time through gonopodial thrusting, they can overcome the disadvantages of small body size.

If it is disadvantageous for females to mate with smaller males, then fertility advertisement would reduce the ability of smaller males to mate successfully. Large males could aggressively prevent smaller ones from mating, and choice of larger males during the fertilizable period would allow their sperm to outcompete sperm from previous matings with smaller males. Although small males persist in natural populations, perhaps the size-frequency distribution is less in their favor than it would be in the absence of fertility advertisement.

These two advantages to fertility advertisement in displaying species are admittedly ad hoc. Because so few displaying species exhibit the phenomenon, comparative study of closely allied species will not shed light on the problem. Unless more species are found to advertise fertility, the only avenue of investigation is more enlightened study of the two available to us. We must begin with more careful documentation of the phenomenon and its behavioral consequences and then proceed with experimental manipulation to determine selective advantages. As always, we must be aware that selection might not have directly favored advertising females, that fertility cues may be incidental by-products of the ovarian cycle, and that selection merely favored males responding to those cues.

Courtship and Secondary Sexual Differentiation

Before speculating on conditions under which females should deviate from the primitive condition of accepting results of intermale competition, I wish to point out a correlation within the family between the presence of courtship and secondary sexual differentiation of males from females. Table 6–1 summarizes, for 55 species, whether males exhibit courtship behavior and whether there are secondary sexual differences. For the remaining species we lack data on either behavior or secondary sexual characters. If the only difference between sexes is a facultative color change in males associated with dominance, I have included the species under the general heading of sexually monomorphic. I have not divided *Xiphophorus* into subspecies.

It is clear that a significant relationship exists between male sexual behavior and secondary sexual differentiation. Only 5 of 34 species (14.7%) lacking male courtship display exhibit appreciable secondary sexual differences, but males of 17 of 22 displaying species (77.3%) are more brightly pigmented or exhibit secondary sexual morphological differences. A 2×2 contingency table analysis (presence or absence of courtship versus presence or absence of secondary sexual differentiation) is highly significant ($\chi^2 = 21.24$, d.f. = 1, P < 0.001). If we accept the assumption that courtship indicates female choice, we can conclude that female choice is correlated with, and perhaps responsible for, the presence of extreme conspicuous male traits. These data thus lend support to the notion that sexual selection, female choice in particular, can result in the evolution of extreme male traits (Fisher 1958; Lande 1980a; Kirkpatrick 1982). Whether the male traits are or were correlated with some aspect of fitness will be addressed below.

The Evolution of Courtship and Female Choice

The existence of courtship and female choice in some poeciliid species indicates that not all species depend wholly on the results of intermale competition for determining male reproductive success. Although the question of why females of a species evolve mechanisms for choosing mates is probably the most important to understanding sexual selection in the Poeciliidae, it is also a question for which we have the least information. I have discussed the evolution of courtship and female choice in two previous works (Farr 1980b, 1984). In one of these (Farr 1984), I examined the evolution of courtship and female choice in the subgenus *Poecilia* (*Limia*), a group in which some species court and others do not. In the earlier work, I examined for the subgenus *Poecilia* (*Lebistes*), the conditions under which females should choose on the basis of male rarity or novelty, a behavior that maximizes outbreeding and maintenance of genetic diversity. The following discussion will focus on the evolution of both courtship and mechanisms that promote outbreeding.

TABLE 6–1. A Summary of the Poeciliid Species that are Sexually Monomorphic or Dimorphic and that Exhibit Courtship or Only Gonopodial Thrusting.

Monomorphic, Thrusting Only	
Tomeurus gracilis	*Xenodexia ctenolepsis*
Girardinus metallicus	*Quintana atrizona*
Carlhubbsia stuarti	*Carlhubbsia kidderi*
Heterandria formosa	*Heterandria bimaculata*
Priapichthys annectens	*Poeciliopsis monacha*
Poeciliopsis lucida	*Poeciliopsis occidentalis*
Poeciliopsis latidens	*Phallichthys amates*
Brachyrhaphis episcopi	*Brachyrhaphis parismina*
Gambusia affinis	*Gambusia nobilis*
Gambusia geiseri	*Gambusia vittata*
Gambusia gaigei	*Gambusia heterochir*
Gambusia aurata	*Alfaro cultratus*
Poecilia vivipara	*Poecilia sphenops*
Poecilia vittata	*Poecilia dominicensis*
Poecilia zonata	

Dimorphic, Thrusting Only	
Neoheterandria tridentiger	*Gambusia manni*
Gambusia atrora	*Poecilia chica*
Xiphophorus maculatus*	

Monomorphic, Displaying	
Belonesox belizanus	*Brachyrhaphis cascajalensis* (?)
Xiphophorus milleri	*Xiphophorus couchianus*
Xiphophorus gordoni	

Dimorphic, Displaying	
Poecilia latipinna	*Poecilia petenensis*
Poecilia velifera	*Poecilia picta*
Poecilia branneri	*Poecilia parae***
Poecilia reticulata**	*Poecilia melanogaster*
Poecilia perugiae	*Poecilia nigrofasciata*
Xiphophorus helleri	*Xiphophorus clemenciae*
Xiphophorus montezumae	*Xiphophorus pygmaeus*
Xiphophorus variatus*	*Xiphophorus cortezi*
Xiphophorus nigrensis**	

* Both sexes highly polymorphic, but males carry patterns not found in females.

** Males polymorphic for secondary sexual coloration.

I have previously argued (Farr 1984) that most poeciliids do not exhibit courtship and female choice because there is no particular male trait indicative of success in a particular environment. Most species are ecological generalists; they are euryphagous and experience a broad range of ecological conditions (Meffe and Snelson, Chapter 2). The tropical to subtropical nature of the group predisposes most species to wet-dry seasonal fluctuations, further subjecting them to significant habitat variability.

A substantial and ever-growing body of theoretical and empirical literature suggests that high levels of genetic heterozygosity can confer significant homeostatic abilities on individuals that experience a wide range of ecological conditions during their lifetimes (Lerner 1954; Bryant 1974; Templeton and Rothman 1978a, 1978b; MacKay 1981; Mitton and Grant 1984). Male sexual vigor, a primary determinant of reproductive success in poeciliids, is often associated with high heterozygosity (Maynard Smith 1956; Jakway 1959; Fulker 1966; McGill 1970; Farr 1983). Beard-more and Shami (1979) demonstrated a positive correlation between fecundity and heterozygosity in guppies; the same relationship occurs in some, but not all, populations of the mosquitofish (Brown 1982). If heterozygosity is indeed advanta-geous, then females should exhibit mating behavior that would most likely result in heterozygous offspring.

It is unlikely that female choice could result in higher heterozygosity in most poeciliid species. As discussed previously, few poeciliids have sufficient phenotypic variability for a female to exercise choice based on negative frequency dependence or negative assortment, two mechanisms that can result in increased offspring heterozygosity. Mating with vigorous males, those that could also be the most heterozygous, is likely but would not necessarily result in more heterozy-gous offspring. At any locus, a double heterozygote mating results in 50% homozy-gotes, as would a mating between a homozygote and a heterozygote. With no phenotypic indicators of male-female genetic differences and no advantage to mating with highly heterozygous males, there is no mechanism by which female choice could maximize offspring heterozygosity. I contend that in most poeciliid species courtship and female choice have not evolved simply because there is no male trait upon which choice could be based that would result in increased offspring fitness. Male and offspring fitness are not correlated, so female choice could not improve upon the subset of males available as a result of intermale competition.

There are three circumstances under which female choice could improve on the subset of males—environmental stability, in which a particular phenotype is most suited to a particular set of physical conditions, ecological specialization not related to habitat stability (e.g., stenophagy), or inhabiting a constantly or intermittently harsh environment in which an adaptive function maximizes fitness under the worst conditions (Templeton and Rothman 1974). In the latter case, if environmental harshness results in small populations, then one would expect male mating success to be determined primarily through aggressive interaction. But in the cases of environmental stability or ecological specialization, a single set of traits could constitute an optimal phenotype and provide a basis for female choice that could maximize offspring fitness.

My hypothesis for the evolution of courtship and female choice is as follows. If some species experienced a change from temporal environmental variability to stability or constancy, or a change that resulted in ecological specialization, then some individuals possessed genotypes that rendered them better able to survive and reproduce in the new environment. Because of environmental stability or ecological specialization, with its concomitant optimal phenotype, a correlation between male fitness and offspring fitness appeared and increased. Females that mated with genetically superior males produced better offspring. In a precise enactment of Fisher's (1958) runaway process of sexual selection, we see the evolution of both female choice of males and male secondary sexual differentiation.

There is almost no evidence to support my hypothesis. A preliminary assessment of the habitats of six species of *Limia* (Farr 1984) indicates that species with a courtship display and female choice exist in more stable conditions than do species with only gonopodial thrusting. Further work on this group could do much to test these ideas. A second group that would provide valuable data is the subgenus *Poecilia* (*Poecilia*), in which high-fin species court and low-fin species do not. A third possibility is the genus *Brachyrhaphis* and *Belonesox belizanus*, the latter being a rather specialized piscivore. Comparative examination of their ecological requirements, including laboratory experimentation of their physiological tolerances and the influence of genetic heterozygosity thereon, are essential. Even if my ideas are incorrect, comparative study of those groups in which some species court and others do not should provide clues to the conditions under which courtship and female choice arose.

The initial behavior associated with female choice was probably similar to that described by Constantz (1975) for *Poeciliopsis occidentalis*, in which females merely remain in the vicinity of preferred males and avoid or flee from nonterritorial males. There is no male courtship display or female response posture associated with female choice. As female preferences became established, males began to evolve stereotyped postures that accentuated phenotypic attributes upon which female choice might be based. I suggest that male courtship displays evolved simultaneously with exaggerated phenotypic traits. There is certainly a tendency for courtship displays in poeciliids to accentuate morphological and pigmentary differences between sexes. Rosen (1960) mentioned how the forward and backward motion of swordtails (*Xiphophorus* spp.) during courtship accentuates the sword. Members of the genus with no sword tend to move from side to side during courtship (Franck 1964). Males of the high-fin species of *Poecilia* (*Poecilia*) have courtship displays that involve spreading the enlarged dorsal fin. Finally, all species with male secondary sexual coloration appear to display that coloration to the fullest extent during courtship.

Female Choice, Outbreeding, and Polymorphism

There are a few species of poeciliids in which males or both sexes are polymorphic for coloration. In the latter case, as in some *Xiphophorus* spp., males can have color patterns not found in females. Little work has been done on the significance of color pattern variation in poeciliids or on possible behavioral mechanisms that might maintain variation. However, the few studies available provide some insight into the adaptive nature of color pattern variation.

Female guppies choose males with rare or novel color patterns (Farr 1977, 1980b). In *Xiphophorus maculatus*, there is a tendency for females to mate disassortatively with respect to color pattern (Borowsky and Kallman 1976), although this species apparently does not court, and mechanisms of female choice have not been documented. Both negative disassortment and choice of rare or novel color patterns can result in an increase in offspring heterozygosity. In *Xiphophorus variatus* there is no evidence of either positive or negative assortative mating (Borowsky and Khouri 1976). Different color morphs appear to be suited to different environmental conditions, indicating that cyclical selection might maintain the polymorphism (Borowsky 1978b, 1984). Males with tail-spot patterns tend to be more successful in mating, whereas females lacking tail-spot patterns have significantly higher levels of multiple insemination (Borowsky and Khouri 1976).

Where data are available, color pattern variation within populations is associated with temporal environmental variation or with behavior patterns that maintain genetic diversity. I have previously suggested (Farr 1980b) that the evolution of the tendency to mate with rare or novel males resulted from reinvasion of temporally variable habitats by species that had previously inhabited conditions leading to the evolution of courtship and secondary sexual differentiation. There are actually two scenarios that could result from reintroduction to variable or unspecialized habitats. Females could cease to choose mates altogether, with a subsequent reversion to male mating success being dependent wholly on the outcome of intermale competition, or female choice could be modified such that choice is based on male traits that promote outbreeding in place of ecological specialization. I speculate that the latter scenario is more likely, because it seems more reasonable to build on an existing system of courtship and choice than to remove the elements of courtship, choice, and secondary sexual differentiation.

To my knowledge there are only two groups that could provide information on the evolution of polymorphisms and behavioral patterns that maximize outbreeding. The first is the subgenus *Poecilia* (*Lebistes*), which includes the highly polymorphic guppy, the trimorphic *Poecilia parae*, and at least two species with no male color pattern variation. The second is the genus *Xiphophorus*, in which *X. variatus* and *X. maculatus* are highly polymorphic, several species have a lesser degree of polymorphism, and other species, particularly the swordtails, exhibit little or no color pattern variation. Even if my hypotheses are incorrect, such a comparative study should provide valuable insight into the evolution of polymorphism and female choice patterns that maximize outbreeding.

SUMMARY AND FUTURE RESEARCH

The family Poeciliidae is an excellent group with which to study the evolution of competition for mates and female choice. The existence of courtship in some species is indicative of the action of female choice, so comparison of species with and without male courtship can provide insight into the workings of sexual selection.

A systematic overview of the family reveals substantial interspecific variation in the determinants of male mating success, both in manifestations of intermale competition and in the existence of female choice. Less than half the species exhibit courtship and female choice. In those lacking courtship, males inseminate females only through gonopodial thrusting with no active choice by females. Most species are not sexually dimorphic, but males of some species exhibit conspicuous secondary sexual coloration or other secondary sexual characters. Some species are highly polymorphic for coloration and/or body size.

Intermale competition manifests itself as aggression or as high levels of sexual activity. Few species develop dominance hierarchies or territoriality in nature because population sizes are not low enough for such aggressive organization to be effective. In species with fertility advertisement, intermale aggression can still determine reproductive success even though dominance or territoriality does not exist. Sexual selection also has resulted in extremely high levels of gonopodial thrusting and courtship display.

Females have several evolutionary options. They can accept the results of intermale competition with no influence on mate choice, they can advertise fertility and thereby strengthen intermale competition, and they can actively choose competing males. I argue that most species are ecological generalists inhabiting temporally variable environments in which heterozygosity is advantageous; female choice has not evolved in these species simply because there is no phenotypic trait upon which choice could be based that would increase offspring fitness. Female choice evolved in species that moved into more stable environments or that became ecological or trophic specialists. There is a strong positive correlation between courtship and the existence of conspicuous male secondary sexual characteristics. Some displaying species with secondary sexual differentiation have reinvaded variable environments, and sexual selection has resulted in disassortative mating or female choice for male rarity or novelty. These latter species are polymorphic for male secondary sexual coloration and body size.

Although there are few data to test my hypotheses, further study of poeciliids could ultimately provide tests of many current ideas of the action of sexual selection. Detailed study should eventually provide data to test several important theoretical problems in evolutionary biology. Once we know the conditions under which courtship and female choice arose, for example, we should be able to determine whether conspicuous male traits were at one time directly associated with fitness, as is inherent in Fisher's (1958) runaway process of sexual selection, or had no particular fitness value, as is suggested by theoretical models of Lande (1980a), Kirkpatrick (1982), and others. The family provides an ideal group for investigations of the adaptive nature of genetic variability, particularly heterozygosity, as a means of coping with temporally variable environments. The separate roles of intermale competition and female choice as determinants of male reproductive success can be easily examined with further study.

Through this synthesis, I have attempted to provide a skeleton upon which future work on sexual selection can be built. I have pointed out where information is available and lacking, and I have focused attention on those evolutionary problems that can be answered by further study. My own hypotheses regarding selective forces are certainly not final answers, but merely represent the state of my thinking at this time. I am fully aware that future researchers will arrive at better answers when more information is available. I only hope that my thoughts will provide direction toward those answers.

ACKNOWLEDGMENTS

The ideas contained in this chapter have evolved over a period of almost 20 years, and it would be impossible to acknowledge everyone who contributed. However, Bill Herrnkind, Chuck Stasek, Glayde Whitney, Dan Simberloff, Don Strong, J. H. Schröder, and Joe Travis have been the most important influences on my thinking and on my ability to make pertinent observations. I acknowledge support at various times from the National Science Foundation, the German Science Foundation, the National Institutes of Health, the Alexander von Humboldt Foundation, the Society of Sigma Xi, the National Geographic Society, the Institut für Biologie of the Gesellschaft für Strahlen-und Umweltforschung, and the Department of Biological Sciences, Florida State University. I thank Joe Travis for his comments on this manuscript and Tim Allen for the loan of his computer. Finally, I thank Joan Crosby for her support and encouragement while I was writing this chapter.

Chapter 7

Review of Life History Patterns In Poeciliid Fishes

DAVID N. REZNICK
DONALD B. MILES

INTRODUCTION

The poeciliids display a great diversity of life history patterns, even within the constraints of viviparity. One dramatic variation is the presence or absence of superfetation, or the ability to simultaneously carry more than one brood (Turner 1937, 1940a, 1940b). A second is the absence (lecithotrophy) or presence (matrotrophy) of maternal provisioning after fertilization (Turner 1940b). Less dramatic but still significant sources of variation include the full spectrum of life history characters, such as body size, age at maturity, offspring size, brood size, and frequency of reproduction (e.g., Constantz 1974, 1979; Reznick and Endler 1982; Stearns 1983b, 1983c). To date, no attempt has been made to synthesize what is known about this diversity. Our goal is to gather available information on poeciliid life histories and go as far as possible to interpret their distribution. Secondarily, we highlight where information is most needed to form a complete picture of poeciliid life history evolution. We also argue that poeciliids hold great promise for future investigations because the emergent patterns are so interesting and the fish are so easy to work with.

Including different species and higher taxa in comparative studies such as this presents a wider range of variation for any trait than would be accessible within a single species. As a statistical consequence, one is more likely to perceive patterns or associations among individual life history traits than could be detected within a species. Such patterns can in turn help make sense out of the overall diversity of life histories. These patterns can also suggest hypotheses for their underlying causes and, with some qualifications, be used to evaluate these hypotheses.

Applying the comparative method incurs a variety of hazards that can compromise or distort the results. The primary difficulty arises from nonindependence of observations (Clutton-Brock and Harvey 1984; Felsenstein 1985), the chief source of which is relatedness among species. For example, all members of the genus *Poeciliopsis* superfetate. If superfetation influences other aspects of the life history, all members of the genus would share these similarities. A likely reason for this pattern is that all species inherited these traits from a common ancestor. Evaluating such similarities is of interest because they imply the imposition of phylogenetic constraints on life history evolution; however, entering each species as an independent observation when evaluating associations or correlations among life history variables would distort results, particularly because this genus is more highly represented than many others. Our data set is too small to employ the recommendations made by Felsenstein or Clutton-Brock and Harvey; however, we will at least apply the spirit of their recommendations when discussing and interpreting our results.

The questions addressed in this chapter are:

1)   What is the phylogenetic distribution of superfetating versus non-superfetating species? Does this distribution imply that superfetation evolved only once, or has it evolved more than once in the family?

2)   What differences in life histories are associated with the two modes of reproduction? In particular, is superfetation strictly associated with matrotrophy, as argued by some authors? More generally, is the mode of reproduction associated with other aspects of the life history, such as offspring size?

3)   Are there any other patterns of association among life history variables in comparisons among species, as often found for other organisms (e.g., Stearns 1983d, 1984b; Dunham et al. 1987)?

4)   What are the patterns of association among life history variables within a species, and what can be deduced about the ultimate and proximate causes of these variations?

5)   How do the patterns of association among life history variables within a species compare with those observed among species?

DATA SELECTION AND ANALYSES

The Data

Our data were derived primarily from values reported in the literature. In some cases, we included our own unpublished observations, values computed from figures or tables contained in published papers, or values computed from raw data provided by colleagues. Because of extreme scarcity of data, we have occassionally combined observations of different authors for a given species. We have, as much as possible, concentrated on papers that provide estimates for a spectrum of life history variables based on large sample sizes. We therefore do not include a complete coverage of papers that report fragmentary results, such as a few observations on fecundity or interbrood interval. We have also exercised discretion in selecting papers to be included. In particular, we include all observations reported by Turner (1937, 1940), because his work has proven consistent with subsequent observations. We exclude many observations by Scrimshaw (1944a, 1944b, 1945) because of the inconsistency of his results with later studies. For example, Scrimshaw reports superfetation in *Poecilia reticulata* and *Gambusia affinis* and matrotrophy in these species plus *Belonesox belizanus*. Subsequent studies with larger sample sizes and samples from multiple localities report that all three species are lecithotrophic and non-superfetating (Thibault and Schultz 1978; Reznick and Endler 1982; Turner and Snelson 1984). Thibault and Schultz (1978) summarize possible reasons for the inconsistency between their observations and Scrimshaw's.

The data set (defined below) includes 1) mode of reproduction, 2) female standard length at first reproduction, 3) mean length of reproducing females, 4) mean brood size, 5) mean offspring weight, 6) mean reproductive allotment, 7) mean interbrood interval, and 8) mean male length. We had also hoped to report estimates of age at maturity, but these data were too limited and too sensitive to rearing conditions to merit inclusion.

1) Mode of reproduction: Species were classified as either superfetating or non-superfetating. We did not attempt to quantify the degree of superfetation (as done by Travis et al. 1987b), nor did we incorporate the few reports of intraspecific variation in this trait (e.g., Monaco et al. 1983). These issues will be raised in the Discussion.

Species were also classified as either lecithotrophic or matrotrophic, based on weight change during development. Lecithotrophy generally involves a 30 to 40% loss of dry mass during development, due to costs of metabolism; matrotrophy is evidenced by either constant or increasing mass during development.

2) Female standard length (SL) at first reproduction: This variable was reported either as the minimum size of reproducing females or as the minimum millimeter size class in which most females were reproducing. We restricted entries to those specifying female size at parturition or minimum size of females with embryos. We did not include figures for minimum size females with eggs, since some ova development can take place longer before a female gives birth than expected from the development time. If results are reported as total lengths (TL), we computed the standard length as 0.8 TL, based on our estimates of TL and SL in *Poecilia reticulata* and *Gambusia affinis*.

3) Mean length (SL) of reproducing females: This includes all females carrying developing embryos or yolking ova (the difference is often not noted).

4) Mean brood size: Mean brood size is reported as the average among all reproducing females or the predicted value for the average female from a length-brood size regression. When multiple data points are reported for a species, we use the adjusted mean brood size, which is the predicted brood size for the

average sized female among all collections for that species. In superfetating species, mean brood size equals the number of embryos in a given or the latest stage of development, or the average number born at one time; it does not equal the total number of developing young in the female. The inclusion of interbrood interval incorporates the discrepency in brood size between these and non-superfetating species.

5) Offspring size: Offspring size is estimated as the dry weight of a newborn or a full term embryo. In some cases, authors only report mean embryo size. Since embryo weight often changes during development, such an average could be either larger or smaller than the true size of newborn young. These figures were also included in our data set.

6) Reproductive allotment: This variable equals the percentage of total weight consisting of developing embryos, generally based on dry weights of somatic and reproductive tissues. In one paper (Milton and Arthington 1983a) it is based on wet weights. In non-superfetating species, the weight of reproductive tissues is equal to the weight of one litter of developing young. In superfetating species, it is the combined weight of all simultaneously developing litters.

7) Interbrood interval: The interval equals the average number of days between subsequent broods. Since this variable is temperature-sensitive, we use only values estimated at "room temperature" or as close as possible to 25°C. Also, the interval is generally estimated in the lab on a small number of females and is paired with variables estimated on a different sample of wild-caught females. When a single value was reported in a study with multiple populations, we included the same value for all populations.

8) Mean male length: This equals the mean length of sexually mature males, or males that have completely developed gonopodia.

If more than one data set was available for a species, we used the means of all sets for interspecific comparisons. We excluded large data sets for *Poecilia reticulata* (Reznick and Endler 1982) and *Gambusia affinis* (Stearns 1983b, 1983c) from these analyses and used them instead for independent analyses of intraspecific variation. *Poecilia reticulata* was represented by data from Thibault and Schultz (1978), whereas *G. affinis* was represented by data from Milton and Arthington (1983a) and Reznick (1981). We also excluded a large number of studies on *G. affinis* that reported partial descriptions of its life history. Doing so excluded much information on seasonal patterns of reproduction. For this species, and all others where seasonal information was available, we chose data that characterized the life history during the height of the reproductive season.

Statistical Analyses

We addressed our questions with the following analyses:

1) We evaluated the phylogenetic distribution of superfetation and the association between superfetation and matrotrophy with contingency tables, using chi square statistics or an equivalent method (Mantel chi-square, Fisher's exact test)

when dictated by small sample sizes. The classification employed follows Parenti and Rauchenberger (Chapter 1).

2)   To evaluate differences associated with the two modes of reproduction, we first considered the association between superfetation/non-superfetation and matrotrophy/lecithotrophy with a chi-square analysis. We used univariate analyses of variance to compare the modes for continuously distributed variables. The independent variable was the mode of reproduction (superfetation versus non-superfetation), and the dependent variable was each of the continuous life history variables. These analyses were done with and without mean female size as a covariate to determine the contribution of body size to any observed differences among modes. We confirmed that the assumption of homogeneous slopes was satisfied before including female body size as a covariate. All results are based on Type III sums of squares (SAS Inst. 1985), which provide conservative tests of hypotheses.

We then compared the two modes with discriminant analysis. Such an analysis is preferable to a series of univariate tests, because it simultaneously considers all dependent variables and accomodates intercorrelations among these variables. However, it has the disadvantage that we could only include species for which all variables were estimated, greatly reducing sample sizes. We performed two such analyses. One included mean female size, brood size, offspring size, and interbrood interval as dependent variables; these variables were available for only eight species. We excluded interbrood interval from the second analysis and were able to increase the sample size to 11 species.

3)   To evaluate associations among life history variables within a mode of reproduction, we first calculated correlations among individual life history traits, then examined the association among life history variables with a principal components analysis. As with the discriminant analysis, principal components analysis has the advantage of simultaneously considering all dependent variables and adjusting for correlations among these variables but has the disadvantage that there are only a few species for which all variables have been estimated. This type of analysis generates a linear function that best describes variation among species and allows inferences about the importance of each dependent variable in accounting for this variance. The analysis was executed for the same dependent variables and species as in the second discriminant analysis and was done separately for each mode of reproduction.

4)   We evaluated patterns of intraspecific variation in life histories with the data sets for *Poecilia reticulata* (Reznick and Endler 1982; Reznick and Bryga 1987) and *Gambusia affinis* (Stearns 1983b). In each study, the authors began with *a priori* hypotheses for potential causes of differences in life history patterns and evaluated them with a series of analyses of variance, comparing fish from different types of localities. Principal components analyses provide a good summary of their results. The dependent variables in these analyses are mean female size, mean fecundity, offspring size, and reproductive allotment. These summaries evaluate the potential of two factors, predation and habitat predictability, for selecting for changes in the life history.

A second analysis evaluates the potential role of food as a proximal source of life history variation. We repeated the principal components analysis of *P. reticulata*, incorporating laboratory data on the response of guppies to different levels of food availability. The objective is to evaluate whether the response to food parallels variation observed among localities.

Data for all analyses are the mean values for these variables for each locality sampled or each level of food availability (summarized in Appendix 4). Analyses of variance of the scores for the first and second principal components evaluate the overall differences among the types of localities.

5)   A third analysis of intraspecific variation is a principal components analysis excluding reproductive allotment so that it is comparable to the three-dependent-variable analysis for interspecific comparisons. This approach evaluates whether patterns of variation within a species are similar to those observed among species.

Data were log transformed for all analyses described in items 2 through 5. We used all available data in the univariate analyses of variance, correlations, and regressions, so the number of degrees of freedom varies among dependent variables. All multivariate analyses were based on correlation matrices, allowing for a direct interpretation of the coefficients (eigenvectors) associated with each dependent variable.

LIFE HISTORY PATTERNS

Means and variances for the continuously distributed variables (Table 7–1) are lumped for the whole family, separated for superfetaters versus non-superfetaters, and separated by tribe. Only three tribes, the Poeciliini, Gambusiini, and Heterandriini, are sufficiently represented to include here. Note: 1) the number of available species ranges from 8 to 18; the amount of information that we have to work with is thus very small; 2) the apparent differences between modes of reproduction in variables such as fecundity, offspring size, and interbrood interval; these values are useful references when considering the results of subsequent analyses; and 3) the range of life history variables among species (Appendices 3 and 4). For example, there is a fourfold range in the minimum size of reproducing females, from 14 mm in some populations of *Poecilia reticulata* to 56 mm in *Belonesox belizanus*, a tenfold range of variation in offspring size, from 0.6 mg in *Poeciliopsis prolifica* to 6.9 mg in *B. belizanus*, and over a thirtyfold range of variation in brood size, from 2.9 offspring in *Poeciliopsis prolifica* to over 100 in *B. belizanus*. There is wide variation even within a genus; for example, mean offspring size in *Poecilia* ranges from 0.7 mg (*P. reticulata*) to 3.7 mg (*P. latipinna*). In general, the range of life history variation in the family is quite large (e.g., compare with Dunham et al. 1987, for a similar analysis of reptile families).

1)   What is the phylogenetic distribution of superfetation? Superfetation is concentrated in, but not exclusive to, the tribe Heterandriini (Table 7–2a). The vast majority of all other species do not superfetate; however, there are reports

TABLE 7-1. Mean Values (One Standard Error in Parentheses) for Selected Life History Variables. (See Data and Analyses section for definition of variables.)

	Minimum Female Size (mm)	Mean Female Size (mm)	Litter Size	Offspring Dry Weight (mg)	Reproductive Allotment (%)	Interval (days)	Mean Male Size (mm)
A. For the Entire Family							
$\bar{X}$(SE)	24.6(2.5)	34.1(4.9)	18.0(5.9)	2.1(0.5)	13.6(1.7)	24.5(3.0)	29.5(5.8)
n	15	16	18	14	8	16	9
B. For Mode of Reproduction							
Non-superfetators							
$\bar{X}$(SE)	25.8(2.6)	38.6(8.2)	28.9(9.3)	2.6(0.8)	16.2(1.4)	32.0(2.4)	32.2(6.3)
n	10	9	10	7	5	10	8
Superfetators							
$\bar{X}$(SE)	22.2(1.6)	28.3(3.3)	4.4(0.6)	1.5(0.4)	9.3(2.6)	12.0(2.0)	16.5
n	5	7	8	7	3	6	1
C. For the Three Tribes Adequately Represented							
Poeciliini							
$\bar{X}$(SE)	22.4(2.7)	30.5(3.8)	28.7(8.5)	1.7(0.9)	15.2(1.1)	29.5(2.3)	27.9(4.1)
n	5	4	5	3	3	5	4
Gambusiini							
$\bar{X}$(SE)	29.2(6.8)	45.1(14.5)	28.9(17.8)	3.3(1.3)	17.7(3.4)	33.1(5.1)	34.4(12.7)
n	5	5	5	5	2	5	4
Heterandriini							
$\bar{X}$(SE)	22.0(1.6)	28.3(3.3)	4.4(0.6)	1.5(0.4)	9.3(2.6)	11.9(2.0)	16.5
n	5	7	8	7	3	6	1

TABLE 7–2.   Tests of Association for Mode of Reproduction.

A. Superfetation/Non-superfetation Versus Tribe.

Tribe	Poeciliini	Cnesterodontini	Gambusiini	Girandinini	Heterandriini
Non-super-fetaters	17	2	7	2	2
Super-fetaters	2	1	1	0	19

p < 0.0001 (Mantel χ^2)

B. Superfetation/Non-superfetation Versus Matrotrophy/Lecithotrophy

	Lecithotrophy	Matrotrophy
Non-super-fetaters	20	0
Super-fetaters	1	9

p < 0.0001 (Fisher's exact text)

of superfetation in three of the other four tribes and four genera represented in this analysis. If we assume that these tribes were derived from a non-superfetating common ancestor and that superfetation evolves from non-superfetation (Turner 1937), then this pattern suggests that superfetation evolved independently multiple times within the family.

This interpretation demands a critical review of the exceptional observations. The two species in the tribe Poeciliini (*Poecilia branneri, Priapella bonita*) and one species in the tribe Cnesterodontini (*Phalloptychus januarius*) were classified as superfetaters by Turner (1937), based on a description by Stoye (1935). Stoye's book was written for the home hobbiest and contained brief descriptions of reproductive mode, such as the following for *P. branneri*: "The young are produced every few days, one or two at a time, with a longer resting period in between" (p. 68). Such an observation, if accurate, argues for superfetation because of the frequent production of small broods. The expected pattern for a non-superfetater is larger broods produced at three- to four-week intervals. *Gambusia vittata* is the only member of the tribe Gambusiini reported to superfetate; it was included in a list of superfetaters by Turner (1940b) with no supporting data. All four of these exceptions therefore rank as compelling and worth further investigation but should not be taken literally at this time.

The non-superfetating members of the tribe Heterandriini are *Priapichthys darienensis* and *Heterandria bimaculatus*. Scrimshaw (1944b) dissected seven and five females, respectively, and found no superfetation. Turner (1937) also reported that *H. bimaculatus* was lecithotrophic and non-superfetating, but no results were presented. In general, the degree of superfetation declines (Travis et al. 1987b) or disappears (Thibault and Schultz 1978) on restricted food, so the failure to find superfetation in a small number of females from one sample does not prove its absence. Again, the observations are compelling but require further investigation.

2) What is the association between mode of reproduction and other aspects of the life history? We found a nearly perfect association between modes of reproduction; superfetaters are almost exclusively matrotrophic and non-superfetators are exclusively lecithotrophic (Table 7–2b). The single exception is *Poeciliopsis monacha* (Thibault and Schultz 1978), whose embryos lose 47 percent of their mass between fertilization and birth, indicating no maternal investment in embryonic growth after fertilization. This conclusion was based on dissections of 45 wild-caught females, which is a sufficiently large sample to make a spurious result highly unlikely.

This single observation is biologically important, because it suggests no strict linkage between these two aspects of the life history. Instead, one of the two traits may be more likely to evolve if the other trait is already present. From a statistical perspective, this association is sufficiently strong to justify including only one reproductive mode in subsequent analyses. We deal only with superfetation versus non-superfetation in all subsequent analyses, because this aspect of reproductive mode was reported more often.

To evaluate associations between mode of reproduction and other aspects of the life history, we first compared superfetaters and non-superfetaters using one-way analyses of variance. Non-superfetaters produce more young per brood and have longer interbrood intervals and larger reproductive allotments than superfetaters (Table 7–3). All of these differences remain significant when mean female body size is included as a covariate. It is noteworthy that superfetation is not associated with larger offspring, contrary to the expectations of previous authors (e.g., Turner and Snelson 1984). The variance attributed to mode of reproduction is reduced to nearly zero when female size is included as a covariate, whereas female size alone remains as a significant determinant of offspring size given the use of Type III sums of squares in these analyses. The consequences of superfetation thus appear to be fewer young per litter, more frequent reproduction, and smaller reproductive allotments than in equal-sized non-superfetating species. The results for litter size and interbrood interval are already well known.

The first discriminant function analysis, with four dependent variables and eight species (Table 7–4; Figure 7–1), resulted in 100% of the species being correctly classified for mode of reproduction but a marginally significant difference between the centroids for each mode ($p = 0.084$; Wilks' lambda); the marginal significance can be attributed to the small sample size. The main source of difference between modes, based on the total structure coefficients (correlations between the discriminant score and the value of the dependent variable for each species), can be attributed to brood size and interbrood interval. The second discriminant function analysis, with 3 dependent variables and 11 species, resulted in 82% of the species being correctly classified to mode and a significant separation between centroids for each mode ($p = 0.045$; Wilks' lambda), with brood size being the dominant

TABLE 7–3. Results From Analyses of Variance
(ANOVA) and Covariance (ANCOVA) Comparing Superfetating and Non-superfetating
Species. Mean female size is the covariate in each ANCOVA.

	ANOVA			ANCOVA		
	df	SS	F	df	SS	F
Minimum Female Size	1	0.0041	0.21ns	1	0.0006	0.30ns
Mean Female Size	—			1	0.1984	103.33***
Residual	11	0.2176		10	0.0192	
Brood Size	1	1.7364	15.22**	1	1.0446	13.25**
Mean Female Size	—			1	0.4726	7.26*
Residual	14	1.5974		13	1.0248	
Offspring Weight	1	0.0954	0.96ns	1	0.0000	0.00ns
Mean Female Size	—			1	0.6905	27.11***
Residual	9	0.8942		8	0.2038	
Reproductive Allotment	1	0.1331	7.92*	1	0.1494	8.93*
Mean Female Size	—			1	0.0173	1.03ns
Residual	6	0.1009		5	0.0837	
Interbrood Interval	1	0.4261	29.88***	1	0.3138	31.20***
Mean Female Size	—			1	0.0479	4.76
Residual	9	0.1283		8	0.0805	
Mean Male Size	1	0.0476	1.26ns	1	0.0021	0.52ns
Mean Female Size	—			1	0.2395	59.24***
Residual	7	0.2637		6	0.2043	

ns – not significant
* – $p < 0.05$
** – $p < 0.01$
*** – $p < 0.001$

TABLE 7–4. Discriminant Function Analysis of Life History Traits, with Superfetation/Non-superfetation as the Class Criterion, Using Species Means: Two Designs, Excluding and Including Interbrood Interval as a Dependent Variable.

	3 Variables		4 Variables	
	Standardized Discriminant Function Coefficient	Total Structure Coefficient	Standardized Discriminant Function Coefficient	Total Structure Coefficient
Mean Female Size	−0.8836	0.4294	−1.3404	0.5480
Brood Size	2.0411	0.9490	3.4556	0.9609
Offspring Weight	0.1999	0.3813	0.1842	0.4737
Interbrood Interval	—	—	0.1443	0.9144
Probability of Correct Classification	82%		100%	

a. Four Variables

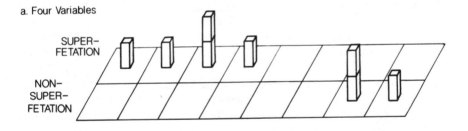

b. Three Variables

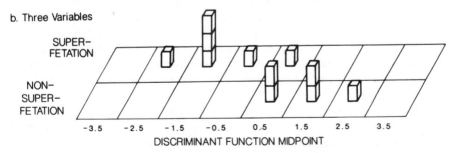

Figure 7–1. Plots of the discriminant function scores for non-superfetating versus superfetating species. a) Plots based on an analysis of 8 species with 4 dependent variables. b) Plots based on an analysis of 11 species with 3 dependent variables.

variable. These multivariate analyses therefore confirm results of the univariate tests and demonstrate independent contributions from interbrood interval and brood size in distinguishing between modes.

3) What are the associations among life history variables within a mode of reproduction? We first analysed the association among life history variables within a mode of reproduction using pairwise correlations among all life history traits (Table 7–5). Because of small sample sizes, we interpret correlations with $p < 0.10$ as significant.

In non-superfetating species, increased body size is associated with larger offspring, larger brood sizes, and longer interbrood intervals. In superfetating species, increased body size is also associated with increased offspring size and longer intervals but is not associated with brood size. Absense of the latter association was also reported by Thibault and Schultz (1978) for intraspecific comparisons in some species of *Poeciliopsis*; however, Travis et al. (1987b) reported a positive correlation for *Heterandria formosa*.

We conclude that there is an association among female body size, offspring size, and interbrood interval within both modes of reproduction, suggesting that evolving a change in one trait should be correlated with changes in the other two. The reproductive modes differ, because in non-superfetaters these traits are also associated with fecundity, while in superfetaters they are independent of fecundity.

Mean female size, brood size, and offspring weight are the only three variables estimated for a sufficient number of superfetaters (six species) and non-superfetaters (five species) for a separate principal components analysis within each mode of reproduction. In non-superfetaters, 91% of the variance is associated with the first principal axis (Table 7–6a). There is an equal, positive loading on all three variables, implying that the main source of life history variation within this mode of reproduction is body size. This suggests that selection for large body size will result in larger offspring and larger broods; bivariate correlations imply that longer interbrood intervals and a larger size at first reproduction are also associated with body size (Table 7–5).

The first principal axis for superfetating species accounts for 61% of the total variance, with large, positive contributions from female size and offspring weight but a small contribution from brood size (Table 7–6a). The second principal axis (34% of variance) is the result of a strong contribution from brood size, but not the other two variables. This suggests that superfetaters differ from non-superfetaters, because in the former mode brood size varies independently of female or offspring size.

4) What are the patterns of life history variation within a species and what can be deduced about their causes? Given such extensive life history variation among species, its causes are of interest. The sources could be genetic, implying that the life histories have evolved in response to some form of selection, or environmental. Comparative investigations within a species provide one means for evaluating such causes. We summarize two case studies suggesting that this

TABLE 7-5. Spearman Rank Order Correlations Among Life History Variables, Using Mean Values for Each Species. The number below each correlation is the number of species. Values above the main diagonal are non-superfetating, and values below are superfetating species.

	Minimum Female Size	Mean Female Size	Brood Size	Offspring Weight	Reproductive Allotment	Interbrood Interval	Mean Male Size
Minimum Female Size		0.93** 9	0.38 10	1.00** 6	-0.20 5	0.61 7	0.74** 8
Mean Female Size	0.95* 4		0.67** 9	1.00** 5	-0.10 5	0.71 6	0.82** 8
Brood Size	-0.15 5	0.11 7		0.60 6	-0.30 5	0.54 7	0.84** 8
Offspring Weight	0.70 5	0.75* 6	-0.16 7		-0.50 3	0.82* 5	1.00** 5
Reproductive Allotment	— 1	-0.50 3	0.50 3	-0.50 3		-1.00** 3	-0.60 5
Interbrood Interval	0.90** 5	0.87* 5	0.20 6	0.89** 6	— 2		0.83** 6
Mean Male Size	— 1	— 1	— 1	— 1	— 1	— 1	

* $0.1 < p < 0.05$
** $p < 0.05$

TABLE 7–6. a) Principal Components Analysis of Life History Traits Using Species Means. (The analysis included five non-superfetating and six superfetating species.)

| | Coefficients of Principal Axes | | | |
| | Non-superfetating | | Superfetating | |
Dependent Variable	1st Axis	2nd Axis	1st Axis	2nd Axis
Female Size	0.5987	−0.0072	0.7050	−0.1485
Brood Size	0.5668	−0.7028	0.0265	0.9827
Offspring Weight	0.5659	0.7114	0.7087	0.1111
% Variance	91.2	7.8	60.6	34.3

b) Principal Components Analysis of Life History Traits for *Poecilia reticulata* (Reznick and Endler 1982; Appendix 4) and *Gambusia affinis* (Stearns 1983a; Appendix 4). Only the first two principal axes are reported, since only these accounted for a significant proportion of the variance.

| | Coefficients of Principal Axes | | | |
| | *P. reticulata* | | *G. affinis* | |
Dependent Variable	1st Axis	2nd Axis	1st Axis	2nd Axis
Female Size	0.4933	0.6984	0.5312	0.6820
Brood Size	−0.4786	0.7157	0.6804	0.0104
Offspring Weight	0.7264	−0.0027	−0.5050	0.7313
% Variance	61.1	36.6	63.5	29.2

variation is an evolved response and illustrate one way in which the environment can influence the life history.

A.   Comparative Studies: If differences among populations are correlated with specific differences in the environment, then those environmental factors are possibly causal in selecting for changes in the life history. Two studies of intraspecific variation in life history patterns of poeciliids (Reznick and Endler 1982; Stearns 1983b) seek such correlations. Constantz (1974, 1979) also performed such comparative studies, but the number of localities is too small for further analysis.

In their study of *Poecilia reticulata*, Reznick and Endler (1982) hypothesize that differences among localities in predation and size-specific mortality can select for changes in the life history, following the theoretical arguments of Gadgil and Bossert (1970), Law (1979), Michod (1979), and Charlesworth (1980). At one series of localities, *P. reticulata* co-occurs with large predators, primarily the pike cichlid (*Crenicichla alta*), which prey selectively on large, sexually mature *P. reticulata* ("*Crenicichla* localities"). At a second type of locality, they co-occur with only *Rivulus harti*, a predator that feeds predominantly on small, immature *P. reticulata* ("*Rivulus* localities"). At a third type of locality, *P. reticulata* co-occurs with *Aequidens pulcher*, an infrequent predator, and lower densities of *Rivulus harti* ("*Aequidens* localities"). These differences in predation are predicted to cause reduced adult survival in *Crenicichla* localities and reduced juvenile survival in *Rivulus* localities. The former will favor earlier maturity and increased reproductive effort, whereas the latter will favor delayed maturity and decreased reproductive effort.

The principal components analysis of the *P. reticulata* data reveals clear separation among the three types of predator communities. The first principal axis separates *Crenicichla* localities from the other two (Table 7–7b, Figure 7–2a). The principal axis coefficients indicate a separation between small females with small offspring, high fecundity, and high reproductive allotments (*Crenicichla* localities) and large females with large offspring, low fecundity, and low reproductive allotments (*Rivulus* and *Aequidens* localities, Table 7–7a). These differences exactly parallel the earlier analyses (Reznick and Endler 1982). The second principal axis separates the *Rivulus* and *Aequidens* localities (Table 7–7b, Figure 7–2a). Coefficients are all positive and similar in magnitude (Table 7–7a), implying that this separation is primarily in body size, with guppies from *Aequidens* localities being larger than guppies from *Rivulus* localities. We conclude that predators, or something closely correlated with predators such as habitat differences (Reznick and Endler 1982; Reznick and Bryga 1987), can select for changes in the life

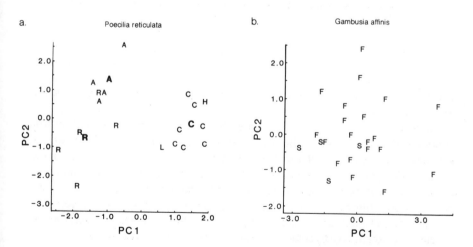

Figure 7–2.   Plots of species' mean values for the first (PC1) and second (PC2) principal component scores based on the analyses summarized in Tables 7–7 and 7–8. a) Results for *Poecilia reticulata.* "A" = *Aequidens* localities, "C" = *Crenicichla* localities, and "R" = *Rivulus* localities. The boldface letters are the centroids for each locality class. "L" = low food, "H" = high food. Note that these points are based on PCA that includes food availability. The plot for the field data alone is very similar in appearance. b) Results for *Gambusia affinis.* "F" = fluctuating reservoirs, "S" = stable reservoirs.

TABLE 7–7.   **a) Summary of Principal Components Analysis of the 16** *Poecilia reticulata* **Localities Studied by Reznick and Endler (1982).**

	Coefficients of Principal Axes			
Dependent Variables	1st Axis	2nd Axis	3rd Axis	4th Axis
Mean Female Size	−0.1999	0.7724	−0.4521	−0.3988
Brood Size	0.6066	0.3008	−0.3331	0.6561
Offspring Weight	−0.5494	0.4169	0.4667	0.5537
Reproductive Allotment	0.5387	0.3730	0.6833	−0.3222
% Variance	56.2	35.3	8.0	0.5

b)   **Analyses of Variance of the First and Second Principal Component Scores for the 16** *P. reticulata* **Localities.**

	df	Sums of Squares	F	P
First PC Score				
Predators	2	31.17	78.77	<0.0001
Residual	13	2.57		
Second PC Score				
Predators	2	10.06	5.89	0.0151
Residual	13	11.10		

A Posteriori Comparisons—solid lines join means that do not differ significantly.

1st axis	Cren	Aequ	Riv

2nd axis	Cren	Aequ	Riv

history. Separate laboratory analyses (Reznick 1982a, 1982b) confirm a genetic basis for these differences.

Stearns (1983a, 1983b) studied the life history patterns of *G. affinis* from reservoirs with either stable or fluctuating water levels. When fluctuating reservoirs were drawn down for irrigation, there was apparently non-size-selective mortality in the resident *G. affinis* populations. One predicted response to such mortality, based on the theory of r- and K-selection (McArthur and Wilson 1967), is that fish from fluctuating reservoirs (r-selected) will mature earlier, have higher reproductive efforts, and more and smaller offspring than fish from stable reservoirs (K-selected). An alternative hypothesis, named "bet-hedging" (Stearns 1976), predicts the opposite changes in life histories.

The principal components analysis for *G. affinis* (Table 7–8, Figure 7–2b) reveals weak separation between fluctuating and stable reservoirs. This separation is primarily along the first axis (Table 7–8b, Figure 7–2b), which separates large females with high fecundity and reproductive allotments but small offspring, from small females with low fecundities and reproductive allotments but large offspring.

TABLE 7–8.   a) Summary of Principal Components Analysis of the 24 *Gambusia affinis* Populations Studied by Stearns (1983a, 1983b).

	Coefficients of Principal Axes	
Dependent Variables	1st Axis	2nd Axis
Mean Female Size	0.3640	0.8292
Brood Size	0.6282	0.0970
Offspring Weight	−0.4387	0.4580
Reproductive Allotment	0.5296	−0.3055
% Variance	61.3	23.5

b)   Analyses of Variance of the First and Second Principal Component Scores for the 24 *Gambusia affinis* Populations.

	df	Sums of Squares	F	P
First PC Score				
Fluctuating versus Stable	1	9.70	4.57	0.0439
Residual	22	46.68		
Second PC Score				
Fluctuating versus Stable	1	0.91	0.96	0.3374
Residual	22	20.75		

These differences generally parallel Stearns's (1983a, 1983b) reported differences for stable versus fluctuating reservoirs. A more prominent feature of the data is the significant differences among reservoirs independent of the stable versus fluctuating contrast. The accompanying genetic analysis (Stearns 1983b) revealed that the degree of water level fluctuation is positively correlated with fecundity and negatively correlated with size at maturity. This pattern is consistent with the predicted response to an uncertain environment, but is not discernible in the field data. It therefore appears that habitat predictability can select for changes in the life history but that, because of complicating factors like environmentally induced changes in the life history, field data alone may not accurately measure these differences.

Both studies illustrate factors that can select for changes in the life history and that are worth assessing when collecting life history data for additional species of poeciliids. They also illustrate the virtues of using poeciliids for such investigations. In each case, the range of variation in all life history variables is substantial. In *P. reticulata*, the differences among populations (e.g., the nearly threefold differences in mean offspring size) are among the largest observed in any vertebrate species. The accompanying laboratory studies illustrate the comparative ease of further evaluating the life history differences observed in the field.

Each of these authors presents more complete discussions of their predictions and alternative hypotheses; the reader should consult the original papers for additional details. Also, consult Boyce (1984) for a commentary on the predictions of r- and K-selection.

B.   Food availability as a proximal influence on life history patterns: One important corollary of the differences in Stearns' results for laboratory versus field data for *G. affinis* is that the life history is plastic and easily modified by the environment. In general, variation in life histories among samples from natural populations can be expected to result from a combination of genetic and environmental influences. The best way to distinguish between environmental and genetic causes is by rearing fish in a common environment, as done in both of these studies, ' or performing reciprocal transplant experiments; however, it may also be possible to qualitatively evaluate these alternatives using a combination of laboratory data and principal components analysis.

Food availability is one factor that can readily vary in nature and that significantly changes components of poeciliid life histories (Reznick 1982a, unpubl. data; Travis et al. 1987b; Reznick and Bryga 1987). To illustrate how such a phenotypic effect could be evaluated in field results, we repeated our principal components analysis of guppy life histories incorporating data for low and high food levels from Reznick and Bryga (1987, unpubl. data; Appendix 4) on the same principal axes as for guppies (Figure 7–2a). A line joining the points for low and high food availability is similar to the pattern of variation within each subset of guppy localities, implying that variation within each of these groups is similar to what could result from differences in food availability alone. Trajectories describing differences between the different classes of guppies can be represented by lines joining the centroids for each type of locality. Such lines indicate that the differences between *Rivulus* and *Aequidens* localities are also quite similar to what could be generated by food differences alone, but differences between these and *Crenicichla* localities are largely independent of food effects; the latter conclusion is consistent with the genetic differences observed in the laboratory (Reznick 1982a, 1982b). Such comparisons only assess whether environmental effects potentially explain variation among natural populations; they are likely to be useful only when comparing organisms that are very similar in morphology and mode of reproduction.

5)   How do the patterns of association among life history variables within a species compare to those observed among species? We repeated the principal components analyses on *P. reticulata* and *G. affinis* with the same three dependent variables as in the analysis among species to make them directly comparable to the results for non-superfetating species. The first principal axis for both species (Table 7–6b) is fundamentally different from the first axis for non-superfetaters (Table 7–6a). Among species, the first axis accounts for over 90% of the variance and is largely a function of body size, in part due to the inclusion of large species like *Belonesox belizanus*. Within *P. reticulata*, the first axis accounts for 61% of the variance and distinguishes among large females with few, large offspring and small females with many, small offspring. This result is in large part due to differences among guppies from the different types of localities; separate analyses on each type of locality had a first axis which was also largely a function of body size (results not summarized here). In *G. affinis*, the first principal axis accounts for 64% of the variance and distinguishes among large females with many, small offspring and small females with few, large offspring. In each case, the primary patterns of variation within a species are not associated with size alone but rather incorporate differences in how resources are allocated to reproduction.

There are many possible interpretations for these differences in patterns of life history variation, in part because the underlying causes represent a combination of genetic and environmental influences. The result may be a consequence of the restricted size range present within a species as opposed to between species (Appendices 3 and 4). This difference would result in a diminution in the influence of size in the intraspecific comparisons. A second possibility is that the broader size range among species is due to a broader ecological diversity; the ecological requirements among populations within these two species are uniform, possibly constraining evolutionary changes in body size and hence limiting the influence of body size on life history patterns.

DISCUSSION

Our discussion and conclusions are based on small sample sizes and an uneven representation of tribes and genera; a more complete data set could significantly alter the results. The spirit of this project is to go as far as possible with the available data and indicate new areas of inquiry.

Phylogeny of Superfetation

The phylogenetic distribution of superfetation suggests that it has evolved independently four or more times within the family. Our reasoning follows that of Blackburn (1982) in his discussion of the evolution of viviparity in lizards. We assume, following Turner (1937), that the common ancestor of all tribes, except Tomeurini, was lecithotrophic and non-superfetating. For the sake of argument, we initially assume that the change is one-way, so that superfetation and matrotrophy are derived from lecithotrophy and that they do not reverse to the ancestral state. Superfetation in multiple, evolutionarily independent tribes, each of which contains both forms of reproduction, suggests that it evolved independently in each. Furthermore, the presence of non-superfetating species within the tribe Heterandriini in genera that also contain superfetating species (*Priaphichthys* and *Heterandria*) suggests multiple evolutionary events within the tribe; alternatively, they suggest that the reverse evolution of these traits may be possible.

If the pattern of multiple, independent origins of viviparity is true, then it would be possible to apply methods suggested by Felsenstein (1985) to evaluate the correlates and possible causes of the trait. A simple application of this method would be a series of paired comparisons between superfetating species and their closest non-superfetating relatives. However, using data in this fashion requires first that the modes of reproduction for all superfetaters outside of Heterandriini and non-superfetaters within Heterandriini be confirmed. More importantly, it also requires development of a phylogenetic tree for the family.

Variation Within Modes of Reproduction

A more detailed consideration of the patterns of reproduction in the family reveals considerable variation within the discrete mode categories. For example, Turner (1937) describes interspecific differences in reproduction as a continuum between non-superfetation and superfetation. Non-superfetaters vary in the amount of time between the birth of one litter and fertilization of the next. In *G. affinis*, there is a pause of several days between these events, while in *Quintana atrizona* the new clutch begins to yolk before, and is fertilized within 24 hours after, the birth of the previous brood. Superfetation varies between the pattern seen in many *Poeciliopsis* spp. and that of *H. formosa*. Many species of *Poeciliopsis* carry only two to three broods, have more young per litter, and longer interbrood intervals than *H. formosa*. The latter can carry up to nine simultaneous broods (Scrimshaw 1944a) with as few as one or two offspring and intervals as short as one to three days. Such extreme superfetation is associated with reduction in yolk sac size and elaboration of tissues for maternal-fetal nutrient transfer (Turner 1940b; Constantz, Chapter 3). Turner (1937) suggests that this continuum represents the evolutionary progression from non-superfetation to superfetation, with the first step being the maturation and fertilization of a new clutch prior to the birth of the previous brood.

Some variation within this progression can be mimicked within a species with manipulations of resource availability. For example, Reznick (1980, unpubl. data) and Snelson et al. (1986b) found that increased food availability caused more rapid yolking and shorter interbrood intervals in well-fed *P. reticulata* and *P. latipinna*, respectively. Travis et al. (1987b) found that increased food availability caused more frequent reproduction and presumably increased the number of simultaneous broods in *H. formosa*. Similarly, Thibault and Schultz (1978) reported that *Poeciliopsis monacha* reduced the number of simultaneous broods from two to one when food was in short supply. These observations suggest that at least some of the progression proposed by Turner could represent environmentally-induced variation, although it is also clear that interspecific differences exist. Demonstration of environmental effects is a cautionary note that fish condition can influence conclusions about reproductive mode.

There is also evidence for intraspecific variation in superfetation. Monaco et al. (1983) argue that some individuals in the unisexual species *Poecilia formosa* and the closely related *P. latipinna* and *P. mexicana* display a form of superfetation. Their evidence includes short interbrood intervals in 5 out of 200 fish, plus embryos in two nonadjacent stages of development in 17 out of 208 wild-caught females.

In most of the 17 females, the majority of embryos were in one stage of development, with only a few in the earlier stage. In a subset, particularly the triploid unisexuals, the litter was divided more evenly between two stages. Such data provide compelling evidence for superfetation. Rosenthal (1955) observed "dysfunctional superfetation" in *P. reticulata* and *X. helleri*; dissections of gravid females revealed some females with a small number of embryos in earlier stages of development than the majority of the litter. He observed the "birth" of apparently undeveloped ova or poorly developed embryos and hypothesized that these individuals are fertilized out of synchrony with the rest of the litter and are ultimately aborted. Rosenthal's observations may well represent a different phenomenon from that reported by Monaco et al. (1983), since the latter make no mention of any abnormalities in the developing embryos or newborn young.

Trexler (1985) presents evidence for variation in maternal provisioning in *P. latipinna*. Some populations display the expected loss of dry mass by embryos between fertilization and the end of development. In one population, the dry mass of the embryos remained constant, implying that there is some transfer of nutrients from mother to offspring during development.

Evidence for intraspecific variation in maternal provisioning (Trexler 1985) and superfetation (Rosenthal 1955; Monaco et al. 1983) suggests genetic variation for these traits. If confirmed, such variation would lend itself to studies of the mechanisms and evolution of both traits.

The Adaptive Significance of Superfetation

Superfetation is associated with more frequent production of young, but a reduced clutch size and a smaller average reproductive allotment. Reduction in reproductive allotment is probably attributable to matrotrophy, so that embryos in earlier stages of development are smaller than more advanced embryos. In contrast, all the young of non-superfetating lecithotrophic species are similar in size. Thibault and Schultz (1978) demonstrate that the fecundity of some superfetaters, averaged over longer time intervals, can be comparable to that of non-superfetaters, so the net effect of the trait is to spread reproduction more evenly over time, thereby changing the distribution of birth ages and the pattern of resource investment by the mother.

From an ecological perspective, superfetation allows for reduction in ovary size and hence improves streamlining (Thibault and Schultz 1978). A streamlined profile would reduce costs of locomotion, particularly in moving water, and possibly improve the ability to escape predators. Species that inhabit deep, moving water (e.g., *Poeciliopsis turneri* or *P. catemaco*) also have reduced litter sizes and in some cases ovoid ovaries oriented along the main axis of the fish; both factors would further reduce the fish's profile (Miller 1975; Thibault and Schultz 1978).

Travis et al. (1987b) summarize energetic arguments for superfetation. The argument best supported by their data is that superfetation reduces peak demand of a litter on the female; by splitting a litter into subsets, the peak energetic demand of each subset is staggered over time. The response to increased food availability—an increase in the number of litters and decrease in interbrood interval—supports this argument, since increased resources presumably reduce energetic constraints on the female.

Thibault and Schultz (1978) argue that matrotrophy requires a more constant supply of food than lecithotrophy. Lecithotrophic species make a single investment when ova are yolked, then little is required to sustain the litter. Meffe and Vrijenhoek (1981) provide experimental support for this interpretation. Matrotrophic species must make a constant investment to sustain development of their young. Meffe and Vrijenhoek therefore argue that lecithotrophy is better suited for unpredictable habitats.

Does Phylogenetic Representation Influence Our Conclusions?

All of our conclusions are based on a small number of species from a few well-studied genera. For example, all comparisons of superfetation with non-superfetation were actually between members of the Heterandriini (superfetaters) and the Poeciliini and Gambusiini (non-superfetaters). We have no representatives from the other tribes and no examples from most genera. This narrow representation means that effects of tribe and reproductive mode are confounded. This may be unavoidable if all superfetaters prove to be restricted to the Heterandriini. If this were the case, then our observations may reflect general differences among tribes rather than effects of reproductive mode. The logical association of life history traits (e.g., multiple broods in different stages of development and shorter interbrood intervals) argues for the differences being attributable to the mode of reproduction. Overlap among the representatives of the Poeciliini and Gambusiini in our second discriminant analysis (Figure 7–1) also argues for the reported trends being attributable to mode rather than tribe.

In conclusion, we do not think that our broad comparisons between modes of reproduction are likely to be affected by phylogenetic representation. However, any arguments for the adaptive significance of these differences in reproductive mode would be greatly strengthened if we had access to independently evolved lineages that displayed each type of reproduction.

SUMMARY AND FUTURE RESEARCH

The results of our original five questions can be summarized as follows:

1) Superfetation is largely confined to the Heterandriini. There are notable exceptions of superfetation in three other tribes and non-superfetating species in the Heterandriini. All of these exceptions require further investigation.

2) All but one of the superfetating species are matrotrophic, while all non-superfetating species are lecithotrophic. This pattern demonstrates a functional

relationship between the two modes of reproduction, but the single exception argues that superfetation and matrotrophy are not strictly linked to one another.

Superfetating species produce fewer young per brood, produce broods more frequently, and tend to have smaller reproductive allotments than non-superfetating species. There are no differences among the two modes of reproduction in size of mature males, the minimum or average size of reproducing females, or offspring size.

3)   Most life history variation among the non-superfetating species can be attributed to body size. Species with larger females tend to produce more and larger offspring, have longer interbrood intervals, and also have larger mature males. The pattern among superfetating species differs because brood size appears independent of female size. All of the remaining associations are similar to the results for non-superfetating species.

Because body size will have an important impact on a species' ecology and evolution independent of its life history, it will always have to be taken into account when performing comparative life history studies. In particular, it is important to consider whether body size alone accounts for life history variations or if there is significant variation independent of body size. In the former case, evolutionary changes in the life history and changes in ecology associated with body size are confounded, making causal interpretations more difficult. In that latter case, the investigator can focus on just the life history changes.

4)   Patterns of intraspecific life history variation demonstrate that in special circumstances this variation can be attributable to specific causes. In the case of *P. reticulata* (Reznick and Endler 1982), predators and/or environmental factors associated with differences in predation proved important. In the case of *G. affinis* (Stearns 1983b, 1983c) habitat predictability appears important. An important feature of both studies is that we readily find substantial intraspecific variation in all aspects of the life history that can be correlated with specific aspects of the environment. A second feature is that it is possible to perform the necessary laboratory experiments to distinguish among genetic and environmental sources of these differences, because the fish are so easily bred and maintained and have short generation times. These two features define the poeciliids as ideal subjects for evaluating general theories of life history evolution.

5)   Patterns of life history variation within *P. reticulata* and *G. affinis* are fundamentally different from the variation observed among species. While much of the variation among species can be attributed to body size, the variation within species is more a function of how resources are allocated to reproduction.

To improve our understanding of life history evolution in this group, the most important progress will be in generating quality life history descriptions of more species. Thibault and Schultz's (1978) work provides a good model, since it combines laboratory observations on variables like age at maturity and interbrood interval with values derived from field collected fish, such as brood size, offspring size, changes in offspring mass during development, and reproductive allotment. These variables, plus observations on reproductive mode, define the species' life history. Where possible, such investigations should also consider intraspecific and seasonal variation for these traits (e.g., Meffe 1985a; Reznick and Braun 1987). Two reasons for considering these sources of variation are: 1) environmentally induced variation in the life history can mask the true mode of reproduction, and 2) they can result in the discovery of genetic differences within species, and thus provide ideal raw material for investigations of life history evolution.

Such investigations should also incorporate information on the species' ecology. Factors that seem important include habitat type, resource utilization, and predators. Habitat can be characterized as standing versus moving water, stream size, and productivity. Habitat predictability, such as the presence of seasonal drought or flooding, is also likely to influence the species' demography. Summaries of resource utilization should include notes on where the species forages (such as in or out of current, surface, substrate, or water column feeder, etc.) and its diet. Finally, the presence and nature of potential predators and competitors should be noted. These features will be of particular interest if several localities are sampled for a given species and if there are differences among localities. A characterization of the habitat will also be of interest in future comparisons among the reproductive modes, since some features have been hypothesized as causal.

The family can be more efficiently characterized with a strategic choice of representative species. First targets should be those species noted previously that appear to have unusual reproductive modes for the tribe. Second targets should be representatives from the Cnesterodontini, Girardinini, and the one species of Xenodexiini. Finally, we should consider representatives from previously unexplored genera, including *Alfaro*, *Priapella*, *Priapichthys*, and *Phallichthys*, all four genera within the Cnesterodontini, and all three genera within the Girardinini. Such a strategic sampling will more quickly characterize the family as a whole.

ACKNOWLEDGMENTS

Gary Meffe, Mary Rauchenberger, Franklin Snelson, Joe Travis, and an anonymous reviewer provided helpful comments on earlier drafts of the manuscript; many of their suggestions were adopted. Sharon Forster, Gary Meffe, Joe Travis, and Joel Trexler generously supplied unpublished data. Heather Bryga and Steve Morey prepared the figures. Georgia Lovely and Debbie Drake prepared the manuscripts. We thank all of these individuals for their help. This project was supported in part by National Science Foundation grants BSR8416599–01 (to DNR) and BSR86–16788 (to DBM).

Chapter 8

Social and Environmental Control of Life History Traits in Poeciliid Fishes

FRANKLIN F. SNELSON, JR.

INTRODUCTION

The first comprehensive life history study of a poeciliid was Louis Krumholz's monograph on *Gambusia affinis* (Krumholz 1948), and it remains one of the most frequently cited papers in the literature on livebearing fishes. In the 40 years since that seminal paper, the accumulation of poeciliid life history information, although still far from complete, has advanced to a point permitting the formulation and testing of hypotheses about causes and consequences of intra- and interspecific differences. Such studies have begun to partition the effects of genetic and nongenetic factors in shaping life histories.

In this chapter I review sex ratios, growth, and age and size at maturity in poeciliid fishes, concentrating on the extent to which variation in these characters is influenced by nongenetic factors. The following chapter by Kallman emphasizes the genetic mechanisms controlling size at maturity and a suite of correlated life history traits. Later chapters by Travis (Chapter 10) and Trexler (Chapter 11) illustrate the progress being made at unraveling the complex interplay between genetic and nongenetic influences on the expression and evolution of life history variables.

Several caveats must be made at the outset. First, little to nothing is known about the natural history of most poeciliid fishes. For each species that has been subjected to even cursory evaluation, there are many others known only from collections on museum shelves. Second, significant progress has been made in recent years at experimentally unraveling the complicated interplay of genetic, biotic, and abiotic factors that influence life history variation (see Chapters 10,

11, and 14). However, these advances have been made with only a handful of species and a limited number of life history traits. For the vast majority of species, we must still interpret field observations in a virtual vacuum of information relative to proximate and ultimate causes. Finally, after life history variation has been reduced to its various components through appropriate controlled experiments, we must again return to the field to understand how those parameters interact in a spatially and temporarily variable natural setting. Although poeciliids are excellent subjects for experimental ecology, this work is only in its infancy.

SEX RATIOS

Primary and Secondary Sex Ratios

I am not aware that the primary sex ratio (sex ratio at fertilization) has been studied in poeciliids. However, the secondary sex ratio (sex ratio at parturition) has been evaluated in several species. Since differential mortality of the sexes during gestation has never been found to be significant, even in cases of skewed sex ratios (Farr 1981), it is likely that secondary accurately reflect primary sex ratios.

The genetics of sex determination in poeciliids is reviewed by Angus (Chapter 4). Mechanisms are not well known except in the genus *Xiphophorus* (Kallman 1984) and in *Poecilia reticulata*. In *X. maculatus* and *P. reticulata*, there are sex chromosomes and autosomal genes that interact to determine sex. Depending on the parental genetic background, some crosses produce sex ratios that depart significantly from unity, and certain inbred laboratory strains consistently produce broods with biased ratios (Farr 1981; Kallman 1984). Sex ratios may also vary widely between individual crosses in the swordtail, *X. helleri*. In this case, gonosomes have not been confirmed but are likely (Angus, Chapter 4; Kallman 1984, Chapter 9).

It is not clear that departure from unity within broods has a significant impact on local population structure. Certainly the best studied species in this regard is the mosquitofish, *Gambusia affinis*. Data from diverse populations over very different time periods show that overall sex ratio in a cohort at birth rarely departs significantly from 1:1 (Geiser 1924; Hildebrand 1927; Dulzetto 1934; Krumholz 1948). Snelson and Wetherington (1980) also showed that overall secondary sex ratio did not depart significantly from unity in wild-caught *Poecilia latipinna*, despite the fact that a few laboratory-born broods were significantly skewed in favor of females. Likewise, in the guppy, overall secondary sex ratios in the wild are typically 1:1 (Haskins et al. 1961).

The sex ratio among juveniles in nature might also be used to approximate the secondary sex ratio in the population at large. In this case, however, factors such as differential mortality, sexual segregation, differential growth rates, or biased sampling could cause the juvenile sex ratio to depart from that at birth. Despite these potential complications, the sex ratio among juveniles in two Florida populations of the sailfin molly departed significantly from 1:1 in only 15 of 47 samples (Snelson and Wetherington 1980), with no clear spatial or temporal pattern in the direction or degree of skewness. The sex ratio among juvenile *P. reticulata* in the wild also is near unity (Haskins et al. 1961).

Adult Sex Ratios in Wild Populations

It has long been known that wild adult populations of many poeciliids are skewed in favor of females. Much of the work on this subject was summarized by Geiser (1924) and Snelson and Wetherington (1980). Other reports of female-biased sex ratios include *Poeciliopsis monacha, P. lucida,* and *P. latidens* (Thibault 1974a), *X. helleri* and *X. maculatus* (Milton and Arthington 1983a), and *Belonesox belizanus* (Turner and Snelson 1984). This observation has been reported for so many species that it seems safe to generalize that female-biased adult sex ratios are characteristic of most species of the family.

Since the few species studied thus far normally have an equal sex ratio at birth, or at least among juveniles, skewed adult sex ratios beg for an explanation. Female dominance may result from sampling bias caused by habitat segregation or by differential susceptibility to capture. Certainly there are cases known where there is habitat segregation by sex (Haskins et al. 1961; Maglio and Rosen 1969; Vrijenhoek 1978; Brown 1985), but in general the segregation is minor and not likely to influence estimates of overall adult sex ratios based on large samples secured by usual methods. A more real concern is that, because mature males are smaller than females in many genera, they pass through the net mesh and are thus under-represented in samples (Krumholz 1948; Hubbs and Springer 1957; Branson et al. 1960; Vrijenhoek 1978). Although most field data are probably biased to some extent by the size differential of the sexes, this bias probably is not large enough to explain the overall preponderance of females noted in most species. For example, female-dominated adult sex ratios are characteristic of *B. belizanus*, where males and females are both large enough to be equally susceptible to normal sampling (Turner and Snelson 1984).

A more reasonable explanation is that males suffer higher mortality, attributable to a variety of causes including predation, greater susceptibility to stress, and accelerated physiological aging. Differential predation on males has been implicated in a number of species in which males are brightly colored and/or conspicuous because of their courtship activities (Krumholz 1963; Baird 1968; Thibault 1974a). This phenomenon has been well investigated only in the guppy, *P. reticulata* (Haskins et al. 1961; Farr 1975; Endler 1978, 1980). In this species, males are more susceptible to predation both because of their conspicuous color patterns and their striking courtship displays. Piscivorous fishes not only drastically reduce the number of males but also have a significant impact on levels of sexual activity and the distribution and relative abundance of the various color morphs (Farr

1975; Endler 1980). It is reasonable to assume that differential predation on males is widespread throughout the Poeciliidae.

Interestingly, one of the few reports of male-biased adult sex ratios is also explained by differential predation. In this case, herons preyed differentially on large female *G. affinis* presumably because of their higher energy content and/or ease of capture. The result was a sex ratio highly skewed in favor of males in shallow marshes where heron predation was high (Britton and Moser 1982). *Gambusia affinis* and other poeciliids such as *P. latipinna* occupy shallow marsh habitats throughout a large part of their vast range. Because wading birds are common to abundant in many such habitats, especially in southeastern United States, it is intriguing that male-biased adult sex ratios have not been reported more often.

It is generally accepted that males succumb more quickly to a variety of stressors. Krumholz (1948) concluded that *G. affinis* males suffer greater mortality when exposed to temperature extremes, overcrowding, and starvation. Males also have greater mortality rates than females at high temperatures (Smoak 1959; Hagen 1964; Bacon et al. 1968; Winkler 1975) and die quicker during hypoxia (Cech et al. 1985). There is evidence that differential mortality exists in other species of *Gambusia*. Hubbs and Springer (1957) found female-biased sex ratios in field samples of all species of the *G. nobilis* complex, yet laboratory stocks had ratios of 1:1. Since predators are uncommon in the spring-head habitats of these species, it is likely that males succumbed quickly to environmental stressors in the field but had higher survivorship under more benign laboratory conditions. Gelbach et al. (1978) subsequently showed that *G. nobilis* males have reduced upper thermal limits compared to females, as is also the case in *G. geiseri* and *G. gaigei* (Hagen 1964). Meffe and Snelson (Chapter 2) present a more detailed discussion of sexual differences in response to abiotic environmental factors.

In the only species examined to date, the routine metabolic rate of *G. affinis* did not differ significantly between the sexes across a variety of temperature and dissolved oxygen conditions (Cech et al. 1985). Thus, speculation that males are genetically predestined to age faster and die younger than females is not supported by physiological data. In most cases, female poeciliids mature later than males (e.g., Kallman and Borkoski 1978), and it is generally assumed that females have greater potential longevity, as is the case in most other fishes. Unfortunately, the most successful method for aging fishes across short time spans, daily increments in otolith growth (Beamish and McFarlane 1987), has not yet been applied to poeciliids to address basic questions concerning age, growth, or longevity. On the basis of preliminary otolith data, however, Haake and Dean (1983) suggest that male *G. affinis* and *Heterandria formosa* are shorter-lived than females in natural populations from the Florida Everglades.

As noted, biased sampling often has been implicated in temporally or spatially variable adult sex ratios, especially when ratios heavily favor larger females. However, at least two pieces of evidence suggest that such variation may not be artifactual but may relate to patterns of maturation. First, male maturation in *P. latipinna* does not proceed uniformly throughout the year but is concentrated in fall and spring (Snelson 1984). This also appears to be the case in mosquitofish in central Florida (Large and Snelson, unpubl. data) and in *Gambusia heterochir* in Texas (Yan 1987). Secondly, the size and age at maturity in males is influenced by both social and genetic mechanisms (see following), with the result that mature males may be recruited into the adult population at variable times and sizes depending upon the interplay of density-dependent and genetic factors. In the case of mosquito-fish, this results in a seasonal trend in the size and abundance of mature males in natural populations (Hubbs 1971; Hughes 1985), perhaps explaining marked fluctuations in adult sex ratios in sequential samples (Hubbs 1964; Snelson and Wetherington 1980).

Consequences of Skewed Adult Sex Ratios

The small proportion of males in most poeciliid populations probably has little impact on reproduction at the population level. First, as is the case in many vertebrates, male-male sexual competition, dominance hierarchies, and alternate male reproductive tactics all suggest that male reproductive fitness is more variable than that of females (Farr, Chapter 6). A single dominant male may fertilize many females, whereas subordinate males may have low reproductive success. Additionally, females can store viable sperm in the oviduct and/or ovary, and a single insemination may suffice for several consecutive broods (Constantz, Chapter 3). Finally, evidence of multiple inseminations in several species (Constantz 1984) suggests that there usually are enough males to service all adult females.

Atretic and apparently unfertilized ova have been noted in developing broods of several species and have been interpreted as indicating that inadequate sperm was present to fertilize all eggs (Tavolga 1949; Vallowe 1953). However, under field conditions, only a small percentage of pregnant females carry broods with unfertilized ova. There are only two cases in which sperm insufficiency or depletion has been reported in nature, and both involve unisexual-bisexual species pairs. In the *Poecilia formosa-P. latipinna* pair in Texas, unisexual *P. formosa* females often are "partially pregnant" and carry many unfertilized eggs in broods with developing embryos, suggesting insufficient sperm are available to fertilize the entire clutch (Hubbs 1964). This situation was caused by the large number of females (both unisexual and bisexual) to be serviced, the small proportion of adult males, and, most importantly, the pattern of mate selection in males. *Poecilia latipinna* males are territorial, and large males dominate small ones and secure most copulations. Males show a decided preference for conspecific females and inseminate heterospecifics after all conspecifics are serviced. The result is that many *P. formosa* females are inseminated either partially, infrequently, or not at all. When male frequency is low, the reproductive potential of the unisexual may be severely reduced, but that of conspecific females is little affected. An almost identical situation occurs in several unisexual-bisexual species pairs in the genus

Poeciliopsis (McKay 1971; Moore and McKay 1971). These are the only two described cases in which males are a limiting resource for females in nature.

Interestingly, *Poecilia mexicana*, the usual sperm donor in the unisexual-bisexual *P. formosa* complex in Mexico, does not mate preferentially with conspecific females. Despite a very low ratio of adult males to females, sperm competition does not appear to limit reproduction in the heterospecific unisexual parasite (Balsano et al. 1981, 1985, Chapter 15). In addition, mate discrimination may change with male size, age, and/or experience (Woodhead and Armstrong 1985). These few case studies illustrate that the significance of skewed sex ratios probably varies among populations and species, and will only be understood through detailed studies of maturation patterns, breeding systems, and courtship preferences.

Environmental Factors Influencing Sex Ratios

Only two environmental factors, pH and temperature, have been shown to have a direct effect on the secondary sex ratio in poeciliids. Rubin (1985) reported that *X. helleri* broods were 100% male at pH 6.2 and 98.5% female at pH 7.8. These results are dramatic but have not been confirmed or repeated either in *X. helleri* or any other poeciliid. Rubin's data leave a number of unanswered questions. The study was based on only four broods, two raised at each experimental pH, and the genetic background of the parents was not controlled. There was no "control" or ambient (normal) pH treatment for comparison, and with only two extremes represented, it is unclear whether the response is a threshold effect or a variable related to changing pH. Also, fish were not sexed until about 180 days after birth, so it is unclear whether pH influenced the secondary sex ratio or whether it produced only a phenotypic response that masked the genetic sex (e.g., Howell et al. 1980). Rubin's results are certainly provocative, but additional experiments are needed with *X. helleri* and other species to determine the generality and relevance of these findings to poeciliid life histories.

Sullivan and Schultz (1986) showed that sex ratio in *Poeciliposis lucida* is influenced by temperature. In this case, the experiments were well designed and the genetic background of the fish was controlled. In one strain, the percentage of males was positively related to temperature as follows: 38% males at 24°C, 54% at 25.5°C, 63% at 27°C, and 92% at 30°C. In a second strain, there was no significant departure from a 1:1 sex ratio at any of the four experimental temperatures. This is significant because it is the first time that temperature-influenced sex ratios, now reported in several poikilothermic vertebrates (Bull and Vogt 1979; Yntema and Mrosovsky 1980; Conover and Kynard 1981), have been shown to be under genetic control. Sullivan and Schultz (1986) hypothesize that temperature-controlled sex ratios in *P. lucida* are adaptive in nature, because sex ratios may be adjusted to match that which is optimum for each "patch" in a patchy environment (Charnov and Bull 1977). As is the case with Rubin's (1985) pH results, it is not clear whether temperature-influenced sex ratios are peculiar to a single strain of *P. lucida* or whether other poeciliids also exhibit labile sex ratios.

GROWTH AND MATURATION

Kallman et al. (1973) discovered that a sex-linked gene controlled age and size at maturity in the platyfish, *X. maculatus*. A similar genetic system operates in other *Xiphophorus* spp. (Schreibman and Kallman 1977; Kallman 1983; Borowsky 1987a) and in *P. latipinna* (Travis et al. 1988b). These subjects are reviewed by Kallman (Chapter 9). The importance of this genetic system to the discussion that follows must be emphasized. Most observations on patterns of growth and maturation in poeciliids are based on natural populations or on laboratory stocks in which the genetic background was unknown or poorly controlled. If a genetic system controlling maturation and growth is widespread in the family, as suggested by Schreibman and Kallman (1977), much of the published information on the relationship of environmental and social factors to growth and maturation may be tainted.

It also seems appropriate to discuss a few methodological issues relative to growth and maturation in livebearers. First, good information on field growth of poeciliids has proven elusive. Length-frequency analysis (e.g., Krumholz 1948; Hubbs 1964; Colson 1969) is generally unsatisfactory because of the protracted reproductive season of most poeciliids. As noted, otolith microstructure is the best available technique for aging short-lived fishes but has been applied to livebearers in only two cases (Haake and Dean 1983; J. Trexler, pers. comm.). Most studies of poeciliid growth have been conducted in the laboratory or under field experimental conditions. Because of the complexity of social, environmental, and genetic factors that may influence growth, experiments must be carefully designed to evaluate only a few parameters at a time, and there is always a question of applicability of experimental results to natural situations (Snelson 1984). In addition, most growth experiments involve sequential measurements from the same individual, requiring that the fish be handled and anesthetized or immobilized. Because of this stress, growth measurements must be taken quickly and with limited accuracy, and they are rarely replicated. Successive size measurements must not be made too frequently, because stress may become an overriding experimental artifact. Finally, there are differences in procedure, with some authors evaluating weight (e.g., McKenzie et al. 1983), some total length (e.g., Farr 1980a; Snelson 1982), and some standard length (e.g., Borowsky 1973a; Kallman and Borkoski 1978). The accuracy of photographic methods for evaluating size and growth (e.g., Stearns 1983c; Trendall 1983) has not been evaluated in the literature.

In male poeciliids, the gonopodium is an accurate and convenient external sign of sexual maturity. Its condition can be easily and accurately evaluated and staged (e.g., Kallman and Schreibman 1973; Snelson 1984) and gonopodial development is closely correlated with testicular maturation (Grobstein 1940; Kallman and Schreibman 1973). The point of maturation in females is much more difficult to determine, because there are no precise external indicators. The best method for determining maturity is autopsy to ascertain the presence of yolked ova (Kallman and Schreibman 1978). However, this is not feasible in most experiments, and authors have used indirect methods such as pigment markers (Farr and Travis 1986) or candling ova (Stearns 1983c) as indicators of maturity. Such measures are likely to be somewhat imprecise.

Juvenile Growth Patterns

Poeciliids are born at a relatively large size and advanced developmental stage and begin feeding immediately. Consequently, juvenile growth begins at once and is fast. Juvenile growth rates in the laboratory range from less than 0.1 mm/day to as high as 0.5 mm/day for the same species, *P. reticulata* (Clemens et al. 1966; Reznick 1983). Growth rates on the order of 0.2 to 0.3 mm/day are perhaps typical, both in laboratory (e.g., Farr 1980; Snelson 1982; Wetherington et al., Chapter 14) and field experiments (Trendall 1983). Unfortunately, such growth rate data are somewhat meaningless in comparative life history studies because of the great diversity of experimental conditions under which they are measured. In general, juveniles of both sexes grow at the same rate over a diversity of experimental conditions (Snelson 1982; Kallman 1983) in marked contrast to their divergent growth rates as adults.

Adult Growth Patterns

The growth pattern of female poeciliids is typical of that of most other fishes, with the rate of increase slowing exponentially as the fish gets older (larger) (Ricker 1979). Males are strikingly different. For many years it was assumed that males ceased growth after becoming sexually mature. However, data from both laboratory and field studies show that male *P. latipinna* continue to grow after maturity, although at a reduced rate (Snelson 1982, 1984). This has since been verified in the sailfin molly (Travis et al. 1988c) and confirmed for *G. affinis* (Hughes 1986), *G. heterochir* (Yan 1987), *X. maculatus* (Kallman and Borkoski 1978), and *H. formosa* (Haake and Dean 1983). In general, males grow after maturity at 20–50% of the rate of females. However, this observation does not necessarily apply to all poeciliids; in some cases, post maturation growth is negligible (e.g., Kallman 1983 for *Xiphophorus montezumae*; Schultz 1961 for *P. lucida*; D. Reznick, pers. comm. for *P. reticulata*) and may differ between laboratory and field conditions for a single species (J. Travis, pers. comm.).

Social Influences on Male Maturation and Growth

One of the most interesting developments in poeciliid biology in recent years is the discovery that growth and maturation of males are influenced by male-male behavioral interactions. Borowsky (1973b) was the first to show that the size at which male maturation begins, and the rate at which it proceeds, is influenced by the presence of a larger juvenile or adult male.

In experiments pairing two juvenile male broodmates of similar size, the first male to mature is usually the larger individual at the start of the experiment. In most cases, it is also the faster growing individual. The growth rate of the early-maturing male slows dramatically after maturity, and thus its size becomes relatively fixed. The second male in each pair delays maturation and continues to grow at a normal rate, eventually exceeding the size of the early-maturing male. Once the second male has exceeded the size of the first, it begins to mature. The same pattern holds for juvenile males paired with larger adult males; juveniles delay maturation until they exceed the size of adults, whereas juveniles raised in isolation mature without delay and at a relatively small size compared to those in experimental pairs. This phenomenon has been termed ''leap-fish'' (Pollack 1977), and by this mechanism a juvenile male whose maturation is delayed by a larger juvenile or adult tankmate will eventually exceed it in size and become the larger adult of the pair.

Since Borowsky's (1973b) original report for the platyfish (*Xiphophorus variatus*), social inhibition of male maturation has been experimentally demonstrated for *X. maculatus* (Sohn 1977a), *Gambusia manni* (Sohn 1977b), and *Girardinus metallicus* (Farr 1980). Indirect evidence indicates that it may operate in natural populations of both *X. variatus* (Borowsky 1978a) and *G. affinis* (Hughes 1985b). ''Leap-fish'' is now known to be mediated through male-male agonistic interactions, with the more aggressive males maturing early and suppressing maturity of subordinates (Sohn 1977a; Farr 1980; Borowsky 1987b). However, social inhibition of maturity should not be generalized to all poeciliids. For example, social interactions between males do not influence size or age at maturity in *P. latipinna* (Farr and Travis, 1989) or *G. heterochir* (Yan 1987). In the sailfin molly, juveniles exhibit almost no aggression, explaining the lack of a social influence (Farr and Travis, 1989).

Environmental Influences on Growth and Maturation

Most experiments measuring the effects of specific environmental parameters on growth and maturation can be grouped into three broad categories.

1) Food: It comes as no surprise that ration has a significant effect on poeciliid growth rates, with fish on reduced rations growing more slowly than those fed high rations or ad libitum. This effect has been demonstrated in the laboratory for the guppy (Reznick 1983), mosquitofish (Wurtsbaugh and Cech 1983; Vondracek et al. 1988), sailfin molly (Smith 1986), variable platyfish (Borowsky 1984), and clones of *Poeciliopsis* (Wetherington et al., Chapter 14), and in field experiments with the mosquitofish (Trendall 1983). Food quality may also affect growth in the direction expected (Meffe and Crump 1987). Differences in habitat productivity and quality and quantity of food probably account for much size variation among local populations of certain poeciliids, although the specific effect of food must be carefully separated from other potential causes in each case (Trexler 1986, Chapter 11). Unfortunately, the requisite parameters for such research are difficult to evaluate directly in the field (Reznick and Bryga 1987).

2) Temperature: Temperature is generally acknowledged to be one of the most important environmental factors influencing growth in fishes. This has been confirmed but not extensively studied in poeciliids. Wurtsbaugh and Cech (1983) showed that growth in juvenile mosquitofish fed ad libitum was zero at 10°C and increased exponentially to a maximum of 21% per day at 30°C. Growth rate declined slightly between 30 and 35°C. Meffe (unpubl. data) found that mosquitofish growth rate in the laboratory was higher at 25°C than at 32°C; growth was in fact inhibited at the higher temperature, but fish matured significantly faster. Gibson and Hurst (1955) examined growth of juvenile guppies at temperatures ranging from 20 to 32°C. In contrast to Wurtsbaugh and Cech's results, they found that guppy growth was fastest at the two intermediate temperatures, 23 and 25°C. However, Gibson and Hurst did not explain how they controlled food intake. In the mosquitofish, food consumption increases exponentially with temperature (Wurtsbaugh and Cech 1983). Thus, if Gibson and Hurst did not make appropriate ration adjustments, the guppies they held at high temperatures may have been underfed, accounting for their slower growth. Yan (1987) found that male *G. affinis* grew faster and matured earlier at 28°C than at 20°C. Food level and temperature have a strong interacting effect on growth in the mosquitofish (Vondracek et al. 1988) and in strains of platyfish (Borowsky 1984).

3) Salinity: Although many poeciliid species are broadly euryhaline (Meffe and Snelson, Chapter 2), the specific effect of salinity on growth is poorly understood. Gibson and Hurst (1955) reported that juvenile guppies acclimated to fresh water grew faster in both 25% and 50% sea water. In contrast, Zimmerer (1983) found no difference in growth of juvenile guppies reared in fresh water and 25% sea water. *Gambusia affinis* from Texas grew more slowly in fresh than in brackish (10 ppt) water (Stearns and Sage 1980), but Zimmerer (1983) found that mosquitofish from southern Florida grew more quickly in fresh water than in 25% sea water.

In euryhaline species of *Poecilia*, individuals from brackish or salt water usually are larger than those inhabiting low-salinity or fresh water (Feltkamp and Kristensen 1970; Sheinbaum 1979). *Poecilia sphenops* juveniles grow faster in normal sea water than in either hypersaline or fresh water, regardless of whether the original stock came from fresh or sea water (Feltkamp and Kristensen 1970). In the sailfin molly, *P. latipinna*, juveniles grew faster in 25% sea water than in fresh water (Zimmerer 1983), although Trexler (1986) was unable to find correlations between size and habitat type in this species.

The Complexity of Controls of Growth and Size

Because the genetic control of sexual maturation and social influences on male maturation and growth were discovered at approximately the same time (Kallman et al. 1973; Borowsky 1973b), there has been considerable interest in the interaction between these influences. It is now known for both *X. maculatus* and *X. variatus* that the social inhibition mechanism operates within maturation genotypes (Sohn 1977a; Borowsky 1987b). If maturation age and/or size is under genetic control in other poeciliids, much of the work on social interactions and the maturation process will need to be reevaluated. As described previously, environmental conditions also influence size and growth in natural populations. Thus, from the viewpoint of the field biologist, the causes and consequences of individual and interdemic differences in growth and size are much more difficult to unravel than we could have imagined just 15 years ago. The magnitude of the problem is well illustrated by two examples. McKenzie et al. (1983) exposed two maturation genotypes of *X. maculatus* to a wide variety of laboratory environmental conditions (food levels, temperature, photoperiod, tank conditions) while holding social influences to a minimum (fish reared in isolation) in order to evaluate the magnitude of environmental influence on the age and size at sexual maturation in males. Some individuals of the late-maturing genotype matured as early as 13 weeks and at a size as large as 1,800 mg, whereas others of the same genotype matured as late as 45 weeks and as small as 100 mg. Travis et al. (1989c) examined postmaturation growth of male *P. latipinna* held in isolation in the laboratory. Postmaturation growth was a function of male size at maturity, but the nature and strength of the relationship was dependent on whether the fish had experienced "summer" or "winter" conditions as juveniles. Under some conditions, large adult males grew as fast as 0.3 mm/day, a rate comparable to that of juveniles; in other cases, large mature males did not grow at all.

Size and growth characteristics of females have received much less attention than those of males. In many poeciliids, adult females are larger-bodied than adult males. Since good data on age structure in poeciliid populations are elusive, it is unclear whether or not females live longer than males. Most of the difference in adult size is probably explained by the fact that females grow faster as adults than do males. Social inhibition of growth has been suggested for juvenile female *Girardinus metallicus* (Farr 1980), but social inhibition of female maturation was not demonstrated. However, Kallman and Borkoski (1978) have shown that the genetic system that determines maturation size in male *X. maculatus* also determines maturation size and fecundity in females. In *P. latipinna*, male and female size usually covary among populations (Snelson 1985; Trexler 1986). This suggests that environmental factors influencing size and growth probably influence both sexes in a similar way. In this species, the genetic system that influences male maturation size is either absent or not expressed in females (J. Travis, pers. comm.).

These examples illustrate that size structure in poeciliid populations may be under a variety of influences, and interactions between genetic, social, and environmental factors are likely to be complex and vary from case to case. Because size may affect a variety of other life history parameters, including susceptibility to predation (Britton and Moser 1982; J. Trexler, pers. comm.), mating behavior (Farr et al. 1986), secondary sexual characters (Snelson 1985), social status (Farr 1980), fecundity (Travis and Trexler 1987), and reproductive success (Zimmerer and Kallman 1988b), the dissection of genetic, social, and environmental influences on size and growth has become a challenging problem in poeciliid biology.

SUMMARY AND FUTURE RESEARCH

The analysis of poeciliid life histories has advanced over the last 40 years from largely a descriptive approach to the point where we are beginning to address questions concerning phenotypic versus genotypic causes of observed patterns and their variation. The dissection of important life history traits into their genetic, social, and environmental components is one of the most significant challenges facing those attempting to understand the evolutionary ecology of these fishes. In this chapter I emphasized what is known about environmental and social components of variation in several important life history traits.

The genetic basis of sex-ratio determination is poorly understood. In a few species, sex ratio is determined by parental genotypes. However, the significance of this variation is unclear at the population level. In most poeciliids, sex ratio appears to be 1:1 at birth, but females usually predominate among adults, probably because males suffer greater mortality from environmental stressors and predation. Only two abiotic environmental parameters, pH and temperature, have been shown to influence sex ratios, and their effects appear to be confined to specific cases and not of broad relevance in the family. Because of the breeding system of most poeciliids, the relative paucity of males in adult populations has little impact on reproductive output. Males may be a limiting resource only in unisexual-bisexual species complexes, where two kinds of females compete for sperm.

Newborn poeciliids begin to feed immediately, and juvenile growth is rapid. Males and females grow at about the same rate until maturity, when male growth slows dramatically. As a result, males typically are smaller than females and are "frozen" near the size at which they mature. Understanding the factors that control size and age at maturity has become a major thrust in poeciliid biology. In some species, maturation is under genetic control, with some genotypes causing maturity at a young age and small size and other genotypes producing the opposite effect. Both social and environmental factors may influence the expression of maturation genes, often in complex ways. Aggressive interactions among juveniles can influence size and age at maturity, with more aggressive individuals suppressing maturity of subordinates. This effect has been demonstrated in all but two species that have been examined. The influence of abiotic environmental factors on growth and maturation is significant but varies from case to case, and the effect of these factors has not been clearly differentiated from possible genetic effects in most instances. Food, temperature, and salinity have all been implicated in causing variation in growth and/or maturation.

Future research should address the aforementioned questions at two levels. First, we need to know more about the expression of life history variables in field populations of a greater diversity of species and genera, especially those from the Caribbean islands and tropical latitudes on the continents. Even in well-known groups such as *Xiphophorus*, we need good descriptive studies based on year-round sampling of wild populations. For political and logistic reasons, these data will be difficult to gather. However, until we have a broader sampling from the family, we must be very cautious about overgeneralizing.

At the second level, we must design relevant field and laboratory experiments to refine our understanding of the expression of life history variables and their importance in the population biology and evolution of wild populations. The phenomenon of "leap-fish" is a good example. In two species recently evaluated, social factors do not seem to influence growth or size at maturity, and this phenomenon may well be limited to only a few species. Some of the early experiments on this subject should be repeated using more robust statistical treatment (Farr and Travis, 1989). Even in those species where the phenomenon is well documented in the laboratory, we need to ask if this mechanism has any general relevance in wild populations, which are usually large, fluid, and unstable in time and space. As a second example, we need to further evaluate the possible influence of environmental variables, especially temperature, salinity, pH, and oxygen, on primary and secondary sex ratios. Because of the broad environmental tolerance of many poeciliids, they are likely candidates for abiotic influences on sex determination. However, the subject needs more detailed analysis with a greater diversity of species, and experiments should be designed to minimize or exclude possible genetic effects.

ACKNOWLEDGMENTS

I thank S. T. Clark for assistance in securing library materials and Barbara Erwin for help in keeping my reprint collection organized.

Chapter 9

Genetic Control of Size at Maturity in *Xiphophorus*

KLAUS D. KALLMAN

INTRODUCTION

Sexual maturation can be viewed as an interaction between the brain, hormonal and neural messengers, and target tissues. Among vertebrates it is the hypothalamic-pituitary-gonadal axis that controls puberty. Timing of maturity can be influenced by a variety of intrinsic and extrinsic factors via peripheral sensory systems. Within populations, most individuals mature at similar sizes and ages, but there may be important differences between populations. The ages at maturity of species within families or orders are more similar to each other than between families and orders. Puberty is a species-specific (genetic) trait that represents the outcome of selection for particular life history strategies over millions of years (Bronson and Rissman 1986). Because life histories encompass virtually an unlimited number of physiological traits, the onset of puberty is a well-buffered polygenic character, yet sufficient genetic variation must exist. Given appropriate selection pressures, changes in the onset of puberty can be achieved over relatively few generations, as indicated by differences between wild and domesticated animals. These differences will have a polygenic basis, because selection does not focus upon any one component of the reproductive axis. Any genetic change, however minor, will be incorporated as long as it is in the right direction.

One of the major unresolved problems in the biology of puberty concerns identification of the precise physiological changes that trigger the onset of maturity. Bronson and Rissman (1986) point out that the reproductive axis consists of many interacting components, and that any of these could represent the final trigger. In

TABLE 9–1.   Sex-Determining Mechanisms and *P* Gene Polymorphism in Ten Species of *Xiphophorus*.

Taxon	Females	Males	P Gene Polymorphism
X. maculatus	WY WX XX	XY YY	on X and Y, W has early factor
X. milleri	XX	XY	on X and Y
X. variatus	XX	XY	restricted to Y
X. andersi	XX	XY	restricted to Y
X. pygmaeus	XX	XY	restricted to Y
X. nigrensis	XX	XY	restricted to Y
X. cf. *montezumae*	XX	XY	restricted to Y
X. cortezi	XX	XY	restricted to Y
X. alvarezi	WY		YY	factors on W and Y not the same
X. helleri		not yet known		Adult size of males is correlated with sex ratio and *P* gene polymorphism

this chapter I discuss the occurrence of discrete sex-linked intraspecific variation in the onset of maturity in fishes of the genus *Xiphophorus*.

Throughout this chapter reference is made to many species of *Xiphophorus*, their sex-determining mechanisms, and their pigment patterns. Taxonomic accounts have been provided by Rosen (1960, 1979). Summaries of the biology and genetics of these fishes have been published by Atz (1962), Kallman (1975), Kallman and Atz (1966), and Zander (1969). An overview of the sex-determining mechanisms is provided in Table 9–1.

SPECIES ACCOUNTS

Xiphophorus maculatus

The genetic polymorphism affecting size and age at sexual maturity was discovered in a stock in which males were homogametic, YY, and females heterogametic, WY, and in which the Y chromosomes carried different marker genes, *Ir* (red iris) and *Br* (red body). From crosses of the type

$$W Y\text{-}Ir\ ♀ \times Y\text{-}Ir\ Y\text{-}Br\ ♂$$

two kinds of males were obtained, *Ir Ir* and *Ir Br*; males homozygous for *Ir* matured earlier and at a smaller size than heterozygotes. From a second cross involving W Y-*Br* females, two classes of males were also obtained, *Ir Br* and *Br Br*. Homozygous *Br* males matured later and at a larger size than heterozygotes

(Kallman and Borkoski 1978). These differences are not controlled by the pigment genes (see following) but by another locus tightly linked to it; this has been termed the *P* (pituitary) locus, because gonad maturation in fishes is controlled by the gonadotropes of the pituitary gland. The gonadotropic zone (ventral caudal pars distalis) of *Ir Ir* males becomes active significantly earlier than that of *Br Br* males.

In a series of crosses, several other X or Y chromosomes were then substituted for either Y-*Br* or Y-*Ir* to determine whether they carried *P* alleles different from the ones on Y-*Ir* or Y-*Br*. At any one time, only a single sex chromosome was changed. Thus, the male progeny of such crosses consisted of two classes, for example, Y-*Ir* Y-*Ir*, which served as the standard against which the unknown Y-*Ir* Y-? was compared. If significantly different, the next step involved comparing Y-*Br* Y-*Br* (the new standard) with Y-*Br* Y-? males. By means of this stepwise substitution, five *P* alleles were identified and reference strains with these alleles have been maintained in the laboratory (Kallman and Borkoski 1978).

P^1 is the allele causing earliest maturation. When raised under standardized conditions in isolation, males homozygous for P^1 mature at 21.3 mm standard length (throughout this chapter, all lengths are standard length) and 8 weeks. P^2P^2 males mature at 29.0 mm and 13.5 weeks; P^4P^4 males at 37.2 mm and 24.7 weeks; and P^5P^5 individuals, which are females, any time between 34 weeks and 2 years (some are still immature at 2 years) and between 31 mm and 50 mm. P^3P^3 individuals have never been raised under these conditions, but it is known from other observations that they mature at somewhat larger sizes and greater ages than P^2 males. In 13 comparisons between P^2 and P^3 using mass cultures, the P^3 class was always larger, significantly so in five tests. Heterozygotes generally mature at ages and sizes intermediate between the two homozygotes, except for P^2P^5 males which represent some of the latest and largest individuals.

Subsequently, the unknown *P* factors on 21 sex chromosomes have been tested against the aforementioned five *P* alleles (Kallman, unpubl. data). P^2 was recovered twice, both Y-linked, and P^3 eight times on Y chromosomes and once on an X, and linked to six pigment markers. The 10 remaining *P* factors were new (Table 9–2). One factor, P^7, was found twice on unmarked Y chromosomes; it causes maturation at sizes intermediate between those stipulated by P^2 and P^3. P^8 was present on four Y chromosomes, all differently marked. Males with P^8 mature at sizes intermediate between P^3 and P^4 fish. A third allele, P^9, occupies a position between P^3 and P^8. It was found once on an unmarked Y and once on an X linked to a melanophore factor. The fourth new allele, P^6, fits between P^8 and P^4; it was present on two Y chromosomes and associated with different color markers in each case. No *P* factor on the W chromosomes was identified. The W of the Belize stock (Bp) carries an "early" factor, but its identity is not known.

No evidence exists for preferential association of certain *P* factors with certain color genes (Table 9–3). Most of this work was done with the Belize River population. This explains why most *P* alleles are of Bp origin and why this should not be taken as evidence that this population is more polymorphic than others. Because

TABLE 9–2.   Identification of Four New P Factors in
Xiphophorus maculatus.

New P Factor and Identity	No. of Experimental Groups*	Comparison With Known P Factor	Males With New P Factor are** Smaller	Larger
P^7	15	P^2	—	15(6)
P^7	19	P^3	18(8)	1
P^9	18	P^3	—	18(11)
P^9	14	P^8	14(8)	—
P^8	23	P^3	—	23(16)
P^8	10	P^4	10(7)	—
P^6	18	P^8	—	18(12)
P^6	9	P^4	9(3)	—

* Experimental group comprises siblings of two genotypes (e.g., P^2P^7 and
P^2P^3 or P^7P^7 and P^7P^3), which were raised together from birth to maturity.
** Parentheses indicate the number of significant differences.

TABLE 9–3.   The Nine Known P Alleles of *X. maculatus*, Their Associated
Pigment Factors, and X or Y Linkage and Geographical Origin.*,** (The
P factors are listed in order of size at sexual maturation.)

P Factor	Pigment Factor, Sex Chromosome, and Origin
P^1+	SP^1-X Jp, $DrSd$-X Jp, Sp^9-Y Cp, N^2-Y Cp
P^2+	$+$-Y Bp (2x), $ArSr$-Y Jp
P^7	Dr-Y Bp, $+$-Y Bp
P^3+	Sp^8-Y Bp (2x), Mr-Y Bp (2x), $MrSd$-Y Bp, Rs-Y Bp, Ay-Y Bp, Ir-Y Bp, $+-$Y Bp, $+$-X Up
P^9	$+$-Y Bp, f-Sd-X Up
P^8	N^1-Y Bp, $TySr$-Y Bp, $CpoSd$-Y Bp, Ir-Y Bp
P^6	Asr-Y Cp, $+$-Y Bp
P^4+	Br-Y BP
P^5+	N^1-X Bp

* The pigment genes have been described previously (Kallman 1976).
** Geographical origin: Jp - Río Jamapa, Cp - Río Coatzacoalcos, Up - Río
Usumacinta system, Bp - Belize River.
+ P factors previously identified.

the X chromosome is uncommon in Belize (Kallman 1970a), mostly Y chromosomes
were surveyed.

Xiphophorus variatus

Adult male size in one stock of *X. variatus* (XX ♀ − XY ♂) is controlled
by a Y-linked factor presumably at the P locus (Borowsky 1987a). No evidence
was obtained that a polymorphism exists at the P locus and the X chromosome.

In my laboratory, females mature at a size and age similar to early maturing males.

Xiphororus andersi

In a stock derived from four males and four females, genetic variation of age and size at maturity was restricted to males, with two genotypes identified. Two males (24.0 and 29.5 mm) belonged to the small, s, and two (26.0 and 36.0 mm) to the large, L, genotype (Kallman, unpubl. data). From these fish, four lines were established and maintained for five generations. Except for the first generation, in which wild virgin females were used, s males were always mated to females of the large male lines and, conversely, L males were always mated to females of the small male lines. In mass cultures, s males (n = 195) matured at 26.7 mm (21 to 34) and 19.1 weeks (11 to 28) and L males (n = 173) at 32.0 mm (22 to 41) and 26.2 weeks (11 to 45). When raised in isolation, size at maturity remained unaffected, but age at maturity decreased significantly (s ♂♂: 26.0 ± 2.8 mm, 12.5 ± 2.4 weeks, n = 20; L ♂♂: 31.6 ± 4.2 mm, 14.7 ± 3.6 weeks, n = 28). No evidence was obtained that variability within the s and L classes of males is due to genetic variation on the X chromosome. The range of adult size of L males totally encompasses that of s males. In mass cultures, females matured at similar ages and sizes as s males, but when raised in isolation these two parameters were much closer to those of L males. The difference in mean adult size between males is due to alternate alleles at the P locus on the Y chromosome.

Xiphophorus milleri

Kallman and Borowsky (1972) documented that adult male size showed Y-linked inheritance (pedigree [ped.] 2669, XY-Sv, n = 17, 21.0 ± 1.33 mm; XY-Gn, n = 21, 22.7 ± 1.95 mm). These relatively minor differences are not due to environmental factors, because these males were produced by the same mating (XX ♀ × Y-Sv Y-Gn ♂) using a rare YY male. Similar observations were made on three other pedigrees, but only small numbers of males were involved.

In a second stock, genetic variation affecting adult male size is X-linked. From a X-Sp X-+ female mated to a X-+ Y-Ty male, two broods were obtained in which the Sp class was significantly larger than the + class (ped. 4667: brood 1, Sp ♂♂, n = 7, 26.1 ± 1.31 mm, + ♂♂, n = 7, 21.4 ± 1.27 mm; brood 2, Sp ♂♂, n = 7, 30.6 ± 1.89 mm, + ♂♂, n = 8, 25.3 ± 3.06 mm). Similar results were obtained in the following pedigree (ped. 4987, Sp ♂♂, n = 18, 21.9 ± 1.44 mm, + ♂♂, n = 10, 19.9 ± 1.35 mm). Differences within classes are of environmental origin, but between classes within broods differences are mostly genetic in nature. In this stock, Y-linked variation is also present, but because of the XX-XY sex-determining mechanism, males with the two Y chromosomes could not be compared within the same pedigree. The mean sizes of 12 experimental

Ty groups ranged from 18.0 to 22.1 mm, and the means of 7 XY-+ groups ranged from 22.0 to 25.3 mm (χ^2 = 8.4, p < 0.01). Only one *Ty* group (22.1 mm) was larger than the smallest + group. The second largest *Ty* group tied the smallest + group in size. Other than *X. maculatus*, *X. milleri* is the only other species in which the *P* gene polymorphism is also present on the X chromosome.

Xiphophorus cf montezumae

Male montezumae swordtails from the Río Valles and Río Tamesi drainages vary from 22 to 45 mm. These differences are, in part, caused by two alleles, *s* and *L*, at the *P* locus on the Y chromosome (Kallman 1983). In the laboratory stock, all X chromosomes carry the *s* allele; males are either *s s* or *s L*. Individual size of the two genotypes of males broadly overlaps (s ♂♂ : 26 − 41 mm, L ♂♂ : 29 − 50 mm), which is attributed to environmental conditions. Females matured at similar sizes and ages as *s* males. With two exceptions, the mean length of 27 groups of *L* males (31 to 45 mm) exceeded the means of 51 groups of *s* males (28 to 37 mm). In one experiment, three exceptional Y-*s* Y-*L* males were mated to X-*s* X-*s* females and the X-*s* Y-*s* and X-*s* Y-*L* progeny of each cross were reared together. The means of the *s* males were 32.2, 33.0, and 33.3 mm, respectively, and those of the *L* males 42.2, 42.9, and 43.1 mm. Individual size of *s* males ranged from 30 to 36 mm (n = 29) and of *L* males from 39 to 49 mm (n = 23). Thus, when raised under identical conditions, males of the two genotypes did not overlap in size.

Xiphophorus montezumae

In natural populations, males range in size from 36 to 61 mm. No evidence was obtained that these differences are genetically controlled (Kallman, unpubl. data).

Xiphophorus cortezi

Adult males in natural populations range in size from 24.0 to 55.0 mm. In the only sample examined (Río Axtla population), the polymorphism is restricted to the Y chromosome. This conclusion is based upon the patroclinous inheritance of mean adult size of the progeny of four wild males raised for up to four generations in mass cultures. Two size genotypes were identified, *s* (small) derived from a 25 mm male and *L* (large) derived from three males, 32.5, 36.0, and 47.0 mm (Kallman, unpubl. data). Although some of the results are still preliminary, it appears that the difference between the two genotypes becomes apparent only when the fish are reared in mass cultures. Under these conditions, *s* males matured at mean sizes between 28.2 and 32.6 mm (individual range 24 to 38) and *L* males between 34.5 and 39.6 mm (range 26 to 48). Age at maturity varied correspondingly. However, when reared in isolation, no difference between the two genotypes could be documented. The average size of the first L males to mature in 11 mass cultures was 30.1 mm (26 to 33), which is close to the size at which L males mature in isolation. The differences within genotypes but between rearing conditions are attributed to social interaction as has been described for other *Xiphophorus* (Borowsky 1973b). The P factors of X. *cortezi* appear to control the degree to which individuals are susceptible to the socially mediated delay of maturation. This condition differs from that in other species of *Xiphophorus* in which the various P genotypes mature at different sizes and ages regardless of whether raised in isolation or mass cultures.

Xiphophorus pygmaeus

Males in natural populations range from 19 to 29 mm, but most of them fall within the 20 to 24 mm range. Besides unmarked (+) males, there also occur some with a solid yellow body coloration (flavus concolor, *con*) or yellow caudal fins (flavus caudipinna, *cp*). A stock has been maintained in the laboratory, derived from three males, +, *cp*, and *con*, respectively. Males with *cp* were alternately mated to females derived from + and *con* males, males with *con* were alternately mated to females derived from *cp* and + males, and + males were similarly mated to females derived from *cp* and *con* males. There was no difference in adult size between + (23.2 ± 0.79 mm, n = 100) and *con* males (23.3 ± 0.79 mm, n = 100), but *cp* males were significantly larger (24.3 ± 1.10, n = 100, $p < 0.001$). Because of the breeding scheme, males with different patterns possess identical genetic backgrounds. The larger size of the *cp* males must be due to a Y-linked factor. It is not known whether large size is always associated with *cp*, because only three males were tested.

Xiphophorus nigrensis

Males inhabiting the Río Choy vary in size from 20 to 41 mm. An extensive series of observations has shown that three Y-linked P alleles are largely responsible for male differences (s - small, 22 to 26 mm; I - intermediate, 24 to 32 mm; L - large, 30 to 41 mm) (Table 9–4). The same variation within genotypes is seen in mass cultures and when fish are raised individually. All X chromosomes carry the same P factor, which codes for maturity at a small size, but this allele appears to be different from s on the Y (see following).

The sex chromosome mechanism of X. *nigrensis* is XX - XY. Therefore, adult male size should show patroclinous inheritance, but this was not always the case (Table 9–5). In 7 of 49 crosses, L or I males sired some s males (22 to 24 mm). This is the result of an autosomal regulatory locus with two alleles, A and a, that acts epistatically to the sex gene on the sex chromosome (Kallman 1984). Individuals that are XX and homozygous for the autosomal factor, aa, develop

TABLE 9–4. Adult Size (mm SL) of Different
Genotypes of Male *Xiphophorus nigrensis*.

Genotype	N	mm	S.D.	Range
Río Choy				
X-*s* Y-*s*	61	24.1	0.88	22–26
X-*s* Y-*I*	154	28.9	1.31	25–32
X-*s* Y-*L*	301	35.5	1.92	30–40
Río Coy				
X-*s* Y-*s*	302	25.3	1.20	22–28
X-*s* Y-*I*	135	27.4	0.12	25–32
X-*s* Y-*II*	216	32.4	2.06	29–38
X-*s* Y-*L*	154	37.5	2.05	32–42

TABLE 9–5. Inheritance of Size and Sex Ratio in *Xiphophorus nigrensis*
(Río Choy). The seven crosses listed by pedigree number were influenced by an
autosomal regulatory locus.

Pedigree or Number of Crosses	Size of ♂ Parent (mm)	No. of Progeny			
		Females	*s* Males <24 mm	*I* Males 25–32 mm	*L* Males >30 mm
3508	35	3	1	—	1
3333	38	14	5	—	32
3267	36	15	5	—	13
3702	38	10	4	—	11
29 crosses*	32–41	227	0	—	242
3415	28	9	5	11	—
3574	29	11	2	11	—
3839	28	13	2	14	—
13 crosses*	24–30	103	0	125	—

	Females	*s* Males	*I* + *L* Males
total of 7 problematical crosses:	75	24	93
	39.1%	12.5%	48.4%
expected:	37.5%	12.5%	50.0%

* Represent combined data from crosses in which no *aa* individuals occur

into functional males (atypical sex determination). The XX males (20 to 24 mm)
average somewhat smaller than XY-*s* males (22 to 26 mm), raising the possibility
that the *s* factors on the X and Y are not identical.

The expectation from a mating involving the following genotypes

$$\text{X-}s \text{ X-}s \ A \ a \ ♀ \times \text{X-}s \text{ Y-}L \ A \ a \ ♂$$

is 50% *L* males (XY *AA*, *Aa* or *aa*), 12.5% *s* males (XX *aa*), and 37.5% females
(XX *AA* or *Aa*). If the male parent is *aa*, the expectation is 50% *L* males (XY

Aa or aa), 25% s males (XX aa), and 25% females (XX Aa). The seven problematical crosses in Table 9–5 best fit the scheme of an XY Aa male ($\chi^2 = 0.22$, p = 0.90).

Support for this interpretation comes from three kinds of observations. 1) The Y chromosomes of the 16 crosses with I males (Table 9–5) were also marked by a dominant Y-linked pigment factor, Flv^{cm}, for yellow caudal fin, or Flv^{en} for yellow sword. These patterns were inherited by all I males 25 mm or larger, whereas the s males (22 to 24 mm) lacked the patterns. 2) When XX males were mated to related females, they often sired males (s) and females in a ratio of 1 : 1, but when bred to unrelated females, apparently AA, all-female broods were produced. 3) The most persuasive evidence comes from a series of crosses in which two s XX males (20 mm) from the Río Choy were crossed to a laboratory stock from which the a factor had been eliminated. The first outcross consisted of females (n = 114) only, which when backcrossed to the two XX males produced a 1 : 1 sex ratio (35 ♀♀, 35 ♂♂; no males were larger than 24 mm). This sequence of outcrossing followed by backcrossing was repeated twice with identical results (second and third outcross: 64 ♀♀, 1 ♂; second and third backcross: 65 ♀♀, 64 ♂♂). These results strongly support the view that a single recessive autosomal factor is involved in the XX male phenomenon, and that the s males generated by L and I males possess the XX genotype.

The males of a second population (Río Coy) range in size from 22 to 42 mm. Male adult size shows patroclinous inheritance. Four P alleles have been identified (Table 9–4). All X chromosomes carry the s factor, whereas the Ys possess one of four P alleles. XX males do not occur in this population.

Xiphophorus helleri

Mature males in natural populations range in size from 24 to well over 60 mm. In each of three wild-derived laboratory strains, both early- and late-maturing males exist. As in the other species, size and age at maturity are correlated (Peters 1964). Females matured at the same age and size as early males. There was a marked tendency of early males to produce male-biased broods and for the late males to sire female-biased broods. A precise genetic analysis was not performed. However, the occurrence of two kinds of males within broods and their apparent correlation with sex ratio suggests, as in X. *nigrensis* and X. cf *montezumae* (Kallman 1983), a P locus polymorphism on the sex chromosomes accompanied by the occurrence of atypical sex determination (Kallman 1984).

Xiphophorus alvarezi

Females of two stocks (Río Dolores and Río Candelaria) mature at an earlier age and smaller size than males, suggesting the location of an early P factor on the W, and a late one on the Y chromosome (Kallman and Bao 1987). A third stock (Río San Ramon) has highly variable sex ratios. Male-biased sex ratios predominate, but occasionally female-biased progeny or even all-female broods are produced. Most males mature late, but some mature as early as females. The sex chromosome mechanism of this stock is still unknown. As in *X helleri*, these observations are not easy to interpret. A working hypothesis is that the sex chromosome mechanism is WY - YY and that the male biased progeny consists of YY and exceptional WY males. If the W carries early and the Y late *P* factors, then the early maturing males would be WY.

Other Species

The remaining nine species of *Xiphophorus* have not been investigated with respect to variation at the *P* locus.

CHANGES IN THE MATURATION SCHEDULE IN INTERSPECIFIC HYBRIDS

Several hybrids show significant changes in maturation schedules compared to the parental species (reviewed by Bao and Kallman 1982). This is most firmly established for *X. helleri* × *X. maculatus* hybrids. Depending on which allele was inherited from *X. maculatus*, F_1 and backcross hybrids to *X. helleri* mature from one to three years after the parental species, and some hybrids fail to mature altogether. By contrast, the backcross hybrids homozygous for the *P* factor (P^h) of *X. helleri* mature at sizes and ages typical for *X. helleri*. A delay has also been observed in hybrids between *X. maculatus* and *X. andersi* with P^3 of *X. maculatus*, which take from 37 to 50 weeks longer to mature than either parental species and grow correspondingly larger (Kallman, unpubl. data).

Conversely, certain hybrids show precocious maturity (Bao and Kallman 1982). This phenomenon is restricted to *X. helleri* × *X. maculatus* hybrids (F_2 backcrosses to *X. maculatus*) that are homozygous for the *P* factors of *X. helleri*, P^hP^h, and homozygous for some autosomes derived from *X. maculatus*. These hybrids often mature as early as five weeks and at sizes smaller than either parental species. A somewhat similar situation occurs in *X. maculatus* × *X. nigrensis* hybrids (Bao and Kallman 1982).

However, not all interspecific hybrids exhibit a change in the maturation schedule. No precocious maturation was encountered in hybrids involving three species of platyfish, *X. maculatus*, *X. variatus*, and *X. xiphidium* (Kosswig 1941). Backcross hybrids between rather dissimilar species, for example, *X. milleri*, a small platyfish, with *X. alvarezi* or *X. clemenciae*, both large swordtails, show no delay or acceleration of maturity (Kallman, unpubl. data). There is also no change in the maturation process in hybrids between $X.$ *helleri* and $X.$ *clemenciae* or $X.$ *alvarezi*.

EVIDENCE FOR REGULATORY GENES

Changes in the maturation schedule of hybrids must be attributed to the interaction of the P factors of one species with regulatory genes of another. The P genes are involved because the magnitude of delay depends, in part, on the P genotype. In $X.$ *maculatus* $\times$ $X.$ *helleri* hybrids, the delay was least in the P^hP^1 males, followed by the P^hP^2, P^hP^4, and P^hP^3 hybrids, in this order (Bao and Kallman 1982). In the F_2 generation, the delay was greater in fish with two P factors of $X.$ *maculatus* than in hybrids with one P factor each from the two species. These observations make it unlikely that the delay in maturation is caused by the interaction between the P factor of the two species.

However, several lines of evidence indicate that other genes are also involved in the change of maturation schedule in species hybrids. If the P genotype is kept constant, the magnitude of delay depends on the number of *helleri* autosomes present. For P^hP^4 and P^hP^3 hybrids, the delay was always least in the F_1 and greatest in the second backcross generations. If the regulatory systems of the two species were identical, there should have been no difference between generations within a genotype.

More evidence for regulatory genes is provided by the maturation schedule of P^hP^h hybrids which, in backcrosses to $X.$ *helleri*, mature at the same age and size as P^hP^h $X.$ *helleri*. However, F_2 hybrids (P^hP^h) mature precociously at sizes smaller than individuals of either species (Kosswig 1941, 1964; Berg and Gordon 1953; Siciliano 1970; Bao and Kallman 1982). Because only the genetic background was changed, differences between the F_2 and the backcrosses to $X.$ *helleri* must be due to autosomal factors. Dwarf males (P^hP^h) also occur in generations produced by crossing backcross hybrids to *maculatus* with themselves (Bao and Kallman 1982). Because the aforementioned investigators worked with different stocks of both species, this phenomenon is of general significance. One property shared by all dwarf P^hP^h males is that they are homozygous for one or more autosomes of $X.$ *maculatus*.

If a single autosomal locus of $X.$ *maculatus* in the homozygous condition were responsible for the dwarf male phenomenon, not more than 25% of the F_2 P^hP^h hybrids would mature precociously. On the other hand, if the specific interaction of several unlinked autosomal loci in homozygous condition were required, the proportion of precocious P^hP^h hybrids would have decreased rapidly, depending on the number of autosomal loci involved (Bao and Kallman 1982). However, every P^hP^h F_2 hybrid matured precociously. Because *Xiphophorus* has 23 pairs of autosomes (Friedman and Gordon 1934), it is unlikely that any two hybrids share the same configuration of autosomes. It appears that most autosomes of *X. maculatus* must carry such regulatory genes. Any one of these genes in homozygous condition can cause precocious maturation, and they must act epistatically to those of *X. helleri*.

SITE OF *P* GENE ACTION

Öztan (1960, 1963) showed that the inability of the *X. maculatus* × *X. helleri* hybrids to mature was caused by a physiological lesion in the nucleus lateralis tuberis (NLT) in the hypothalamus, and that gonads of the hybrids would develop after administration of gonadotropic hormone. The action of the *P* gene has now been traced to certain higher centers of the brain. One of the main differences between P^1P^2 (early) and P^2P^5 (late) males of *X. maculatus* concerns the age at which gonadotropin releasing hormone (GnRH) can be detected in the nucleus olfactoretinalis (NOR) and the NLT (Halpern-Sebold et al. 1986). GnRH controls the synthesis and release of gonadotropic hormone from the caudal pars distalis of the pituitary gland, and gonadotropic hormone, in turn, is necessary for maturation of the ovary and testis (Reiter and Grumbach 1982). Differences in GnRH activity between P^1P^2 and P^2P^5 males can be detected as early as five weeks in the NOR, long before either of the two genotypes initiates maturation. At maturity, only the perikarya of the NLT of P^1P^2 males exhibit GnRH activity, whereas in P^2P^5 males it is restricted to the fibers. Halpern-Sebold et al. (1986) advanced two explanations. The late-maturing P^2P^5 individuals may produce the neuropeptide in such low quantities that it cannot be detected or it may be rapidly released. The authors appeared to favor the first possibility, because they detected only a faint basophilia, suggestive of less peptide synthesis in the NLT perikarya of P^2P^5 than of P^1P^2 males.

However, Bao and Kallman (1982) suggested that the *P* locus controls the fate of GnRH rather than its production. When synthetic LH-RH was administered to immature males of different *P* genotypes, they responded differently. A direct correlation existed between the age at which the various genotypes mature spontaneously and the rapidity of their response to hormone administration. The earliest genotype tested (P^2P^5) initiated maturity at age 13 weeks (injections began at 6 weeks) and the latest genotype (P^hP^3) at age 38 weeks (injections began at 12 weeks).

If it were only a question of the production of GnRH, the different genotypes should not have differed in their response. Administration would have been downstream from the site of gene action in the chain of developmental events leading to the onset of maturity. The *P* locus could control the fate or physiological function of GnRH by means of substances that inactivate or degrade GnRH. The *P* locus could be concerned with the rate and timing at which such substances are produced.

The onset (gonopodial stage 2) and completion (stage 6) of male maturation can be measured precisely (Kallman and Schreibman 1973). The time required to pass from stage 2 to stage 6 also depends on the P genotype. Early genotypes complete the maturation process in less than 3 weeks, whereas late genotypes require 20 weeks (Kallman and Borkoski 1978; Bao and Kallman 1982). Some males of genotype P^hP^4 entered stage 2 around the age of one year but two years later had still not attained stage 6. Again, it appears that there is insufficient GnRH for differentiation and functional activity of the gonadotrops. The slow rate of response to LH-RH administration and the protracted spontaneous maturation process of the late genotypes is not an age phenomenon because, for the LH-RH treatments, age was kept constant. In another experiment, immature males of different P genotypes were administered gonadotropic hormone. All fish responded equally rapidly; clearly this treatment is developmentally below the site of gene action of the P locus (Bao 1981).

GENETIC AND DEVELOPMENTAL CORRELATES OF SIZE DIFFERENCES

A number of morphological, physiological, and behavioral traits are correlated with size. Some of them are undoubtedly an indirect effect of the age at which an individual of a given P genotype matures, and others are due to genes (hitchhiking genes) closely linked to certain P alleles. There are some traits that are difficult to assign to one of these two categories; conceivably, they could be under direct control of the P gene.

Indirect Effects of the P Alleles

The P genes are involved in the physiology of LH-RH and the timing of gonadotropin secretion. The beginning of androgen production is thus an indirect effect upon which, in turn, depend cessation of growth in males (adult size) and appearance of male secondary sex characters (pigmentation, caudal appendage).

Hitchhiking Genes

Several pigmentary traits are controlled by genes closely linked to certain P factors. The two genotypes of male X. *andersi* differ by a melanophore pattern that has been dubbed the "pseudo-gravidity spot" (Kallman, unpubl. data). The gravidity spot in mature female *Xiphophorus* spp., as in other poeciliid fishes, is caused by a dense accumulation of melanophores in the lining of the posterior part of the peritoneum.

The genetically large males, L, show an extensive area of black pigment on the flank above the gonopodium. This pattern suggests a gravidity spot, but it is located more posteriorly in the connective tissue sheath that surrounds the gonacti-nostal complex and the gonapopheses. In the size range where s and L males overlap, appearance of the pseudo-gravidity spot shows a perfect correlation with genotype and not with size. Presumably, this pattern has an epigamic function. Superficially, L males resemble females in body shape and pigmentation. It may be more than a coincidence that female X. *andersi* have one of the largest gravidity spots in the genus, a pattern that is mimicked by a pattern in L males. Genetic analysis has shown that the pseudo-gravidity spot is a polygenic character. The Y chromosome with the s allele carries a suppressor gene for this trait. The suppression is absent from the X chromosomes and the Y with L (Kallman, unpubl. data).

Two pigment patterns in the Río Coy population of X. *nigrensis* are always associated with the s factor on the Y. Approximately 10% of the s males exhibit a solid yellow coloration controlled by the dominant Y-linked factor, Flv^{con}. None of the more than 2,000 females and males with the I, II, or L alleles collected in the field possessed this pattern. No crossover occurred among the more than 600 progeny of X-s Y-s *con* males. There is an obligatory linkage between the sex-determining locus, the s factor, and *con*.

The second pigmentary trait concerns the vertical bar pattern. All I, II, and L males exhibit well-developed bars, which are also present in many other *Xiphophorus* spp. and also in other genera, but in s males the pattern is poorly developed or absent (Zimmerer and Kallman 1988). This trait has a polygenic basis, and the absence of bars in small males is due to a suppressor gene linked to s on the Y chromosome. All other Y and X chromosomes lack the suppressor. Absence of this pattern from the Río Choy population of X. *nigrensis* is due to absence of the polygenic basis for this pigmentation and not to presence of the suppressor gene (Zimmerer and Kallman 1988).

The vertical bar pattern plays an important role during agonistic behavior, when it darkens significantly, especially in dominant fish. In subordinate individuals pigment becomes concentrated in the center of the melanophores, and the bars fade. Existence of the suppressor gene linked to s on the Y chromosome appears to be advantageous in a population where small males have little chance to gain dominance and in which large males prevent small males from having access to females. One of the tactics of s males is to be inconspicuous and avoid challenging larger males (Zimmerer and Kallman 1989).

Males of the three large size genotypes of X. *nigrensis* (Río Coy) exhibit an identical courtship behavior that consists of a frontal display with spread fins, lasting up to 36 seconds. Copulation attempts are rare after these displays. The s males also exhibit this courtship behavior, but it is of significantly shorter duration. In addition, s males engage in a behavior termed sneak-chase, during which they dart toward the female, usually from behind, followed by a copulation attempt. In the laboratory, frequency of the two behaviors depends on whether or not larger males are present. The behavioral shift appears to be adaptive during competitive conditions, because large males prevent small males from having access to females. Therefore, s males may attempt to increase their mating success by a change in tactics.

The difference in behavior between s males on the one hand and I, II, and

L males on the other is under direct genetic control and is not an indirect ontogenetic effect related to size. The difference between s and I males remains when size is standardized by testing the largest s males and the smallest I males. Because males of the four genetic size classes have the same genotype except for the Y chromosome, the behavioral differences must be attributed to Y-linked factors. Most behaviors have a polygenic basis (Manning 1967); the presence of a given behavior in one P genotype and its absence in another must be due to a suppressor gene.

Additional insight into this problem is provided by consideration of two other behaviors, "orient" and "circle," which are commonly exhibited by s males but never by L males. In the absence of large congeners, orient behavior is only rarely shown by I males, and circle behavior is never seen. But under competitive conditions with L males, the frequency of orient behavior by I males is significantly increased, and some instances of circle behavior are observed. Thus, given the proper motivational stimulus, a behavioral trait surfaces, albeit very rarely. I males, therefore, must possess the genetic basis for circle behavior. Because the orient and circle trait frequencies differed between I and s males, even when size was standardized, Zimmerer and Kallman (1989) suggested that gene loci on the Y chromosomes govern the threshold at which particular behaviors appear. The alleles at these loci are not the same on Y chromosomes with the s, I, and L factors. Farr (1983) came to similar conclusions in *Poecilia reticulata*, where the frequency of various components of the male courtship behavior show patroclinous inheritance.

Sneak-chase may represent a basic poeciliid behavior, because it is also present in three other species of *Xiphophorus* (Franck 1964, 1968), and behavior that resembles sneak-chase has been reported in subordinate male *Poeciliopsis occidentalis* (Constantz 1975). Absence of this trait in certain species or genotypes of *Xiphophorus* could be due to genetic factors that set the threshold for this behavior rather high. These factors can then be regarded as repressor genes.

In *Poecilia latipinna*, the only species outside *Xiphophorus* with a P gene polymorphism, similar strong correlates exist between a number of behaviors and adult male size (Travis et al. 1989a, 1989b). As in *X. nigrensis*, display behavior is common in large males, whereas forced insemination attempts—a behavior that may be analogous to sneak-chase—is predominantly exhibited by smaller males. Contrary to *X. nigrensis*, no evidence was obtained that major variations in the behaviors are directly due to a Y-linked factor.

Polygenic Basis for Allometric Growth

The L males of *X. nigrensis* of both populations possess a habitus quite different from s males. In this respect, the P genotypes of *X. nigrensis* differ from those of the other species in which the late-maturing males are essentially larger versions of the small morphs. Greatest depth and least depth in *X. nigrensis* increase at a faster rate than standard length. The s males appear rather slender and elongate, while L males are stout and deep-bodied. The dorsal fin of s males is low in height, and their dorsal fin index (height of dorsal fin/length of caudal peduncle) is 0.74. (All measurements are for the Choy stock.) The dorsal fin of L males is relatively higher. The most posterior fin fays are especially long and, when depressed, extend beyond the origin of the caudal fin (dorsal fin index 1.1). The erected dorsal fin contitutes an important signal during frontal display and agonistic behavior. The sword of s males is short with a sword index (length of sword/standard length) of 0.04, whereas in L males the sword index is 0.41. Overall, the difference between L and s males is just as great as between males of different species. The difference in body shape develops gradually as the immature L males increase in size. However, allometric growth of the dorsal fin and sword are secondary sex characters. Prior to maturation, large L males have dorsal fins relatively as small as s males.

Differences in shape and size of the dorsal fin and sword between L and s males of X. *nigrens* are a consequence of the P gene polymorphism but are not controlled by it. This conclusion is based on observing the effect of the L factor X. *nigrensis* after introgression into X. *pygmaeus*. The two species are sister taxa, and the s males of X. *nigrensis* closely resemble those of X. *pygmaeus* (Rosen 1979). The L hybrids (second backcross generation to X. *pygmaeus*) are as large as L males of X. *nigrensis*, but they have short dorsal fins (index 0.6), and the sword is virtually absent (index 0.05). The F_1 and first-generation hybrids are intermediate for these parameters. Allometric growth of the dorsal fin and sword of X. *nigrensis* is a species-specific polygenic trait that is absent from X. *pygmaeus*.

A similar strong correlation between dorsal fin morphology and adult size is present in P. *latipinna*. Variation in dorsal fin height when adult size is kept constant appears to be due to a number of autosomal modifiers (Travis et al. 1989b).

Direct Control of Growth Rate by the *P* Locus of *X. nigrensis*

In all but one species of *Xiphophorus*, immature males and females grow at the same rate regardless of P genotype. Kallman (1975) showed this for X. *maculatus*, and Peters (1964) demonstrated it for X. *helleri*. Data are available for 10 additional species of *Xiphophorus* and, in 3 of them, the comparison was between early maturing females and genetically late-maturing males (Kallman, unpubl. data). No significant differences were present in 116 comparisons; in 3 comparisons males were significantly smaller, and in 9 tests males were significantly larger.

There are references to juvenile growth in four other poeciliid species (*Poecilia reticulata*, Ryman 1972; Vanelli et al. 1984; *P. latipinna*, Snelson 1982; Travis et al. 1989b; *Girardinus metallicus*, Farr 1980a; *Gambusia manni*, Krumholz 1963). In each, the sexes grow at the same rate prior to maturation. In *P. latipinna*, in which male size and age at maturity are inherited as a Y-linked trait, the growth rate of females and early and late males is the same (Travis et al. 1989a). Therefore, an equal growth rate of immature males and females is the basic poeciliid growth pattern.

However, in *X. nigrensis*, growth rate of immature fish depends on the *P* genotype (Table 9–6). The *s* genotypes grow at the slowest rate and *I*, *II*, and *L* males grow increasingly faster, in this order. In all but 1 of 26 comparisons between *s* males and females, males were smaller, significantly so in 11 instances. Males of 16 of these groups had the XX genotype and, therefore, the same *P* genotype as females. The slightly smaller size of the males at eight weeks must ultimately be attributed to hormonal differences. Eight weeks is near the age at which *s* males initiate maturation, and sufficient androgenic hormone may already have been present to slow their growth rate. However, the anal fin rays had not yet begun to elongate.

At eight weeks, the males of all but 1 (*I*) of 37 experimental groups involving *I*, *II*, and *L* males were larger than females. In the Río Choy stock, all eleven groups of *L* males and six groups of *I* males differed from females at the p = 0.05 or p = 0.01 levels. Five groups of *I* males were larger and one group smaller than females, but not significantly so. Five experimental groups consisted of both *L* (XY) and *s* (XX) males, and this made a direct comparison between the two

TABLE 9–6. Comparison of Size of Immature Male and Female *Xiphophorus nigrensis* at Eight Weeks within Experimental Groups.

River and Genotype	Number of experimental groups	Males significantly smaller at p<		Size difference not significant	Males significantly larger at p<	
		0.01	0.05		0.05	0.01
Río Choy						
s (XX)	16	—	5	11	—	—
s (XY)	3	1	—	2	—	—
s (XX) versus *I*	2	1	1	—	—	—
s (XX) versus *L*	5	5	—	—	—	—
Río Choy I (XY)	12	—	—	6	4	2
Río Choy L (XY)	11	—	—	—	—	11
Río Coy s (XY)	7	3	2	2	—	—
Río Coy I (XY)	4	—	—	4	—	—
Río Coy II (XY)	6	—	—	4	—	2
Río Coy L (XY)	4	—	—	1	1	2

classes of males possible. *L* males were significantly larger, and this difference was already present at five weeks. Similarly, a comparison between *I* (XY) and *s* (XX) males in two groups showed that *I* males grew significantly faster. A similar relationship exists in the Coy population.

Because the growth pattern of the *I*, *II*, and *L* males of *X. nigrensis* is more differentiated than that of other poeciliid fishes, it represents a derived condition. Females and *s* males, therefore, have retained the basic (plesiomorphic) condition. In both populations, a perfect positive correlation exists between growth rate and the genetically controlled size at maturity. The fast growth rate of *L* males is adaptive, because it partially negates the disadvantage of having to grow for long periods of time to attain the genetically controlled size for maturity. If growth rate differences were controlled by a separate gene, it must also exist in several allelic states. (Preliminary evidence indicates that the *P* factors of the Coy and Choy populations are not identical.) There is no reason to assume that a mutation from the original condition (slow growth rate) at the putative growth locus always gave rise to an allele for intermediate growth rate, if linked to *I*, or to an allele for fast growth rate, if linked to *L*. If *s*, *I*, and *II* males grew at the maximum possible rate, they would then mature still earlier and compound their advantage over *L* males. Because this did not occur, growth rates may be directly controlled by the *P* factors.

SPECIES SPECIFICITY OF THE *P* FACTORS

Ten of the 20 species of *Xiphophorus* are known to be polymorphic at the *P* locus. Even those taxa that are monomorphic must possess the *P* locus but, because of absence of genetic variation, it is not possible to demonstrate formally its existence. Nine *P* alleles have been identified in *X. maculatus*, 3 or 4 in each of the two populations of *X. nigrensis* and 2 each in 8 additional species. Therefore, a large number of *P* factors may exist in the genus.

Are certain *P* factors shared by more than one species? This question was examined by comparing the phenotypes produced by *P* alleles derived from different species on a common genetic background under identical environmental conditions (Bao and Kallman 1982). The potentially large number of *P* factors clearly sets a limit to such an undertaking. Only rather general statements can be made concerning species differences in the maturation schedule. The nine species of platyfish or the early genotypes of those that are polymorphic at the *P* locus undergo maturation at similar ages and sizes and would be prime candidates to share certain *P* factors. The four species of southern swordtails (*X. clemenciae*, *X. alvarezi*, *X. helleri*, *X. signum*) and four northern swordtails in the Panuco basin (*X. montezumae*, *X.* cf. *montezumae*, *X. cortezi*, and *X.* cf. *cortezi*) mature at larger sizes than the platyfishes but not always at a much greater age, because swordtails have a higher growth rate.

The P^1, P^2, P^3, and P^4 factors of *X. maculatus* are different from P^h of the

Bx stock of *X. helleri*. Hybrid $P^h P^h$ males mature at different sizes and ages than their siblings with P^h and one of the P factors of *X. maculatus*. It is also certain that none of the P factors present in the stocks of *X. maculatus* and *X. helleri* used by various investigators were identical with each other, because the $P^h P^h$ hybrids always had a different maturation schedule than the hybrids heterozygous for P^h and the P factor derived from *X. maculatus*. Bao and Kallman (1982) have suggested that the P factors may be species-specific.

The early P factors, P^s, of the two populations of *X. nigrensis* are not identical with P^l (the early P factor) of *X. maculatus* (Bao and Kallman 1982). Preliminary evidence indicates that the P factors of the Río Choy and Río Coy populations are not the same (Zimmerer and Kallman, unpubl. data). The P^3 factor of *X. maculatus* is not identical with either the early or late P factors of *X. andersi*. After introgression into *X. andersi*, males with P^3 mature significantly later and at larger sizes than either of the two P genotypes of *X. andersi* (Kallman, unpubl. data).

Is the *P* Locus Involved in Speciation Events?

The polymorphism at the P locus appears to provide a mechanism for the punctuated equilibrium model of speciation (Gould and Eldredge 1977). A substitution of one P allele by another, especially when their phenotypic effects are large, can significantly change adult size and age at maturity. Assume that two founder stocks are formed from a heterozygous population, and that one stock becomes fixed for the early factor and the other becomes homozygous for the late factor. Thus, in one step, two populations will have been formed that differ significantly in size and age at maturity. The two populations, by virtue of their different life histories, will be exposed to very different selection pressures and rapidly diverge. What began as a single locus difference will rapidly evolve additional genetic differences that may ultimately lead to speciation. Has an allele substitution at the P locus been involved in any speciation event in *Xiphophorus*? This possibility can be examined by a cladistic analysis, and candidates for such a process would be two closely related sister groups that differ significantly in size.

I see no evidence for such a process among the nine species of platyfish, the early genotypes of which mature at roughly the same age and size. The four species of southern swordtails mature at significantly larger sizes than platyfish, but the age at maturity (at least of the early genotypes) is not much greater. The swordtails have faster growth rates, but there is no evidence that the difference in growth rates between platyfish and swordtails is controlled by the P locus.

Among the northern swordtails, four taxa of relatively large size are represented. *Xiphophorus montezumae* is the largest species and differs significantly in size from *X.* cf. *montezumae* (Kallman 1983). I had suggested earlier that size differences between the two species may be due to the presence of different P alleles, with *s* (small) and *I* (intermediate) factors present in *X.* cf. *montezumae* and *I* and *L* factors present in *X. montezumae*. This view now has to be abandoned;

the differences within X. cf. *montezumae* can be attributed to two alleles as reported earlier (Kallman 1983), but the differences between the two species appear to be polygenic in nature (Kallman, unpubl. data).

The three species of pygmy swordtail in the Panuco basin (X. *pygmaeus*, X. *nigrensis*, X. cf. *pygmaeus*) differ from all other northern swordtails by small adult size and slow growth rate of females and s males. It is possible that a polymorphism at the P locus was responsible for the split of the pygmy swordtail group from the larger X. *montezumae* and/or X. *cortezi* groups.

Within the pygmy swordtails, the P locus may have been involved in the speciation event between X. *pygmaeus* and X. *nigrensis*. *Xiphophorus pygmaeus* lacks the polygenic basis for allometric growth of the sword and dorsal fin, the suppressor factor for the vertical bar pattern (Zimmerer and Kallman 1988), and the polygenic basis for this pattern and the gravid spot, a pigment pattern that forms part of the dorsal pigmentation of the sword (Kallman and Atz 1966). In other words, X. *pygmaeus* does not exhibit a trace of any character associated with large size. For this reason, X. *nigrensis* and X. *pygmaeus* may have shared a common ancestor with a habitus close to that of the small morphs of pygmy swordtails. Females and s males of these taxa resemble each other closely, and they exhibit the basic *Xiphophorus* growth pattern. Accelerated growth of the I, II, and L males is considered a derived condition, as is allometric growth of the sword and dorsal fin. The origin of the I, II, and L factors is obscure; presumably they arose by mutation but, once present, they could have provided the impetus for further genetic differentiation of the population that has evolved into X. *nigrensis*. The Río Coy population of X. *nigrensis* subsequently became distinct from the Río Choy fish by acquiring the vertical bar pattern and the suppressor gene linked to s.

POSSIBLE PRESENCE OF A *P* GENE POLYMORPHISM IN OTHER GENERA

Widespread occurrence of the P gene polymorphism in *Xiphophorus* raises the question of whether similar variation is present in other genera; *Poecilia latipinna* is the best candidate. Adult male size of *P. latipinna* in natural populations varies from 19 to over 55 mm, and laboratory-reared fish show a similar broad spread (Snelson et al. 1986b; Farr and Travis 1986; Travis et al. 1989a). As in *Xiphophorus*, age at maturity is closely correlated with size. In an experimental design in which males were mated to two females, size variation among half sibs was significantly less than between the progeny of different males (Travis et al. 1989a). No effect of females on male size could be detected. Although relatively few fish comprised this study and the analysis was not pursued through a second generation, the results nevertheless resemble those of several species of *Xiphophorus* in which male size shows paternal inheritance. Travis et al. (1989a) pointed out that *P. latipinna* has an XX − XY sex-determining mechanism (Schröder 1964) and that their results best fit a model of allelic variation restricted to a Y-linked locus. They infer that the locus of *P. latipinna* is homologous to the *P* locus of *Xiphophorus* in view of the extensive conservation of linkage groups in poeciliid fishes (Morizot and Siciliano 1984). This would also constitute the first bit of evidence that the sex chromosomes in species belonging to different genera of poeciliid fishes are homologous (derived from a common ancestral form) and not independently derived as postulated by the polygenic theory of sex determination (for review see Kallman 1984). The case for homology would be further strengthened if it could be shown that, in *Poecilia* as in *Xiphophorus*, the locus for carbonic anhydrase is sex-linked (Morizot and McEntire 1988).

Other possible examples of species in which a *P* gene polymorphism may exist are *Poeciliopsis occidentalis* (Constantz 1975), *Gambusia affinis* and *G. manni* (Krumholz 1948, 1963), and *Phalloceros caudimaculatus* (Philippi 1908). In populations of these species, a few large and late-maturing males occur. Miller (1975) described two populations of *Poecilia chica* in which males attain very different adult sizes, but the basis for these differences are not known. Miller also stated that marked variation in adult male size is a general phenomenon in the Poeciliidae. However, without experimentation it will never be known whether the delay in achieving sexual maturity is caused by genetic or environmental factors.

SUMMARY AND FUTURE RESEARCH

The *P* gene polymorphism is found in 10 of 20 species of the genus *Xiphophorus*, and presumably was present in the ancestral form. Only a small number of the nearly 200 species of this family have been studied alive in the laboratory. Therefore, the extent to which this genetic polymorphism occurs in other genera is not known. A good way to screen candidate species would be by examining museum collections. The best prospects are species in which the spread of adult male size is especially large. The presence of a sex-linked size polymorphism in *Poecilia latipinna* suggests that it may also exist in other genera, and that it represents a plesiomorphic condition for the family.

With the exception of *X. maculatus*, *X. milleri*, and the two populations of *X. nigrensis*, no other species of *Xiphophorus* was extensively examined. Most samples of these other species were comprised of less than 10 fish and, in each case, came from a single population. The demonstration of a genetic size polymorphism in most of these samples indicates that alternate alleles at the *P* locus occur at a high frequency in these species.

The genetic mechanism controlling adult size and age at maturity (a locus closely linked to the sex-determining gene) is the same in all species of *Xiphophorus*, but significant phenomenological differences exist among species as to how this polymorphism expresses itself. In *X. maculatus*, nine alleles have been identified that can be present on both X and Y chromosomes. Because of the mechanism of sex determination, adult male size shows no paternal inheritance in this species.

Assuming that each of the alleles occurs in a given population, potentially 45 *P* genotypes can exist. Bearing in mind that the largest and smallest adult males of *X. maculatus* do not differ by more than 25 mm, many genotypes will give rise to virtually identical size phenotypes. Moreover, late *P* factors are quite uncommon in natural populations, and individuals homozygous for them or carrying two different late factors will be exceedingly rare. There also exists a large genotype-environment interaction that affects adult size. For these reasons, definitive genetic size classes are not present in natural populations.

A different situation exists in *X. nigrensis*. Although the range of adult male size is virtually identical to that of *X. maculatus*, only three and four *P* alleles, respectively, are present in the two populations. The polymorphism is restricted to the Y chromosome in *X. nigrensis*, and as a result of its sex-determining mechanism, male size shows patroclinous inheritance. This and the absence of significant genotype-environment interaction causes the existence of well-defined genetic size classes. The patroclinous inheritance of size has provided the opportunity for other genes affecting pigmentation and behavior to become closely linked to specific *P* factors. For this reason, a number of traits are restricted to certain genetic size classes.

A third variation of *P* gene expression is present in *X. cortezi*. In this form, no difference between genotypes can be demonstrated in the absence of social interaction. The two genotypes differ in their response to the socially mediated delay in maturation.

Future research should be concerned with even earlier and later genotypes in order to maximize key physiological differences between the two kinds of fish and pinpoint the exact site of gene action. This work should also encompass other species, for example *X. nigrensis*, in order to discover the physiological basis for the link between enhanced growth rate and age and size at maturity. On the population level, research must involve both field observations and laboratory experiments to determine how this polymorphism is maintained. Several species should be studied, because the answer to these questions are presumably not the same for different taxa.

ACKNOWLEDGMENTS

This study was supported in part by National Institutes of Health grant GM 19934. I thank the Mexican Government, Dirección General de Regiónes Pesqueras, Secretaría de Pesca (Permiso No. 1497, No. 1818, No. 3789, No. 130287–113–01) for permission to collect in the Río Panuco basin.

Chapter 10

Ecological Genetics of Life History Traits in Poeciliid Fishes

JOSEPH TRAVIS

INTRODUCTION

The Study of Life History Traits

Life history traits are phenotypic characters that affect the age- or stage-specific rates of natality and mortality in a population and the developmental events that determine transitions between ages or stages (after Lande 1982). A wide variety of characters can be considered life history traits under this definition, including (but not limited to) egg size or size at parturition, juvenile growth rate, age at maturity, age-specific body size, age-specific reproductive effort, and age-specific fecundity. This definition emphasizes the connection between an individual's phenotypic value for such traits and its contribution to future population growth. That connection is why the study of these characters occupies a central position in population biology: an individual's contribution to future population growth is its absolute fitness (Caswell 1980; Charlesworth 1980; Doyle and Myers 1982; Lande 1982). The study of life history traits enables ecological geneticists to examine the contribution of individual traits to fitness and to determine how selection molds genetic variation for those traits into the best available phenotype for a given environment (Dingle and Hegmann 1982; Rose 1982, 1985; Istock 1983). In this chapter I focus on the value of studying life history traits for examining fitness structure in poeciliid populations. Appendix 5 presents a brief review of concepts and terminology in population genetics that may be unfamiliar to some readers.

It is important to place life history traits in the context of evolutionary theory, so that the goals of empirical study are brought into focus. In a population near genetic equilibrium (a population that has adapted to its ecological conditions), we expect to see little heritable variation in fitness. The reason is that selection drives the additive genetic variance in fitness toward zero, regardless of the genetic system involved in generating fitness differences (Ewens 1976). This result does not imply that we should not expect to see phenotypic variation in fitness. In natural populations, individuals rarely contribute equally to the next generation (Lomnicki 1988). We expect these differences among individuals to be based either on environmental effects (Crow 1958) or on nonadditive genetic differences (Mackay 1985). The first goal of ecological genetic studies is to quantify the inequality among individuals and to dissect its genetic and environmental sources.

The possible patterns of genetic variation in life history traits that are the components of fitness are more varied. If the genetic variation in each trait were independent of every other trait (that is, no pleiotropic gene action or close linkage that would generate a genetic correlation between traits), then there should be no heritable trait variation other than that generated by recurrent mutation (Crow and Nagylaki 1976; Turelli 1985). However, pleiotropic gene action appears to be commonplace (Wallace 1981), and the effects of pleiotropy can result in heritable variation for individual traits but negative genetic correlations among traits such that there is no genetic fitness variation. This theory is well established (Dickerson 1955) and has considerable empirical support (Antonovics 1976; Falconer 1981; Istock 1983). A third pattern is substantial nonadditive genetic variation in individual traits. This pattern is expected after directional selection has operated for a sufficient time that nonaddictive genetic variance in fitness accounts for most observable variation (Robertson 1955; Fisher 1958) regardless of the level of pleiotropy (Rose 1985). This pattern also has empirical support (Lynch and Sulzbach 1984; Travis et al. 1987b). A second goal of ecological genetic studies is to dissect the nature of the genetic variation in life history traits that contribute to fitness.

These expectations do not hold for observations made during periods of adaptive gene substitution, during a return toward equilibrium genetic configuration after a perturbation, or during a short time interval excerpted from a longer sequence of fluctuating selection pressures. Thus, a final goal of ecological genetics is to investigate how often populations appear to be near genetic equilibrium, what factors preclude genetic equilibrium, and which traits are affected in nonequilibrial situations.

The Focus on Poeciliid Fishes

Poeciliid fishes exhibit a wide diversity of life histories (Reznick and Miles, Chapter 7). There may be striking differences among conspecific populations, among closely related species, and among taxa at higher levels. Life history evolution may proceed independently in each gender. *Heterandria formosa*, for example, has a highly derived female life history (extensive viviparity, superfetation; Constantz, Chapter 3) but a primitive male life history (no male polymorphisms, no elaboration of secondary sex characters, lack of courtship; Farr, Chapter 6). *Poecilia latipinna* females have a primitive reproductive pattern (ovoviviparity or slight viviparity [Trexler 1985], single brood development) but a highly derived male life history (extensive polymorphism, elaborate development of secondary sex characters, extensive variation in courtship behaviors).

Poeciliids also exhibit extensive, persistent variation in life history traits within populations, and this chapter focuses on these observations. The ease with which poeciliids can be raised in experimental settings has allowed investigators to make progress in dissecting sources of variation and uncovering the genetic architecture of fitness and its components.

THE NATURE OF VARIATION WITHIN POPULATIONS

Phenotypic Variation

Phenotypic variation in life history traits is extensive. Offspring size varies enormously among female *Gambusia affinis* and *Heterandria formosa* (Reznick 1981; Cheong et al. 1984; Meffe 1987b, unpubl. data; Travis et al. 1987a). Adult male body size and its correlate, age at maturity, vary widely within populations of several species of *Xiphophorus* (Kallman, Chapter 9), *Poecilia latipinna* (Kilby 1955; Hubbs 1964; Luckner 1979; Snelson 1985; Farr et al. 1986; Travis and Trexler 1987, and Brhacki), and *Brachyrhaphis episcopi* (Turner 1938). Female body size usually varies widely within populations, but most of that variation is attributable to age structure (Haake and Dean 1983).

Less well noted are populations in which there is little variation in life history traits. It would be interesting to compare species whose populations display much variation with those that display little, but this cannot be done because the literature is one-sided: most reports about variation document its presence and not its absence.

Most poeciliid populations display enormous brood size variation among individual females. In ovoviviparous and moderately viviparous species, female body size explains about one-half of the variance among females in brood size (Reznick and Endler 1982; Trexler 1985; Reznick and Bryga 1987). In the more viviparous species, especially those with superfetation, female body size explains a much smaller fraction of brood size variance (Thibault and Schultz 1978; Travis et al. 1987a).

A few cases have been sufficiently studied to reveal that such extensive variation is not a transient phenomenon: both the mean value of the trait and the magnitude of variance around that mean persist across many generations. Kallman (1984, Chapter 9) and Borowsky (1984, 1987a) discuss persistence of body size variation within *Xiphophorus* populations. The dramatic variation in male body size in *P. latipinna* persists through long time periods as an essentially constant statistical distribution, despite different populations having different characteristic

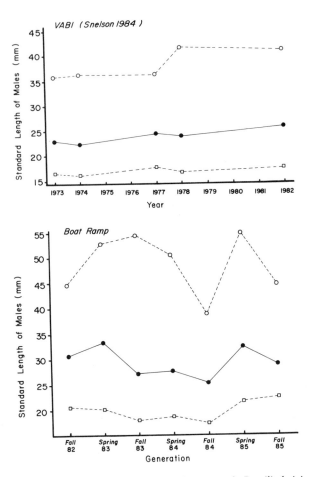

Figure 10–1. Distribution of standard length of mature male *Poecilia latipinna* across time in two populations. Average values are indicated by closed circles, minimum standard lengths by open squares, and maximum standard lengths by open circles. The upper figure is drawn from data extracted from Snelson (1985) at the VABI population in east central Florida; the lower figure is based on unpublished data of the author taken in north Florida at the Boat Ramp population. Sample sizes at VABI are at least 100 for each time period, and those at Boat Ramp are at least 50.

distributions (Figure 10–1). Repeated sampling of a large number of populations showed that despite annual variation in average male body size, populations maintained their characteristic "rank orders" and characteristic levels of phenotypic variation (Trexler 1986). Offspring size variation in one population of *H. formosa* did not change in either mean or variance across five to seven generations, including three generations of laboratory breeding (Table 10–1).

TABLE 10-1. Average Values of Brood Size and Offspring Size in the Wacissa River, Florida Population of *Heterandria formosa* Estimated Across Five to Seven Generations (standard deviations in parentheses).

Collection	Reference	Brood Size	Offspring Size Dry Weight (mg)	Number of Females
Sept. 1982	Cheong et al. 1984	3.17 (1.38)	0.86 (0.15)	18
Sept. 1983	Travis et al. 1987 b	3.71 (1.36)	0.85 (0.23)	48
Spring 1985*	Henrich 1985	4.22 (1.89)	0.86 (0.24)	78

* After 3 generations of lab breeding.

Genetic and Environmental Effects

Size and Age at Maturity and Juvenile Growth Rate

Adult male size has received more attention than any other trait. Males grow little after maturity (Kallman and Borkoski 1978; Snelson 1982, 1985; Hughes 1986), so patterns in adult size can be understood by examining sources of variation in body size at maturity. In several species of *Xiphophorus* (Kallman, Chapter 9) and in *P. latipinna* (Travis et al. 1989b) male body size variation is determined primarily by a series of sex-linked allelic variants. Autosomal modifiers that act in sex-limited fashion appear to influence body size in some species (Kallman 1984, Chapter 9; Borowsky 1987a; Travis et al. 1989a). The heritability of body size generated by these effects appears quite high, indicating that most phenotypic variation in natural populations is based on persistent additive genetic variation. The same genes affect age at maturity, so heritabilities for this trait are comparably high.

A proportion of the phenotypic variation in male body size at maturity in other species has a genetic basis. Busack and Gall (1983) estimated heritabilities of 25% and 41%, respectively, for length and age at maturity in *P. reticulata*. These data are problematic in interpretation; the estimates were based on full-sib families and therefore include nonadditive genetic effects and effects of common maternal environments. Additionally, their laboratory populations exhibited a dramatic drop in size over time (Busack 1983). The results are provocative, however, because different heritability levels for each trait may indicate a genetic control different from the sex-linked pleiotropic genes of *Xiphophorus* spp. and *P. latipinna*.

Stearns's (1984a) study of contrasting populations of *G. affinis* offers equally provocative but more reliable data. Male length at maturity had high heritability in a population from a fluctuating reservoir, but age at maturity exhibited no heritability. Neither age nor size at maturity was heritable in a population from a stable reservoir. These results indicate that the pleiotropic effects that tie these two traits together in *Xiphophorus* spp. and *P. latipinna* are absent in these populations of *G. affinis*. The presence of discrete size classes in *B. episcopi* (Turner

1938; A. Meyer, pers. comm.) and the apparent correlation of age with size at maturity (Turner 1938) suggest that a genetic system similar to that in *Xiphophorus* and *P. latipinna* may operate in this species. This result is intriguing, because *Brachayraphis* is more closely related to *Gambusia* than it is to the Poeciliini (Parenti and Rauschenberger, Chapter 1), and one might expect its genetic control to be more similar to that in *Gambusia*.

Female size and age at maturity have been examined in several species, and they appear to be less heritable than the homologous male traits. Kallman and Borkoski (1978) and Kallman (1984) indicate that there is much less additive variation for age and size in female *Xiphophorus* spp. than in males in natural populations. Travis et al. (1989a) found no evidence for any heritable variation in female *P. latipinna* despite a sample size twice that with which they found substantial heritability in males. In Stearns's (1984a) study of *G. affinis*, female size at maturity had more genetic variation than male size at maturity in the "fluctuating-reservoir" population. However, most genetic variation in females was due either to nonaddictive genetic variance or to common maternal environments (Travis et al. 1989a found similar effects in *P. latipinna*), whereas that in males was truly heritable. Busack and Gall (1983) estimated heritabilities for size at maturity in female *P. reticulata* that were three times the values for males, but these were based on full-sib families (confounding nonadditive genetic effects and effects of common maternal environments with the potential additive effects). They found no evidence for heritability for age at maturity in females, despite high heritability of the trait in males. The results of a selection experiment for larger fish generated estimates of heritability for size at maturity that were comparable between genders (Busack 1983), but this conclusion is plagued by problems of the laboratory regime previously mentioned. Ryman (1972, 1973) failed to find evidence of heritability for age and size at maturity in either gender of *P. reticulata*.

Stearns (1984a) and Travis et al. (1989a) found evidence clearly implicating either nonadditive genetic variation or effects of a common maternal environment as an important source of variation in growth rate of juvenile female *G. affinis* and *P. latipinna*, respectively. None of the studies examining male juvenile growth rates have found evidence for any genetic variation, additive or nonadditive (Stearns 1984a; Travis et al. 1989a; Kallman, Chapter 9). This result implicates nonadditive sex-limited genetic variation as the source of variance in female growth rates, because it is difficult to envision the effects of a common maternal environment acting on juveniles of only one gender. This would be an interesting pattern if verified, because it may implicate a sex difference in the actual targets of selection and consequent differences in norms of reaction (Stearns and Koella 1986; Trexler, Chapter 11).

Other Traits

Few other life history traits have been investigated genetically, despite the wide levels of phenotypic variation such traits exhibit. Henrich and Travis (1988) found that, within one population of *H. formosa*, additive genetic variation explained

20 to 25% of phenotypic variance in offspring size, total number of offspring, and number of broods produced during a female's lifetime. Age and size at maturity, age at first reproduction, interbrood intervals, and net fertility were not heritable, although some traits showed either nonadditive genetic effects or nongenetic maternal sources of variation. Stearns (1984a) found that offspring size in G. affinis (inferred from growth curves) varied significantly in the "fluctuating reservoir" population due either to nonadditive genetic variation or to the effects of maternal environment. There was no variation of this sort in the population from the stable reservoir. Variation among female X. maculatus in size-specific fecundity rates has an additive genetic basis by means of the pleiotropic effects of sex-linked genes that generate variation in age and size at maturity (Kallman and Borkoski 1978). There is unlikely to be much heritable variation in natural populations from this effect, because there is little allele frequency variation in females (Kallman 1984). Busack and Gall (1983) found no evidence that brood size variation for a given female body size in P. reticulata was heritable.

A number of studies have used correlative evidence to suggest that a significant fraction of residual variation in brood size (the variation remaining after accounting for female body size variation) has a nonadditive genetic basis. These studies have used correlations of brood size or body size-specific brood size with the level of allozyme heterozygosity. These correlations are central to several problems in population biology (Vrijenhoek 1985) and thus deserve careful scrutiny. Correlations have been reported from laboratory populations of P. reticulata (Beardmore and Shami 1979) and natural populations of G. affinis (Brown 1982; Feder et al. 1984). The correlations in G. affinis appear to be inconsistent (Kennedy et al. 1986), and the generality of the phenomenon is unclear. There are considerable difficulties with analysis and interpretation of such data; however, the ease with which they can be obtained and their potential usefulness warrant detailed discussion.

It is important to separate any correlation of heterozygosity with female size from potential correlations of heterozygosity with brood size. It is tempting to do so by dividing the total number of embryos by female size and thereby obtaining a measure of "size-specific fecundity" that can be examined for correlations with heterozygosity (Brown 1982). This procedure will only be reliable if the relationship between female size and brood size is isometric; unfortunately this does not seem to be the case very often (Travis and Trexler 1987). This procedure can also introduce a sampling bias even when isometry is true in the population (Cochran 1977). One way to avoid these problems is to employ analyses of covariance, using heterozygosity level as a class variable and female body size as a covariate.

This procedure can be illustrated with raw data on 80 gravid female P. latipinna drawn from 7 localities (Table 10–2; data extracted from Trexler 1986). The number of heterozygous loci is based on electrophoretic analysis of 26 loci that displayed high levels of overall variation (Trexler 1988). Data on brood sizes and female body sizes were log-transformed for analysis. The 7 localities differed significantly in average female body sizes ($F_{[6,73]} = 10.76$, $p < 0.001$, 47% of

TABLE 10–2.   Descriptive Data for Average Values of Fecundity, Female Size, and Number of Heterozygous Loci for Female *P. latipinna* from Seven Localities. Adjusted average numbers of embryos are backtransformed from logarithms.

(a) Summary by Locality

Locality	n	Standard Length X̄ (mm)	No. of Embryos	No. Embryos Adjusted for Female Size	Average No. Heterozygous Loci
Sapelo Island	12	33.6	20.0	28.3	3.18
Skidaway Island	11	42.8	40.0	30.3	1.91
Ossabaw Island	11	66.8	56.6	67.1	2.18
Mounds Pond	9	36.1	16.9	20.5	2.78
Live Oak Island	19	44.9	48.0	28.0	3.47
Big Pine Key	9	36.6	8.9	9.8	2.22
C-111 Canal	9	42.4	24.8	17.5	2.90

(b) Summary by Degree of Heterozygosity

Locality	Number of Heterozygous Loci 0–1	2	3	4–6
Sapelo Island	0	3	6	3
Skidaway Island	4	4	2	1
Ossabaw Island	2	5	3	1
Mounds Pond	1	3	4	1
Live Oak Island	1	4	4	10
Big Pine Key	1	5	3	0
C-111 Canal	2	2	3	2
Average female size (mm)	38.9	39.6	38.2	42.5
Average number of embryos	33.2	35.4	27.0	39.7

variance explained), but there were no detectable differences among the four levels of heterozygosity in average female size ($F_{[3,76]} = 1.88$). Thus, heterozygosity and female size are not associated in the samples, so their effects on brood size can be clearly separated. This is not true for location and female size, nor is it strictly true for location and level of heterozygosity, because different locations have different distributions of individuals in the four heterozygosity levels. The method of analysis must anticipate these possible confounding effects (other data sets may have additional confounding factors).

There is no evidence that heterozygosity level affects brood size (Table 10–3). Analysis of variance (a) ignores all of the potential confounding effects. Analysis (b) ignores locality effects but tests heterozygosity level after female size effects are removed. Analysis (c) tests heterozygosity levels in the presence of all other effects. These procedures are equivalent to stepwise regression using female size and dummy variables for location and heterozygosity level, entering heterozygosity level first (a), second (b), or last (c). These multiple analyses are standard, recom-

TABLE 10–3.   Alternative Analyses of Variance and Covariance for Fecundity Data of Table 10–2. Sums of squares in each table were extracted in the order presented. Asterisks indicate significance at the 0.0001 level.

(a) Ignoring Female Size and Locality Effects

Source	df	SS	F
Heterozygosity	3	1.89	1.09
Residual	76	43.83	—
TOTAL	79	45.72	—

(b) Ignoring Locality Effects but Accounting for Female Size

Source	df	SS	F	Proportion of Variance Explained
Female size	1	15.82	40.15*	0.35
Heterozygosity	3	0.35	0.89	—
Residual	75	29.55	—	—
Slope differences	3	0.90	0.75	—
Error	72	28.65	—	—
TOTAL	79	45.72	—	0.35

(c) Accounting for Female Size and Locality Effects

Source	df	SS	F	Proportion of Variance Explained
Female size	1	15.82	122.63*	0.35
Locality	6	20.88	161.86*	0.46
Heterozygosity	3	0.12	0.93	—
Residual	69	8.90	—	—
Size x Locality	6	1.22	1.66	—
Error	63	7.68	—	—
TOTAL	79	45.72	—	0.81

mended methods for dealing with confounded variables and should always be employed. This approach offers a comprehensive examination of the association of heterozygosity with brood size in the presence or absence of a variety of other factors. The approach does not presume a linear relationship of heterozygosity to brood size and is therefore powerful with respect to a variety of alternative statistical and genetical hypotheses.

There is little evidence for any genetic basis to the extensive "residual" variation in brood size, but several environmental effects appear to be important. Two environmental sources of brood size variation have been reported in several species. Female age affects brood size: female *X. maculatus* that are older at a given body size produce smaller broods (Kallman and Borkoski 1978), and brood size in *H. formosa* changes regularly with female age (Cheong et al. 1984; Travis et al. 1987a; Henrich 1988). In ovoviviparous species or moderately viviparous species, females in better nutritional condition have higher brood sizes for their body size (Wootten 1979, Reznick 1983). This pattern was not found for the highly viviparous *H. formosa* (Travis et al. 1987a); in this case females in better nutritive condition produce more broods but do not alter individual brood sizes.

There are other environmental effects that have been described in only one or two species but may be of general significance. Dahlgren (1979) found that increased population densities in *P. reticulata* resulted in smaller female body sizes but also produced smaller brood sizes for a given female body size. This result is interesting because Dahlgren provided the same amount of food per individual at all densities. This husbandry procedure should have minimized scramble competition for food, and therefore the results implicate an important role for

TABLE 10–4. Gestation Times and Brood Sizes for Female *P. latipinna* Under Laboratory Conditions. Gestation class refers to the 4 nonoverlapping groups into which females could be placed with reference to the gestation time. Females in classes 2, 3, and 4 were pooled for analysis of covariance on log-transformed data. Asterisk denotes significance at or below the 0.01 critical level.

(a) Data Description

Variable		Gestation Class			
		1	2	3	4
Sample size		39	5	3	2
Standard length at birth of brood (mm)	$\bar{X}$	38	40	42	44
	s.d.	2.8	2.9	8.0	3.2
Gestation time (days)	$\bar{X}$	35	67	92	122
	s.d.	4.1	3.1	4.0	7.7
Brood size	$\bar{X}$	22	41	50	43
	s.d.	15.4	6.5	40.2	21.9
Brood size adjusted for body size	$\bar{X}$	18	30	30	30

(b) Analysis of Variance

Source	df	MS	F	Proportion of Variance Explained
Female size	1	8.81	38.3*	0.45
Gestation class	1	1.77	7.8*	0.09
Residual	40	0.23	—	—
Female size x gestation class	1	0.22	0.98	—
Error	39	0.23	—	—

social interactions in determining fecundity. Social interactions are known to affect gonadal activity and endocrine function in a variety of fish (Lam 1983), so Dahlgren's result is very likely due to social effects.

We have found two additional environmental sources of brood size variation in *P. latipinna*. First, females with longer gestation times produce larger broods (Table 10–4). These data indicate that, if a female does not produce a brood after a normal (approximately 30-day) cycle, she will not do so for another 30 days, at which time the brood size will be larger by an average of 67%. The second source of variation is related to mating experience. Wild-caught female *P. latipinna* with multiply sired broods are larger on average and also have 50% more embryos for the same body size than females with single-sired broods (paternity exclusion data of M. Mulvey, J. Trexler, and J. Travis based on 14 loci: Table 10–5). A similar but more precise relationship between brood size and number of sires was reported by Borowsky and Kallman (1976) in *X. maculatus*, although no such relationship was found in *X. variatus* (Borowsky and Khouri 1976).

There are two hypotheses for the effect of mating status on brood size. The simpler one is that enhanced fecundity is a cumulative effect of breeding activity

TABLE 10–5. Effect of Paternity Level on Brood Size in *P. latipinna*. Analysis of variance performed on log-transformed data. Asterisk denotes significance at or below the 0.01 critical level.

(a) Data Description

Variable		Single Sire	Two or More Sires
n		11	11
Standard length	X̄	40	49
(mm)	s.d.	4.7	3.8
Brood size	X̄	28	65
	s.d.	10.5	17.0
Brood size adjusted for body size	X̄	33	49

(b) Analysis of Variance

Source	df	MS	F	Proportion of Variance Explained
Female size	1	5.14	23.4*	0.78
Level of insemination	1	0.44	8.2*	0.07
Residual	19	0.05	—	—
Female size x level of insemination	1	0.001	0.01	—
Error	18	1.022	—	—

in older females (female size is correlated with age: Haake and Dean 1983). Enhanced brood size is not an immediate consequence of multiple insemination but is the eventual consequence of cumulative mating activity. Current knowledge of the control of oocyte maturation and ovulation in the Poeciliini indicates that any immediate brood size changes at fertilization or afterward can only be reductions, not increases (Grier 1973).

The second hypothesis is that increased brood size is an immediate consequence of multiple insemination via one of two mechanisms. First, multiple insemination could cause a female to withhold fertilization of the mature ova, proceed through another cycle of oocyte maturation and vitellogenesis, and then simultaneously fertilize the "old brood" and the "new brood." Second, multiple insemination could induce accelerated maturation of a second brood, producing a temporary overlap of two broods. Such limited superfetation has been reported in several species (Reznick and Miles, Chapter 7). We saw no evidence of this pattern in *P. latipinna*.

There is endocrinological evidence that fecundity can be affected by mating activity. Chemical signals from males can exert priming effects on females (Liley and Stacey 1983), and a variety of social factors are known to affect gametogenesis, steroidogenesis, and ovulation (Lam 1983). Female sexual behavior can be affected by a variety of experiential factors (Liley and Wishlow 1974). It is also possible that multiple siring is not solely the cause of higher fecundity but is in part the outcome of it. More fecund females can signal their status by means of a pheromonal signal produced by ripe ova (Liley and Stacey 1983). Males can perceive the signal and may focus their competitive interactions on the more fecund females.

ORGANIZATION OF GENETIC VARIATION

Pleiotropic Effects Within Genders

The best known pleiotropic genes are those that control size and age at maturity in male *Xiphophorus* spp. and *P. latipinna*. Kallman (Chapter 9) describes in detail the action of these genes and how they produce a strong positive genetic correlation between these traits. In a species with a striking range in age at maturity, such as *P. latipinna* (from 50 to 200+ days; Travis et al. 1989a), the variation in body mass that results from this polymorphism is enormous. A small male (~ 20 mm SL) will have a somatic dry mass around 60 mg, whereas a large male (~ 58 mm SL) will weigh around 1,600 mg. This range in body size is large enough to generate a substantial range in physiological parameters (Schmidt-Nielsen 1984); consequently, there may be a number of physiological characteristics that exhibit strong genetic correlations with age and size at maturity.

Genetic correlations between size and age at maturity appear to exist in other species, but the sign of the correlation varies. The data for *B. episcopi* (Turner 1938) implicate a positive correlation, and Kallman (Chapter 9) suggests other species that may exhibit a positive correlation. Busack and Gall (1983) found a strong positive genetic correlation in *P. reticulata* between length and weight at maturity for both genders, but a selection experiment for heavier fish produced earlier maturity as a by-product, indicating a negative genetic correlation between size and age at maturity (Busack and Gall 1983). The generality of this correlation is unknown because of the husbandry problems previously mentioned. Such a correlation would support the hypothesis that genetic control of size and age at maturity in *P. reticulata* is different from that of the species with the P-allele system (Kallman, Chapter 9).

There are few data on genetic correlations in female poeciliids. Different P-allele genotypes in female *X. maculatus* differ not only in age and size at maturity (the genetic correlation is positive as in males) but also in their age- and size-specific fecundities (Kallman and Borkoski 1978). The strength of any genetic correlations that these effects would generate in natural populations is likely to be weak because of the low level of allelic diversity in females. Henrich and Travis (1988) found that the average size of individual offspring in the first brood of a female *H. formosa* had a negative genetic correlation with the number of broods that the female could produce over her lifetime. There are negative phenotypic correlations among life history traits that indicate a cost of reproduction in females (Reznick 1983; Henrich 1988), but there are no data on whether those correlations are also genetic (Reznick et al. 1986). Circumstantial evidence for pleiotropic constraints on the evolution of life history traits is provided by studies on genetic differences in life history traits among populations (Reznick 1982a; Stearns 1983a).

Genetic correlations are also produced by close linkage, and several genetic correlations between traits in poeciliids arise because the controlling genes are linked on the sex chromosomes. Kallman (1984, Chapter 9) discusses traits known to be correlated through such linkage. This effect generates genetic correlations between life history traits, such as age and size at maturity, and a variety of other traits, including offspring sex ratio (Kallman 1984). The role that these linked traits may play in constraining the evolution of life history traits is largely unknown. Constraints resulting from linkage can play roles different from those resulting from pleiotropy if some recombination can occur (Lande 1980b, 1984); thus the roles of these variously linked traits and their actual linkage relationships to life history traits is an important area for future research.

Gender Effects

Genetic Correlations Across Genders

Genetic correlations of homologous traits between genders reveal the extent to which adaptive evolution in one gender will be constrained by the other. Such correlations may be due to sex-linked or autosomal genes (Griffing 1966). In poeciliids, major sex-linked polymorphisms are largely restricted to males (Kallman, Chapter 9). This restriction means that variation in life history traits governed primarily by such genes will show small correlations between genders. Data on

P. latipinna (Travis et al. 1989a) reflect such a pattern: genetic correlations were strong within males, small and statistically insignificant within females, and negligible even in magnitude between genders for homologous and nonhomologous traits.

Genetic correlations between genders produced by autosomal genes can also constrain life history evolution, but there are no data for poeciliids. Data from other systems indicate that such effects can play major roles. Genetic correlations due to such genes can be very high in mammals (Eisen and Legates 1966; Eisen and Johnson 1981) and *Drosophila* (Frankham 1968; Luckinbill et al. 1988) and can involve morphological, physiological, and behavioral traits (Lynch et al. 1988).

Dimorphism and Secondary Sex Characters

Poeciliids vary enormously in degree of sexual dimorphism (Farr, Chapter 6), yet there are no data on the genetic basis of the level of dimorphism. This problem is likely to be a complex one, if data from other groups are indicative. Control of dimorphic characters is not limited to sex-linked genes; autosomal genes may play major roles in governing dimorphism, and they may interact epistatically with sex-linked genes (Frankham 1968; Bird and Shaffer 1972; Luckinbill et al. 1988; Lynch et al. 1988).

Some information is available on the control of secondary sex characters and their expression in males. Kallman (Chapter 9) points out that dorsal fin morphology in *X. nigrensis* is governed by an interaction between autosomal genes and the sex-linked alleles that determine male age and size at maturity. Male sexual behavior is genetically correlated with male size and appears to be controlled by genes linked to the controlling elements for male size on the Y chromosome. Autosomal modifiers appear to influence male behavior rates. Dorsal fin size in *P. latipinna* had a strong positive genetic correlation with body size, but the data cannot exclude a complex inheritance like that for the fin of *X. nigrensis* (Travis et al. 1989b). Male sexual behavior in *P. latipinna* has both an ontogenetic and a direct genetic component: males are capable of a wide range of behaviors but exhibit only a narrow range, determined primarily by their body size phenotype (regardless of genotype). There is heritable variation in courtship display rate around the value predicted for a given male body size. Local populations of *P. latipinna* vary in body size, dorsal fin shape, and behavioral profiles (Farr et al. 1986), and these data indicate that both sex-linked and autosomal factors are involved in that local differentiation.

SUMMARY AND FUTURE RESEARCH

The data in hand indicate that many poeciliid populations exhibit stable levels of genetic variation for life history traits. These patterns imply that such populations are near genetic equilibrium and therefore offer exciting possibilities for ecological genetic analyses. However, it is nearly impossible to follow individuals over their lifetimes in natural populations, and estimates of the extent of individual variation in fitness and its genetic and environmental sources may not be possible.

Analyses of trait variation can be made, and some qualified insights into the genetics of components of fitness are possible. Males possess more heritable variation in life history traits than do females. Females have higher levels of nonadditive genetic variation than males. The persistent heritable variation in males may reflect the importance of alternative male strategies and consequent frequency-dependent selection in the family (Zimmerer and Kallman 1989; Farr, Chapter 6), whereas the potential role of nonadditive genetic variation may reflect a traditional prediction of the outcome of consistent directional selection. The negative genetic correlation between offspring size and number of broods in *H. formosa* found by Henrich and Travis (1988), coupled with lack of heritability for overall fertility, is consistent with a traditional prediction of population genetics theory. The consistently higher heritabilities for several traits in *G. affinis* populations from reservoirs with fluctuating water levels, compared with levels in populations from stable reservoirs, is entirely consistent with the expectation that fluctuating selection pressures somehow protect genetic variation in key components of fitness (Stearns 1984a). Although this expectation has some theoretical support and considerable support from naturalists' intuition, the issue is a complicated one (Travis and Mueller 1988), and Stearns's study is perhaps the only quantitative support for it in natural populations.

Several intriguing results indicate where more confirmatory research is needed. The sex-linked nature of the major controlling elements for some traits and the apparent sex-limitation of the autosomal modifiers of many male life history traits would imply that life history evolution can proceed independently in each gender. Patterns of variation among species support this suggestion, but more research on the genetic correlations between genders and the genetic control of dimorphic characters is necessary. The genetic architecture of male traits in *Gambusia* spp. and other groups that do not appear to have the P-allele series is largely unknown except for Stearns's work on Hawaiian populations. A comparison of the genetics of the Hawaiian populations with the genetics of presumably ancestral populations in southern United States would contribute enormously to our understanding of the genetic changes that occur in colonizing populations.

So little is known about the genetic control of traits that vary in females that almost any study would make an important contribution. This gap in our knowledge is especially striking given the extensive phenotypic variation that persists in many populations. There is some indication that the organization of life history trait variation will differ among species with different levels of viviparity and superfetation (Travis et al. 1987a; Reznick and Miles, Chapter 7). The only data in hand about the genetics of female reproductive traits are based on too few species to draw any conclusions. The most useful future research should focus on species that occupy key positions on the continuum of reproductive modes within the family; a strategy focusing on such target species is likely to be more productive than one that attacks species indiscriminately.

The general importance of nonadditive genetic variation deserves more investigation given its prominence in other fishes, especially for juvenile growth rate (Gall 1975, Kincaid 1976; Moav et al. 1978). The extensive variation in life history traits among clones within populations of hybridogenetic and gynogenetic forms of *Poeciliopsis* appears to have a high nonadditive genetic component (R. C. Vrijenhoek, pers. comm.). The viviparous nature of poeciliid reproduction, however, does not allow one to infer nonadditive genetic effects directly from maternal effects, because differential nongenetic maternal effects may well be operating (Trexler 1985). The separation of these two potential sources of maternal effects is an important avenue for future research.

A myopic focus on genetics may hinder the pursuit of equally profitable lines of inquiry into environmental sources of variation in life history traits within populations. The variation in brood size for a given female body size appears to be determined solely by environmental factors, some of which are poorly understood. In particular, the role of social interactions, mating experience, and the factors that might induce longer gestation times (skipping whole brood cycles) deserve much more attention. Variation in nutritive condition appears to affect different traits in species with different reproductive modes; further exploration in targeted species could contribute enormously to our understanding of how the diversity of poeciliid reproductive systems has evolved.

ACKNOWLEDGMENTS

I thank James Farr, Sabine Henrich, and Joel Trexler for their intellectual stimulation and companionship in the field and the lab. I am not sure where their ideas end and mine begin. I have benefited over the years from the generous sharing of ideas, criticism, and husbandry tips of D. Reznick, R. J. Schultz, and F. F. Snelson, Jr. The Department of Biological Science at Florida State University has provided excellent intellectual and material support, and the staff of the St. Marks National Wildlife Refuge has been exceptionally cooperative over the years. This chapter was improved enormously by the comments of S. C. Stearns and an anonymous reviewer. My research has been supported by National Science Foundation grants BSR 83–05823 to J. Travis and J. A. Farr, BSR 84–15529 to J. Travis, BSR 86–12528 to J. Travis and S. L. Forster, and State of Florida Non-Game Wildlife Research Grant 84–022 to J. Travis and J. C. Trexler.

Chapter 11

Phenotypic Plasticity in Poeciliid Life Histories

JOEL C. TREXLER

INTRODUCTION

An organism's phenotype is the product of its genotype and environment, although the relative contribution of each is often debatable (James 1983). Phenotypic plasticity, the influence of environment on phenotype, is not necessarily constant across genotypes of a species. Genetic variation for phenotypic plasticity is important because it is necessary if plasticity is to evolve. There is an increasing appreciation of plasticity of life history traits and its potential role in adaptation (Stearns 1983a; Policansky 1983; Caswell 1983). However, more data are needed before generalizations regarding the role of plasticity in evolution and ecotypic variation can be made (Meyer 1987; Vrijenhoek et al. 1987).

   In this chapter, I review experimental evidence for plasticity in poeciliids, with emphasis on genetic variation for plasticity in life history traits. In addition, I evaluate the role of phenotypic plasticity in poeciliid evolution and ecotypic variation. Finally, I discuss data needed to assess the role of phenotypic plasticity in adaptation.

PHENOTYPIC PLASTICITY BACKGROUND

Phenotypic plasticity is a description of the extent to which environmental conditions modify the phenotype. Though phenotypic plasticity has been described as an "epi-genetic" phenomenon, uncoupling of environment from genotype is an unrealistic view of inheritance (Bradshaw 1965; Lewontin 1974; Sultan 1987). A complete description of the genetic variation for any trait requires that it be studied in the full range of conditions experienced by the organism. An analogy from analysis of variance encapsulates this view of phenotypic variation:

$$P_{ij} = G_i + E_j + GE_{ij}$$

where P_{ij} is the phenotypic value of the ith genotype in the jth environment, G_i is the genetic contribution for the ith genotype, E_j is the environmental deviation resulting from the jth environment, and GE_{ij} is the environmental deviation caused by interaction of the jth environment and the ith genotype (Hedrick 1983). This model sets out two ways in which environment influences phenotype: a main effect, consistent across all genotypes, and an interaction effect, unique to each genotype. The latter influence represents genetic variation that must be present for selection to influence phenotypic plasticity (Bulmer 1985).

Genotype-environment interactions may be documented in two ways, through selection experiments conducted in different environments (e.g., Robertson 1960) or through experiments in which individuals of several genotypes are reared in one or more common environments (e.g., Stearns 1983c). The latter approach is called a "common garden experiment" after Clausen, Keck, and Heisey's pioneering work (Clausen et al. 1948). A reciprocal transplant experiment is a special case in which individuals from two or more populations are reciprocally reared under conditions experienced by each (e.g., Via 1984). These experimental designs allow one to document genetic variation for a trait if multiple individuals of two or more clones, families, or populations can be raised in each environment. They do not allow estimates of heritability but do provide for partitioning of phenotypic variation into relative environmental and genetic components.

When individuals from a common genetic stock are reared in two or more environments, a "norm of reaction" can be drawn to characterize the phenotypes produced by that genotype (Schmalhausen 1949). The norm of reaction is a profile of the performance of that genotype across a range of conditions. Nonparallel norms of reaction for different genotypes indicate genotype-environment interactions.

These interactions have significant consequences for evolutionary study (Lewontin 1974; Gupta and Lewontin 1982). I have redrawn a figure from Gupta and Lewontin's (1982) paper to illustrate their observations with norms of reaction for size at maturity from two hypothetical genotypes of a poeciliid fish (Figure 11-1). The hypothetical norms of reaction are indicative of results I obtained for wild stocks of female *Poecilia latipinna*. Three evolutionary issues are demonstrated by imagining a population composed solely of fishes with these two genotypes (Gupta and Lewontin 1982):

1) The genotypic variance estimated for a population in a given environment depends on the diversity of shapes of norms of reaction of its members and the environment studied. In our hypothetical population, the two genotypes yield identical progeny where norms of reaction cross. Thus, genetic variance for size at

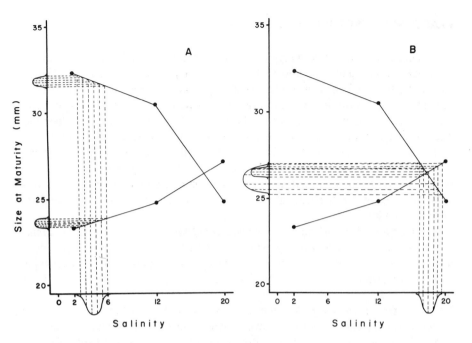

Figure 11-1. Reaction norm curves showing the relationship of size at maturity to salinity for two hypothetical genotypes of female *P. latipinna*. Bell curves on horizontal axes indicate distribution of salinities experienced by a hypothetical population. Salinities are projected to bell curves on vertical axes to indicate phenotypes produced. Note that the distribution of environments experienced during development can yield dramatically different phenotypic distributions. Further details explained in text.

maturity estimated at 16 to 20 ppt salinity (Figure 11-1b) would be underestimated by classical inheritance study based on analysis of variance. Also, heritability estimates at these salinities would be different from those made at lower salinities.

2)   The rank and magnitude of phenotypic differences between populations can change with environment (see also Gill et al. 1983). In our hypothetical population, a phenotypic description at 2 to 6 ppt salinity (Figure 11-1a) would be quite different from that at 16 to 20 ppt salinity (Figure 11-1b). This might be described as ecotypic variation, though two such populations would be composed of the same mix of genotypes.

3)   The outcome of selection would also be influenced by environment. The "opportunity for selection" (Crow 1958) depends on phenotypic variance, which changes from Figure 11-1a to Figure 11-1b. Selection could remove those individuals most fit under all but current circumstances, possibly even decreasing mean fitness of a population. Consider the case of wading birds selecting the largest fish as prey. The birds' preferred prey would be of different genotypes at 20 and 2 ppt in this example.

PLASTICITY RESEARCH IN POECILIIDS

To evaluate the role of phenotypic plasticity in poeciliid life histories, several basic questions need to be addressed. Foremost is the prevalence of genetic variation for plasticity in life history traits. Assuming genetic variation for plasticity is present, how is it partitioned within and among populations? Specifically, is plasticity locally adapted? Questions regarding the nature of plasticity are also important. Theorists suggest that there may be combinations of traits where plasticity in one buffers another (Caswell 1983). The existence and significance of this buffering is poorly documented. Other issues relevant to poeciliids include consistency of plasticity between the sexes and possible phylogenetic patterns of plasticity. Answers to these questions will shed light on how phenotypic plasticity influences life history evolution.

Xiphophorus maculatus, X. variatus, Gambusia affinis, Poecilia reticulata, P. latipinna, and Poeciliopsis spp. have received almost all the attention of experimental biologists studying the role of genotype and environment in phenotypic variation of poeciliids. I review the findings for each and summarize results for the group.

1) Xiphophorus spp. Xiphophorus maculatus, X. pygmaeus (X. nigrensis), X. montezumae, and X. variatus have a genetic factor, the P-gene, influencing size and timing of sexual maturity (Borowsky 1987a; Kallman, Chapter 9). The homology of this locus across species remains to be demonstrated (Borowsky 1987a) but seems likely. P-gene variation is limited in expression to males (Kallman 1983); with rare exception, females are fixed for one allele.

McKenzie et al. (1983) demonstrated that environmental conditions can greatly influence two of the P-genotypes of X. maculatus males. Notably, the two genotypes, though raised in a wide variety of conditions, remained distinct in weight and age at maturity. Kallman and Borkoski (1978) found growth of male and female X. maculatus to be influenced by their social environment, but only in females did this change size at maturity.

A variety of environmental conditions slow juvenile growth rates but do not ultimately alter size at maturity in X. variatus. There are probably autosomal genes modifying growth rates in both males and females (Borowsky 1987a). Their action does not alter size at maturity in males because slow growth is compensated by an extended juvenile period. Social context does alter size at maturity in X. variatus, since the order of maturation of siblings determines their relative sizes at maturity (Borowsky 1973b). It is not known if the P-genotypes remain distinct across environments as in X. maculatus.

Borowsky and colleagues documented genotype-environment interactions for males with different tailspot genotypes (Borowsky 1984). The faster growing of two genotypes at a high food level was the slower growing at low food. When this experiment was repeated at a lower temperature, the interaction disappeared: the same genotype was fastest growing at both food levels. Borowsky (1984) interprets this result by differences in metabolic rate of the two genotypes. Interactions of the tailspot genotypes and P-genotypes have yet to be studied.

In summary, size at maturity in male *X. variatus*, *X. maculatus*, and possibly all *Xiphophorus* spp. has a strong genetic component, but the combination of timing and size at maturity is plastic across environmental conditions. It appears that plasticity of age at maturity may "screen" (in Caswell's [1983] terminology) size at maturity in *X. variatus*. The relative size at a given age at maturity remains distinct for males of two P-genotypes, at least in *X. maculatus*. Female *X. maculatus* are plastic in both size and age at maturity.

2) *Gambusia affinis*. Plasticity in size and age at maturity does not appear to differ between sexes in *G. affinis*. Stearns and Sage (1980) raised fish from two adjacent Texas populations from birth to sexual maturity at two salinities; they found a consistent influence of salinity on growth rate and size at maturity in both sexes. Males suffered higher mortality in fresh water than did females. There was no difference in plasticity between the populations, even though one inhabited a brackish, and the other a freshwater habitat. Offspring from both populations grew most rapidly and matured at the largest size in salt water. Interestingly, offspring of *G. affinis* from Hawaiian reservoirs displayed no plasticity for maturation size between salt and fresh water treatments. Hence, Stearns and Sage (1980) observed a genotype-environment interaction between Texas and Hawaiian populations, but not between local Texas populations.

A variety of environmental factors yield main effects on life history traits in this species. For example, food quality influences growth rates, reproductive condition, and embryo size (Meffe and Crump 1987; Meffe 1987b). Brood size is influenced by food level (Trendall 1983). Conspecific density influences juvenile growth rates, especially in females (Busack and Gall 1983). However, these studies were generally not done in a manner that permits testing for genotype-environment interactions.

3) *Poecilia reticulata*. Reznick and Bryga (1987) observed genotype-environment interactions for male and female age and size at maturity in *P. reticulata* from Trinidad streams. They transplanted *P. reticulata* from a population experiencing size-selective predation from *Crenicichla alta* into a pool lacking *C. alta*. Genetic differentiation of these populations (genotype-environment interactions) arose over the subsequent two years of isolation. Food level was studied as the environmental factor and produced a strong main effect in addition to the interaction.

Males and females differed in their response to selection. Male norms of reaction indicated that one population was consistently larger and older at maturity than the other and that observed differences were greatest at low food level. Female norms of reaction crossed, so that the population maturing at the largest size and oldest age changed between low and high food.

4) *Poecilia latipinna*. Inheritance of size and age at maturity in *P. latipinna* is similar to the P-genotypes of *Xiphophorus* (Travis, Chapter 10). Size at maturity is highly heritable in males but not in females.

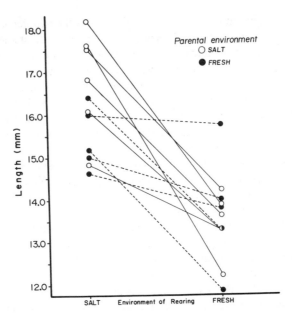

Figure 11–2. Norms of reaction for size at three weeks of age from 10 family groups of *P. latipinna* collected from two populations. The crossing of reaction norms indicated by this figure is typical of results for this species. Offspring of females collected in a salt water pond are indicated by open circles and from females collected in a fresh water pond by closed circles. Lines connect results obtained from broodmates raised in different ponds, and points plotted represent the average results from nine fish spread equally in three cages. Note that open circles plotted over the salt environment indicate that fish experienced a habitat similar to that of their mother, while those over fresh did not. The converse is true for closed circles.

Field reciprocal transplant experiments document extensive variation in the effect of environmental conditions on prematuration growth rate and size and age at maturity in *P. latipinna* (Figure 11–2) (Trexler 1986; Trexler and Travis, unpubl. data). Norms of reaction frequently differed among family groups within populations but seldom differed between populations. This experiment was repeated four times and consistently documented extensive interfamilial variation. Apparently, there is much genetic variation for phenotypic plasticity within populations, but this has not led to divergence of norms of reaction between populations.

Probability of survival to three weeks of age differed among family groups in field experiments (Trexler 1986; Trexler, Travis, and McManus, unpubl. data). Also, survival probability differed between environments among family groups (family genotype-environment interactions). Fish were more likely to survive to sexual maturity in a freshwater than a saltwater pond in one of two years they were followed to maturity. Hence, environmental influences on survival differed among family groups and over time.

Field studies provide a realistic view of nature but cannot be tightly controlled;

TABLE 11–1.   Approximate Percentage of Variance in Size at Maturity (Size),
Age at Maturity (Age), and Growth Rate (GR) Explained in Laboratory Experiment
with *Poecilia latipinna*. Results obtained from nested analysis of variance. All two-
way interactions were tested, as well as all three-way interactions involving
population. "Pop" indicates differences among population means, "temp" indicates
differences in temperature, "sal" is salinity, "ns" indicates that the term is not
statistically significant, and "df" indicates degrees of freedom for each test.

Source of Variation	df	Males			Females		
		Size	Age	GR	Size	Age	GR
Pop	3,17	22.0	17.2	ns	ns	10.4	ns
Temp	1,20	ns	8.4	ns	9.2	56.4	47.8
Sal	2,40	3.9	4.5	4.6	6.7	4.1	4.0

laboratory experiments are necessary to assess the action of specific environmental factors. I conducted an experiment in which offspring of females from four populations were reared in all possible combinations of two temperatures (23°C and 29°C), three salinities (2, 12, 20 ppt), and two food levels (maximum ration and half-maximum ration). This study was designed to detect genotype-environment interactions among populations, should they exist, and interactions among the various environmental factors. Because the field study indicated that families within populations were heterogeneous, I nested families within population (Trexler 1986).

The laboratory experiment provided results consistent with the notion that sailfin mollies have P-gene-like genetic control of maturity. Most variation in male size and age at maturity was attributable to interpopulation differences, whereas most female variation was environmentally induced (Table 11–1; Figure 11–3). Populations may differ in the frequency or range of male P-genotypes present, thus yielding interpopulation differences in size and age at maturity in that sex. In females, only age at maturity varied among populations, and both that trait and pre-maturation growth rate were greatly influenced by temperature. Consistent with the field study, no population-environment interactions were documented; all environmental effects were main effects (family-environment interactions could not be tested).

The food levels used did not differ enough to yield detectable growth variation. Food level is an important factor in many studies of fish growth (Brett 1979) and can influence growth in *P. latipinna* when set well below half-maximum ration (M. McManus, pers. comm.).

In general, both males and females grow faster and mature earlier in warm, relatively salty water (Figure 11–3). Females also mature smaller under these conditions but males do not. Temperature in particular, and environmental factors in general, have a more pronounced influence on females than on males (Table 11–1; Figure 11–3). The genetics of maturation in *P. latipinna*, including patterns of genetic variation for plasticity, are very similar to those of *X. maculatus* and *X. variatus*.

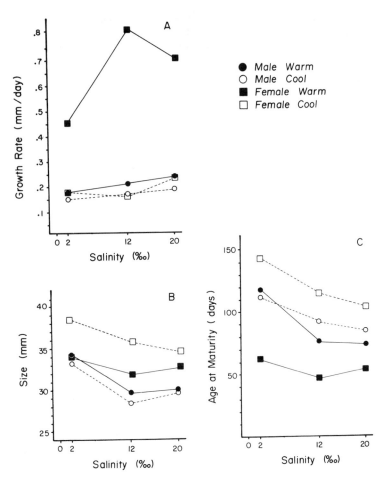

Figure 11–3. Norms of reaction for *P. latipinna* raised in a laboratory experiment. Open symbols indicate results from a 23°C room, and closed symbols indicate those from a 29°C room. Circles indicate results for males, and squares indicate results for females. (A) Growth rate prior to maturity. (B) Size at maturity. (C) Age at maturity.

5) *Poeciliopsis* spp. Schultz and Fielding (1988) reported a genotype-environment interaction for the effect of temperature on two hemiclones of *P. monacha-lucida* (see also Wetherington et al., Chapter 14). The rank order of growth rate in the two clones studied switched between 20°C and 27°C. Food quality also affected growth differently in these clones, probably because of different dietary preferences (Schultz and Fielding 1988). Crowding influenced growth rate in *P. monacha-lucida*, but rank order of growth rate among clones did not change (Schultz 1982; Schultz and Fielding 1988). The relative growth rate difference increased when an aggressive and a nonaggressive clone were reared together (duoculture) compared to rearing at the same density with members of the same clone (monoculture). However, the difference was not great. Differences between monoculture and duoculture seemed to result from energy diverted from growth to agonistic behavior in the aggressive clone.

Survival under temperature stress and sex of offspring are differentially influenced by environment in different *Poeciliopsis* clones. A triploid clone of *P. monacha-2 lucida* was superior in survival at low temperatures but poorest of all clones screened at high temperature survival (Bulger and Schultz 1979). The influence of temperature on offspring sex ratio differs between two strains of *P. lucida* (Sullivan and Schultz 1986).

OVERVIEW OF PLASTICITY IN POECILIIDS

Prevalence of Plasticity

There are many experimental studies documenting environmental effects in poeciliids (Appendix 6). Of 29 studies noted, only 9 attempted to differentiate main effects from genotype-environment interactions. These nine examine the six species discussed in the previous section. Assessment of the prevalence and patterns of genotypic variation for the influence of environmental conditions on life history traits must await studies in a greater diversity of species. Some conclusions can be drawn, however.

Norms of reaction may differ between sexes and between interrelated traits such as size and age at maturity. In *X. maculatus* (Kallman and Borkoski 1978) and *P. latipinna* (Trexler 1986), plasticity in size and age at maturity differs between sexes. It appears that variation in male size at maturity is minimized by plasticity in the timing of maturation. Females of these species are plastic in both size and timing of maturation. In *P. reticulata*, the sexes also differed in the way their norms of reaction diverged in a selection experiment (Reznick and Bryga 1987). Female norms of reaction were less influenced by the transplant treatment than were males. This could have resulted from selection acting antagonistically on traits correlated with size and age at maturity (Reznick and Bryga 1987). Divergence between sexes suggests some sex limitation of genetic control of maturation (Lande 1980a).

Plasticity has been found to vary among genotypes. Norms of reaction for juvenile growth rate diverge between genotypes of *G. affinis*, *P. latipinna*, and *P. monacha-lucida*. In *P. monacha-lucida*, divergence is related to metabolic and behavioral differences between clones. In *G. affinis*, the genotypes probably differ in some component of osmotic physiology. Populations of *P. latipinna* may also differ in osmotic abilities (Gustafson 1981), although the proper experiment to eliminate physiological acclimation through maternal effects remains to be conducted.

Genetic variation for norms of reaction has been documented both within and among poeciliid populations. Only *X. variatus*, *P. latipinna*, and *P. monacha-*

lucida have been examined for genetic variation within populations, and it was documented in each case. Such variation must be present at some point during evolution of a species for norms of reaction of populations to diverge. Interpopulation variation in norms of reaction has been noted in *G. affinis* and *P. reticulata*.

Plasticity and Evolution

Spatially divergent selective regimes can yield genotype-environment interactions (Via and Lande 1985); Reznick and Bryga's (1987) selection experiment provides an example. However, if genetic variation for plasticity is present, locally adapted norms of reaction may be observed only when little or no gene flow occurs (Via and Lande 1985). *Poecilia reticulata* populations from different streams are generally considered isolated; according to theory, Reznick and Bryga's (1987) results could only have arisen if such isolation obtains. Stearns and Sage's (1980) study of *G. affinis* is also consistent with theory, as local populations did not differ but distant populations did. On the other hand, I have found no evidence for differentiation in norms of reaction among populations of *P. latipinna* in north Florida; this result might be expected for a species characterized by high gene flow (Trexler 1988). It remains to be seen whether geographically isolated populations of *P. latipinna* differ in plasticity. One would expect that they could differ, given the extensive genetic variation for plasticity within populations.

Variation at the P-locus may constrain evolution of plasticity in size at maturity. This sex-linked locus may have arisen before the splitting of the tribe Poeciliini (see Travis, Chapter 10). Male size at maturity appears to be a relatively canalized trait when compared to age at maturity in *X. variatus*, *X. maculatus*, and *P. latipinna*. Size at maturity in females is not as constrained in *X. maculatus* and *P. latipinna* (*X. variatus* females have not been studied in this way). Therefore, lack of plasticity in male size at maturity in these species may stem from historical rather than current ecological circumstances (Stearns 1983d, 1984b; see also Vitt and Seigel 1985). This is not to say that current conditions are unimportant. Autosomal genes that influence the P-genotypes and on which selection could operate may be present in *X. variatus* (Borowsky 1987a). Autosomal genes that modify size at maturity in males may also be present in *P. latipinna*.

Recent advances in life history theory suggest that phenotypic plasticity may be an adaptive response to stressful or unpredictable environments (Stearns 1983a; Policansky 1983; Caswell 1983; Kaplan and Cooper 1984). Stearns and Crandall (1984) proposed a model that predicts norms of reaction for size and age at maturity in environments with a range of physiological stressfulness. Their model indicates that the relationship of juvenile to adult mortality and the gain in fecundity with size are important in determining what norms of reaction will evolve. Only for *P. reticulata* are such data available (Reznick and Endler 1982; Reznick and Bryga 1987), but they have not been applied to Stearns and Crandall's model.

Given that genetic variation for phenotypic plasticity in life history traits is present, both current ecological conditions and historical factors influence its evolution. It cannot be assumed that genetic variation will yield to selection pressures if it is present. Gene flow establishes minimal levels of selection necessary for evolution to occur and determines how genetic variation is partitioned within and among breeding units. This is borne out in the three species of poeciliids for which there are data. In addition, patterns of plasticity like that between sexes in *P. latipinna* may have arisen before the species diverged from its ancestral stock and may not represent adaptations to current conditions. Demographic schedules probably dictate the shapes of norms of reaction that evolve if genetic variation is present.

Plasticity and Ecotypic Variation

There is extensive variation in life history traits among poeciliid populations (Stearns 1983b; Snelson 1985; Reznick and Miles, Chapter 7). To what extent is this explained by physiologically mediated phenotypic plasticity in response to environmental conditions? Stearns and Sage (1980) concluded that local Texas populations of *G. affinis* differed in average size because of phenotypic plasticity in growth rate due to osmotic stress. Stearns (1983b) noted variation in life history traits in *G. affinis* from Hawaii, which he attributed to phenotypic plasticity. In a subsequent experiment, Stearns (1983c) documented genetic variation among populations for some of the same traits. However, design of the latter study did not permit partitioning of variation into genetic and environmental sources.

Poecilia reticulata populations differ in life history traits such as female size at maturity, male adult size, offspring size, and size-specific fecundity (Reznick and Endler 1982). These differences are maintained in second-generation laboratory-reared fishes (Reznick 1982b), indicating that plasticity alone does not explain variation for these traits in natural populations of this species.

It is likely that selection, rather than plasticity, maintains geographic variation in *P. latipinna*. Average male size varies dramatically among local *P. latipinna* populations, and the relative differences are maintained over time (Snelson 1985; Trexler and Travis, unpubl. data). Two surveys of local size variation in *P. latipinna* suggest that salinity and male size are related (Swift et al. 1977; Loftus and Kushlan 1987); in two other surveys this is not the case (Kilby 1955; Snelson 1985). The former studies implicate phenotypic plasticity in size variation, and the latter are consistent with differential survival from predation associated with refuges or simple habitat preferences by different sized fish.

I examined *P. latipinna* size variation in Georgia and Florida populations in spring and fall 1984, spring 1985, and spring 1986. I found that 20% of variation in male size was attributable to differences among local populations, 7% to regional differences, and less than 1% to temporal variation (Trexler 1986). There was no north-south clinal variation in male size. Average male size and salinity were not correlated (Pearson's r ranged from 0.08 to 0.29 over four different sampling periods, with 26 to 44 populations sampled each period). Mantel analyses (Manly 1985) were also used to test for correlations of size and habitat variation described by principal components analysis based on 12 habitat variables (Trexler 1986). This did not indicate a relationship between habitat type and either average male size or the coefficient of variation of male size in any collections. My survey, encompassing a larger geographic area than those cited earlier, did not support phenotypic plasticity as an explanation for geographic variation.

I addressed phenotypic size plasticity directly through a laboratory experiment. As discussed earlier, male size was weakly influenced by environmental conditions in the laboratory (Trexler 1986) in contradiction to the plasticity hypothesis. In that study, large males were raised in the laboratory from populations where no large males were collected in a five-year monthly sampling effort (Trexler 1986). I interpret this as indicative of differential survival of size genotypes in nature, possibly from size-selective predation. High gene flow (Trexler 1988) would maintain the large male genotype in such a population, only to be removed by predators each generation before reaching maturity. The cumulative predation risk is much greater for the large male genotype, which takes almost one year to reach sexual maturity, than for the smallest male genotype, which matures in less than 30 days.

Phenotypic plasticity is not completely excluded, however. In the laboratory, we have found that temperature stress (the first 120 days of life at 20°C) can induce plasticity in male size at maturity (Travis, Trexler, and Farr, unpubl. data). Males stressed in this way matured at a uniformly small size after being transferred to 25°C. However, this result is inadequate to explain small male size in many populations year-round. Additionally, in natural *P. latipinna* populations, male and female size co-varies (Travis and Trexler 1987) even though the sexes differ in environmentally induced plasticity. This supports the notion that processes linked to survival, rather than plasticity, explain interpopulation variation in *P. latipinna* (see also Snelson [1985]). More work is needed before the relative roles of survival and development can be conclusively separated in this species.

In summary, the genetic basis of ecotypic variation in life history traits has been explored in three poeciliid species. In one of these, plasticity seems a likely explanation, in another the populations are clearly genetically differentiated, and in the final case selectively maintained genetic differences are implicated. More case studies are needed before any generalities about the sources of variation can be made.

SUMMARY AND FUTURE RESEARCH

Poeciliids are an excellent group for study of phenotypic plasticity, because they are readily maintained in the laboratory and have a short generation time. Phenotypic plasticity has been documented in many poeciliid species, and genetic variation for plasticity has been observed in several of these. I suggest that research into the genetic basis of plasticity in more species is needed to determine the prevalence of genetic variation for plasticity. As new species are studied, traits likely to be interrelated, such as size and age at maturity, should be examined together. Size at maturity is less plastic than age at maturity in some members of the tribe Poeciliini with genetic variation at the P-locus. It will be interesting to learn if this genetic system is present in other poeciliid tribes (see also Kallman, Chapter 9 and Travis, Chapter 10).

Norms of reaction for fish with different alleles at the P-locus should be studied. For example, my data from *Poecilia latipinna* suggest that small and large males may differ in patterns of plasticity; stressed small males mature later but not smaller, whereas relatively large males may actually be smaller and younger at maturity when conditions are stressful. The genetic correlation between size and age at maturity may differ across environments for the different P-locus alleles. If this proves to be true, predictions about the evolutionary trajectories of these life history traits would be influenced (Arnold 1987).

Clonal poeciliids, such as the triploid *Poeciliopsis* spp. and *Poecilia formosa*, provide special opportunities to explore the genetics of phenotypic plasticity. In these species, the multilocus genotype of individuals can be identically replicated, permitting detailed study of the interaction of genes and environment. This is significant for norms of reaction, because they are likely to involve polygenic inheritance. Sibling bisexuals may differ at some of the constituent loci, dependent upon gene linkage and parental genotypes. However, because the vast majority of poeciliids are bisexual, the importance of phenotypic plasticity must ultimately be assessed by its prevalence in, and relevance to, their biology.

Studies designed to explain or predict the evolution of norms of reaction should include several types of information. Genetic variation for plasticity within the range of environmental circumstances experienced in nature should be documented. Field data on demographic schedules (mortality and fertility tables) of natural populations are needed to predict the shape of expected reaction norms. Gene flow should be estimated to determine the selection intensities necessary for localized adaptation in norms of reaction and the spatial scale over which evolutionary responses are expected.

The significance of phenotypic plasticity can be viewed from two perspectives: its role in adaptation and as an explanation of ecotypic variation. In addition, phenotypic plasticity can complicate the estimation of genetic variance and alter the outcome of selection. These issues have received little empirical scrutiny in animals, probably because their study requires controlling the environment of organisms during development or selection experiments. Few animals are as conducive to such research as poeciliids. It is thus likely that this group will play a central role in expanding our understanding of phenotypic plasticity in natural populations.

ACKNOWLEDGMENTS

I thank Drs. Joseph Travis for his teaching and support over several years and R. Jack Schultz for sharing an unpublished manuscript. Melanie Trexler frequently helped with field and laboratory work and drew all figures presented in this paper.

Dr. John Reynolds made helpful comments on a draft of this chapter, and Roberta Dimouro helped with manuscript preparation. The studies reported here were funded by National Science Foundation grants BSR 83–05823 to J. Travis and J. A. Farr, BSR 84–15529 to J. Travis, and State of Florida Non-Game Wildlife Research Grant GFC–84–022 to J. Travis and J. Trexler.

Section III

Evolutionary Genetics and Ecology

Small size and laboratory adaptability render poeciliids important subjects for genetic and ecological study and manipulation. In this respect, poeciliids are the "white mice" of the fish world, and provide an opportunity to unravel the complicated interplay of genetics and environment in shaping adaptations to ecological conditions. These investigations are facilitated by a wealth of visible genetic markers in some species. Furthermore, unisexual forms constitute a natural genetic control system with which to test hypotheses involving genetics and genotype-environment interactions.

In Chapter 12, Echelle et al. present a comprehensive review of electrophoretic studies of allozyme variation in poeciliids. Their analyses of heterozygosity relative to geographic distribution and ecological conditions reveal significant relationships. They also indicate the potential importance of genetic variation to individual fitness, discuss hybridization in nature, and point out the need to apply genetic data in phylogenetic studies.

In Chapter 13, Smith et al. use biochemical genetic data to argue that there are two species and three major genetic groups of mosquitofish in southeastern United States. They further explore temporal and spatial genetic structure of *Gambusia holbrooki* (the eastern mosquitofish) and find a complex situation that must be analyzed on several spatial scales. Genetic drift, selection, and inbreeding all probably interact to produce the tremendous genetic variance evident over the range of the species.

Wetherington et al. (Chapter 14) use unisexual poeciliids to examine questions of niche partitioning and ecological coexistence. They argue that new clones are repeatedly synthesized in nature and serve to "freeze" subsets of the genetic variation present in their sexual ancestors. Since foraging modes, growth rates, and other ecological traits are a reflection of genotype, coexistence among clones is possible due to among-clonal genetic differences.

Balsano et al. (Chapter 15) complete this section with a review of the first known unisexual vertebrate, *Poecilia formosa*, and its triploid associate. They present details of spatial and temporal aspects of the distribution of the complex and discuss clonal diversity and paternal inheritance. They summarize a variety of data suggesting that the coexistence of unisexuals and bisexuals is not a function of the breeding system but, as in the genus *Poeciliopsis*, is due to resource partitioning. Their work reiterates the great potential of unisexual livebearers in the analysis of broad ecological questions.

Chapter 12

Allozyme Studies of Genetic Variation in Poeciliid Fishes

ANTHONY A. ECHELLE
DAVID M. WILDRICK
ALICE F. ECHELLE

INTRODUCTION

A quarter of a century ago, Hewitt et al. (1963) published the first electrophoretic study of protein variation in poeciliids. Shortly thereafter, Lewontin and Hubby (1966) and Harris (1966) demonstrated the usefulness of enzyme electrophoresis, coupled with histochemical staining methods, as a tool for the study of genetic variation. In this chapter, we review electrophoretic studies of genetic variation in poeciliid fishes and the contributions such studies have made to our understanding of poeciliid evolution.

Two recent publications give thorough introductions to protein electrophoresis and its use in research on genetic variation (Richardson et al. 1986; Ryman and Utter 1987). The techniques are conducted with standard laboratory equipment and are relatively inexpensive and easily mastered compared with other biochemical methods such as mitochondrial DNA analyses (see Lansman et al. 1981). Using protein electrophoresis as a basis for studies of genetic variation depends on the assumption that different forms of a given isozyme (allozymes) or nonenzymatic protein (hemoglobin, albumins, etc.) are products of alternative alleles at the same gene locus. Although direct evidence for this assumption is rarely presented, especially strong support is available from laboratory crosses with poeciliids (Angus, Chapter 4).

In number of gene loci resolved, the broadest electrophoretic survey of poeciliids has been that of Morizot and Siciliano (1984) in which some 100 loci were assayed in *Xiphophorus* spp. Sixty-three showed intraspecific and/or interspecific electrophoretic variation. Because it provides a readily accessible source of single-gene markers, protein electrophoresis has been especially useful in laboratory genetics and other topics in experimental biology.

Early studies of the genetic structure of poeciliid populations and other organisms relied primarily upon morphology and experimental crosses (e.g., Hubbs and Hubbs 1932; Miller and Schultz 1959) or on tissue-graft experiments (e.g., Kallman 1962a). Protein electrophoresis, by providing a rapid method of assaying relatively large numbers of gene products, stimulated a virtual explosion of information on genetic variation in natural populations (Avise and Aquadro 1982; Smith and Fujio 1982; Nevo et al. 1984). Other biochemical approaches, such as restriction endonuclease analyses of nuclear and mitochondrial DNA, are contributing valuable insights into genetic variation of natural populations. However, while such analyses may provide levels of resolution and certain unique insights not available with protein electrophoresis (Avise et al. 1987; Hillis 1987; Moritz et al. 1987), none is likely, in the near future at least, to supplant protein electrophoresis as our primary data source for understanding genetic variation in natural populations.

VARIATION IN GENE-LINKAGE RELATIONSHIPS

Experimental crosses coupled with protein electrophoresis in *Xiphophorus* spp. (Morizot and Siciliano 1984) and *Poeciliopsis* spp. (Leslie 1982) have demonstrated linkage groups involving two to six protein-coding genes. In *Xiphophorus*, these linkage groups are conserved among species examined, although some linkages have diverged in recombination rate. Interestingly, there is good evidence of homology between linkage groups of *Xiphophorus* and *Poeciliopsis*. Some evidence even suggests homologous linkage groups between poeciliids and animals as divergent as salmonid fishes, frogs, pigeons, and man (Morizot and Siciliano 1984). As emphasized by Morizot and Siciliano, such data eventually should contribute detailed insight into regulatory functions, rates of change in the genetic architecture, and organization of the vertebrate genome.

UNISEXUAL POECILIIDS

Among poeciliids, two genera, *Poeciliopsis* and *Poecilia*, are known to include unisexual all-female clones (Schultz, Chapter 5). Electrophoretic surveys (in combination with morphological and karyological markers) have clearly demonstrated that unisexual poeciliids, like most if not all unisexual vertebrates, arise as interspecific hybrids between congeneric parents (Vrijenhoek 1972; Vrijenhoek et al. 1977, 1978; Turner et al. 1980a; Turner 1982). Because of their hybrid origins, unisexuals typically are several times more heterozygous than their bisexual relatives (Turner et al. 1980a). Hybridity and heightened heterozygosity have contributed heuristically to theoretical considerations regarding evolutionary interactions between unisexuals and their bisexual relatives (Moore 1984; Schultz, Chapter 5).

Allozymically detected clonal variation in unisexual poeciliids typically corresponds with allozyme polymorphisms in the parent species (Schultz 1977; Vrijenhoek 1979; Turner et al. 1980a). Thus, each of the recognized unisexual forms comprises a complex of different lineages, many of which originated through separate hybridization events (Schultz 1977; Vrijenhoek 1979a). Multiple origins is the foundation of Vrijenhoek's (1979a) "frozen-niche variation" hypothesis as an explanation of coexistence and geographic patterns of relative abundance in unisexual-bisexual complexes (Wetherington et al., Chapter 14).

Electrophoretic markers have greatly facilitated other research areas critical to understanding the origin and maintenance of genetic variation in unisexual poeciliids, such as modes of reproduction (Vrijenhoek 1972; Schultz 1977), parental genomic contributions in triploid forms (Balsano et al. 1972; Vrijenhoek 1972; Vrijenhoek and Schultz 1974), mutation in clonal genomes (Leslie and Vrijenhoek 1978), interclonal histocompatibility (Moore and Eisenbrey 1979), and niche differentiation (Schenck and Vrijenhoek 1986). The resulting body of knowledge, only partially reviewed here, is an excellent example of how experimental biology, in combination with detailed knowledge of natural history, can contribute to our understanding of the proximate mechanisms and ultimate evolutionary explanations of natural phenomena.

POPULATION VARIABILITY IN BISEXUAL (GONOCHORISTIC) SPECIES

Studies by M. H. Smith and co-workers on natural and semi-natural populations of *Gambusia affinis* represent perhaps the most extensive effort to document demographic, geographic, and temporal patterns of allozymic variation in a vertebrate. Their work has provided an unusually detailed background of data for tests of theory and mechanisms involved in populational variation (Smith et al., Chapter 13). Our purpose here is to review patterns of genetic variation among species, exclusive of unisexual forms.

Heterozygosity and Polymorphism

Two measures of genetic variability are typically reported from electrophoretic data: average frequency of heterozygotes per locus per individual ($\overline{H}$), and proportion of loci polymorphic (P). Of the two, $\overline{H}$ is less arbitrary and more precise because it is relatively insensitive to number of individuals sampled (Nei 1975).

This section focuses on our largely unpublished results from assays of 23 to 26 loci in 20 species of *Gambusia*. Although conducted in two different laboratories, these assays include essentially identical horizontal starch-gel conditions, and a total of 18 loci were common to both surveys. The tissues used were either skeletal muscle alone (Wildrick) or a mixture of head, epaxial muscle, and liver (Echelles). Enzymes were resolved on two different buffer systems described by

Siciliano and Shaw (1976): TC (Tris-citrate, pH 7) and TVB (Tris-versene-borate, pH 8). In the following list, the name of each protein system assayed is followed by its code (assigned by the International Union of Biochemistry), the number of loci scored, the buffer system used with each, and the laboratory in which it was assayed (E = Echelle, W = Wildrick, EW = both): Adenosine deaminase (EC 3.5.4.4), 1, TVB, W; adenylate kinase (EC 2.7.4.3), 1, TC, E; aspartate aminotransferase (EC 2.6.1.1), 1, TC, E; creatine kinase (EC 2.7.3.2), 3, TVB, EW; general proteins (no EC number), 4, TVB, EW; glucose-6-phosphate dehydrogenase (EC 1.1.1.49), 1, TVB, W; glucose-6-phosphate isomerase (EC 5.3.1.9), 2, TVB, EW; glyceraldehyde-3-phosphate dehydrogenase (EC 1.2.1.12), 2, TVB, EW; isocitrate dehydrogenase (EC 1.1.1.42), 2, TC, E; L-lactate dehydrogenase (EC 1.1.1.27), 2–3, TC, E (all three loci) W (eye-specific locus not examined); malate dehydrogenase (EC 1.1.1.37), 3, TC, EW; malic enzyme (EC 1.1.1.40), 1, TVB, W; mannose-6-phosphate isomerase (EC 5.3.1.8), 1, TVB, EW; peptidase (EC 3.4.13, LGG substrate), 2, TVB, W; phosphoglucomutase (EC 5.4.2.2), 1, TVB, EW; phosphogluconate dehydrogenase (EC 1.1.1.44), 1, TC, W; triose phosphate isomerase (EC 5.3.1.1), 2, TVB, W. Our statistical analysis for *Gambusia* also includes data on two additional species (Milstead 1980) assayed for 16 or 17 loci in one of our laboratories (Echelle).

The 22 species of *Gambusia* examined include forms occupying a great range of environments, including temperate rivers, isolated desert springs, tropical rivers, islands, and marine environments (Table 12–1). The relationships between genetic variability and four variables associated with the occurrence of the 22 species were explored by analyses of variance, with $\bar{H}$ or P as dependent variables. The independent variables included whether or not the species is strictly a spring dweller, and three other variables summarized in Table 12–1.

General Patterns

Local population history can have profound effects on electrophoretic estimates of heterozygosity. For example, the range of values in 22 species of *Gambusia* from extremely divergent environments (Table 12–1) is not markedly greater than that reported by Vrijenhoek et al. (1985) for *Poeciliopsis occidentalis* from a single river drainage, the Río Sonora ($\bar{H} = 0.00$–0.09).

Our data for *Gambusia* provide no evidence for two trends noted in surveys by Nevo et al. (1984) and Smith and Fujio (1982): 1) there is no tendency for subtropical-tropical species to be more variable than temperate species (F-ratio = 0.4, p = 0.52; 2) there is no significant difference between presumed habitat specialists (species restricted to springs) and presumed habitat generalists (all others; F-ratio = 0.2, p = 0.68). In a search for correlates of allozyme variability in a single species (*Poecilia latipinna*), Simanek (1978a) found no association between heterozygosity and 13 habitat/climatic variables.

Interestingly, Nevo et al. (1984) and Smith and Fujio (1982) obtained opposite trends in comparisons of habitat generalists and specialists. In *Gambusia*, the most extreme habitat generalists, *G. affinis* and *G. holbrooki*, consistently exhibit relatively high variability. However, high variability also occurred in two of the most highly restricted spring-dwellers, *G. georgei* and *G. heterochir* (Table 12–1), both of which are among the most geographically restricted of all vertebrate species. The role of introgressive hybridization, however, is unknown. Several spring-dwellers from Texas and New Mexico, including *G. georgei* and *G. heterochir*, occur in sympatry with the wide-ranging species, *G. affinis*. In nearly all such instances, hybridization has been described (Hubbs and Peden 1969; Peden 1970; Rutherford 1980). However, it is worth noting that in Simanek's (1978a) survey of *P. latipinna*, the highest variability ($\overline{H}$ = 0.10) occurred in the only spring population surveyed, and there was no opportunity for hybridization.

As emphasized by Soulé (1976), interspecific comparisons of patterns in $\overline{H}$ and *P* should control for population size and the history of genetic drift due to founder events and population bottlenecking. Those variables are poorly understood for most species. Heterozygosity differences between *G. affinis* and *G. holbrooki* illustrate a possible example of historical effects (Wooten et al. 1988). In the southeastern United States, these closely related taxa both occupy diverse waters where they have similar ecological roles. However, over large areas, heterozygosity in *G. holbrooki* is consistently higher than in *G. affinis*.

Another possible historic effect is the consistently low variabilities in the marine populations we examined (Table 12–1). Two of the three species involved, *G. yucatana* and *G. puncticulata* were, until recently, considered a single species (Greenfield and Wildrick 1984). Conceivably, their low variability reflects a common, genetically depauperate ancestor and lack of time for accrual of new diversity. (See Echelle and Echelle 1984 for a similar argument involving reduced variability in several species of atherinid fishes.) The survey by Nevo et al. (1984) revealed no heterozygosity differences between marine and freshwater organisms.

Desert Species

One major pattern emerges from the data in Table 12–1: species of *Gambusia* restricted to desert habitats tend to have reduced variability compared with other populations ($\overline{H}$ = 0.016 vs 0.047, F-ratio = 6.3, p = 0.02; *P* = 0.050 vs 0.167, F-ratio = 8.2, p = 0.01). The only examples of zero variability ($\overline{H}$ = 0.00; *P* = 0.00) involved highly restricted desert-dwelling populations: 1) *G. alvarezi*, endemic to Ojo de San Gregorio, a small spring and associated spring run less than 300 m long in Chihuahua, Mexico; 2) *G. longispinis*, endemic to springs in the Cuatro Ciénegas basin, Coahuila, Mexico; 3) a disjunct population of *G. marshi* occurring widely in Cuatro Ciénegas (the species also occupies the Río Salado, a tributary to the Río Grande in northern Mexico); and 4) a seminatural population of *G. gaigei* from Big Bend National Park, Texas. Because *G. gaigei* is an artificially maintained population (Johnson and Hubbs, Chapter 16), it was excluded from statistical analyses.

Although based on single geographic samples, our assessments of zero variability are reasonably representative of the entire species for both *G. alvarezi* and *G. gaigei*. Each species occupies a small spring and is effectively restricted to

TABLE 12-1. Polymorphism (*P*), Heterozygosity ($\overline{H}$), Overall Occurrence, and Variables Associated with Occurrence of 22 Species of *Gambusia*. A locus was considered polymorphic if two or more alleles were detected. Heterozygosity is Nei's (1978) unbiased estimate. When more than one locality was sampled, the means (above) and ranges (parentheses) of *P* and $\overline{H}$ are given. L = number of localities sampled; (N) = number of specimens per sample; R = restricted to single system of springs (= 1) versus more widely distributed (= 2); D = restricted to desert areas (= 1) versus occurs primarily in other physiographic areas (= 2); T = occurrence in temperate regions (= 1) versus occurrence south of 23.5° N (= 2, "subtropical-tropical" herein). Data sources: 1 = AAE and AFE (unpubl.); 2 = AFE et al. (in review); 3 = Milstead (1980); 4 = DMW (unpubl.).

Occurrence/Species	L(N)	P	$\overline{H}$	R	D	T	Source
Temperate region							
Desert springs only							
G. alvarezi	1 (9)	0.000	0.000	1	1	1	1
G. gaigei	1(10)	0.000	0.000	1	1	1	1
G. hurtadoi	1(10)	0.120	0.046	1	1	1	1
G. longispinis	1(10)	0.000	0.000	1	1	1	1
G. nobilis*	16(12–34)	0.128	0.027	2	1	1	2
		(0.042–0.208)	(0.004–0.060)				
G. krumholzi	1(10)	0.040	0.021	1	1	1	1
Desert rivers and springs							
G. marshi	1(10)	0.000	0.000	2	1	1	1
G. senilis	2(11–20)	0.100	0.021	2	1	1	1
		(0.08–0.12)	(0.011–0.031)				
Non-desert springs							
G. geiseri**	1(19)	0.235	0.047	2	2	1	3
G. georgei	1 (2)	0.120	0.060	1	2	1	1
G. heterochir	1(19)	0.320	0.093	1	2	1	1

		P	$\overline{H}$				
Others							
G. affinis	5(21–41)	0.276 (0.188–0.438)	0.070 (0.018–0.155)	2	2	1	3
G. holbrooki	1(4)	0.192	0.089	2	2	1	4
Subtropical-tropical regions							
River drainages							
G. atrora	2(9,4)	0.039 (0.038–0.040)	0.014 (0.010–0.017)	2	2	2	1,4
G. luma	1(29)	0.308	0.069	2	2	2	4
G. panuco	2(4,10)	0.175 (0.080–0.269)	0.079 (0.028–0.129)	2	2	2	1,4
G. regani	1(4)	0.077	0.019	2	2	2	4
G. sexradiata	1(26)	0.269	0.042	2	2	2	4
G. vittata	1(10)	0.040	0.004	2	2	2	1
Marine-mainland (Mexico, Central America)***							
G. nicaraguensis	1(4)	0.077	0.032	2	2	2	4
G. yucatana	4(28–30)	0.096	0.026	2	2	2	4
Marine-islands (Caribbean)							
G. puncticulata	3(28–30)	0.115 —	0.016 (0.015–0.026)	2	2	2	4

* For G. nobilis, the values of 0.128 and 0.027 for P and $\overline{H}$, respectively, are the averages of the means of values from four disjunct systems of springs.

** The population represented is from the Guadalupe River, San Marcos, Texas; the other populations for which data are available (see Table 12–3) are presumably introduced (Hubbs and Springer 1957).

*** Two of the G. yucatana samples were from freshwater sites.

the sample locality. In *G. gaigei*, Hubbs et al. (1986) also found no variability in an assay of 60 protein-coding loci in two different samples. Neither *G. longispinis* nor the Cuatro Ciénegas population of *G. marshi* is restricted to a single location (Minckley 1977); thus, the single-sample estimates of zero variability for these species refer only to local populations.

The existing *G. gaigei* population has gone through a series of severe population bottlenecks, including one with three individuals in 1956 (Johnson and Hubbs, Chapter 16). Since 1960, the population has been maintained at modest to large sizes (hundreds to thousands) in various artificial refugia. It seems likely that low variability was present in *G. gaigei* prior to the recorded bottlenecking. Nei et al. (1975) found that even the most extreme bottleneck possible, down to an effective population size of two individuals, contains more than 65% of the original genetic variation, and brief bottlenecks of 10 individuals have little effect on variability. The consequence of such events on long-term variability is minimal when followed by rapid increase in population size (Nei et al. 1975), as seems likely in the refuge populations of *G. gaigei*. Therefore, although the recorded bottlenecks may be a contributing factor, the absence of detected heterozygosity in extensive electrophoretic surveys indicates low heterozygosity at earlier times as well.

Two groups of closely related desert-dwellers provide evidence of a positive association between spring size and level of genetic variability. 1) Two species having $\bar{H}$ values of 0.00, *G. gaigei* and *G. alvarezi*, are very similar (Peden 1973a) to a third desert-spring dweller, *G. hurtadoi*. *Gambusia hurtadoi* occupies a spring of sufficient size to be used in large-scale agricultural irrigation, whereas the other two species occupy much smaller springs (Hubbs and Springer 1957). Perhaps as a result, variability in *G. hurtadoi* is relatively high (Table 12–1). 2) Among the four isolated, desert-spring populations of *G. nobilis*, the highest $\bar{H}$ values (0.051 to 0.060) were in those from a complex of large artesian springs in the vicinity of Balmorhea, Reeves Co., Texas, whereas lower values (0.004 to 0.031) occurred in those from three smaller, less complex spring systems (Echelle et al. 1989). The Balmorhea spring system also supports an endemic pupfish, *Cyprinodon elegans*, having high heterozygosity relative to three other geographically restricted pupfishes in the Chihuahuan Desert (Echelle et al. 1987). Thus, the relatively high $\bar{H}$ values in populations of the Balmorhea area probably are not artifacts of chance.

As noted by Vrijenhoek et al. (1985) for another desert-dwelling species, *Poeciliopsis occidentalis*, electrophoretic surveys of poeciliids provide empirical support for the suggestion (Soulé 1973) that peripheral populations exhibit reduced variability relative to more centrally located populations. In their survey of 25 loci in 21 populations of *P. occidentalis*, Vrijenhoek et al. (1985) obtained $\bar{H}$ values of 0.00 in 7 populations, all of which were at the northern periphery of the distribution or in upstream portions of rivers. In contrast, a broad geographic survey of 26 samples of *G. affinis* and 50 samples of *G. holbrooki* found no $\bar{H}$ value of 0.00, even though only 13 loci were assayed (Wooten et al. 1988).

None of those samples were from "peripheral" areas; all were from large rivers and reservoirs of southeastern United States.

Reduced heterozygosity in peripheral populations of poeciliids is not restricted to desert-dwellers. In a survey of 29 loci in 13 populations (seven species) of *Poecilia*, Brett and Turner (1983) obtained two $\bar{H}$ values of 0.00: one was in the only island population examined (*P. vanderpolli* on Curacao) and the other was in a Costa Rican population of *P. mexicana* at the southern periphery of the species' range.

Population Structure

When species exist with little spatially structured genetic heterogeneity (as may occur in a species endemic to a single spring), the heterozygosity estimate ($\bar{H}$) from a single sample will closely approximate Nei's (1977) "total gene diversity" (H_T) for the species. However, most species exhibit some degree of genetic heterogeneity among subpopulations. Thus, total gene diversity is expected to exhibit a hierarchical structure in which the number of levels varies depending on population structure (Nei 1977).

In a species composed of subpopulations, total gene diversity can be expressed as $H_T = H_S + D_{ST}$, where H_S is gene diversity within subpopulations (unweighted average of H across subpopulations) and D_{ST} is diversity due to differences between subpopulations. If groups of subpopulations exist, $H_T = H_S + D_{SG} + D_{GT}$, where D_{SG} is gene diversity due to differences between subpopulations within groups and D_{GT} is gene diversity due to differences between groups. The various components of diversity generally are expressed as proportions of H_T; for example, D_{ST}/H_T is Wright's (1978) standardized variance or F_{ST} statistic. Similarly, gene diversity due to differences at one level (e.g., between subpopulations) in the hierarchy can be expressed as a proportion of the total gene diversity at any higher level (e.g., groups of subpopulations); such proportions are referred to as "standardized variances" in Tables 12–2 and 12–3. In assessing biases associated with sampling and alternative methods of computing hierarchical gene diversity, Chakraborty and Leimar (1987) found that it is "probably more important for an investigator to be aware of the limitations that are due to an incomplete sampling of the species than to use a particular method of analysis."

Smith et al. (Chapter 13) examine the various evolutionary models for patterns of genetic differentiation among populations. Our purpose here is primarily restricted to comparing species for levels of heterogeneity among populations. For the available studies, Tables 12–2 and 12–3 summarize Wright's (1978) standardized variances for subpopulations defined at different levels (F_{XY}) and, where appropriate, the percent of total gene diversity at different hierarchical levels ($\%H_T$). In all instances, the analysis was performed with the BIOSYS-1 computer program (Swofford and Selander 1981).

Table 12–2 compares genetical population structure in a desert-dwelling spe-

TABLE 12–2.   Standardized Variances (F_{XY}) and Percent of Total Gene Diversity ($\%H_T$) at Different Hierarchical Levels in Mosquitofishes (*Gambusia affinis* and *G. holbrooki*) and Sonoran Topminnows (*Poeciliopsis occidentalis*). The notation "Locality:River" = localities within rivers, etc. Using Locality:River as an example, F_{XY} is the proportion of the total gene diversity within the average river that is due to allele frequency differences between localities (= sample sites), and $\%H_T$ is the proportion of total gene diversity in the species that is explained by differences between localities within rivers. Data sources: mosquitofish = M. C. Wooten (pers. comm.) from data reported by Wooten et al. (1988); Sonoran topminnow = Vrijenhoek et al. (1985) and Vrijenhoek (pers. comm.).

Hierarchical Level	Mosquitofishes		Sonoran Topminnow	
	F_{XY}	$\%H_T$	F_{XY}	$\%H_T$
Locality:River	0.108	7	0.544	26
Locality:Biotype	0.280	—	0.548	—
Locality:Total	0.431	57	0.787	21
River:Biotype	0.194	15	0.008	0.4
River:Total	0.362	—	0.532	—
Biotype:Total	0.209	21	0.528	53

Sample Design:
Mosquitofishes: 13 loci sampled, 13 polymorphic; 4 localities in each of 19 coastal drainages in SE U.S.; two closely related species (subspecies of some authors) sampled in nonoverlapping areas. Topminnow: 25 loci sampled, 12 polymorphic; 1–6 localities in each of six Sonoran Desert rivers; three biotypes sampled in nonoverlapping areas; two biotypes represent recognized subspecies.

cies, *Poeciliopsis occidentalis*, with that in a complex of two mosquitofishes, *G. affinis* and *G. holbrooki*, from the southeastern United States. These two data sets include the same hierarchical levels, thus facilitating comparison. However, the comparison is biased by differences in sampling design, a factor that must be carefully considered although it is often ignored (Chakraborty and Leimar 1987). In this instance, the data for *P. occidentalis* include peripheral populations within each river drainage, whereas the mosquitofish data do not. At the level of local populations ("Locality" in Table 12–2), this sampling bias would elevate the F_{XY} statistics for *P. occidentalis* relative to the mosquitofish. Correspondingly, those F_{XY} values for *P. occidentalis* are two to five times larger than for the mosquitofishes (Table 12–2). Mosquitofish are abundant and seem rather continuously distributed in the southeastern United States. Thus, they would be expected to show low F_{XY} values at the local population level. However, the differences illustrated in Table 12–2 represent a sampling bias of unknown magnitude.

At hierarchical levels above the local population, the F_{XY} statistics should be less affected by sampling bias. At those levels, the statistics are computed from the average allele frequencies among local populations. Those averages should be reasonable approximations of the average allele frequencies in, for example, a given river or biotype.

Comparison of these species above the local population level produces two

TABLE 12–3. Standardized Variances (F_{XY}) and Percent of Total Gene Diversity ($\%H_T$) at Different Hierarchical Levels in Four Species of *Gambusia*. Number of loci shows number examined (left) and number polymorphic (right). See Table 12–2 for further explanation. Data sources: 1 = McClenaghan et al. (1985); 2 = computations from Milstead's (1980) data; 3 = A. F. Echelle et al. (1989).

Species	No. Loci	F_{XY}	$\%H_T$	Sample Design	Source
G. holbrooki Locality:Total	5/5	0.196	80	70 locations, Savannah River drainage	1
G. affinis Locality:Total	16/8	0.294	71	5 widely separated lo- calities, 4 in springs of Pecos R. drainage, Texas, and New Mexico, 1 in Brazos River drainage, Texas	2
G. geiseri Locality:Total	17/5	0.272	73	4 widely separated springs, 3 in Pecos R. drainage, Texas, 1 in Guadalupe R., Texas	2
G. nobilis Locality:Total	17/4	0.603	40	4 widely separated springs, Pecos R. drainage, New Mex- ico and Texas	2
G. nobilis Locality:Spring Spring:Area Locality:Area Area:Total Spring:Total Locality:Total	24/6	0.009 0.251 0.257 0.348 0.512 0.516	0.4 16 — 35 — 48	2–6 localities in each of four widely separated spring systems (ar- eas), Pecos River drainage, New Mex- ico, and Texas	3

interesting results. 1) Populations in different rivers within the range of a biotype are more heterogeneous in the mosquitofishes than in *P. occidentalis*. This may be partly explained by the greater geographic range and numbers of rivers occupied by the mosquitofishes. Also, Wooten et al. (1988) recognized two allopatric forms within *G. holbrooki*, whereas in Table 12–2 the two are considered a single biotype. 2) Gene diversity due to differences between the closely-related mosquitofish species ($F_{XY} = 0.21$) is less than half of that between "subspecies" of *P. occidentalis* ($F_{XY} = 0.53$). Two of the three biotypes of *P. occidentalis* occur in the Río Mayo, Sonora; thus, studies of geographic variation in that system would be especially interesting from the standpoint of whether the two biotypes are reproductively isolated. There is some question about whether *P. occidentalis* represents a single species (Vrijenhoek et al. 1977).

The data presented in Tables 12–2 and 12–3 allow comparisons of heterogeneity in *P. occidentalis* and another desert species, *Gambusia nobilis*. These species represent contrasting models of population structure that Meffe and Vrijenhoek

(1988) recognized for desert fishes: the "Death Valley" model (*G. nobilis*) and the "Stream Hierarchy" model (*P. occidentalis*). *Gambusia nobilis* is restricted to four small areas of a single river basin in the Chihuahuan Desert of New Mexico and Texas, whereas *P. occidentalis* occupies several dendritic river systems of the Sonoran Desert. Within each river drainage, *P. occidentalis* generally is more continuously distributed than is *G. nobilis*, although northern populations of the former species have become fragmented due to human-induced environmental changes (Meffe and Vrijenhoek 1988).

The most appropriate comparisons for these species are the "Locality:Total" F_{XY} values for *G. nobilis* (Table 12–3) and the "Locality:River" value for *P. occidentalis* (Table 12–2). Contrary to expectation (Meffe and Vrijenhoek 1988), gene diversity due to differences between localities apparently is no greater in *G. nobilis* (0.516 to 0.603) than in *P. occidentalis* (0.544). The F_{XY} values for both species are among the largest reported for fishes (see reviews by Gyllensten 1985 and Zimmerman 1987). Thus, local populations of *P. occidentalis* within a given river apparently are more strongly isolated than expected relative to *G. nobilis*.

Milstead's (1980) data for *G. nobilis* and *G. affinis* compare two cohabiting species with highly contrasting overall distributions. Unlike *G. nobilis*, which consists of four strongly isolated populations, natural populations of *G. affinis* are widely distributed. Thus, Milstead was able to sample both species from some of the same spring systems in the Pecos River drainage. As predicted, the F_{XY} values for spring-dwelling populations of *G. affinis* were much lower than those for *G. nobilis* (Table 12–3). This difference is even more striking than it appears, because Milstead's five samples of *G. affinis* included two subspecies (4 = *G. a. affinis*, 1 = *G. a. speciosa* [considered a full species by Rauchenberger, Appendix 1]), and one sample of *G. a. affinis* was from another river system (Brazos River, central Texas). The comparison of *G. nobilis* with *G. holbrooki* from the Savannah River drainage in South Carolina and Georgia gives a similar result (Table 12–3). These data are consistent with expectations from the theory that disrupted gene flow is a major factor in allowing populational differentiation.

Milstead's (1980) data also included *G. geiseri*, a highly restricted spring-dweller occupying two of the spring systems supporting *G. nobilis*. Her samples of *G. geiseri* included three populations from isolated springs in the Pecos River drainage and a sample from the San Marcos River on the opposite side of the Edwards Plateau in central Texas. The relatively low F_{XY} values for this species compared with *G. nobilis* (Table 12–3) agree with Hubbs and Springer's (1957) hypothesis that Pecos River populations of *G. geiseri* represent introductions from the San Marcos River area.

Conclusions

Assuming selective neutrality or near neutrality of most allozymes (Chakraborty 1980; Nei 1983), variability within and between populations is determined by the effective population size (N_e) and the migration rate between populations (m).

On average, these parameters will be relatively small in peripheral populations of wide-ranging species and in species with highly restricted geographic ranges. Genetic drift and inbreeding in combination with restricted gene flow would cause reduced genetic variability within, and increased divergence between, populations. Such effects would be greatest in populations susceptible to bottlenecking. Correspondingly, among species of *Gambusia* restricted to springs, desert-dwellers showed reduced variability while others did not. Furthermore, among the desert-dwellers there was evidence of a positive association between variability and spring size.

In his survey of *Poecilia latipinna*, Simanek (1978a) found an inverse relationship between heterozygosity and the ratio of females to dominant (sailfin) males. Territoriality and social dominance are expected to reduce N_e. This effect probably acts in concert with environmental factors to heighten genetic drift and inbreeding during periods of population bottlenecking.

Because poeciliids are livebearers with multiple insemination and sperm storage (Constantz, Chapter 3), N_e of founder populations generally should not be small enough to cause severe losses of genetic variability. Accordingly, Brown (1987) found no evidence of reduced heterozygosity in recently established populations of *G. affinis* in Kansas. Introduced Hawaiian populations of *G. affinis* also show little evidence of reduced variability (M. C. Wooten, pers. comm.). Thus, founder effect seems an unlikely explanation for low variability in peripheral populations and restricted desert-dwellers. Rather, extended periods of isolation, coupled with repeated population bottlenecking, is more likely. Motro and Thomson (1982) demonstrated that the effect of repeated bottlenecking on genetic variability may be even greater than generally expected from classical theory.

The relationship between heterozygosity and variables indicative of fitness in animals (e.g., growth rates, developmental stability, etc.) has received considerable attention (reviewed by Allendorf and Leary 1986). For poeciliids, the following associations have been found: 1) positive correlation between heterozygosity and body size in *Gambusia affinis* (Feder et al. 1984); 2) positive association between heterozygosity and growth rate in *Poeciliopsis occidentalis* (R. C. Vrijenhoek, pers. comm.); 3) negative association between heterozygosity and degree of bilateral asymmetry in *P. monacha* (Vrijenhoek and Lerman 1982) and *G. holbrooki* (G. K. Meffe, pers. comm.); 4) a weak negative association between heterozygosity and morphological variability in *P. lucida* (Angus and Schultz 1983); and 5) a negative correlation between heterozygosity and morphological variation in *Poecilia reticulata* (Beardmore and Shami 1979, cited by Allendorf and Leary 1986). With some qualifications (Allendorf and Leary 1986), all of these effects can be interpreted as indicating reduced fitness in more homozygous individuals.

ALLOZYMIC DIFFERENTIATION VERSUS TAXONOMIC LEVEL

A variety of indices have been devised to convert allozyme data into estimates of genetic similarity and genetic distance (difference) between populations. In this review, we use Nei's (1978) index of genetic identity (I) to summarize allozymic

TABLE 12–4. Genetic Differentiation at Various Taxonomic Levels in Four Groups of Poeciliids. Values are unweighted means and (in brackets) ranges of Nei's index of genetic identity, and (in parentheses) number of comparisons. Data sources: *Xiphophorus*, computed from data on the 25 loci examined in all samples assayed by Morizot and Siciliano (1982); *Poecilia sphenops* complex, Brett and Turner (1983); Gambusiines, unpublished data on species listed in Table 12–1 and D. M. Wildrick's unpublished data on the gambusiine genera *Belonesox* and *Brachyrhaphis*; *P. occidentalis*, R. C. Vrijenhoek (pers. comm.) from the study by Vrijenhoek et al. (1985). All three "geographic groups" recognized by Vrijenhoek et al. (1985) are treated as subspecies; two of the groups coincide with formally recognized subspecies.

| | Group | | | |
| | | *Poecilia sphenops* | | *Poeciliopsis* |
Taxonomic Level	*Xiphophorus*	complex	Gambusiines	*occidentalis*
Within subspecies	0.93 (135) [0.76–1.0]	—	—	0.98 (69) [0.90–1.0]
Within species	0.86 (212) [0.55–1.0]	0.90 (13) [0.62–0.97]	0.96 (12) [0.78–1.0]	0.93 (190) [0.80–1.0]
Between subspecies, same species	0.75 (89) [0.55–0.88]	—	—	0.89 (121) [0.80–0.97]
Between species	0.66 (568) [0.48–0.84]	0.74 (65) [0.55–0.90]	0.73 (246) [0.42–1.0]	—
Between genera	—	—	0.43 (31) [0.28–0.57]	—

differentiation at different taxonomic levels in poeciliids. To our knowledge, broad allozyme surveys encompassing more than one taxonomic level are available for only four groups of poeciliids (Table 12–4): *Xiphophorus*, the *Poecilia sphenops* complex, *Gambusia* and two closely allied genera, and *Poeciliopsis occidentalis*. These four groups show approximately the same levels of allozyme differentiation at different taxonomic levels (Table 12–4). The data for *Xiphophorus* were taken mostly from highly inbred laboratory strains, and this might explain the indication of somewhat lower identity at different taxonomic levels in that group. The averages of genetic identity among species of the four groups and among the genera *Gambusia*, *Brachyrhaphis*, and *Belonesox* are well within the range of means given for those two levels in a review of fishes by Avise and Aquadro (1982).

The relationship between genetic divergence and speciation has been of interest to evolutionists at least since Mayr (1954) suggested that speciation was associated with "genetic revolutions." There was early optimism that level of allozyme divergence might correspond with speciation. However, it is clear for a variety of organisms (Barigozzi 1983), including fishes (Buth 1984a; Echelle and Kornfield 1984), that allozyme divergence beyond that expected for local populations of the same species does not necessarily accompany speciation. Nonetheless, interspecific similarity generally is below $I = 0.90$. Among poeciliids, there are only two known exceptions to this rule: 1) the "*Gambusia gaigei* complex" of three allopatric species, *G. gaigei*, *G. hurtadoi*, and *G. alvarezi* ($I = 0.95$–1.00), and 2) three of five comparisons of *Poecilia mexicana* and *P. gracilis* ($I = 0.90$; Brett and Turner 1983). Although differentiation levels should not be used to delimit species (Buth 1984a), such high similarity indicates potential taxonomic problems.

PHYLOGENETIC RELATIONSHIPS

The methodology of using electrophoretic data to reconstruct phylogenetic trees is highly controversial (see Farris 1981; Felsenstein 1981; Buth 1984b; Nei 1987). Dendrograms based on the unweighted pairgroup method with arithmetic averaging (UPGMA) are popular and convenient methods of summarizing genetic similarities or distances among forms. However, such dendrograms represent phylogenetic trees only if it is assumed that rates of change along different branches are sufficiently similar that rate differences do not distort genealogical relationships. Most systematists are not comfortable with this assumption (Swofford 1981; Buth 1984b; Hillis 1987).

With one exception, published summaries of genetic relationships among poeciliids are based on UPGMA dendrograms (Morizot and Siciliano 1982; Brett and Turner 1983). The exception consists of preliminary electrophoretic data on relationships within the *Gambusia puncticulata* species group (Greenfield and Wildrick 1984). That study used the "allele as character" approach (Buth 1984b), in which relationships are inferred from presence-absence of alleles. However, there was no outgroup perspective for the assignment of evolutionary polarity (primitive or derived) to alleles. Thus, as Greenfield and Wildrick (1984) noted, alleles uniquely shared by different taxa were not well-substantiated synapomorphies (uniquely shared, derived traits). In a reanalysis of the *G. puncticulata* species group, one of us (Wildrick) is using the poeciliid genera *Belonesox* and *Brachyrhaphis* as outgroups.

An unpublished phylogenetic analysis of electrophoretic data (Echelles) supports Peden's (1973a) suggestion of a close relationship between *G. senilis* and the *G. gaigei* complex of three recognized species (*G. hurtadoi*, *G. alvarezi*, and *G. gaigei*). These four forms seem to represent a monophyletic group that has evolved in the Río Grande drainage of southern Texas and northern Mexico.

HYBRIDIZATION IN NATURAL POPULATIONS

Protein electrophoresis is perhaps more useful than any other technique for studying genetic interaction between different populations. Mendelian segregation and co-dominant expression of protein-coding alleles and the frequent occurrence of fixed interspecific differences at individual loci typically allow high confidence in recognition of first-generation hybrids and products of backcrossing. We are aware of only two available allozyme studies of natural hybridization in poeciliids (Yardley and Hubbs 1976; Rutherford 1980), although M. C. Wooten (pers. comm.) is analyzing contact zones between *G. affinis* and *G. holbrooki*.

Yardley and Hubbs (1976) examined a hybrid zone between *G. affinis* and the highly restricted spring-dweller, *G. heterochir*. Electrophoretic markers demonstrated hybridization and probable backcrossing to *G. heterochir*. Hubbs' (1959, 1971) extensive morphological and ecological data on this system and more recent surveys of microdistribution of the various forms (C. Hubbs and R. J. Edwards, pers. comm.) provide an unusually detailed background for studies of this hybridization system.

Rutherford (1980) combined morphological and electrophoretic data in an analysis of hybridization among three species of *Gambusia* in west Texas springs. The analysis indicated various levels of genetic interaction between *G. affinis* and *G. nobilis*, depending on the spring. In one system, evidence of hybridization and introgression of *G. nobilis* occurred in areas downstream from spring outflows; in another system there was virtually no hybridization, although microdistributions of the two species overlapped extensively. In two other springs, *G. affinis* and *G. nobilis* exhibited only minimal contact, and hybrids were uncommon. Evidence of hybridization between *G. geiseri* and the other two species was rare, although small numbers of apparent backcross hybrids between *G. nobilis* and *G. geiseri* were detected.

SUMMARY AND FUTURE RESEARCH

Although other molecular techniques are coming to the fore, none is likely to soon replace protein electrophoresis as the primary data source on genetic variation in natural populations. This technique has contributed significantly to studies of variation in gene linkages in poeciliids. Continued work in this area should provide considerable insight into the organization of the vertebrate genome. Protein electrophoresis also has contributed enormously to studies of the origins and maintenance of genetic variation in unisexual poeciliids. This body of information eventually should help resolve the elusive question, "Of what use is sex?".

Poeciliid populations restricted to desert springs, and populations in peripheral areas of species' ranges, tend to have reduced levels of intrapopulational gene diversity and heightened levels of interpopulational diversity. This presumably reflects susceptibility to repeated population bottlenecking and the attendant heightened effects of genetic drift and inbreeding. The literature provides a number of comparisons between heterozygosity and factors that may be interpreted as components of individual fitness (growth rate, developmental stability, etc.). In general, low heterozygosity seems associated with reduced fitness.

Data summarized herein for poeciliids and elsewhere for pupfishes (Turner 1974; Echelle et al. 1987) indicate that reduced variability may be common in isolated desert fishes. This evokes concern for both the short-term fitness and the long-term evolutionary viability of such fishes. Many populations of desert fishes are declining in response to pressures from introduced species (Schoenherr 1981; Meffe 1989). Thus, it would be of both theoretical and practical value to have a better understanding of the relationship between heterozygosity and survival abilities in desert fishes. R. C. Vrijenhoek (pers. comm.) and his students are pursuing this topic in studies of *Poeciliopsis occidentalis*. Although populations experiencing repeated bottlenecks may be selected for tolerance of high homozygosity (Angus and Schultz 1983), their fitness may, nonetheless, be relatively low. Such knowledge is essential for management of existing populations (Johnson and Hubbs, Chapter 16).

The sympatric occurrences of *G. affinis* and a number of spring-dwelling species (Peden 1970; Johnson and Hubbs, Chapter 16) provide a largely unexploited opportunity (but see Hubbs 1971) for tests of theory regarding maintenance of hybrid zones (e.g., Moore 1977a; Barton and Hewitt 1985). In those springs, sharp environmental gradients and associated changes in fish distributions typically occur within a few hundred meters (Hubbs 1971; Echelle and Echelle 1980), thus offering relatively small model systems for studies of temporal and spatial dynamics of interspecific interaction.

The paucity of electrophoretic studies of natural hybridization in poeciliids is surprising given their livebearing habit. Viviparity offers obvious advantages to genetic studies of evolutionary dynamics in hybridization systems. For example, different electrophoretic classes of females could be characterized for relative fecundity and, with unusually high confidence, frequency of hybrid offspring. Also, cohort analyses aimed at estimating relative fitness of hybrids and parental forms (e.g., Dowling and Moore 1985) could use the population of developing embryos as a separate cohort.

Molecular studies of phylogenetic relationships may represent the most important research need revealed herein, as there is a virtual absence of such studies on poeciliids. By providing independent data sets, molecular studies can furnish important tests of phylogenetic relationships inferred from morphology (Parenti and Rauchenberger, Chapter 1). Also, the use of multiple data sets can give unusually high confidence in the resulting phylogenetic hypothesis (Hillis 1987). Well-corroborated phylogenetic hypotheses would provide an important genealogical perspective for interpretation of the wealth of knowledge summarized in this volume on poeciliid biology.

ACKNOWLEDGMENTS

We wish to thank D. R. Edds for help with computer analyses, R. J. Edwards, D. W. Greenfield, T. A. Greenfield, and D. C. Morizot for help in obtaining specimens, M. C. Wooten for the analysis of gene diversity in southeastern mosquitofishes and an unpublished manuscript, J-T Chang for laboratory assistance, E. G. Zimmerman for consultation on data analysis, R. C. Vrijenhoek for consultation and help with the data on *Poeciliopsis*, G. K. Meffe for an unpublished manuscript, and B. L. Brett for helpful discussions. This review was written while Echelles were on leave at the Dexter National Fish Hatchery. We wish to thank the hatchery personnel for their hospitality and helpful discussions during our stay. Partial support was provided by the US Fish and Wildlife Service and by National Science Foundation grants to AAE and AFE (DEB 79–12227) and D. W. Greenfield (BMS 75–08684 and DEB 79–23443).

Chapter 13

Demographic, Spatial, and Temporal Genetic Variation in *Gambusia*

MICHAEL H. SMITH
KIM T. SCRIBNER
J. DAVID HERNANDEZ
MICHAEL C. WOOTEN

INTRODUCTION

A major challenge in evolutionary biology is to describe and understand patterns of genetic variation in natural populations (Lewontin 1974b). Such patterns are likely the result of complex interactions among many causal variables. Interpretation is difficult, because surveys of genetic characteristics are often made without accompanying life history data or other pertinent information. Such surveys can result in incomplete descriptions or erroneous conclusions concerning patterns of genetic variation and the evolutionary forces accounting for them. Simple explanations based on general theory, although appealing, often account for little observed variation.

Life history characteristics underlie short-term population processes and determine evolutionary responses to selection, dispersal, drift, and mutation. Evolution is a change in allele frequencies over time in response to these four factors. To understand these relationships, it is necessary to first describe patterns of genetic variation and then to determine which factors contribute to that variation. Although evolution occurs continually with individual births and deaths, this type of change is not normally considered significant, because the net change in allele frequency is slight in a large, randomly breeding population. However, these changes could be relatively large in populations that are reduced in number but later expand rapidly. Population size, structure, and growth rate are critical characteristics that partially determine the outcome of the evolutionary process.

Most freshwater fishes are not organized into large, randomly breeding populations but occur as a series of smaller semi-isolated groups (Altukhov 1982). The amount of gene flow among groups determines the extent of genetic differentiation. When fish from neighboring locations have different allele frequencies but experience some gene exchange, they may be envisioned as a series of subpopulations organized within a larger metapopulation. If the genetic characteristics of these subpopulations are not correlated, subpopulations are equivalent to populations. Whereas genetic characteristics may change considerably over time within and among subpopulations, these changes are averaged over the metapopulation of which they are a part. The metapopulation represents the effective gene pool over long periods of time.

Genetic variation in mosquitofish occurs as a result of taxonomic differentiation of various forms, and variation at the sub- and metapopulation levels. Genetic variation within populations results from differences among individuals, sex-age classes, or among semi-isolated subpopulations. Patterns of genetic variation within and among populations change over time in response to the evolutionary forces of drift, dispersal, selection, and mutation. While the last force is important, its effects in natural populations have not been determined.

Evolution at each level should not be assessed independently because of influences on genetic variation at other levels. The interpretation of spatial and temporal patterns of genetic variation requires an integration of information from several different disciplines, including population ecology and genetics, behavior, and biogeography.

Geographical isolation between metapopulations is important in speciation and biogeography. Understanding the effects of drift, demographic processes, selection, and the extent of gene flow among subpopulations within each metapopulation is critical in interpreting long-term evolutionary change and in evaluating current patterns of genetic variation. Our primary purpose in this chapter is to describe patterns of genetic variation within and among subpopulations of mosquitofish over space and time. Spatial analyses are based on data taken over several geographic scales, from within localized areas of single drainages to comparisons from multiple drainages across southeastern United States. Changes in genetic characteristics within subpopulations over periods of several weeks to several years are also presented.

Several causal factors and their interactions should be considered in explaining the observed spatial and temporal divergence. The ephemeral environment occupied by mosquitofish makes it more likely that effects of drift and gene flow will be of prime importance. Without evidence of a selective basis for the patterns of genetic differentiation, drift and dispersal would be emphasized. Strong divergence among adjacent subpopulations cannot be explained by weak selection if drift and high gene flow occur. Selection at some level seems likely though, and the effects of its interaction with dispersal and drift probably keep genetic characteristics of subpopulations from becoming homogeneous on a regional scale. The model developed here to explain the evolution of mosquitofish populations may be generally applicable to other poeciliids.

SYSTEMATICS AND BIOGEOGRAPHY

The population ecology and genetics of mosquitofishes (*Gambusia* spp.) are best understood within historical constraints placed on the evolution of regional gene pools, as well as proximal factors causing changes within these gene pools. Regional and taxonomic patterns of genetic variation are the result of recent geological processes, divergence, and subsequent introgression in certain areas. *Gambusia* spp. occur naturally over most of Central America, Mexico, the southeastern United States, and all major islands of the Caribbean (Rivas 1963; Lee et al. 1981). Within the United States, there are two major categories of *Gambusia* spp.: forms that occupy relatively limited geographic areas because of historical isolation or habitat specialization, and ubiquitous forms. The latter forms include *G. affinis* and *G. holbrooki*, which until recently were considered subspecies of *G. affinis* (Wooten et al. 1988).

Spatial patterns of allele frequencies within the ubiquitous forms across southeastern United States (Figure 13–1) suggest the following: 1) at least three genetically distinct forms exist (*G. affinis*, *G. holbrooki* Type I and II); 2) a zone of potential interspecific hybridization exists in the Mobile River drainage; 3) the regions of

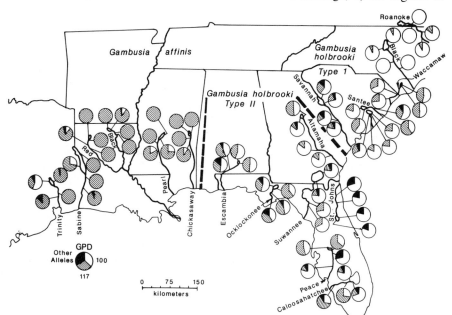

Figure 13–1. Allele frequencies at alpha glycerophosphate dehydrogenase (GPD) for 75 samples from 19 drainages across southeastern United States. Frequencies are given by the proportion of the circle representing each allele. The approximate ranges of three forms of *Gambusia* as proposed by Wooten et al. (1988) are delineated by the dotted lines. (Modified from Wooten et al. [1988]).

major taxonomic separation and hybridization are similar to those for other freshwater fishes in southeastern United States (e.g., *Esox americanus*, Lee et al. 1981; *Amia calva*, Bermingham and Avise 1986; and several species of *Lepomis*, Avise and Smith 1974; Bermingham and Avise 1986); and 4) regional patterns of genetic divergence cannot be explained simply by degree of geographic isolation between subpopulations. Further evidence suggests that there may be two major forms of *G. holbrooki* Type I (Hernandez 1988). The present forms have probably resulted from isolation caused by past geographic barriers to dispersal.

The eastern form of *Gambusia* historically occurred in headwaters of rivers draining into the Atlantic Ocean, and the western form in southern rivers draining into what was to become the Gulf of Mexico. Isolation was probably due to elevated ocean levels and the intervening Appalachian Mountains. Once divergence of *G. holbrooki* and *G. affinis* occurred, *G. holbrooki* probably invaded drainages in the lower Coastal Plain and Florida. This range extension would have followed the receding ocean levels. A second vicariant event was probably associated with divergence of the third form (*G. holbrooki* Type II; Figure 13–1) in the Florida highlands. The presence of Type II eastern mosquitofish as far west as the Escambia River, throughout Florida and into Mobile Bay, and northward into the Altamaha River in Georgia suggests that this group dispersed from a Pleistocene Florida refuge and came into contact with the other two forms.

The potential area of introgression between *G. affinis* and *G. holbrooki* is not limited to the Mobile River drainage as proposed by Wooten et al. (1988). Based on subsequent allozyme and morphological data, the zone of intergradation is widespread and consistent with reports of earlier studies that species contact is extensive in this region (Hubbs 1955; Black and Howell 1979). Another important finding from allozyme and morphological studies is that populations of *G. affinis* exist in headwater regions of both the Chattahoochee and Savannah rivers, well within the range of *G. holbrooki* proposed by Wooten et al. (1988). These isolated *G. affinis* populations are repeatedly found only in headwater sites and probably represent relicts of a wider historical distribution.

Introgression between *G. holbrooki* Type I and Type II may also occur in the mouths of some eastern rivers; this could explain increased heterozygosities in populations near the mouth of the Savannah River (Smith et al. 1983) but not in the mouths of the Pee Dee and Broad-Santee drainages in South Carolina (Hernandez 1988). The propensity for interspecific hybridization by *G. affinis* (Hubbs 1955; Getter 1976; Yardley and Hubbs 1976) and the presence of multiple areas of contact between forms complicate interpretation of spatial genetic patterns within certain areas.

SPATIAL PATTERNS

Fisheries biologists have focused considerable attention during the last two decades on patterns of intraspecific differentiation (MacLean and Evans 1981; Allendorf et al. 1985). Large amounts of allelic and genotypic data have been collected for many species, including poeciliids, primarily through the use of starch gel electrophoresis (Echelle et al., Chapter 12). Most species may be subdivided into more or less distinct groups based on differences in allele frequency. Genetic diversity expressed as variation among populations, individuals, or subpopulations within populations is important to a species' adaptability to future environmental conditions and should be the focus of conservation and management. Appreciation of the forces underlying maintenance or loss of genetic diversity is critical to an understanding of the long-term evolution of local gene pools.

Mosquitofish are highly variable genetically. On average, between 47.3 and 76.5% of loci surveyed may be polymorphic at a location (Table 13–1). Estimates of mean individual heterozygosity $(\overline{H})$ range from an average of 0.055 for *G. affinis* to 0.124 for *G. holbrooki* collected from the Broad-Santee and Pee Dee drainages in North and South Carolina (Table 13–1). Higher levels of $\overline{H}$ have been described for Texas populations of *G. affinis* $(\overline{H} = 0.126$ to 0.146; Scribner, unpubl. data) based on an extended series of loci. These high estimates of $\overline{H}$ exceed those for most vertebrates (e.g., $\overline{H} = 0.063$ over all fishes, Nevo et al. 1984). Average multilocus heterozygosity is observed for *Poeciliopsis monacha* $(\overline{H} = 0.058$; Vrijenhoek 1979b). Heterozygosity in *Poeciliopsis* seems to be maintained by dispersal among seasonally isolated subpopulations and by sperm storage and multiple insemination.

Gambusia spp. are characterized by extensive spatial genetic differentiation. Genetic distance $(D$, Rogers 1972) between *G. affinis* and *G. holbrooki* was estimated to be 0.39 (Wooten et al. 1988). High estimates of genetic distance among subpopulations occur over the ranges of both species $(D = 0.152$ and 0.218 for *G. affinis* and *G. holbrooki*, respectively, Table 13–1) and within two intensively sampled drainages in North and South Carolina $(D = 0.149)$ for subpopulations in the Piedmont. Lower genetic distances were observed among populations in close proximity $(D = 0.045$ for locations from the Savannah River Plant; Table 13–1). These estimates of genetic differentiation suggest a high degree of spatial structuring of the gene pool throughout the ranges of both species.

Mosquitofish may be viewed as spatially structured subpopulations within groups of larger size, with individuals of the same group being more similar genetically than those from different groups. Hierarchical arrangements of groups of increasing size can be constructed. For example, subpopulations may be grouped within metapopulations, which occur within drainages. Subpopulations are composed of individuals that together constitute a breeding unit. Local samples may represent subpopulations, because differences in allele frequency among them are usually significant for most variable loci (McClenaghan et al. 1985; Hernandez 1988). The evolutionary forces that determine these patterns and their maintenance over time are best understood when studied on local as well as regional scales.

Surveys reveal genetic associations of fish within regions or drainages based on widely divergent allele frequencies or alternate fixation of alleles. These patterns are shown for alpha glycerophosphate dehydrogenase (GPD) for both *G. holbrooki* and *G. affinis* (Figure 13–1). The species are characterized by near-alternate fixation

TABLE 13–1. Parameters Describing Mean Levels of Genetic Variation (P and $\overline{H}$) and Genetic Differentiation Among Locations (D) for Three Levels of Spatial Subdivision (See also Figures 13–1, 13–2a, and 13–2b).

| Variable | *Gambusia holbrooki /affinis* from southeastern U.S.* | | | Broad-Santee and Pee Dee Drainages** | 64 Locations on the Savannah River Plant*** |
	75 Populations	*G. holbrooki*	*G. affinis*		
Number of loci	14	14	14	21	17
Mean Individual Heterozygosity ($\overline{H}$)	0.095	0.113	0.055	0.124	0.116
Proportion of Loci Polymorphic (P)	0.554	0.585	0.487	0.473	0.765
Mean Genetic Distance (D)****	0.390	0.218	0.152	0.149	0.045

* Locations were sampled across 19 drainages throughout southeastern United States (Wooten et al. 1988).

** Data for *G. holbrooki* summarized from Hernandez (1988; Figure 13–2a).

*** Data for *G. holbrooki* summarized from Zimmerman (pers. comm.; Figure 13–2b).

**** Genetic distances were calculated as described by Rogers (1972).

of alleles at the GPD locus. Large differences in allele frequency also exist among subpopulations from different geographic regions and among drainages. These genetic differences emphasize the importance of isolation by distance at this geographic scale.

Extensive variation in allele frequency is observed even over more limited geographic areas (Figure 13–2). Significant clustering of allele frequencies occurs

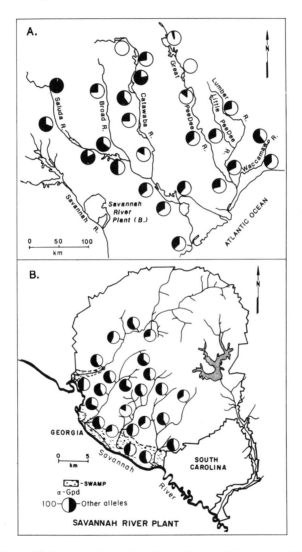

Figure 13–2.   Allele frequencies at alpha glycerophosphate dehydrogenase (GPD) for samples from (a) the Broad-Santee and Pee Dee drainages in North and South Carolina, and (b) 64 locations from a section of the Savannah River drainage. Frequencies are indicated by the proportion of the circle representing each allele.

TABLE 13-2. Hierarchical Analysis of Genetic Diversity (Fst: Nei 1977; Wright 1978) Describing Components of Spatial Variance in Allele Frequency for Three Levels of Spatial Subdivision (see also Figures 13-1, 13-2a, and 13-2b). The percentage of total genetic variance explained at each hierarchical level is presented in parentheses.

Comparison x (within):y	Gambusia holbrooki/affinis from southeastern U.S.*			64 Locations on the Savannah River Plant***, ****
	75 Populations**	G. holbrooki	G. affinis	
Drainage:Total	0.377 (0.250)	0.204 (0.304)	0.137 (0.288)	0.016 (0.113)
Location:Drainage	0.083 (0.150)	0.084 (0.150)	0.108 (0.227)	0.055 (0.387)
Location:Total	0.428 (0.284)	0.271 (0.484)	0.230 (0.484)	0.071 (0.500)

* Locations were sampled across 19 drainages throughout southeastern United States (Wooten et al. 1988).

** Other hierarchical levels not presented from the analysis of 75 populations include Drainage:Species = 0.204 (0.148); Location:Species = 0.326 (0.183); and Species:Total = 0.152 (0.101).

*** Data for G. holbrooki summarized from Zimmerman (pers. comm.; Figure 13-2b).

**** Drainage in this hierarchical analysis refers to upper stream locations versus lower stream locations for several small tributaries of the Savannah River in South Carolina (Figure 13-2b).

for populations within individual rivers and for those from the upper (Piedmont) versus lower (Coastal Plain) portions of two Carolina drainages (Hernandez 1988). However, the major result of comparisons of samples from adjacent locations is striking differences in allele frequency. Common allele frequency for GPD varied from 1.00 to 0.00 among subpopulations in seven North and South Carolina rivers and from 0.81 to 0.30 among samples from streams within the Savannah River Plant (Figures 13–2a and 13–2b, respectively). The magnitude of allelic variation among subpopulations is partially a function of distance among samples.

Significant allele frequency differences among subpopulations occur even on a microgeographic scale (Figure 13–2b; McClenaghan et al. 1985; Kennedy et al. 1985, 1986). Allele frequencies differ even over a few hundred meters within the same stream (Kennedy et al. 1986) or over slightly longer distances within a reservoir (Kennedy et al. 1985). Differentiation over short distances is also observed in genotypic frequencies and multilocus heterozygosities. Variation at this level cannot be due to geographic distance and lack of gene flow among subpopulations. Drift or demographic factors must be partially involved in causing spatial genetic heterogeneity at this level.

Patterns of spatial relatedness among subpopulations can be shown using variance partitioning and spatial autocorrelation (Table 13–2 and Figure 13–3, respectively). Hierarchical analyses (e.g., F_{st}, Wright 1978; Table 13–2) partition components of genetic diversity relative to nested levels of increasing distance. Most genetic variance is contained within subpopulations. For example, within the Broad-Santee and Pee Dee drainages in South and North Carolina, 84.1% of the total genetic variance is found within subpopulations, and 15.9% can be attributed to all other levels of organization (Hernandez 1988). This within-subpopulation variance is above the average for freshwater fish (68.2%) which range from 23.8 to 94.5% (Gyllensten 1985). The portion of total genetic variance explained by differences among subpopulations consistently accounts for greater variance than higher levels of organization.

Spatial autocorrelation provides a measure (Moran's I) of the correlation of allele frequencies in samples from locations separated by similar distances (Sokal and Oden 1978a, 1978b). Similar deterministic or stochastic processes (e.g., parental dispersal affecting neighborhood size) should generate similar spatial distributions of allele frequencies and autocorrelative patterns (Sokal and Wartenberg 1983). Positive autocorrelation of allele frequencies for subpopulations separated by specific distances implies that fish within these distances are nonrandomly clustered and are probably part of the same gene pool. General autocorrelation patterns show positive interlocation correlation of allele frequencies over short distances, with a decrease in correlation toward negative values at greater distances (Figure 13–3). Autocorrelograms for the seven North and South Carolina river samples (Figure 13–3a; Hernandez 1988) and for the 64 samples from the Savannah River Plant (Figure 13–3b) both show decreasing correlations with increasing distance, as expected in Wright's (1969) isolation by distance model. The decline in interlocation

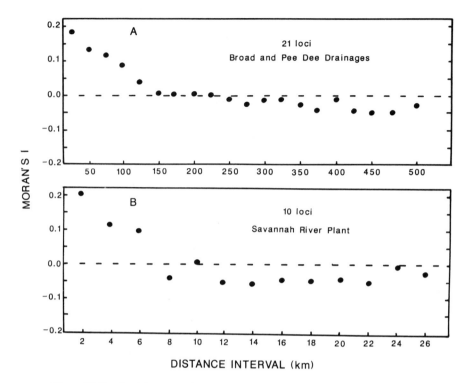

Figure 13–3. Spatial autocorrelograms representing Moran's *I*. (A) averaged over 21 loci for 85 samples in the Broad-Santee and Pee Dee drainages (modified from Hernandez 1988); (B) averaged over 10 loci for 64 samples on the Savannah River Plant (Zimmerman, pers. comm.).

genetic association is linear over short distances; negative correlations occur at longer distance intervals.

High positive autocorrelation is observed at distances up to 150 km for subpopulations from the Broad-Santee and Pee Dee drainages, which were analyzed using an interlocation distance interval of 25 km. High positive spatial autocorrelation up to 150 km indicates that subpopulations are nonrandomly associated within this distance. Subpopulations sampled from the 64 sites on the Savannah River Plant were separated at 2 km distance intervals to a maximum interlocation distance of 26 km (Figure 13–3b). Positive autocorrelation occurs at distances up to 6 km at this scale of analysis. Positive autocorrelation is not observed when the analyses are conducted on an even smaller distance scale. Inter-subpopulation correlation in allele frequency is not different from zero in most cases and is occasionally negative at distance intervals less than 100 m (Kennedy et al. 1986).

The range of allele frequencies characterizing subpopulations increases with geographical scale of analysis, which partially determines the extent of positive autocorrelation and determination of patch size (distance where Moran's *I* goes from positive to negative). Changes in sampling distances among subpopulations will change patch size (Sokal and Wartenberg 1983), although the underlying process(es) that affects allele frequency surfaces (i.e., gene flow) and the resulting autocorrelative patterns remains the same. Over large and intermediate distances, the patterns observed are of isolation by distance. Spatial autocorrelation to 150 km or even 6 km suggests that the effects of gene flow extend over distances much greater than may be realized by dispersal in a single generation.

When spatial comparisons are made within limited areas characterized by small or intermediate subpopulation differences in allele frequency, the high genetic variance within subpopulations exceeds inter-subpopulation variance. High within-subpopulation variance is probably the primary factor responsible for the lack of spatial association over very short distances. The effects of demographic processes are probably greater than those of gene flow when spatial comparisons are made among adjacent subpopulations. Local differences in subpopulation size, demographic structure, breeding structures that are complicated by multiple insemination and sperm storage (Smith and Chesser 1981; Robbins et al. 1987), and differential dispersal by fish from different age and sex classes among subpopulations (Brown 1985; Robbins et al. 1987) all serve to confound our ability to predict microgeographic spatial patterns. These factors help explain the lack of significant positive spatial autocorrelations observed within distances in which gene flow should be effective over short time periods (hundreds of meters; Kennedy et al. 1986).

Some type of population structuring is implied by the frequent occurrence of relatively large differences in allele frequencies among adjacent subpopulations (Smith et al. 1983; McClenaghan et al. 1985; Kennedy et al. 1985, 1986; Hernandez 1988). Although the majority of genetic variation is accounted for within subpopulations, the second most important source of variation is among locations. The low amount of variation accounted for by species, drainages, or creeks is striking (Table 13–2; Figures 13–1 and 13–2a) given regional differences in allele frequency. Processes at the microgeographical level must have a major impact on spatial patterning of genetic characteristics of mosquitofish and occur despite substantial gene flow among subpopulations.

Gene flow normally results in homogeneous allele frequencies over space (Wright 1931). Estimates of the number of individuals migrating between subpopulations each generation (Nm; Slatkin 1981) within South Carolina rivers and in the small interconnected tributaries of the Savannah River are high (15 to 20 fish per generation). The number of dispersers is much lower when gene flow is estimated within and between drainages ($Nm = 1.35$; Hernandez 1988). Although confidence intervals are not available for Nm, effective migration at all levels is quite high compared to that in most other vertebrates (Slatkin 1985). An Nm value of 1 is sufficient to ensure qualitative but not necessarily quantitative equivalence of subpopulations between drainages (Crow and Kimura 1970; Allendorf and Phelps 1981).

A simple explanation of how relatively large differences in allele frequency are observed among subpopulations in close proximity with high rates of gene flow is difficult. One of the assumptions of most population genetic models is that populations are in demographic equilibrium and do not vary substantially in size among generations. These assumptions are not accurate for natural populations of mosquitofish, and gene flow estimates may be inflated. Gene flow (*Nm*) may reflect movement among subpopulations as well as effects of extinction and recolonization. Furthermore, calculation of Nm takes into account multiple insemination of females, which increases estimates of gene flow with lower numbers of migrating fish.

Genetic and demographic implications of dispersal in mosquitofish have been examined for subpopulations on the Savannah River Plant (Brown 1985; Robbins et al. 1987) and in recently colonized drainages in the Midwest (Brown 1987). Dispersal of *G. holbrooki* in Pond C on the Savannah River Plant is not random with respect to sex-age class or genotype. Adults disperse more often than juveniles (Brown 1985; Robbins et al. 1987). Dispersing adults are significantly larger than nondispersers of the same sex and have different allele frequencies than resident individuals collected before and after dispersal occurred (Brown 1985). These genetic and demographic differences between dispersing and nondispersing individuals can cause the short-term temporal and microgeographic heterogeneity in allele frequency commonly observed among subpopulations.

A number of characteristics, including demographic and temporal heterogeneity in allele and genotypic frequencies, suggest that subpopulations are not in equilibrium. A trend for heterozygote deficiency has been observed across subpopulations in some but not all studies of mosquitofish, as indicated by relatively high positive F_{is} values (Feder et al. 1984; Kennedy et al. 1986; Hernandez 1988). Different groups within subpopulations differ in their genetic characteristics (Feder et al. 1984; Brown 1986), and samples usually contain more fish of certain sexes and ages than others. Spatial and temporal variation in allele frequency could then be partially due to demographic differences in genetic characteristics and a type of Wahlund effect produced by the mixing of individuals with different genetic characteristics. Another explanation might involve nonrandom dispersal of fish with genotypic characteristics that differ on average from those in the population of origin (Brown 1985, 1987; Kennedy et al. 1985). Selection on a microgeographic scale could also account for differences among subpopulations (Kennedy et al. 1985), but there is no evidence for selection of the magnitude necessary to produce the degree of divergence observed.

Spatial autocorrelation of allele frequencies over large distances suggests that the effective gene pool or metapopulation may be quite large. Autocorrelation of allele frequency and high estimates of gene flow are contrasted by genetic differentiation among subpopulations collected over short distances. Autocorrelation defines spatial structure resulting from proximate as well as historical gene flow among subpopulations. Metapopulations are divided into ephemeral subpopulations whose size and permanence is a function of the temporary nature of habitats, exchange of individuals between subpopulations, and reproductive recruitment. High estimates of gene flow probably reflect high dispersal rates and local extinction and recolonization. For example, recolonization of vacant habitats by a few large, multiply-inseminated females would carry most of the founding population's genetic diversity (Robbins et al. 1987) and raise estimates of gene flow. The potential for drift in allele frequencies leading to differentiation among adjacent subpopulations would also be high because of low numbers of founding or overwintering individuals. These differences among local subpopulations probably are not stable over time because of high gene flow. The characteristics of subpopulations with extreme frequencies should regress over time toward regional average frequencies for the metapopulation.

DRIFT AND TEMPORAL VARIATION

Studies of *Gambusia* spp. consistently describe mosquitofish as being adapted in many ways to temporally heterogeneous environments (Krumholz 1948; Smith et al. 1983; Lui et al. 1985; Zimmerman et al. 1987). Subpopulations must also be quite variable in size due to changes in available habitat and varying levels of predation. While quantitative estimates of population size are not available for most natural mosquitofish populations, assessments based on catch per unit effort indicate that numbers fluctuate dramatically on a seasonal basis. Similar environmental variability and corresponding variations in population size and distribution occur for several species of *Poeciliopsis* living in Mexican streams (Vrijenhoek et al. 1977; Vrijenhoek 1979b). Drift and dispersal are the predominant forces determining genetic characteristics of subpopulations under these conditions.

Drift causes fixation of alleles, while dispersal maintains variability at polymorphic loci. If subpopulation size is small, the effects of these processes should result in temporal variation in allele frequencies. The magnitude of this variation depends on regional average frequencies, size and permanence of subpopulations, and the relative importance of drift and dispersal over time. Our perception of these changes depends on what part of the metapopulation is sampled. Subpopulation size and demographic composition can change rapidly, and there is a greater chance of detecting temporal genetic variation at this level than in the metapopulation.

The effects of drift are often seen when subpopulations rapidly expand from low numbers of founding or overwintering adults. Drift effects are further enhanced because the effective number of breeders is reduced by female-biased sex ratios (Hildebrand 1921; Smoak 1959; Ferens and Murphy 1974; Snelson, Chapter 8). However, this effect of skewed sex ratios on effective population size may be reduced by sperm storage (Robbins et al. 1987).

Significant temporal variation in allele frequency over several weeks to years is observed at many locations. Temporal variation at the glucose phosphate isomerase-2 (GPI-2) locus has been reported for mosquitofish sampled from two of six subpopulations during 1973 and 1977 (Yardley et al. 1974; Smith et al. 1983, respectively). Spatial and temporal variability in allele frequency also has been documented for sexual forms of *Poeciliopsis*, principally due to drift within small, seasonally isolated populations (Vrijenhoek 1979b).

Fish were repeatedly sampled from a series of locations along the Savannah

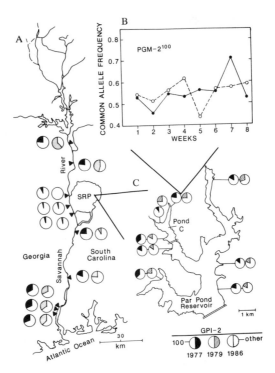

Figure 13–4. Allele frequencies for locations repeatedly sampled over years or weeks within a year. Frequencies are given by the proportion of the circle representing each allele: (A) glucophosphate isomerase-2 (GPI-2) from the Savannah River, South Carolina and Georgia, sampled 1977 and 1986; (B) phosphoglucomutase-2 (PGM-2) at two locations within Pond C, Savannah River Plant over an eight-week period; (C) GPI-2 in Pond C, sampled in 1977 and 1979.

River and on the Savannah River Plant in South Carolina. Allele frequency changes for GPI-2 are described for several Savannah River subpopulations sampled during 1977 and 1986 (Figure 13–4a), for Par Pond subpopulations sampled during 1977 and 1979 (Figure 13–4b; McClenaghan et al. 1985), and for two Pond C subpopulations over a period of eight weeks during 1985 (Figure 13–4c; L.W. Robbins, pers. comm.). Variation in allele frequency is noted between years for some of the Savannah River and Par Pond subpopulations, and significant variability is seen over shorter time periods for Pond C subpopulations.

Significant temporal variation at GPI-2 and phosphoglucomutase-2 (PGM-2) occurred for samples collected from seven Pond C locations during eight consecutive weeks. Data for two of the seven populations were chosen to illustrate the general trend (Figure 13–4b). Spatial and temporal variation was also observed in proportions of adult males and females within these locations. Time and demography are frequently confounded, and attempts to explain this variation need to consider both.

Changes in allele frequencies over years are not surprising given the dynamic demographic characteristics of poeciliids. Most of the significant temporal heterogeneity occurred among subpopulations inhabiting an intensively sampled reservoir and a thermally impacted area in Pond C (McClenaghan et al. 1985). Other examples of temporal variation are documented for subpopulations inhabiting flowing water habitats subject to periodic flooding (Figure 13–4a). Changes in allele frequency for most of these subpopulations are probably random in direction, and their net effect is further reduced over time by gene flow. Subpopulations inhabiting fluctuating environments may be particularly prone to temporal genetic variation as a result of local declines or extinctions. However, the average change in allele frequency for all subpopulations should result in little or no net change in the larger metapopulation.

High levels of genetic variability observed for *Gambusia* spp. would not be expected if subpopulations were subjected to prolonged reductions in size. However, *Gambusia* spp. have high dispersal rates (Hernandez 1988), high frequency of multiple insemination and sperm storage (Chesser et al. 1984), and high reproductive rates, which reduce or reverse effects of temporary reductions in population size. Loss of alleles and reductions in heterozygosity depend on the magnitude and duration of reduction in numbers (Nei et al. 1975). Populations do fluctuate seasonally and certainly become low enough, at least for short periods, to produce changes in allele frequency and heterozygosity among fish of different sex-age classes. Genetic characteristics do differ among sex-age classes, but the high levels of heterozygosity observed for *Gambusia* spp. across the southeastern United States suggest that, although drift alters allele frequencies, it does not normally operate over sufficient time for allelic fixation and loss of genetic variation to occur.

DEMOGRAPHIC VARIATION

Gambusia populations undergo seasonal and short-term demographic changes in sex ratio, age composition, population size, reproductive biology, and dispersal among subpopulations. All of these changes can influence genetic characteristics. Reproductive activity is not continuous throughout the year but varies in initiation, duration, and intensity (Bennett and Goodyear 1978). Mosquitofish are reproductively active during warmer portions of the year, and females may give birth from four to five times annually (Krumholz 1948). The size of overwintering subpopulations is low compared to that during the reproductive season due to continuing mortality without recruitment during winter.

Winter population reductions may result in genetic drift leading to differences in allele frequency and heterozygosity for fish produced at various times of the year. This is frequently seen as significant allelic and genotypic differences between adult males, females, and juvenile mosquitofish. Genotypic frequencies are significantly different among sex-age classes in each of five subpopulations sampled in

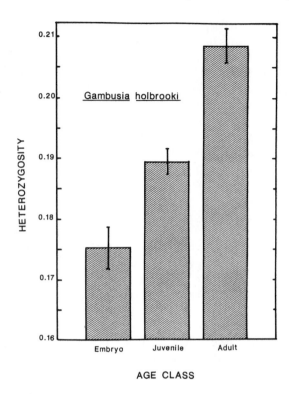

Figure 13–5. Mean and 95% confidence intervals for multilocus heterozygosity calculated from five loci for three life history stages (N = 3443) of *Gambusia holbrooki* from 11 southeastern drainages.

a South Carolina reservoir (Feder et al. 1984). Within the same subpopulation, genotypic proportions at several variable loci differed from Hardy-Weinberg expectations for adult males and juveniles due to a deficiency of heterozygotes.

Genetic changes among sex-age classes are further reflected by differences in multilocus heterozygosity, which occur between juveniles and adults within a reservoir in South Carolina. Heterozygosity for juveniles was 90% that of the adults (Feder et al. 1984). Increasing heterozygosity with increasing age is consistently observed for *G. holbrooki* throughout southeastern United States. Mean individual heterozygosity increases from embryo to juvenile (individuals <20 mm in length) and from juvenile to adult age classes (Figure 13–5). This increase is accentuated in fish from running water habitats (Scribner, unpubl. data).

Drift in small isolated populations can result in localized inbreeding and lower heterozygosity of resulting offspring. Selection can also account for this reduction. Regardless of the mechanism, these differences enhance the probability of fish of different genetic characteristics entering the breeding population and causing temporal variation in allele or genotypic frequencies.

SELECTION

Adaptation via selection is expected under most circumstances, but the extent of local adaptation is also dictated by drift and dispersal. The genetic factors underlying a particular adaptation are strongly influenced by drift and may differ over time and space (Wright 1970). The effects of selection are determined by its magnitude, consistency, and duration. The net results of selection on mosquitofish probably differ considerably at the level of subpopulations versus the metapopulation.

Selection is difficult to demonstrate in natural populations (Endler 1986). However, mosquitofish exhibit a number of characteristics that suggest natural selection may be operating. These include: genetic differences among fish from various sex-age classes within the same subpopulation; allele frequency and multilocus heterozygosity differences among fish of different lengths; genetic differences of fish inhabiting different environments; temporal changes in allele frequencies; correlations between inter-subpopulation differences in environmental and genetic characteristics; correlations between allele frequencies or heterozygosities in various areas; and results from direct tests for selection. Demonstration of whether or not selection is occurring is critical to choice of an appropriate model for interpreting genetic patterns in field data and for predicting temporal change in natural populations.

Populations consist of various groups with different demographic characteristics, which should have similar allele frequencies and heterozygosities if the population is randomly breeding and in equilibrium. Embryos, juveniles, and adults sampled from subpopulations in 11 southeastern drainages differ in levels of multilocus heterozygosity (Figure 13–5). This effect is generally observed across the species range, and a similar difference has been reported for embryos and adults in a South Carolina reservoir (Feder et al. 1984). The populations are not in equilibrium, and the effect is probably due in part to selection. Inbreeding can also reduce multilocus heterozygosity within local subpopulations, but the level necessary to account for the difference between adults and embryos would have to be high, with an inbreeding coefficient of 0.16. This is equivalent to the level of inbreeding produced by matings between first cousins. Reproduction in small subpopulations may lead to this level of inbreeding over short periods of time, but it is more likely that selection and inbreeding are both responsible for the age-specific differences in heterozygosity observed among demographic groups.

Differences in allele frequencies and heterozygosities among adults of different body lengths have also been observed for a number of loci (Smith and Chesser 1981; Feder et al. 1984). Larger adults are more heterozygous than those of smaller size (Figure 13–6). Fish were sampled during different years and at various sites, and the genotypic proportions of fish within subpopulations did not deviate from Hardy-Weinberg expectations. These considerations make it likely that natural selection of some unknown cause(s) operates in populations to first produce a

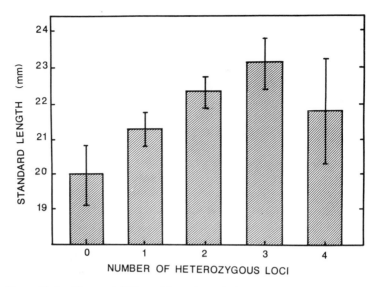

Figure 13–6. Mean and 95% confidence intervals for adult female standard length among *G. holbrooki* differing in number of heterozygous loci.

decrease in heterozygosity during early life history and then to increase heterozygosity in later stages. Similar age-specific differences in heterozygosity have been described for white-tailed deer (Cothran et al. 1983), and other age-related genetic changes occur in other vertebrates (e.g., Fujino and Kang 1968; Tinkle and Selander 1973). Individuals with higher heterozygosities also have greater tolerance for mercury (S. A. Diamond, pers. comm.). Phenol resistance in mosquitofish inhabiting polluted areas may have a genetic basis (Angus 1983b). Selection for varying levels of heterozygosity seems to operate during different life history stages.

Genetic characteristics do not occur randomly over space but differ among fish occurring in different environments. For example, allele frequencies for several loci and multilocus heterozygosity vary according to whether *G. holbrooki* occur in lotic or lentic environments, in elevated or ambient thermal conditions, high or low elevations (Smith et al. 1983; Hernandez 1988), and estuarine versus freshwater habitats (Stearns and Sage 1980). Thermal tolerance is high in *G. holbrooki* (Smoak 1959), and *G. affinis* may have adapted to heated waters from electric generating stations in Texas (Dean 1981). Allele frequencies for PGM-2 also change seasonally in a small, isolated Carolina bay in South Carolina. The allele that increases in frequency during the summer is the same as that most prevalent in habitats receiving thermal effluents (M. W. Smith, unpubl. data). Thus, mosquitofish show genetic changes in response to local environmental conditions.

Selection is inferred by correlations between interlocation genetic and environmental differences. A series of 16 water quality variables and variation at 28 loci were measured for each of 17 populations of *G. affinis* in Hawaii. Correlation was observed between the matrices of genetic and environmental differences for these 17 populations (Scribner, unpubl. data). In this area, various allelic combinations are emphasized in different environments, as might be predicted from Wright's (1970) Shifting Balance Model of evolution. There are also strong correlations between allele frequencies of various loci within different rivers in Georgia, South Carolina, and North Carolina (Smith et al. 1983; Hernandez 1988), suggesting coadapted sets of alleles. Most of these correlations for allele frequencies are not due to linkage but might be due to introgression of the various types of mosquitofishes in the Southeast. Similar relationships have been documented for *Lepomis macrochirus* across the same area (Avise and Smith 1974). It is harder to use this explanation for environmental-genetic correlations and differences in tolerances. All of the preceding observations indirectly indicate selection operating on mosquitofish.

One of the most rigorous ways of testing for selection in natural populations is through Selection Component Analysis (Christian and Frydenburg 1973). Analyses are based on genotypic data from mother-offspring combinations and other adults in the populations, and deviations from expected genotypic proportions are used to infer selection. The genotypic proportions of all demographic groups within a population should be the same. For example, if breeding and nonbreeding adult females do not have the same genotypic proportions, some form of reproductive selection must be operating. Six different subpopulations of mosquitofish (N = 1,200+ each) from the Savannah River Plant have been analyzed for three to four variable loci; one population was sampled twice in different years.

Twenty-six selection component analyses were conducted. All subpopulations sampled showed evidence of selection operating on one or more loci, and 50% of the locus-population combinations showed evidence of selection (M.J. Godt and C. Fisher, pers. comm.). These results for *G. holbrooki* are in contrast to the very few rejections observed for several loci tested over a series of years in the eel pout (*Zoarces viviparous*; Christiansen et al. 1984). Mosquitofish populations show evidence of selection, but selection operates on the loci in different ways in each population. For example, two populations in South Carolina sampled during 1985 differed in the occurrence of female sexual selection at the mannose phosphate isomerase (MPI-1) locus, because genotypic proportions were different between pregnant and nonpregnant adult females in only one population. Selection may not be operating on the loci considered but on some other linked loci, and the cause(s) of selection is not known. Selection and/or differential dispersal between subpopulations are possible sources for these departures from equilibrium, and the latter may be a special form of selection.

Selection seems to be operating within natural populations of mosquitofish, but its magnitude is probably small. Although significant, the correlation between environmental and genetic distance matrices is small, the amount of variation in genetic characteristics associated with different environments is low, and significances of most orthogonal tests for selection are low $(0.05 \leq P \leq 0.01)$ even though sample sizes are large. Selection interacts with drift and dispersal to produce the genetic associations observed among and within natural populations, but drift and dispersal are the predominant factors influencing allele frequencies. High dispersal rates of the most genetically variable adults result in high effective metapopulation size and are the likely cause for high multilocus heterozygosity observed in *G. affinis* and *G. holbrooki* by Wooten et al. (1988).

GENERAL DISCUSSION

Any model of population structure and evolution for mosquitofish must account for several of the more conspicuous characteristics of the species. These include high multilocus heterozygosity, relatively large interpopulation differences in allele frequencies, high estimated dispersal rates, and low divergence among different types of environments. These characteristics need to be understood in terms of the relative influences of drift, dispersal, and selection while considering the constraints imposed by the general life history of the species. The apparent contradiction that the model must explain is high multilocus heterozygosity in subpopulations subject to drift and high genetic divergence among subpopulations separated by short distances but with high gene flow among them.

The simplest explanation involves chance processes, but it is difficult to explain how chance alone increases population divergence without decreasing heterozygosity. *Gambusia* spp. live in highly variable lentic environments characterized by seasonally changing water levels. Individuals that find ideal habitat conditions with few or no predators probably expand their numbers rapidly. The timing of demographic processes could be instrumental in causing spatial divergence by allowing fish in certain sex-age classes to quickly increase representation of their genetic characteristics in the subpopulation. If a few females inseminated by several males found new subpopulations, genetic variability could be maintained, but allele frequencies would show high variability across these subpopulations because of the limited number of breeders. Higher tendency to disperse and greater heterozygosity among large adults than among fish of earlier life history stages would further ensure maintenance of heterozygosity in expanding subpopulations. High reproductive potential of *Gambusia* spp. makes rapid expansion in founding subpopulations likely, thus decreasing the loss of genetic variability through bottlenecks.

Under this model, many *Gambusia* subpopulations would be ephemeral in space and time. Founding subpopulations would have to be small enough to cause allele frequencies to diverge, but the size and duration of bottlenecks would not be sufficient to decrease heterozygosity. The effective size of subpopulations and bottleneck duration would determine the extent of drift and divergence in allele frequency.

Stochastic processes will constantly create new genetic combinations for selection to act upon. These combinations do exist in natural populations, as evidenced by high divergence, the presence of unique alleles in certain areas but not in others (Hernandez 1988), correlations of allele frequencies within various parts of the range of *G. holbrooki* (Smith et al. 1983; Hernandez 1988), or genetic differences among fish of different body lengths or sexes (Feder et al. 1984). These are some of the conditions required under Wright's (1970) Shifting Balance Model of evolution. In this model, selection must also be operative, as is likely for *Gambusia*. The interaction of selection and drift in producing local adaptations is essential to Wright's model.

There are problems in applying this model to mosquitofish evolution and rigorously testing it. First, mosquitofish exist in a series of subpopulations that are highly interconnected by dispersal . The average condition of the overall metapopulation is probably relatively stable in terms of genetic characteristics. Secondly, drift and inbreeding within subpopulations occur only during short intervals relative to seasonal or other environmental effects. Selection in highly variable environments probably operates in different directions over relatively short time periods and on fish at different stages of their life history.

Wright (1970) describes a species as occupying an adaptive landscape having a series of peaks with intervening valleys. For Wright's model to apply to mosquitofish, adaptive peaks and valleys must exist, and the peaks must emphasize different genetic characteristics as important determinants of fitness. High dispersal rates in mosquitofish would result in very broad and only slightly elevated adaptive peaks. This makes the demonstration of peaks difficult. Despite these problems, Wright's model is the most parsimonious explanation of the data, and it can serve as an intellectual focal point in considering population dynamics and evolution in mosquitofish and other poeciliids.

Evolutionary theories have generally considered populations as either large and panmictic, with selection the most important factor, or as small, subdivided, and subjected to drift and selection (Provine 1971). Most major controversies in biology are resolved by incorporating features of both points of view in formulating an explanation of the phenomenon. In this case, the explanation for patterns of genetic variation depends upon the level of biological organization being examined. At the local subpopulation level, drift apparently predominates, and rapid population expansion amplifies stochastic effects. At this level, Wright's emphasis on drift and small populations seems correct. On a broader scale, perhaps at the metapopulation level, dispersal rates are so high that the metapopulation must be quite large, and selection operating over long periods may be the driving source of evolution. Thus, both evolutionary points of view may be correct but apply to different levels of biological organization over space. Mosquitofish may not be unusual in terms of the relative importance of drift, dispersal, and selective effects on its population structure and short-term evolution, and a similar model may be needed to explain the patterns of genetic variation in natural populations of other fishes and vertebrates.

SUMMARY AND FUTURE RESEARCH

Genetic variability in mosquitofish is among the highest found for vertebrates. High divergence in allele frequencies among subpopulations occurs even over short distances despite high estimated gene flow. High dispersal rates result in large effective metapopulation sizes, which, along with selection for higher heterozygosities among adults, could account for the high genetic variability.

Relatively large differences in genotypic proportions and multilocus heterozygosity frequently occur among fish of the various sex-age classes. Subpopulations that undergo frequent bottlenecks and subsequent expansions are not likely to be in equilibrium. There is a trend for a deficiency of heterozygotes, especially among embryos and juveniles. Such a deficiency is at least partially due to inbreeding during the early expansion phase following temporary bottlenecks. Sperm storage, multiple insemination, and high reproductive potential, however, ameliorate the effects of reduced population size on genetic characteristics. Drift and demographic differences are probably the primary causes of temporal and spatial heterogeneity.

Drift effects amplified by rapid population expansion create spatial divergence in allele frequencies that dispersal is not totally able to counteract. Dispersal is also not random with respect to genotype, and this could further increase spatial heterogeneity in allele frequencies. Even though local divergence is high, the average effect of dispersal results in spatial autocorrelation over distances of 6 to 150 km.

Low-level selection must also operate on the new allelic combinations continuously generated by drift and gene flow, but high dispersal rates make it difficult to produce strong microgeographic adaptation. Geographical isolation and subsequent evolution have resulted in speciation and differentiation of genetically distinct forms in southeastern United States. Two previously recognized subspecies are actually species (*G. affinis* and *G. holbrooki*), and there are probably three forms of *G. holbrooki*. On a finer scale, drift, dispersal, and selection produce a dynamic equilibrium between the subpopulations that form larger metapopulations.

Future research on the population biology of poeciliids should concentrate on the causes of genetic and demographic heterogeneity as well as interrelationships between them. Long-term studies of population dynamics and genetics must be conducted jointly. Annual and seasonal changes in effective population size and in the genetic and demographic composition of populations should also be documented. Methods are needed to directly measure dispersal and to evaluate its causes and genetic effects. Population growth rates during the early expansion phase need to be measured under a variety of conditions. These data will better evaluate the general evolutionary model proposed.

Experiments are necessary to evaluate the relative importance of selection, gene flow, and drift in determining characteristics of natural populations. Hypotheses should be tested concerning potential sources of selection and possible cause and effect relationships between genetic variability and demographic performances.

Additional data are also needed to confirm biogeographic hypotheses about the origin of different types of mosquitofishes. Finally, the generality of the results of studies on *Gambusia* spp. should be tested with other poeciliids to increase our understanding of the short-term dynamics and evolution of these species.

ACKNOWLEDGMENTS

We thank P. Leberg, J. Novak, and an anonymous reviewer for commenting on earlier drafts of the manuscript. Jean Coleman is gratefully acknowledged for her graphical assistance. We thank M. J. Godt, C. Fisher, S. A. Diamond, C. Lydeard, L. Robbins, M.W. Smith and E. Zimmerman for allowing us to quote their results prior to publication. This work was supported by contract DE-AC09-76SROO 819 between the University of Georgia's Institute of Ecology and the US Department of Energy.

Chapter 14

The Origins and Ecological Success of Unisexual *Poeciliopsis*: The Frozen Niche-Variation Model

JEFFREY D. WETHERINGTON
RUSSELL A. SCHENCK
ROBERT C. VRIJENHOEK

INTRODUCTION

In 1932, Hubbs and Hubbs reported the first all-female vertebrate, *Poecilia formosa*, and suggested that this small Mexican topminnow arose as an interspecific hybrid (Schultz, Chapter 5). Since this pioneering study, more than 50 unisexual vertebrates have been discovered. Nearly all are the equivalent of F_1 hybrids between two or more sexually reproducing species (Schultz 1969; Moore 1984). All-female reproduction precludes normal genetic recombination and the variability it engenders. Thus, theoreticians often suggest that such organisms are "evolutionary deadends" with minimal adaptive potential and a high extinction probability (Mayr 1970; White 1973; Maynard Smith 1978). Nevertheless, in an ecological context, unisexual poeciliids are remarkably successful, often coexisting with, and in many localities outnumbering, the sexual lineages from which they arose (Schultz 1977; Vrijenhoek 1979a, 1984a, 1984b; Moore 1984).

Unisexuality and hybridity are intimately coupled in the vertebrates. Thus, it has proven difficult to distinguish the individual contributions of unisexuality and hybridity to the ecological success of unisexual vertebrates. Moore (1984) provides a thoughtful critique of alternative hypotheses regarding ecological success of unisexual vertebrate lineages; however, the search for broad generalities has been complicated by the discovery that many populations are actually composed of diverse assemblages of genetically distinct clones (Vrijenhoek et al. 1977, 1978; Angus and Schultz 1979; Parker 1979; Angus 1980). The Frozen Niche-Variation Model was developed to account for coexistence of genetically related clones with one another and with sexual relatives (Vrijenhoek 1979, 1984a, 1984b).

Accordingly, multiple origins of clones from genetically variable sexual ancestors produce a broad array of phenotypically diversified unisexual genotypes. Interclonal selection eliminates clones with substantial niche overlap. The result is a structured assemblage of clonal genotypes that exploit the breadth of available resources in heterogeneous environments. Ecological differences among surviving clones account for coexistence. Thus, the success of natural unisexuals results from the selection of clones from a broad spectrum of genotypes that arose via multiple clonal origins. Similar models based on interclonal resource partitioning have been explored by Bell (1982) and by Case and Taper (1986).

The Frozen Niche-Variation Model is based on two assumptions. First, distinct clones had independent origins from sexual ancestors. Although mutation has played a role in generating some clonal diversity (Leslie and Vrijenhoek 1980; Spinella and Vrijenhoek 1982), electrophoretic evidence from many unisexual populations supports multiple origins as the primary source of clonal diversity (Parker and Selander 1976; Vrijenhoek et al. 1977, 1978; Moore 1984). Second, the sexual progenitors of clonal lineages possess genetic variability for phenotypic characters that affect niche breadth (see Roughgarden 1972). Different clones are "frozen" genotypes that existed in the sexual gene pool.

In this chapter, we review the results of recent laboratory and field studies of *Poeciliopsis* spp. First, our success at synthesizing many new unisexual strains in the laboratory demonstrates the feasibility of multiple clonal origins. Second, our laboratory studies of these synthetic clones demonstrate that ecologically relevant genetic variation can be frozen from the gene pool of the sexual ancestors. Finally, field studies demonstrate ecological differences among coexisting clones and their sexual ancestors. These differences reduce competition and thereby facilitate coexistence.

EXPERIMENTAL ANIMAL

The genus *Poeciliopsis* comprises approximately 18 species that inhabit rivers of western Mexico. *Poeciliopsis monacha*, the common sexual ancestor to all the unisexual biotypes (Schultz, Chapter 5), is restricted to headwater springs and arroyos near the border of the states of Sinaloa and Sonora. *Poeciliopsis lucida*, *P. occidentalis*, and *P. latidens* inhabit broader and more permanent rivers from southern Arizona through southern Sinaloa. In zones of overlap between *P. monacha* and these riverine species, multiple hybridization events have given rise to an array of diploid and triploid all-female biotypes.

The laboratory studies described herein were performed with the diploid hybridogenetic biotypes *P. monacha-lucida* (**ML**) and *P. monacha-occidentalis* (**MO**) (Schultz 1969, 1971). The oogenetic process in *P. monacha-lucida* transmits only the *monacha* chromosome set (**M**) to each ovum (Figure 14–1a). The paternal *lucida* set (**L**) is expelled in a premeiotic cell division, thereby precluding synapsis and recombination (Cimino 1972a). In nature, the haploid **M** ova produced by

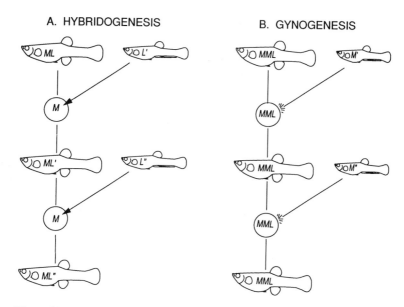

Figure 14–1. Hybridogenetic (A) and gynogenetic (B) reproduction in *Poeciliopsis*. The letters **M** and **L** denote *monacha* and *lucida* genomes, and the primes denote different markers for the paternal *lucida* genome.

ML females are fertilized by *lucida* sperm (**L′**) and a new **ML′** hybrid expressing traits encoded by both parental genomes is formed (Schultz 1966; Vrijenhoek 1972). Only the maternal **M** genome of a hybridogenetic strain is cloned; the paternal genome is substituted in each generation. We refer to distinct haploid **M** genotypes as hemiclones (Vrijenhoek et al. 1977). Oogenesis in *P. monacha-occidentalis* is identical except that a paternal *occidentalis* (**O**) genome is substituted in each generation.

Our field studies focused on ecological relationships among clones of the triploid gynogenetic biotype *P. 2 monacha-lucida* (Schultz 1969). These clones possess two haploid sets of *P. monacha* chromosomes and one set of *P. lucida* chromosomes. Gynogenesis is a strictly clonal mode of reproduction; the entire triploid genome is faithfully replicated (Figure 14–1b). Gynogenetic females require sperm from sexual males in order to initiate egg cleavage; however, the sperm makes no genetic contribution to the offspring (Cimino 1972b).

Sperm dependence forces hybridogenetic and gynogenetic unisexuals to coexist with a closely related sexual species. Competitively excluding the sexual host, or escaping interactions with it by colonizing new environments, would result in local extinction of the unisexual. Analytical models suggest that some form of density- or frequency-dependent mating success is required for stable coexistence between a sperm-dependent parasite and its sexual host (Moore 1976; Stenseth et al. 1985). Niche partitioning between these clones and related sexual forms is not a prerequisite in these models. While undoubtedly playing an important role in the evolution of unisexual populations, sperm-dependence alone cannot explain the coexistence of numerous genetically distinct clones. Our approach has been to treat each genetic lineage, sexual or clonal, as a potentially unique ecological phenotype.

MULTIPLE ORIGINS OF CLONES

According to the Frozen Niche-Variation Model, ecologically distinct clones arise independently from hybridizations between sexual ancestors. Electrophoretic studies provided the earliest conclusive evidence for multiple hybrid origins of unisexual vertebrates (Vrijenhoek 1972; Parker and Selander 1976; Vrijenhoek et al. 1977, 1978). Most of the allozymes that distinguished among clones also occurred in sympatric populations of the sexual species. Thus, each clone froze a different combination of alleles present in the founding sexual populations. Tissue grafting studies also provided support for multiple clonal origins (Kallman 1964c; Angus and Schultz 1979; Moore and Eisenbrey 1979; Angus 1980).

The feasibility of multiple origins was demonstrated directly through laboratory crosses. Schultz (1973a) synthesized viable and fertile unisexuals by crossing *P. monacha* females with *P. lucida* males. More than 67 matings produced only five viable hybrid strains, but they were all females and spontaneously hybridogenetic. Difficulties with this cross derive primarily from a disparity between a large-egged (*P. monacha*) and small-egged (*P. lucida*) species (see Schultz, Chapter 5). To increase the likelihood of successful hybridizations, Wetherington et al. (1987) crossed *P. monacha* females (hereafter referred to as foundresses) with *P. occidentalis* males (Figure 14–2, cross 1). Egg sizes in these species are more similar (Thibault and Schultz 1978). Thirty percent of 69 crosses produced viable **MO** hybrids. Seventy percent of 148 **MO** progeny survived to sexual maturity (approximately 120 days postpartum), and all were females.

To determine whether the **MO** females were spontaneously hybridogenetic, we crossed them with an isogenic strain of *P. lucida* (strain S68–4 PC) (Figure 14–2, cross 2). Forty-three percent of 70 females tested were fertile hybridogens producing **ML** progeny. The remaining 57% were either sterile or incapable of producing viable progeny. Viability and fertility of the **MO** hybrids depended on geographic origin of the *P. monacha* foundress; nevertheless, all fertile **MO** hybrids were spontaneously hybridogenetic. The diagnostic dorsal fin spot and allozymes encoded by the *occidentalis* genome were replaced by *lucida* alleles in the **ML** generation. Thus, the ability to synthesize new clonal lineages in the laboratory supports the idea that recurrent clonal synthesis in nature can provide a continuous source of new clones. Clearly, what we can accomplish in the laboratory has probably occurred many times in nature during the past few thousand years. Nevertheless, many developmental, behavioral, and ecological constraints limit the successful establishment of new clones in nature (reviewed in Vrijenhoek 1989).

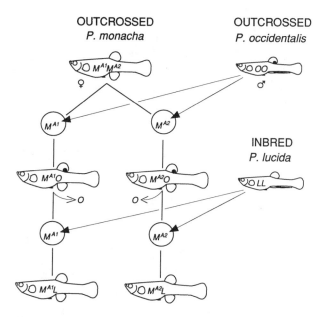

Figure 14–2. Experimental crosses used to synthesize hemiclones of *Poeciliopsis*. The letters **M, L,** and **O**, respectively, represent the *monacha, lucida,* and *occidentalis* genomes. Different haploid *monacha* genomes (**A1, A2, . . . , An**) produced by a *monacha* foundress are "frozen" in synthetic hemiclones ($M^{A1}O$, $M^{A2}O$, . . . , $M^{An}O$) in cross 1. In cross 2, the haploid *monacha* genome is transmitted intact in the egg; however, the *occidentalis* genome is replaced by *lucida*. This is visually evident in the progeny by loss of the dorsal fin spot characteristic of *P. occidentalis* (modified from Wetherington et al. 1987).

GENETIC VARIATION FROZEN FROM SEXUAL ANCESTORS

The second assumption of the Frozen Niche-Variation Model is that ecologically relevant variation can be frozen from the gene pool of the sexual ancestors. For this to be valid, the sexual ancestors must maintain considerable genetic variation for traits that affect niche breadth and life history characteristics. For *Poeciliopsis*, this variation must reside in *P. monacha*, the common ancestor to all unisexual biotypes. Analysis of diversity among naturally occurring clones does not provide a sufficient test of this assumption, because extant clones may represent a highly select subset of unisexual lineages and not exhibit the range of phenotypic variation that could be frozen from the sexual gene pool. Furthermore, original differences frozen among clones cannot be distinguished from postformational divergence due to mutation.

To test the second assumption, Wetherington et al. (1989) examined phenotypic variation in birth length, birth weight, and juvenile growth rate among 14 synthetic *P. monacha-lucida* hemiclones derived from Río Fuerte and Río

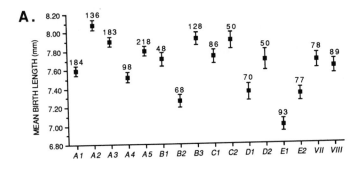

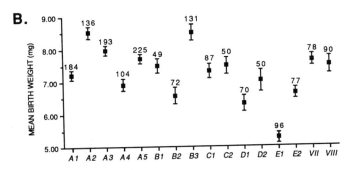

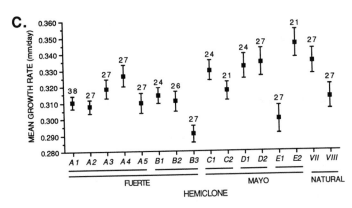

Figure 14–3. Mean birth length (A), mean birth weight (B), and mean juvenile growth rate under a high-quality diet (C) for 14 strains of synthetic hemiclones of *Poeciliopsis*. Natural hemiclones **ML/VII** and **ML/VIII** are shown for comparison. Vertical bars denote two standard errors about the mean. Sample sizes are given above the bars for each strain (modified from Wetherington et al. 1989).

Mayo *P. monacha* foundresses. Natural hemiclonal strains **ML/VII** (strain S68–4 Cw) and **ML/VIII** (strain T70–3 Cw) were included for comparative purposes. These two hemiclones coexist with *P. monacha* and *P. lucida* in the Río Fuerte (Schenck and Vrijenhoek 1986). The substitutable paternal genome of all strains was standardized by using an isogenic strain of *P. lucida* (S68–4 PC, Angus and Schultz 1983). Thus, genetic differences among strains were attributable to only the clonal *monacha* genome.

Wetherington et al. (1989) examined offspring of two to three broods produced by each of three females of each strain. Standard length and wet weight of all offspring from each brood were determined at birth. For analysis of growth rates, three offspring from each brood were randomly selected and raised individually. They were fed a diet of high protein commercial trout chow twice daily. Standard lengths were determined from photographic negatives of individual fish on the day of birth and at weekly intervals for nine weeks. The growth rate of each fish was estimated by the slope of the regression line of standard length on age (in days). Wetherington et al. (1989) provide details of rearing procedures and statistical methodology.

Synthetic and natural hemiclones exhibited substantial phenotypic variation for each of the three life history traits (Figure 14–3). For the synthetic hemiclones, we hierarchically partitioned phenotypic variation into genetic and environmental components (Table 14–1). The genetic variance (V_G) was estimated from the difference among hemiclonal strains and was hierarchically partitioned into three components. First, $V_{G(r)}$, the variance among rivers (Río Fuerte versus Río Mayo), was not significant for any of the life history traits. Second, $V_{G(f)}$, the variance among *P. monacha* foundresses, was also not significant for any trait. Finally, $V_{G(h)}$, the variance among hemiclones synthesized from the same *P. monacha* foundress (hereafter referred to as sibling hemiclones), was significant for all three traits, accounting for 24% of the total phenotypic variation in birth length, 23% in birth weight, and 9% in growth rate. The environmental variance (V_E) was estimated from differences among offspring within a hemiclonal strain and was hierarchically partitioned into three components. $V_{E(m)}$ is the variance among mothers within a strain, $V_{E(b)}$ is the variance among broods within mothers, and $V_{E(o)}$ is the variance within broods. These nongenetic factors ($V_{E(m)} + V_{E(b)} + V_{E(o)}$) accounted for the remaining 53%, 59%, and 85% of the total phenotypic variance in birth length, birth weight, and growth rate, respectively (Table 14–1). Because there was relatively little variation attributable to differences among mothers within hemiclonal strains ($V_{E(m)}$), the rearing conditions used in this experiment probably made only a minor contribution to the total environmental variance.

Natural hemiclonal strains **ML/VII** and **ML/VIII** were generally encompassed within the range of phenotypic variation exhibited by the synthetic hemiclones for each of the three life history traits. There were no phenotypic differences between natural hemiclones in mean birth length or birth weight; however, mean growth rate of **ML/VII** was greater than that of **ML/VIII** (Figure 14–3). Schultz

TABLE 14–1. Analysis of Variance for Hemiclonal Genotypes Derived from the Ríos Fuerte and Mayo. River = variation between rivers; Foundress = variation among founding *P. monacha* females nested within rivers; Hemiclone = variation among sibling hemiclones nested within foundresses; Mother = variation among mothers nested within hemiclonal genotypes; Brood = variation among broods nested within mothers; and Offspring = variation among offspring nested within broods.

Source	d.f.	SS	M#	F-Ratio	F	P	Variance Components
A. Standard length at birth ($R^2 = 0.67$)							
Model	131	171.56			20.58	0.000	—
River $V_{G(r)}$	1	10.32	M1	M1/M7	1.06	0.379	0.000 (0%)
Foundress $V_{G(f)}$	3	29.25	M2	M2/M3	2.01	0.183	0.042 (23%)
Hemiclone $V_{G(h)}$	9	43.58	M3	M3/M4	11.52	0.000	0.044 (24%)
Mother $V_{E(m)}$	35	14.71	M4	M4/M5	0.99	0.499	0.001 (1%)
Brood $V_{E(b)}$	83	35.26	M5	M5/M6	6.67	0.000	0.034 (18%)
Offspring $V_{E(o)}$	1325	84.34	M6	M6/M7			0.064 (34%)
			M7				
B. Wet weight at birth ($R^2 = 0.62$)							
Model	132	1670.67			17.15	0.000	—
River $V_{G(r)}$	1	174.94	M1	M1/M7	4.35	0.128	0.323 (16%)
Foundress $V_{G(f)}$	3	120.60	M2	M2/M3	0.85	0.500	0.046 (3%)
Hemiclone $V_{G(h)}$	9	425.18	M3	M3/M4	7.94	0.000	0.467 (23%)
Mother $V_{E(m)}$	35	208.25	M4	M4/M5	1.24	0.212	0.058 (3%)
Brood $V_{E(b)}$	84	403.59	M5	M5/M6	6.51	0.000	0.375 (19%)
Offspring $V_{E(o)}$	1391	1026.26	M6	M6/M7			0.738 (37%)
			M7				
C. Juvenile growth rate ($R^2 = 0.42$)*							
Model	124	207.67			1.96	0.000	—
River $V_{G(r)}$	1	18.94	M1	M1/M7	7.92	0.067	0.100 (8%)
Foundress $V_{G(f)}$	3	7.18	M2	M2/M3	0.56	0.655	−0.026 (−2%)
Hemiclone $V_{G(h)}$	9	38.50	M3	M3/M4	2.69	0.019	0.102 (9%)
Mother $V_{E(m)}$	31	49.30	M4	M4/M5	1.45	0.094	0.062 (5%)
Brood $V_{E(b)}$	80	87.57	M5	M5/M6	1.28	0.078	0.082 (7%)
Offspring $V_{E(o)}$	242	206.60	M6	M6/M7			0.854 (73%)
			M7				

* SS $\times\ 10^{-3}$; variance components $\times\ 10^{-3}$

and Fielding (1989) also reported that **ML/VII** grows significantly faster on average than **ML/VIII**.

In addition to differences in length and weight at birth and juvenile growth rate, newly synthesized hemiclones also freeze differences in phenotypic plasticity. Wetherington (1988) assessed effects of variation in food quality on growth rates. Four strains of synthetic hemiclones were raised on a low-quality diet (commercial catfish chow fed three times per week); natural hemiclones **ML/VII** and **ML/VIII** also were compared. To estimate growth rate under this low-quality diet, the offspring of two broods produced by each of three females were examined. Six offspring from each brood were randomly selected and raised individually. Standard lengths were determined at birth from photographic negatives, and at three-week intervals for nine weeks. The growth rate of each fish was estimated by the slope of the regression of standard length on age (in days). Wetherington (1988) provides details of rearing procedures and statistical methodology.

As expected, mean daily growth rates of the synthetic hemiclones were reduced on the low-quality diet; however, not all hemiclonal genotypes responded equally. A significant genotype by environment interaction was found. Consequently, the changes in growth rates of synthetic hemiclones under the two diets were not parallel (Figure 14-4). In contrast, no genotype by environment interaction was found for growth rates of the two natural hemiclones; **ML/VII** grew faster than **ML/VIII** under both diets. Schultz and Fielding (1989) reported a significant genotype by environment interaction in growth rate when these two hemiclones were reared at different temperatures.

Experiments with synthetic hemiclones clearly demonstrate that significant genetic variation in birth size and juvenile growth rate under a single uniform diet are frozen during the origin of new clones. Additionally, newly synthesized hemiclones freeze significant genetic variability for plasticity of growth rate. Since the substitutable paternal genome was standardized, this variation in ecologically relevant traits must be attributable to the clonally inherited *monacha* genomes. Thus, the raw material for the Frozen Niche-Variation Model appears to exist in *P. monacha*. However, caution must be exercised in extending these results to natural hemiclones. The substitutable paternal genome of natural hemiclones adds to the nonheritable variation, thus obscuring some of the heritable differences identified in our controlled laboratory studies.

ECOLOGICAL VARIATION AMONG SEXUAL AND CLONAL FORMS

Because each cloning event captures a different portion of genetic variation from the sexual ancestors, recurrent hybrid origins should freeze a wide range of ecologically different phenotypes. Recent studies of *Poeciliopsis* identified ecological differences among natural clones and their sexual ancestors. Schenck and Vrijenhoek (1986, 1989) examined the spatial segregation and foraging behavior of sexual

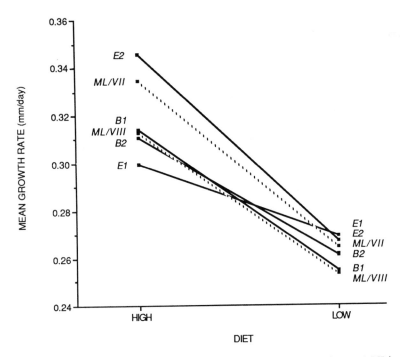

Figure 14–4. Growth rate reaction norms of natural hemiclones **ML/VII** and **ML/VIII** and four strains of synthetic hemiclones reared under high- and low-quality diets. Differences in elevation of the lines indicate genetic variation. Nonparallelism is an expression of genotype by environment interaction (see also Trexler, Chapter 11).

and clonal *Poeciliopsis* forms living in the Arroyo de los Plátanos, a small montaine tributary of the Río Fuerte. This short (approximately 1 km) stream, which traverses a steep gradient through a rocky crevice, consists of a series of small bedrock pools, each typically with a single current input and outflow. Substrates consist of rock, gravel, sand, and detritus. *Poeciliopsis* are the only fish in this stream. Male and female *P. monacha* coexist with all-female clones **MML/I** and **MML/II** of *P. 2 monacha-lucida*, a triploid gynogenetic biotype (together, the *monacha* complex).

The possibility of resource partitioning between clones **MML/I, MML/II,** and *P. monacha* was inferred from dentitional differences and preliminary dietary analysis (Vrijenhoek 1978). Schenck and Vrijenhoek (1986) observed that *Poeciliopsis* forms in the Arroyo de los Plátanos often exhibit distinct feeding modes. Some fish peck foods from substrates or feed at the surface in areas of still water (pool feeders), whereas others feed in the riffle of water flowing into pools (drift feeders). We sampled fish with these different feeding modes through one year (June and October 1980, and January and March 1981) and found that sexual and clonal fish were not equally represented in the two feeding modes (Table 14–2). Clones **MML/I** and **MML/II** were overrepresented as drift feeders, and

TABLE 14–2. Microhabitat Selection Among Adult and Juvenile Fishes of the *monacha* Complex in the Arroyo de los Plátanos. The hypothesis of no association between fish forms and microhabitats was examined among adults and juveniles with contingency tests. Juvenile males and females (<15 mm standard length) could not be distinguished, so all juvenile *P. monacha* were pooled in the female group. (Modified from Schenck and Vrijenhoek 1986.)

Group Habitat	Percent of Collection				N	χ^2
	P. monacha Females	Clone MML/I	Clone MML/II	*P. monacha* Males		
Adults						
Current	55.3	28.7	6.9	9.1	1,000	108.4 (d.f. = 3) P < 0.001
Pool	74.3	14.4	3.1	8.2	1,407	
Total (N)	1598	490	112	207	2,407	
Juveniles						
Current	39.6	38.4	22.0	—	152	10.2 (d.f. = 2) P < 0.01
Pool	43.3	53.3	3.3	—	60	
Total (N)	80	90	35	—	212	

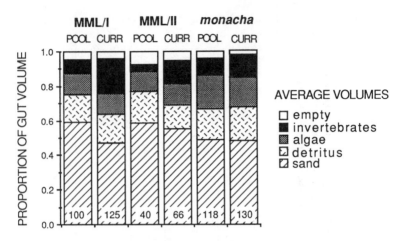

Figure 14–5. Average volumes for four broadly defined food categories consumed by *monacha* complex fishes of the Arroyo de los Plátanos. Data were pooled from fish collected during four seasons of a yearly period. Seasonal variation in *Poeciliopsis* diets is treated in detail elsewhere (Schenck and Vrijenhoek 1989).

P. monacha females were overrepresented as pool feeders. This pattern of microhabitat segregation was repeated in collections taken during each of four seasons. The magnitude of spatial segregation is particularly striking because current and still-water subsamples were never taken from more than 3 m apart in the same pool.

High recruitment in June, 1983, permitted similar microhabitat subsampling of juveniles (< 15 mm SL). Clone **MML/II** juveniles exhibited the same pattern of microhabitat selection as adults, but clone **MML/I** juveniles reversed the adult pattern, being overrepresented as pool feeders (Table 14–2). The possibility that different clones have frozen distinct developmental programs for foraging behavior is tantalizing and remains to be tested.

Ecological segregation based on spatial heterogeneity appears to be a widespread phenomenon among other mixed reproductive assemblages within *Poeciliopsis*. Schenck and Vrijenhoek (1986) reported microhabitat segregation among members of the *monacha* and *lucida* complex, including sexual *P. lucida* and hemiclones **ML/VII** and **ML/VIII,** in the Arroyo Jaguari at Agua Caliente. Current and still-water segregation also occurs between the sexual species *P. occidentalis* and hybridogenetic hemiclones of *P. monacha-occidentalis* in the ríos Concepcion, Sonora, Matape, and Yaqui (Vrijenhoek 1984a).

Microhabitat segregation was a strong determinant of diets of the two clones in the Arroyo de los Plátanos (Schenck and Vrijenhoek 1989). Both clones (particularly **MML/I**) increased the volume (Figure 14–5) and frequency (Table 14–3) of invertebrates in their diets by drift feeding. In contrast, *P. monacha* females had similar diets in both microhabitats.

TABLE 14–3. Frequencies of Occurrence of the Six Invertebrate Taxa Most
Commonly Consumed by *monacha* Complex Fishes in the Arroyo de los Plátanos.
Fisher's exact chi-square tests were performed to test the statistical significance
of microhabitat differences exhibited by each fish form. (From Schenck and
Vrijenhoek 1989.)

	MML/I		MML/II		*P. monacha*	
Microhabitat	Pool	Current	Pool	Current	Pool	Current
N	100	125	40	66	118	130
Food item						
Ephemeroptera	24.0	48.8**	12.5	25.8	27.1	35.9
Chironomids	25.0	38.4*	25.0	30.3	33.9	31.3
Ostracods	19.0	32.8*	15.0	27.2	18.6	25.2
Terrestrials	15.0	24.0	12.5	24.2	17.0	21.4
Trichopterans	9.0	24.8**	0.0	12.1*	2.5	16.8**
Copepods	2.0	9.6*	0.0	1.5	12.7	4.5*
All invertebrates	33.0	56.8**	22.5	43.9*	46.6	49.6

* = P < 0.05
** = P < 0.001

We initiated a field experiment to assess changes in foraging behavior in
response to manipulation of these microhabitat characteristics (Schenck and Vrijenhoek 1989). Individually marked fish were observed in pools covered with reference
grids. Fish were first observed in natural current, then observed again after the
current was diverted from the pool. Each member of the *monacha* complex shifted
its foraging and spatial behavior in response to manipulation. Clone **MML/I** dramatically increased its feeding rate on rocky substrates, and both clones decreased
feeding at the surface or in the water column (Table 14–4). In contrast, female
P. monacha did not change foraging behavior in response to the current manipulation.

The fish also shifted their use of current and pool microhabitats in response
to current manipulation. Under natural conditions, the triploid clones fed most
frequently in shallow water with relatively swift water currents, whereas *P. monacha*
females foraged almost exclusively in deep water with relatively slow currents.
When the current was diverted, *P. monacha* and clone **MML/II** responded oppo-
sitely: clone **MML/II** moved into deeper waters in which currents had previously
been absent, and *P. monacha* females moved into shallower areas that previously
had swift currents. Although clone **MML/I** showed the greatest changes in foraging
behavior as a result of this manipulation (Table 14–4), its use of current and
pool microhabitats was least affected by the manipulation.

The differences in foraging behavior and use of space exhibited by members
of the *monacha* complex can facilitate coexistence by reducing direct competition
(Schenck, unpubl. data). Our observations suggest that microhabitat selection reduces behavioral interactions among these fish. In the presence of microhabitat

TABLE 14-4. **Feeding Rates for Each Foraging Behavior, Presented as the Mean Number of Feeding Events per Individual per Minute. P-values from two-way analysis of variance for fish form and current manipulation are presented for effects that were significant (P < 0.05). (From Schenck and Vrijenhoek 1989.)**

	Fish Form						Analysis of Variance		
	MML/I		MML/II		P. monacha				
No. of Individuals	25	32	37	33	37	35			
Current Condition	FLOW	NO FLOW	FLOW	NO FLOW	FLOW	NO FLOW	Fish Forms	Current	Fish X Current
Mean Observation Time (sec.)	120.6	160.8	100.8	156.3	132.8	144.4			
Variable									
ROCK	1.55	15.94	2.86	10.95	2.33	0.20	0.0390	0.0033	0.0221
DETRITUS	10.33	11.59	6.87	11.27	5.86	8.65	NS	0.0021	NS
ALGAE	0.74	0.00	1.19	0.00	0.34	0.00	NS	0.0013	NS
MIDDLE	0.38	0.14	1.35	0.70	0.29	0.52	0.0194	NS	NS
SURFACE	1.41	0.09	1.71	0.12	0.22	0.12	0.0473	0.0001	0.0459

heterogeneity in the form of varying currents, estimates of competitive interactions revealed them to be weak or nonexistent. Removal of current resulted in stronger pairwise competitive interactions. Competition between coexisting sexual and clonal fish should be most severe during the dry season when currents are absent from most residual pools. Fish examined from such conditions consistently show effects of resource depletion and are often in poor somatic and reproductive condition.

SUMMARY AND FUTURE RESEARCH

Our studies of all-female *Poeciliopsis* clearly support the assumptions of the Frozen Niche-Variation Model. First, synthesis of many new hemiclones in the laboratory demonstrates the feasibility of multiple origins of new clonal lineages in nature. New clones can arise as siblings from a single hybridization or as nonsiblings from independent hybridizations. Genetic variation among sibling hemiclones was generally greater than that found among nonsibling hemiclones founded by different *P. monacha* females. This result was surprising, because sibling hemiclones are more closely related. Sibling hemiclones are identical by descent, on average, for 50% of their *monacha* alleles and 100% of their *lucida* alleles. Thus, their coefficient of relatedness (r) is 0.75. In contrast, independent hemiclonal strains are not identical by descent for any *monacha* alleles and share only the standardized *lucida* genome; therefore, r = 0.50. Thus, independent hybrid origins might not be necessary for generating clonal diversity. Single hybrid events may produce considerable hemiclonal diversity as a consequence of recombination in the founding sexual mothers.

Second, our experiments with laboratory-synthesized hemiclones demonstrate that substantial genetic variation for ecologically relevant traits is present in the sexual ancestors. Genetic variation in survival, fertility, birth size, juvenile growth rate, and phenotypic plasticity can be frozen during clonal synthesis. Although these synthetic strains do not occur in nature, the *P. monacha* foundresses from which they were "frozen" did exist in nature. Perhaps the differences observed among these strains accurately represent heritable differences in the ecologically relevant traits of the sexual ancestor. The phenotypes of natural hemiclones **ML/VII** and **ML/VIII** were generally within the range of variation exhibited by our synthesized hemiclones. Thus, the synthetic hemiclones probably represent the range of variation from which natural hemiclones **ML/VII** and **ML/VIII** were selected.

Laboratory and field studies demonstrate ecological differentiation among coexisting clones of *Poeciliopsis* in nature. In the laboratory, differences in aggressive behavior (Keegan-Rogers 1984; Keegan-Rogers and Schultz 1984), predation efficiency (Spindler, Schenck, and Vrijenhoek, unpubl. data), and juvenile growth rate (Wetherington 1988; Schultz and Fielding 1989) were found among coexisting natural hemiclones. Life history variation and physiological differences have been found among other coexisting natural clones (Bulger and Schultz 1979, 1982;

Schultz 1982). We observed spatial segregation on a local scale and found substantial differences in natural diets and feeding behavior.

Our studies of unisexual *Poeciliopsis* forms demonstrate that differences in use of food and space, life history traits, and phenotypic plasticity can contribute to resource partitioning and, presumably, to niche diversification among clones. According to the Frozen Niche-Variation Model, these differences are fixed from the range of genetic variation for niche-related characters present in the gene pool of the sexual ancestor. Ironically, the success of these nonrecombinant clonal forms depends on the recombinational genetic variation in their sexual ancestors. Recruitment of frozen sexual genotypes into unisexual populations permits the interclonal selection and resource partitioning that lead to the ecological success of unisexual populations. Without an opportunity for the origin of new clones, unisexual populations have only mutation and migration as sources of variation. These processes cannot generate sufficient phenotypic variation for ecological differentiation, and thus hamper the opportunity for the unisexual population to usurp a major portion of the niche of the sexual ancestor (Vrijenhoek 1979a, 1984a, 1984b).

Because of the diversity of breeding modes, the ease in which they can be manipulated in the laboratory and field, and the relative ease with which new clones can be synthesized, *Poeciliopsis* complexes provide an ideal system for studying a variety of ecological questions regarding unisexual species. In the laboratory, we are determining whether variation for other ecologically relevant traits exists in the gene pool of the sexual ancestor, *P. monacha*. We are examining phenotypic variation of trophic morphology, foraging behavior, predation efficiency, and egg production in the synthetic *P. monacha-lucida* strains. We are also examining phenotypic covariances of these characters so we can determine if new clones arise with the appropriate combination of trophic morphology and feeding behavior. Additionally, we will be able to determine if there is an energetic trade-off between growth and egg production. Because natural hybridogens can substitute paternal alleles, the results obtained with standard-bred **ML** strains might not be indicative of variation in natural populations. We are examining the contribution of paternal substitution to the phenotypic variance of ecologically relevant characters by varying the *lucida* genome of synthetic and natural **ML** strains. Finally, we are examining *P. monacha* and *P. lucida* to determine if these sexual species express greater phenotypic variation in their niche requirements, life history characters, and behavior than the individual **ML** clones to which they gave rise.

Poeciliopsis complexes also provide an ideal system for studying a spectrum of evolutionary phenomena. Attempts to estimate the genetic basis for ecologically relevant phenotypes in sexual species are complicated by the existence of unique individuals produced by genetic recombination in each generation. Replication of individual genotypes through cloning or vegetative propagation is more reliable, because genetic and environmental sources of variation can be estimated from the phenotypic variation within and between clones. Inbred sexual strains are most often used for such studies, but inbreeding depression may alter the physiological and developmental homeostasis of a normally outcrossed species through exposure of deleterious alleles (Falconer 1981). Conclusions based on specially constructed inbred strains may have little relevance to natural populations of outcrossed organisms. On the other hand, since cloning is impossible for most vertebrates, inferences from unisexual *Poeciliopsis* must be extrapolated cautiously to the sexual ancestors. Although our experiments demonstrate that *P. monacha* contains considerable genetic variation for ecologically relevant traits, these results cannot be used to estimate heritabilities. Dominance and epistatic components will be confounded with additive variation frozen among the clones. Also, hybridization itself might inflate estimates of genetic variation. Incompatibilities between different structural and regulatory genes in *P. monacha* and *P. lucida* genomes may alter developmental pathways in the hybrids, and thus, unisexual hybrids might exhibit unusual phenotypes produced by novel gene interactions.

We are continuing our field and laboratory studies of coexistence among naturally successful clones. Long-term studies of population dynamics are needed to characterize ecological interactions that facilitate coexistence. Although the ecological differences identified thus far are consistent with the Frozen Niche-Variation Model, a carefully executed removal experiment is needed to examine clonal competition under field conditions. In addition, niche parameters of adults should be compared to those of juveniles to determine whether ecological shifts are associated with development. Water current preferences and foraging behavior of juveniles might be critical to success, since juveniles are subject to entirely different feeding constraints, microhabitat availability, and predation pressures.

Finally, multivariate comparisons of ecological phenotypes of natural and synthesized laboratory clones are needed. If naturally occurring clones represent a highly select subset, then phenotypic differences between any two natural clones will be greater than that between any two randomly chosen synthetic clones. For the growth-related characters reported herein, this prediction is clearly not met. Normalizing selection might act on such life history characters in populations inhabiting a fluctuating environment (Lynch 1984). These characters probably do not directly affect niche relationships. In an effort to better test the Frozen Niche-Variation Model, our next goal is to study trophic morphology and feeding behaviors of these synthetic and natural clones. The variances and covariances among these traits should be highly illuminating in this regard.

ACKNOWLEDGMENTS

We thank Mike Bell for thoughtful suggestions regarding an earlier draft of the manuscript, and we especially thank Kathy Wetherington, Karen Kotora, and Carl Sadowski for their assistance in the care and breeding of fish. Research was supported by a Charles and Johanna Busch Predoctoral Fellowship and grants from the National Science Foundation (BSR 82–12150 and BSR 86–00661).

Chapter 15

The Evolutionary Ecology of *Poecilia formosa* and Its Triploid Associate

JOSEPH S. BALSANO
ELLEN M. RASCH
PAUL J. MONACO

INTRODUCTION

Poecilia formosa is a diploid unisexual of hybrid origin (Hubbs and Hubbs 1932; Abramoff et al. 1968; Schultz, Chapter 5), one of several unisexual vertebrates that reproduce by gynogenesis. Sperm from a related bisexual species are needed to initiate development of eggs (Hubbs and Hubbs 1946), but inheritance is strictly maternal (Kallman 1962a, 1962b, 1964c; Darnell et al. 1967). Females produce diploid eggs by apomixis (Rasch et al. 1982; Monaco et al. 1984), which involves suppression of meiosis I and results in no reduction division and no bivalents. Premeiotic endoduplication followed by normal meiosis occurs in most other gyno-genetically reproducing unisexuals (Moore 1984). This was also thought to be the case in *P. formosa* until the early 1980s, when that hypothesis was clearly falsified (Rasch et al. 1982; Monaco et al. 1984).

 Poecilia formosa occurs naturally in southeastern Texas and northeastern Mexico where it is a sexual parasite on sympatric bisexual congeners *P. latipinna* in coastal rivers and *P. mexicana* in inland rivers (Darnell and Abramoff 1968). Although *P. formosa* normally produce diploid offspring, triploids, which include the entire male genome in diploid eggs, have been reported for both laboratory-reared and wild-caught individuals (Rasch et al. 1965; Schultz and Kallman 1968; Rasch and Balsano 1974; Strömmen et al. 1975a, 1975b). Once formed, these unisexuals persist as triploids, apparently reproducing by gynogenesis, since they can be maintained in the laboratory only by matings with congeneric males (Rasch and Balsano 1974; Strömmen et al. 1975a, 1975b). We are unaware of reports of diploid offspring appearing in broods from known triploids.

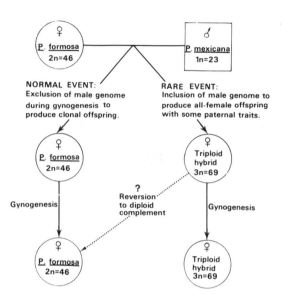

Figure 15–1. Relationship of the diploid *Poecilia formosa* to its triploid associate.

The putative parental species of *P. formosa* have yet to be confirmed by laboratory synthesis as has been done for unisexual *Poeciliopsis monacha-lucida* (Schultz, Chapter 5). In addition, biochemical evidence indicates that the taxonomic status of one of the putative parental species, *P. mexicana*, needs revision (Turner 1982). Since *P. formosa* was originally described as a diploid, it is inconsistent to include triploids under the same species. Furthermore, it is premature to follow the *Poeciliopsis* style of nomenclature and refer to triploids as *P. latipinna-* 2 *mexicana*, because the two *mexicana* genomes may be distinct. Consequently, we use the expression "triploid associate of *P. formosa.*" Pertinent information about the relationship of *P. formosa* to its triploid associate is summarized in Figure 15–1. These triploids comprise a significant, but highly variable, component of the natural populations of *Poecilia* in northeastern Mexico (Balsano et al. 1972, 1981).

Prevailing Questions and Hypotheses

Throughout our review there is a recurrent theme: different results are obtained from populations of *P. formosa* from different parts of its range. At times these discrepancies cannot be reconciled. Furthermore, results often differ from what is known about unisexual *Poeciliopsis* forms. Consequently, it is difficult to generalize some of the hypotheses concerning the evolutionary ecology of unisexuals.

Since gynogenetic unisexuals must mate with closely related bisexual males, they must not only coexist but also need to seduce males of the bisexual species. Two hypotheses have been advanced to account for bisexual-unisexual coexistence:

the behavioral regulation hypothesis and the resource partitioning (frozen niche-variation) hypothesis.

The behavioral regulation hypothesis is based upon well-developed mate preference by males for conspecific females and dominance hierarchies that restrict access of subordinate males to preferred conspecifics (McKay 1971; Moore and McKay 1971). During heightened sexual activity, these subordinates become indiscriminate and mate with unisexuals. Since such matings would be inversely proportional to the frequency of bisexual females, a negative feedback mechanism regulates bisexual and unisexual frequencies. In addition, mate preference is, in part, a learned behavior, and immature males may err during learning.

According to the resource partitioning (frozen niche-variation) hypothesis, bisexual and unisexual taxa are sufficiently distinct that they do not compete for common limiting resources. The beauty of this hypothesis is that it also accounts for other facets of the evolutionary ecology of unisexuals such as clonal diversity, geographic variation in bisexual/unisexual ratio, and so forth (Wetherington et al., Chapter 14).

DISTRIBUTION, ABUNDANCE, AND ASSOCIATIONS

Poecilia Complexes at the Center of *P. formosa*'s Range in Northeastern Mexico

Distribution and Abundance

The native distribution of *P. formosa* was summarized by Darnell and Abramoff (1968). The range includes the lower Río Grande valley of Texas and headwaters of all the intervening drainages as far south as the Río Tamesi near Tampico, Mexico. The species is also found in lowland coastal streams and lagoons around Tampico as far south as the mouth of the Río Tuxpan, and has been introduced into several other localities (Courtenay and Meffe, Chapter 17). Phenotypic male *P. formosa*, although very rare and uзually nonfunctional, were reported in several populations (Darnell and Abramoff 1968).

Triploid unisexuals were initially documented in five Mexican populations by Balsano et al. (1972) and subsequently confirmed by Menzel and Darnell (1973b) and Rasch and Balsano (1974). These reports all indicate that triploids are a significant proportion of the *Poecilia* populations in northeastern Mexico. Triploids near the periphery of *P. formosa*'s range have only recently been documented (Rasch and Balsano 1989), and their frequencies are extremely low. Because the Soto la Marina drainage is at the center of *P. formosa*'s distribution and has some of the highest triploid frequencies, we have studied the *Poecilia* complexes in this drainage most extensively.

Over 10,000 females from 20 locations in the Soto la Marina drainage were sampled from 1970 to 1978. Care was taken to obtain multiple and representative samples from as many locations as possible. The data, summarized in Figure

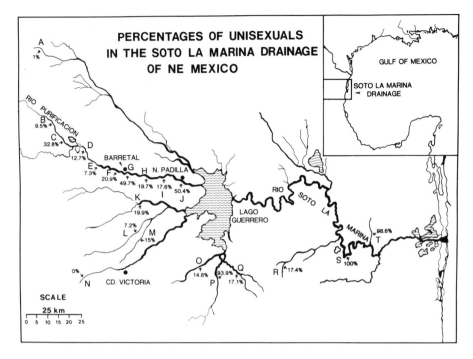

Figure 15–2. Percentages of unisexuals among female *Poecilia* from 20 locations in the Soto la Marina drainage, northeastern Mexico. Percentages are based on sample sizes of 4 to 2,225 ($\overline{X}$ = 514) collected during one to thirteen field trips including winter, spring, summer and autumn seasons from 1970 to 1978.

15–2, show that 32.1% of *Poecilia* females are unisexuals: 12.1% *P. formosa*, and 20% triploids. Great variation occurs within and among sites. Generally, female *P. mexicana*, the bisexual species, were more abundant in headwater localities: the correlation of percent female *P. mexicana* and distance downstream was − 0.793 (p = 0.06). Conversely, unisexuals increased downstream.

Locations A, B, D, E, L, M, and N in Figure 15–2 are all headwater habitats (shallow water over gravel), and all had at least 85% bisexual females and < 5% diploid unisexuals. Although site C is between two headwater locations, it had many diverse habitats due to a gravel pit that produced deeper-water pools with several cul-de-sacs. Similar sites were found at F, H, I, K, Q, and R, which showed 17 to 33% unisexuals but with triploids far more abundant than *P. formosa*. The deepest water, and sites with highest habitat diversity, are downstream at sites such as G (Barretal) and J (Nuevo Padilla) where unisexuals accounted for about 50% of *Poecilia* females. The Nuevo Padilla site is the furthest downstream collection for the Río Purificacion and had the highest frequency of *P. formosa* (30.4%). Arroyo Grande (P) and Arroyo Ratón (T) are anomalies: the former is a very silty bottom, turbid-water stream in which mollies have never been very abundant; the latter is a typical headwater arroyo no more than a meter wide in parts and often dries to a series of intermittent pools or desiccates completely.

We have previously reported considerable microhabitat variation in unisexual frequencies (Balsano et al. 1981), but unisexuals tend to be more abundant in the cul-de-sacs and deeper-water pools, whereas bisexuals are more abundant in shallows of the main river channel. These observations, coupled with increasing abundance of triploid and diploid unisexuals downstream, suggest at least a degree of resource partitioning among these three types of females that may account for their coexistence. Since triploids have two doses of the bisexual *mexicana* genome, it is reasonable to assume they are better adapted to headwater habitats than is *P. formosa*, with only a single dose. Geographic variation in bisexual/unisexual ratio may simply be a function of habitat diversity at any given location, which tends to increase downstream.

Seasonal Fluctuations

Seasonal fluctuations in frequencies of the three types of females are extensive, and chance phenomena can be quite dramatic (Balsano et al. 1983). Samples taken from the same sites during January, April, and June or July of 1974 were compared (Table 15–1). The seven collecting localities represent different degrees of habitat diversity. The upper three, Arroyo la Presa, Río Cobe, and Arroyo Moro have lowest habitat diversity and more headwater-like microhabitats consisting of shallow water flowing over large gravel with intermittent pools. When the dry season extends into early July, only intermittent pools remain, and on occasion they also are dry. The Río Corona has intermediate habitat diversity, and the two Río Purificacion localities have the highest. Only once in 22 field trips was the Río Purificacion not a flowing river at Barretal and Padilla. The Arroyo Grande is quite different from all other sites: it has turbid water flowing over a silty bottom; in some areas there is gravel just below the silt, and in other areas the silt is over 40 cm deep. It is similar to streams in a coastal plain.

There is no pattern to seasonal fluctuations in unisexual frequencies (Table 15–1). The 21.5% frequency of *P. formosa* for the June/July collection from the Río Corona is noteworthy, because none were collected in the previous two seasons. Chance is the most likely explanation: we may have missed them in previous collections or by chance happened upon them in June/July. In another situation, a collection of 80 mollies from a 100 m long, narrow, and isolated pool in the Río Purificacion at Barretal yielded 35.2% triploids in January, 1974. As the dry season progressed, this became two separate pools by April: 60 fish from one pool yielded 91.7% triploids, whereas 40 mollies from the second pool yielded none. The two Río Purificacion sites have the highest habitat diversity and routinely have the highest percentages of unisexuals in this tributary, from about 30% to over 75%, with a long-term average of 50%. Although we indicated that unisexual frequencies increased downstream within a tributary, this pattern was only evident

TABLE 15–1.   Seasonal Variation in Unisexual Frequency Among Female *Poecilia* Collected in 1974 from Seven Localities in the Soto la Marina Drainage of Northeastern Mexico. Letters within parentheses refer to localities in Figure 15–2.

Locality and Season	n	% Triploid	% P. formosa
Arroyo la Presa (M)			
January	96	8.3	0
April	66	21.2	0
June/July	90	11.1	1.1
Río Cobe (L)			
January	70	7.1	0
April	53	0	0
June/July	45	8.9	0
Arroyo Moro (Q)			
January	403	14.1	0.7
April	323	4.5	3.6
June/July	567	2.6	1.6
Río Corona (K)			
January	31	6.5	0
April	43	25.6	0
June/July	65	7.7	21.5
Río Purificacion at Barretal (G)			
January	128	35.2	7.0
April	279	38.4	11.1
June/July	512	21.1	8.4
Río Purificacion at Nuevo Padilla (J)			
January	90	45.6	28.9
April	228	28.5	47.8
June/July	595	15.6	24.5
Arroyo Grande (P)			
January	107	31.8	52.3
April	58	41.4	51.7

when data from different microhabitats at a location were pooled for all seasons and over several years. Apparently, random fluctuations between seasons and between microhabitats are so high that any pattern is obscured during a given year.

Poecilia Complexes Near the Periphery of *P. formosa*'s Range

The *Poecilia* complexes at the northern and southern limits of *P. formosa*'s range are characterized by extreme rarity or absence of triploids. Rasch and Balsano (1989) reported only four triploids out of almost 5,000 mollies (0.08%) collected from 1964 to 1982 from various habitats in the vicinity of Brownsville, Texas. One triploid was collected in 1967 and three in 1977. The 10-year absence is noteworthy because 11 collection trips were made, including 1 whose specific objective was to sample extensively in search of triploids. Frequencies of *P. formosa* fluctuated from 17% to 60% of *Poecilia* females with a long-term average of 37%. Hubbs (1964) made extensive molly collections from the Brownsville area but never reported triploids. Kallman (1962a, 1962b), who did the original tissue compatibility studies with *P. formosa*, obtained his stocks from the Brownsville area and reported no triploids.

Why are triploids so rare at the periphery of the range? Three alternatives include clonal variation in *P. formosa*, the type of host species, and the physical environment. Although clonal variability in *P. formosa* is extensive, it is an unlikely explanation for triploid paucity. Triploids occur with *P. formosa* in several drainages in addition to the Soto la Marina (Balsano et al. 1972). Triploids occur with mollies in the Río Santa Catarina (also called the Río Cadereyta), a headwater tributary of the Río Grande east of Monterrey, Mexico. In this locality, however, *P. mexicana* is the host species—an observation that suggests that the bisexual host is a contributing, if not the causative, factor.

Triploids are also rare at the southern end of *P. formosa*'s distribution from Tampico, Mexico, south to the Tuxpan drainage. Several hundred fish collected from lagoons and ditches in the vicinity of Tampico have been examined over many years, with no triploids found. Both *P. latipinna* and *P. mexicana* are host species in these coastal locations. Samples of *P. mexicana* include both northern and southern subspecies, *P. m. limantouri* and *P. m. mexicana*, respectively (Menzel and Darnell 1973a), as well as their hybrids. Triploid absence may be related to low frequency of *P. m. limantouri*, which is the subspecies found in all the northern upstream tributaries where triploids are abundant. The one triploid that was found, however, most likely resulted from syngamy of a diploid egg of *P. formosa* with a sperm from a male of the southern subspecies, *P. m. mexicana* (Rasch and Balsano 1989). This triploid was collected from the Río Tihuatlan, a headwater tributary of the Río Tuxpan drainage south of Tampico.

Do upstream, headwater habitats where *P. formosa* is found provide an environment conducive to the production and survival of triploids? Triploids are abundant in such localities but are rare in the silt-laden ditches, lagoons, and streams of the coastal areas around Brownsville and Tampico. Perhaps on rare occasions triploids arise *de novo* throughout *P. formosa*'s range, but they survive and are perpetuated only in the clear waters of upstream habitats.

Experimental Analysis of Fish Associations and Habitat Preference

Several studies were conducted to determine factors responsible for maintaining diploid and triploid unisexuals within breeding populations of bisexuals (Balsano et al. 1981, 1983, 1985). The first factor pertains to association of the three types of females in nature. About two-thirds of the time (210 out of 356 observations) a female *P. mexicana* was positioned nearest to her own kind, and over half of the time (173 out of 332) a triploid was closest to another triploid. Similarly, *P. formosa* were nearest each other slightly more than half of the time (173 out of 308). Females appeared to associate in subgroups of two or three of their own kind within larger groups that might include all three types (Balsano et al. 1981).

Two other field experiments were conducted to confirm and clarify behavioral interactions seen in laboratory aquaria (Balsano et al. 1985). Dominance hierarchies were routinely observed in all microhabitats that contained several males. All activities in laboratory experiments were observed in the field, but frequencies differed. Larger males characteristically occupied deeper or more shaded areas. Smaller males were more often in shallows or open areas of a pool or stream. Dominant males chased subordinate males out of their home range,[1] but subordinates were able to move freely in other areas of the pool and regularly court and mate. Subordinates did mate within the dominant male's home range while he was chasing another male or when he was less active.

When 30 tagged *P. formosa* were added to an 8 m × 4 m pool, they dispersed throughout and exhibited the same preferences for some sections as did resident fish. Not only were these alien unisexuals incorporated into schools of residents, but resident males courted and mated with them. Since the vast majority, if not all, of the resident females were bisexuals, the willingness of males to mate with the unisexuals may be attributable to their "foreignness." For example, male *Poeciliopsis lucida* are likely to mate with unisexuals of unfamiliar clones (Keegan-Rogers 1984); this may translate into a rare-female advantage in nature.

Habitat preference experiments were carried out sequentially in the laboratory and the field (Balsano et al. 1981). In a high-density situation (30 females in a 1.2 m × 2.4 m pool in a greenhouse), female *P. mexicana* preferred sandy substrate and both unisexuals preferred gravel. At low density (15 females/pool), all 3 females preferred shade regardless of substrate. In a low-density field experiment using an isolated, 6 m × 4 m pool with 24 tagged females and 3 males, all fish preferred shady zones with gravel substrate.

The fish association and habitat preference studies yield three major conclusions. First, all females showed a stronger preference to be in a group, even when "foreign" females composed the group, than to be in a particular habitat. Second, nearest neighbors were usually of the same type. Finally, habitat segregation occurs only at higher densities.

---

[1] In this study, the terms "home range" and "territory" can be thought of as ends of a range of related phenomena (Morse 1980). Individual males displayed characteristics of both ends of such a range while occupying the same area. Since territoriality implies that an area is occupied by one male, we decided to routinely use the term home range. It should be understood, however, that sometimes a given male excluded other males from this area.

REPRODUCTIVE BEHAVIOR AND MAINTENANCE
OF UNISEXUALS

Dominance Hierarchies, Sperm Production and Courting
Activities for Male *P. mexicana*

Other investigators have postulated that male dominance hierarchies are responsible for restricting access of subordinate males to conspecific females. Consequently, subordinates mate with unisexual females (McKay 1971; Moore and McKay 1971). We wanted to test whether this hypothesis applies to bisexual/unisexual breeding complexes of *Poecilia* and studied male/male and male/female interactions in both the laboratory and the field.

Balsano et al. (1985) showed that male/male interactions establish linear dominance hierarchies like those described in other poeciliids (Noble 1939; Braddock 1945; Baird 1968; Gorlick 1976; Farr, Chapter 6) and appear to function in home-range defense. Observation of an undisturbed stream and an experimental pool showed typical male behavior in defining and defending his home range from other males. There was also evidence that a home range was initially established by a dominant female who nipped at and chased males away from her favored feeding area.

Males are reproductively competent throughout the year (Monaco et al. 1981). Males of many poeciliids exhibit nearly continuous and vigorous sexual behavior, much of which is promiscuous (Constantz 1984). Males retain a large proportion of mature sperm in winter, a time when reproductive activity of females is minimal. This suggests that female reproductive schedules are more critical than those of males in maintaining a balance between unisexuals and bisexuals.

Quantitative analyses (Balsano et al. 1985) of four males and four bisexual females indicated that dominant males directed only 37% of their activities toward females and 63% toward other males. These statistically significant differences were inversely correlated with male rank in the hierarchy: females received more attention from males ranked lower in the hierarchy. The third subordinate directed two-thirds of his activity toward females and only one-third toward other males.

The repertoire of courting activities in *P. mexicana* is limited and the courting sequence short. Typically, the male initiates one to two activities prior to attempting to mate: dominant males showed 1.99 ± 0.12 courting events, whereas subordinates exhibited 1.79 ± 0.12 ($\overline{X} \pm SE$ based on 244 and 63 sequences, respectively). Absence of an elaborate courting sequence may explain why male dominance hierarchies do not prevent subordinates from mating with any receptive female. Occasionally a female would apparently try to attract the attention of a particular male, but she allowed other males to court and mate with her as well. Such behavior was observed in both bisexual and unisexual females. Most males (19 of 23 observed in aquaria) showed a preference for a particular bisexual female, but these males routinely courted and mated with other females, both bisexual and unisexual. Similar results were observed in the field. In one instance, a tagged male followed a tagged female in an experimental pool for five days: we observed no mating attempts during the first four days, but he did mate with other females; on the fifth day he mated with her several times. On that day she was also involved in several mating frenzies, which the dominant male unsuccessfully tried to break up, but the subordinates persisted until the female took shelter under a rock.

A series of laboratory experiments was carried out to determine the preference of male *P. mexicana* for two different females (Balsano et al. 1981). These studies indicated that males do not show a consistent mating preference for conspecific females. Males were promiscuous, and courted and attempted to mate with a bisexual or unisexual, whichever was more receptive at the time.

Although dominant males in an aquarium initiate more activity than all subordinates combined, subordinates may be as effective or more so in inseminating females (Balsano et al. 1985). Over 25% of dominant males' activities were erect fin displays, whereas displays involved only 13% of the activities of subordinates ($P < 0.01$). Conversely, 25% of the subordinate male's, but less than 14% of the dominant male's activities were mating attempts ($P < 0.01$). Subordinate males mated 170 times, whereas dominant males mated 132 times. Woodhead and Armstrong (1985) observed similar results for male *P. latipinna* and *P. sphenops*. Display, territoriality, and chasing occupied a significant proportion of large males' time, allowing small males greater access to conspecific females and more mating attempts. Parzefall (1968) previously noticed a distinction between early and late maturing male *P. latipinna*. Only large males display for females, and small males compensate for their size disadvantage by "ambushing" females (Parzefall 1979). Most mating attempts in poeciliid fishes do not result in successful insemination (Liley 1966). The proportion of mating attempts that do yield insemination, however, are assumed to be about equal for all types of males.

Reproductive Behavior in Other Species

Other investigators studying male reproductive behavior in bisexual/unisexual complexes, including *P. formosa*, have obtained results different from ours. Hubbs and Delco (1960) and Hubbs (1964) showed that both in the wild and the laboratory, male *P. latipinna* showed a significant preference for conspecifics over the Amazon molly; males typically directed 65 to 75% of mating attempts to conspecifics. Hubbs (1964) suggested that males from populations coexisting with the Amazon molly would devote only a few mating attempts to unisexuals, whereas allopatric males might be more indiscriminate. Woodhead and Armstrong (1985) reported that male *P. latipinna* or *P. sphenops* reared with their own, or with their own plus female *P. formosa* paid little attention to the Amazon mollies when the females were presented separately. Males reared only with Amazons, however, courted them as much as they did their own females. Furthermore, large dominant males ignored Amazons as long as conspecifics were available; small males were more indiscriminate, with a simpler courtship behavior. Woodhead and Armstrong (1985) concurred with Hubbs and Delco (1960) in suggesting that experience and learning may play a large role in mate preference. McKay (1971) made the same suggestion to explain the maintenance of *Poeciliopsis* unisexuals; adult *P. lucida* males show a marked preference for conspecific females, whereas small, subordinate males are indiscriminate. Moore and McKay (1971) reported that over 90% of unisexual *Poeciliopsis* females were pregnant when the female population was at least 22% bisexual. Moore (1976) estimated that at bisexual frequencies less than 20%, the probability of unisexual pregnancy was 0.3 or less, whereas it was almost 1.0 for the bisexuals.

Such studies raise several interesting questions. Are male *P. latipinna* and *P. sphenops* more discriminating in mate preference than male *P. mexicana*? Are males more discriminating when unisexuals are abundant and less so when they are rare? Are males more discriminating when reared and observed in laboratory aquaria than they are in nature?

When a female is receptive in nature, all males in her vicinity will attempt to mate with her. This results in mating frenzies that include subordinates and dominants. During an 8-day observation of an isolated pool with all tagged fish, 13 females were involved in mating frenzies: 5 bisexuals, 3 triploids, 1 diploid unisexual, and 4 that could not be identified. During these frenzies, males were not aggressive toward each other, but rather took turns thrusting at the receptive female. Furthermore, if males are present while a female delivers her brood, they will attempt to mate with her (Farr and Travis 1986), and if several males are present, a frenzy will occur. Persistent following and courting activity, however, was definitely biased in favor of bisexual females, 13 times versus only 3 times for both unisexuals.

Asynchrony of Egg Development and Reproductive Output

The first clue to the mechanism for maintenance of unisexual *Poecilia* forms was provided by a study of seasonal variation in percentages of various stages of oocyte development. Monaco et al. (1978) showed that, after oocytes progress beyond the earliest developmental stages, the percentages at each subsequent stage differed among the three types of females from a given locality at the same season and for different seasons. These patterns reflect asynchronous initiation of reproductive activity and/or rates of egg maturation. These presumably result in subsequent asynchrony in reproductive readiness. In other words, at any given time particular females, either bisexual or unisexual, can become reproductively competent and thus receptive. Due to the protracted breeding season, all three types of females are periodically serviced by available males. Similar data were reported for *P. latipinna* and *P. formosa* populations near Brownsville, Texas (Hubbs 1964). That situation was also characterized by 1) a highly skewed sex ratio, with a low, genetically-determined proportion of males; 2) comparable fertility in bisexuals and unisexuals but with different seasonal peaks; and 3) wide fluctuations in female fertility during the breeding season. We infer that these cycles of receptivity are responsible for the mating frenzies with all types of females.

Certainly one of the best ways to compare success of the two unisexuals in attracting males is to determine their reproductive output and compare it with that of bisexuals. We examined about 5,000 females from nine localities along the Río Purificacion, collected in winter, spring, and summer over an eight-year period (Balsano et al. 1985). Only during winter do female bisexuals show a significantly higher pregnancy percentage than the two unisexuals. When weighted by their respective sample sizes and combined for the entire year, there were no differences among the three types of females. The mean number of embryos was calculated for 1,524 pregnant females. During winter, triploids had significantly fewer embryos, but there were no significant differences for spring or summer, or for the entire year.

The product of the proportion of pregnant females and the mean number of embryos yields "reproductive output". Triploid and possibly diploid unisexuals have significantly lower values than *P. mexicana* in winter. Values for spring are about equal for all three types. Although reproductive outputs of both unisexuals for summer and for the entire year are slightly reduced, the production of females is about equal for all three types, if one assumes that 10 to 20% of bisexual offspring are males. Furthermore, triploid offspring may have higher survival rates: a two-year study showed that an average of 20.3% of adult females were triploids but only 8.7% of juveniles from the same samples were triploids (Balsano et al. 1983).

Since all females depend upon male *P. mexicana* for sperm, and since males typically account for less than 20% of the total *Poecilia* spp. at a given locality, we thought that sperm competition would be very keen. However, males are always reproductively competent, and no significant differences are observed in testicular maturation values associated with body size, hierarchial rank, or localition within the Río Purificacion. Males retain a large proportion of mature sperm in winter, when female reproductive activity is minimal. Females are asynchronous in initiating reproduction or egg maturation, which presumably is responsible for asynchrony in reproductive receptivity and mating frenzies observed in the field. Although dominant males prefer to court particular females (usually conspecifics), attempted matings occur with any receptive female. Since the proportion of gonopodial thrusting is significantly higher in subordinates than in dominants (at least in aquaria), subordinates may inseminate as many females as do dominant males despite their reduced activity. In nature the subordinate's access to a dominant male's home range is restricted, but the subordinate's hierarchical position does not determine access to receptive females. Consequently, our field observations indicate that competition among the three types of females for male services does not exist.

CLONAL DIVERSITY AND RELATEDNESS TO
SYMPATRIC BISEXUALS

Clonal Diversity: Río Grande and
Río Guayalejo Populations

Tissue transplantation techniques have been used extensively to demonstrate the clonal structure of natural populations of unisexual vertebrates. When Kallman (1962b, 1964c) examined *P. formosa* in the Río Grande drainage northwest of Brownsville, Texas, he found that all 45 females belonged to three histocompatibility clones. He subsequently found 8 additional, rare clones (K. D. Kallman, pers. comm.). *Poecilia formosa* from Brownsville had been introduced to the San Marcos River south of Austin, Texas, about 20 years earlier; all 133 San Marcos females tested belonged to the 2 most common Brownsville clones. The Brownsville population of *P. formosa* is noteworthy for ecological persistence and genetic stability of some clones, and absence of triploid unisexuals.

When Darnell et al. (1967) examined *P. formosa* from the Río Guayalejo (Río Tamesi drainage), they found that seven females belonged to one clone and five belonged to at least one other clone. Since all fish were collected from a single site in the shallows of the main river, nothing can be said about clonal diversity in relation to extensive habitat diversity at this location. Triploids occur at this location, but they were not studied by Darnell et al. (1967).

Clonal Diversity: Río Soto la Marina Populations

Our tissue transplantation studies of offspring of unisexuals from seven localities within the Soto la Marina drainage indicated that clonal diversity increases downstream where there is greater habitat diversity. Triploids have as diverse a clonal structure as do diploids. Paternal inheritance via *de novo* origin of triploids from diploid unisexuals was a rare but routine event, and some type of paternal inheritance also occurred without ploidy change. Consequently, we postulate that paternal inheritance is a major generator of the clonal variation observed in the Soto la Marina drainage; we describe several types of evidence for this interpretation after a brief discussion of clonal diversity.

Two results from our histocompatibility experiments (Figure 15–3) illustrate that clonal diversity is extensive and that mechanisms in addition to mutation are responsible. The Arroyo Moro sample of six diploids and three triploids came from two sites about 1 km apart. Lineages B, C, N, and O may be derived from the same *P. formosa* clone, which was distributed over at least 1 km of this arroyo; F and G represent another one or two clones. Since a C graft was also accepted by triploid host A, the triploid A clone was likely derived from diploid clone C. The most surprising observation was acceptance of triploid donor E

Arroyo Moro sample (1975)

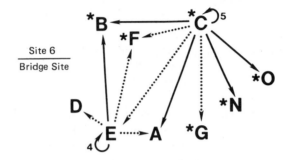

Site 6
Bridge Site

Rio Purificacion sample from Nuevo Padilla (1975)

Site 5 | Site 4

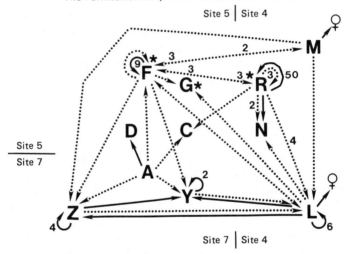

Site 5
Site 7

Site 7 | Site 4

Figure 15–3. Clonal diversity among unisexuals from two localities in the Soto la Marina drainage in northeastern Mexico (see Figure 15–2 for locations). Each letter indicates the offspring of a different wild-caught unisexual. Arrows point from donor to recipient of transplant; a solid line indicates acceptance for the lifetime of the host and a dotted line indicates rejection; numbers are shown for those transplants done more than once; ♀ indicates that a transplant from an offspring was made to the wild-caught mother of the lineage; * indicates diploid lineages of *P. formosa*. Arroyo Moro is a headwater location with the two sites about 1 km apart; the Nuevo Padilla location is the most downstream location in Río Purificacion with its three sites less than 250 m apart.

grafts by diploid host B; the graft setup was repeated and both grafts survived for the life of their hosts, 345 and 107 days. This suggests that either triploid E clone was derived by autopolyploidization from diploid clone B with some deletion of a histocompatibility locus, or that histocompatibility genes in the third genome of the triploid were not expressed. Consequently, there were at least two diploid and two triploid clones coexisting in a 10 m × 4 m pool, a site that is very often dry. Offspring of eight unisexuals collected from the same site in 1978 indicated at least three different clones.

The vast majority of grafts (86.2%) among offspring of wild-caught females from Nuevo Padilla were rejected. The intraclonal rejections involving diploid clones F and R (Figure 15–3) warrant further comment. Host 7F rejected three sequentially transplanted grafts in 134, 136, and 128 days indicating it probably had a deletion or mutation in a histocompatibility locus. Fifty-three grafts were made over six generations of R lineage fish. The three rejections all involved the same brood of third-generation fish: two hosts rejected a graft from a sibling, and black-mottled fish also occurred in this brood. Thus, this brood had something wrong with the normal gynogenetic mechanism that excludes paternal involvement in offspring. The peculiarity of clone R was also indicated by results of transplants between it and triploid N. Since one graft was accepted by host N while another graft was rejected, a third graft was made to the same host. This graft was rejected while the first R graft remained healthy on host N. At least two diploid and five triploid clones were represented in this collection of 11 fish from three sites within a 250 m section of the Río Purificacion. The extensive clonal diversity at Nuevo Padilla was confirmed in 1982 when 13 grafts among offspring from 10 wild-caught females were rejected.

The histocompatibility studies indicated higher clonal diversity in downstream localities such as Nuevo Padilla than in headwaters such as Arroyo Moro. This was correlated with habitat diversity. The unanswered question is how three or four clones can coexist with the bisexual species in such a limited area. Furthermore, some clones persist for a number of years and over a considerable length of the Río Purificacion, suggesting a broad niche, which further confounds the question of how so many clones can coexist.

Evidence for Paternal Inheritance

De novo *Origin of Triploids*

Several reports document paternal inheritance in triploid hybrids from diploid unisexuals inseminated by commercial black male *Poecilia* spp. (Rasch et al. 1965; Schultz and Kallman 1968; Rasch and Balsano 1974; Strömmen et al. 1975a, 1975b). We obtained 11 more cases and observed a higher occurrence of *de novo* triploids when *P. m. limantouri* males were used. When other males (*P. m. mexicana*, *P. latipunctata*, and *P. latipinna*) were used in matings for three years, no triploids were produced. Although over 2,000 triploids were collected from three drainages where *P. m. limantouri* is the host species, only 1 triploid involving

P. m. mexicana was recently collected (Rasch and Balsano 1989), 1 possibly involving *P. latipunctata* was reported (Balsano et al. 1972), and 4 triploids involving *P. latipinna* were found out of almost 5,000 *Poecilia* spp. collected from the Río Grande. Consequently, it appears that sperm from *P. m. limantouri* are more effective in stimulating *de novo* triploids than other types of molly sperm. This observation warrants further study to elucidate the basic mechanism of egg/sperm interaction. Laboratory data suggest that 1.5% of offspring of diploid unisexuals are triploid, and that 10.8% of *P. formosa* clones include triploids. Although the occurrence of *de novo* triploidy is rare, it must undoubtedly be a significant contributor to clonal diversity of the triploid unisexuals.

Electrophoretic Evidence

Poecilia formosa are highly heterozygous ($\overline{H} = 31$ to 33%, 35 loci; Turner et al. 1980b). This is not surprising, because *P. formosa* most likely arose via hybridization. However, the relatively low variation encountered within populations was not expected; only three genotypes were detected. In contrast, Turner et al. (1983) reported that variability among triploids was rather high; eight distinct allozyme genotypes were detected among 48 individuals. Furthermore, these triploid genotypes do not represent a random combination of host and *P. formosa* genomes; some loci from *P. mexicana* are overrepresented among triploids. Simanek (1978b) reported that samples of *P. formosa* uniformly had the B2 allele for phosphoglucomutase which was found in *P. mexicana* from the Río Purificacion but not in *P. latipinna* nor *P. mexicana* from other localities; a similar pattern occurs at the LDH locus. All these studies suggest that the host species do contribute genetically to both unisexuals.

Experimental Breeding

To verify paternal inheritance in these unisexuals, a series of mating experiments was set up using all-black male *Poecilia* spp. as sires. We obtained more than a dozen cases of mottled offspring from wild-caught diploid unisexuals or their laboratory-reared progeny and one from a triploid lineage; two sets are shown in Figure 15–4. The majority of offspring from these matings had wildtype coloration, but a few fish were mottled or spotted. Brood A_1 (Figure 15–4) is noteworthy, because it came from a diploid unisexual *P. formosa* collected from the Río Grande drainage near Brownsville; C_1 fish are *P. formosa* offspring from Arroyo la Presa in the Soto la Marina drainage. Despite expectations that these black-mottled offspring would be triploid hybrids like those previously reported, all these fish had scale epithelial nuclei with diploid amounts of DNA. There was no difference in DNA values of the wildtypes and any mottled fish. Similarly, the one mottled triploid had the same DNA value as its wildtype mother and three wildtype siblings. Thus, among offspring of triploid as well as diploid unisexuals, there are rare occurrences of expression of paternal traits without addition of an entire haploid genome. Kallman (1964c) had described similar pigmentation in *P. formosa* offspring.

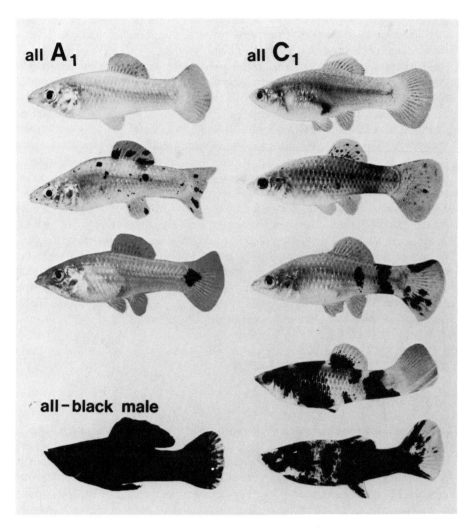

Figure 15–4.   Variation in expression of black pigmentation in offspring *Poecilia formosa* sired by commercial all-black males (*Poecilia* spp.). The mother of A_1 fish was collected from Brownsville, Texas. She had a brood of 9 offspring: 7 were wildtype, as illustrated by the top fish and two showed black spotting. The C_1 fish were derived from an Amazon molly collected from Arroyo la Presa, a headwater tributary in the Soto la Marina drainage. There were 43 offspring in this brood: 37 were wildtype females similar to the uppermost fish, and 6 were melanistic to various degrees, of which four are shown. All specimens shown had diploid amounts of DNA in scale epithelial nuclei. Seven other broods, including a triploid lineage, contained 1 or more spotted or mottled fish.

One of the most interesting aspects of these breeding experiments is the observation that all 87 F_2 offspring obtained from mottled or speckled F_1 daughters mated with wildtype males show no signs of black spotting but exhibit the characteristic wildtype phenotype. Consequently, black spotting is not perpetuated during gynogenesis. Since all fish were maintained at the same constant temperature throughout these experiments, it is unlikely that our observations can be accounted for by the temperature-sensitive melanistic allele described by Angus (Chapter 4) for *P. latipinna*. Furthermore, the expression of melanism in commercially derived stocks of all-black mollies is not sensitive to temperature (R. A. Angus, pers. comm.).

There are several potential explanations for these anomalous breeding results. One or two small paternal chromosomes may have been incorporated with maternal chromosomes in production of mottled offspring; absence of mottling in F_2's argues against this. Alternatively, somatic mutations, particularly of regulatory genes for the time and place of melanin production, may account for these observations. These aberrant results may also be due to transposable genetic elements that can restructure the genome at various levels, from a few nucleotides to entire segments of chromosomes. These breeding experiments clearly indicate that the genomes of *P. formosa* and its triploid associate are susceptible to invasion of new genetic material. Obviously, more breeding experiments are needed to elucidate the basic mechanism of this "on-again/off-again" pigment pattern.

SUMMARY AND FUTURE RESEARCH

Poecilia formosa as a Model System

Unisexual forms of *Poecilia* are perpetuated as fixed heterozygotes (Hubbs and Hubbs 1946; Abramoff et al. 1968; Monaco et al. 1982). Heterozygosity resulting from hybridization is not necessarily coupled to ecological success (Wetherington et al. 1987), but it provides a broad array of genotypes upon which selection can operate. By clonal reproduction, unisexuals can perpetuate advantageous gene complexes without suffering the usual cost of meiosis. Clonal evolution is thought to be due primarily to mutation (Kallman 1964c; Turner et al. 1980b, 1983). We believe, however, that clones also originate from the rare transfer of paternal genetic material to the genome of both unisexuals, and that this is a major contributor to clonal diversity.

Understanding the biology of unisexuals such as *P. formosa* will ellucidate an array of evolutionary and ecological phenomena beyond unisexuals. The varied reproductive modes provide unique experimental opportunities to evaluate gene/environment interactions, origin and role of gene duplication, the role of hybridization and polyploidy in animal speciation, and the adaptive value of sexual reproduction. *Poecilia formosa* provides an excellent model for addressing the question of how clonal diversity is maintained. If the nature of clonal coexistence were understood, we would gain insight into ecological aspects of niche specialization, resource partitioning, and adaptive radiation. Furthermore, *P. formosa* is an ideal model system to elucidate some aspects of developmental genetics. Since variation occurs in expression of paternal pigment genes within a single brood, understanding the mechanism of paternal leakage may provide new insights into gene expression.

Where Do We Go From Here?

Clonal Diversity and Coexistence

Two explanations have been proposed to account for bisexual/unisexual coexistence. First, male dominance hierarchies regulate sperm availability to unisexuals such that they are not likely to competitively exclude their bisexual host species (McKay 1971; Moore and McKay 1971; Moore 1976, 1984). Second, bisexuals and unisexuals are sufficiently different that they do not compete for a common limiting resource, and therefore coexist by resource partitioning (Vrijenhoek 1978; Schenck and Vrijenhoek 1986; Wetherington et al., Chapter 14). Our summaries for the bisexual/unisexual *Poecilia* complexes clearly support the resource partitioning hypothesis while falsifying the sperm competition hypothesis. Despite the highly skewed sex ratio in favor of females, sperm availability is not a limiting resource.

There appears to be greater clonal diversity in the Soto la Marina drainage than in the Río Grande or the Río Guayalejo. Although this could be because more habitats were sampled, we feel it is due to *de novo* triploidy. Furthermore, paternal inheritance data indicate that new clones can occur without a change in ploidy level in both diploids and triploids. Schenck and Vrijenhoek (1986) succinctly stated the selective advantage:

> Cloning effectively freezes and faithfully replicates multilocus genotypes which may encode ecologically relevant differences already existing in the gene pool of the sexual progenitors. Polyphyletic origins of new clones from a genetically variable sexual ancestor provide a wide base of variability upon which interclonal selection can act. . . . Given sufficient recruitment of new clones from a genetically variable sexual ancestor, interclonal selection should produce locally structured assemblages of differentiated clones that effectively subdivide resources. (p. 1060)

Remaining questions deal with the resources that have been subdivided and the nature of clonal specialization. Habitat diversity and the ephemeral nature of many headwater streams are, no doubt, important factors in maintenance of this clonal diversity (as well as contributing to clonal extinction). Differential response to temperature stress (Bulger and Schultz 1979), variation in female aggressiveness (Keegan-Rogers and Schultz 1984), differences in feeding behavior and diet (Schenck and Vrijenhoek 1986; Wetherington et al., Chapter 14), and differences in the onset of female receptivity (Woodhead and Carlson 1986) are some promising avenues for future research.

Mate Discrimination versus Promiscuity

Are male *P. latipinna* more discriminating in mate choice than male *P. mexicana*? That is the question raised by the review of reproductive behavior of these species. Studies dealing with female choice and receptivity as well as sexual experience, similar to studies in guppies (Farr 1980a, 1980b), need to be conducted with these bisexual/unisexual complexes before we can resolve these apparent differences.

Furthermore, we need to know what happens in the field (see also Farr, Chapter 6). We would have interpreted the "aquarium role" of dominance hierarchies in *P. mexicana* as a mechanism restricting access of subordinates to conspecific females, but that clearly did not occur in nature, where all fish had more space. Furthermore, mating frenzies were a prevalent aspect of reproductive behavior observed in the field and subsequently in aquaria. This prompts us to ask two questions: Do male *P. latipinna* engage in mating frenzies? How successful in terms of insemination are these mating frenzies?

Abundance and Paucity of Triploids

Why are triploids common in the Soto la Marina drainage but rare at the northern and southern periphery of the range? This question warrants further study, because it will not only provide insight into ecological relationships but also enhance our understanding of egg/sperm interactions.

It is possible that headwater habitats are more conducive to production or survival of triploids or the sexual species. Higher triploid frequencies were found among adults than among juveniles in the same samples (Balsano et al. 1983) despite triploid annual reproductive output being slightly less than that of the sexual species or the diploid unisexual. Since triploids contain an additional genome of *P. mexicana*, they should be intermediate between *P. mexicana* and *P. formosa* in various aspects of their niche dimensions. Their distribution and relative frequencies in the Soto la Marina support this hypothesis. In fact, relative frequencies in various microhabitats at the same locality indicate that resource partitioning is finely tuned.

An alternative explanation for triploid abundance relates to the host species. More *de novo* triploids occur when the northern subspecies of *P. mexicana* is used as the sire than any other source of males. We suspect that this relates to the hybrid origin of *P. formosa*, an event that involved the two sexual species, *P. latipinna*, and *P. mexicana* from northeastern Mexico. Some evidence suggests that the northern subspecies was involved (Abramoff et al. 1968; Simanek 1978b), whereas other evidence implicates the southern subspecies (Monaco et al. 1982). Subspecific intergrades are common in coastal lagoons around Tampico, Mexico (Menzel and Darnell 1973a).

Since Brett and Turner (1983) suggest that these two subspecies are highly differentiated, intergrades may experience gametic abnormalities that could have set the stage for the origin of *P. formosa*. We hypothesize that *P. formosa* developed from an intergrade egg with *P. m. limantouri* surface features and albumin phenotype but a muscle protein phenotype of *P. m. mexicana*; the egg was fertilized by a *P. latipinna* sperm. A survey of mitochondrial DNA from these various forms could evaluate this hypothesis. Such a hybridization event would provide *P. formosa* with a *limantouri*-like egg surface which may be less likely to exclude *limantouri* sperm than sperm from other host species. This could account for the abundance of triploids as well as the extensive *de novo* clonal diversity in the Soto la Marina drainage. It would also account for all the past failures of several laboratories to synthesize *P. formosa* from its putative parental species. To our knowledge, no attempts have used an intergrade female and a *P. latipinna* male; this warrants investigation.

ACKNOWLEDGMENTS

We thank the Mexican government for permission to carry out the field aspects of this research, which was supported by grants from the National Science Foundation, the National Geographic Society, the University of Wisconsin-Parkside Committee on Research and Creative Activity, and the Whitehall Foundation. The competent typing of the secretarial staff of the Science Division at University of Wisconsin-Parkside is also acknowledged.

Section IV

Conservation and Impacts of Poeciliids

With regard to conservation and ecological impacts, poeciliids have assumed an importance that belies their small size. Several North American species are endangered and one, *Gambusia amistadensis*, recently became extinct. Some species are exceptionally vulnerable due to limited natural ranges and extreme isolation. In contrast, other poeciliids have been widely introduced outside of their native ranges and are causing severe ecological disturbances. A great deal of time and money is being spent on both types of problems, but efforts often directly conflict: despite deleterious effects associated with introductions, many agencies and individuals continue to stock poeciliids under the mistaken and damaging notion that they effectively control disease vectors.

Conservation of North American poeciliids is reviewed by Johnson and Hubbs in Chapter 16; almost all efforts have been concentrated in the arid Southwest, where problems are most severe. They discuss present conservation efforts in light of conservation genetics theory and conclude that most species are probably not in danger of immediate extinction although long-term survival is less certain. Unfortunately, almost nothing is known about the status of poeciliids inhabiting areas outside the United States and Mexico.

The worldwide pattern and effects of poeciliid introductions are reviewed by Courtenay and Meffe (Chapter 17), who list all known introductions. They discuss positive and negative impacts of such practices and conclude that, other than for conservation purposes, there is no reason to spread these fish beyond their native distributions. They further argue that mosquitofish are ineffective mosquito control agents, and have had major and predictably negative impacts where introduced.

In Chapter 18, Arthington and Lloyd present a southern hemisphere perspective of poeciliid introductions with a review of introductions in Australia and New Zealand. Although a similar chapter could be written for most continents, more detailed work has been done in Australia, a country that has clearly recognized the dangers of exotic species. The authors corroborate experiences in other parts of the world and provide further details on the ecology of misplaced poeciliids.

Chapter 16

Status and Conservation of Poeciliid Fishes

JAMES E. JOHNSON
CLARK HUBBS

INTRODUCTION

Worldwide distribution of poeciliid fishes centers in New World tropical and subtropical areas (Rosen and Bailey 1963) and reaches its northern boundary in south-central United States. Species richness is highest in tropical regions of Central America, northern South America, and the Caribbean, all of which are under tremendous development pressures and are rapidly being degraded. Unfortunately, virtually nothing is known of conservation aspects of those faunas.

Of 14 poeciliids native to the United States, 8 are endemic to the Southwest (Texas, New Mexico, Arizona; Lee et al. 1980) (Table 16–1). The native southwestern fish fauna is largely composed of endemic freshwater species, a large proportion of which are protected as threatened or endangered (Johnson and Rinne 1982). Six of the 73 fishes protected under the federal Endangered Species Act are southwestern poeciliids (Johnson 1987). Five of those have recovery plans (Table 16–1) and one species (*Gambusia amistadensis*) has recently become extinct (Hubbs and Jensen 1984; USFWS 1987). A seventh, *Gambusia senilis*, is protected by state (Texas) but not federal law. *Gambusia geiseri* is the only southwestern poeciliid not protected by endangered species legislation, the result of its being successfully introduced into several Texas habitats.

Although most conservation efforts for poeciliids are being implemented at the periphery of their familial range, recovery actions are applicable to generic threats such as loss of habitat and interaction with nonnative species. In this chapter we review specific threats to poeciliids native to the Southwest and discuss legal and biological efforts to assist their survival and conservation.

TABLE 16–1. Poeciliid Fishes Native to the United States, Their Legal Protection, Status, and Distribution.

Species	Common Name	Status	Recovery Plan	Native US Distribution
*Gambusia affinis**	Western mosquitofish	abundant	none	Slowly flowing waters of central US from Mobile Bay west to NM, north to IL and IN
Gambusia amistadensis	Amistad gambusia	extinct	US, TX	Endemic to Goodenough Spring, Val Verde Co., TX. Extinct
Gambusia gaigei	Big Bend gambusia	endangered	US, TX (USFWS 1984b)	Original: Boquillas Spring, Brewster Co., TX. Present: 2 artificial ponds, Big Bend National Park
Gambusia geiseri	Largespring gambusia	restricted	none	Endemic to San Marcos and Comal springs; widely introduced into large TX springs
Gambusia georgei	San Marcos gambusia	endangered; perhaps extinct	US, TX (USFWS 1984a)	Endemic to San Marcos Spring and River, Hays Co., TX
Gambusia heterochir	Clear Creek gambusia	endangered	US, TX (USFWS, 1982)	Endemic to Clear Creek Spring, Menard Co., TX
Gambusia holbrooki	Eastern mosquitofish	abundant	none	Slowly flowing waters of eastern and southern US, east of Mobile Bay
Gambusia nobilis	Pecos gambusia	endangered	US, TX, NM (USFWS 1983)	Endemic to springs in Pecos Valley, NM, TX. Presently found in 4 spring areas
Gambusia rhizophorae	Mangrove gambusia	locally abundant	none	Brackish waters of south FL
Gambusia senilis	Blotched gambusia	restricted	TX	Devil's River, TX (possibly extinct); Rio Conchos, Mexico.
Heterandria formosa	Least killifish	abundant	none	Coastal waters of southeastern US
*Poecilia formosa***	Amazon molly	locally abundant	none	Lower Río Grande Valley of TX
Poecilia latipinna	Sailfin molly	abundant	none	Fresh to salt waters along southeastern coast from NC through TX
Poeciliopsis occidentalis	Sonoran topminnow	endangered	US, AZ, NM (USFWS 1984c)	Gila and Yaqui River drainages, AZ, NM

*This taxon includes the subspecies *G. a. speciosa*, considered a full species (*G. speciosa*) by Rauchenberger (Appendix 1).

**This is a unisexual form of hybrid origin and thus not a "species" in the usual sense.

CAUSES OF POECILIID DECLINES

Habitat Threats

Anthropogenic environmental changes, including dewatering, diversion, and channelization, threaten southwestern poeciliids (Miller 1961; Minckley 1973; Pister 1974; Deacon et al. 1979; Johnson and Rinne 1982). Most of these species have narrow habitat requirements and are often dependent upon one or a few springs for survival. Even minor impacts on these isolated habitats may jeopardize species that evolved in constant environments and may possess reduced genetic abilities to adapt to change. However, most alterations in southwestern aquatic habitats are not subtle: for example, 63 of the 281 major springs in Texas have ceased to flow due to human activities (Brune 1975).

Poeciliids formerly with wide distributions (e.g., *Poeciliopsis occidentalis*, *Gambusia nobilis*) have been extirpated throughout much of their range and are isolated in small springs and streams. Restricted endemics have gone extinct when their limited habitats were drastically altered (e.g., *Gambusia amistadensis*). The southwestern poeciliids that survive do so principally by chance; their remaining habitats have not been impacted, or changes are subtle enough not to have resulted in immediate extinctions. Three major premises for conserving these remnant populations are that their genetic base is sufficient for survival, habitats exist that can support them, and, with proper biological information and sufficient funding, those habitats can be preserved.

Threats From Nonnative Fishes

Native poeciliids are frequently impacted by a broad array of nonnative fishes, often resulting in competition or predation. Introductions occur for biological control of disease vectors, sport fishing, the aquarium trade, and protein supplement (Courtenay and Meffe, Chapter 17). Any nonnative fish introduction may negatively impact poeciliids, but some species appear particularly susceptible. For example, most southwestern poeciliids evolved in isolated springheads, with only a few (three to five) sympatric fish species, none of which are predaceous (Meffe 1985b). A new, larger, and predaceous fauna typically results in rapid losses of poeciliids.

CONSERVATION OF SOUTHWESTERN POECILIIDS

Conservation of any rare organism involves both egocentric and philosophical arguments. Kellert (1985) discussed many of these, relating protection an organism receives to values society derives; these include naturalistic, ecological, moral, scientific, aesthetic, utilitarian, and cultural values. The actual effort to conserve any natural resource depends on a number of diverse attributes, some of which are intrinsic to the resource while others are dependent upon societies that must decide if conservation is worthwhile. In 1973, the United States passed the Endangered Species Act to preserve species facing extinction as a result of economic growth and development. Under the Act and similar legislation by most states, rare organisms, including poeciliid fishes, are presently receiving protection.

Recovery plans, developed for endangered and threatened species by the US Fish and Wildlife Service, are documents to coordinate conservation efforts by private, state, and federal organizations. All five poeciliid recovery plans call for protection of existing populations and habitats, reintroduction into historic waters, maintenance of a refuge population in case wild stocks are lost, and publication of the plight of the species. Recovery efforts in each of these areas are discussed in general terms in this section and more specifically in individual case histories that follow.

The success of a recovery effort depends on how well recovery actions are thought out, how biologically sound they are, and how drastically they impact socioeconomic values. For species dependent upon a single spring, protection of the area and its aquifer are vital. Endangered species habitats on federal lands receive direct protection through the Endangered Species Act. No federal agency may fund, authorize, or carry out any action that jeopardizes the continued existence of a threatened or endangered species. On private lands, protection can vary from outright purchase of habitat to less specific actions like conservation agreements or easements that allow habitat management for the species. A refuge population is normally recommended in case the wild population is lost. To date, one poeciliid (*G. gaigei*) was extirpated from the wild and then "resurrected" through its refuge population when a suitable habitat was recreated. A second poeciliid (*G. amistadensis*) lacked suitable reintroduction habitat and became extinct when its refuge population was lost (see following).

The time scale is important in conservation of rare species. It is difficult to think and plan in terms of evolutionary or geological time scales, but such long-term planning must at least be considered when working with endangered species (Frankel and Soulé 1981). Survival over short time scales (years or decades) dominates most recovery plans in order to remove immediate threats. Long-term threats to habitats and gene pools are more difficult to anticipate due to changes in societies and their values over centuries and millennia.

Dexter National Fish Hatchery

Dexter National Fish Hatchery (DNFH) in southeastern New Mexico is operated by the US Fish and Wildlife Service solely as a native species refuge and hatchery. Constructed in the early 1930s as a hatchery for production of game species, it has proved suitable for rearing many of the warm-water endangered southwestern fishes. DNFH began endangered species work in 1974 when C. Hubbs and A. A. Echelle brought six Texas species to the facility to test its suitability as a native fishes rearing center. From that initial trial, DNFH has become entirely devoted to protection and propagation of native fishes (Rinne et al. 1986).

At present, 14 species are maintained at DNFH, including 2 poeciliids, but over its 13-year history as a native fishes hatchery, 22 rare species have been housed. The purpose of the hatchery is threefold: refuge, production, and research. The first species were brought to the facility because they were threatened with extinction in the wild, and a secure refuge population was necessary to restock habitats in case wild populations were lost. Production and research efforts have been added more recently. Presently, a permanent staff of nine produces over 3,000,000 native fish each year for reintroductions and research topics as diverse as interspecific competition, early life history feeding habits, artificial spawning methods, and allele frequency changes in captive populations.

Conservation in artificial environments is recognized as an important short-term measure to protect a limited portion of the gene pool from immediate extinction (Maitland and Evans 1986). However, long-term conservation measures must center around protection of the species within natural ecosystems.

Conservation Biology

Conservation biology combines ecology, population biology, genetics, behavior, modeling, statistics, and other disciplines into an in-depth study of a species, its habitat, threats to its continued survival, and its place in society. Concepts of conservation biology have been detailed by Soulé and Wilcox (1980), Frankel and Soulé (1981), Schonewald-Cox et al. (1983), and Soulé (1986, 1987), with certain aspects applied specifically to fisheries management by Ryman and Utter (1987). The results help biologists understand conservation from an expanded viewpoint and time scale.

A principal concern of conservation biology is the use of a few individuals to found new populations, whether in a refuge or in the wild. Central to this concern is the genetically effective population size (N_e), or "the size of an idealized population that would have the same amount of inbreeding or of random gene frequency drift as the population under consideration" (Kimura and Crow 1963). N_e is typically smaller than the census population size (N) due to uneven sex ratio of breeding adults, unequal progeny distribution among breeders, or large population fluctuations (Meffe 1986a). Small N_e can result in inbreeding depression and loss of genetic diversity through drift. To minimize these effects, founder populations should be as large as practically possible. Frankel and Soulé (1981) suggested a minimum N_e of 50 to minimize loss of variation through several generations, and 500 for longer periods. Other factors, of course, must enter into consideration, including historic levels of inbreeding, gene flow, and population differentiation (Meffe and Vrijenhoek 1988).

Large populations tend to retain high levels of genetic diversity or heterozygosity. High heterozygosity is often correlated with higher levels of fitness-related parameters such as size, growth rate, developmental stability, or fecundity (reviewed by Mitton and Grant 1984), although this is not always the case. Generally, loss of heterozygosity (or conversely, increased homozygosity) is thought to be detrimental to the individual and thus to the population (Allendorf and Leary 1986).

Most conservation genetics examples are derived from amniotic vertebrates. Poeciliids differ from amniotes in many reproductive parameters including larger brood sizes and shorter generation times (Williams 1966). Such rapid reproduction can allow quick recovery from population bottlenecks and reduce the extent of inbreeding depression and genetic drift following major population declines. Annual population cycles that produce many individuals and several generations during summer months and then decline to few individuals during winter seem likely to increase homozygosity and result in populations well adapted to their present habitats but not readily able to withstand habitat alterations. High homozygosity has been recorded in two of the endangered poeciliids discussed below (*Poeciliopsis occidentalis* and *G. gaigei*) (Vrijenhoek et al. 1985; Hubbs et al. 1986). Echelle et al. (Chapter 12) record three additional populations of spring endemics with high homozygosity.

Heterozygosity may be most important in a changing or severe environment, in that more diverse biochemical pathways are available in more heterozygous individuals. If the environment changes, it is more likely that a highly heterozygous individual (or its lineage) could physiologically adjust to new conditions more rapidly than could a highly homozygous individual (or lineage). Consequently, a problem may exist for any organism homozygous for attributes that promote survival in a specific time and place: if circumstances change, there is less opportunity for adjustment. As a result, a management goal for southwestern poeciliids is to maintain existing levels of genetic variation both within and among populations.

Meffe (1987a) raised the question of the proper taxonomic level with respect to conservation efforts: species, subspecies, populations, or even unique alleles. The species is the basic level of legislation for the Endangered Species Act and perhaps the lowest level to which most nonbiologists can relate, but the Act defines "species" as any species, subspecies, or population in danger of extinction throughout all or a significant portion of its range. Variation within and among populations of a taxon is perhaps the most difficult variable with which to deal when determining what should be saved. For example, Echelle et al. (1983) found that the four known populations of *Gambusia nobilis* differed electrophoretically more among themselves than do some recognized pairs of species. Vrijenhoek et al. (1985) reported that genetic diversity across the geographic range of *Poeciliopsis occidentalis* could best be interpreted as representing three subspecies. Some of these populations are highly heterozygous and are thus better candidate stocks for reintroductions, whereas others have little or no demonstrable variation but may be well suited to their existing habitat and are valuable for their genetic uniqueness.

Procedures at DNFH attempt to conform to many of the conservation biologists' recommendations. Originally, when new species were brought into the hatchery, an effort was made to obtain between 30 and 200 individuals. Now, a minimum of 500 fish are used (in both hatchery and field stockings) to provide a broad genetic basis for local adaptation. Of course, it is sometimes impossible to obtain 500 fish from the wild in species that are on the brink of extinction (e.g., *G. gaigei*, following). In these cases, we continue to work with what is available and closely monitor the population. Suggestions to increase heterozygosity of captive populations by mixing stocks from different localities, or even mixing subspecies, continue to be discouraged (but see Meffe and Vrijenhoek [1988] for exceptions).

The US Fish and Wildlife Service has just begun to investigate the genetic composition of species at DNFH, with some of the most interesting information pertaining to *P. occidentalis*. The initial DNFH stock came from Monkey Spring, Santa Cruz County, Arizona. Electrophoretic evaluation of five wild stocks in the United States (Vrijenhoek et al. 1985) indicated that most were homozygous for the loci tested, including the Monkey Spring stock, but that the nearby Sharp Spring population had higher heterozygosity. Between 1981 and 1984, DNFH stocked over 100 new sites with *P. occidentalis* derived from the Monkey Spring source (Simons 1987). Starting in 1985, that stock was replaced with more heterozygous fish from Sharp Spring, and since 1986 all new stockings have been made with that lineage. We eventually hope to compare survival of the two genetic groups to determine if the heterozygous populations are more successful. Results of stockings in constant versus fluctuating environments will also be evaluated to determine if the homozygous Monkey Spring fish are better adapted to the former situation.

SPECIES ACCOUNTS

We now detail the status of six southwestern poeciliids, chosen for the following reasons: 1) *Gambusia heterochir*—survival depends on a privately owned, one-spring system; 2) *Gambusia georgei*—recovery efforts incorporate an ecosystem approach; 3) *Gambusia gaigei*—endemic to federally protected lands; frequent low populations; 4) *Gambusia nobilis*—a widely distributed, spring-adapted species; 5) *Poeciliopsis occidentalis*—a widely distributed species now restricted to a few isolated habitats; and 6) *Gambusia amistadensis*—so others may learn from our failure with this extinct species.

Clear Creek Gambusia (*Gambusia heterochir*)

The Clear Creek gambusia is restricted to privately owned headspring waters of Clear Creek, Menard County, Texas (Hubbs 1957). When the fish was discovered (1953), Clear Creek had already been significantly altered by four dams approximately 100 m, 1.5 km, 3.1 km, and 3.5 km from the headsprings. The upstream-most dam (hereafter, the dam) was constructed before 1900, the other three in the 1930s. Prior to 1930, Clear Creek was a cypress-lined stream with numerous large pools separated by short riffles. Later, the creek became a series of four pools approximately 100 m wide. Flow from Clear Creek (Wilkerson) Springs has varied from 7 to 25 cfs during the latter half of this century, depending upon aquifer recharge (Brune 1975).

During the 1960s and 1970s, *Gambusia heterochir* was essentially restricted to the upper headspring pool (approximately 100 × 100 m) where it was abundant along the shallow, heavily vegetated margins. The dam impounding this pool was in disrepair, with water flowing through two breaches. Extensive hybridization with native *Gambusia affinis* was centered above and below the breaches. *Gambusia heterochir* was abundant in the upper pool, with *G. affinis* abundant in equivalent habitats in the adjacent lower pool (Hubbs 1959). Two somewhat distinct biotic assemblages occurred, with *G. affinis*, *Hyalella azteca*, and *Myriophyllum* in the relatively eurythermal, high pH waters below the dam, and *G. heterochir*, *Hyalella texana*, and *Ceratophyllum* in the stenothermal, relatively low pH waters above (Stevenson and Peden 1973).

Presumably, the free-running Clear Creek originally had stenothermal headwaters and eurythermal downstream flow. The interface between habitat types was relatively wide, with a gradation between extremes. Impoundment brought the two habitat types in close proximity and may have led to the high frequency of hybridization between *G. heterochir* and *G. affinis*. Regardless of duration and extent of hybridization, there is no evidence that the two gene pools have become more similar (Edwards and Hubbs 1971), indicating selection against hybrids.

In the upper pool, extensive hybridization was attributed to migration of *G. affinis* through the dam breaches, a low level of courtship preferences, and some overlap of activity peaks. However, Peden (1975) showed gonopodial thrusts of male *G. heterochir* were directed posteriorly to match the posteriorly directed urogenital sinus of conspecific females, whereas those of *G. affinis* were reversed, a morphological-behavioral difference that would reduce hybridization.

The dam continued to deteriorate during the 1970s and was finally repaired in 1978. We predicted that closure would reduce hybridization frequency in the upper pool, thus preserving genetic integrity of the endangered *G. heterochir*. Hybrid frequency had been about 10% in prior samples and diminished to about 1% by 1984. Similarly, *G. affinis* abundance in the upper pool went from about 35% to below 10% during the same interval, in response to elimination of immigrants.

Shortly after the 1978 renovation, rainwater killifish (*Lucania parva*) were found in the lower pool. They are members of a related family (Cyprinodontidae) but are reproductively isolated from poeciliids. Food and habitats of *L. parva* resemble those of *G. affinis* with which they appear to compete most strongly. Consequently, *G. heterochir* abundance has increased dramatically in the lower pool adjacent to the dam, and hybrid *G. heterochir* x *G. affinis* now occur throughout the lower pool. These changes appear to be the result of expansion of *G. heterochir* into a less physically suitable habitat due to reduction of *G. affinis* caused by interaction with *L. parva*.

At the present time, *G. heterochir* abounds in the upper pool along with a few hybrids or *G. affinis*. The lower pool has numerous *G. affinis* and *L. parva* at eurythermal locations, while many *G. heterochir* and *L. parva* occupy the more stenothermal waters. *Dionda episcopa* (an omnivore), *Micropterus salmoides* (a piscivore), various *Lepomis* species, and *Ictalurus natalis* are also common in the spring waters. None have extensive feeding overlap with the invertebrate-feeding *Gambusia* spp. or *L. parva*.

The Clear Creek Gambusia Recovery Plan (USFWS 1982) recognizes the extremely limited distribution of *G. heterochir* and recommends that the headspring habitat and its aquifer be protected through purchase or easement. Although the new owner of Clear Creek is aware of the unique fish inhabiting the spring, he is unwilling to relinquish ownership of any property rights due to their aesthetic and financial values. As long as the current, informal agreement continues to benefit *G. heterochir*, the US Fish and Wildlife Service will concentrate on monitoring and research objectives of the recovery plan.

San Marcos Gambusia (*Gambusia georgei*)

The Sam Marcos Gambusia is an endemic poeciliid from the San Marcos River in central Texas (Hubbs and Peden 1969). Its historic range extends from the San Marcos headsprings downstream for about 4 km. No *G. georgei* have been collected since 1983 despite repeated attempts, and the species may be extinct.

San Marcos Springs in Hays County, Texas, is the second largest spring in Texas, with discharge averaging 150 cfs and a maximum recorded flow of 300 cfs (Brune 1975). Additional endemics to the San Marcos system include the fountain darter (*Etheostoma fonticola*), San Marcos salamander (*Eurycea naua*), and Texas wild-rice (*Zyzania texanus*), all listed by the US Fish and Wildlife Service and Texas Parks and Wildlife Department as endangered species. Additional native poeciliids include the largespring gambusia (*G. geiseri*) and *G. affinis*; introduced *Poecilia latipinna* and *P. formosa* are also present.

Numerous changes in the San Marcos system, including introduction of exotic fishes and vegetation, damming, eutrophication, and increased siltation from streamside activities have led to possible extinction of the San Marcos gambusia. Hybridization with native *G. affinis* has also been recorded (Hubbs and Peden 1969) but was not considered important until only hybrids could be found.

Perhaps the major threat to the San Marcos system and its endemic species is the continual decline of the Edwards Aquifer, a result of groundwater pumping. Local recharge provides about one-half of the flows from San Marcos Springs, with the remainder coming from the Edwards Aquifer (Ogden et al. 1985). Twice in the past 30 years, flow from San Marcos Springs has dropped to less than 30 cfs. Comal Springs, also of the Edwards Aquifer and the largest spring in Texas, ceased flowing entirely in 1957 after seven years of drought (Brune 1975).

The San Marcos Recovery Plan (USFWS 1984a) approaches recovery on the ecosystem level, rather than concentrating on individual species, and recommends specific steps to protect and manage the entire river and its flora and fauna as an integrated system. Careful coordination with Southwest Texas State University and the City of San Marcos is necessary, as the river flows directly from the privately owned and highly modified headsprings (Aquarena Springs Resort) directly through the campus and town. Recovery efforts to date include a city ordinance to protect riverbanks from construction and erosion, experimental removal of the exotic, semiaquatic plant *Colocasia asculenta* (elephant ears) that lines both banks of the river, reestablishment of Texas wild-rice for its own recovery and to provide habitat for *G. georgei*, attempts to capture and rear *G. georgei* in captivity, and thorough modeling of the local recharge areas for San Marcos Springs to prevent contamination and determine consistency of flow.

Recovery efforts as outlined in the San Marcos Recovery Plan provide both short- and long-term recommendations. Short-term actions include habitat improvements for the San Marcos River that will benefit all endemic species, continued and increased protection of the existing areas, and removal of some of the alterations and exotic species. Long-term recovery goals are to obtain habitat management authority for the San Marcos River and to establish limits for groundwater pumping of the Edwards Aquifer. The most immediate recovery goal for the San Marcos gambusia is to determine if the species is still extant and to bring it into a refuge.

Big Bend Gambusia (*Gambusia gaigei*)

The Big Bend gambusia is known only from the vicinity of Boquillas in Big Bend National Park, Texas. The original specimens were from Boquillas Spring (Hubbs 1929), which was dry in 1954 (Hubbs and Springer 1957); post-1960 samples contained numerous *G. affinis* (native to the Río Grande) and no *G. gaigei*. Subsequent samples of the Big Bend gambusia were collected from Graham Ranch Warm Springs, approximately 2 km from the type locality.

The initial Graham Ranch Warm Springs samples were collected after spring outflow had been altered to provide a fishing pool in 1953. In 1954, this open pool was inhabited by a few *G. affinis* and many *G. gaigei*. Sixteen months later, poeciliid abundance had been reversed, with *G. affinis* dominant. This led to initial recovery efforts in April 1956, when the now-modified Graham Ranch Warm Springs was treated with rotenone in a futile effort to eradicate *G. affinis*. More than half of the sequestered Big Bend gambusia (N = 25) were distributed to four locations within the Park, and two juvenile females and two males were taken to Austin, Texas and maintained in aquaria. By the following winter, all fish retained in the Park were dead, as was one of the females in Austin. All *G. gaigei* alive today are descendants of the three surviving Austin fish!

Big Bend gambusia from Austin were used to restock a refuge pond 100 m from Graham Ranch Warm Springs, where the species flourished between 1957 and 1960. By April 1960, the refuge pool had been colonized by *G. affinis*, and two sampling efforts obtained 15 and 8 *G. gaigei*. Six months later, 14 of these fish (plus 13 young from two captive broods) were placed in a second, adjacent refuge pond (Hubbs and Broderick 1963). No further contamination by *G. affinis* has occurred. A flow-through system was installed at the second pond after a winter kill in 1975 again decimated the *G. gaigei* population. The species now flourishes at Big Bend National Park.

Prior to construction of the fishing pool, Graham Ranch Warm Springs flowed through a gentle valley for about 100 m to the Río Grande; the spring was diverted upon pool construction. The old streambed was dry between 1954 and 1972, but by 1980 a small stream developed from a water leak through the pool dike (USFWS 1984b). On 20 August 1984, Big Bend gambusia were found to occupy running (= stenothermal) but not stagnant (= eurythermal) water in this valley. Since 1984, this population has consistently been found in the stenothermal overflow waters, whereas *G. affinis* abounds in a eurythermal beaver pond immediately downstream.

Heavy rains in December 1983 apparently transported *G. gaigei* from the nearby refuge pool to the fishing pool and the outlet stream. Samples from the fishing pool in 1985 and 1986 are exclusively Big Bend gambusia; when examined in 1957, 1960, 1961, 1972, and 1976, only *G. affinis* were found there. Conditions in the 1980s, when *G. gaigei* replaced *G. affinis*, are somewhat different from those during the 1950s, when *G. affinis* replaced *G. gaigei*. The most obvious difference is the dense growth of *Typha* throughout the pond, which isolates the water from ambient air, reducing thermal oscillations and resulting in a habitat more commonly associated with spring-adapted *G. gaigei*. The underwater *Typha* stems also add environmental heterogeity. The only other change is leakage of the dike; this makes the pool more stenothermal due to constant passage of spring water.

Big Bend gambusia have passed through several severe bottlenecks: 1) 3 individuals in 1955; 2) 27 individuals in 1960; 3) an unknown reduction via green sunfish predation in 1968; 4) a major winter kill in 1975, from which fewer than 1% of the population survived; and 5) the fishing pool and outlet stream populations must have been founded by a small fraction of the refuge populations. Both the refuge pond and pool populations of *G. gaigei* are homozygous for 60 enzymes (Hubbs et al. 1986). This extensive homozygosity is in full accord with inbreeding, bottlenecking, or a founder effect. Yet both populations appear healthy, with no signs of abnormalities, and the fishing pool population was able to replace *G. affinis* under conditions similar to original springhead habitats. Unfortunately, we do not know heterozygosity levels prior to the bottlenecks. It is possible that this species has historically existed in small populations with frequent bottlenecks.

The Big Bend Gambusia Recovery Plan (USFWS 1984b) calls for continued protection in springs within Big Bend National Park. The National Park Service is given responsibility for maintaining these spring habitats and monitoring *G. gaigei* populations. The springs are also used as a water supply for Río Grande Village Campgrounds. As long as sufficient water of adequate quality exists for *G. gaigei*, there will be no conflict. However, if drought reduces spring flows, fish will have first priority for water. In addition, the recovery plan calls for reclamation of additional springs in Big Bend National Park and maintenance of a refuge population of *G. gaigei* at DNFH. While Big Bend gambusia have been at DNFH since 1974, they do not survive well in the outdoor ponds during the coldest winters and have been lost from the hatchery five times, making *G. gaigei* the only species not to have flourished there. After each loss, new stocks from the refuge pond at Big Bend National Park have been obtained. Now, each winter a small portion of the hatchery population of *G. gaigei* (n = 500) is brought indoors and maintained in large aquaria.

Pecos Gambusia (*Gambusia nobilis*)

Once found along the Pecos River as far north as Fort Sumner, New Mexico and as far south as Fort Stockton, Texas, the Pecos gambusia is now restricted to four series of springs: 1) Bitter Lake National Wildlife Refuge, a series of spring-fed sinkholes near Roswell, New Mexico; 2) Blue Springs, a privately owned spring near Carlsbad, New Mexico; 3) a series of large private, state, and federally owned springs that flow into Toyah Creek near Toyahvale, Texas; and 4) Diamond Y Spring and Leon Creek, private springs near Fort Stockton, Texas. Populations in Leon Springs, Comanche Springs, Tunis Springs, Pecos River near Fort Sumner, and North Spring River (near Roswell, New Mexico) have been extirpated. In each of the remaining spring systems, downstream eurythermal waters are occupied by native *G. affinis*. The two species hybridize extensively in Leon Creek. The two Texas localities are also inhabited by introduced populations of another spring-adapted poeciliid, the largespring gambusia (*Gambusia geiseri*).

The Pecos River mainstream has been influenced by man for more than 100 years, first through irrigation withdrawals and more recently through construction of mainstream dams for irrigation and flood control (USFWS 1983). Presently, five major dams and at least three lesser dams are on the mainstream Pecos River, and another is under construction. These actions have severely depleted natural flows in the river and caused dramatic salinity increases in remaining reaches.

Although the mainstream Pecos River probably was never important as a permanent habitat for *G. nobilis*, it must have served as a dispersal route between tributary springs and streams. These vital lateral habitats began to be impacted by extensive groundwater pumping in the mid-1950s, resulting in cessation of flow from Leon Springs, Comanche Springs, Tunis Springs, and North Spring River and reduced flow with habitat loss in other areas. Consequently, populations of *G. nobilis* became isolated in a few disjunct permanent waters and are now totally dependent on spring flow (USFWS 1983). However, Hubbs and Springer (1957) believed a strongly fragmented distribution has existed since at least Pleistocene times, with little gene flow and much opportunity for divergence among the various populations. This divergence was confirmed by Echelle and Echelle (1986) and Echelle et al. (1989) who studied population variation electrophoretically and morphologically. Principal components analysis distinguished three groups: 1) Blue Springs; 2) Bitter Lake NWR and Leon Creek; and 3) the remaining Texas localities, centered around Toyah Creek. On the basis of mensural, meristic, and electrophoretic characters, the Toyah Creek populations were most divergent. Major recovery efforts outlined in the Pecos Gambusia Recovery Plan (USFWS 1983) include protection and monitoring of existing habitats, reintroduction into historic habitats, and maintaining a refuge population in case of catastrophic loss in the wild. Many of those actions are now being implemented. Monitoring and reintroduction has occurred in Bitter Lake NWR over the past 10 years (Bednarz 1975; Hatch and Conway 1980; Echelle and Echelle 1980; Bouma 1984), with Pecos gambusia now found in at least 7 of the more than 40 springs and sink holes (Brooks 1988). Twice-annual monitoring of Texas springs includes all endangered species in these habitats (*Cyprinodon elegans*, *C. bovinus*, several snails).

A major renovation of Leon Creek took place in 1976 to remove the nonnative sheepshead minnow (*Cyprinodon variegatus*) that threatened to genetically swamp the Leon Springs pupfish (*C. bovinus*). Attempts were made to remove representatives of all Leon Creek biota prior to application of rotenone, and were reintroduced after detoxification (Hubbs et al. 1978). Such a major management effort in an endangered species habitat is to be avoided unless absolutely necessary due to potential long-term changes to the habitat and sympatric species. The extreme rarity of *C. bovinus* made this effort necessary (Hubbs 1980), and reestablishment of all of the known vertebrates and invertebrates, including the *G. nobilis/G. affinis* hybrid zone, indicates no long-term impacts to *G. nobilis* (Hubbs et al. 1978).

In further recovery efforts, Eddy County (New Mexico) Public Health officials investigated the use of *G. nobilis* in stock ponds within the Pecos River drainage to control mosquitoes, but the project was stopped when stocked fish failed to survive. A small stock of *G. nobilis* was taken from nearby Giffin Springs (near Toyahvale, Texas) and stocked into the Comanche Springs Pupfish (*Cyprinodon elegans*) Refuge at Balmorhea State Recreation Area (Texas), where they continue to flourish. Future plans call for removal of nonnative fishes on Bitter Lake National Wildlife Refuge and devotion of all aquatic habitats to native species.

To date, recovery of this unusually diverse species has retained the genetic distinctiveness of each group through geographic isolation. No *G. nobilis* have been stocked into waters of another genetic group, and the Fish and Wildlife Service has rejected a suggestion to combine all three genetic groups into a "super guppy" at DNFH in order to maintain highest heterozygosity in the smallest space. However, protection of all three *G. nobilis* groups at DNFH was also refused for lack of space. Protection of the total genetic identity of *G. nobilis* has yet to be fully addressed by conservation agencies already overburdened with protecting many full species.

Sonoran Topminnow (*Poeciliopsis occidentalis*)

The Sonoran topminnow is endemic to the Sonoran Desert of southern Arizona, western New Mexico, and northwestern Mexico and includes two subspecies, the Gila topminnow (*P. o. occidentalis*) and the Yaqui topminnow (*P. o. sonoriensis*) endemic to adjacent Gila and Yaqui drainages, respectively. The species is protected as endangered under the Endangered Species Act and by Arizona and New Mexico Departments of Game and Fish.

Gila topminnows were once common in springs, streams, and marshy pools bordering the Gila River and its tributaries below 1,800 m elevation. Decline of the subspecies resulted from modification of surface waters for flood control and municipal use for the rapidly growing desert cities of Phoenix and Tucson. Between 1910 and 1962, a series of mainstream dams constructed on the Colorado, Gila, Salt, and Verde rivers dramatically changed the nature of riverine aquatic habitats in the Sonoran Desert (Miller 1961; Minckley 1973; Johnson and Rinne 1982). Springs and smaller streams were also altered for agricultural and domestic water supplies through smaller dams, diversions, and groundwater pumping. Changes in these systems resulted in loss of most Gila topminnow habitats, thus isolating the remaining eight wild populations in small (0.1 to 1.0 cfs) springheads and streams (Minckley et al. 1977; Meffe et al. 1983). Habitat loss is also the principal reason for decline of Yaqui topminnows in the United States. That subspecies was confined to reaches of two small permanent streams in extreme southeastern Arizona (Hendrickson et al. 1980). In Mexico, both subspecies remain abundant but are also threatened by overutilization and modification of aquatic habitat.

The second major threat to *P. occidentalis* is the introduction of nonnative species, especially *G. affinis*, into their remaining habitats. Miller (1961) described replacement of Gila topminnows by *G. affinis* in Arivaca Creek, Pima County, Arizona, between April 1957 and March 1959. Schoenherr (1981) and Meffe (1985b) have described predation as the primary replacement mechanism.

In 1980, the US Fish and Wildlife Service, US Forest Service, and Arizona Department of Game and Fish signed a cooperative agreement to stock Gila topminnows into habitats within the Gila River drainage in Arizona. While such an agreement seems basic to recovery of an endangered species, earlier agreement attempts had failed due to the legal protection such habitats might then receive under the Endangered Species Act. The 1980 agreement recommended that no legal efforts be used to protect stocked habitats but instead encouraged all signatory agencies to work toward betterment of the endangered species. From 1982 to 1985, nearly 100 sites on national forests in Arizona were stocked with Gila topminnows (Brooks 1985; see also previous section, Conservation Biology). By late 1987, 35 of those introduced populations survived, with 30 populations persisting at least three years and 23 populations for at least five years (Simons 1987). The oldest known reintroduction site (Hidden Waters) has maintained *P. o. occidentalis* since 1976.

The Sonoran Topminnow Recovery Plan was approved in 1984 (USFWS 1984c), setting specific downlisting and delisting goals for both Gila and Yaqui topminnows. Gila topminnows may be downlisted to threatened when 20 populations have been reestablished and have survived for at least three years, and delisted when all wild populations have been protected and 50 reestablished populations have survived three years or 30 populations for five years. Yaqui topminnows may be delisted when their limited habitat in the US is under Federal protection, stable populations persist for at least five years, and exotic predators are eliminated from topminnow habitats.

Downlisting goals have already been met for the Gila topminnow, as were most of the delisting goals for the Yaqui topminnow when the two permanent water habitats in the United States were purchased by the US Fish and Wildlife Service and The Nature Conservancy. The rulemaking package to downlist *P. occidentalis* to threatened status awaits publication. Questions have arisen about the short-term survival goals (three to five years) for reintroduced Gila topminnow populations, especially since there has recently been a prolonged period of abundant rainfall in the Southwest. It is difficult to plan and manage actions on long-term, evolutionary, or geologic time scales. In place of perpetuity, governments obtain management control of areas and develop continuing management plans or obtain legal agreements to coordinate management efforts on private lands. As long as cooperating agencies agree to manage topminnow populations actively, with new locations constantly being considered and established localities monitored and re-stocked if they fail, topminnows have an opportunity for survival. No method has yet been devised to assure survival on any longer time scales.

Amistad Gambusia (*Gambusia amistadensis*)

The original description of the Amistad gambusia (Peden 1973a) recognized that extinction had probably already occurred. John Van Conner obtained a relatively large sample of the fish from Goodenough Spring, Val Verde County, Texas, on 11 April 1968; on 3 August, Alex Peden revisited the site to learn more about the habitat. His visit coincided with the rise of Amistad Reservoir over Goodenough Spring. Conner and Peden observed that the gambusia were restricted to stenothermal spring water. Consequently, Peden brought live fish to Austin, Texas, to establish a stock of the species; subsequent stocks were transferred to DNFH in 1974. Peden's prediction of extinction in nature was verified, as no wild individuals have since been found.

When Amistad Reservoir covered Goodenough Spring, outflow ceased and water in the aquifer found alternate outflows, many of which were already small springs in the vicinity of Del Rio, Texas, and Villa Acuna, Mexico. The Texas locations were examined as possible alternate release sites for Goodenough gambusia, but those sites contained substantial populations of *G. affinis speciosa* (considered a full species [*G. speciosa*] by Rauchenberger, Appendix 1), which is otherwise scarce in the United States. Consequently, release of *G. amistadensis* was delayed until further information on *G. a. speciosa* (and unknown invertebrates) was obtained. In the interim, refuge stocks at both Austin and DNFH failed, and *G. amistadensis* was declared extinct (USFWS 1987).

SUMMARY AND FUTURE RESEARCH

Threats to the survival of southwestern poeciliids have been recognized (habitat destruction and introduction of nonnative fishes) and methods of reducing or counteracting them proposed in individual recovery plans. Plans are being implemented with enough success to be guardedly optimistic about short-term survival of most species. Projecting current conservation trends, *Poeciliopsis occidentalis* and *Gambusia nobilis* will survive into the twenty-first century. Genetic diversity of both species will likely be reduced, however, due to loss of wild populations. *Gambusia nobilis* will survive through careful protection of remaining high-quality habitats. Conservation of *P. occidentalis* will also depend on protection of wild habitats, but because remaining springs are small, efforts will concentrate on high numbers of introduced populations in selected habitats that are periodically monitored and restocked or replaced quickly if they fail. Neither species will need refuge protection, as existing populations will supply individuals to found new populations or replace failed stocks.

We believe that both *G. gaigei* and *G. heterochir* will also survive, but the extreme endemism of both species reduces their chances appreciably and will make continued refuge populations necessary. Genetic bottlenecks may continue to reduce heterozygosity but are not expected to result in extinctions. Even limited spring failure might not result in extinction because of refuge populations.

Gambusia amistadensis is already extinct, but destruction of Goodenough Spring may not have occurred if the Endangered Species Act had been in force. The Act and similar state legislation will continue to provide protection for extant poeciliids. *Gambusia amistadensis* also demonstrates the dangers of depending solely on refuges as means of protecting a species.

Gambusia georgei may also be extinct. If a remnant population can be found, it may be possible to produce large populations under refuge conditions for reintroduction into the San Marcos River. However, a restocking program alone will not suffice. Only one wild habitat exists for *G. georgei*, and at present the San Marcos River is either failing to support the species or at best supporting it minimally. A major effort will be needed to determine factors limiting the species in its native habitat, and a second effort initiated to reduce or eliminate those problems. Private ownership of the San Marcos River will complicate conservation actions, even though the City of San Marcos supports the efforts. It seems unlikely that *G. georgei* will survive.

A growing problem in conservation of endangered species is the schism between theory and practice of conserving rare species. Conservation biologists continue to learn more about the importance of protecting genetic diversity for the long-term well-being of species. This usually requires broadening the concept of what must be protected and is difficult to explain to managers already protecting single habitats or populations they have been told represent the species. In a world of fiscal and political priorities, it does not seem realistic to protect three separate populations of one species when it costs the same to protect one population each of three species. Managers accustomed to making decisions with limited or conflicting data feel pressured to concentrate on projects that directly and immediately benefit species. This results in goals that reduce short-term threats but may fail to consider long-term consequences.

The solution to this dilemma includes increased education and funding. We are just now learning to apply sound biological and ecological principles to the conservation of rare species, and immediate action must sometimes be taken in order to save a species from an imminent threat, even though the actions may result in future problems. Hopefully, we will be able to improve short-term remedies in order to incorporate long-term biological needs and repair long-term problems before they become lethal. In spite of occasional misunderstandings between conservation biologists and wildlife managers it is unlikely that, without both groups, any of the rare southwestern poeciliids would survive even short-term threats into the twenty-first century.

Chapter 17

Small Fishes in Strange Places: A Review of Introduced Poeciliids

WALTER R. COURTENAY, JR.
GARY K. MEFFE

INTRODUCTION

Nineteen species of poeciliids have been reported as introduced beyond their known historical ranges. Their ability to survive and successfully establish reproducing populations in alien warmwater ecosystems probably is paralleled only by certain cichlids (particularly tilapiines) and some cyprinids and salmonids in colder waters. For many poeciliids, success has been spectacular, even in the presence of predators.

Poeciliids have been intentionally introduced for biological control of insects (particularly mosquitos), to protect species from extinction (species conservation; see Johnson and Hubbs, Chapter 16), and to dispose of unwanted pet or experimental fishes. Some have also escaped from ornamental aquarium fish culture facilities. Many introductions were intended to have positive impacts (biological control and species conservation). Nevertheless, positive effects have been few (except in species conservation efforts) and are usually outweighed by negative impacts on other organisms. Because many introductions have not been reported in the scientific literature and may exist only in agency reports, our review should not be considered complete; in that regard, one of our purposes is to solicit records of which we are unaware.

IMPACTS OF INTRODUCTIONS

Measuring impacts is subjective, an anthropocentric activity usually based on a paucity of ecological knowledge and "best guesses" as to how we manage resources. A spectrum of opinions results, ranging from positive to negative; conclusions as to where in the spectrum impacts will occur or have occurred depend on what the evaluator considers more important—man or the resource.

A major source of information on introductions and impacts outside of North America has been Welcomme (1981) and new data he supplied to us in 1987 from his revision in progress of "Register of International Transfers of Inland Fish Species." His data are based on results of questionnaires sent to regional bodies of the Food and Agriculture Organization of the United Nations. Those bodies asked for replies from individual nations, and answers were received from most. One of the questions regarded "effects" of the introductions, which, unfortunately, was often not answered, probably due to lack of evaluation.

Positive Impacts

Positive impacts are measured against goals of the transfer, which necessitates evaluating purposeful introductions. Some transfers are for conservation and are discussed by Johnson and Hubbs (Chapter 16); the remainder are usually associated with pest control.

Mosquito Control

Welcomme (1981 and pers. comm.) recorded introductions of *Gambusia affinis*, *Poecilia latipinna*, and *P. reticulata* for biological control of mosquitos. Of the 19 nations and 1 US territory indicating purposeful introductions of *G. affinis*, only 4 (Argentina, Brazil, Italy, and Yugoslavia) indicated positive results. Brazil termed the introduction successful but undesirable. Egypt stated there was no evident effect on mosquitos, similar to Papua New Guinea's reply that this species was of little value in mosquito control. None of the eight nations that introduced *P. latipinna* or *P. reticulata* indicated favorable results; in fact, four of the eight called the introductions undesirable due to negative impacts on native fishes. Considering that most introductions of these purported mosquito control agents were made three to five or more decades ago, one would expect a greater number of positive replies had these fishes met intended goals.

Negative Impacts

Most negative impacts of introduced poeciliids appear to involve predation on larvae, juveniles, or small adults of other fishes. Hybridization poses a threat to some native species. Behavioral interactions and introduction of parasites and diseases may also play a role but are yet to be investigated. Because more is known regarding impacts of *Gambusia affinis* and *G. holbrooki* than any other species, they are treated in a separate section.

Deacon et al. (1964), Hubbs and Deacon (1965), Courtenay and Deacon (1982), and Courtenay et al. (1985) listed *Poecilia mexicana* and *P. reticulata* as threats to continued existence of several endemic fishes in southern Nevada. Courtenay et al. (1988) suggested that introduced *P. reticulata* and *Xiphophorus helleri* may have played a role in decline of the Utah sucker (*Catostomus ardens*) in a thermal spring in northwestern Wyoming. Contreras and Escalante (1984) cited introduced *Xiphophorus helleri* and *X. variatus* as responsible for "massive hybridization with . . . the endangered endemic *X. couchianus*." Belshe (1961) indicated that introduced *Belonesox belizanus* in southeastern Florida feed preferentially on *G. affinis*. Miley (1978) reported *B. belizanus* as having severely impacted native *G. affinis* in Florida canals where vegetation cover was sparse, noting that this exotic also preys on other fishes.

In comments provided by various nations on negative impacts (Welcomme 1981 and pers. comm.), Malawi listed *Phalloceros caudimaculatus* as "successful but undesirable" following introduction for mosquito control. Kenya and Uganda cited introduced *Poecilia reticulata* as responsible for declining populations of native cyprinodontids, and Australia considered exotic *Poecilia latipinna* as "undesirable."

Gambusia affinis and *G. holbrooki*—Species of Particular Concern[1]

No poeciliid has had ecological impacts close to those of the mosquitofish. This species is present on all continents except Antarctica and is the topic of more scientific and management papers than any other poeciliid. The mosquitofish has been touted as a savior of humanity from mosquito-borne disease and cursed as the bane of natural ecosystems and conservation efforts. It is at once propagated and stocked in a variety of aquatic habitats by government health departments and actively eliminated by the same government's wildlife and conservation groups.

Whatever its role, there is no question that the mosquitofish has been extraordinarily successful as an introduced species, a subject we pursue here. We start by asking why this fish in particular is so successful. Ehrlich (1986) provided clues when he listed eight characteristics often possessed by highly successful invaders. Seven of the eight are applicable to mosquitofish (abundant in original range, polyphagous, short generation times, a single female can colonize, broad physiological tolerances, closely associated with man, and high genetic variability), and only one does not (large size). Lloyd (1984) and Arthington and Mitchell (1986) also discuss these issues. Two additional characteristics, not listed by Ehrlich, contribute specifically to the success of *Gambusia affinis* as an exotic:

1) Specialized reproduction—Mosquitofish produce moderate numbers of advanced offspring several times per year. They need no particular spawning condi-

---

[1] Recent evidence, in combination with previously recognized distinctions, clearly supports the elevation of the western and eastern mosquitofishes to full species status, *Gambusia affinis* and *G. holbrooki*, respectively (Wooten et al. 1988). Both forms have been introduced worldwide, although the sources of stocks established in most places are usually unknown and/or unreported. Consequently, most literature on mosquitofish introductions uses the name *Gambusia affinis*. Except where otherwise noted, we use the species name *affinis* and the common name mosquitofish to refer in an inclusive sense to what is known about the distribution, biology, and impacts of these two forms outside their native ranges.

TABLE 17–1.   **Reports of Unsuccessful Mosquito Control by** *Gambusia affinis/holbrooki.*

Locality	Comments	Reference
Australia	It is arguable whether mosquitofish offer better mosquito control than some native fishes.	Grant 1978
Australia	"I believe their effect on mosquitoes has been negligible."	Lake 1971
California	Mosquitofish can increase mosquito populations by eliminating other mosquito predators.	Moyle 1976
California	Experiment. Pupfish more effective mosquito predator in emergent vegetation; mosquitoes a problem in Owens Valley after Owens Pupfish eliminated, despite mosquitofish introduction.	Danielson 1968
California	Experiment. Native *Cyprinodon macularius* is equal in mosquito control and not as dangerous.	Walters and Legner 1980
Iraq	Native fish also consumes mosquitoes; mosquitofish lose efficiency in presence of other organisms. Males are poor consumers.	Sharma and Al-Daham 1979
Italy	Mosquitofish unsuccessful in eliminating *Anophales* from running waters.	Hildebrand 1930
Japan	Mosquitofish reduced the number of larval, but not adult mosquitoes.	Hirose et al. 1980
Missouri	Mosquitofish are little more effective in mosquito control than the natives it replaces.	Pflieger 1975

tions other than seasonally appropriate temperatures and daylengths. Offspring are protected within the mother until "hatching," with consequent low prenatal mortality. Newborns are precocious and independent of the parents after birth.

2)   High aggression levels—Adult mosquitofish are extremely aggressive toward other species, including fishes much larger than themselves. Females, in particular, attack other fishes, shredding fins, and sometimes killing them (Meffe 1983, 1985b). Predation on juveniles of other species may be intense (Myers 1965), resulting in high mortality and replacement by mosquitofish.

Thus, success of the mosquitofish is attributable to a combination of biological characteristics that preadapt the species for colonization. Other poeciliids also possess many of these traits and have been successful colonists as well. However, active and widespread stocking of mosquitofish in particular has vastly increased its opportunity to gain access to a diversity of habitats around the world.

Mosquito Control

Although mosquitofish have been widely introduced for mosquito control, they accomplish little toward this goal while having major detrimental impacts on native biota. There is no convincing evidence that mosquitofish have desired effects on mosquito populations and a great deal of information to the contrary. A number of authors have commented on the ineffectiveness of mosquitofish in controlling mosquito populations (Table 17–1), although some evidence exists for moderate control capabilities (e.g., Cech and Linden 1986, 1987). In total, mosquitofish have a far greater negative impact where introduced (loss of native biota, including other larvivores) with little to no mosquito control effectiveness. The continued, indiscriminate introduction of mosquitofish for biological control should cease in lieu of development of biological control by native species.

Impacts of Gambusia affinis/holbrooki on Natural Systems

The biological impacts of introduced *G. affinis* on natural systems are usually clear and often drastic. Fishes and invertebrates in a diverse array of ecosystems have been significantly reduced or eliminated after mosquitofish introductions (Table 17–2), including impacts on such unlikely species as largemouth bass (*Micropterus salmoides*) and introduced common carp (*Cyprinus carpio*). These effects are likely the result of predation by *Gambusia* on eggs, larvae, juveniles, or even adults of native forms (Myers 1965; Meffe 1985b).

Impacts at the ecosystem level are less clear but likely important as well. Hildebrand (1930) noted that mosquitofish densities in Italian ponds were so high that cattle could not drink the water. In an experimental pond study, Hurlbert et al. (1972) reported a series of system changes following mosquitofish introduction; ponds with *G. affinis* had large phytoplankton blooms, decreased optical transmission, higher water temperatures, and decreased dissolved inorganic phosphorus. Hurlbert and Mulla (1981) also found that experimental systems with mosquitofish had higher pH and oxygen levels than those without.

Although impacts of introduced mosquitofish on natural systems are often

TABLE 17–2.   Examples of Negative Impacts of Nonnative *Gambusia affinis/holbrooki* Populations on Local Fishes.

Native Species	Effect	Reference
20 Taxa: Cyprinidae (1), Cyprinodontidae (6), Poeciliidae (9), Neostethidae (3), Gasterosteidae (1)	Reduction or elimination	Schoenherr 1981
Cyprinus carpio	No reproduction	Sreenivasan and Natarajan 1962
Crenichthys baileyi	Reduction	Deacon et al. 1964
Cyprinodon calaritanus	Elimination	Missiroli 1948
Cyprinodon bovinus, Gambusia gagei, Lepidomeda mollispinis pratensis	Elimination partially due to mosquitofish	Miller 1961
Rhinichthys osculus	Elimination	Deacon et al. 1964
Hypereleotris galii, Melanotaenia fluviatilis	Reduction	Arthington et al. 1983
Eleotridae, *Ambassus castelnaui, Nannoperca australis, Craterocephalus* spp., *Melanotaenia fluviatilis, Pseudomugil signifer, Retropinna semoni*	Reduction	Lloyd 1984

clear, mechanisms are more equivocal, and typically speculative and anecdotal. Hybridization is a possible danger to the integrity of at least one species, *Gambusia heterochir* (reviewed by Johnson and Hubbs, Chapter 16). Competition has often been invoked by default—mosquitofish appear, native species disappear, so it is concluded that they must have been outcompeted. There is, to our knowledge, no experimental evidence that competition is important in replacement of native fishes by *G. affinis*. Competition may occur, but it has not been demonstrated.

Evidence indicates that predation is the primary mechanism by which mosquitofish deplete or eliminate native species. First, mosquitofish have the anatomical structures to be effective predators. With strong, conical teeth, short gut length (Meffe et al. 1983), and open cephalic canals (Rosen and Mendelson 1960), they can efficiently detect, capture, and subdue many invertebrate and vertebrate prey. Their small size also allows access to areas that would otherwise provide prey with refuge from larger predators. Second, *G. affinis* are known predators of many fishes (Table 17–2) and invertebrates (e.g., Hurlbert et al. 1972; Farley and Younce 1977b; Hurlbert and Mulla 1981) and have been observed to feed upon smaller fishes and harass larger adults (Meffe et al. 1983). One of the authors (WRC) and several associates were "attacked" by large numbers of mosquitofish while snorkeling in a rockpit near Fort Lauderdale, Florida; mosquitofish nipped and pulled at body hairs, structures not too different in size from certain invertebrates or many fish larvae. Finally, experimental evidence in laboratory and natural settings indicates that predation is the primary mode of impact in at least one case, local elimination of the endangered *Poeciliopsis occidentalis* in Arizona (Meffe 1983, 1985b).

Patterns of Success of Mosquitofish Invasions

Although sometimes appearing to be invincible, mosquitofish do not always establish wherever transplanted. The species is most successful in habitats modified or disturbed by man and fares poorly under many natural conditions. A variety of disturbed habitats, such as dammed, diverted, or channelized rivers, or heavily grazed or artificial aquatic systems, have proved quite suitable to introduced *G. affinis*, in some cases resulting in huge swarms or monocultures (Table 17–3). Densest populations are usually in artificial habitats, polluted areas, or thermally elevated systems where few or no other fishes survive.

Conversely, certain aspects of natural habitats inhibit mosquitofish success. In particular, cold water, springhead conditions, heavy flooding, and natural predators all reduce or preclude introduced mosquitofish. Cold water limits the range of the species (e.g., Cadwallader 1979), although some populations have adapted to rigorous winter conditions in northern states (Krumholz 1944, 1948). Springheads with low pH and high dissolved CO_2 in southwestern United States typically serve as refugia for native fishes in the face of mosquitofish invasion (Hubbs 1971; Deacon and Bradley 1972; Minckley et al. 1977; Williams and Sada 1985). We do not know why mosquitofish do poorly under these conditions. Flash flooding in American deserts has reduced or eliminated introduced mosquitofish and other

TABLE 17–3.   Examples of Successful Use of Modified Habitats by _Gambusia affinis/holbrooki._

Locality	Modification	Reference
Arizona	Stabilized reservoirs, golf courses	Minckley 1969b, 1973
Australian streams	General habitat change	Arthington et al. 1983
Australian streams	Thermal, polluted streams	McKay 1984
Australia (Brisbane)	Disturbed, urban streams	Milton and Arthington 1983a
California	Cattle grazing, damming, siltation, reduced stream flows	Moyle and Nichols 1973, 1974
Europe, Asia	Thermal pollution	Vooren 1972
Hawaii, Oceania	Modified stream channels	Maciolek 1984
Japan	Ponds and irrigation ditches	Hirose et al. 1980
San Francisco Bay	Drainage ditches	Balling et al. 1980
San Francisco Bay	Disturbed, intermittent habitats	Leidy 1984

exotics native to mesic lowland habitats that do not experience heavily erosive floods (Meffe 1984b; Minckley and Meffe 1987); mosquitofish are washed out by catastrophic, erosive flooding, whereas native species often persist. Winter floods in Western Australia reduce mosquitofish populations each year (Arthington, pers. comm.).

Because mosquitofish populations generally do not expand to excessive or problematic sizes within their native range, it seems likely that predation or other interactions in biotically rich systems inhibit mosquitofish. In biotically depauperate habitats, the species is free to expand to large populations. Moreover, predation by native fishes or other exotics often inhibits the success of introduced _Gambusia_ (Bhasker and Ramod 1942; Cross 1976).

In summary, mosquitofish almost invariably present a multitude of problems when introduced beyond their native range and offer no real compensatory or biological control advantages. The species should not be used as a larvivore, with native species much preferable in that role whenever possible (e.g., Lloyd 1984). Mosquitofish are far too aggressive and predatory to be indiscriminately spread throughout the world without recognition of dangers to native biota. An international ban on their use as a control agent is biologically appropriate and warranted.

SYNOPSIS OF INTRODUCED POECILIIDS

In this section, we review introduced poeciliids alphabetically by genus and species. Not included are four species introduced beyond their native ranges for conservation purposes (see Johnson and Hubbs, Chapter 16).

Belonesox belizanus—The pike killifish is native to the Atlantic slope of Middle America from Laguna San Julian, northwest of Ciudad Veracruz, Mexico, to Costa Rica (Caldwell et al. 1959; Miller 1966). It was introduced into southwestern

Dade County, Florida, in November 1957 after termination of medical research (Belshe 1961; Miley 1978) and subsequently became established. Three decades later, *Belonesox* had a range of approximately 116 km². A separate population was found in a borrow pit on North Key Largo in 1984 (F. Cichocki, pers. comm.), but apparently did not establish (J. N. Taylor, pers. comm.). A previously established population in the San Antonio River, Texas (Barron 1964) apparently is no longer extant (Hensley and Courtenay, in Lee et al. 1980).

Cnesterodon decemmaculatus—This native of Argentina was introduced into Chile (Welcomme 1981) where it is established (R. L. Welcomme, pers. comm.). Date of and rationale for introduction are unknown.

Gambusia affinis—Native to the Mississippi River drainage southward from southeastern Iowa (Harlan et al. 1987), coastal drainages of the Gulf of Mexico south to Veracruz, Mexico, and the Atlantic slope of the US north to southern New Jersey (Lee and Burgess, in Lee et al. 1980), this species may be the most widely introduced fish in the world (Krumholz 1948). Two subspecies, *G. affinis affinis* and *G. affinis holbrooki*, have been recognized, and we recommend future recognition as full species (Wooten et al. 1988, and footnote 1). Both forms were available for introduction, and presumably both are widely dispersed.

Introductions beyond its natural range in the United States include Arizona (Minckley 1973), California (Moyle 1976), most Hawaiian islands (Maciolek 1984), Idaho (Simpson and Wallace 1978), Montana (Brown 1971), Nevada (Deacon and Williams 1984), New Mexico (Koster 1957), Oregon (Bond 1961), Utah (Sigler and Miller 1963), Washington (Wydoski and Whitney 1979), and Wyoming (Baxter and Simon 1970).

In Canada it was released in Alberta, possibly British Columbia, and Manitoba, but persisted only in thermal outflows in Alberta (Crossman 1984; Nelson 1984). It is established in Sonora, Baja California Sur, and Chihuahua in Mexico (Contreras and Escalante 1984). Erdman (1984) recorded this species from two reservoirs in Puerto Rico and indicated minor range expansion since 1935.

In South America *G. affinis* is established in Argentina, Bolivia, Chile, and Peru (Welcomme 1981). On the African subcontinent, it is established in the Central African Republic, Egypt, Madagascar, South Africa (Jubb 1977; Bruton and van As 1986), Sudan, Zimbabwe, and has been reported (reproductive status unknown) from Ghana and the Ivory Coast (Welcomme 1981). It also occurs in the crater lake on Annobon Island, Gulf of Guinea, off Africa, where it was introduced by the Spanish military (C. R. Robins, pers. comm.). In Europe, it is established and "widespread" in Italy and Yugoslavia, and in thermal ponds in Hungary (Welcomme 1981).

Oceania has also been the recipient of *G. affinis* releases, with established populations in American Samoa, Australia (McKay 1984; Arthington and Lloyd, Chapter 18), Cook Islands, Federated States of Micronesia, Fiji, Guam, Kiribati (Marshall and Line Islands) (Maciolek 1984), New Zealand (McDowall 1984; Arthington and Lloyd, Chapter 18), northern Mariana Islands, Papua New Guinea, Tahiti, and Western Samoa (Welcomme 1981 and pers. comm.). C. R. Robins (pers. comm.) indicated that the US Army Air Corps (now the US Air Force) took *G. affinis* into many new localities during World War II for mosquito control, dropping it into remote waters from aircraft.

Gambusia panuco—Native to the Río Panuco, Mexico, Hubbs and Miller (1977) and Contreras and Escalante (1984) record the Panuco gambusia as having been introduced to La Media Luna Springs, San Luis Potosi, Mexico. Its status there and rationale for introduction are unknown (Contreras and Escalante 1984).

Limia vittata—Maciolek (1984) recorded the Cuban limia, native to Cuba and the Isle of Pines (Franz and Rivas 1983), as introduced and established in Oahu, Hawaii, perhaps as a release of unwanted pet fish.

Phalloceros caudimaculatus—This poeciliid is native from extreme southern Brazil (Río de Janeiro) into Uruguay and Paraguay. It was introduced into Malawi from Brazil and became established at Bwumbwe Dam and the Ruo River (Jubb 1977; Welcomme 1981). Trendall and Johnson (1981) and Arthington and Lloyd (Chapter 18) noted its establishment in Western Australia. Dates of and rationale for introductions are unknown.

Poecilia formosa—Native to the lower Río Grande Valley of Texas southward in coastal streams and lagoons to the Río Tuxpan estuary, Mexico, and possibly native to the coastal Nueces River, Texas, the Amazon molly is introduced and established in the San Marcos and San Antonio rivers in Texas (Martin, in Lee et al. 1980). Introduction rationale is unknown.

Poecilia latipinna—The sailfin molly is native to fresh, brackish, and some inshore marine waters of Gulf of Mexico drainages from northwestern Yucatan peninsula, Mexico, northward and eastward, the estuarine and inshore waters of peninsular Florida, and coastal drainages northward to southeastern North Carolina (Burgess, in Lee et al. 1980). It is locally established in Arizona (Minckley 1973), California (Moyle 1976), Nevada (Deacon and Williams 1984), Texas (San Marcos River, and San Antonio Spring; C. Hubbs, pers. comm.), Alberta, Canada (Crossman 1984; Nelson 1984), and Hildago and Sonora, Mexico (Contreras and Escalante 1984).

Welcomme (1981) reported *P. latipinna* as introduced and established, except as noted, in Central America, Singapore (status unknown), Australia (McKay 1984; Arthington and Lloyd, Chapter 18), and New Zealand (McDowall 1984; Arthington and Lloyd, Chapter 18). Welcomme (pers. comm.) recently added the Philippines to this list. Maciolek (1984) and Welcomme (pers. comm.) included Guam and Hawaii as sites of establishment.

Some US records of introduced populations are of the black molly, a popular aquarium fish. R. B. Socolof (pers. comm.), in the early 1970s, indicated that the black molly is often a hybrid of *P. latipinna* and *P. velifera* Regan.

Although known to be largely or completely herbivorous, the sailfin molly has, ironically, been introduced for mosquito control (Welcomme 1981 and pers. comm.). Most introductions in North America appear to be releases of unwanted pet fish.

Poecilia mexicana—The shortfin molly is native to the Atlantic slope of

Middle America from the Río San Juan (Río Grande basin), Nuevo Leon, Mexico, and the Pacific slope from Río del Fuerte basin, Sonora, Mexico, southward to the Caribbean slope of Colombia, the Pacific slope of eastern Panama (Río Tuira), and the Netherlands and Colombian West Indies (Miller 1966; Rosen and Bailey 1963).

Introduced populations exist north of the Río Grande basin in California (Hubbs et al. 1979; W. R. Courtenay, pers. observ.), Bruneau River, Idaho (Courtenay et al. 1988), and in certain springs and most of the Moapa River and Hiko Spring, Nevada (Deacon et al. 1964; Courtenay and Deacon 1982; Deacon and Williams 1984). A population, formerly established in Trudau Pond, Montana (Brown 1971), is no longer extant (W. R. Courtenay, pers. observ.). Status of the population reported by Hahn (1966) in Saguache County, Colorado, remains unknown. Minckley and Deacon (1968) and Minckley (1973) cited one collection of this species from Maricopa County, Arizona, but establishment did not occur. Fishes of the "species complex" to which *P. mexicana* belongs (Rosen and Bailey 1963; Schultz and Miller 1971) were reported from Florida (Courtenay and Robins 1973; Courtenay et al. 1974), but there have been no recent reports or findings.

Welcomme (pers. comm.) included American Samoa, Fiji, Tahiti, Western Samoa, and Hawaii (Oahu) as sites where this species has become established. Maciolek (1984) lists a member of the species complex, *P. sphenops* Valenciennes, as established on Oahu, Hawaii, and suggests that another, *P. butleri* Jordan, may be established in certain islands of Oceania; until specialists verify species identification, we include them with this account.

Poecilia reticulata—The guppy occurs naturally in the Netherlands Antilles, Venezuelan islands, Trinidad, Windward (Barbados) and Leeward (St. Thomas and Antigua) islands, and from western Venezuela to Guyana; records from the Lesser Antilles may represent introductions (Rosen and Bailey 1963). Endler (1980) included northeastern Venezuela, Margarita, and Tobago as part of the natural range. It is a highly popular aquarium species and the second most widely introduced poeciliid worldwide; it also has been sold as a purported mosquito control agent. All introductions in North America apparently were made to dispose of unwanted pet fish; elsewhere, most releases were intentional for mosquito control.

Established populations have been reported in the US from Arizona (Minckley 1973), Florida (Courtenay et al. 1974; W. King, pers. comm.), Idaho (Simpson and Wallace 1978), Nevada (Deacon et al. 1964; Williams et al. 1980; Courtenay and Deacon 1982, 1983), Texas (Hubbs et al. 1978; Hubbs 1982), and Wyoming (Baxter and Simon 1970). Populations in Florida do not appear to be self-sustaining, and Minckley (pers. comm.) has indicated the same for this fish in Arizona. Moyle (1976) suggested established populations may exist in sewage settling ponds in California, and Courtenay et al. (1988) confirmed persistence in thermal springs of Idaho and Wyoming.

McAllister (1969) reported an established population from thermal outflows in Alberta, Canada, but that population disappeared in the 1970s (Crossman 1984;

Nelson 1984). Contreras and Escalante (1984) cited established populations in several states of Mexico.

Welcomme (1981) included Colombia, Kenya, Nigeria, Uganda, Netherlands, and the United Kingdom (in thermal waters), Sri Lanka, Australia, New Zealand, and Papua New Guinea as localities where *P. reticulata* was introduced and became established. McKay (1984) and McDowall (1984) confirmed establishment in Australia and New Zealand. It was introduced for mosquito control in South Africa in 1912 but failed to survive; later releases by aquarists, however, resulted in local establishment (Bruton and van As 1986). Welcomme (pers. comm.) added Peru, Puerto Rico (Erdman 1984), Fiji, Guam, Hawaii, Palau, Tahiti, and Western Samoa (Maciolek 1984) to this list.

Poeciliopsis gracilis—The porthole livebearer, native to the Atlantic and Pacific slopes of Middle America from southern Mexico to Honduras, has been established for two decades in an agricultural drain south of Mecca, California (Mearns 1975; Moyle 1976; Hubbs et al. 1979; Courtenay et al. 1984). It probably escaped from or was released by an adjacent aquarium fish farm. The drain where established is overgrown with vegetation (W. R. Courtenay, pers. observ.), and the population's status as of March 1988 was unknown. Welcomme (pers. comm.) reported this species as established in Venezuela, an apparent pet fish release.

Xiphophorus helleri—Native distribution includes mostly lotic habitats on the Atlantic slope of Middle America from Río Nautla, Veracruz, Mexico, to northwestern Honduras (Rosen 1960; Rosen and Kallman 1969). The green swordtail and its congeners, along with numerous hybrids and color varieties, are staples of the international aquarium fish industry. Most introductions are presumed to be releases of unwanted pet fishes; some releases, however, may have been made on the assumption that they would control mosquitos.

Xiphophorus helleri was introduced and became established in Florida (Courtenay et al. 1974; Dial and Wainright 1983) where populations are probably impermanent, in two thermal outflows in Idaho (Courtenay et al. 1988), in thermal Trudau Pond, Montana (Brown 1971) where it persists (W. R. Courtenay, pers. observ.), as a hybrid with *X. maculatus* at Indian Spring, Nevada (Courtenay and Deacon 1982), and in Kelly Warm Spring, Wyoming (Courtenay et al. 1988). LaRivers (1962) recorded it from two springs upstream from the Overton Arm of Lake Mead, Nevada, but Courtenay and Deacon (1982, 1983) found it to be absent. Specimens, without evidence of establishment, have been collected in Arizona (Minckley 1973) and California (St. Amant and Hoover 1969; Moyle 1976). It was reproducing in thermal outflows in Alberta, Canada, but has not been collected in recent years (Crossman 1984; Nelson 1984). The species remains established in Hawaii (Maciolek 1984) and Puerto Rico (Erdman 1984).

Contreras and Escalante (1984) reported *X. helleri* as introduced in Michoacan, Morelos, Nuevo Leon, and Coahuila in Mexico. Welcomme (1981) recorded reproducing populations from Transvaal, South Africa (Jubb 1977; Bruton and van As 1986), Sri Lanka, and Australia (McKay 1984; Arthington and Lloyd, Chapter

18). Welcomme (pers. comm.) has added Fiji and Guam (Maciolek 1984) to the list of established populations.

Xiphophorus maculatus—Occurring naturally in lentic habitats on the Atlantic slope of Middle America from just south of Ciudad Veracruz, Mexico, to northern Belize, the southern platyfish has become established in several foreign locales. All introductions appear to have been released pet fishes.

In the US, a reproducing population (a hybrid with *X. helleri*) exists in a thermal spring in Nevada (Courtenay and Deacon 1982; Deacon and Williams 1984). It is locally, but often impermanently, established in Florida (Courtenay et al. 1974; Dial and Wainwright 1983). It has been collected in Orange County, California (St. Amant and Hoover 1969) and in Texas (Hubbs 1972) without evidence of establishment. It is established on three islands in Hawaii (Maciolek 1984) and in springs in Coahuila, Guanajuato, Nuevo Leon, and Sonora, Mexico (Contreras and Escalante 1984).

Welcomme (1981) recorded *X. maculatus* as established in Puerto Rico (confirmed by Erdman [1984] at three locations), possibly established in Nigeria, and reproducing in Australia (McKay 1984; Arthington and Lloyd, Chapter 18). Maciolek (1984) added Kiribati (Palau), and Welcomme (pers. comm.) included Colombia as additional establishment sites.

Xiphophorus variatus—The variable platyfish is native to Mexico, from southern Tamaulipas to eastern San Luis Potosi and northern Veracruz (Rosen 1960). All releases appear to be from disposal of unwanted pet fish.

Burgess et al. (1977) reported an established population in Alachua County, which remained extant in 1985 (G. K. Meffe, pers. observ.), and Courtenay et al. (1984, 1986) indicated locally-reproducing but impermanent populations elsewhere in Florida. Brown (1971) recorded established populations in thermal spring outflows in three Montana counties, and those in Beaverhead County were extant in 1985 (W. R. Courtenay, pers. observ.). This species was established in the Salt River at Tempe, Arizona but was destroyed by a flood in 1965; it had also been collected near Yuma without evidence of establishment (Minckley 1973). St. Amant and Hoover (1969) and St. Amant and Sharp (1971) recorded possible establishment in Orange and Riverside counties, California, but Moyle (1976), Hubbs et al. (1979), and J. A. St. Amant (pers. comm.) expressed doubt that it remained extant; Shapovalov et al. (1981) listed these populations as extinct. Maciolek (1984) cited the species as possibly established on Oahu, Hawaii. Welcomme (pers. comm.) noted an established population in Colombia.

SUMMARY AND FUTURE RESEARCH

Eighteen species of poeciliids are recorded as introduced beyond their native ranges. Except for conservation (Johnson and Hubbs, Chapter 16), impacts on native fishes have been negative to perhaps neutral. Beneficial effects in biological control of target pests are rare to nonexistent.

As is true for nearly all introduced fishes, detailed analyses of impacts and impact mechanisms are needed. Although it is important to note that an introduction occurred and changes in native fish populations followed, this is merely correlational and does not prove cause and effect, nor does it document impact mechanisms. Often, introductions occur with, or subsequent to, other environmental perturbations that may confuse the situation. We should focus on comparisons of factors having negative impacts and ask whether they act independently or synergistically.

Documentary field studies (population censusing) can provide important data but should be coupled with underwater observations and behavioral ecology studies wherever feasible. More importantly, innovative experimental manipulations in the field and laboratory are needed to define and critically evaluate potential mechanisms involved in species replacement.

Before any nonnative fish is considered for approval as a biological control agent, research should be conducted with native species having similar potential. Even more critical, the real and potentially undesirable effects of the species proposed for introduction should be investigated and understood. Once an introduction is made, its effects—positive or negative—must be studied and reported in mainstream literature. Recognizing that it is virtually impossible to eradicate a fish once it becomes established and expands it range signals the need for strong caution prior to introduction.

Finally, public education as to the dangers of nonnative fish releases is sorely needed. Most laypersons are simply not aware that their unwanted pets can pose great problems for native ecosystems. This is pointedly illustrated in a quote regarding *Belonesox belizanus* in an aquarists' magazine. After dwelling on the predaceous nature of the fish, the author makes the amazing statement that:

> . . . the species is one of those on the restricted list in the State of Texas, and aquarists wishing to keep *Belonesox* there must obtain a permit for them and presumably for each one of the young that may come along in time. To further compound this nonsense, the State also requires notification in writing should the aquarist decide to get rid of his *Belonesox*. What fools some mortals be! (Connely 1968, p. 50).

With such ignorance of ecological systems among the general public, our task remains formidable.

ACKNOWLEDGMENTS

We thank A. H. Arthington, M. L. Bruton, I. de Moor, A. A. Echelle, C. Hubbs, W. L. Minckley, J. A. St. Amant, L. H. Simons, P. H. Skelton, C. R. Robins, and R. L. Welcomme for their contributions of information used in this chapter.

Chapter 18

Introduced Poeciliids in Australia and New Zealand

ANGELA H. ARTHINGTON
LANCE N. LLOYD

INTRODUCTION

Australian inland waters have been successfully colonized by 19 freshwater fish species introduced to the continent. Of these, 6 are poeciliids, 3 are salmonids, 5 are cyprinids, 4 are cichlids, and 1 is a percid (Arthington and Mitchell 1986). New Zealand also has 19 introduced species—4 poeciliids, 7 salmonids, 6 cyprinids, 1 percid, and 1 ictalurid (McDowall 1987). The salmonids, although not without adverse impacts on endemic fishes (see Fletcher 1986; McDowall 1987), are considered beneficial in both countries, but the poeciliids, cichlids, and cyprinids are regarded as ecological pests (McKay 1984; Arthington and Mitchell 1986; Lloyd et al. 1986; McDowall 1987).

Australian and New Zealand experiences with introduced poeciliids are similar in that *Gambusia affinis* is the most widely distributed species, with a relatively long history of deliberate introductions for mosquito control, whereas other poeciliids have become established accidentally and more recently through the aquarium trade. A major difference is that the aquarium species have only been able to persist in New Zealand in geothermally heated waters, while in Australia most of these species thrive in suitable natural waters from the subtropics northward. Ecological impacts are therefore of greater concern in Australia, and accordingly more work has been done on poeciliids there than in New Zealand.

Another important difference is that in Australia *G. affinis* occurs from cold temperate to tropical climates with strikingly different hydrologic and water quality regimes. This provides an opportunity to compare the processes of invasion and differential adaptation to environment, as well as ecological impacts, in very diverse aquatic systems with different endemic fish communities. Such comparisons have begun in Australia and are reviewed here.

We present an Australian perspective on the use of *G. affinis* for mosquito control and suggest that a new common name is needed for the "mosquitofish" to prevent the uncritical use of this species in mosquito abatement; this disassociation of ideas could help to encourage the use of endemic fish species, which in Australia are more effective than *G. affinis*. However, an appropriate common name has eluded us.

Our chapter concludes with two predictions: first, that poeciliids will spread in northern Australia, and second, that the widely distributed carnivorous guppy, *Poecilia reticulata*, may prove to be as troublesome as *G. affinis*. We outline critical gaps in poeciliid biology in Australia and New Zealand and discuss the research needed to address questions such as the genetic, morphometric, and physiological divergence of stocks since introduction, natural population controls, and interactions with endemic fish species and invertebrates. Finally, we suggest a simple measure to reduce the spread of poeciliids via the aquarium trade.

INTRODUCED POECILIIDS

Courtenay and Meffe (Chapter 17) review the natural and introduced range of poeciliids. We give a more detailed account of the history of species introductions in Australia and New Zealand; although reproducing populations exist for most species in outdoor ornamental ponds and artificially heated waters, we will not regard them as feral fish.

Gambusia affinis was the first poeciliid to be introduced into Australian waters. The history of introductions is poorly documented, but it is known that the mosquitofish originally entered the country as an aquarium species in the early 1920s and was subsequently widely released to control mosquito larvae (Lloyd 1986). The present distribution and dates of major introductions have been summarized by Lloyd et al. (1986) (Figure 18–1). It appears that all feral mosquitofish in Australia belong to the subspecies (now species) *holbrooki* (Lloyd and Tomasov 1985), which indicates that the original Australian stocks came from southeastern United States (Smith et al., Chapter 13).[1]

The mosquitofish was introduced into New Zealand in 1930 to control mosquitoes and for many years was known only from a few swampy lakes in the Northland region of the North Island (Figure 18–2). Now it is widespread, "verging on ubiquitous in waters north of the Waikato and east into the Bay of Plenty" (McDowall 1987; Figure 18–2). It is also abundant in geothermally heated waters near Lake Taupo (Vincent and Forsyth 1987).

[1] Although recent information indicates clear taxonomic separation at the species level, we choose to retain the former designation (*G. a. affinis* and *G. a. holbrooki*) to avoid confusion with the literature. We thus refer to introduced mosquito fishes in Australia and New Zealand as *Gambusia affinis*. Preliminary evidence indicates that the form feral in New Zealand is *G. a. affinis* (see later).

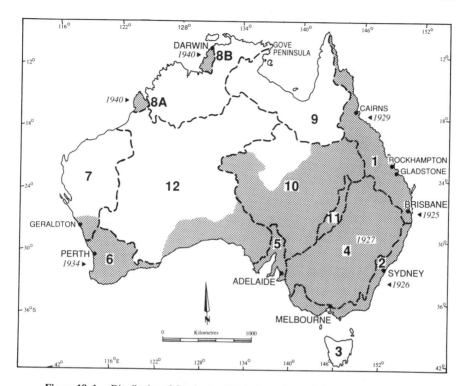

Figure 18–1. Distribution of *Gambusia affinis* in Australia, with dates of major introductions. Numbers 1 through 12 refer to the drainage divisions recognized by the Australian Water Resources Council. Shaded areas indicate the presence of mosquitofish within at least parts of the drainage division (from Lloyd et al. 1986, modified and redrawn). 1) Northeast Coast Division; 2) Southeast Coast Division; 3) Tasmanian Division; 4) Murray-Darling Division; 5) South Australian Gulf Division; 6) Southwest Coast Division; 7) Indian Ocean Division; 8) Timor Sea Division—(A) Cape Levesque Coast, (B) Finnis River; 9) Gulf of Carpentaria Division; 10) Lake Eyre Division; 11) Bulloo-Bancannia Division; 12) Western Plateau Division.

Gambusia "dominicensis" (=*hispaniolae*), a poeciliid native to Haiti, was thought to be present in central Australia (Lake 1971). However, Lloyd and Tomasov (1985) have shown that the fish were *G. affinis holbrooki* with atypical scale counts.

Phalloceros caudimaculatus, the one-spot livebearer, has been recorded in creeks and drains around Perth, Western Australia (Griffiths 1972; Trendall and Johnson 1981). While this species does not appear to have established feral populations elsewhere in Australia or New Zealand, outdoor pond populations occur in South Australia (L. N. Lloyd, unpubl. data). The first specimens caught in Australia were thought to be *G. a. holbrooki* (Griffiths 1972), but gel electrophoresis and gonopodium morphology unequivocally confirmed their correct identity (Trendall and Johnson 1981).

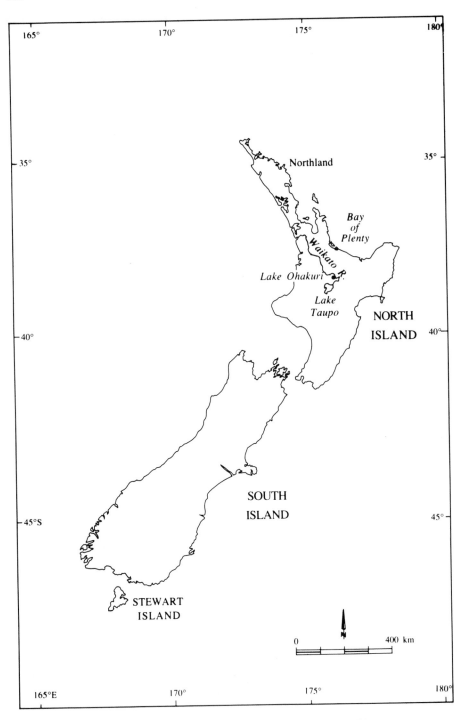

Figure 18–2. Major New Zealand locations supporting poeciliids.

Populations of the sailfin molly, *Poecilia latipinna*, have been established in a few creeks and drains at Hervey Bay and in Sandgate Lagoon (Figure 18–3), north of Brisbane, Queensland, since approximately 1968 (McKay 1978). In New Zealand, sailfin mollies occur only in geothermally heated swamps near Tokaanu at the southern limit of Lake Taupo (McDowall 1987). A population recorded in Waipahihi Stream, flowing into Lake Taupo, has recently been replaced by the swordtail, *Xiphophorus helleri*; the temperature range in these thermal waters is 22 to 48°C (Vincent and Forsyth 1987).

The guppy, *Poecilia reticulata*, is widespread in eastern Queensland in urban and suburban creeks and drains around Cairns, Innisfail, Ingham, Mackay, Rockhampton, and Gladstone (McKay 1978; Figure 18–3). Further south, the guppy is more patchily distributed, occurring in clear, freshwater springs flowing into Barambah Creek, a tributary of the Burnett River, and in a few Brisbane creeks (Figure 18–3). Between 1977–78 and 1981–82, some Brisbane populations of this species disappeared (Arthington et al. 1983). In the Australian Northern Territory, guppies are found in the Gove town lagoon and in Sadgroves Creek near Darwin (McKay 1987). Some of the spread of the guppy in Australia was due to releases for mosquito control (Lloyd 1986).

Poecilia reticulata was once recorded in Waipahihi Stream flowing into Lake Taupo in New Zealand (Figure 18–2), but this population did not persist. However, populations of guppies were rediscovered more recently in thermal streams flowing into the Waikato River (McDowall 1987) and at a thermal site in Lake Ohakuri (Howard-Williams et al. 1987). These populations may have originated from ornamental ponds at Golden Springs thermal resort, which empty into a stream flowing into the lake (McDowall 1979; Howard-Williams et al. 1987).

The earliest records of the swordtail, *Xiphophorus helleri*, in Brisbane date back to about 1966. McKay (1978) recorded swordtails in 19 creeks around Brisbane in 1977–78, and most of these populations have persisted to the present. One introduction has been traced to the escape of juvenile fish from an aquarist's fish ponds located near the headwaters of a creek, and many other feral populations are undoubtedly due to release of unwanted aquarium fish or flooding of outdoor ornamental ponds during cyclonic rains (McKay 1978). Some of the subsequent spread of swordtails around Brisbane is due to movement by school children. This species has also been found at Gladstone, Queensland (Figure 18–3). In New Zealand, the swordtail occurs only in Waipahihi Stream flowing into Lake Taupo (Vincent and Forsyth 1987).

The platyfish, *Xiphophorus maculatus*, is known from a few creeks and swampy sites in and north of Brisbane (Figure 18–3). Original establishment of the platyfish in the upper Brisbane River may have been due to deliberate stocking of a deep, isolated pool for breeding large numbers of aquarium fish and subsequent spread to the river during floods (McKay 1978). The platyfish has spread naturally in the upper Brisbane River in recent years (Arthington et al. 1983; McKay 1984). At Hervey Bay the species was introduced from an aquarium fish farm in the late 1960s (McKay 1978). It does not occur in New Zealand waters.

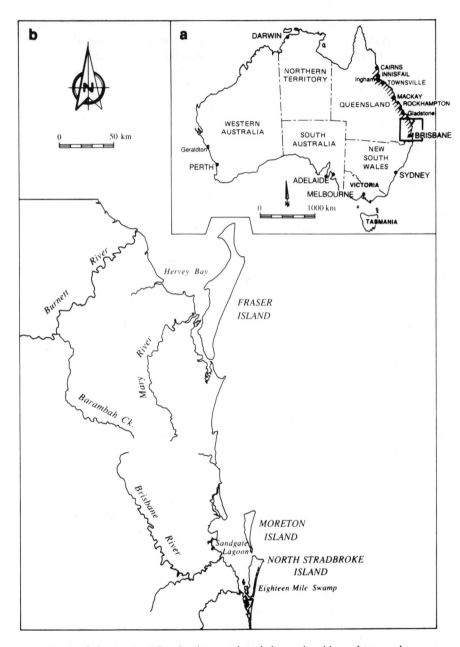

Figure 18–3. (a) Australia, showing state boundaries, major cities and towns where *Xiphophorus helleri* occurs, and the distribution of *Poecilia reticulata* (crosshatched area). (b) Southeastern Queensland, showing Barambah Creek and Sandgate Lagoon (colonized by *P. reticulata*), and Eighteen-Mile Swamp, North Stradbroke Island, where an endemic rainbowfish may have been eliminated by *G. affinis.*

HABITATS AND ENVIRONMENTAL
TOLERANCES OF POECILIIDS

Gambusia affinis is locally abundant in inland and coastal streams and rivers within 10 major drainage divisions on the Australian mainland (Figure 18–1). It is most often found in warm, slowly flowing or still waters among aquatic vegetation and in backwaters and billabongs (small oxbow lakes) of lotic systems (McDowall 1980; Shiel 1980; Arthington et al. 1983; McKay 1984; Lloyd and Walker 1986). Mosquitofish have also been recorded in freshwater ponds, swamps, lagoons, lakes, salt lakes (Chessman and Williams 1974), thermal springs (Bayly and Williams 1973) and various artificially heated waters (e.g., the cooling pond of the Hazelwood power station in Victoria [Cadwallader et al. 1980]). Colonization of estuaries does not appear to be widespread, but mosquitofish are clearly capable of surviving in such environments (Griffiths 1972; Booth 1980).

In southeastern Queensland, *G. affinis* is particularly abundant in modified and/or polluted urban and suburban creeks overgrown with introduced grasses, water hyacinth, and *Azolla*, and in more degraded creeks may comprise over 90% of the total fish population (Arthington et al. 1983). Creek headwaters may support up to 14 species of native freshwater fishes; in these lower-order creeks the mosquitofish and swordtail are usually absent, because they are unable to pass natural barriers and weirs and cannot tolerate fast-flowing waters (Meffe 1984b). Also, there have probably been few, if any, accidental or deliberate introductions in such inaccessible areas.

Although most often found in disturbed habitats in Queensland, *G. affinis* has become established in environments that are almost pristine, such as Eighteen-Mile Swamp on North Stradbroke Island and freshwater creeks on Fraser Island, Queensland (Arthington 1984; Figure 18–3). Coastal swamps and creeks on these islands have dilute, acidic waters and are limnologically similar to dystrophic dune lakes. The endemic fish faunas of these insular ecosystems are depauperate (Arthington 1984; Arthington et al. 1986b).

Mosquitofish occur in almost every conceivable aquatic habitat in southeastern Australia. They are present in the relatively pristine Cooper Creek and Finke River systems (Glover 1982; Puckridge and Drewien 1988) in central Australia, waterholes in the arid regions of central and southern Australia (L. N. Lloyd, unpubl. data), in flowing permanent streams and other urban wetlands around Adelaide, Melbourne, and Sydney (Marshall 1966; Lloyd et al. 1986), polluted drains and lakes (Tomasov 1981), and saline evaporation basins adjacent to the River Murray (Lloyd et al. 1984; Lloyd 1987a). Along the Coorong, a hypersaline lagoon at the mouth of the River Murray, mosquitofish are found in freshwater soaks (small freshwater ponds fed by groundwater; J. Glover, pers. comm.).

In the lower River Murray, only two streams were not colonized by *G. affinis* in 1984 (Lloyd and Walker 1986), but subsequent invasion in 1986 into one of them suggested their absence was due to lack of access rather than environmental conditions (Lloyd 1987a). In the southeast of South Australia, mosquitofish distribution is limited, probably due to the temporary nature of many waterbodies. Lack of introductions may also play a part as *G. affinis* is absent from several locations which could presumably support it (Glover 1983). In montane locations, the mosquitofish is probably restricted by intolerance of high flows (Reddy and Pandian 1974).

In Western Australia, *G. affinis* is common in both lotic and lentic habitats throughout the southwest of the state (Griffiths 1972; Mees 1977; Sarti and Allen 1978; Christensen 1982; Lloyd and Tomasov 1985). Its range extends along the west coast from the Hay River to the Greenough River system north of Perth, and there are a few records from unspecified habitats near Broome and Derby (Mees 1977; Lloyd and Tomasov 1985). Many of the shallow lakes that surround Perth provide excellent mosquitofish habitat (Davis et al. 1987). Sarti and Allen (1978) found mosquitofish in all lentic habitats in their survey of the Northern Swan Coastal Plain and noted that native fishes were uncommon and their distributions patchy. However, in several lotic habitats (Moore River, Ellen Brook, Canning River, and North Dandalup River) mosquitofish coexist with a diverse assemblage of endemic fishes, including most species expected in these systems (Pusey et al. 1989). In the Canning and Dandalup rivers, *G. affinis* achieves large populations by the end of summer but is nearly eliminated by high river discharges in winter; according to B. Pusey (pers. comm.) discharge predictability in southwestern rivers is high and removal of mosquitofish appears to be an annual event. This situation parallels the long-term coexistence of mosquitofish and Sonoran topminnows (*Poeciliopsis occidentalis*) in the Sonoran Desert of Arizona, where flash floods periodically remove disproportionate numbers of *G. affinis* before it can eliminate the topminnow (Meffe 1984b).

Data from Australia and New Zealand provide further evidence of wide environmental tolerances of mosquitofish. For instance, salinities at introduction sites range from 40 mg/l (dystrophic swamps) to 30 g/l (salt lakes); large populations have survived in stagnant, oily waters of urban creeks and drains, in creeks receiving pesticide runoff from crops in the Brisbane Valley, and in many waters treated with herbicides (Johnson 1978). *Gambusia affinis* has also been collected from a Brisbane creek polluted with zinc, lead, chromium, nickel, and cadmium. In the Torrens River near Adelaide, a mosquitofish population exhibits resistance to the piscicide rotenone (B. E. Pierce, pers. comm.).

Xiphophorus helleri is frequently found in the same habitats as *G. affinis* in Queensland waters, although some isolated populations exist around Brisbane. It also flourishes in disturbed habitats and weed-infested creeks with degraded water quality, and it is not uncommon to find that 80 to 90% of the fish in highly modified urban creeks are poeciliids (Arthington et al. 1983). However, swordtails are more sensitive to low water temperatures than are mosquitofish and barely tolerate the coldest winters in Brisbane. Laboratory determination of the critical thermal minimum showed that *G. affinis* was capable of spasmodic movements at 1.79°C, but *X. helleri* was stressed at 7.70°C and lost its righting ability at 5.26°C (Arthington et al. 1986a). This difference may partly account for greater abundance of *G. affinis* in creeks around Brisbane. The swordtail does not occur in estuarine or brackish waters in Queensland, although a few of the sites colonized are subject to tidal influence.

In Australia, platyfish, guppies, sailfin mollies, and one-spot livebearers have been found in urban creeks, drains, swamps, lagoons, and outdoor ornamental ponds. In New Zealand, poeciliids other than *G. affinis* are associated only with geothermally heated waters and have not been able to survive in cooler natural waters (McDowall 1979, 1987).

IMPACTS OF POECILIIDS

Mechanisms of Impact

Potential impacts of introduced fishes may involve hybridization with endemics, habitat disruption, competition for space or food, predation, and introduction of exotic parasites and diseases (Courtenay and Stauffer 1984). Hybridization with endemic species cannot occur in Australia and New Zealand, because neither country has an endemic poeciliid fauna. Hybridization between two species, subspecies, or genetic strains of poeciliids is a possibility but has not been recorded in either country.

Most evidence of ecological impacts in Australia and New Zealand is speculative, anecdotal, or supported mainly by patterns of distribution and abundance; information on the fish fauna of aquatic systems before the introduction of exotics is largely unavailable (McKay 1984; McDowall 1987). Although research on this problem has increased in the last decade, most work has concentrated on describing trends and documenting the biology and ecology of poeciliids and the endemic species most likely to be affected (e.g., Arthington et al. 1983; Milton and Arthington 1983a, 1983b, 1984, 1985; Lloyd and Walker 1986; Lloyd 1987a). Rigorous analyses of species interactions under different environmental conditions and in experimental systems have only just begun (see Lloyd 1987a).

Habitat Disruption

There is little evidence that introduced livebearing fishes have disrupted aquatic habitats in Australia and New Zealand. Although *X. helleri* is predominantly herbivorous (A. H. Arthington, unpubl. data), there is no clear evidence that swordtails have contributed to changes in aquatic macrophyte or algal communities in streams. Loss of native macrophytes from Brisbane's urban creeks has resulted from dredging, channel modifications, siltation, dumping by riparian landowners, bank erosion, and invasion of exotic plants (Arthington et al. 1983). Herbicide control of water hyacinth and other nuisance plants may also have contributed to decline of some native macrophytes.

Water quality changes, such as increased turbidity or substrate disturbance, have coincided with proliferation of exotic fishes but cannot be attributed to their activities. For example, such changes have been attributed to introduced European carp, *Cyprinus carpio*, in Australia, but studies in the Goulburn River, Victoria do not support this (Fletcher et al. 1985). Poeciliids seem unlikely to have any direct effect on benthic substrates, but increased algal densities have resulted from selective feeding by mosquitofish in experimental ponds (Hurlbert et al. 1972).

Impacts of Competition on Fish

Resource competition, mediated by interference and aggression, seems a likely mechanism of impact by *G. affinis* in many areas of introduction. Taylor et al. (1984) and Arthington and Mitchell (1986) pointed out that successful exotic fish typically exhibit generalist feeding habits and trophic opportunism. There is considerable overlap in diets of mosquitofish, guppies, and representatives of several Australian fish families, particularly melanotaeniids, retropinnids, eleotrids, atherinids, and galaxiids (Lloyd 1987a; A. H. Arthington, unpubl. data).

The diet of rainbowfish, *Melanotaenia duboulayi*, in Brisbane Creeks changes when large populations of mosquitofish are present. Algae become more important and terrestrial insects less important in rainbowfish diets; these changes are accompanied by selective feeding on larger prey than that eaten in habitats without mosquitofish. These differences reduce dietary overlap between the rainbowfish and *G. affinis*, which actively selects small prey (Bence and Murdoch 1986; A. H. Arthington, unpubl. data) and does not consume algae in these creeks. Precisely how dietary niche shifts affect growth, reproduction, and recruitment of *M. duboulayi* is unknown.

There is both field and experimental evidence that some fishes in the Murray-Darling River shift feeding niches and expand niche breadth in the presence of *G. affinis* (Lloyd 1987a). While competition theory (O'Connor et al. 1975) predicts that niche breadth should decrease as a result of interspecific competition, optimal foraging theory states that, given equal exploitation of the resource by the competitors, niche breadth should expand (Pyke et al. 1977).

As a corollory of niche shifts in the presence of *G. affinis*, some native fishes shift distribution and abundance (Lloyd 1987a). A mutually exclusive pattern exists between mosquitofish and the pigmy perch, *Nannoperca australis*, in the lower Murray River (Lloyd 1984; Lloyd and Walker 1986). Other species show lower abundances in the presence of *G. affinis* and *X. helleri* than do populations of the same species in habitats without poeciliids (Arthington et al. 1983; Lloyd 1987a).

Interference competition is also important, because the mosquitofish is an aggressive species that nips the fins of other fishes (Myers 1965; Meffe 1983, 1985b). However, the ecological impact of such aggression is largely unquantified. Lloyd (1987a) showed that mosquitofish would attack native fish twice their size and could inflict caudal fin damage, leaving fish susceptible to disease. Schoenherr

(1981) interpreted aggressive behaviour of mosquitofish leading to the suppression of reproduction in the Gila (Sonoran) topminnow as interspecific competition for space. Meffe (1985b), however, disputed this interpretation and stated that, while some interference does occur, predation by mosquitofish has been the important mechanism of decline. McKay (1978, 1984) suggested that the sheer numbers of mosquitofish and swordtails in creek habitats could adversely affect the endemic fish fauna.

Impacts of Predation

Myers (1965) called *G. affinis* the "fish destroyer", because it attacks the eggs and fry of important sport fishes and is a known piscivore. Australian dietary studies provide only incidental evidence of piscivory (Cadwallader 1979; Lloyd 1987a; Arthington 1988), but this is probably an artifact of standard methods of gut content analyses, which underestimate rapidly-digested foods such as fish (Meffe 1985b). Aquarium studies show conclusively that *G. affinis* will attack and eat juvenile fish (Johnson 1976b; Meffe 1985b; Lloyd 1987a), and Meffe (1985b) calculated that, even at low predation rates, a mosquitofish female could eat the entire annual reproductive output of a single Sonoran topminnow, *P. occidentalis*. He concluded that rare predation on fry could easily have a significant impact on a species with lower fecundity, such as *P. occidentalis*. Several of the small-bodied native fishes possibly affected by the mosquitofish in eastern Australia (e.g., melanotaeniids, atherinids, and a retropinnid) have low fecundity (Milton and Arthington 1983b, 1984, 1985), but others do not.

Regardless of the mechanisms involved, there is good evidence from Australia that several endemic species have declined in habitats where swordtails and/or mosquitofish are abundant (e.g., melanotaeniids, eleotrids, ambassids, kuhlids, atherinids, and a retropinnid; Arthington et al. 1983; Lloyd and Walker 1986). In Brisbane, decline of native fishes is due partly to habitat degradation, invasion of introduced plants, and poor water quality, conditions that poeciliids are able to exploit. In the River Murray, *G. affinis* is held at least partly responsible for reduction or absence of endemic fishes, because some species exist only in suitable habitats without mosquitofish (Lloyd 1987a).

There is at least one Australian instance where *G. affinis* may have eliminated a native fish from a near pristine system. The rainbowfish *Rhadinocentris ornatus* is a common species in swamps and lakes on Queensland's dune islands but is rare in Eighteen Mile Swamp on North Stradbroke Island (Arthington 1984; Figure 18–3); *G. affinis* is abundant in this swamp. The rainbowfish, like *G. affinis*, feeds predominantly on terrestrial insects at the water's surface (Bayly et al. 1975), and this may be a case of competitive displacement. However, predation on eggs and young fish may also be involved. *Gambusia affinis* was introduced to control mosquito larvae, but sedge swamps of this type breed few mosquitoes. The major pest mosquitoes on the island originate from brackish salt marshes, where *G. affinis* does not occur (Bensink and Burton 1975; Arthington 1984).

Impacts on Invertebrates

Mosquitofish have had destructive effects on invertebrate populations in various field situations (Stephanides 1964; Legner and Medved 1974), and controlled experiments support these observations. Taxa such as beetles (Walters and Legner 1980), back swimmers (Hurlbert and Mulla 1981), rotifers, Crustacea (Hurlbert et al. 1972), and molluscs (Rees 1979) have been affected by the mosquitofish. In Australian streams, *G. affinis* feeds on small terrestrial insects and immature stages of aquatic insects in the drift and among aquatic plants (Lloyd 1987a; Arthington 1988). In environments where terrestrial insects are scarce (where there is little overhanging riparian vegetation), *G. affinis* may feed predominantly on aquatic invertebrates. We speculate that this, coupled with active selection of small prey (Arthington 1988), might affect the structure of invertebrate communities by altering recruitment of various taxa. Davis et al. (1987) showed that in lakes without *G. affinis*, there were 11 species of Odonata, but only 3 to 4 species in lakes with this poeciliid. More work is required on this aspect of poeciliid impacts.

Introduction of Parasites and Diseases

Biologists who oppose liberal introduction of aquarium species into Australia are concerned that exotic diseases and parasites may also be introduced (Hoffman 1970; McKay 1984). There is some evidence that disease organisms such as goldfish ulcer disease (Trust et al. 1980) have entered Australia via the aquarium trade. This disease has spread rapidly from aquarium stocks to wild populations. A new viral disease of introduced European perch (*Perca fluviatilis*) has been described (Langdon 1986; Langdon and Humphrey 1987). Concern that diseases can easily be introduced has led to quarantine facilities at major ports handling aquarium stocks (McKay 1984).

Other fish introductions were responsible for importing fish parasites such as fish louse (*Argulus* sp.) (Williams 1980) and anchor worm (*Lernaea cyprinacea*) (Roberts 1978; Hoffman and Schubert 1984). Although *G. affinis* is host to 23 species of parasites in North America (Lloyd 1987a), there is only one record of parasitism from Australia. *Lernaea cyprinacea* occurs in fish from the River Murray and other sites in South Australia (Lloyd 1984, 1987a). The incidence of exotic parasites in other poeciliids and endemic fishes is unknown.

ROLE OF *GAMBUSIA AFFINIS* IN MOSQUITO CONTROL

Although *G. affinis* was introduced worldwide to control mosquitoes, releases were not based on firm evidence that this species would be especially effective (see Lloyd 1986, 1987a, 1987b). Studies in Australia have shown that *G. affinis*

TABLE 18–1.   Comparative Mosquito Predation by *Gambusia affinis* and
Endemic Fish Species from the Lower River Murray, South Australia
(from Lloyd 1986).

Species	% in Diet by Volume	% Frequency of Occurrence
Retropinna semoni	33	71
Melanotaenia fluviatilis	17	48
Philypnodon grandiceps	16	30
Galaxias olidus	11	36
Gambusia affinis	10	28
Craterocephalus stercusmuscarum	6	18

is in fact a poor mosquito predator. In the lower River Murray, only 10% of its diet consists of mosquito larvae, whereas four endemic fish species consume more mosquitoes (Table 18–1). Mosquito larvae are rarely eaten by *G. affinis* in Brisbane creeks, even though several mosquito species breed in the sheltered, vegetated margins of pools and backwaters (A. H. Arthington, unpubl. data).

Review of the world literature on mosquito control has not supported the view that *G. affinis* has reduced mosquito problems or the incidence of mosquito-borne diseases in Australia or elsewhere (Lloyd 1986; Courtenay and Meffe, Chapter 17), apart from moderate control in parts of California (e.g., Cech and Linden, 1986). Where good larval control has been reported (Krumholz 1948; Wilson 1960; Miura et al. 1984) the evidence was largely anecdotal or derived from poorly designed experiments (see Lloyd 1986 for details).

Many Australian biologists believe that endemic fish provide a preferable alternative to *G. affinis*, because mosquitofish are relatively ineffective and have adverse ecological impacts (McKay 1978; McDowall 1980; Lloyd 1984, 1986). Recent changes in the attitude of local health authorities are encouraging, in that endemic fish are being considered for mosquito control. However, the spread of *G. affinis* continues (Lloyd 1987a).

The early acceptance and subsequent entrenchment of *G. affinis* as a suitable mosquito control agent was greatly assisted by its common name, the "mosquito-fish." This immediately identified *G. affinis* as the "logical" choice for the solution to mosquito problems, to the extent that endemic fish were often ignored as potential vector controls (Lloyd 1987b). The previous common name, "topminnow," is nondescript and unsuitable as a substitute, because it also refers to other endemic American poeciliids and cyprinodontids; additionally, *G. affinis* is not a minnow. We suggest that these common names, both misnomers, be replaced by a suitable, nonevocative common name in the interests of discouraging use of *G. affinis* for mosquito control.

SUMMARY AND FUTURE RESEARCH

Six species of poeciliids have been introduced into Australian waters and four into New Zealand. Declines of native fishes frequently occur in habitats where exotics, particularly *Gambusia affinis*, are abundant, but mechanisms of decline are difficult to unequivocally demonstrate. Often, declines are associated not only with exotic fishes, but also with severe habitat disruption. Likely biotic mechanisms of species replacement include resource competition and predation by aggressive poeciliids.

We predict that future spread of poeciliids is inevitable in subtropical and tropical areas of Australia, and effects on endemic fish and aquatic ecosystems are likely (McKay 1978; Balla et al. 1985). Given the experience with *G. affinis*, widespread carnivorous species such as *P. reticulata* are of most concern. In New Zealand, natural water temperatures are too low for survival of poeciliids (excluding *G. affinis*) except where geothermal heating occurs (McDowall 1979, 1987). Nevertheless, the impact of introduced poeciliids on the specialized invertebrate fauna of geothermal systems (Vincent and Forsyth 1987) will be of scientific interest.

All *G. affinis* in Australia are the subspecies *holbrooki*, and there is no possibility that subspecific crosses will occur with their attendant implications for the ecology of this fish (Black and Howell 1979; Reznick 1981). The subspecific status of *G. affinis* in New Zealand is incompletely known. Lloyd and Tomasov (1985) found two populations to be *G. a. affinis*, but populations throughout the species' range in New Zealand have not been examined.

The presence of only *G. a. holbrooki* in Australia presents an opportunity, possibly a rare one, to study genetic and phenotypic divergence of this subspecies in a country where a wide latitudinal range of environments has been colonized. Tomasov (1981) has shown that populations as far apart as Melbourne and Perth, and Sydney and Darwin were phenotypically more similar than populations closer together (in Sydney and Melbourne, and in Sydney and Brisbane); also, genotypic differences between populations were not consistently manifest in morphometic differences, and vice versa. Such differences may be the result of local selection. More critical studies on divergence since introduction of *G. affinis* populations in Queensland are in progress and are needed for all poeciliids in Australia and New Zealand.

The critical physiological tolerances of poeciliids, particularly temperature tolerance, must be investigated to determine if exposure to extreme conditions has shifted response spectra. *Gambusia affinis* exists as "warm-adapted" and "cold-adapted" strains in the United States (Otto 1973), and a similar shift of thermal tolerance could occur in fish from southern and northern Australia. *Xiphophorus helleri* may be undergoing selection for cold tolerance in southern Queensland, the species' southern limit; low winter temperatures have intermittently killed many fish in local populations (McKay 1978). That shifts in physiological tolerances occur means that the future range of an introduced species can never be predicted with certainty. Appreciation of this and other problems has led Australian fisheries authorities to restrict introduction of aquarium species and to reject the introduction of Nile perch (*Lates niloticus*) into northern waterbodies for recreational fishing (Barlow and Lisle 1987). However, we believe more stringent restrictions on fish imports are warranted.

Whereas *G. affinis* may form part of the diet of endemic piscivores (although it is avoided when there is a choice, Lloyd 1987a) and perhaps water birds, factors limiting poeciliid population growth in Australia and New Zealand are poorly understood. The roles of parasitism and disease are unknown. Fortunately, flooding and low water temperatures reduce local *G. affinis* populations in the lower River Murray (Lloyd 1987a) and in southwestern Australia (Pusey et al. 1989); summer floods probably achieve some population control in Queensland waters. However, biological population control in conjunction with density independent mortality to restrict *G. affinis* is well beyond present capabilities. Thus, eradication of *G. affinis* and other poeciliids may never be possible except in the most restricted circumstances.

Obviously, further spread of poeciliids must be discouraged. The major problem for the future lies with poeciliids already established in northern Australia, where temperatures permit extended breeding (Milton and Arthington 1983a), and further spread is likely. A major problem with aquarium fish of all types is that people are reluctant to destroy unwanted fish and instead release them into some "suitable" environment (Balla et al. 1985). An important step that all state governments in Australia should take is to provide repositories for unwanted fish to prevent repeated releases of potentially damaging species (Balla et al. 1985). This simple approach has not yet been applied.

Gambusia affinis has been in Australia and New Zealand for nearly 60 years, and many ecosystems are already affected. We have conducted research on population genetics, ecology, and the impact of this most troublesome poeciliid, as well as other carnivorous species, and will use this knowledge to argue for greater restrictions on the importation and trade of poeciliids and aquarium fishes in general. Support for such research in Australia and New Zealand has to date largely been limited to more conspicuous immigrants such as salmonids, European carp, and tilapia. "Small fishes in strange places" in the southern hemisphere must receive more attention.

ACKNOWLEDGMENTS

A. H. Arthington acknowledges two research grants from the Australian National Parks and Wildlife Service for the study of introduced fishes in Queensland, and the assistance of R. J. McKay, D. A. Milton, and M. English in these studies. B. Pusey and J. M. Hughes contributed to this manuscript and A. Chandica redrew the figures from original published versions. L. N. Lloyd acknowledges research funds from the University of Adelaide, the Peter Till Environmental Laboratory (A.W.D.C., Albury), the Department of Environment and Planning, South Australia and the National Water Resources Council (Department of Resources and Energy, Canberra). Thanks are to K. F. Walker, G. Lloyd, and all members of the River Murray Laboratory for support and assistance in the course of this research.

Section V

Conclusions and Future Research

We use the final chapter to consolidate impressions and viewpoints that surfaced during the many discussions and long hours devoted to the planning, organization, and production of this book. A number of deficiencies are now apparent in both our understanding of and our approach to these fishes. However, a bright perspective emerges that reflects great potential for innovative directions and ideas. We hope that this chapter will stimulate renewed efforts to use fishes in this family to fullest advantage in evolutionary and ecological research.

Chapter 19

Poeciliid Biology: Where We Are and Where We Should Be Going

FRANKLIN F. SNELSON, JR.
GARY K. MEFFE*

INTRODUCTION

The previous 18 chapters addressed a variety of general to specialized topics in poeciliid biology. Although a number of themes have been sounded, one in particular occurs in virtually every chapter: the prevalence of huge gaps in our knowledge of the family and the need for further research in every topical area. There remains a wealth of information to be gleaned from this scientifically appealing group, from basic natural history and zoogeography to complex details of genetics and reproductive physiology. The poeciliids potentially can be one of the most important groups of animals with which to explore myriad details of evolution and ecology, but this will first require greater understanding of their natural history, distribution, physiology, development, and genetics. Synthesis across these research areas should provide the greatest rewards and insights.

We discuss five aspects of poeciliid research that have become evident to us during this project as areas needing attention. Rigorous pursuit of these endeavors will advance progress in poeciliid research and conservation and could result in a group of organisms unsurpassed in their value toward understanding pattern and process in nature.

---

* Order of authorship randomly determined.

GAPS IN OUR KNOWLEDGE

Most of the preceding chapters indicate where gaps lie in our knowledge of poeciliid biology and why they are important to fill. We choose several ideas to illuminate here, with the hope that researchers will be stimulated to pursue them in an organized and rigorous fashion. Literally hundreds of other questions await attention.

1) Basic natural history—The basic natural history of most poeciliids is virtually or completely unknown. Probably more important than any other endeavor, we must expand this seriously deficient data base. We are especially in need of information on South American and Caribbean species to balance our present North and Central American, subtropical to temperate biases. It is impossible to make sense out of the biology of individual species, or of the group in general, unless basic information is gathered regarding distribution, habitat preferences, trophic dynamics, population structure, physiological ecology, and so forth. Such information is lacking for the vast majority of species, and would be most valuable when studies are designed to provide good, comparative data, making cross-taxon comparisons meaningful. We feel a growing sense of urgency about these problems, since the well-documented destruction of tropical communities threatens to reduce many poeciliid species to museum jar curiosities, forever eliminating our opportunity to understand them as living entities.

2) Community ecology—The role of poeciliids on the community level has essentially not been studied. In particular, these fish, which often exist in large populations, may be significant vectors of energy flow across trophic levels as both consumers and prey. Their importance as a food source for predaceous invertebrates, fishes, water snakes, and wading birds needs to be further analyzed. Their interactions with invertebrates and other fishes should also be examined in context of niche and competitive relationships.

3) Allotopic distributions of poeciliids—Based on the few studies conducted (Meffe and Snelson, Chapter 2) there appears to be strong microhabitat segregation in poeciliids. Is there a high degree of competition among these fishes, or would they select (prefer) different microhabitats even in the absence of competitive interactions? Questions about the allotopic distribution of closely related species need to be addressed experimentally in the field and under controlled laboratory conditions.

4) The dimunitive size of poeciliids—What are the ecological and evolutionary implications of the small size of poeciliids? This question has not been addressed. We speculate, with no evidence, that viviparity may constrain size in this family. This is a very basic question that may have interesting answers, providing insights into evolution of the group.

5) Control of parturition in poeciliids—Although descriptive aspects of reproduction and life histories are well developed for some species, the physiology of reproduction is poorly known. We do not even know, for example, how parturition is initiated. This would be particularly interesting to pursue in superfetators, because only a few of the many developing embryos are selectively delivered. Does the mother or the embryo "signal" that development is complete? Many other aspects of poeciliid reproductive physiology, including ovarian microstructure, hormonal control of reproduction, maternal-fetal transfer of materials, and sources and importance of pheromones, are all poorly known.

THE SEARCH FOR PROXIMATE MECHANISMS

In this family, we have the opportunity to evaluate proximate mechanisms for factors important to life history evolution, especially those dealing with reproduction. Although elegant theories abound for many aspects of poeciliid life history and evolution, the ability of the organism to respond through appropriate physiological or behavioral mechanisms is not always addressed. Ultimate, evolutionary-oriented questions must be paired with proximate, mechanistically-based responses.

A number of questions concerning reproduction and life history theory present themselves and provide excellent avenues of study for physiologically-oriented researchers:

1)   What controls the "decision" to initiate reproduction? Under what conditions does a female begin the vitellogenic process? Obviously, an individual must be in good physiological condition in order to reproduce, but some apparently healthy fish skip a reproductive episode (Travis, Chapter 10). It would be informative to know the hormonal basis for vitellogenesis, as well as other physiological conditions that must be met for reproduction to occur.

2)   How are "choices" made regarding the number and size of offspring in a brood? How is energy allocated between individuals within a brood, or between successive broods? These questions are particularly relevant to contrasting theories of offspring size such as optimality arguments and the adaptive coin-flipping principle (Meffe 1987b). Before one or another theory can be reasonably accepted as an evolutionary interpretation of a life history pattern, a plausible mechanism must be available. Thus, the question of how tightly a female can control energy flow to offspring is critical.

3)   What are the physical mechanisms that enable viviparity (matrotrophy) to work? That is, how does the female provision ova or embryos with nutrients? Little has been done to explain mechanisms of nutrient transfer between mother and offspring, or even to identify the nutrients. Detailed physiological and biochemical studies employing radioactive tracers would greatly improve our understanding of viviparity.

4)   What are the histological and biochemical details of development? There was no chapter on poeciliid developmental biology in this book, because little has been done since descriptive work earlier this century. Obviously, it is difficult to study development in a fish that retains embryos until "hatching." Development and wider use of existing *in vitro* techniques (Depeche 1962, 1964, 1976) to raise poeciliid embryos outside of the mother would allow experimental and descriptive analyses of nutrition and development. This could have great impact on under-

standing the evolution of viviparity and the range of its expression within the family.

5) How might facultative viviparity (Trexler 1985) work? How and under what circumstances might a female "decide" to shunt additional resources to developing embryos? This interesting theory begs for mechanistic and deterministic studies. The results of such research could have a bearing on the question of facultative superfetation (Monaco et al. 1983).

REEVALUATION OF DOGMA

The accuracy of some early poeciliid research has come under suspicion as contemporary authors critically evaluate that work or repeat the research and draw new conclusions. For example, Medlen (1951) is frequently cited in reference to photoperiod and thermal control of reproduction in mosquitofish (*Gambusia affinis*). Based on a small laboratory study, Medlen concluded that temperature is more critical than photoperiod in initiation of reproduction. Although this may be true, his "experiment" was poorly designed and has no bearing on the question. It is absurd to expect mosquitofish to reproduce at 48°F, one of Medlen's experimental temperatures, no matter how long the daylength. Medlen also had no replicates and no formal data analysis; he did not even present a relevant data table. We feel that the paper's conclusions are invalid due to poor experimental design and misinterpretation of results; yet, it is repeatedly cited in current literature as evidence of the importance of temperature in poeciliid brood cycling.

Reznick and Miles (Chapter 7) question the validity of much of Scrimshaw's work on poeciliid reproduction, because more recent and extensive data disagree with his results published in the 1940s. For example, Scrimshaw (1945) reported that mature ova of *Belonesox belizanus* averaged almost 20 mg in weight, whereas the largest weighed by Turner and Snelson (1984) was 12 mg and the average was less than 10 mg. Similarly, Snelson (1982) challenged the widely-held dogma that male poeciliids cease growing at sexual maturity. Since that report, several other authors have confirmed that males of some species continue to grow, albeit slowly, after maturation (Snelson, Chapter 8). Other areas of "classical" poeciliid research may be similarly suspect.

Although superficially we appear to have a rich data base in selected aspects of poeciliid biology, little has been corroborated by other researchers. Instead, we cite and re-cite the same papers, somewhat like constructing a large building on an uncertain foundation. The definitive works on most topics have not been completed or even attempted. Reexamination of some basic dogma regarding poeciliid biology (particularly with respect to reproduction) would constitute a major contribution. We need more family-wide reviews of selected topics, such as Reznick and Miles' (Chapter 7) treatment of superfetation or Farr's (Chapter 6) analysis of behavior and sexual selection. Another good model is Thibault and Schultz's (1978) effort, which provided a solid, comparative analysis of reproduction in five poeciliid species. Similar studies with other groups or on other topics would be welcomed.

SYNTHESIS ACROSS DISCIPLINES

The greatest advances in evolutionary ecology will undoubtedly come from synthesis across disciplines as diverse as systematics, genetics, development, ecology, behavior, physiology, and life history evolution. We encourage poeciliid biologists to approach their specific area of interest in context of other disciplines and to ask whether there is concordance among them. In particular, systematics can be an organizational theme for all poeciliid research. Testing ideas in context of proposed evolutionary relationships (Parenti and Rauchenberger, Chapter 1; Rauchenberger, Appendix 1) will provide a more rigorous framework for understanding the chosen phenomenon than will myopic, single-species approaches. By organizing research around proposed phylogenetic relationships, we can ask whether new genetic or behavioral data, for example, are concordant or suggest new interpretations. Alternatively, do phylogenetic constraints dictate other aspects of poeciliid biology, such as behavior or life history pattern?

We are intrigued by Parenti's suggestion (1981, Chapter 1) that the closest relatives of the poeciliids are not other viviparous cyprinodontiforms but are certain oviparous groups from both the Old and New World tropics. This hypothesis casts a novel light on our attempts to understand the origin and diversity of reproductive modes in this group. Our understanding of reproduction in egg-laying cyprinodontiforms is based primarily on members of the family Cyprinodontidae, especially the genus *Fundulus*. It is now unclear whether we can use what we know about cyprinodontids to bridge the gap from oviparity to primitive ovoviviparity, such as practiced by *Tomeurus gracilis*.

Comprehensive surveys across broad taxonomic categories would serve to rigorously outline problems in an evolutionary context and would permit more thorough analyses of biological phenomena. For example, Farr (Chapter 6) examined sexual selection and male mating strategies across poeciliid taxa and uncovered patterns that would have gone unnoticed in a study lacking a systematic perspective. Likewise, Reznick and Miles (Chapter 7) systematically approached life history evolution to suggest patterns across taxa. Echelle et al. (Chapter 12) suggest that proposed phylogenetic relationships be tested by genetic analyses; we agree that such a study would prove most beneficial in understanding poeciliid evolution.

Huge gaps exist in our most basic knowledge of certain taxa. We suspect, for example, that almost any biological information on the most primitive poeciliid, *Tomereus gracilis*, would cast new light on problems ranging from relationships and biogeography to evolution of the gonopodium. To have such large gaps within certain taxonomic categories greatly cripples our abilities to use poeciliids to understand evolutionary and ecological processes.

Poeciliid trophic levels could be another organizing theme. Analysis of behavior, life histories, reproduction, conservation, and physiological ecology could be approached from the perspective of energy acquisition. The particular trophic level at which a species functions may influence or constrain other aspects of its biology. Farr (Chapter 6), for example, suggests that the predatory nature of *Belonesox belizanus*, with its need for secrecy and stealth, so constrains its reproductive behavior that males do not exhibit gonopodial thrusting or the sexual vigor so characteristic of most poeciliid species. Similarly, the herbivorous nature of other species may influence reproductive mode and general physiology. Does the presumed continuous availability of food to detritivorous species result in more uniform reproductive output than in carnivores?

The merging of population ecology and population genetics is an exciting and promising development that will have tremendous future impact on subdisciplines of evolutionary ecology. Livebearers can play a central role in these developments due to their abundance, natural occurrence in a wide variety of habitats, broad life history differences, and the ease with which they can be bred and manipulated in the laboratory or the field. The most exceptional contribution from poeciliids, however, and potentially the greatest contributor to the field of ecological genetics, is the availability of unisexual clones. Clonal and hemiclonal poeciliids have already been used to address questions of niche partitioning (Wetherington et al., Chapter 14). The use of known, fixed genotypes to investigate life history theory, optimality arguments, the genetic basis of plasticity, and so forth is an efficient way to separate genetic from environmental influences on the phenotype. Clonal livebearers should even prove valuable in testing aspects of conservation genetics theory due to our ability to control genetic background of the fishes and evaluate their success in different environments. However, caution must be exercised in direct extrapolation from clonal to sexual organisms.

Finally, one of the most interesting results of the blending of behavior and evolutionary biology in recent years is our increased understanding of the evolution of animal breeding systems, and especially alternative male mating strategies. Alternative male strategies abound in vertebrates; indeed, they are found in almost every group that has been critically evaluated, including poeciliids. Livebearers provide an ideal vehicle to further understand the complexities of fish breeding systems because of the diversity of alternatives that have evolved and our ability to track the outcome of sexual selection through well-defined genetic markers. Recent studies by Travis, Farr, Woodhead, and coworkers on *Poecilia latipinna* are on the leading edge of this exciting subject (Farr, Chapter 6; Travis, Chapter 10).

NEED FOR A NATIONAL REPOSITORY OF POECILIID STOCKS

The primary factor responsible for our ignorance of most poeciliid fishes is certainly their unavailability to most researchers. The vast majority of species occur only in Central or South America, or on Caribbean islands. These areas are often physically or politically inaccessible to most researchers or are at least expensive to access. Greater availability of stocks of species from these regions would be a boon to poeciliid research. We suggest that, at minimum, researchers informally make stocks available to colleagues for nonconflicting or collaborative research. Ideally, a national or international repository for living stocks, combined with active pursuit of as many species as possible, would enable tremendous research strides. A model for such a repository is available in the form of Dexter National Fish Hatchery (Johnson and Hubbs, Chapter 16), where several endangered or threatened poeciliids are held for research, as a hedge against against extinction, and for propagation and return to the wild. Expansion of the spirit of such an effort to include more abundant but inaccessible taxa seems appropriate at a time when information on, and preservation of, global biological diversity is finally becoming appreciated.

CONCLUSIONS

Although we often state that certain aspects of the family Poeciliidae are well known and that the group is a popular and powerful research "tool," we are really at an embryonic stage in our knowledge of poeciliid biology. Some groundwork has been laid, and we know enough to realize that poeciliids are excellent animals with which to probe processes of ecology and evolution. However, we remain far from a powerful synthesis and understanding of these fishes. This is at once a sobering and a stimulating thought; we know less than we would like to admit, but there is much to learn, and many exciting and unexplored avenues to pursue. This should be particularly appealing to young researchers who sometimes feel that all of the interesting questions in biology have already been answered.

The time is right for a renaissance of thought in poeciliid biology. A systematic overhaul in our approach is appropriate, one that begins with healthy skepticism of what has come before and proceeds with a broad and synthetic view of the group. Some very basic data need to be collected, and large gaps need to be filled. Concentration on basic ecology and natural history, reproductive physiology, ecological and developmental genetics, and population and community processes will then permit synthetic treatment of more sophisticated topics in evolutionary ecology.

We caution, however, that new workers must recognize both the strengths and weaknesses of the group as research organisms, and exploit the former. Although we have repeatedly touted poeciliids throughout this text as excellent study animals, they do have some drawbacks. They may be outstanding for life history and reproductive investment studies but are poor subjects for population analyses such as those involving mark-recapture techniques. They are excellent for population genetic or laboratory heritability studies but present problems for *in vivo* developmental research, largely because it is difficult to precisely determine time of fertilization and follow the progress of ontogeny. Finally, we caution that poeciliids may not constitute "the" model group for studies concerning the evolution of cyprinodonti-form viviparity. Parenti's (1981, Chapter 1) phylogenetic analysis suggests that viviparity may have evolved several times in the order. If so, differences such as follicular gestation in poeciliids versus ovarian gestation in goodeids (Wourms 1981) may represent fundamental dichotomies of ancient evolutionary origin. Poeciliids would then constitute only one of several groups we need to study in order to completely understand the evolutionary ecology of viviparous reproduction.

We reiterate that poeciliids offer promising and exciting opportunities as a model group for advances in evolutionary ecology. Despite wide information gaps and the fact that they live underwater, they are one of the best vertebrate groups for diverse research opportunities. If this book has stimulated a resurgence of thought and energy to use the Poeciliidae to better advantage in ecological and evolutionary research, then we will have succeeded in accomplishing one of our main objectives.

Appendix 1

Annotated Species List
of the Subfamily Poeciliinae

MARY RAUCHENBERGER

This annotated species list augments the classification presented in Chapter 1. When Parenti (1981) examined relationships within the Order Cyprinodontiformes, she delineated a family Poeciliidae that included not only the livebearing subjects of this book, but also their South American (*Fluviphylax*) and Old World (*Pantanodon* and the procatopines) relatives. The group under consideration, whether called the family Poeciliidae of Rosen and Bailey (1963), or the subfamily Poeciliinae of Parenti (1981) and Chapter 1, is the same. Thus, the group described by all chapters in this book (other than Chapter 1) as the family Poeciliidae, and vernacularly referred to as "poeciliids," is equivalent to the subfamily Poeciliinae of this classification.

Rosen and Bailey (1963) listed all recognized poeciliid species as of that date. The following list includes newly described species and references to taxonomic works since 1963. Where recent generic revisions contain all pertinent references to current literature for a genus, only that reference is given. Areas of dispute, particularly with regard to recognition of genera synonymized by Rosen and Bailey (1963), are noted; in most cases, phylogenetic analyses, generally not yet available, will ultimately decide the validity of these taxa. Because species concepts differ among revisors, taxa recognized as subspecies by some authors may be called species by others (particularly in *Xiphophorus* and *Gambusia*). Taxonomic decisions of the most recent revisors are generally followed herein. This listing encompasses 194 species, including the unisexual "species" *Poecilia formosa* and one fossil species, *Poeciliopsis maldonadoi*.

Subfamily Poeciliinae
  Supertribe Tomeuriini
    Genus *Tomeurus*
      Tomeurus gracilis Eigenmann, 1909, p. 53
  Supertribe Poeciliini
  Tribe Poeciliini
    Genus *Alfaro*
      Alfaro cultratus (Regan, 1908, p. 462)
      Alfaro huberi (Fowler, 1923, p. 27)
    Genus *Poecilia*

> Note: Subgeneric classification of *Poecilia* follows Rosen and Bailey (1963). Subgenus *Poecilia*
> Note: Miller (1975) recognized another subgenus, *Mollienesia*; this is contained here within the subgenus *Poecilia*. Within that subgenus, he defined two species complexes, listed below, with *Poecilia formosa* judged to be phylogenetically intermediate (Miller 1983).

      Poecilia caucana (Steindachner, 1880, pp. 87, 93)
      Poecilia elegans (Trewavas, 1948, p. 409)
      Poecilia montana Rosen and Bailey, 1963, p. 4

> = *Poecilia dominicensis* (Evermann and Clark, 1906). This would be a valid name if the recommendation of Rivas (1978) to recognize *Limia* as a genus, rather than a subgenus of *Poecilia*, was adopted. *Poecilia dominicensis* Valenciennes, 1846, in the subgenus *Limia*, has priority over *Poecilia dominicensis* Evermann and Clark, 1906, and the replacement name *Poecilia montana* proposed by Rosen and Bailey is valid.

      Poecilia hispaniolana Rivas, 1978, pp. 101
      Poecilia vivipara Bloch and Schneider, 1801, p. 452
      Mollienesia group:
      Poecilia formosa (Girard, 1859b, p. 115)

> Note: Following the recommendations of Schultz (1969) for nomenclature of taxa of hybrid origin, this might be referred to as *Poecilia latipinna mexicana*.

      Poecilia sphenops complex:

> Note: See Schultz and Miller (1971) for a review of the Mexican species of this complex.

      Poecilia sphenops Valenciennes, *In* Cuvier and Valenciennes, 1864, p. 130
      Poecilia chica Miller, 1975, pp. 2–13
      Poecilia catemaconis Miller, 1975, pp. 13–19
      Poecilia mexicana Steindachner, 1863, p. 178

> Note: Menzel and Darnell (1973) recognize two subspecies, *P. m. mexicana,* and *P. m. limantouri* Jordan and Snyder, 1900, 116–17, 129–31.

Poecilia gilli (Kner and Steindachner, 1864, p. 25)
  Note: Miller (1983) notes that this may be synonymous with *P. mexicana*, but needs further study.
Poecilia butleri Jordan, 1889, p. 330
Poecilia sulphuraria (Alvarez, 1948b, pp. 276, 279–80)
Poecilia latipunctata Meek, 1904, pp. 150–51
Poecilia maylandai Meyer, 1983a, pp. 56–58
Poecilia orri Fowler, 1943, pp. 1–3
  Poecilia latipinna complex:
Poecilia latipinna (LeSueur, 1821, p. 3)
Poecilia petenensis (Günther, 1866, p. 348)
Poecilia velifera (Regan, 1914a, p. 338)
Subgenus *Lebistes*
Poecilia reticulata Peters, 1859, p. 412
Poecilia parae Eigenmann, 1894, p. 628
Poecilia picta Regan, 1913, p. 1007
Poecilia branneri Eigenmann, 1894, p. 629
Poecilia amazonica Garman, 1895, p. 64
Poecilia scalpridens (Garman, 1895, p. 45)
Subgenus *Pamphorichthys*
Poecilia minor (Garman, 1895, p. 92)
Poecilia hollandi (Henn, 1916, pp. 95, 104, 138)
Poecilia hasemani (Henn, 1916, pp. 116–17)
Poecilia heterandria (Regan, 1913, p. 1017)
Subgenus *Limia*
  Note: Rivas (1978) treats this subgenus as a genus, and defined two subgenera, *Odontolimia* and *Limia* (Rivas 1980).
  Odontolimia group:
Poecilia ornata (Regan, 1913, p. 1016)
Poecilia fuscomaculata (Rivas, 1980, p. 31)
Poecilia garnieri (Rivas, 1980, pp. 31–32)
Poecilia grossidens (Rivas, 1980, pp. 29–31)
Poecilia immaculata (Rivas, 1980, pp. 32–33)
Poecilia miragoanensis (Rivas, 1980, pp. 33–34)
  Limia group:
Poecilia vittata Guichenot, 1853, pp. 2, 146
Poecilia perugiae (Evermann and Clark, 1906, pp. 851–53)
Poecilia nigrofasciata (Regan, 1913, p. 1015)
Poecilia melanotata (Nichols and Myers, 1923, p. 1)
Poecilia melanogaster Günther, 1866, pp. 345–46
Poecilia dominicensis Valenciennes, *In* Cuvier and Valenciennes, 1846, p. 131

Poecilia zonata (Nichols, 1915, p. 603)
Poecilia versicolor (Günther, 1866, p. 352)
Poecilia tridens Hilgendorf, 1889, p. 52
Poecilia caymanensis (Rivas and Fink, 1970, pp. 271–73)
Poecilia pauciradiata (Rivas, 1980, pp. 34–35)
Poecilia sulphurophila (Rivas, 1980, pp. 36–38)
Poecilia yaguajali (Rivas, 1980, pp. 35–36)
Poecilia rivasi (Franz and Burgess, 1983, pp. 51–54)
Genus *Priapella*
  Priapella bonita (Meek, 1904, p. 132)
  Priapella intermedia Alvarez, 1952a, pp. 284–86, 289
  Priapella compressa Alvarez, 1948a, pp. 334–35, 338–40
Genus *Xiphophorus*
  Note: The most recent revision of the genus is Rosen (1979), with the "*montezumae-cortezi* species complex" treated by Lechner and Radda (1987).
  Xiphophorus couchianus (Girard, 1859b, p. 116)
  Xiphophorus gordoni Miller and Minckley, 1963, pp. 540–48
  Xiphophorus variatus (Meek, 1904, pp. 146–47)
  Xiphophorus evelynae Rosen, 1960, pp. 87–89
  Xiphophorus xiphidium (Gordon, 1932, p. 287)
  Xiphophorus maculatus (Günther, 1866, pp. 350–51)
  Xiphophorus milleri Rosen, 1960, pp. 89–92
  Xiphophorus andersi Meyer and Schartl, 1980, pp. 148–51
  Xiphophorus montezumae Jordan and Snyder, 1900, pp. 131–33
  Xiphophorus cortezi Rosen, 1960, pp. 96–98
  Xiphophorus birchmanni Lechner and Radda, 1987, pp. 190–96
    Note: Lechner and Radda (1987) treat *X. birchmanni* and *X. cortezi* as subspecies of *X. montezumae.*
  Xiphophorus pygmaeus Hubbs and Gordon, 1943, pp. 31–33
  Xiphophorus nigrensis Rosen, 1960, pp. 100–102
  Xiphophorus clemenciae Alvarez, 1959, pp. 69–71
  Xiphophorus alvarezi Rosen, 1960, pp. 126–27
  Xiphophorus helleri Heckel, 1848, p. 127
  Xiphophorus signum Rosen and Kallman, 1969, pp. 5–15
Tribe Cnesterodontini
  Genus *Phallotorynus*
    Phallotorynus fasciolatus Henn, 1916, pp. 95, 129
    Phallotorynus jucundus von Ihering, 1930, pp. 98–99
    Phallotorynus victoriae Oliveros, 1983, pp. 17–27
  Genus *Phalloceros*
    Phalloceros caudimaculatus (Hensel, 1868, p. 362)
  Genus *Phalloptychus*
    Phalloptychus januarius (Hensel, 1868, p. 360)
    Phalloptychus eigenmanni Henn, 1916, pp. 95, 121

Genus *Cnesterodon*
  Cnesterodon decemmaculatus (Jenyns, 1843, pp. 115–16)
  Cnesterodon carnegiei Haseman, 1911, pp. 385–86
Tribe Scolichthyini
  Genus *Scolichthys*
    Scolichthys greenwayi Rosen, 1967, pp. 4–9
    Scolichthys iota Rosen, 1967, pp. 9–12
Tribe Gambusiini
  Genus *Brachyrhaphis*
    Brachyrhaphis terrabensis (Regan, 1907a, p. 260)
    Brachyrhaphis hartwegi Rosen and Bailey, 1963, pp. 87–88
    Brachyrhaphis rhabdophora (Regan, 1980, p. 457)
    Brachyrhaphis episcopi (Steindachner, 1878, p. 387)
    Brachyrhaphis punctifer (Hubbs, 1926, p. 49)
    Brachyrhaphis cascajalensis (Meek and Hildebrand, 1913, p. 86)
    Brachyrhaphis parsimina (Meek, 1912, p. 71)
    Brachyrhaphis holdridgei Bussing, 1967, pp. 223–27
  Genus *Belonesox*
    Belonesox belizanus Kner, 1860, pp. 419–22
      Note: Two subspecies are recognized, *B. b. belizanus* and *B. b. maxillosus* Hubbs, 1936, pp. 229–30.
  Genus *Gambusia*
    Note: The classification of *Gambusia* follows Rauchenberger (1988).
    Subgenus *Heterophallina*
      Gamgbusia vittata Hubbs, 1926, pp. 22, 26–27
        Note: Some authors treat *Gambusia vittata* as a monotypic genus, *Flexipenis* Turner, 1940a (e.g., Rivas 1963; Meyer et al. 1985a).
        panuco species group:
      Gambusia marshi Minckley and Craddock, *In* Minckley, 1962, pp. 392–96
      Gambusia panuco Hubbs, 1926, pp. 22, 30–32
      Gambusia regani Hubbs, 1926, pp. 28–29
        rachowi species group:
      Gambusia rachowi (Regan, 1914b, p. 66)
      Gambusia echeagayari (Alvarez, 1952b, pp. 95–97)
        Note: Some authors treat the members of the *rachowi* species group as a separate genus, *Heterophallus* Regan, 1914b (e.g., Rivas 1963; Meyer et al. 1985a).
    Subgenus *Arthrophallus*
        affinis species group:
      Gambusia affinis (Baird and Girard, 1853, p. 390)
        Note: The following two taxa are treated by many authors as subspecies of *G. affinis.*
      Gambusia holbrooki Girard, 1859a, pp. 61–62
      Gambusia speciosa Girard, 1859b, p. 121

Gambusia aurata Miller and Minckley, 1970, pp. 249–59
Gambusia lemaitrei Fowler, 1950, p. 2
  Note: A second Colombian species of *Gambusia*, *G. meadi*, was described by Dahl and Medem (1964, pp. 80–83). This was treated as a synonym of *G. lemaitrei* by Meyer et al.(1985a). No other authors have commented on *G. meadi*, and I have not yet seen the type material.
    nobilis species group:
Gambusia nobilis (Baird and Girard, 1853, p. 390)
Gambusia georgei Hubbs and Peden, 1969, pp. 357–64
Gambusia heterochir Hubbs, 1957, pp. 3–16
Gambusia krumholzi Minckley, 1963, pp. 154–60
Gambusia sexradiata Hubbs, 1936, pp. 225–26
Gambusia eurystoma Miller, 1975, pp. 19–27
    senilis species group:
Gambusia senilis Girard, 1859b, p. 122
Gambusia gaigei Hubbs, 1929, pp. 3–6
Gambusia alvarezi Hubbs and Springer, 1957, pp. 279–321
Gambusia hurtadoi Hubbs and Springer, 1957, pp. 279–321
Gambusia amistadensis Peden, 1973a, pp. 211–20
Gambusia geiseri Hubbs and Hubbs, *In* Hubbs and Springer, 1957, pp. 279–324
Gambusia longispinis Minckley, 1962, pp. 391–93
Gambusia atrora Rosen and Bailey, 1963, pp. 102–3
Subgenus *Gambusia*
    nicaraguensis species group:
Gambusia nicaraguensis Günther, 1866, pp. 336–337
Gambusia wrayi Regan, 1913, p. 988
Gambusia melapleura (Gosse, 1851, pp. 84–85)
    puncticulata species group:
Gambusia yucatana Regan, 1914b, p. 67
  Note: Two subspecies are recognized, *G. y. yucatana* and *G. y. australis-*(Greenfield 1985, pp. 375–76).
Gambusia hispaniolae Fink, 1971a, pp. 51, 57–61
  Note: Fink (1971b) places this species in the *nicaraguensis* species group. Specimens identified as *Gambusia dominicensis* are probably all *G. hispaniolae*.
Gambusia hubbsi Breder, 1934, pp. 1, 3 (uncertain status)
  Note: This species, and the following eight species, were synoymized as *G. puncticulata* by Fink (1971b). Greenfield and Wildrick (1984) and Rauchenberger (1988) discussed evidence indicating that this synonymization might have been premature; however, no specific taxonomic actions were taken in either of those two works. Therefore, the taxa in question are listed as "uncertain status."
Gambusia manni Hubbs, 1927, pp. 62, 64 (uncertain status)

Gambusia monticola Rivas, 1971, pp. 6–9 (uncertain status)
Gambusia baracoana Rivas, 1944, p. 46 (uncertain status)
Gambusia bucheri Rivas, 1944, pp. 42, 44–45 (uncertain status)
Gambusia puncticulata Poey, 1854, p. 381
Gambusia oligosticta Regan, 1913, p. 988 (uncertain status)
Gambusia caymanensis Regan, 1913, p. 990 (uncertain status)
Gambusia howelli Rivas, 1944, pp. 41, 44, 46 (uncertain status)
    punctata species group:
Gambusia luma Rosen and Bailey, 1963, pp. 99–101
Gambusia beebei Myers, 1935, pp. 305, 307–10
Gambusia pseudopunctata Rivas, 1969, pp. 781, 784–86
Gambusia punctata Poey, 1854, pp. 376–80, 384, 390
Gambusia rhizophorae Rivas, 1969, pp. 781, 791–94
Gambusia xanthosoma Greenfield, 1983, pp. 459–64
Tribe Girardinini
  Genus *Carlhubbsia*
    Carlhubbsia stuarti Rosen and Bailey, 1959, pp. 5–8
    Carlhubbsia kidderi (Hubbs, 1936, pp. 232–38)
  Genus *Girardinus*
    Note: Rivas (1958) recognized the eight species listed herein (and in Rosen
    and Bailey 1963) in five genera: *Toxus* Eigenmann, 1903, for *G. serripenis*
    and *G. creolus*; *Glaridichthys* Garman, 1895, for *G. uninotatus* and *G.*
    falcatus; *Allodontium* Howell-Rivero and Rivas, 1944, for *G. cubensis*;
    Girardinus Poey, 1854, limited to *G. microdactylus* and *G. metallicus*;
    and *Dactylophallus* Howell-Rivero and Rivas, 1944, for *G. denticulatus*.
    Whereas most workers have followed Rosen and Bailey's (1963) synonymy,
    some works are still being published using the junior synonyms (e.g.,
    Barus et al. 1981b, 1986a, 1986b.)
    Girardinus serripenis (Rivas, 1958, pp. 282, 286–87, 289)
    Girardinus creolus Garman, 1895, p. 47
      Ref: Barus et al. (1981b, 1986a).
    Girardinus uninotatus Poey, 1860, p. 309
    Girardinus falcatus (Eigenmann, 1903, p. 224)
    Girardinus cubensis (Eigenmann, 1903, p. 227)
    Girardinus denticulatus Garman, 1895, p. 47
      Ref: Barus et al. (1986b).
    Girardinus microdactylus Rivas, 1944, p. 51
    Girardinus metallicus Poey, 1854, p. 387
  Genus *Quintana*
    Quintana atrizona Hubbs, 1934, pp. 1–8
      Ref: Barus et al. (1981a).
Tribe Heterandriini
  Genus *Priapichthys*
    Note: Radda (1987) recognizes the genus *Pseudopoecilia* Regan, 1913

(which Rosen and Bailey [1963] synonymized with *Priapichthys*) for *P. fria* and *P. austrocolombianus* (which would be *Pseudopoecilia austrocolombiana* if that recommendation were followed).

Priapichthys annectens (Regan, 1907a, p. 259)

Priapichthys panamensis Meek and Hildebrand, 1916, pp. 322–23

Priapichthys darienensis (Meek and Hildebrand, 1913, p. 88)

Priapichthys chocoensis (Henn, 1916, pp. 95, 104–5, 114–15)

Priapichthys nigroventralis (Eigenmann and Henn, *In* Eigenmann, 1912, p. 26)

Priapichthys caliensis (Henn, 1916, pp. 95–113)

Priapichthys fria (Eigenmann and Henn, *In* Eigenmann et al., 1914, pp. 13–14)

Priapichthys austrocolombianus (Radda, 1987)

Genus *Neoheterandria*

Neoheterandria elegans Henn, 1916, p. 118

Neoheterandria tridentiger (Garman, 1895, p. 89)

Neoheterandria cana (Meek and Hildebrand, 1913, p. 87)

Neoheterandria umbritalis (Meek, 1912, p. 70)

Note: *Neoheterandria umbritalis* is treated as a monotypic genus, *Xenophallus* Hubbs, 1924, by some authors (e.g., Radda and Meyer 1981; Meyer et al. 1985a).

Genus *Heterandria*

Note: The classification of *Heterandria* follows Rosen (1979), the most recent revision of the genus.

Subgenus *Heterandria*

Heterandria formosa Agassiz, 1855, p. 136

Subgenus *Pseudoxiphophorus*

Note: Radda (1985) treats this as a separate genus.

Heterandria attenuata Rosen, 1979, pp. 315–19

Heterandria jonesi (Günther, 1874, p. 371)

Heterandria litoperas Rosen and Bailey, *In* Rosen, 1979, pp. 320–21

Heterandria obliqua Rosen, 1979, pp. 321–24

Heterandria anzuetoi Rosen and Bailey, *In* Rosen, 1979, pp. 324–28

Heterandria cataractae Rosen, 1979, pp. 328–29

Heterandria dirempta Rosen, 1979, pp. 329–30

Heterandria bimaculata (Heckel, 1848, p. 296)

Genus *Poeciliopsis*

Note: Subgenera in the genus *Poeciliopsis* were defined by Miller (1960). Meyer et al. (1986) divide the genus into complexes; their *Poeciliopsis elongata* complex corresponds to the subgenus *Aulophallus*, and the other complexes are listed under the subgenus *Poeciliopsis*. Note that three species do not belong to any complex.

Subgenus *Poeciliopsis*

Poeciliopsis turrubarensis complex:

Poeciliopsis turrubarensis (Meek, 1912, p. 71)

Poeciliopsis maldonadoi Alvarez and Aguillar, 1957, pp. 167–68 (fossil)
Poeciliopsis presidionis (Jordon, 1895, pp. 412–14)
Poeciliopsis scarlli Meyer, Riehl, Dawes, and Dibble, 1985b, p. 26
  Poeciliopsis gracilis complex:
Poeciliopsis gracilis (Heckel, 1848, pp. 300–302)
  Note: Meyer et al. (1986) feel that *Poeciliopsis lutzi* (Meek, 1902), which
  was synonymized with *Poecilipis gracilis* by Rosen and Bailey (1963),
  might be a valid species.
Poeciliopsis catemaco Miller, 1975, pp. 35–41
Poeciliopsis hnilickai Meyer and Vogel, 1981, pp. 358–60
  Poeciliopsis occidentalis complex:
Poeciliopsis infans (Woolman, 1894, pp. 56, 62)
Poeciliopsis viriosa Miller, 1960, pp. 4–5
Poeciliopsis lucida Miller, 1960, pp. 2–3
  Note: The populations of hybrid origin derived from various combinations
  of this and the following two species are not included in this species list.
  See Chapter 5 for details of these populations.
Poeciliopsis occidentalis (Baird and Girard, 1853, p. 390)
  Note: Two subspecies are recognized (Minckley 1973), *P. o. occidentalis*
  and *P. o. sonoriensis* (Girard, 1895b, p. 120).
Poeciliopsis monacha Miller, 1960, pp. 3–4
  Poeciliopsis latidens-fasciata complex:
Poeciliopsis fasciata (Meek, 1904, p. 129)
Poeciliopsis latidens (Garman, 1895, p. 42)
Poeciliopsis baenschi Meyer, Radda, Riehl, and Feichtinger, 1986, pp.
  80–84
  Not placed in any complex:
Poeciliopsis prolifica Miller, 1960, pp. 5–6
Poeciliopsis turneri Miller, 1975, pp. 27–34
Poeciliopsis balsas Hubbs, 1926, p. 66
Subgenus *Aulophallus*
Poeciliopsis elongata (Günther, 1866, p. 342)
Poeciliopsis retropinna (Regan, 1908, p. 458)
Poeciliopsis paucimaculata Bussing, 1967, pp. 227–29
  Genus *Phallichthys*
  Phallichthys amates (Miller, 1907, p. 108)
    Note: Two subspecies are recognized, *P. a. amates* and *P. a. pittier* (Meek
    1912, pp. 71–72).
  Phallichthys fairweatheri Rosen and Bailey, 1959, pp. 24–29
  Phallichthys quadripunctatus Bussing, 1979, pp. 1–8
  Phallichthys tico Bussing, 1963, pp. 3–13
Tribe Xenodexiini
  Genus *Xenodexia*
    Xenodexia ctenolepis Hubbs, 1950, pp. 1–28

Appendix 2

List of Accepted Common Names of Poeciliid Fishes

GARY K. MEFFE

The following is a compilation of common names generally used for poeciliid fishes. Although use of common names is usually discouraged due to geographic variation and imprecision, poeciliid common names are often so deeply engrained and widely used that familiarity with them is important. These names were compiled from Rosen and Bailey (1963), Lee et al. (1980, 1983), Robins et al. (1980), Miller (1983), and Smith et al. (Chapter 13).

Scientific Name	Common Name
Belonesox belizanus	Pike killifish
Gambusia affinis	Western mosquitofish
Gambusia amistadensis	Amistad gambusia
Gambusia beebei	Miragoane gambusia
Gambusia gaigei	Big Bend gambusia
Gambusia geiseri	Largespring gambusia
Gambusia georgei	San Marcos gambusia
Gambusia heterochir	Clear Creek gambusia
Gambusia hispaniolae	Hispaniolan gambusia
Gambusia holbrooki	Eastern mosquitofish
Gambusia melapleura	Striped gambusia
Gambusia nobilis	Pecos gambusia
Gambusia pseudopunctata	Tiburon Peninsula gambusia
Gambusia punctata	Cuban gambusia
Gambusia puncticulata	Caribbean gambusia
Gambusia rhizophorae	Mangrove gambusia
Gambusia senilis	Blotched gambusia
Gambusia wrayi	Wray's gambusia

Scientific Name	Common Name
Gambusia xanthosoma	Cayman gambusia
Girardinus creolus	Creole topminnow
Girardinus cubensis	Cuban topminnow
Girardinus denticulatus	Toothy topminnow
Girardinus falcatus	Goldbelly topminnow
Girardinus metallicus	Metallic topminnow
Girardinus microdactylus	Smallfinger topminnow
Girardinus serripenis	Serrated topminnow
Girardinus uninotatus	Singlespot topminnow
Heterandria formosa	Least killifish
Poecilia butleri	Pacific molly
Poecilia catemaconis	Catemaco molly
Poecilia chica	Dwarf molly
Poecilia elegans	Elegant molly
Poecilia formosa	Amazon molly[1]
Poecilia hispaniolana	Hispaniola molly
Poecilia latipinna	Sailfin molly
Poecilia latipunctata	Tamesí molly
Poecilia mexicana	Atlantic molly
Poecilia montana	Dominican molly
Poecilia orri	Mangrove molly
Poecilia petenensis	Peten molly
Poecilia reticulata	Guppy
Poecilia sphenops	Mexican molly
Poecilia velifera	Yucatan molly
Poecilia (Limia) caymanensis	Grand Cayman limia
Poecilia (Limia) dominicensis	Tiburon Peninsula limia
Poecilia (Limia) fuscomaculata	Blotched limia
Poecilia (Limia) garnieri	Garnier's limia
Poecilia (Limia) grossidens	Largetooth limia
Poecilia (Limia) immaculata	Plain limia
Poecilia (Limia) melanogaster	Blackbelly limia
Poecilia (Limia) melanonotata	Blackbanded limia
Poecilia (Limia) miragoanensis	Miragoane limia
Poecilia (Limia) nigrofasciata	Humpback limia
Poecilia (Limia) ornata	Ornate limia
Poecilia (Limia) pauciradiata	Few-rayed limia
Poecilia (Limia) perugiae	Perugia's limia
Poecilia (Limia) rivasi	Rivas's limia
Poecilia (Limia) sulphurophilia	Sulfur limia
Poecilia (Limia) tridens	Trident limia
Poecilia (Limia) versicolor	Varicolored limia
Poecilia (Limia) vittata	Cuban limia
Poecilia (Limia) yaguajali	Yaguajal limia
Poecilia (Limia) zonata	Striped limia
Poeciliopsis gracilis	Porthole livebearer
Poeciliopsis occidentalis	Sonoran topminnow[2]
Quintana atrizona	Barred topminnow
Xiphophorus clemenciae	Yellow swordtail
Xiphophorus couchianus	Northern platyfish
Xiphophorus helleri	Green swordtail

Scientific Name	Common Name
Xiphophorus maculatus	Southern platyfish
Xiphophorus milleri	Catemaco livebearer
Xiphophorus montezumae	Montezuma swordtail
Xiphophorus pygmaeus	Pygmy swordtail
Xiphophorus variatus	Variable platyfish

[1] I include the common name for this unisexual, although it is not considered a true species due to its hybrid origin.

[2] Consists of two subspecies with recognized common names, *P. occidentalis occidentalis* (Gila topminnow) and *P. occidentalis sonoriensis* (Yaqui topminnow).

Appendix 3

Poeciliid Life History Patterns

DAVID N. REZNICK
DONALD B. MILES

Summary of data used in analyses of mode of reproduction and interspecific variation in life histories. MODEA = maternal provisioning (1 = lecithotrophic, 2 = matrotrophic); MODEB = number of litters (1 = nonsuperfetating, 2 = superfetating); MINFEM = minimum standard length of reproducing females (mm); MEANFEM = mean standard length of reproducing females (mm); NEMB = average number of developing embryos; ADJNEMB = average number of embryos, adjusted for average female size (only used when there was more than one sample per species); OFFWT = average dry weight of developing embryos (mg); RA = reproductive allotment, or the percentage of total weight which consisted of developing embryos; INTERVAL = mean interval between broods (days); MEANMALE = average standard length of mature males (mm). Sources: (1) Breder and Rosen 1966; (2) Cheong et al. 1985; (3) Constantz 1974 (4) Constantz 1979; (5) S. Forster, pers. comm.; (6) Henn 1916; (7) Hubbs 1971; (8) Krumholz 1963; (9) Meffe 1985; (10) G. K. Meffe, pers. comm.; (11) Miller 1960; (12) Miller 1975; (13) Milton and Arthington 1983; (14) Monaco et al. 1983; (15) Reznick 1981; (16) D. N. Reznick, unpubl. data; (17) D. N. Reznick and S. Winslow, unpubl. data; (18) Schultz 1961; (19) Scrimshaw 1944b; (20) Snelson et al. 1986; (21) Stearns 1978; (22) Stoye 1935; (23) Thibault and Schultz 1978; (24) J. Travis, pers. comm.; (25) Trexler 1985; (26) Turner 1937; (27) Turner 1938; (28) Turner 1940b; (29) Turner and Snelson 1984.

Tribe	Genus	Species	MODEA	MODEB	MINFEM
Poeciliini	*Poecilia*	*latipinna*	1	1	34.1
"	"	"	1	1	27.8
"	"	"	1	1	34.6
"	"	"	1	1	37.1
"	"	"	1	1	35.6
"	"	"	1	1	31.0
"	"	"	1	1	28.1
"	"	*sphenops*	1	1	—
"	"	*reticulata*	1	1	21.0
"	"	*vivipara*	1	1	—
"	"	*picta*	1	1	16.0
"	"	"	1	1	16.0
"	"	"	1	1	17.0
"	"	"	1	1	19.0
"	"	*parae*	1	1	—
"	"	*vittata*	1	1	—
"	"	*branneri*	2	–	—
"	"	*velifera*	1	–	—
"	"	*chica*	1	–	—
"	"	*caucana*	1	–	—
"	"	*formosa*	1	1	—
"	"	*mexicana*	1	–	—
"	"	*hollandi*	1	–	—
"	*Priapella*	*bonita*	2	–	—
"	*Xiphophorus*	*helleri*	1	1	22.8
"	"	*h. strigatus*	1	1	—
"	"	*maculatus*	1	1	18.6
"	"	*variatus*	1	1	—
Cnesterodontini	*Phalloceros*	*caudimaculatus*	1	–	—
"	*Phalloptychus*	*januarius*	2	–	—
"	*Cnesterodon*	*decemmaculatus*	1	–	—
Gambusiini	*Brachyrhaphis*	*episcopi*	1	1	25.0
"	*Gambusia*	*affinis*	1	1	21.3
"	"	"	1	1	24.0

MEANFEM	NEMB	ADJNEMB	OFFWT	RA	INTERVAL	MEANMALE	SOURCE
38.8	40.5	37.3	—	—	34.8	38.9	20,24,25,26
30.0	14.9	25.0	—	—	34.8	26.5	20,24,25,26
40.1	27.7	22.9	—	—	34.8	33.1	20,24,25,26
45.2	35.4	21.1	3.0	—	34.8	48.4	20,24,25,26
40.0	22.7	19.4	3.6	—	34.8	32.4	20,24,25,26
35.9	16.9	19.0	3.7	—	34.8	32.4	20,24,25,26
30.9	6.4	10.1	3.5	—	34.8	26.8	20,24,25,26
—	—	—	—	—	—	—	26
—	24.2	—	0.9	—	21.9	—	23,26
—	—	—	—	—	—	—	6,26
20.2	—	8.4	0.8	17.1	—	18.1	17,26
20.9	—	8.6	0.8	15.6	—	18.0	17,26
20.4	—	7.0	0.8	14.0	—	18.5	17,26
22.4	—	11.5	0.9	22.3	—	18.8	17,26
—	—	—	—	—	—	—	26
—	—	—	—	—	—	—	26
—	—	—	—	—	—	—	22
—	—	—	—	—	—	—	1
—	—	—	—	—	—	—	12
—	—	—	—	—	—	—	1
—	—	—	—	—	—	—	14
—	—	—	—	—	—	—	14
—	—	—	—	—	—	—	6
—	—	—	—	—	—	—	22
35.6	60.1	—	—	15.2	29.2	34.9	13,26
—	—	—	—	—	—	—	26
28.2	27.3	—	—	13.3	33.6	23.6	13,26
—	—	—	—	—	28.0	—	26
—	—	—	—	—	—	—	6
—	—	—	—	—	—	—	22
—	—	—	—	—	40.0	—	1,6
33.4	7.4	7.4	—	—	—	—	26,27
29.9	22.8	—	—	17.7	23.9	21.0	13,26
31.9	17.5	11.5	1.3	18.1	—	23.2	15,16,26

Tribe	Genus	Species	MODEA	MODEB	MINFEM
Gambusiini	*Gambusia*	*affinis*	1	1	21.0
"	"	"	1	1	22.0
"	"	"	1	1	25.0
"	"	*panuco*	1	1	—
"	"	*vittata*	2	–	—
"	"	*heterochir*	1	1	—
"	"	*marshi*	1	1	28.0
"	"	"	1	1	23.0
"	"	"	1	1	23.0
"	"	"	1	1	22.0
"	"	*manni*	1	–	20.0
"	"	"	1	–	19.2
"	"	"	1	–	16.0
"	*Belonesox*	*belizanus*	1	1	56.0
Girardinini	*Quintana*	*atrizona*	1	1	—
"	*Carlhubbsia*	*kidderi*	1	–	—
Heterandriini	*Priapichthys*	*fria*	2	–	—
"	"	*chacoensis*	2	–	—
"	"	*darienensis*	1	–	—
"	*Neoheterandria*	*tridentiger*	2	2	—
"	"	"	2	2	—
"	*Heterandria*	*bimaculata*	1	1	—
"	"	*formosa*	2	2	18.8
"	*Poeciliopsis*	*infans*	2	–	—
"	"	*balsas*	2	–	—
"	"	*fasciata*	2	–	—
"	"	*retropinna*	2	2	—
"	"	*elongata*	2	2	—
"	"	*occidentalis*	2	2	—
"	"	"	2	2	—
"	"	"	2	2	—
"	"	"	2	2	—
"	"	*prolifica*	2	2	20.0
"	"	*monacha*	2	1	22.4
"	"	*lucida*	2	2	21.6
"	"	*turneri*	2	2	28.2
"	"	*catemaco*	2	2	—
"	"	*gracilis*	2	–	—
"	"	"	2	–	—
"	"	"	2	–	—
"	*Phallichthys*	*fairweatheri*	2	–	—

MEANFEM	NEMB	ADJNEMB	OFFWT	RA	INTERVAL	MEANMALE	SOURCE
26.5	23.7	28.3	0.7	24.5	—	19.1	15,16,26
27.2	29.1	34.1	0.7	27.8	—	19.7	15,16,26
33.2	13.5	8.5	1.5	17.0	—	23.7	15,16,26
—	—	—	—	—	—	—	26
—	—	—	—	—	—	—	28
—	—	—	2.8	—	42.0	—	7
37.4	8.4	5.3	2.9	11.6	—	21.7	9,10
32.2	14.4	14.8	2.1	17.8	—	21.8	9,10
32.9	9.0	9.1	2.3	15.8	—	23.0	9,10
32.6	6.3	7.4	2.4	12.0	—	21.6	9,10
26.9	6.2	6.7	—	—	24.5	23.2	8
23.6	5.6	7.3	—	—	24.5	23.3	8
24.2	6.4	9.7	—	—	24.5	19.6	8
102.9	99.4	99.4	6.9	—	42.0	72.4	29
—	—	—	—	—	—	—	26
—	—	—	—	—	—	—	19
23.8	3.0	—	—	—	—	—	6
—	—	—	—	—	—	—	6
—	—	—	—	—	—	—	19
20.0	—	5.6	1.3	17.0	—	—	21
19.7	—	8.1	0.7	12.0	—	—	11
—	—	—	—	—	—	—	19,26
21.8	3.1	—	1.1	6.3	8.7	16.5	2,5,19,26
—	—	—	—	—	—	—	26
—	—	—	—	—	—	—	28
—	—	—	—	—	—	—	28
—	—	—	—	—	—	—	28
—	—	—	—	—	—	—	28
—	4.7	4.7	2.2	6.3	21.0	—	4,19
—	13.6	13.6	1.6	13.5	21.0	—	4,19
35.7	9.6	9.6	2.8	—	21.0	—	3,19
29.9	2.4	2.4	2.8	—	21.0	—	3,19
—	4.0	—	0.6	—	6.9	—	11,23
27.1	2.9	—	1.3	—	11.6	—	23
27.1	4.0	—	0.7	—	10.3	—	18,23
46.0	3.6	—	3.4	—	13.0	—	12,23
—	—	—	—	—	—	—	12
—	—	—	—	—	—	—	26
—	—	—	—	—	—	—	26
—	—	—	—	—	—	—	28
—	—	—	—	—	—	—	19,28

Appendix 4

Intraspecific Life History Variation

DAVID N. REZNICK
DONALD B. MILES

A summary of intraspecific data for *Poecilia reticulata* (Reznick and Endler 1982), *Gambusia affinis* (Stearns 1983b), and influence of food availability on *Poecilia reticulata* (Reznick and Bryga 1987). Abbreviations for dependent variables are the same as in Appendix 3. Conditions—C = *Crenicichla*, R = *Rivulus*, A = *Aequidens*, S = stable, F = fluctuating, Low = low food, High = high food.

OBS	Tribe	Genus	Species	Predators	MINFEM
1	Poeciliini	*Poecilia*	*reticulata*	C	13
2	"	"	"	C	16
3	"	"	"	C	15
4	"	"	"	C	15
5	"	"	"	C	14
6	"	"	"	C	17
7	"	"	"	C	12
8	"	"	"	R	16
9	"	"	"	R	20
10	"	"	"	R	15
11	"	"	"	R	18
12	"	"	"	R	18
13	"	"	"	A	20
14	"	"	"	A	18
15	"	"	"	A	18
16	"	"	"	A	18
17	Gambusiini	*Gambusia*	*affinis*	S	—
18	"	"	"	S	—
19	"	"	"	S	—
20	"	"	"	S	—
21	"	"	"	F	—
22	"	"	"	F	—
23	"	"	"	F	—
24	"	"	"	F	—
25	"	"	"	F	—
26	"	"	"	F	—
27	"	"	"	F	—
28	"	"	"	F	—
29	"	"	"	F	—
30	"	"	"	F	—
31	"	"	"	F	—
32	"	"	"	F	—
33	"	"	"	F	—
34	"	"	"	F	—
35	"	"	"	F	—
36	"	"	"	F	—
37	"	"	"	F	—
38	"	"	"	F	—
39	"	"	"	F	—
40	"	"	"	F	—
41	Poeciliini	*Poecilia*	*reticulata*	Low	—
42	"	"	"	High	—

MEANFEM	NEMB	ADJNEMB	OFFWT	RA	INTERVAL	MEANMALE
18.3	6.0	8.0	0.8	16.7	—	13.0
20.3	5.8	5.7	1.1	18.2	24.1	16.2
19.4	6.4	7.3	0.8	16.6	—	14.8
19.7	6.1	6.6	1.1	18.3	—	15.2
19.8	6.3	6.7	0.8	14.0	—	14.8
19.6	5.5	5.8	0.7	13.4	—	15.6
18.6	5.5	6.4	0.8	14.9	23.9	14.8
20.0	3.5	3.9	1.3	13.5	—	15.7
21.2	3.2	3.0	1.7	14.4	26.9	18.4
17.7	2.0	2.8	1.2	11.4	—	16.2
19.8	2.3	2.4	1.4	10.6	—	14.6
19.4	2.7	2.6	1.7	12.6	25.7	17.2
24.3	5.7	2.3	1.7	15.0	—	17.0
21.1	3.3	3.2	1.6	13.9	—	18.4
22.3	3.5	2.9	1.7	13.6	—	18.5
21.6	4.1	2.9	1.6	13.3	24.3	17.2
34.3	7.7	6.6	1.4	9.6	23.5	17.3
34.1	18.9	21.1	1.9	23.7	22.0	16.6
31.7	5.5	5.9	2.1	11.4	—	—
30.1	13.3	12.5	1.8	15.4	—	—
34.8	27.7	31.9	1.7	29.0	—	—
34.4	17.6	18.7	2.0	20.8	—	—
30.8	14.0	17.7	2.0	28.1	—	—
35.5	23.0	22.1	1.5	19.5	—	—
40.7	27.3	20.3	2.1	20.7	—	—
33.8	7.2	7.5	2.0	13.8	19.3	18.6
39.4	37.4	33.9	1.9	29.3	—	—
43.1	109.2	70.0	1.1	36.1	23.8	18.5
31.9	11.0	11.8	1.8	18.5	—	—
43.6	31.4	25.8	2.1	16.8	22.5	18.5
31.1	24.9	36.4	1.5	30.3	—	—
32.5	14.1	17.4	1.9	21.9	—	—
36.7	24.0	25.8	2.0	23.6	—	—
35.6	15.3	15.9	2.0	18.5	—	—
37.1	17.0	15.9	2.1	18.4	—	—
34.0	24.5	26.5	1.8	25.6	—	—
35.7	72.6	67.9	1.1	44.0	18.3	17.1
38.6	15.0	5.4	1.8	12.6	—	—
33.1	9.6	10.9	2.0	14.6	—	—
35.4	27.2	27.3	1.8	28.2	—	—
18.4	4.9	6.1	1.0	14.5	25.1	13.5
20.8	8.3	7.2	0.8	15.9	24.5	14.7

Appendix 5

Ecological Genetics: Definitions and Terminology

JOSEPH TRAVIS

Genetic analysis begins with partitioning the phenotypic variance of a trait into three components. **Genotypic variance** is produced by differences among distinct genotypes in their average phenotypic values of the trait. The magnitude of this effect is a function of actual difference among genotypes in their average phenotypic values and the relative frequencies of each genotype. **Environmental variance** is produced by differences in phenotypic values among individuals with the same genotype. These differences are generated by different ontogenetic experiences in factors like temperature and nutrition. The **genotype-environment interaction variance** is produced by different levels of susceptibility among genotypes to environmental influences. This effect is discussed in more detail by Trexler (Chapter 11).

Genotypic variance in a trait can be further partitioned in sexually reproducing species. **Additive genetic variance** is the variation produced by allelic diversity at the loci that govern the trait. Some alleles produce an increase in phenotypic value above the population average, and some produce a decrease. The magnitude of additive genetic variance is a function of the marginal effect of each allele on the trait (the effect of the allele calculated as a weighted average of its effects when paired with all other alleles in diploid genotypes, with the weights being the frequencies of each pairing) and its relative frequency. Thus, with little allelic diversity, even if the allelic effects themselves are large in magnitude, there will be little additive genetic variance. **Heritability** of a trait is the additive genetic variance for that trait divided by the total phenotypic variance. This term is also referred to as the "narrow-sense heritability" or "the proportion of phenotypic variance that is heritable." This component of variance is what selection acts on in large, randomly mating populations: directional selection will act to fix the allele with the most favorable effect on the trait. If "fitness" itself is considered a trait, then selection acts to eliminate allelic diversity in fitness.

The other components of genotypic variance are often referred to collectively as **non-additive genetic variance.** This quantity is not acted upon by selection in large, randomly mating populations, although it does contribute to the total response to selection in small populations and populations with appreciable inbreeding. This variance in turn can be partitioned. **Dominance variance** is the component of genotypic variance produced when heterozygotes do not possess phenotypic values of a trait that are exactly intermediate between the values of the homozygotes for the same alleles. This definition encompasses partial or complete dominance, overdominance, and underdominance. The magnitude of dominance variance will be a function of the dominance relations among alleles and their relative frequencies. **Epistatic variance** is the component of genotypic variance produced by interlocus interactions, phenomena that cause the average phenotypic trait value of an individual with a genotype at locus A to depend on its genotype at one or more other loci.

Correlations of trait values with heterozygosity reveal the possibility of non-additive genetic variance in the trait (these are correlative analyses, not experimental crosses that can indicate causation). At a single locus, such correlations suggest the presence of dominance variance. The extent to which multiple-locus heterozygosity increases the trait value above or below what would be expected on the basis of the effects of heterozygosity at the constituent loci reflects one form of epistasis. In general, it is quite difficult to make accurate partitions of the non-additive genetic component of variance.

Gene action is the general term for the way in which alleles interact to generate genotypic variance. **Additive gene action** is the case where there is no dominance at the polymorphic loci that affect the trait and no epistasis. In **pleiotropic gene action**, segregating alleles affect more than one trait. Pleiotropy can be positive (alleles that increase the value of one trait above the population average also increase the value of the second trait) or negative (alleles that increase the value of one trait decrease the value of the other). If the pleiotropic effect is strong for a number of alleles, and if there is appreciable allelic diversity, then this gene action will generate a **genetic correlation** between the two affected traits. A genetic correlation can be thought of as the correlation between two phenotypic trait values produced by concordant genetic effects on the traits. Genetic correlation can be positive (alleles increase values of both traits) or negative (alleles increase one trait value and decrease the other). Genetic correlations can also be produced without pleiotropy. In this case, adjacent loci each affect a single trait, but there are nonrandom associations of alleles at those loci such that an allele that increases the value of trait A is bound to an allele that increases (decreases) the value of trait B, generating a positive (negative) genetic correlation through this **linkage disequilibrium.** Only detailed genetic analyses can distinguish true pleiotropy from the effects of linkage disequilibrium.

Appendix 6

Traits Known to Be Plastic in Poeciliids

JOEL C. TREXLER

Each study includes some form of a common garden experiment. Asterisks mark those studies where genetic variation for plasticity of the trait was noted. Age at maturity and growth rate are combined in the first category, because most studies addressing the former relate it to juvenile growth rate. Generally, studies in the growth rate category did not follow the fish to sexual maturity. Environmental factors are as follows: 1 = temperature, 2 = salinity, 3 = food level, 4 = photoperiod, 5 = social context, 6 = oxygen level, 7 = food quality, 8 = unidentified.

Trait	Environmental Factor	Species
Age at maturity	1,2	*Poecilia latipinna*: Trexler 1986*
& growth	3	*Xiphophorus variatus*: Borowsky 1984
rate	5	*X. variatus*: Borowsky 1973b; Borowsky 1978b
	5	*Xiphophorus maculatus*: Kallman and Borkoski 1978*; Sohn 1977a*; Borowsky 1987b
	5 (age only)	*Gambusia manni*: Sohn 1977b
	5	*Xiphophorus helleri*: Scott and Currie 1980
	5	*Girardinus metallicus*: Farr 1980a
	3 (age only)	*Poecilia reticulata*: Reznick and Bryga 1987*
	1	*Gambusia affinis*: Vondracek et al. 1988
Growth rate	1,3	*X. variatus*: Tzall, cited in Borowsky 1984*
	6*	*X. variatus*: Borowsky and Bao, cited in Borowsky 1984

Trait	Environmental Factor	Species
	1,3	*Poeciliopsis monacha-lucida*: Schultz and Fielding 1988*
	5	*P. monacha-lucida*: Schultz 1982*
	5	*G. affinis*: Busack and Gall 1983
	1	*G. affinis*: Wurtsbaugh and Cech 1983
	1,3	*G. affinis*: Wurtsbaugh and Cech 1983
	3	*G. affinis*: Vondracek et al. 1988
	7	*G. affinis*: Meffe and Crump 1987
	3	*P. reticulata*: Silliman 1968
Size at maturity	5	*G. manni*: Sohn 1977b
	5	*Girardinus metallicus*: Farr 1980a
	5	*X. maculatus*: Kallman and Borkoski 1978*; Sohn 1977a*; Borowsky 1987b
	5	*X. variatus*: Borowsky 1973b; Borowsky 1987a
	2	*G. affinis*: Stearns and Sage 1980*
	3	*P. reticulata*: Reznick and Bryga 1987*
	1,2	*P. latipinna*: Trexler 1986*
Reproductive condition	1,3	*X. variatus*: Tzall, cited in Borowsky 1984*
	7	*G. affinis*: Meffe and Crump 1987
	4	*P. latipinna*: Grier 1973
Sex Ratio	1	*Poeciliopsis lucida*: Sullivan and Schultz 1986*
Number of embryos	4	*Poeciliopsis gracilis, Poecilia sphenops*: Burns 1985*
	3	*P. reticulata*: Hester 1964; Reznick and Bryga 1987*
	5	*P. reticulata*: Dahlgren 1979
	3	*G. affinis*: Trendall 1983
Interbrood interval	3	*P. reticulata*: Reznick and Bryga 1987*
	1	*G. affinis*: Vondracek et al. 1988
	1	*P. latipinna*: Snelson et al. 1986
Testis size	4	*P. gracilis, P. sphenops*: Burns 1985
Survival to maturity	2	*G. affinis*: Stearns and Sage 1980
	8	*P. latipinna*: Trexler 1986*
Coloration	1	*P. latipinna*: Angus 1983*
	5	*X. variatus*: Borowsky 1973b
Adrenocortical activity	5	*X. helleri*: Scott and Currie 1980
Superfetation	3	*Heterandria formosa*: Travis et al. 1987b

LITERATURE CITED

ABRAMOFF, P., R. M. DARNELL, AND J. S. BALSANO. 1968. Electrophoretic demonstration of the hybrid origin of the gynogenetic teleost *Poecilia formosa*. Amer. Natur. 102:555–58.

AGASSIZ, J. L. R. 1855. Remarks on Dr. B. Dowler's paper "Discovery of viviparous fishes in Louisiana." Amer. J. Sci. Arts 2:133–36.

AHO, J. M., J. W. GIBBONS, AND G. W. ESCH. 1976. Relationship between thermal loading and parasitism in the mosquitofish. Pp. 213–18 *In*: G. W. Esch and R. W. McFarlane (eds.), Thermal Ecology II. ERDA Symp. Ser., CONF-750425.

AHUJA, M. R., M. SCHWAB, AND F. ANDERS. 1980. Linkage between a regulatory locus for melanoma cell differentiation and an esterase locus in *Xiphophorus*. J. Heredity 71:403–7.

AL-DAHAM, N. K. AND M. N. BHATTI. 1977. Salinity tolerance of *Gambusia affinis* (Baird and Girard) and *Heteropneustes fossilis* (Bloch). J. Fish. Biol. 11:309–13.

AL-HUSSAINI, A. H. 1949. On the functional morphology of the alimentary tract of some fishes in relation to differences in their feeding habits. Anatomy and histology. Quart. J. Micros. Sci. 90:109–39.

ALLENDORF, F. W. AND R. F. LEARY. 1986. Heterozygosity and fitness in natural populations of animals. Pp. 57–76 *In*: M. E. Soulé (ed.), Conservation Biology: The Science of Scarcity and Diversity. Sinauer Assoc., Inc., Sunderland, MA, USA.

ALLENDORF, F. W. AND S. R. PHELPS. 1981. Use of allele frequencies to describe population structure. Can. J. Aqua. Fish. Sci. 38:1507–14.

ALLENDORF, F. W., N. RYMAN, AND F. UTTER. 1985. Genetics and fisheries management: past, present, and future. Pp. 1–20 *In*: N. Ryman and F. Utter (eds.), Population Genetics and Fisheries Management, Univ. of Wash. Press, Seattle, WA, USA.

ALTUKHOV, V. P. 1982. Biochemical population genetics and speciation. Evolution 36:1168–81.

ALVAREZ, J. 1948a. Contribución al conocimiento del genero *Priapella* y descripción de una nueva especie (Pisces, Poeciliidae). Rev. Soc. Mexicana Hist. Natur. 9:331–40.

ALVAREZ, J. 1948b. Descripción de una nueva especie de *Mollienesia* capturada en Baños del Azufre, Tabasco (Pisces, Poeciliidae). Ann. Esc. Nac. Cien. Biol. 5:275–81.

ALVAREZ, J. 1952a. Cuatro especies nuevas de peces dulcaecuilcolas del sureste de Mexico. Ciencia 11:281–89.

ALARVEZ, J. 1952b. Dicerophallini, nueva tribu de Poeciliidae de Chiapas. Ciencia 12:95–97.

ALVAREZ, J. 1959. Nueva especies de *Xiphophorus* e *Hyporamphus* procedents del Río Coatzocoalcos. Ciencia 19:69–73.

ALVAREZ, J. AND F. AGUILLAR. 1957. Contribución al estudio de la suspensión gonopodica del genero *Poeciliopsis* con descripción de una nueva especie fosil procedente de El Salvador, Centro America. Rev. Soc. Mexicana Hist. Natur. 18:153–72.

AMOROSO, E. C. 1960. Viviparity in fishes. Symp. Zool. Soc. London 1:153–81.

AMOURIQ, L. 1964. L'activite et le phenomene social chez *Lebistes reticulatus* (Poeciliidae, Cyprinodontiformes). Compt. Rend. Acad. Sci. Paris 259:2701–2.

AMOURIQ, L. 1965. Origine de la substance dynamogene emise par *Lebistes reticulatus* femelle (Poisson, Poeciliidae, Cyprinodontiformes). Compt. Rend. Acad. Sci. Paris 260:2334–35.

AMOURIQ, L. 1967. Sensibilite des *Lebistes reticulatus* male a la substance dynamogene emise par des femelles de Poeciliidae et de Gasterosteidae. Rev. Comp. Anim. 4:83–86.

ANDERS, A. AND F. ANDERS. 1978. Etiology of cancer as studied in the platyfish-swordtail system. Biochim. Biophys. Acta 516:61–95.

ANDERS, A., F. ANDERS, AND K. KLINKE. 1973. Regulation of gene expression in the Gordon-Kosswig melanoma system. I. The distribution of the controlling genes in the genome of the xiphophorin fish *Platypoecilus maculatus* and *Platypoecilus variatus*. Pp. 33–52 *In*: J. H. Schröder (ed.), Genetics and Mutagenesis of Fish. Springer-Verlag, New York, NY, USA.

ANDERS, F., A. ANDERS, AND U. VIELKIND. 1974. Regulation of tumor expression in the Gordon-Kosswig melanoma system, and the origin of malignancy. P. 305 *In*: Abstracts XIth Inter. Cancer Congr., Florence, Italy.

ANDERS, F., H. DIEHL, AND E. SCHOLL. 1980. Differentiation of normal melanophores and neoplastically transformed melanophores in the skin of fishes of the genus *Xiphophorus*. Pp. 211–24 *In*: R. I. Spearman and P. A. Riley (eds.), The Skin of Vertebrates. Academic Press, New York, NY, USA.

ANDERS, F., M. SCHARTL, AND A. BARNEKOW. 1984a. *Xiphophorus* as an *in vivo* model for studies on oncogenes. Nat. Cancer Inst. Monogr. 65:97–109.

ANDERS, F., M. SCHARTL, A. BARNEKOW, AND A. ANDERS. 1984b. *Xiphophorus* as an *in vivo* model for studies on normal and defective control of oncogenes. Adv. Cancer Res. 42:191–275.

ANDERSON, R. S. 1980. Geographic variation and aspects of the life history of *Belonesox belizanus* Kner (Pisces: Poeciliidae) from Central America. M. S. Thesis, Northern Illinois Univ., DeKalb, IL, USA.

ANDERSSON, M. 1986. Evolution of condition-dependent sex ornaments and mating preferences: sexual selection based on viability differences. Evolution 40:804–16.

ANGUS, R. A. 1980. Geographic dispersal and clonal diversity in unisexual fish populations. Amer. Natur. 115:531–50.

ANGUS, R. A. 1983a. Genetic analysis of melanistic spotting in sailfin mollies. J. Heredity 74:81–84.

ANGUS, R. A. 1983b. Phenol tolerance in populations of mosquitofish from polluted and nonpolluted waters. Trans. Amer. Fish. Soc. 112:794–99.

ANGUS, R. A. AND R. J. SCHULTZ. 1979. Clonal diversity in the unisexual fish *Poeciliopsis monacha-lucida*: a tissue graft analysis. Evolution 33:27–40.

ANGUS, R. A. AND R. J. SCHULTZ. 1983. Meristic variation in homozygous and heterozygous fish. Copeia 1983:287–99.

ANTONOVICS, J. 1976. The nature of limits to natural selection. Ann. Missouri Bot. Gard. 63:224–47.

ARNOLD, S. J. 1987. Genetic correlation and the evolution of physiology. Pp. 189–215 *In*: M. E. Feder, A. F. Bennett, W. W. Burrgren, and R. B. Huey (eds.), New Directions in Ecological Physiology. Cambridge Univ. Press, New York, NY, USA.

ARTHINGTON, A. H. 1984. Freshwater fishes of Stradbroke, Moreton and Fraser Island. Pp. 279–82 *In*: J. Covacevich and J. Davie (eds.), Focus on Stradbroke. Boolarong Press, Brisbane, Australia.

ARTHINGTON, A. H. 1988. Diet of *Gambusia affinis holbrooki* (Baird and Girard) in streams of the Brisbane region, southeastern Queensland, Australia. Proceedings (Verhandlungen) of the Societe Internationale Limnologie 1987.

ARTHINGTON, A. H. AND D. S. MITCHELL. 1986. Aquatic invading species. Pp. 34–52 *In*: R. H. Grooves and J. J. Burdon (eds.), Ecology of Biological Invasions: An Australian Perspective. Aust. Acad. Sci., Canberra, Australia.

ARTHINGTON, A. H., R. J. MCKAY, AND D. A. MILTON. 1986a. The ecology and management of exotic and endemic freshwater fishes in Queensland. Pp. 93–103 *In*: T. Hundloe (ed.), Fisheries Management. Theory and Practice in Queensland. Griffith Univ. Press, Brisbane, Australia.

ARTHINGTON, A. H., D. A. MILTON, AND R. J. MCKAY. 1983. Effects of urban development and habitat alterations on the distribution and abundance of native and exotic freshwater fish in the Brisbane region, Queensland. Aust. J. Ecol. 8:87–101.

ARTHINGTON, A. H., H. B. BURTON, R. W. WILLIAMS, AND P. M. OUTRIDGE. 1986b. Ecology of humic and non-humic dune lakes, Fraser Island, with emphasis on the effects of sand infilling in Lake Wabby. Aust. J. Mar. Freshwater Res. 37:743–64.

ATZ, J. W. 1962. Effects of hybridization on pigmentation in fishes of the genus *Xiphophorus*. Zoologica 47:153–81.

AVISE, J. C. AND C. F. AQUADRO. 1982. A comparative summary of genetic distances in the vertebrates. Evol. Biol. 15:151–85.

AVISE, J. C. AND M. H. SMITH. 1974. Biochemical genetics of sunfish. I. Geographic variation and subspecific intergradation in the bluegill, *Lepomis macrochirus*. Evolution 33:42–56.

AVISE, J. C., J. ARNOLD, R. M. BALL, E. BERMINGHAM, T. LAMB, J. E. NEIGEL, C. A. REEB, AND N. C. SAUNDERS. 1987. Intraspecific phylogeography: the mitochondrial DNA bridge between population genetics and systematics. Annu. Rev. Ecol. Syst. 18:489–522.

BACON, E. J., JR., W. H. NEILL, AND R. V. KILAMBI. 1968. Temperature selection and heat resistance of the mosquito fish, *Gambusia affinis*. Proc. 21st Annu. Conf. Southeastern Assoc. Game & Fish Comm. 1967:411–16.

BAERENDS, G. P., R. BROWER, AND H. T. J. WATERBOLK. 1955. Ethological studies on *Lebistes reticulatus* (Peters). I. An analysis of the male courtship pattern. Behaviour 8:249–335.

BAGNARA, J. T., J. MATSUMOTO, W. FERRIS, S. K. FROST, W. A. TURNER, JR., T. TCHEN, AND J. D. TAYLOR. 1979. Common origin of pigment cells. Science 203:410–15.

BAILEY, R. J. 1933. The ovarian cycle in the viviparous teleost *Xiphophorus helleri*. Biol. Bull. 64:206–25.

BAIRD, R. C. 1968. Aggressive behavior and social organization in *Mollienesia latipinna* (LeSueur). Texas J. Sci. 20:157–76.

BAIRD, R. C. 1974. Aspects of social behavior in *Poecilia latipinna* (LeSueur). Rev. Biol. Trop. 21:399–416.

Baird, S. F. and C. Girard. 1853. Descriptions of new species of fishes collected by Mr. John H. Clark, on the U.S. and Mexican Boundary Survey, under Lt. Col. Jas. D. Graham. Proc. Acad. Natur. Sci. Philadelphia 6:387–90.

Balla, S. A., L. N. Lloyd, and B. E. Pierce. 1985. Unwanted aquarium fish. Search 16:300–301.

Ballin, P. J. 1973. Geographic variation of courtship behaviour in natural populations of the guppy, Poecilia reticulata (Peters). M. S. Thesis, Univ. British Columbia, Vancouver, British Columbia, Canada.

Balling, S. S., T. Stoehr, and V. H. Resh. 1980. The effects of mosquito control recirculation ditches in the fish community of a San Francisco Bay salt marsh. Calif. Fish & Game 66:25–34.

Balon, E. K. 1975. Reproductive guilds of fishes: a proposal and definition. J. Fish. Res. Bd. Canada 32:821–64.

Balon, E. K. 1981. Additions and amendments to the classification of reproductive styles in fishes. Env. Biol. Fish. 6:377–89.

Balsano, J. S. and E. M. Rasch. 1974. Microspectrophotometric and enzymatic analyses of fish plasma proteins electrophoretically separated in thin polyacrylamide gels. J. Fish Biol. 6:51–59.

Balsano, J. S., R. M. Darnell, and P. Abramoff. 1972. Electrophoretic evidence of triploidy associated with populations of the gynogenetic teleost Poecilia formosa. Copeia 1972:292–97.

Balsano, J. S., E. M. Rasch, and P. J. Monaco. 1983. Reproductive interactions within bisexual/unisexual complexes of Poecilia from the Río Purificacion in northeastern Mexico. Nat. Geogr. Soc. Res. Repts., 1976 Projects:113–35.

Balsano, J. S., E. J. Randle, E. M. Rasch, and P. J. Monaco. 1985. Reproductive behavior and the maintenance of all-female Poecilia. Env. Biol. Fish. 12:251–63.

Balsano, J. S., K. Kucharski, E. J. Randle, E. M. Rasch, and P. J. Monaco. 1981. Reduction of competition between bisexual and unisexual females of Poecilia in northeastern Mexico. Env. Biol. Fish. 6:39–48.

Bao, I. Y. 1981. The genetic and endocrine control of sexual maturation and sterility in hybrids between Xiphophorus helleri and X. maculatus. Ph.D. Dissertation, New York University, New York, NY, USA.

Bao, I. Y. and K. D. Kallman. 1982. Genetic control of the hypothalamo-pituitary axis and the effect of hybridization on sexual maturation (Xiphophorus, Pisces, Poeciliidae). J. Exp. Zool. 220:297–309.

Barigozzi, C. (ed.). 1983. Mechanisms in Speciation. Alan R. Liss, New York, NY, USA.

Barlow, C. G. and A. Lisle. 1987. Biology of the nile perch Lates niloticus (Pisces: Centropomidae) with reference to its proposed role as a sport fish in Australia. Biol. Conserv. 39:269–89.

Barrington, E. J. W. 1957. The alimentary canal and digestion. Pp. 109–61 In: W. S. Hoar and D. J. Randall (eds.), Fish Physiology, Vol. 1. Academic Press, New York, NY, USA.

BARRON, J. C. 1964. Reproduction and apparent overwinter survival of the suckermouth catfish, *Plecostomus* sp., in the headwaters of the San Antonio River. Texas J. Sci. 16:449–50.

BARTON, N. H. AND G. M. HEWITT. 1985. Analysis of hybrid zones. Annu. Rev. Ecol. Syst. 16:113–48.

BARUS, V. AND J. LIBOSVARSKY. 1986. Some new data on *Dactylophallus denticulatus* (Poeciliidae) from Cuba. Folia Zool. 35:357–62.

BARUS, V., J. LIBOSVARSKY, AND F. P. GUERRA. 1981a. Observations on *Quintana atrizona* (Poeciliidae) from Cuba, reared in aquaria. Folia Zool. Brno 30:203–14.

BARUS, V., J. LIBOSVARSKY, AND F. P. GUERRA. 1981b. Notes on *Toxus creolus* (Poeciliidae) from Cuba. Folia Zool. Brno 30:363–70.

BARUS, V., J. LIBOSVARSKY, AND A. M. PEREZ. 1986a. Supplements to the description of *Girardinus microdactylus* (Pisces, Poeciliidae). Folia Zool. Brno 35:173–81.

BARUS, V., J. LIBOSVARSKY, AND A. M. PEREZ. 1986b. Some new data on *Dactylophallus denticulatus* (Poeciliidae) from Cuba. Folia Zool. Brno 35:357–362.

BATEMAN, A. J. 1948. Intra-sexual selection in *Drosophila*. Heredity 2:349–68.

BAXTER, G. R. AND J. R. SIMON. 1970. Wyoming Fishes. Bull. Wyoming Game & Fish Dept. 4:1–168.

BAYLY, I. A. E. AND W. D. WILLIAMS. 1973. Inland Waters and Their Ecology. Longman, Australia Ltd., Hawthorn, Victoria, Australia.

BAYLY, I. A. E., P. EBSWORTH, AND F. W. HANG. 1975. Ecology of Fraser Island lakes. Aust. J. Mar. Freshwater Res. 24:1–13.

BEAMISH, R. J. AND G. A. McFARLANE. 1987. Current trends in age determination methodology. Pp. 15–42 *In*: R. C. Summerfelt and G. E. Hall (eds.), Age and Growth of Fish. Iowa State Univ. Press, Ames, IA, USA.

BEARDMORE, J. A. AND S. A. SHAMI. 1976. Parental age, genetic variation and selection. Pp. 3–22 *In*: S. Karlin and E. Nevo (eds.), Population Genetics and Ecology. Academic Press, New York, NY, USA.

BEARDMORE, J. A. AND S. A. SHAMI. 1979. Heterozygosity and the optimum phenotype under stabilizing selection. Aquilo Ser. Zool. 20:100–110.

BEDNARZ, J. C. 1975. A study of the Pecos gambusia. New Mexico Dept. Game & Fish, Santa Fe, NM, USA.

BELL, G. 1982. The Masterpiece of Nature: The Evolution and Genetics of Sexuality. Univ. Calif. Press, Berkeley, CA, USA.

BELLAMY, A. W. 1924. Bionomic studies on certain teleosts (Poeciliidae). I. Statement of problems, description of material, and general notes on life histories and breeding behavior under laboratory conditions. Genetics 9:513–29.

BELLAMY, A. W. AND M. L. QUEAL. 1951. Heterosomal inheritance and sex determination in *Platypoecilus maculatus*. Genetics 36:93–107.

BELSHE, J. F. 1961. Observations of an introduced tropical fish (*Belonesox belizanus*) in southern Florida. M. S. Thesis, Univ. Miami, Coral Gables, FL, USA.

BENCE, J. R. AND W. W. MURDOCH. 1986. Prey size selection by the mosquitofish: relation to optimal diet theory. Ecology 67:324–36.

BENNETT, D. H. AND C. P. GOODYEAR. 1978. Response of mosquitofish to thermal effluent. Pp. 498–510 In: J. H. Thorp and J. W. Gibbons (eds.), Energy and Environmental Stress in Aquatic Systems. DOE Symp. Ser., CONF-771114.

BENSINK, A. H. A. AND H. BURTON. 1975. North Stradbroke Island. A place for freshwater invertebrates. Proc. Royal Soc. Queensland 80:29–45.

BERG, O. AND M. GORDON. 1953. Relationship of atypical pigment cell growth to gonadal development in hybrid fishes. Pp. 43–71 In: M. Gordon (ed.), Pigment Cell Growth. Academic Press, New York, NY, USA.

BERMINGHAM, E. AND J. C. AVISE. 1986. Molecular zoogeography of freshwater fishes in the southeastern United States. Genetics 133:939–65.

BHASKER, R. R. AND H. RAMOD. 1942. Some notes on the practical aspects of mosquito control in wells and tanks by the use of larvivorous fish. J. Malaria Inst. India 4:341–47.

BILLARD, R. 1986. Spermatogenesis and spermatology of some teleost fish species. Reprod. Nutr. Dev. 26:877–920.

BIRD, M. A. AND H. E. SCHAFFER. 1972. A study of the genetic basis of the sexual dimorphism for wing length in *Drosophila melanogaster*. Genetics 72:475–87.

BLACK, D. A. AND W. M. HOWELL. 1979. The North American mosquitofish, *Gambusia affinis*: a unique case in sex chromosome evolution. Copeia 1979:509–13.

BLACKBURN, D. G. 1982. Evolutionary origins of viviparity in the Reptilia. I. Sauria. Amphibia-Reptilia 3:185–205.

BLOCH, M. E. AND J. O. G. SCHEINDER. 1801. Systema Ichthyologiae, Vols. 1, 2. Berlin, Germany.

BOND, C. E. 1961. Keys to Oregon freshwater fishes. Oregon St. Univ. Agric. Exp. Sta. Tech. Bull. 58:1–42.

BOOTH, D. J. 1980. Investigations into the extent and mechanisms of prey-size selection by the fish species *Pseudomugil signifer* Kner and *Gambusia affinis* (Baird and Girard). B. S. Thesis, Univ. Sydney, Sydney, Australia.

BOROWSKY, R. L. 1973a. Relative size and the development of fin coloration in *Xiphophorus variatus*. Physiol. Zool. 46:22–28.

BOROWSKY, R. L. 1973b. Social control of adult size in males of *Xiphophorus variatus*. Nature 245:332–35.

BOROWSKY, R. L. 1978a. Social inhibition of maturation in natural populations of *Xiphophorus variatus* (Pisces: Poeciliidae). Science 201:933–35.

BOROWSKY, R. L. 1978b. The tailspot polymorphism of *Xiphophorus* (Pisces: Poeciliidae). Evolution 32:886–93.

BOROWSKY, R. L. 1984. The evolutionary genetics of *Xiphophorus*. Pp. 235–310 In: B. J. Turner (ed.), Evolutionary Genetics of Fishes. Plenum Press, New York, NY, USA.

BOROWSKY, R. L. 1987a. Genetic polymorphism in adult male size in *Xiphophorus variatus* (Atheriniformes: Poeciliidae). Copeia 1987:782–87.

BOROWSKY, R. L. 1987b. Agonistic behavior and social inhibition of maturation in fishes of the genus *Xiphophorus* (Poeciliidae). Copeia 1987:792–96.

BOROWSKY, R. L. AND K. D. KALLMAN. 1976. Patterns of mating in natural populations of *Xiphophorus* (Pisces: Poeciliidae). I. *X. maculatus* from Belize and Mexico. Evolution 30:693–706.

Borowsky, R. L. and J. Khouri. 1976. Patterns of mating in natural populations of *Xiphophorus*. II. *X. variatus* from Tamaulipas, Mexico. Copeia 1976:727–34.

Botsford, L. W., B. Vondracek, T. C. Wainwright, A. L. Linden, R. G. Kope, D. E. Reed, and J. J. Cech, Jr. 1987. Population development of the mosquitofish, *Gambusia affinis*, in rice fields. Env. Biol. Fish. 20:143–54.

Bouma, R. W. 1984. A contribution to the management of *Gambusia nobilis* at Bitter Lake National Wildlife Refuge. Final Rept., US Fish & Wildl. Serv., Albuquerque, NM, USA.

Bourliere, F. 1954. The Natural History of Mammals. Alferd A. Knopf, New York, NY, USA.

Bowden, B. S. 1969. A new method for obtaining precisely timed inseminations in viviparous fishes. Prog. Fish-Cult. 31:229–30.

Bowden, B. S. 1970. The relationship of light and temperature to reproduction in the guppy, *Poecilia reticulata* Peters. Ph.D. Dissertation, Univ. Connecticut, Storrs, CT, USA.

Boyce, M. S. 1984. Restitution of r- and K-selection as a model of density-dependent natural selection. Ann. Rev. Ecol. Syst. 15:427–47.

Braddock, J. C. 1945. Some aspects of the dominance-subordination relationship in the fish *Platypoecilius maculatus*. Physiol. Zool. 18:176–95.

Bradshaw, A. D. 1965. Evolutionary significance of phenotypic plasticity in plants. Adv. Genet. 13:115–55.

Branson, B. A., C. J. McCoy, Jr., and M. E. Sisk. 1960. Notes on the freshwater fishes of Sonora with an addition to the known fauna. Copeia 1960:217–20.

Breder, C. M., Jr. 1934. A new *Gambusia* from Andros Island, Bahamas. Amer. Mus. Novitates 719:1–3.

Breder, C. M., Jr. and C. W. Coates. 1932. A preliminary study of population stability and sex ratio of *Lebistes*. Copeia 1932:147–55.

Breder, C. M., Jr. and C. W. Coates. 1934. Sex recognition in the guppy, *Lebistes reticulatus*. Zoologica 19:187–207.

Breder, C. M. and D. E. Rosen. 1966. Modes of Reproduction in Fishes. American Museum of Natural History Press, New York, NY, USA.

Breider, H. 1938. Die Gesetze der Vererbung und Züchtung in Versuchen mit Aquariehfischen. Gustav Wenzel & Sohn, Braunschweig, Germany.

Brett, B. L. H. and D. J. Grosse. 1982. A reproductive pheromone in the Mexican poeciliid fish *Poecilia chica*. Copeia 1982:219–23.

Brett, B. L. H. and B. J. Turner. 1983. Genetic divergence in the *Poecilia sphenops* complex in middle America. Biochem. Syst. Ecol. 11:127–37.

Brett, J. R. 1956. Some principles in the thermal requirements of fishes. Quart. Rev. Biol. 31:75–87.

Brett, J. R. 1979. Environmental factors and growth. Pp. 599–675 *In*: W. S. Hoar, D. J. Randall, and J. R. Brett (eds.), Fish Physiology, Vol. 8. Academic Press, New York, NY, USA.

Britton, R. H. and M. E. Moser. 1982. Size specific predation by herons and its effect on the sex-ratio of natural populations of the mosquito fish *Gambusia affinis* Baird and Girard. Oecologia 53:146–51.

BRONSON, F. H. AND E. F. RISSMAN. 1986. The biology of puberty. Biol. Rev. 61:157–95.

BROOKS, J. E. 1985. Factors affecting the success of Gila topminnow (*Poeciliopsis o. occidentalis*) introductions on four Arizona national forests. US Fish & Wildl. Serv., Albuquerque, NM, USA.

BROOKS, J. E. 1988. A survey of the fishes of Bitter Lake National Wildlife Refuge, with a historic overview of the game and non-game fishes. US Fish & Wildlife Serv., Albuquerque, NM, USA.

BROWN, C. J. D. 1971. Fishes of Montana. Big Sky Books, Montana State Univ., Bozeman, MT, USA.

BROWN, C. J. D. AND A. C. FOX. 1966. Mosquito fish (*Gambusia affinis*) in a Montana pond. Copeia 1966:614–16.

BROWN, K. L. 1982. Demographic and genetic characteristics of dispersal in the mosquitofish, *Gambusia affinis* (family Poeciliidae). Ph.D. Dissertation, Univ. Georgia, Athens, GA, USA.

BROWN, K. L. 1985. Demographic and genetic characteristics of dispersal in the mosquitofish, *Gambusia affinis* (Pisces: Poeciliidae). Copeia 1985:597–612.

BROWN, K. L. 1987. Colonization by mosquitofish (*Gambusia affinis*) of a Great Plains river basin. Copeia 1987:336–51.

BRUNE, G. 1975. Major and Historical Springs of Texas. Texas Water Develop. Bd. Rept. 189, Austin, TX, USA.

BRUTON, M. N. AND J. G. VAN AS. 1986. Faunal invasions of aquatic ecosystems in southern Africa, with suggestions for their management. Pp. 47–62 *In*: I. A. W. Macdonald, F. J. Kruger, and A. A. Ferrar (eds.), The Ecology and Management of Biological Invasions in Southern Africa. Oxford Univ. Press, Cape Town, South Africa.

BRYANT, E. H. 1974. On the adaptive significance of enzyme polymorphisms in relation to environmental variability. Amer. Natur. 108:1–19.

BULGER, A. J. AND R. J. SCHULTZ. 1979. Heterosis and interclonal variation in thermal tolerance in unisexual fish. Evolution 33:848–59.

BULGER, A. J. AND R. J. SCHULTZ. 1982. Origin of thermal adaptations in northern versus southern populations of a unisexual hybrid fish. Evolution 36:1041–50.

BULL, J. J. 1983. The Evolution of Sex Determining Mechanisms. Benjamin Cummings, Menlo Park, CA, USA.

BULL, J. J. AND R. C. VOGT. 1979. Temperature dependent sex determination in turtles. Science 206:1186–88.

BULMER, M. G. 1985. The Mathematical Theory of Quantitative Genetics. Clarendon Press, Oxford, England.

BURGESS, G. H., C. R. GILBERT, V. GUILLORY, AND D. C. TAPHORN. 1977. Distributional notes on some north Florida freshwater fishes. Fla. Sci. 40:33–41.

BURNS, J. R. 1985. The effect of low-latitude photoperiods on the reproduction of female and male *Poeciliopsis gracilis* and *Poecilia sphenops*. Copeia 1985:961–65.

BUSACK, C. A. 1983. Four generations of selection for high 56-day weight in the mosquitofish (*Gambusia affinis*). Aquaculture 33:83–87.

BUSACK, C. A. AND G. A. E. GALL. 1983. An initial description of the quantitative genetics of growth and reproduction in the mosquitofish, *Gambusia affinis*. Aquaculture 32:123–40.

BUSSING, W. A. 1963. A new poeciliid fish, *Phallichthys tico*, from Costa Rica. Contrib. Sci. Los Angeles County Mus. 77:1–13.

BUSSING, W. A. 1967. New species and new records of Costa Rican freshwater fishes with a tentative list of species. Rev. Biol. Trop. 14:205–49.

BUSSING, W. A. 1979. A new fish of the genus *Phallichthys* (family Poeciliidae) from Costa Rica. Contrib. Sci. Los Angeles County Mus. 301:1–8.

BUTH, D. G. 1984a. Allozymes of the cyprinid fishes: variation and application. Pp. 561–90 *In*: B. J. Turner (ed.), Evolutionary Genetics of Fishes. Plenum Press, New York, NY, USA.

BUTH, D. G. 1984b. The application of electrophoretic data in systematic studies. Annu. Rev. Ecol. Syst. 15:501–22.

CADWALLADER, P. L. 1979. Distribution of native and introduced fish in the Seven Creeks River system, Victoria. Aust. J. Ecol. 4:361–85.

CADWALLADER, P. L., G. N. BACKHOUSE, AND R. FALLU. 1980. Occurrence of tropical fish in the cooling pondage of a power station in temperate south-eastern Australia. Aust. J. Mar. Freshwater Res. 31:541–46.

CALDWELL, M. C. AND D. K. CALDWELL. 1962. Monarchistic dominance in small groups of captive male mosquitofish, *Gambusia affinis patruelis*. Bull. Southern Calif. Acad. Sci. 61:37–43.

CALDWELL, D. K., L. H. OGREN, AND L. GIOVANNOLI. 1959. Systematic and ecological notes on some fishes collected in the vicinity of Tortuguero, Caribbean coast of Costa Rica. Rev. Biol. Trop. 7:7–33.

CAMPOS, H. H. AND C. L. HUBBS. 1971. Cytomorphology of six species of gambusiine fishes. Copeia 1971:566–69.

CARLSON, D. R. 1969. Female sexual receptivity in *Gambusia affinis* (Baird and Girard). Texas J. Sci. 21:167–73.

CARTER, H. J. 1981. Aspects of the physiological ecology of species of *Gambusia* from Belize, Central America. Copeia 1981:694–700.

CASE, M. L. AND T. J. TAPER. 1986. On the coexistence and coevolution of asexual and sexual competitors. Evolution 40:366–87.

CASWELL, H. 1980. On the equivalence of maximizing reproductive value and maximizing fitness. Ecology 61:19–24.

CASWELL, H. 1983. Phenotypic plasticity in life-history traits: demographic effects and evolutionary consequences. Amer. Zool. 23:35–46.

CECH, J. J., JR. AND A. L. LINDEN. 1986. Comparative mosquito predation efficiency of mosquitofish and juvenile Sacramento blackfish in experimental rice paddies. Proc. Pap. Annu. Conf. California Mosq. Vector Control Assoc. 54:89.

CECH, J. J., JR. AND A. L. LINDEN. 1987. Comparative larvivorous performance of mosquitofish, *Gambusia affinis*, and juvenile Sacramento blackfish, *Orthodon microlepidotus*, in experimental paddies. J. Amer. Mosq. Control Assoc. 3:35–41.

CECH, J. J., JR., M. J. MASSINGILL, AND T. E. WRAGG. 1980. The food demands of mosquitofish, *Gambusia affinis*. Proc. Pap. Annu. Conf. California Mosq. Vector Control Assoc. 48:45–47.

CECH, J. J., JR., M. J. MASSINGILL, B. VONDRACEK, AND A. L. LINDEN. 1985. Respiratory metabolism of mosquitofish, *Gambusia affinis*: effects of temperature, dissolved oxygen, and sex difference. Env. Biol. Fish. 13:297–307.

CHAKRABORTY, R. 1980. Gene-diversity analysis in nested subdivided populations. Genetics 96:721–23.

CHAKRABORTY, R. AND O. LEIMAR. 1987. Genetic variation within a subdivided population. Pp. 89–120 *In*: N. Ryman and F. Utter (eds.), Population Genetics and Fishery Management. Univ. Washington Press, Seattle, WA, USA.

CHAMBERS, J. 1987. The cyprinodontiform gonopodium, with an atlas of the gonopodia of the fishes of the genus *Limia*. J. Fish. Biol. 30:389–418.

CHARLESWORTH, B. 1980. Evolution in Age-structured Populations. Cambridge Univ. Press, New York, NY, USA.

CHARNOV, E. L. AND J. J. BULL. 1977. When is sex environmentally determined? Nature 266:828–30.

CHEN, T. R. 1967. Comparative karyology of selected deep-sea and shallow-water teleost fishes. Ph.D. Dissertation, Yale Univ., New Haven, CT, USA.

CHEONG, R. T., S. HENRICH, J. A. FARR, AND J. TRAVIS. 1984. Variation in fecundity and its relationship to body size in a population of the least killifish, *Heterandria formosa* (Pisces: Poeciliidae). Copeia 1984:720–26.

CHESSER, R. K., M. W. SMITH, AND M. H. SMITH. 1984. Biochemical genetics of mosquitofish. III. Incidence and significance of multiple insemination. Genetica 64:77–81.

CHESSMAN, B. C. AND W. D. WILLIAMS. 1974. Distribution of fish in inland saline waters in Victoria, Australia. Aust. J. Mar. Freshwater Res. 25:167–72.

CHRISTENSEN, P. 1982. The distribution of *Lepidogalaxias salamandroides* and other small freshwater-fishes in the lower south-west of Western Australia. J. Royal Soc. Western Aust. 65:131–41.

CHRISTIANSEN, F. B. AND O. FRYDENBURG. 1973. Selection component analysis of natural polymorphisms using population samples including mother-offspring combinations. Theor. Pop. Biol. 4:425–45.

CHRISTIANSEN, F. B., O. FRYDENBURG, AND V. SIMONSEN. 1984. Genetics of *Zoarces* populations. XII. Variation at the polymorphic loci PGI-1, PGM-2, HB-1, and EST-2. Hereditas 101:37–48.

CIMINO, M. C. 1972a. Egg production, polyploidization and evolution in a diploid all-female fish of the genus *Poeciliopsis*. Evolution 26:294–306.

CIMINO, M. C. 1972b. Meiosis in a triploid all-female fish (*Poeciliopsis*, Poeciliidae). Science 175:1484–86.

CIMINO, M. C. 1974. The nuclear DNA content of diploid and triploid *Poeciliopsis* and other poeciliid fishes with reference to the evolution of unisexual forms. Chromosoma (Berl.) 47:297–307.

CLARK, E. AND L. R. ARONSON. 1951. Sexual behavior in the guppy, *Lebistes reticulatus* (Peters). Zoologica 36:49–65.

CLARK, E., L. R. ARONSON, AND M. GORDON. 1954. Mating behavior patterns in two sympatric species of Xiphophorin fishes: their inheritance and significance in sexual isolation. Bull. Amer. Mus. Natur. Hist. 103:135–226.

CLAUSEN, J., D. D. KECK, AND W. M. HEISEY. 1948. Experimental studies on the nature of species. III. Environmental responses of climatic races of *Achillea*. Carnegie Inst. Wash. Publ. 581:1–129.

CLEMENS, H. P., C. McDERMITT, AND T. INSLEE. 1966. The effects of feeding methyl testosterone to guppies for sixty days after birth. Copeia 1966:280–84.

CLUTTON-BROCK, T. H. AND P. H. HARVEY. 1986. Comparative approaches to investigating adaptation. Pp. 7–29 *In*: J. R. Krebs and N. B. Davies (eds.), Behavioral Ecology. Sinauer Associates, Sunderland, MA, USA.

COCHRAN, W. G. 1977. Sampling Techniques. 3rd ed. John Wiley & Sons, New York, NY, USA.

COLE, L. C. 1954. The population consequences of life history phenomena. Quart. Rev. Biol. 29:103–37.

COLLIER, A. 1936. The mechanism of internal fertilization in *Gambusia*. Copeia 1936:45–53.

COLLINS, J. P., C. YOUNG, J. HOWELL, AND W. L. MINCKLEY. 1981. Impact of flooding in a Sonoran Desert stream, including elimination of an endangered fish population (*Poeciliopsis o. occidentalis*, Poeciliidae). Southwest. Natur. 26:415–23.

COLSON, C. M. 1969. Effects of daylength and temperature on the reproduction of *Heterandria formosa*. Ph.D. Dissertation, Univ. Florida, Gainesville, FL, USA.

CONNELLY, H. 1968. The pike livebearer. The Aquarium 2:4–5, 46–50.

CONOVER, D. O. AND B. E. KYNARD. 1981. Environmental sex determination: interaction between temperature and genotype in a fish. Science 213:577–79.

CONSTANTZ, G. D. 1974. Reproductive effort in *Poeciliopsis occidentalis* (Poeciliidae). Southwest. Natur. 19:47–52.

CONSTANTZ, G. D. 1975. Behavioral ecology of mating in the male gila topminnow, *Poeciliopsis occidentalis* (Cyprinodontiformes: Poeciliidae). Ecology 56:966–73.

CONSTANTZ, G. D. 1976. Life history strategy of the Gila topminnow, *Poeciliopsis occidentalis*: a field evaluation of theory on the evolution of life histories. Ph.D. Dissertation, Arizona St. Univ., Tempe, AZ, USA.

CONSTANTZ, G. D. 1979. Life history patterns of a livebearing fish in contrasting environments. Oecologia 40:189–201.

CONSTANTZ, G. D. 1980. Energetics of viviparity in the Gila topminnow (Pisces: Poeciliidae). Copeia 1980:876–78.

CONSTANTZ, G. D. 1984. Sperm competition in poeciliid fishes. Pp. 465–75 *In*: R. L. Smith (ed.), Sperm Competition and the Evolution of Animal Mating Systems. Academic Press, New York, NY, USA.

CONTRERAS-B., S. AND M. A. ESCALANTE-C. 1984. Distribution and known impacts of exotic fishes in Mexico. Pp. 102–30 *In*: W. R. Courtenay, Jr. and J. R. Stauffer, Jr. (eds.), Distribution, Biology, and Management of Exotic Fishes. Johns Hopkins Univ. Press, Baltimore, MD, USA.

COTHRAN, E. G., R. K. CHESSER, M. H. SMITH, AND P. E. JOHNS. 1983. Influences of genetic variability and maternal factors on fetal growth in white-tailed deer. Evolution 37:282–91.

COURTENAY, W. R., JR. AND J. E. DEACON. 1982. The status of introduced fishes in certain spring systems in southern Nevada. Great Basin Natur. 42:361–66.

COURTENAY, W. R., JR. AND J. E. DEACON. 1982. Fish introductions in the American southwest: a case history of Rogers Spring, Nevada. Southwest. Natur. 28:221–24.

COURTENAY, W. R., JR. AND C. R. ROBINS. 1973. Exotic aquatic organisms in Florida with emphasis on fishes: a review and recommendations. Trans. Amer. Fish. Soc. 102:1–12.

COURTENAY, W. R., JR. AND J. R. STAUFFER, JR. (eds.). 1984. Distribution, Biology and Management of Exotic Fishes. Johns Hopkins Univ. Press, Baltimore, MD, USA.

COURTENAY, W. R., JR., D. A. HENSLEY, J. N. TAYLOR, AND J. A. McCANN. 1984. Distribution of exotic fishes in the continental United States. Pp. 41–77 In: W. R. Courtenay, Jr. and J. R. Stauffer, Jr. (eds.), Distribution, Biology, and Management of Exotic Fishes. Johns Hopkins Univ. Press, Baltimore, MD, USA.

COURTENAY, W. R., JR., D. A. HENSLEY, J. N. TAYLOR, AND J. A. McCANN. 1986. Distribution of exotic fishes in North America. Pp. 675–98 In: C. H. Hocutt and E. O. Wiley (eds.), The Zoogeography of North American Freshwater Fishes. John Wiley & Sons, New York, NY, USA.

COURTENAY, W. R., JR., C. R. ROBINS, R. M. BAILEY, AND J. E. DEACON. 1988. Records of exotic fishes from Idaho and Wyoming. Great Basin Natur. 47:523–26.

COURTENAY, W. R., JR., H. F. SAHLMAN, W. W. MILEY, II, AND D. J. HERREMA. 1974. Exotic fishes in fresh and brackish waters of Florida. Biol. Conserv. 6:292–302.

COURTENAY, W. R., JR., J. E. DEACON, D. W. SADA, R. C. ALLAN, AND G. L. VINYARD. 1985. Comparative status of fishes along the course of the pluvial White River, Nevada. Southwest. Natur. 30:503–24.

COX, C. R. AND B. J. LEBOEUF. 1977. Female incitation of male competition: a mechanism in sexual selection. Amer. Natur. 111:317–35.

CROSS, J. N. 1976. Status of the native fish fauna of the Moapa River (Clark Co., Nevada). Trans. Amer. Fish. Soc. 105:503–08.

CROSSMAN, E. J. 1984. Introduction of exotic fishes into Canada. Pp. 78–101 In: W. R. Courtenay, Jr. and J. R. Stauffer, Jr. (eds.), Distribution, Biology, and Management of Exotic Fishes. Johns Hopkins Univ. Press, Baltimore, MD, USA.

CROW, J. F. 1958. Some possibilities for measuring selection intensities in man. Human Biol. 30:1–13.

CROW, J. F. AND M. KIMURA. 1970. An Introduction to Population Genetics Theory. Harper and Row Publ., New York, NY, USA.

CROW, J. F. AND T. NAGYLAKI. 1976. The rate of change of a character correlated with fitness. Amer. Natur. 110:207–13.

CROW, R. T. AND N. R. LILEY. 1979. A sexual pheromone in the guppy, *Poecilia reticulata* (Peters). Can. J. Zool. 57:184–88.

CUELLAR, O. 1971. Reproduction and the mechanism of meiotic restitution in the parthenogenetic lizard *Cnemidophorus uniparens*. J. Morphology 133:139–66.

CUVIER, M. LE B. AND M. A. VALENCIENNES. 1846. Histoire Naturelle des Poissons, Vol. 18. Paris, France.

DAHL, G. AND F. MEDEM. 1964. Informe sobre la fauna acuática del Río Sinu. Corporación autonoma regional de los valles del Magdelena y del Sinu, Departamento de Investigaciónes Ictiologicas y Faunisticas. 160 pp.

DAHLGREN, B. T. 1979. The effects of population density on fecundity and fertility in the guppy, *Poecilia reticulata* (Peters). J. Fish Biol. 15:71–91.

DANIELSEN, T. L. 1968. Differential predation on *Culex pipiens* and *Anopheles albimanus* mosquito larvae by two species of fish (*Gambusia affinis* and *Cyprinodon nevadensis*) and the effects of simulated reeds on predation. Ph.D. Dissertation, Univ. California, Riverside, CA, USA.

DARNELL, R. M. AND P. ABRAMOFF. 1968. Distribution of the gynogenetic fish, *Poecilia formosa*, with remarks on the evolution of the species. Copeia 1968:354–61.

DARNELL, R. M., P. ABRAMOFF, AND E. LAMB. 1967. Matroclinous inheritance and clonal structure of a Mexican population of the gynogenetic fish, *Poecilia formosa*. Evolution 21:168–73.

DARWIN, C. 1871. The Descent of Man, and Selection in Relation to Sex. John Murray, London, England.

DAVIS, J. A., S. W. ROLLS, AND S. A. BALLA. 1987. The role of the Odonata and aquatic Coleoptera as indicators of environmental quality in wetlands. Pp. 31–42 In: J. D. Majer (ed.), The Role of Invertebrates in Conservation and Biological Survey. Rept. Western Australia Dept. Conserv. & Land Mgt., Perth, Western Australia.

DAVIS, J. R. 1978. Reproductive seasons in *Gambusia affinis* and *Gambusia geiseri* (Osteichthys: Poeciliidae) from southcentral Texas. Texas J. Sci. 30:97–99.

DAWLEY, R. M., R. J. SCHULTZ, AND K. A. GODDARD. 1987. Clonal reproduction and polyploidy in unisexual hybrids of *Phoxinus eos* and *Phoxinus neogaeus* (Pisces; Cyprinidae). Copeia 1987:275–83.

DEACON, J. E. AND W. G. BRADLEY. 1972. Ecological distribution of fishes of Moapa (Muddy) River in Clark County, Nevada. Trans. Amer. Fish. Soc. 101:408–19.

DEACON, J. E. AND J. E. WILLIAMS. 1984. Annotated list of the fishes of Nevada. Proc. Biol. Soc. Washington 97:103–18.

DEACON, J. E., C. HUBBS, AND B. J. ZAHURANEC. 1964. Some effects of introduced fishes on the native fish fauna of southern Nevada. Copeia 1964:384–88.

DEACON, J. E., G. KOBETICH, J. WILLIAMS, AND S. CONTRERAS. 1979. Fishes of North America endangered, threatened, or of special concern: 1979. Fisheries 4(2):29–44.

DEAN, S. M. 1981. The evolutionary adaptation of the mosquitofish, *Gambusia affinis* to heated effluent waters of steam electric generated stations. Ph.D. Dissertation, Univ. Texas, Austin, TX, USA.

DEPECHE, J. 1962. Le developpment in vitro des oeufs de Poeciliidae (Cyprinodontes vivipares). Compt. Rend. Acad. Sci. Paris 225(Ser. D):2670–72.

DEPECHE, J. 1964. Les rapports anatomiques maternoembryonnaires au cours de la gestation des Poeciliidae (Cyprinodontes Vivipares). Bull. Assoc. Anat. (Paris) 49:536–44.

DEPECHE, J. 1976. Acquistion et limites de l'autonomie trophique embryonnaire au cours du development du poisson teleosteen vivipare *Poecilia reticulata*. Bull. Biologique France Belgique 110:45–97.

DeVlaming, V. 1974. Environmental and endocrine control of teleost reproduction. Pp. 13–83 In: C. B. Schreck (ed.), Control of Sex in Fishes. Extension Div., Virginia Polytechnic Inst. & St. Univ., Blacksburg, VA, USA.

Dial, R. S. and S. C. Wainright. 1983. New distributional records for non-native fishes in Florida. Fla. Sci. 46:8–15.

Dickerson, G. E. 1955. Genetic slippage in response to selection for multiple objectives. Cold Spring Harbor Symp. Quant. Biol. 20:213–24.

Dildine, G. C. 1936. The effect of light and temperature on the gonads of Lebistes. Anat. Rec. 67(Suppl. 1):61–66.

Dingle, H. and J. P. Hegmann (eds.). 1982. Evolution and Genetics of Life Histories. Springer-Verlag, New York, NY, USA.

Dowling, T. E. and W. S. Moore. 1985. Evidence for selection against hybrids in the family Cyprinidae (genus Notropis). Evolution 39:152–58.

Doyle, R. W. and R. A. Myers. 1982. The measurement of the direct and indirect intensities of natural selection. Pp. 157–76 In: H. Dingle and J. P. Hegmann (eds.), Evolution and Genetics of Life Histories. Springer-Verlag, New York, NY, USA.

Dressler, R. L. 1971. Local polymorphism in Brachyrhaphis episcopi (Poeciliidae). Copeia 1971:170–71.

Drewry, G. E. 1964. Appendix I-Chromosome number. Pp. 67–70 In: C. Hubbs, Interactions between a bisexual fish species and its gynogenetic sexual parasite. Bull. Texas Memorial Mus. 8:1–72.

Dulzetto, F. 1928. Osservationi sulla vita sessuale della Gambusia holbrooki (Grd.). Atti Rend. Accad. Naz. Lincei (Rome) 8:96–101.

Dulzetto, F. 1934. Osservationi sulla vita e sul rapporto sessuale dei nati Gambusia holbrooki (Grd.). Arch. Zool. Ital. 20:45–65.

Dunham, A. E., D. B. Miles, and D. N. Reznick. 1987. Life history patterns in Squamate reptiles. Pp. 442–522 In: C. Gans and R. B. Huey (eds.). Biology of the Reptilia, Vol. 16, Ecology B. Alan R. Liss, Inc., New York, NY, USA.

Dussault, G. V. and D. L. Kramer. 1981. Food and feeding behavior of the guppy, Poecilia reticulata (Pisces: Poeciliidae). Can. J. Zool. 59:684–701.

Dzwillo, M. 1959. Genetische Untersuchungen an domestizierten Stammen von Lebistes reticulatus (Peters). Mitt. Hamburg Zool. Mus. Inst. 57:143–86.

Dzwillo, M. 1962. Über künstliche Erzeugung funktioneller Männchen weiblichen Genotyps bei Lebistes reticulatus. Biol. Zentralbl. 81:575–84.

Dzwillo, M. 1966. Über den Einfluss von Methyltestosteron auf primäre und sekundäre Geschlechtsmerkmale während verschiedener Phasen der Embryonalentwicklung von Lebistes reticulatus. Verh. Dtsch. Zool. Ges. Jena 29:471–76.

Echelle, A. A. and A. F. Echelle. 1980. Status of the Pecos Gambusia. Endangered Species Rept. No. 10. US Fish & Wildlife Serv., Albuquerque, NM, USA.

Echelle, A. A. and A. F. Echelle. 1984. Evolutionary genetics of a "species flock": atherinid fishes on the Mesa Central of Mexico. Pp. 93–110 In: A. A. Echelle and I. Kornfield (eds.), Evolution of Fish Species Flocks. Univ. Maine Press, Orono, ME, USA.

Echelle, A. A. and I. Kornfield (eds.). 1984. Evolution of Fish Species Flocks. Univ. Maine Press, Orono, ME, USA.

ECHELLE, A. A., A. F. ECHELLE, AND D. R. EDDS. 1983. Genetic structure of three species of endangered desert fishes. Final Rept., US Fish & Wildl. Serv., Albuquerque, NM, USA.

ECHELLE, A. A., A. F. ECHELLE, AND D. R. EDDS. 1987. Population structure of four pupfish species (Cyprinodontidae: *Cyprinodon*) from the Chihuahuan Desert region of New Mexico and Texas: allozymic variation. Copeia 1987:668–81.

ECHELLE, A. F. AND A. A. ECHELLE. 1986. Geographic variation in morphology of a spring-dwelling desert fish, *Gambusia nobilis* (Poeciliidae). Southwest. Natur. 31:459–68.

ECHELLE, A. F., A. A. ECHELLE, AND D. R. EDDS. 1989. Conservation genetics of a spring-dwelling desert fish, the Pecos gambusia, *Gambusia nobilis* (Poeciliidae). Conserv. Biol., in press.

EDWARDS, R. J. AND C. HUBBS. 1971. Temporal changes in the *Gambusia heterochir* X *G. affinis* hybrid swarm following dam reconstruction. Endangered Species Rept. No. 13, US Fish & Wildl. Serv., Albuquerque, NM, USA.

EHRLICH, P. 1986. Which animal will invade? Pp. 79–95 *In*: H. A. Mooney and J. A. Drake (eds.), Ecology of Biological Invasions of North America and Hawaii. Springer-Verlag, New York, NY, USA.

EIGENMANN, C. H. 1894. Notes on some South American fishes. Ann. New York Acad. Sci. 7:625–37.

EIGENMANN, C. H. 1903. The fresh-water fishes of western Cuba. Bull. US Fish Comm. 1902 (22):211–36.

EIGENMANN, C. H. 1909. Reports on the expedition to British Guiana of the Indian University and the Carnegie Museum, 1908. Some new genera and species of fishes from British Guiana. Ann. Carnegie Mus. 6:4–54.

EIGENMANN, C. H. 1912. Some results of an ichthyological reconnaissance of Colombia, South America. Indiana Univ. Studies 1(8):1–27.

EIGENMANN, C. H., A. HENN, AND C. WILSON. 1914. New fishes from western Colombia, Ecuador and Peru. Indiana Univ. Studies 19:1–15.

EISEN, E. J. AND B. H. JOHNSON. 1981. Correlated responses in male reproductive traits in mice selected for litter size and body weight. Genetics 99:513–24.

EISEN, E. J. AND J. E. LEGATES. 1966. Genotype-sex interaction and the genetic correlation between the sexes for body weight in *Mus musculus*. Genetics 54:611–23.

ENDLER, J. A. 1978. A predator's view of animal color patterns. Evol. Biol. 11:319–64.

ENDLER, J. A. 1980. Natural selection on color patterns in *Poecilia reticulata*. Evolution 34:76–91.

ENDLER, J. A. 1982. Convergent and divergent effects of natural selection on color patterns in two fish faunas. Evolution 36:178–88.

ENDLER, J. A. 1983. Natural and sexual selection on color patterns in poeciliid fishes. Env. Biol. Fish. 9:173–90.

ENDLER, J. A. 1986. Natural Selection in the Wild. Princeton Univ. Press, Princeton, NJ, USA.

ERDMAN, D. S. 1984. Exotic fishes in Puerto Rico. Pp. 162–76 *In*: W. R. Courtenay, Jr. and J. R. Stauffer, Jr. (eds.), Distribution, Biology, and Management of Exotic Fishes. Johns Hopkins Univ. Press, Baltimore, MD, USA.

EVERMANN, B. W. AND H. W. CLARK. 1906. New fishes from Santo Domingo. Proc. US Nat. Mus. 30:851–55.

EWENS, W. J. 1976. Remarks on the evolutionary effect of natural selection. Genetics 83:601–7.

FALCONER, D. 1981. Introduction to Quantitative Genetics. 2nd ed. Longman Press, New York, NY, USA.

FARLEY, D. G. AND L. C. YOUNCE. 1977a. Stocking density versus efficacy of *Gambusia affinis* in Fresno County rice fields. Proc. Pap. Annu. Conf. California Mosq. Vector Control Assoc. 45:83–86.

FARLEY, D. G. AND L. C. YOUNCE. 1977b. Some effects of *Gambusia affinis* (Baird & Girard) on selected non-target organisms in Fresno County rice fields. Proc. Pap. Annu. Conf. California Mosq. Vector Control Assoc. 45:87–94.

FARR, J. A. 1975. The role of predation in the evolution of social behavior of natural populations of the guppy, *Poecilia reticulata* (Pisces: Poeciliidae). Evolution 29:151–58.

FARR, J. A. 1976. Social facilitation of male sexual behavior, intrasexual competition, and sexual selection in the guppy, *Poecilia reticulata* (Pisces: Poeciliidae). Evolution 30:707–17.

FARR, J. A. 1977. Male rarity or novelty, female choice behavior, and sexual selection in the guppy, *Poecilia reticulata* Peters (Pisces: Poeciliidae). Evolution 31:162–68.

FARR, J. A. 1980a. The effects of juvenile social interaction on growth rate, size and age at maturity, and adult social behavior in *Girardinus metallicus* Poey (Pisces: Poeciliidae). Z. Tierpsychol. 52:247–68.

FARR, J. A. 1980b. Social behavior patterns as determinants of reproductive success in the guppy, *Poecilia reticulata* Peters (Pisces: Poeciliidae): an experimental study of the effects of intermale competition, female choice, and sexual selection. Behaviour 74:38–91.

FARR, J. A. 1980c. The effects of sexual experience and female receptivity on courtship-rape decisions in male guppies, *Poecilia reticulata* (Pisces: Poeciliidae). Anim. Behav. 28:1195–1201.

FARR, J. A. 1981. Biased sex ratios in laboratory strains of guppies, *Poecilia reticulata*. Heredity 47:237–48.

FARR, J. A. 1983. The inheritance of quantitative fitness traits in guppies, *Poecilia reticulata* (Pisces: Poeciliidae). Evolution 37:1193–1209.

FARR, J. A. 1984. Premating behavior in the subgenus *Limia* (Pisces: Poeciliidae): sexual selection and the evolution of courtship. Z. Tierpsychol. 65:152–65.

FARR, J. A. AND W. F. HERRNKIND. 1974. A quantitative analysis of social interaction of the guppy, *Poecilia reticulata* (Pisces: Poeciliidae), as a function of population density. Anim. Behav. 22:582–91.

FARR, J. A. AND K. PETERS. 1984. The inheritance of quantitative fitness traits in guppies, *Poecilia reticulata* (Pisces: Poeciliidae). II. Tests for inbreeding effects. Heredity 52:285–96.

FARR, J. A. AND J. TRAVIS. 1986. Fertility advertisement by female sailfin mollies, *Poecilia latipinna* (Pisces: Poeciliidae). Copeia 1986:467–72.

FARR, J. A. AND J. TRAVIS. 1989. The effect of ontogenetic experience on variation in growth, maturation, and sexual behavior in the sailfin molly, *Poecilia latipinna* (Pisces: Poeciliidae). Env. Biol. Fish, in press.

FARR, J. A., J. TRAVIS, AND J. C. TREXLER. 1986. Behavioural allometry and interdemic variation in sexual behaviour of the sailfin molly *Poecilia latipinna* (Pisces: Poeciliidae). Anim. Behav. 34:497–509.

FARRIS, J. S. 1981. Distance data in phylogenetic analysis. Pp. 3–23. *In*: V. A. Funk and D. R. Brooks (eds.), Advances in Cladistics. New York Botanical Garden, Bronx, NY, USA.

FEDER, J. L., M. H. SMITH, R. K. CHESSER, M. J. W. GODT, AND K. ASBURY. 1984. Biochemical genetics of mosquitofish. II. Demographic differentiation of populations in a thermally altered reservoir. Copeia 1984:108–19.

FELSENSTEIN, J. 1981. Evolutionary trees from gene frequencies and quantitative characters: finding maximum likelihood estimates. Evolution 35:1229–42.

FELSENSTEIN, J. 1985. Phylogenies and the comparative method. Amer. Natur. 125:1–15.

FELTKAMP, C. A. AND I. KRISTENSEN. 1970. Ecology and morphological characters of different populations of *Poecilia sphenops vandepolli*. Stud. Fauna Curacao & Other Caribbean Islands 120:102–30.

FERENS, M. C. AND T. M. MURPHY, JR. 1974. Effects of thermal effluents on populations of mosquitofish. Pp. 237–45 *In*: J. W. Gibbons and R. R. Sharitz (eds.), Thermal Ecology. AEC Symposium Series, CONF-730505.

FINK, W. L. 1971a. A revision of the *Gambusia puncticulata* complex (Pisces: Poeciliidae). Publ. Gulf Coast Res. Lab. Mus. 2:11–46.

FINK, W. L. 1971b. A revision of the *Gambusia nicaraguensis* species group (Pisces: Poeciliidae). Publ. Gulf Coast Res. Lab. Mus. 2:47–77.

FISHER, R. A. 1958. The Genetical Theory of Natural Selection. 2nd ed. Dover Publ., New York, NY, USA.

FLETCHER, A. R. 1986. Effects of introduced fish in Australia. Pp. 231–38 *In*: P. DeDeckker and W. D. Williams (eds.), Limnology in Australia. CSIRO, Melbourne, Australia.

FLETCHER, A. R., A. K. MORRISON, AND D. J. HUME. 1985. Effects of carp, *Cyprinus carpio* L., on communities of aquatic vegetation and turbidity of waterbodies in the Lower Goulburn River Basin. Aust. J. Mar. Freshwater Res. 36:311–27.

FOSTER, N. R. 1967. Trends in the evolution of reproductive behavior in killifishes. Stud. Trop. Oceanog. 5:549–66.

FOWLER, H. W. 1923. Fishes from Nicaragua. Proc. Acad. Natur. Sci. Philadelphia 75:23–32.

FOWLER, H. W. 1943. A new poeciliid fish from Honduras. Notulae Natur. 117:1–3.

FOWLER, H. W. 1950. Colombian zoological survey. Pt. VI. Fishes obtained at Totumo, Colombia, with descriptions of two new species. Notulae Natur. 222:1–8.

FRANCK, D. 1964. Vergleichende Verhaltensstudien an lebendgebärenden Zahnkarpfen der Gattung *Xiphophorus*. Zool. Jb. Physiol. 71:117–70.

FRANCK, D. 1968. Weitere Untersuchungen zur vergleichenden Ethologie der Gattung *Xiphophorus* (Pisces). Behaviour 30:76–95.

FRANKEL, O. H. AND M. E. SOULÉ. 1981. Conservation and Evolution. Cambridge Univ. Press, Cambridge, England.

FRANKHAM, R. 1968. Sex and selection for a quantitative character in *Drosophila*. II. The sex dimorphism. Aust. J. Biol. Sci. 21:1225–37.

FRANZ, R. AND G. H. BURGESS. 1983. A new poeciliid killifish, *Limia rivasi*, from Haiti. Northeast Gulf Sci. 6:51–54.

FRANZ, R. AND L. R. RIVAS. 1983. *Limia vittata* (Guichenot). P. 45 *In*: D. S. Lee, S. P. Platania and G. H. Burgess (eds.), Atlas of North American Freshwater Fishes, 1983 Supplement. North Carolina Biol. Surv. Contrib. 1983–6, Raleigh, NC, USA.

FRASER, E. A. AND R. M. RENTON. 1940. Observations on the breeding and development of the viviparous fish, *Heterandria formosa*. Quart. J. Micros. Sci. 81:479–516.

FRIEDMAN, B. AND M. GORDON. 1934. Chromosome numbers in xiphophorin fishes. Amer. Natur. 58:446–55.

FUJII, R. 1969. Chromatophores and pigments. Pp. 307–53 *In*: W. S. Hoar and D. J. Randall (eds.), Fish Physiology, Vol. 3. Academic Press, New York, NY, USA.

FUJINO, K. AND T. KANG. 1968. Transferrin groups in tunas. Genetics 59:79–91.

FULKER, D. W. 1966. Mating speed in male *Drosophila melanogaster*: a psychogenetic analysis. Science 153:203–5.

GADGIL, M. AND W. H. BOSSERT. 1970. Life historical consequences of natural selection. Amer. Natur. 104:1–24.

GALL, G. A. E. 1975. Genetics of reproduction in domesticated rainbow trout. J. Anim. Sci. 40:19–28.

GANDOLFI, G. 1969. A chemical sex attractant in the guppy *Poecilia reticulata* Peters (Pisces, Poeciliidae). Monitore Zool. Ital. 3:89–98.

GANDOLFI, G. 1971. Sexual selection in relation to the social status of males in *Poecilia reticulata* (Teleostei: Poeciliidae). Bol. Zool. 38:35–48.

GARDINER, D. M. 1978. Utilization of extracellular glucose by spermatozoa of two viviparous fishes. Comp. Biochem. Physiol. 59A:165–68.

GARMAN, S. 1895. The cyprinodonts. Mem. Mus. Comp. Zool. 19:1–179.

GEISER, S. W. 1924. Sex-ratios and spermatogenesis in the topminnow, *Gambusia holbrooki* Grd. Biol. Bull. 47:175–207.

GELBACH, F. R., C. L. BRYAN, AND H. A. RENO. 1978. Thermal ecological features of *Cyprinodon elegans* and *Gambusia nobilis*, endangered Texas fishes. Texas J. Sci. 30:99–101.

GEORGE, C. 1960. Behavioral interaction of the pickerel (*Esox niger* LeSueur and *Esox americanus* LeSueur) and the mosquitofish (*Gambusia patruelis* Baird and Girard). Ph.D. Dissertation, Harvard Univ., Cambridge, MA, USA.

GERKING, S. D. AND D. V. PLANTZ. 1980. Size-biased predation by the Gila topminnow, *Poeciliopsis occidentalis* (Baird and Girard). Hydrobiologica 72:179–91.

GETTER, C. D. 1976. The systematics and biology of the poeciliid fish, *Gambusia rhizophorae*, with an account of its hybridization with *Gambusia affinis* and *Gambusia punctata*. M. S. Thesis, Univ. Miami, FL, USA.

GIBSON, M. B. 1954. Upper lethal temperature relations of the guppy, *Lebistes reticulatus*. Can. J. Zool. 32:393–407.

GIBSON, M. B. AND B. HIRST. 1955. The effect of salinity and temperature on the pre-adult growth of guppies. Copeia 1955:241–43.

GILL, D. E., K. A. BERVEN, AND B. A. MOCK. 1983. The environmental component of evolutionary biology. Pp. 1–36 *In*: C. E. King and P. S. Dawson (eds.), Population Biology. Retrospect and Prospect. Columbia Univ. Press, New York, NY, USA.

GIRARD, C. 1859a. Ichthyological notices. Proc. Acad. Natur. Sci. Philadelphia 11:56–68.

GIRARD, C. 1859b. Ichthyological notices. Proc. Acad. Natur. Sci. Philadelphia 11:113–22.

GLOVER, C. J. M. 1982. Adaptations of fishes in arid Australia. Pp. 241–46 *In*: W. R. Barker and P. J. M. Greensland (eds.), Evolution of the Flora and Fauna of Arid Australia. Peacock Publications, Adelaide, Australia.

GLOVER, C. J. M. 1983. Freshwater and marine fishes. Pp. 157–67 *In*: M. J. Tyler, C. R. Twidale, J. R. King, and J. W. Holmes (eds.), Natural History of the South East. Royal Soc. South Aust., Adelaide, Australia.

GOODRICH, H. B. 1929. Mendelian inheritance in fish. Quart. Rev. Biol. 4:83–99.

GOODYEAR, C. P. 1973. Learned orientation in the predator avoidance behavior of mosquito-fish, *Gambusia affinis*. Behaviour 45:191–224.

GORDON, H. AND M. GORDON. 1957. Maintenance of polymorphism by potentially injurious genes in eight natural populations of the platyfish, *Xiphophorus maculatus*. J. Genet. 55:1–44.

GORDON, M. 1927. The genetics of the viviparous top-minnow *Platypoecilus*: the inheritance of two kinds of melanophores. Genetics 12:253–83.

GORDON, M. 1931. Hereditary basis of melanosis in hybrid fishes. Amer. J. Cancer 15:1495–1523.

GORDON, M. 1932. Dr. Myron Gordon going on expedition. Aquatic Life 15:287–88.

GORDON, M. 1937a. Heritable color variations in the Mexican swordtail fish. J. Heredity 28:222–30.

GORDON, M. 1937b. Genetics of *Platypoecilus*. 3. Inheritance of sex and crossing over of the sex chromosomes in the platyfish. Genetics 22:376–92.

GORDON, M. 1938. The genetics of *Xiphophorus helleri*: heredity in Montezuma, a Mexican swordtail fish. Copeia 1938:19–29.

GORDON, M. 1943. Genetic studies of speciation in the swordtail-platyfish group and of the experimentally produced hybrids. Trans. NY Acad. Sci., Ser. II, 5:63–71.

GORDON, M. 1946. Introgressive hybridization in domesticated fishes. 1. The behavior of comet, a *Platypoecilus maculatus* gene in *Xiphophorus helleri*. Zoologica 31:77–88.

GORDON, M. 1948. Effects of five primary genes on the site of melanoma in fishes and the influence of two color genes on their pigmentation. Pp. 216–68 *In*: The Biology of Melanomas. Spec. Publ. NY Acad. Sci., Vol. 4.

GORDON, M. 1950. Heredity of pigmented tumors in fish. Endeavour 9:26–34.

GORDON, M. 1951a. The variable expressivity of a pigment cell gene from zero effect to melanotic tumor induction. Cancer Res. 11:676–86.

GORDON, M. 1951b. Genetic correlated studies of normal and atypical pigment cell growth. Growth Symp. 10:153–219.

GORDON, M. 1955. Those puzzling "little toms." Anim. Kingdom 58:50–55.

GORDON, M. 1956. An intricate genetic system that controls nine pigment cell patterns in the platyfish. Zoologica 41:153–62.

GORDON, M. 1957. Physiological genetics of fishes. Pp. 431–501 *In*: M. E. Brown (ed.), The Physiology of Fishes, Vol. 2. Academic Press, New York, NY, USA.

GORLICK, D. L. 1976. Dominance hierarchies and factors influencing dominance in the guppy *Poecilia reticulata* (Peters). Anim. Behav. 24:336–46.

GOSSE, P. H. 1851. A naturalist's sojourn in Jamaica. Longman, Brown, Green, and Longmans, London, England.

GOULD, S. J. AND N. ELDREDGE. 1977. Punctuated equilibria: the tempo and mode of evolution reconsidered. Paleobiology 3:115–51.

GRANT, E. M. 1978. Guide to Fishes. Dept. Harbors & Marine, Brisbane, Queensland, Australia.

GREENFIELD, D. W. 1983. *Gambusia xanthosoma*, a new species of poeciliid fish from Grand Cayman Island, BWI. Copeia 1983:457–64.

GREENFIELD, D. W. 1985. Review of the *Gambusia yucatana* complex (Pisces: Poeciliidae) of Mexico and Central America. Copeia 1985:368–78.

GREENFIELD, D. W. AND D. M. WILDRICK. 1984. Taxonomic distinction of the Antilles *Gambusia puncticulata* complex (Pisces: Poeciliidae) from the *G. yucatana* complex of Mexico and Central America. Copeia 1984:921–33.

GREENFIELD, D. W., T. A. GREENFIELD, AND S. L. BRINTON. 1983a. Spatial and trophic interactions between *Gambusia sexradiata* and *Gambusia puncticulata yucatana* (Pisces: Poeciliidae) in Belize, Central America. Copeia 1983:598–607.

GREENFIELD, D. W., T. A. GREENFIELD, AND D. M. WILDRICK. 1982. The taxonomy and distribution of the species of *Gambusia* (Pisces: Poeciliidae) in Belize, Central America. Copeia 1982:128–47.

GREENFIELD, D. W., C. F. RAKOCINSKI, AND T. A. GREENFIELD. 1983b. Spatial and trophic interactions in wet and dry seasons between *Gambusia luma* and *Gambusia sexradiata* (Pisces: Poeciliidae) in Belize, Central America. Fieldiana Zool. 14:1–16.

GREENWOOD, P. H., D. E. ROSEN, S. H. WEITZMAN, AND G. S. MYERS. 1966. Phyletic studies of teleostean fishes, with a provisional classification of living forms. Bull. Amer. Mus. Natur. Hist. 131:339–456.

GRIER, H. J. 1973. Reproduction in the teleost *Poecilia latipinna*, an ultrastructural and photoperiodic investigation. Ph.D. Dissertation, Univ. South Florida, Tampa, FL, USA.

GRIER, H. J. 1980. The morphology of enclosed testicular tubules in a teleost fish, *Poecilia latipinna*. Trans. Amer. Micros. Soc. 99:268–76.

GRIER, H. J. 1981. Cellular organization of the testis and spermatogenesis in fishes. Amer. Zool. 21:345–57.

GRIFFING, B. 1966. Influence of sex on selection. III. Joint contributions of sex-linked and autosomal genes. Aust. J. Biol. Sci. 19:775–93.

GRIFFITHS, K. 1972. A study of the depredations incurred among endemic Australian fishes by introduced fishes with particular reference to *Gambusia affinis*. Teacher's Higher Certificate Thesis, Dept. Education, Perth, Western Australia.

GROBSTEIN, D. 1940. Endocrine and developmental studies of gonopod differentiation in certain poeciliid fishes. I. The structure and development of the gonopod in *Platypoecilus maculatus*. Univ. Calif. Publ. Zool. 47:1–22.

GRUBB, J. C. 1972. Differential predation by *Gambusia affinis* on the eggs of seven species of anuran amphibians. Amer. Midl. Natur. 88:102–8.

Guichenot, A. 1853. Zoologie. Poissons. *In*: D. Ramón de la Sagra (ed.), Histoire Physique, Politique et Naturelle de l'Qle de Cuba, Vol. 2. Paris, France.

GUNTER, G. 1950. Distributions and abundance of fishes on the Aransas National Wildlife Refuge, with life history notes. Publ. Inst. Marine Sci. 1:89–101.

GÜNTHER, A. 1866. A catalogue of the fishes in the British Museum, Vol. 6. London, England.

GÜNTHER, A. 1874. Descriptions of new species of fishes in the British Museum. Ann. Mag. Natur. Hist. 4:368–71.

GUPTA, A. P. AND R. C. LEWONTIN. 1982. A study of reaction norms in natural populations of *Drosophila pseudoobscura*. Evolution 36:934–49.

GUSTAFSON, D. L. 1981. The influence of salinity on plasma osmolality and routine oxygen consumption in the sailfin molly, *Poecilia latipinna* (LeSueur), from a freshwater and an estuarine population. M. S. Thesis, Univ. Florida, Gainesville, FL, USA.

GYLLENSTEN, U. 1985. The genetic structure of fish: differences in the intraspecific distribution of biochemical genetic variation between marine, anadromous, and freshwater species. J. Fish. Biol. 26:691–99.

HAAKE, P. W. AND J. M. DEAN. 1983. Age and growth of four Everglades fishes using otolith techniques. Report SFRC-83/03, Nat. Park Serv., South Florida Res. Center, Everglades Nat. Park, Homestead, FL, USA.

HAGEN, D. W. 1964. Evidence of adaptation to environmental temperatures in three species of *Gambusia*. Southwest. Natur. 9:6–19.

HAHN, D. E. 1966. An introduction of *Poecilia mexicana* (Osteichthyes: Poeciliidae) into Colorado. Southwest. Natur. 11:296–312.

HALPERN-SEBOLD, L. R., M. P. SCHREIBMAN, AND H. MARGOLIS-NUNNO. 1986. Differences between early- and late-maturing genotypes of the platyfish (*Xiphophorus maculatus*) in the morphometry of their immunoreactive luteinizing hormone releasing hormone-containing cells: a developmental study. J. Exp. Zool. 240:245–57.

HARLAN, J. R., E. B. SPEAKER, AND J. MAYHEW. 1987. Iowa Fish and Fishing. Iowa Dept. Natur. Res., Des Moines, IA, USA.

HARRINGTON, R. W., JR. 1974. Sex determination and differentiation in fishes. Pp. 4–12 *In*: C. B. Schreck (ed.), Control of Sex in Fishes. Sea Grant Extension Div., Virginia Polytechnic Inst. & State Univ., Blacksburg, VA, USA.

HARRINGTON, R. W., JR. AND E. S. HARRINGTON. 1961. Food selection among fishes invading a high subtropical salt marsh: from onset of flooding through the progress of a mosquito brood. Ecology 42:649–65.

HARRINGTON, R. W., JR. AND E. S. HARRINGTON. 1982. Effects on fishes and their forage organisms of impounding a Florida salt marsh to prevent breeding by salt marsh mosquitoes. Bull. Mar. Sci. 32:523–31.

HARRIS, H. 1966. Enzyme polymorphisms in man. Proc. Royal Soc., Ser. B, 164:298–310.

HART, J. S. 1952. Geographic variations of some physiological and morphological characters in certain freshwater fish. Univ. Toronto Biol. Ser. 60:1–79.

HASEMAN, J. D. 1911. Some new species of fishes from the Río Iguassu. Ann. Carnegie Mus. 7:374–87.

HASKINS, C. P. AND E. F. HASKINS. 1949. The role of sexual selection as an isolating mechanism in three species of poeciliid fishes. Evolution 3:160–69.

HASKINS, C. P. AND E. F. HASKINS. 1950. Factors governing sexual selection as an isolating mechanism in the poeciliid fish *Lebistes reticulatus*. Proc. Nat. Acad. Sci. 36:464–76.

HASKINS, C. P. AND E. F. HASKINS. 1951. The inheritance of certain color patterns in wild populations of *Lebistes reticulatus* in Trinidad. Evolution 5:216–25.

HASKINS, C. P. AND E. F. HASKINS. 1954. Note on a "permanent" experimental alteration of genetic constitution in a natural population. Proc. Nat. Acad. Sci. (USA) 40:627–35.

HASKINS, C. P., E. F. HASKINS, J. J. A. MCLAUGHLIN, AND R. E. HEWITT. 1961. Polymorphism and population structure in *Lebistes reticulatus*, an ecological study. Pp. 320–95 *In*: W. F. Blair (ed.), Vertebrate Speciation. Univ. Texas Press, Austin, TX, USA.

HASKINS, C. P., P. YOUNG, R. E. HEWITT, AND E. F. HASKINS. 1970. Stabilized heterozygosis of supergenes mediating certain Y-linked color patterns in populations of *Lebistes reticulatus*. Heredity 25:575–89.

HATCH, M. D. AND M. C. CONWAY. 1980. Management plan for the Pecos gambusia, *Gambusia nobilis* (Baird and Girard, 1853) on the Bitter Lakes National Wildlife Refuge. US Fish & Wildl. Serv., Albuquerque, NM, USA.

HAÜSSLER, G. 1928. Über Melanombildungen bei Bastarden von *Xiphophorus maculatus* var rubra. Klin. Wochenschr. 7:1561–62.

HECKEL, J. 1848. Eine neue Gattung von Poecilien mit rochenartigem Anklammerungs-Organe. Sitzber. K. Akad. Wiss. Wien, Math. Nat. Cl. 1:289–303.

HEDRICK, P. W. 1983. Genetics of Populations. Van Nostrand Reinhold Co., New York, NY, USA.

HEISLER, I. L. 1984. A quantitative genetic model for the origin of mating preferences. Evolution 38:1283–95.

HENDRICKSON, D. A., W. L. MINCKLEY, R. R. MILLER, D. J. SEIBERT, AND P. H. MINCKLEY. 1980. Fishes of the Rio Yaqui Basin, Mexico and the United States. J. Arizona-Nevada Acad. Sci. 15:65–106.

HENN, A. W. 1916. On various South American poeciliid fishes. Ann. Carnegie Mus. 10:93–142.

HENNIG, W. 1966. Phylogenetic Systematics. Univ. Illinois Press, Urbana, IL, USA.

HENRICH, S. 1988. Variation in offspring sizes of the poeciliid fish *Heterandria formosa* (Pisces: Poeciliidae) in relation to fitness. Oikos 51:13–18.

HENRICH, S. AND J. TRAVIS. 1988. Quantitative genetic analysis of fecundity in *Heterandria formosa* (Pisces: Poeciliidae). J. Evol. Biol. 1:275–80.

HENSEL, R. 1868. Beiträge zur Kenntniss der Wirbelthiere Sudbrasiliens. Arch. Naturgesch. 34:356–75.

HERNANDEZ, D. 1988. Genetic variation in eastern mosquitofish (*Gambusia holbrooki* Girard) from the Piedmont and Coastal Plain of the Altamaha, Broad-Santee and Pee Dee drainages. M. S. Thesis, Univ. Georgia, Athens, GA, USA.

HESS, A. D. AND C. M. TARZWELL. 1942. The feeding habits of *Gambusia affinis affinis*, with special reference to the malaria mosquito, *Anopheles quadrimaculatus*. Amer. J. Hygiene 35:142–51.

HESTER, F. J. 1964. Effects of food supply on fecundity in the female guppy, *Lebistes reticulata* (Peters). J. Fish. Res. Bd. Canada 21:757–64.

HEUGEL, B. R., G. R. JOSWIAK, AND W. S. MOORE. 1977. Subcutaneous diazo film tag for small fishes. Prog. Fish-Cult. 39:98–99.

HEUTS, B. A. 1968. A presumed case of territoriality in poeciliids (Pisces—Cyprinodontiformes). Rev. Can. Biol. 27:297–312.

HEWITT, R. E., L. W. WORD, E. F. HASKINS, AND C. P. HASKINS. 1963. Electrophoretic analysis of muscle proteins in several groups of poeciliid fishes, especially the genus *Mollienesia*. Copeia 1963:296–303.

HILDEBRAND, S. F. 1921. Top minnows in relation to mosquito control, with notes on their habits and distribution. Publ. Health Bull. 114:3–34.

HILDEBRAND, S. F. 1927. Sex ratio in *Gambusia*. Biol. Bull. 53:390–404.

HILDEBRAND, S. F. 1930. *Gambusia* in foreign lands. Science 74:655–56.

HILDEMANN, W. H. 1954. Effects of sex hormones on secondary sex characters of *Lebistes reticulatus*. J. Exp. Zool. 126:1–15.

HILDEMANN, W. H. AND E. D. WAGNER. 1954. Intraspecific sperm competition in *Lebistes*. Amer. Natur. 88:87–91.

HILGENDORF, F. 1889. Fischsammlung von Haiti, welche 2 neue Arten, *Poecilia* (subg. *Acropoecilia*) *tridens* und *Eleotris maltzani*, enthllt. Sitzber. Ges. Naturf. Freunde Berlin 2:51–55.

HILLIS, D. M. 1987. Molecular versus morphological approaches to systematics. Annu. Rev. Ecol. Syst. 18:23–42.

HIROSE, Y., S. KASUGA, AND S. OKUBO. 1980. Ecological studies of the mosquitofish (*Gambusia affinis*) in Tokushima City, Japan. Japanese J. Sanit. Zool. 31:41–48.

HOAR, W. S. 1969. Reproduction. Pp. 1–72 *In*: W. S. Hoar and D. J. Randall (eds.), Fish Physiology, Vol. 3. Academic Press, New York, NY, USA.

HOFFMAN, G. L. 1970. Intercontinental and transcontinental dissemination and transfaunation of fish parasites with emphasis on whirling disease (*Myxosoma cerebralis*). Pp. 69–81 *In*: S. F. Snieszko (ed.), A Symposium on Diseases of Fishes and Shellfishes. Special Publ. No. 5, Amer. Fish. Soc., Washington, DC, USA.

HOFFMAN, G. L. AND G. SCHUBERT. 1984. Some parasites of exotic fishes. Pp. 233–61 *In*: W. R. Courtenay, Jr. and J. R. Stauffer, Jr. (eds.), Distribution, Biology and Management of Exotic Fishes. Johns Hopkins Univ. Press, Baltimore, MD, USA.

HOGARTH, P. J. 1972a. Immune relations between mother and foetus in the viviparous poeciliid fish *Xiphophorus hellerii* Haeckel. I. Antigenicity of the foetus. J. Fish Biol. 4:265–69.

HOGARTH, P. J. 1972b. Immune relations between mother and foetus in the viviparous poeciliid fish *Xiphophorus hellerii* Haeckel. II. Lack of status of the ovary as a favourable site for allograft survival. J. Fish Biol. 4:271–75.

HOGARTH, P. J. 1973. Immune relations between mother and foetus in the viviparous poeciliid fish *Xiphophorus hellerii* Haeckel. III. Survival of embryos after ectopic transplantation. J. Fish Biol. 5:109–13.

HOGARTH, P. J. AND C. M. SURSHAM. 1972. Antigenicity of *Poecilia* sperm. Experientia 28:463.

HOLSINGER, K. E. AND N. C. ELLSTRAND. 1984. The evolution and ecology of permanent translocation heterozygotes. Amer. Natur. 24:48–71.

HOPPER, A. F., JR. 1943. The early embryology of *Platypoecilus maculatus*. Copeia 1943:218–24.

HOUDE, A. E. 1987. Mate choice based upon naturally occurring color-pattern variation in a guppy population. Evolution 41:1–10.

HOWARD-WILLIAMS, C., J. S. CLAYTON, B. T. COFFEY, AND I. M. JOHNSTONE. 1987. Macrophyte invasions. Pp. 307–31 *In*: A. B. Viner (ed.), Inland Waters of New Zealand. Sci. Information Publ. Centre, Dept. Scientific & Indust. Res., Wellington, New Zealand.

HOWELL, W. M., D. A. BLACK, AND S. A. BORTONE. 1980. Abnormal expression of secondary sex characters in a population of mosquitofish, *Gambusia affinis holbrooki*: evidence for environmentally-induced masculinization. Copeia 1980:676–81.

HUBBELL, S. P. AND L. K. JOHNSON. 1987. Environmental variance in lifetime mating success, mate choice, and sexual selection. Amer. Natur. 130:91–112.

HUBBS, C. 1957. *Gambusia heterochir*, a new poeciliid fish from Texas, with an account of its hybridization with *G. affinis*. Tulane Stud. Zool. 5:3–16.

HUBBS, C. 1959. Population analysis of a hybrid swarm between *Gambusia affinis* and *G. heterochir*. Evolution 13:236–46.

HUBBS, C. 1964. Interactions between a bisexual fish species and its gynogenetic sexual parasite. Bull. Texas Memorial Mus. 8:1–72.

HUBBS, C. 1971. Competition and isolation mechanisms in the *Gambusia affinis* × *G. heterochir* hybrid swarm. Bull. Texas Memorial Mus. 19:1–46.

HUBBS. C. 1972. A checklist of Texas freshwater fishes. Texas Parks & Wildl. Dept., Tech. Ser. 2:1–11.

HUBBS, C. 1980. The solution to the *Cyprinodon bovinus* problem: eradication of a pupfish genome. Proc. 10th Desert Fishes Council:9–14.

HUBBS, C. 1982. Occurrence of exotic fishes in Texas waters. Pearce-Sellards Ser., Texas Memorial Mus. 36:1–19.

HUBBS, C. AND H. J. BRODERICK. 1963. Current abundance of *Gambusia gaigei*, an endangered fish species. Southwest. Natur. 8:46–48.

HUBBS, C. AND J. E. DEACON. 1965. Additional introductions of tropical fishes into southern Nevada. Southwest. Natur. 9:249–51.

HUBBS, C. AND E. A. DELCO, JR. 1960. Mate preference in males of four species of gambusiine fishes. Evolution 14:145–52.

HUBBS, C. AND E. A. DELCO, JR. 1962. Courtship preferences of *Gambusia affinis* associated with the sympatry of the parental population. Copeia 1962:396–400.

HUBBS, C. AND B. L. JENSEN. 1984. Extinction of *Gambusia amistadensis*, an endangered fish. Copeia 1984:529–30.

HUBBS, C. AND A. E. PEDEN. 1969. *Gambusia georgei* sp. nov. from San Marcos, Texas. Copeia 1969:357–64.

HUBBS, C. AND V. G. SPRINGER. 1957. A revision of the *Gambusia nobilis* species group, with descriptions of three new species, and notes on their variation, ecology, and evolution. Texas J. Sci. 9:279–327.

HUBBS, C., G. HODDENBACH, AND C. M. FLEMING. 1986. An enigmatic population of *Gambusia gaigei*. Southwest. Natur. 31:121–23.

HUBBS, C., T. LUCIER, E. MARCH, G. P. GARRETT, R. J. EDWARDS, AND E. MILSTEAD. 1978a. Results of an eradication program on the relationships of fishes from Leon Creek, Texas. Southwest. Natur. 23:487–96.

HUBBS, C., T. LUCIER, G. P. GARRETT, R. J. EDWARDS, S. M. DEAN, E. MARSH, AND D. BELK. 1978b. Survival and abundance of introduced fishes near San Antonio. Texas J. Sci. 30:369–76.

HUBBS, C. L. 1924. Studies of the fishes of the order Cyprinodontes. I-IV. Misc. Publ. Mus. Zool., Univ. Michigan 13:1–31.

HUBBS, C. L. 1926. Studies of the fishes of the order Cyprinodontes. VI. Material for a revision of the American genera and species. Misc. Publ. Mus. Zool., Univ. Michigan 16:1–87.

HUBBS, C. L. 1927. Studies of the fishes of the order Cyprinodontes. VII. *Gambusia manni*, a new species from the Bahamas. Copeia 1927:61–65.

HUBBS, C. L. 1929. Studies of the fishes of the order Cyprinodontes. VIII. *Gambusia gaigei*, a new species from the Río Grande. Occas. Pap. Mus. Zool., Univ. Michigan 198:1–11.

HUBBS, C. L. 1933. Species and hybrids of *Mollienisia*. Aquarium 1:263–68, 277.

HUBBS, C. L. 1934. Studies of the fishes of the order Cyprinodontes. XIII. *Quintana atrizona*, a new poeciliid. Occas. Pap. Mus. Zool., Univ. Michigan 301:1–8.

HUBBS, C. L. 1936. Fishes of the Yucatan Peninsula. Pp. 157–287 *In*: A. S. Pearse, E. P. Creaser and F. G. Hall (eds.), The Cenotes of Yucatan, a Sociological and Hydrographic Survey. Carnegie Inst. Washington Publ. 457.

HUBBS, C. L. 1946. Experimental breeding of the Amazon molly. Aquarium J. 17:4–6.

HUBBS, C. L. 1950. Studies of cyprinodont fishes. XX. A new subfamily from Guatemala, with ctenoid scales and a unilateral pectoral clasper. Misc. Publ. Mus. Zool., Univ. Michigan 78:1–28.

HUBBS, C. L. 1955. Hybridization between fish species in nature. Syst. Zool. 4:1–20.

HUBBS, C. L. AND M. GORDON. 1943. Studies of cyprinodont fishes. XIX. *Xiphophorus pygmaeus*, new species from Mexico. Copeia 1943:31–33.

HUBBS, C. L. AND L. C. HUBBS. 1932. Apparent parthenogenesis in nature in a form of fish of hybrid origin. Science 76:628–30.

HUBBS, C. L. AND L. C. HUBBS. 1946. Experimental breeding of the Amazon molly. Aquarium J. 17:4–6.

HUBBS, C. L. AND R. R. MILLER. 1941. Studies of the fishes of the order Cyprinodontes. XVII. Genera and species of the Colorado River System. Occas. Pap. Mus. Zool., Univ. Michigan 433:1–9.

HUBBS, C. L. AND R. R. MILLER. 1954. Studies of cyprinodont fishes. XXI. *Glaridodon latidens*, from northwestern Mexico, redescribed and referred to *Poeciliopsis*. Zoologica 39:1–12.

HUBBS, C. L. AND R. R. MILLER. 1977. Six distinctive cyprinid fish species referred to *Dionda* inhabiting segments of the Tampico embayment drainage of Mexico. Trans. San Diego Soc. Natur. Hist. 18:267–336.

HUBBS, C. L., W. I. FOLLETT, AND L. J. DEMPSTER. 1979. List of the fishes of California. Occas. Pap. California Acad. Sci. 133:1–51.

HUGHES, A. L. 1985a. Seasonal changes in fecundity and size at first reproduction in an Indiana population of the mosquitofish *Gambusia affinis*. Amer. Midl. Natur. 114:30–36.

HUGHES, A. L. 1985b. Seasonal trends in body size of adult male mosquitofish, *Gambusia affinis*, with evidence for their social control. Env. Biol. Fish. 14:251–58.

HUGHES, A. L. 1986. Growth of adult mosquitofish *Gambusia affinis* in the laboratory. Copeia 1986:534–36.

HUMPHRIES, C. J. AND L. R. PARENTI. 1986. Cladistic Biogeography. Oxford Monographs on Biogeography No. 2. Clarendon Press, Oxford, England.

HUNT, B. P. 1953. Food relationships between Florida spotted gar and other organisms in the Tamiami Canal, Dade County, Florida. Trans. Amer. Fish. Soc. 82:13–33.

HURLBERT, S. H. AND M. S. MULLA. 1981. Impacts of mosquitofish (*Gambusia affinis*) predation on plankton communities. Hydrobiologica 83:125–51.

HURLBERT, S. H., J. ZEDLER, AND D. FAIRBANKS. 1972. Ecosystem alteration by mosquitofish (*Gambusia affinis*) predation. Science 175:639–41.

ISHII, S. 1963. Some factors involved in the delivery of the young of the top-minnow, *Gambusia affinis*. J. Faculty Sci., Univ. Tokyo 10:181–87.

ISTOCK, C. A. 1983. The extent and consequences of heritable variation for fitness characters. Pp. 61–96 *In*: C. E. King and P. S. Dawson (eds.), Population Biology: Retrospect and Prospect. Columbia Univ. Press, New York, NY, USA.

ITZKOWITZ, M. 1971. Preliminary study of the social behavior of male *Gambusia affinis* (Baird and Girard) (Pisces: Poeciliidae) in aquaria. Chesapeake Sci. 12:219–24.

JACOBS, K. 1969. Die lebendgebärenden Fische der Süssgewässer. Verlag Harri Deutsch, Frankfurt/Main, West Germany.

JAKWAY, J. S. 1959. Inheritance of patterns of mating behaviour in the male guinea pig. Anim. Behav. 7:150–62.

JAMES, F. C. 1983. Environmental component of morphological differentiation in birds. Science 221:184–86.

JASKI, C. J. 1939. Ein oestruszyklus bei *Lebistes reticulatus* (Peters). Proc. Koninkl. Ned. Akad. Wetenschap. 42:201–7.

JENYNS, L. 1843. Fish. *In*: C. Darwin (ed.), The Zoology of the Voyage of H. M. S. "Beagle," During the Years 1832–1836. Part 4. London, England.

JOHANSEN, P. H. AND J. A. CROSS. 1980. Effects of sexual maturation and sex steroid hormone treatment on the temperature preference of the guppy, *Poecilia reticulata* (Peters). Can. J. Zool. 58:586–88.

JOHNSON, C. R. 1976a. Diel variation in the thermal tolerance of *Gambusia affinis*. Comp. Biochem. Physiol. 55:337–40.

JOHNSON, C. R. 1976b. Observations on growth, breeding and fry survival of *Gambusia affinis affinis* under artificial rearing conditions. Proc. Pap. Annu. Conf. California Mosq. Vector Control Assoc. 44:48–51.

JOHNSON, C. R. 1978. Herbicide toxicities in the mosquitofish, *Gambusia affinis*. Proc. Royal Soc. Queensland 89:25–27.

JOHNSON, J. E. 1987. Protected Fishes of the United States and Canada. Amer. Fish Soc., Bethesda, MD, USA.

JOHNSON, J. E. AND J. N. RINNE. 1982. The Endangered Species Act and Southwest fishes. Fisheries 7(4):2–8.

JORDAN, D. S. 1889. List of fishes collected by Alphonse Forrer about Matzatlan, with descriptions of two new species—*Heros beani* and *Poecilia butleri*. Proc. US Nat. Mus. 11:329–34.

JORDAN, D. S. 1895. The fishes of Sinaloa. Proc. California Acad. Sci. 2:337–514.

JORDAN, D. S. AND J. O. SNYDER. 1900. Notes on a collection of fishes from the rivers of Mexico, with descriptions of twenty new species. Bull. US Fish Comm. 1899:115–47.

JUBB, R. A. 1977. Notes on exotic fishes introduced into South African waters. II. Live-bearing tooth carps. Piscator 98:132–34.

KADOW, P. C. 1954. An analysis of sexual behavior and reproductive physiology in the guppy, *Poecilia reticulata* (Peters). Ph.D. Dissertation, New York Univ., New York, NY, USA.

KALLMAN, K. D. 1960. Dosage and additive effects of histocompatibility genes in the teleost *Xiphophorus maculatus*. Ann. NY Acad. Sci. 87:10–43.

KALLMAN, K. D. 1962a. Population genetics of gynogenetic teleost, *Mollienesia* (*Poecilia*) *formosa*. Evolution 16:497–504.

KALLMAN, K. D. 1962b. Gynogenesis in the teleost, *M. formosa*, with discussion of the detection of parthenogenesis in vertebrates by tissue transplantation. J. Genet. 58:7–21.

KALLMAN, K. D. 1964a. An estimate of the number of histocompatibility loci in the teleost *Xiphophorus maculatus*. Genetics 50:583–95.

KALLMAN, K. D. 1964b. Genetics of tissue transplantation in isolated platyfish populations. Copeia 1964:513–22.

KALLMAN, K. D. 1964c. Homozygosity in a gynogenetic fish, *Poecilia formosa*. Genetics 50:260–62.

KALLMAN, K. D. 1965. Genetics and geography of sex determination in the poeciliid fish, *Xiphophorus maculatus*. Zoologica 50:151–90.

KALLMAN, K. D. 1968. Evidence for the existence of transformer genes for sex in the teleost *Xiphophorus maculatus*. Genetics 60:811–28.

KALLMAN, K. D. 1970a. Sex determination and the restriction of pigment patterns to the X and Y chromosomes in populations of a poeciliid fish, *Xiphophorus maculatus*, from the Belize and Sibun Rivers of British Honduras. Zoologica 55:1–16.

KALLMAN, K. D. 1970b. Stable changes in pigment patterns after crossing over in the teleost *Xiphophorus maculatus*. Genetics 64, Suppl. 32.

KALLMAN, K. D. 1971. Inheritance of melanophore patterns and sex determination in the Montezuma swordtail, *Xiphophorus montezumae cortezi* Rosen. Zoologica 56:77–94.

KALLMAN, K. D. 1973. The sex-determining mechanism of the platyfish, *Xiphophorus maculatus*. Pp. 19–28 *In*: J. H. Schröder (ed.), Genetics and Mutagenesis of Fish. Springer-Verlag, New York, NY, USA.

KALLMAN, K. D. 1975. The platyfish, *Xiphophorus maculatus*. Pp. 81–132 *In*: R. C. King (ed.), Handbook of Genetics, Vol. 4. Plenum Publ. Corp., New York, NY, USA.

KALLMAN, K. D. 1976. Control of size in *Xiphorphorus pygmaeus* (Poeciliidae, Pisces). Amer. Zool. 16:260.

KALLMAN, K. D. 1983. The sex determining mechanism of the poeciliid fish, *Xiphophorus montezumae*, and the genetic control of the sexual maturation process and adult size. Copeia 1983:755–69.

KALLMAN, K. D. 1984. A new look at sex determination in poeciliid fishes. Pp. 95–171 *In*: B. J. Turner (ed.), Evolutionary Genetics of Fishes. Plenum Publ. Co., New York, NY, USA.

KALLMAN, K. D. AND J. W. ATZ. 1966. Gene and chromosome homology in fishes of the genus *Xiphophorus*. Zoologica 51:107–35.

KALLMAN, K. D. AND I. Y. BAO. 1987. Female heterogamety in the swordtail, *Xiphophorus alvarezi* Rosen (Pisces, Poeciliidae), with comments on a natural polymorphism affecting sword coloration. J. Exp. Zool. 243:93–102.

KALLMAN, K. D. AND V. BORKOSKI. 1978. A sex-linked gene controlling the onset of sexual maturity in female and male platyfish (*Xiphophorus maculatus*), fecundity in females and adult size in males. Genetics 89:79–119.

KALLMAN, K. D. AND R. BOROWSKY. 1972. The genetics of gonopodial polymorphism in two species of poeciliid fish. Heredity 28:297–310.

KALLMAN, K. D. AND V. BRUNETTI. 1983. Genetic basis of three mutant color varieties of *Xiphophorus maculatus*: the gray, gold and ghost platyfish. Copeia 1983:170–81.

KALLMAN, K. D. AND M. P. SCHREIBMAN. 1971. The origin and possible genetic control of new, stable pigment patterns in the poeciliid fish *Xiphophorus maculatus*. J. Exp. Zool. 176:147–68.

KALLMAN, K. D. AND M. P. SCHREIBMAN. 1973. A sex-linked gene controlling gonadotrop differentiation and its significance in determining the age of sexual maturation and size of the platyfish, *Xiphophorus maculatus*. Gen. Comp. Endrocrinol. 21:287–304.

KALLMAN, K. D., M. P. SCHREIBMAN, AND V. BORKOSKI. 1973. Genetic control of gonadotrop differentiation in the platyfish, *Xiphophorus maculatus* (Poeciliidae). Science 181:678–80.

KAPLAN, R. H. AND W. S. COOPER. 1984. The evolution of developmental plasticity in reproductive characteristics: an application of the "adaptive coin-flipping" principle. Amer. Natur. 123:393–410.

KEEGAN-ROGERS, V. 1984. Unfamiliar-female advantage among clones of unisexual fish (*Poeciliopsis*, Poeciliidae). Copeia 1984:169–74.

KEEGAN-ROGERS, V. AND R. J. SCHULTZ. 1984. Differences in courtship aggression among six clones of unisexual fish. Anim. Behav. 32:1040–44.

KEEGAN-ROGERS, V. AND R. J. SCHULTZ. 1988. Sexual selection among clones of unisexual fish (*Poeciliopsis*, Poeciliidae): genetic factors and rare-female advantage. Amer. Natur. 132:846–68.

KEENLEYSIDE, M. 1979. Diversity and Adaptation in Fish Behaviour. Springer-Verlag, Berlin, Germany.

KELLERT, S. R. 1985. Social and perceptual factors in endangered species management. J. Wildl. Mgt. 49:528–39.

KENNEDY, P. K., M. L. KENNEDY, AND M. H. SMITH. 1985. Microgeographic genetic organization of populations of largemouth bass and two other species in a reservoir. Copeia 1985:118–25.

KENNEDY, P. K., M. L. KENNEDY, E. G. ZIMMERMAN, R. K. CHESSER, AND M. H. SMITH. 1986. Biochemical genetics of mosquitofish. V. Perturbation effects on genetic organization of populations. Copeia 1986:937–45.

KILBY, J. D. 1955. The fishes of two Gulf coastal marsh areas of Florida. Tulane Stud. Zool. 2:175–247.

KIMURA, M. AND J. F. CROW. 1963. The measurement of effective population number. Evolution 17:279–88.

KINCAID, H. L. 1976. Inbreeding in rainbow trout. J. Fish. Res. Board Canada 33:2420–26.

KIRKPATRICK, M. 1982. Sexual selection and the evolution of female choice. Evolution 36:1–12.

KIRKPATRICK, M. 1986. The handicap mechanism of sexual selection does not work. Amer. Natur. 127:222–40.

KIRPICHNIKOV, V. S. 1981. Genetic Bases of Fish Selection. Springer-Verlag, New York, NY, USA.

KNER, R. 1860. Über Belonesox belizanus, nov. gen. et spec. aus der Familie der Cyprinodonten. Sitzber. K. Akad. Wiss. Wien, Math. Nat. Cl. 40:419–22.

KNER, R. AND F. STEINDACHNER. 1864. Neue Gattungen und Arten von Fischen aus Central-Amerika; gesammelt von Prof. Moritz Wagner. Abhandl. Bayerischen Akad. Wiss., Math. Phys. Cl. 10:1–62.

KODRIC-BROWN, A. AND J. H. BROWN. 1984. Truth in advertising: the kinds of traits favored by sexual selection. Amer. Natur. 124:309–23.

KOFRON, C. P. 1978. Foods and habitats of aquatic snakes (Reptilia, Serpentes) in a Louisiana swamp. J. Herpetology 12:543–54.

KOSSWIG, C. 1929. Melanotische Geschwulstbildung bei Fischbastarden. Verh. Deutsche Zool. Ges. 1929:90–98.

KOSSWIG, C. 1939. Die Geschlechtsbestimmung in Kreuzungen zwischen Xiphophorus und Platypoecilus. Rev. Fac. Sci. Univ. Istanbul, New Ser. 4:1–54.

KOSSWIG, C. 1941. Mitteilungen zum Geschlectsbestimmungs-problem bei Zahnkarpfen. Rev. Fac. Sci. Univ. Istanbul, Ser. B. 6:1–32.

KOSSWIG, C. 1961. Über sogenannte homologe Gene. Zool. Anz. 166:333–56.

KOSSWIG, C. 1964. Polygenic sex determination. Experientia 20:190–99.

KOSSWIG, C. 1965. 40 Jahre genetische Untersuchungen an Fischen. Abh. Verh. Naturwiss. Ver Hamburg 10:13–39.

KOSTER, W. J. 1957. Guide to the Fishes of New Mexico. Univ. New Mexico Press, Albuquerque, NM, USA.

KRAMER, D. L. AND J. P. MEHEGAN. 1981. Aquatic surface respiration, an adaptive response to hypoxia in the guppy, Poecilia reticulata (Pisces, Poeciliidae). Env. Biol. Fish. 6:299–313.

KRISTENSEN, I. 1969. Competition in three cyprinodont fish species in the Netherlands Antilles. Stud. Fauna Curacao & Other Caribbean Islands 32:82–101.

KRUMHOLZ, L. A. 1944. Northward acclimatization of the western mosquitofish, *Gambusia affinis affinis*. Copeia 1944:82–85.

KRUMHOLZ, L. A. 1948. Reproduction in the western mosquitofish *Gambusia affinis affinis* (Baird & Girard) and its use in mosquito control. Ecol. Monogr. 18:1–43.

KRUMHOLZ, L. A. 1963. Relationships between fertility, sex ratio, and exposure to predation in populations of the mosquito fish *Gambusia manni* Hubbs at Bimini, Bahamas. Int. Rev. ges. Hydrobiol. 48:201–56.

KULKARNI, C. V. 1940. On the systematic position, structural modification, bionomics and development of a remarkable new family of cyprinodont fishes from the province of Bombay. Rec. Indian Mus. 42:379–423.

KUNTZ, A. 1913. Notes on the habits, morphology of the reproductive organs, and embryology of the viviparous fish *Gambusia affinis*. Bull. US Bur. Fisheries 33:177–90.

KUSHLAN, J. A. 1973. Bill-vibrating: a prey-attracting behavior of the snowy egret, *Leucophoyx thula*. Amer. Midl. Natur. 89:509–12.

KUSHLAN, J. A. 1980. Population fluctuations of Everglades fishes. Copeia 1980:870–74.

LAGLER, K. F., J. E. BARDACH, R. R. MILLER, AND D. R. M. PASSINO. 1977. Ichthyology. John Wiley & Sons, New York, NY, USA.

LAKE, J. S. 1971. Freshwater Fishes and Rivers of Australia. Thomas Nelson (Australia) Ltd., Sydney, Australia.

LAM, T. J. 1983. Environmental influences on gonadal activity in fish. Pp. 65–116 *In*: W. S. Hoar, D. J. Randall and E. M. Donaldson (eds.), Fish Physiology, Vol. 9B. Academic Press, New York, NY, USA.

LAMBERT, J. G. D. 1970. The ovary of the guppy *Poecilia reticulata*. The granulosa cells as sites of steroid biosynthesis. Gen. Comp. Endocrinol. 15:464–76.

LANDE, R. 1980a. Sexual dimorphism, sexual selection, and adaptation in polygenic characters. Evolution 34:292–305.

LANDE, R. 1980b. The genetic covariance between characters maintained by pleiotropic mutations. Genetics 94:203–15.

LANDE, R. 1982. A quantitative genetic theory of life-history evolution. Ecology 63:607–15.

LANDE, R. 1984. The genetic correlation between characters maintained by selection, linkage, and inbreeding. Genet. Res. 44:309–20.

LANGDON, J. 1986. A new viral disease of redfin perch. Aust. Fisheries 45:35–36.

LANGDON, J. AND J. D. HUMPHREY. 1987. Epizootic hematopoietic necrosis, a new viral disease in redfin perch, *Perca fluviatilis* L., in Australia. J. Fish. Dis. 10:289–97.

LANSMAN, R. A., R. O. SHADE, J. F. SHAPIRA, AND J. C. AVISE. 1981. The use of restriction endonucleases in natural populations: III. Techniques and potential applications. J. Molec. Evol. 17:214–26.

LANZA, J. 1983. Microhabitat use by bisexual and unisexual fishes (*Poeciliopsis*: Poeciliidae) in an artificial stream. Oecologia 57:142–47.

LARGE, H. L. 1985. Life history tactics of the sailfin molly (*Poecilia latipinna*) in contrasting environments. M. S. Thesis, Univ. Central Florida, Orlando, FL, USA.

LARIVERS, I. 1962. Fishes and Fisheries of Nevada. Nevada State Fish & Game Comm., Reno, NV, USA.

Laudien, H. and V. Schlieker. 1981. Temperature dependence of courtship in the male guppy, *Poecilia reticulata*. J. Thermal Biol. 6:307–14.

Law, R. 1979. Optimal life histories under age-specific predation. Amer. Natur. 114:399–417.

Lechner, P. and A. C. Radda. 1987. Revision des *Xiphophorus montezumae/cortezi* Komplexes und Neubeschreibung einer subspezies. Sonderdruck aus Aquaria 39:189–96.

Lee, D. S., S. P. Platania, and G. H. Burgess. 1983. Atlas of North American Freshwater Fishes: 1983 Supplement. Occas. Pap. North Carolina Biol. Surv. 1983-3:1–67.

Lee, D. S., C. R. Gilbert, C. H. Hocutt, R. E. Jenkins, D. E. McAllister, and J. R. Stauffer, Jr. 1980. Atlas of North American Freshwater Fishes. North Carolina State Mus. Natur. Hist., Raleigh, NC, USA.

Legner, E. F. and R. A. Medved. 1974. The native desert pupfish, *Cyprinodon maculatus*, a substitute for *Gambusia* in mosquito control. Proc. Pap. Annu. Conf. California Mosq. Vector Control Assoc. 42:58–59.

Leidy, R. A. 1984. Distribution and ecology of stream fishes in the San Francisco Bay drainage. Hilgardia 52:1–175.

Lerner, I. M. 1954. Genetic Homeostasis. Dover Publications, New York, NY, USA.

Leslie, J. F. 1982. Linkage analysis of seventeen loci in poeciliid fish (genus *Poeciliopsis*). J. Heredity 73:19–23.

Leslie, J. F. and R. C. Vrijenhoek. 1977. Genetic analysis of natural populations of *Poeciliopsis monacha*. J. Heredity 68:301–6.

Leslie, J. F. and R. C. Vrijenhoek. 1978. Genetic dissection of clonally inherited genomes of *Poeciliopsis*. I. Linkage analysis and preliminary assessment of deleterious gene loads. Genetics 90:801–11.

Leslie, J. F. and R. C. Vrijenhoek. 1980. Consideration of Muller's ratchet mechanism through studies of genetic linkage and genomic compatibilities in clonally reproducing *Poeciliopsis*. Evolution 34:1105–15.

LeSueur, C. A. 1821. Description of a new genus, and several species of fresh water fish, indigenous to the United States. J. Acad. Natur. Sci. Philadelphia 2:2–8.

Lewontin, R. C. 1965. Selection for colonizing ability. Pp. 77–91 *In*: H. G. Baker and G. L. Stebbins (eds.), The Genetics of Colonizing Species. Academic Press, New York, NY, USA.

Lewontin, R. C. 1974a. The analysis of variance and the analysis of causes. Amer. J. Hum. Genet. 26:400–411.

Lewontin, R. C. 1974b. The Genetic Basis of Evolutionary Change. Columbia Univ. Press. New York, NY, USA.

Lewontin, R. C. and J. L. Hubby. 1966. A molecular approach to the study of genic heterozygosity in natural populations. II. Amount of variation and degree of heterozygosity in natural populations of *Drosophila pseudoobscura*. Genetics 54:595–609.

Liley, N. R. 1966. Ethological isolating mechanisms in four sympatric species of poeciliid fishes. Behaviour, Suppl. 13:1–197.

Liley, N. R. 1968. The endocrine control of reproductive behaviour in the female guppy, *Poecilia reticulata* (Peters). Anim. Behav. 16:318–31.

LILEY, N. R. AND B. H. SEGHERS. 1975. Factors affecting the morphology and behavior of guppies in Trinidad. Pp. 92–118 *In*: G. P. Baerends, C. Beer and A. Manning (eds.), Function and Evolution in Behavior. Oxford Univ. Press, Oxford, England.

LILEY, N. R. AND N. E. STACEY. 1983. Hormones, pheromones, and reproductive behavior in fish. Pp. 1–63 *In*: W. S. Hoar, D. J. Randall and E. M. Donaldson (eds.), Fish Physiology, Vol. 9B. Academic Press, New York, NY, USA.

LILEY, N. R. AND W. P. WISHLOW. 1974. The interaction of endocrine and experiential factors in the regulation of sexual behaviour in the female guppy *Poecilia reticulata*. Behaviour 48:185–214.

LIU, E. H., M. H. SMITH, M. J. GODT, R. K. CHESSER, A. K. LETHCO, AND D. J. HENZLER. 1985. Enzyme levels in natural mosquitofish populations. Physiol. Zool. 58:242–52.

LLOYD, L. N. 1984. Exotic fish—useful additions or 'animal weeds.' Fishes of Sahul 1:31–34, 39–42.

LLOYD, L. N. 1986. An alternative to insect control by "Mosquitofish," *Gambusia affinis* (Baird and Girard 1854). Pp. 156–63 *In*: T. D. St. George, B. H. Kay and J. Blok (eds.), Arbovirus Research In Australia. Proc. Fourth Aust. Arbovirus Symp., Brisbane, Australia.

LLOYD, L. N. 1987a. Ecology and distribution of small native fish of the lower River Murray, South Australia and their interactions with exotic mosquitofish, *Gambusia affinis holbrooki* (Girard). M.Sc. Thesis, Univ. Adelaide, Adelaide, Australia.

LLOYD, L. N. 1987b. Biological control of insects with fish. Pp. 115–23 *In*: P. F. S. Liehne (ed.), Mosquito Vector Control in Australia: Current Status and Future Prospects. Commonwealth Dept. Health, Canberra, Australia.

LLOYD, L. N. AND J. TOMASOV. 1985. Taxonomic status of the mosquitofish, *Gambusia affinis* (Poeciliidae), in Australia. Aust. J. Mar. Freshwater Res. 36:447–51.

LLOYD, L. N. AND K. F. WALKER. 1986. The distribution and conservation status of small fish in the River Murray in S.A. Trans. Royal Soc. South Aust. 110:49–57.

LLOYD, L. N., A. H. ARTHINGTON, AND D. A. MILTON. 1986. The mosquitofish, *Gambusia affinis*, a valuable mosquito control agent or a pest? Pp. 6–25 *In*: R. L. Kitching (ed.), The Ecology of Exotic Animals and Plants in Australasia. Jacaranda Wiley Press, Brisbane, Australia.

LODI, E. 1979. Induction of atypical gonapophyses within the gonopodial suspensorium of the palla mutant male of *Poecilia reticulata* Peters (Poeciliidae: Osteichthyes). Monit. Zool. Ital. 13:95–104.

LOFTUS, W. F. AND J. A. KUSHLAN. 1987. Freshwater fishes of southern Flordia. Bull. Florida State Mus. Biol. Sci. 31:147–344.

LOMNICKI, A. 1988. Population Ecology of Individuals. Princeton Univ. Press, Princeton, NJ, USA.

LUCKINBILL, L. S., J. L. GRAVES, A. H. REED, AND S. KOETSAWANG. 1988. Localizing genes that defer senescence in *D. melanogaster*. Heredity 60:367–74.

LUCKNER, C. L. 1979. Morphological and behavioral polymorphism in *Poecilia latipinna* males (Pisces: Poeciliidae). Ph.D. Dissertation, Louisiana State Univ., Baton Rouge, LA, USA.

LYNCH, C. B. AND D. S. SULZBACH. 1984. Quantitative genetic analysis of temperature regulation in *Mus musculus*. II. Diallele analysis of individual traits. Evolution 38:527–40.

LYNCH, C. B., D. S. SULZBACH, AND M. S. CONNOLLY. 1988. Quantitative-genetic analysis of temperature regulation in *Mus domesticus*. IV. Pleiotropy and genotype-by-environment interactions. Amer. Natur. 132:521–537.

LYNCH, M. 1984. Destabilizing hybridizations, general-purpose genotypes, and geographic parthenogenesis. Quart. Rev. Biol. 59:257–90.

MACARTHUR, R. H. AND E. O. WILSON. 1967. The Theory of Island Biogeography. Princeton Univ. Press. Princeton, NJ, USA.

MACGREGOR, H. C. AND T. M. UZZELL. 1964. Gynogenesis in salamanders related to *Ambystoma jeffersonianum*. Science 143:1043–45.

MACIOLEK, J. A. 1984. Exotic fishes in Hawaii and other islands of Oceania. Pp. 131–61 *In*: W. R. Courtenay, Jr. and J. R. Stauffer, Jr. (eds.), Distribution, Biology, and Management of Exotic Fishes. Johns Hopkins Univ. Press, Baltimore, MD, USA.

MACKAY, T. F. C. 1981. Genetic variation in varying environments. Genet. Res. 37:79–93.

MACKAY, T. F. C. 1985. A quantitative genetic analysis of fitness and its components in *Drosophila melanogaster*. Genet. Res. 47:59–70.

MACLEAN, J. A. AND D. O. EVANS. 1981. The stock concept, discreteness of fish stocks, and fisheries management. Can. J. Fish. Aqua. Sci. 38:1889–98.

MAGLIO, V. J. AND D. E. ROSEN. 1969. Changing preference for substrate color by reproductively active mosquitofish, *Gambusia affinis* (Baird and Girard) (Poeciliidae, Atheriniformes). Amer. Mus. Novitates 2397:1–37.

MAITLAND, P. S. AND D. EVANS. 1986. The role of captive breeding in the conservation of fish species. Inter. Zoo. Yearbook (1986) 24/25:66–74.

MANLY, B. F. J. 1985. The Statistics of Natural Selection. Chapman and Hall, New York, NY, USA.

MANNING, A. 1967. Genes and the evolution of insect behavior. Pp. 44–60 *In*: J. Hirsch (ed.), Behaviour-Genetics Analysis. McGraw-Hill, New York, NY, USA.

MARSHALL, A. J. (ed.). 1966. The Great Extermination. Heinemann, Melbourne, Australia.

MARTIN, R. G. 1975. Sexual and aggressive behavior, density, and social structure in a natural population of mosquitofish, *Gambusia affinis holbrooki*. Copeia 1975:445–54.

MARTIN, R. G. 1977. Density dependent aggressive advantage in melanistic male mosquitofish *Gambusia affinis holbrooki* (Girard). Florida Sci. 40:393–400.

MARTIN, R. G. 1984. Proportion of melanistic offspring resulting from crossing melanistic male mosquitofish and normal female mosquitofish, *Gambusia affinis holbrooki*. J. Elisha Mitchell Sci. Soc. 100:221–23.

MAYER, F. 1948. A contribution to the *Micropoecilia* problem. Aquarium 17:172–74.

MAYNARD SMITH, J. 1956. Fertility, mating behaviour, and sexual selection in *Drosophila subobscura*. J. Genet. 54:261–79.

MAYNARD SMITH, J. 1978. The Evolution of Sex. Cambridge Univ. Press, Cambridge, England.

MAYR, E. 1954. Change of genetic environment and evolution. Pp. 157–80 *In*: J. Huxley, A. C. Hardy and E. B. Ford (eds.), Evolution as a Process. Macmillan Press, New York, NY, USA.

MAYR, E. 1970. Populations, Species, and Evolution. Belknap Press, Cambridge, MA, USA.

MCALLISTER, D. E. 1969. Introduction of tropical fishes into a hotspring near Banff, Alberta. Can. Field-Natur. 83:31–35.

MCALLISTER, W. H. 1958. The correlation of coloration with social rank in *Gambusia hurtadoi*. Ecology 39:477–82.

MCCLENAGHAN, L. R., JR., M. H. SMITH, AND M. W. SMITH. 1985. Biochemical genetics of mosquitofish. IV. Changes of allele frequencies through time and space. Evolution 39:451–59.

MCDOWALL, R. M. 1979. Exotic fishes in New Zealand—dangers of illegal releases. New Zealand Ministry of Agric. & Fish., Fisheries Information Leaflet 9:1–17.

MCDOWALL, R. M. 1980. Freshwater Fishes of South-eastern Australia. Reed, Sydney, Australia.

MCDOWALL, R. M. 1984. Exotic fishes: the New Zealand experience. Pp. 200–214 *In*: W. R. Courtenay, Jr. and J. R. Stauffer, Jr. (eds.), Distribution, Biology, and Management of Exotic Fishes. Johns Hopkins Univ. Press, Baltimore, MD, USA.

MCDOWALL, R. M. 1987. Impacts of exotic fishes on the native fauna. Pp. 333–48 *In*: A. B. Viner (ed.), Inland Waters of New Zealand. Science Information Publishing Centre, Dept. Scientific and Indust. Res., Wellington, New Zealand.

MCGILL, T. E. 1970. Genetic analysis of male sexual behavior. Pp. 57–88 *In*: G. Lindzey and D. D. Thiessen (eds.), Contributions to Behavior-Genetic Analysis: The Mouse as a Prototype. Appleton Press, New York, NY, USA.

MCKAY, F. E. 1971. Behavioral aspects of population dynamics in unisexual-bisexual *Poeciliopsis* (Pisces: Poeciliidae). Ecology 52:778–90.

MCKAY, R. J. 1978. The exotic freshwater fishes of Queensland. Rept. to Australian Nat. Parks & Wildl. Serv., Canberrra, Australia.

MCKAY, R. J. 1984. Introductions of exotic fishes in Australia. Pp. 177–99 *In*: W. R. Courtenay, Jr. and J. R. Stauffer, Jr. (eds.), Distribution, Biology, and Management of Exotic Fishes. Johns Hopkins Univ. Press, Baltimore, MD, USA.

MCKAY, R. J. 1987. It's your problem too! Part 4. The Australian introductions. Aquarium Life Aust. 2:39–40.

MCKENZIE, W. D., JR., D. CREWS, K. D. KALLMAN, D. POLICANSKY, AND J. J. SOHN. 1983. Age, weight and the genetics of sexual maturation in the platyfish, *Xiphophorus maculatus*. Copeia 1983:770–74.

MCPHAIL, J. D. 1978. Sons and lovers: the functional significance of a sexual dichromism in a fish, *Neoheterandria tridentiger* (Garman). Behaviour 64:329–39.

MEARNS, A. J. 1975. *Poeciliopsis gracilis* (Heckel), a newly introduced poeciliid fish in California. Calif. Fish & Game 61:251–53.

MEDLEN, A. B. 1951. Preliminary observations on the effects of temperature and light upon reproduction in *Gambusia affinis*. Copeia 1951:148–52.

MEEK, S. E. 1902. A contribution to the ichthyology of Mexico. Publ. Field Columbian Mus., Zool. Ser. 3:63–128.

MEEK, S. E. 1904. The fresh-water fishes of Mexico north of the Isthmus of Tehuantepec. Publ. Field Columbian Mus., Zool. Ser. 5:1–252.

MEEK, S. E. 1912. New species of fishes from Costa Rica. Publ. Field Columbian Mus., Zool. Ser. 10:69–75.

MEEK, S. E. AND S. F. HILDEBRAND. 1913. New species of fishes from Panama. Publ. Field Mus. Natur. Hist., Zool. Ser. 10:77–91.

MEEK, S. E. AND S. F. HILDEBRAND. 1916. The fishes of the fresh waters of Panama. Publ. Field Mus. Natur. Hist., Zool. Ser. 10:217–374.

MEES, G. F. 1977. The status of *Gambusia affinis* (Baird and Girard) in south western Australia. Rec. West. Aust. Mus. 6:27–31.

MEFFE, G. K. 1983. Attempted chemical renovation of an Arizona spring brook for management of the endangered Sonoran topminnow. N. Amer. J. Fisheries Mgt. 3:315–21.

MEFFE, G. K. 1984a. Density-dependent cannibalism in the endangered Sonoran topminnow (*Poeciliopsis occidentalis*). Southwest. Natur. 29:500–503.

MEFFE, G. K. 1984b. Effects of abiotic disturbance on coexistence of predator-prey fish species. Ecology 65:1525–34.

MEFFE, G. K. 1985a. Life history patterns of *Gambusia marshi* (Poeciliidae) from Cuatro Ciénegas, Mexico. Copeia 1985:898–905.

MEFFE, G. K. 1985b. Predation and species replacement in American southwestern fishes: a case study. Southwest. Natur. 30:173–87.

MEFFE, G. K. 1986a. Conservation genetics and the management of endangered fishes. Fisheries 11(1):14–23.

MEFFE, G. K. 1986b. Cannibalism, food availability, and reproduction in mosquitofish: a critique. Amer. Natur. 127:897–901.

MEFFE, G. K. 1987a. Conserving fish genomes: philosophies and practices. Env. Biol. Fish. 18:3–9.

MEFFE, G. K. 1987b. Embryo size variation in mosquitofish: optimality vs plasticity in propagule size. Copeia 1987:762–68.

MEFFE, G. K. 1989. Fish utilization of springs and ciénegas in the arid southwest. *In*: R. R. Sharitz and J. W. Gibbons (eds.), Freshwater Wetlands and Wildlife: Perspectives on Natural, Managed, and Degraded Ecosystems. Office of Scientific and Technical Information, US Dept. Energy, Oak Ridge, TN, USA. (in press).

MEFFE, G. K. AND M. L. CRUMP. 1987. Possible growth and reproductive benefits of cannibalism in the mosquitofish. Amer. Natur. 129:203–12.

MEFFE, G. K. AND R. C. VRIJENHOEK. 1981. Starvation stress and intraovarian cannibalism in livebearers (Atheriniformes: Poeciliidae). Copeia 1981:702–5.

MEFFE, G. K. AND R. C. VRIJENHOEK. 1988. Conservation genetics in the management of desert fishes. Conserv. Biol. 2:157–69.

MEFFE, G. K., D. A. HENDRICKSON, W. L. MINCKLEY, AND J. N. RINNE. 1983. Factors resulting in decline of the endangered Sonoran topminnow (Atheriniformes: Poeciliidae) in the United States. Biol. Conserv. 25:135–59.

MENZEL, B. W. AND R. M. DARNELL. 1973a. Systematics of *Poecilia mexicana* (Pisces: Poeciliidae) in northern Mexico. Copeia 1973:225–37.

MENZEL, B. W. AND R. M. DARNELL. 1973b. Morphology of naturally occurring triploid fish related to *Poecilia formosa*. Copeia 1973:350–52.

MEYER, A. 1987. Phenotypic plasticity and heterochrony in *Cichlasoma managuense* (Pisces, Cichlidae) and their implications for speciation in cichlid fishes. Evolution 41:1357–69.

MEYER, M. K. 1983a. Une nouvelle espece de *Poecilia* du Guerrero, Mexique. Rev. Fr. Aquariol. 10:55–58.

MEYER, M. K. 1983b. *Xiphophorus*-Hybriden aus Nord-Mexico, miteiner Revision der Taxa *X. kosszanderi* und *X. roseni*. Zool. Abh. Mus. Tierk. Dresden 38:285–91.

MEYER, M. K. AND M. SCHARTL. 1980. Eine neue *Xiphophorus*-Art aus Vera Cruz, Mexiko (Pisces: Poeciliidae). Senckenbergiana Biol. 60:147–51.

MEYER, M. K. AND D. VOGEL. 1981. Ein neuer *Poeciliopsis* aus Chiapas, Mexiko (Pisces: Poeciliidae). Senckenbergiana Biol. 61:357–61.

MEYER, M. K. AND L. WISCHNATH. 1981. Zwei neue *Xiphophorus*-Arten aus Nuevo Leon, Mexiko. Aquaria 28:129–34.

MEYER, M. K., L. WISCHNATH, AND W. FOERSTER. 1985a. Lebendgebärende Zierfische Arten der Welt. Mergus-Verlag, Melle, West Germany.

MEYER, M. K., A. C. RADDA, R. RIEHL, AND W. FEICHTINGER. 1986. *Poeciliopsis baenschi* n. sp., un nouveau taxon de Jalisco, Mexique (Teleostei, Poeciliidae). Rev. Fr. Aquariol. 12:79–84.

MEYER, M. K., R. RIEHL, J. A. DAWES, AND I. DIBBLE. 1985b. *Poeciliopsis scarlii* spec. nov., a new taxon from Michoacan, Mexico (Teleostei: Poeciliidae). Rev. Fr. Aquariol. 12:23–26.

MICHOD, R. E. 1979. Evolution of life histories in response to age-specific mortality factors. Amer. Natur. 113:531–50.

MILEY, W. W. 1978. Ecological impact of the pike killifish, *Belonesox belizanus* Kner, (Poeciliidae) in southern Florida. M.S. Thesis, Florida Atlantic Univ., Boca Raton, FL, USA.

MILLER, N. 1907. The fishes of the Motagua River, Guatemala. Bull. Amer. Mus. Natur. Hist. 23:95–123.

MILLER, R. R. 1960. Four new species of viviparous fishes, genus *Poeciliopsis*, from northwestern Mexico. Occas. Pap. Mus. Zool., Univ. Michigan 619:1–11.

MILLER, R. R. 1961. Man and the changing fish fauna of the American southwest. Pap. Mich. Acad. Sci., Arts and Lett. 46:365–404.

MILLER, R. R. 1966. Geographic distribution of Central American freshwater fishes. Copeia 1966:773–802.

MILLER, R. R. 1974. Mexican species of the genus *Heterandria*, subgenus *Pseudoxiphophorus* (Pisces: Poeciliidae). Trans. San Diego Soc. Natur. Hist. 17:235–50.

MILLER, R. R. 1975. Five new species of Mexican poeciliid fishes of the genera *Poecilia*, *Gambusia*, and *Poeciliopsis*. Occas. Pap. Mus. Zool., Univ. Michigan 672:1–44.

MILLER, R. R. 1979. Ecology, habits and relationships of the Middle American cuatro ojos, *Anableps dowi* (Pisces: Anablepidae). Copeia 1979:82–91.

MILLER, R. R. 1983. Checklist and key to the mollies of Mexico (Pisces: Poeciliidae: *Poecilia*, subgenus *Mollienesia*). Copeia 1983:817–22.

MILLER, R. R. AND W. L. MINCKLEY. 1963. *Xiphophorus gordoni*, a new species of platyfish from Coahuila, Mexico. Copeia 1963:538–46.

MILLER, R. R. AND W. L. MINCKLEY. 1970. *Gambusia aurata*, a new species of poeciliid fish from northeastern Mexico. Southwest. Natur. 15:249–59.

MILLER, R. R. AND R. J. SCHULTZ. 1959. All-female strains of the teleost fishes of the genus *Poeciliopsis*. Science 130:1656–57.

MILSTEAD, E. 1980. Genetic differentiation among subpopulations of three *Gambusia* species (Pisces: Poeciliidae) in the Pecos River, Texas and New Mexico. M.S. Thesis, Baylor Univ., Waco, TX, USA.

MILTON, D. A. AND A. H. ARTHINGTON. 1983a. Reproductive biology of *Gambusia affinis* Baird and Girard, *Xiphophorus helleri* (Gunther) and *X. maculatus* (Heckel) (Pisces: Poeciliidae) in south-eastern Queensland, Australia. J. Fish Biol. 23:23–41.

MILTON, D. A. AND A. H. ARTHINGTON. 1983b. Reproduction and growth of *Craterocephalus marjoriae* and *C. stercusmuscarum* (Pisces: Atherinidae) in south-eastern Queensland, Australia. Freshwater Biol. 13:589–97.

MILTON, D. A. AND A. H. ARTHINGTON. 1984. Reproductive strategy and growth of the crimson-spotted rainbow fish, *Melanotaenia splendida fluviatilis* (Castelnau) (Pisces: Melanotaeniidae) in south-eastern Queensland. Aust. J. Mar. Freshwater Res. 35:75–83.

MILTON, D. A. AND A. H. ARTHINGTON. 1985. Reproductive strategy and growth of the Australian smelt, *Retropinna semoni* (Weber) (Pisces: Retropinnidae), and the olive perchlet, *Ambassis nigripinnis* (de Vis) (Pisces: Ambassidae), in Brisbane, south-eastern Queensland. Aust. J. Mar. Freshwater Res. 36:329–41.

MINCKLEY, W. L. 1962. Two new species of fishes of the genus *Gambusia* (Poeciliidae) from northeastern Mexico. Copeia 1962:391–96.

MINCKLEY, W. L. 1963. A new poeciliid fish (genus *Gambusia*) from the Río Grande drainage of Coahuila, Mexico. Southwest. Natur. 8:154–61.

MINCKLEY, W. L. 1969a. Environments of the bolson of Cuatro Ciénegas, Coahuila, Mexico. Texas Western Press, Sci. Ser. 2:1–65.

MINCKLEY, W. L. 1969b. Attempted reestablishment of the Gila topminnow within its former range. Copeia 1969:193–94.

MINCKELY, W. L. 1973. Fishes of Arizona. Arizona Dept. Game & Fish, Phoenix, AZ, USA.

MINCKLEY, W. L. 1977. Endemic fishes of the Cuatro Ciénegas Basin, northern Coahuila, Mexico. Pp. 383–404. *In*: R. H. Wauer and D. H. Riskind (eds.), Transactions of the Symposium on the Biological Resources of the Chihuahuan Desert Region. Nat. Park Serv. Transactions & Proceedings Series, No. 3, US Dept. Interior, Washington, DC, USA.

MINCKLEY, W. L. 1984. Cuatro Ciénegas fishes: research review and a local test of diversity versus habitat size. J. Arizona-Nevada Acad. Sci. 19:13–21.

MINCKLEY, W. L. AND J. E. DEACON. 1968. Southwestern fishes and the enigma of "endangered species." Science 159:1424–32.

MINCKLEY, W. L. AND G. K. MEFFE. 1987. Differential selection by flooding in stream-fish communities of the arid American southwest. Pp. 93–104 *In*: W. J. Matthews and D. C. Hines (eds.), Community and Evolutionary Ecology of North American Stream Fishes. Univ. Oklahoma Press, Norman, OK, USA.

MINCKLEY, W. L., J. N. RINNE, AND J. E. JOHNSON. 1977. Status of the Gila topminnow and its co-occurrence with mosquitofish. US Dept. Agric., Forest Serv. Res. Pap. RM-198:1–8.

MISSIROLI, A. 1948. Prevention of malaria in practice. Riv. Malariol. 9:667–705.

MITTON, J. B. AND M. C. GRANT. 1984. Associations among protein heterozygosity, growth rate and developmental homeostasis. Annu. Rev. Ecol. Syst. 15:479–99.

MITTWOCH, U. 1973. Genetics of Sex Differentiation. Academic Press, Orlando, FL, USA.

MIURA, T., R. M. TAKAHASHI, AND W. H. WILDER. 1984. Impact of the mosquitofish (*Gambusia affinis*) on a ricefield ecosystem when used as a mosquito control agent. Mosquito News 44:516–17.

MOAV, R., T. BRODY, AND G. HULATA. 1978. Genetic improvement of wild fish populations. Science 201:1090–94.

MONACO, P. J., E. M. RASCH, AND J. S. BALSANO. 1978. Cytological evidence for temporal differences during the asynchronous ovarian maturation of bisexual and unisexual fishes of the genus *Poecilia*. J. Fish Biol. 13:33–44.

MONACO, P. J., E. M. RASCH, AND J. S. BALSANO. 1981. Sperm availability in naturally occurring bisexual-unisexual breeding complexes involving *Poecilia mexicana* and the gynogenetic teleost, *Poecilia formosa*. Env. Biol. Fish. 6:159–66.

MONACO, P. J., E. M. RASCH, AND J. S. BALSANO. 1983. The occurrence of superfetation in the Amazon molly, *Poecilia formosa*, and its related sexual species. Copeia 1983:969–74.

MONACO, P. J., E. M. RASCH, AND J. S. BALSANO. 1984. Apomictic reproduction in the Amazon molly, *Poecilia formosa*, and its triploid hybrids. Pp. 311–28 *In*: B. J. Turner (ed.), Evolutionary Genetics of Fishes. Plenum Press, New York, NY, USA.

MONACO, P. J., E. M. RASCH, J. S. BALSANO, AND B. J. TURNER. 1982. Muscle protein phenotypes and the probable evolutionary origin of a unisexual fish, *Poecilia formosa*, and its triploid derivatives. J. Exp. Zool. 221:265–74.

MOORE, W. S. 1974. A mutant affecting chromatophore proliferation in a poeciliid fish. J. Heredity 65:326–30.

MOORE, W. S. 1976. Components of fitness in the unisexual fish *Poeciliopsis monacha-occidentalis*. Evolution 30:564–78.

MOORE, W. S. 1977a. An evaluation of narrow hybrid zones in vertebrates. Quart. Rev. Biol. 52:263–77.

MOORE, W. S. 1977b. A histocompatibility analysis of inheritance in the unisexual fish *Poeciliopsis 2 monacha-lucida*. Copeia 1977:213–23.

MOORE, W. S. 1984. Evolutionary ecology of unisexual fishes. Pp. 329–98 *In*: B. J. Turner (ed.), Evolutionary Genetics of Fishes. Plenum Press, New York, NY, USA.

MOORE, W. S. AND A. B. EISENBREY. 1979. The population structure of an asexual vertebrate, *Poeciliopsis 2 monacha-lucida* (Pisces: Poeciliidae). Evolution 33:563–78.

MOORE, W. S. AND F. E. McKAY. 1971. Coexistence in unisexual-bisexual species complexes of *Poeciliopsis* (Pisces: Poeciliidae). Ecology 52:791–99.

MORITZ, C., T. E. DOWLING, AND W. M. BROWN 1987. Evolution of animal mitochondrial DNA: relevance for population biology and systematics. Annu. Rev. Ecol. Syst. 18:269–92.

MORIZOT, D. C. AND K. D. McENTIRE. 1988. Sex linkage of carbonic anhydrase-1 in poeciliid fishes. Isozyme Bull. 21:201.

MORIZOT, D. C. AND M. J. SICILIANO. 1982. Protein polymorphisms, segregation in genetic crosses and genetic distances among fishes of the genus *Xiphophorus* (Poeciliidae). Genetics 102:539–56.

MORIZOT, D. C. AND M. J. SICILIANO. 1983a. Comparative gene mapping in fishes. Isozymes 10:261–85.

MORIZOT, D. C. AND M. J. SICILIANO. 1983b. Linkage group V of platyfishes and swordtails of the genus *Xiphophorus* (Poeciliidae): linkage of loci for malate dehydrogenase-2 and esterase-1 and esterase-4 with a gene controlling the severity of hybrid melanomas. J. Nat. Cancer Inst. 71:809–13.

MORIZOT, D. C. AND M. J. SICILIANO. 1984. Gene mapping in fishes and other vertebrates. Pp. 173–234 *In*: B. J. Turner (ed.), Evolutionary Genetics of Fishes. Plenum Press, New York, NY, USA.

MORRIS, D. 1956. The function and causation of courtship. Pp. 261–86 *In*: P. P. Grasse (ed.), L'Instinct dans le Comportement des Animaux et de l'Homme. Masson, Paris, France.

MORSE, D. H. 1980. Behavioral Mechanisms in Ecology. Harvard Univ. Press, Cambridge, MA, USA.

MOTRO, U. AND G. THOMSON. 1982. On heterozygosity and the effective size of populations subject to size changes. Evolution 36:1059–66.

MOYLE, P. B. 1976. Inland Fishes of California. Univ. California Press, Berkeley, CA, USA.

MOYLE, P. B. AND R. D. NICHOLS. 1973. Ecology of some native and introduced fishes of the Sierra Nevada foothills in central California. Copeia 1973:978–90.

MOYLE, P. B. AND R. D. NICHOLS. 1974. Decline of the native fish fauna of the Sierra Nevada foothills, central California. Amer. Midl. Natur. 92:72–83.

MULLER, J. J. 1964. The relation of recombination to mutational advance. Mutation Res. 1:2–9

MUSHINSKY, H. R. AND J. J. HEBRARD. 1977. Food partitioning by five species of water snakes in Louisiana. Herpetologica 33:162–66.

MYERS, G. S. 1935. An annotated list of the cyprinodont fishes of Hispaniola, with descriptions of two new species. Zoologica 10:301–16.

MYERS, G. S. 1965. *Gambusia,* the fish destroyer. Trop. Fish Hobbyist 13:31–32, 53–54.

NATALI, V. F. AND A. I. NATALI. 1931. On the problem of localization of genes in the X and Y chromosomes of *Lebistes reticulatus*. Z. Exp. Biol. 7:41–70.

NAYUDU, P. L. 1979. Genetic studies of melanic color patterns and atypical sex determination in the guppy, *Poecilia reticulata*. Copeia 1979:225–31.

NEEDHAM, J. 1931. Chemical Embryology. Cambridge Univ. Press, Cambridge, England.

NEI, M. 1975. Molecular Population Genetics and Evolution. North-Holland Publ., Amsterdam, Holland.

NEI, M. 1977. F-statistics and analysis of gene diversity in subdivided populations. Ann. Human Genet. 41:225–33.

NEI, M. 1978. Estimation of average heterozygosity and genetic distance from a small number of individuals. Genetics 89:583–90.

NEI, M. 1983. Genetic polymorphism and the role of mutation in evolution. Pp. 165–90 *In*: M. Nei and R. K. Koehn (eds.), Evolution of Genes and Proteins. Sinauer Assoc., Sunderland, MA, USA.

NEI, M. 1987. Genetic distance and molecular phylogeny. Pp. 193–223 *In*: N. Ryman and F. Utter (eds.), Population Genetics and Fishery Management. Univ. Washington Press, Seattle, WA, USA.

NEI, M., T. MARUYAMA, AND R. CHAKRABORTY. 1975. The bottleneck effect and genetic variability in populations. Evolution 29:1–10.

NELSON, J. S. 1984. The tropical fish fauna in Cave and Basin hotsprings drainage, Banff National Park, Alberta. Can. Field-Natur. 97:255–61.

NEVO, E. 1978. Genetic variation in natural populations: patterns and theory. Theor. Popul. Biol. 13:121–77.

NEVO, E., A. BEILES, AND R. BEN-SHLOMO. 1984. The evolutionary significance of genetic diversity: ecological, demographic and life history correlates. Lect. Notes Biomath. 53:13–213.

NICHOLS, J. T. 1915. On *Heterandria zonata* sp. nov. and *Heterandria versicolor* (Günther) from the island of Santo Domingo. Bull. Amer. Mus. Natur. Hist. 34:603–4.

NICHOLS, J. T. AND G. S. MYERS. 1923. A new *Limia* from San Domingo. Amer. Mus. Novitates 79:2 pp.

NOBLE, G. K. 1939. The experimental animal from a naturalist's point of view. Amer. Natur. 73:113–21.

NOLTIE, D. B. AND P. H. JOHANSEN. 1986. Laboratory studies of microhabitat selection by the guppy, *Poecilia reticulata* (Peters). J. Freshwater Ecol. 3:299–307.

NORLAND, R. L. AND J. R. BOWMAN. 1976. Population studies of *Gambusia affinis* in rice fields: sampling design, fish movement and distribution. Proc. Pap. Annu. Conf. California Mosq. Vector Control Assoc. 44:53–56.

O'CONNOR, R. J., P. J. S. BOADEN, AND R. SEED. 1975. Niche breadth in Bryozoa and a test of competition theory. Nature 25:307–9.

O'DONALD, P. 1962. The theory of sexual selection. Heredity 17:541–52.

O'DONALD, P. 1967. A general model of sexual and natural selection. Heredity 22:499–518.

O'DONALD, P. 1980. Genetic Models of Sexual Selection. Cambridge Univ. Press, Cambridge, England.

OGDEN, A. E., A. J. SPINELLI, AND J. HORTON. 1985. Hydrologic and hydrochemical data for the Edwards Aquifer in Hays and Comal Counties (TX). Final Rept., US Fish & Wildl. Serv., Albuquerque, NM, USA.

OHNO, S. AND N. B. ATKIN. 1966. Comparative DNA values and chromosome complements of eight species of fishes. Chromosoma (Berl.) 18:455–66.

ÖKTAY, M. 1964. Über genbedingte rote Farbmuster bei *Xiphophorus maculatus*. Mitt. Hamburg. Zool. Mus. Inst. (Kosswig Festschrift):133–57.

OLIVEROS, O. B. 1983. *Phallotorynus victoriae* sp. nov. de la cuenca del Río Parana Medio, Argentina (Pisces, Poeciliidae). Rev. Asoc. Ciencias Natur. Litoral 14:17–27.

OTTO, R. G. 1973. Temperature tolerance of the mosquitofish, *Gambusia affinis* (Baird and Girard). J. Fish. Biol. 5:575–85.

OTTO, R. G. 1974. The effects of acclimation to cyclic thermal regimes on heat tolerance of the western mosquitofish. Trans. Amer. Fish. Soc. 103:331–35.

ÖZTAN, N. 1960. The effects of gonadotropin and steroid hormones on the gonads of sterile hybrid fishes. Rev. Fac. Sci. Univ. Istanbul, Ser. B, 25:27–56.

ÖZTAN, N. 1963. The hypothalamic neurosecretory system of a poeciliid fish, *Platypoecilus maculatus*, and its sterile hybrid backcross with *Xiphophorus helleri*. Gen. Comp. Endocrinol. 3:1–14.

PARENTI, L. R. 1981. A phylogenetic and biogeographic analysis of cyprinodontiform fishes (Teleostei, Atherinomorpha). Bull. Amer. Mus. Natur. Hist. 168:335–557.

PARENTI, L. R. 1984. Biogeography of the Andean killifish genus *Orestias* with comments on the species flock concept. Pp. 85–92 *In*: A. A. Echelle and I. Kornfield (eds.), Evolution of Fish Species Flocks. Univ. Maine at Orono Press, Orono, ME, USA.

PARKER, E. D. 1979. Ecological implications of clonal diversity in parthenogenetic morphospecies. Amer. Zool. 19:753–62.

PARKER, E. D. AND R. K. SELANDER. 1976. The organization of genetic diversity in the parthenogenetic lizard *Cnemidophorus tesselatus*. Genetics 84:791–805.

PARTRIDGE, L. 1980. Mate choice increases a component of offspring fitness in fruit flies. Nature 283:290–91.

PARZEFALL, J. 1969. Zur vergleichenden Ethologie verschiedener *Mollienesia*-Arten einschliesslich einer Höhlenform von *M. sphenops*. Behaviour 33:1–37.

PARZEFALL, J. 1970. Morphologische untersuchungen an einer höhlenform von *Mollienesia sphenops* (Pisces, Poeciliidae). Z. Morphol. Tiere 68:323–42.

PARZEFALL, J. 1973. Attraction and sexual cycle of poeciliids. Pp. 177–83 *In*: J. H. Schröder (ed.), Genetics and Mutagenesis of Fish. Springer-Verlag, Berlin, Germany.

PARZEFALL, J. 1979. Zur genetik und biologischen bedeutung des aggressionsueshaltens von *Poecilia sphenops* (Pisces, Poeciliidae). Z. Tierpsychol. 50:399–422.

PEDEN, A. E. 1970. Courtship behaviour of *Gambusia* (Poeciliidae) with emphasis on isolating mechanisms. Ph.D. Dissertation, Univ. Texas, Austin, TX, USA.

PEDEN, A. E. 1972a. The function of gonopodial parts and behavioral pattern during copulation by *Gambusia* (Poeciliidae). Can. J. Zool. 50:955–68.

PEDEN, A. E. 1972b. Differences in the external genitalia of female gambusiin fishes. Southwest. Natur. 17:265–72.

PEDEN, A. E. 1973a. Virtual extinction of *Gambusia amistadensis* n. sp., a new poeciliid fish from Texas. Copeia 1973:210–21.

PEDEN, A. E. 1973b. Variation in anal spot expression in gambusiin females and its effect on male courtship. Copeia 1973:250–63.

PEDEN, A. E. 1975. Differences in copulatory behavior as partial isolating mechanisms in the poeciliid fish *Gambusia*. Can. J. Zool. 53:1290–96.

PETERS, G. 1964. Vergleichende Untersuchungen an drei Subspecies von *Xiphophorus helleri* Heckel (Pisces). Z. Zool. Syst. Evolutionforsch. 2:185–271.

PETERS, G. AND B. MADER. 1964. Morphologische veranderungen der gonadenausfuhrgange sich fortpflanzender schwerttragerweibchen (*Xiphophorus helleri* Heckel). Zool. Anz. 173:243–57.

PETERS, W. 1859. Hr. W. Peters legte eine neue von Hrn. Jagor im atlanischen Meere gefangene Art der Gattung *Leptocephalus* vor und fügte Mittheilungen über einige andere neue Fische des zoologischen Museums hinzu. Monatsber. K. Preussischen Akad. Wiss. (Berlin), pp. 411–12.

PFLIEGER, W. L. 1975. The Fishes of Missouri. Missouri Dept. Conserv., Jefferson City, MO, USA.

PHILIPPI E. 1908. Fortpflanzungsgeschichte der viviparen teleosteer *Glaridichthys januarius* und *G. decem-maculatus* in ihrem einfluss auf lebensweise, makroskopische und mikroskopische anatomie. Zoologische Jahrbucher Abt. f. Anat. 27:1–94.

PISTER, E. P. 1974. Desert fishes and their habitats. Trans. Amer. Fish. Soc. 102:531–40.

POEY, F. 1854. Los guajacones, pecesillos de agua dulce. *In*: F. Poey, Memorias sobre la historia natural de la Isla de Cuba. Havana(1):374–92.

POEY, F. 1860. Poisson de Cuba, espèces nouvelles. *In*: F. Poey, Memorias sobra la historia natural de la Isla de Cuba, acompañadas de sumarios latinos y extractos en frances. Havana(2):115–336.

POLICANSKY, D. 1983. Size, age, and demography of metamorphosis and sexual maturation in fishes. Amer. Zool. 23:57–60.

POLLACK, E. I. 1977. Social behavior, growth and health of tropical fishes. Trop. Fish Hobbyist 25:68–70.

PREHN, L. M. AND E. M. RASCH. 1969. Cytogenetic studies of *Poecilia* (Pisces). 1. Chromosome numbers of naturally occurring poeciliid species and their hybrids from eastern Mexico. Can. J. Genet. Cytol. 11:880–95.

PROVINE, W. R. 1971. The Origins of Theoretical Population Genetics. Univ. Chicago Press, Chicago, IL, USA.

PUCKRIDGE, J. P. AND M. DREWIEN. 1988. The aquatic fauna of the north-west branch of Cooper Creek: synecology of fishes, with preliminary notes on macroinvertebrate taxonomy and distribution. Pp. 69–107 *In*: J. O. Reid and J. Gillen (eds.), The Coongie Lakes Study. Dept. Environment & Planning, Adelaide, South Australia.

PURSER, G. L. 1938. Reproduction in *Lebistes reticulatus*. Quart. J. Micros. Sci. 81:151–58.

PUSEY, B. J., A. W. STOREY, P. M. DAVIES AND D. H. D. EDWARD. 1989. Spatial variation in fish communities in two southwestern Australian river systems. J. Royal Soc. West. Aust, in press.

PYKE, G. H., H. R. PULLIAM, AND E. L. CHARNOV. 1977. Optimal foraging: a selective review of theory and tests. Quart. Rev. Biol. 52:138–55.

RADDA, A. C. 1980. Synopsis der gattung *Xiphophorus* Heckel. Aquaria 27:39–44.

RADDA, A. C. 1985. Revalidisierung der Gattung *Pseudoxiphophorus* Bleeker 1860 (Poeciliidae, Osteichthyes). Aquaria 32:126–28.

RADDA, A. C. 1987. Poeciliiden-Studien en Equador und Kolumbien. Aquaria 34:169–77.

RADDA, A. C. AND M. K. MEYER. 1981. Revalidisierung der Gattung *Xenophallus* Hubbs (Poeciliidae, Osteichthyes). Aquaria 28:115–18.

RASCH, E. M. AND J. S. BALSANO. 1973. Cytogenetics of *Poecilia* (Pisces). III. Persistence of triploid genomes in the unisexual progeny of triploid females associated with *Poecilia formosa*. Copeia 1973:810–13.

RASCH, E. M. AND J. S. BALSANO. 1974. Biochemical and cytogenetic studies of *Poecilia* from eastern Mexico. II. Frequency, perpetuation, and probable origin of triploid genomes in females associated with *Poecilia formosa*. Rev. Biol. Trop. 21:351–81.

RASCH, E. M. AND J. S. BALSANO. 1989. Trihybrids related to the unisexual molly fish, *Poecilia formosa*. *In*: R. M. Dawley and J. P. Bogart (eds.), The Evolution and Ecology of Unisexual Vertebrates. State Univ. NY Press, Albany, NY, USA. (in press).

RASCH, E. M., P. J. MONACO, AND J. S. BALSANO. 1978. Identification of a new form of triploid hybrid fish by DNA-Feulgen cytophotometry. J. Histochem. Cytochem. 26:218.

RASCH, E. M., P. J. MONACO, AND J. S. BALSANO. 1982. Cytophotometric and autoradiographic evidence for functional apomixis in a gynogenetic fish, *Poecilia formosa*, and its related triploid hybrids. Histochemistry 73:515–33.

RASCH, E. M., L. M. PREHN, AND R. W. RASCH. 1970. Cytogenetic studies of *Poecilia* (Pisces). II. Triploidy and DNA levels in naturally occurring populations associated with the gynogenetic teleost *Poecilia formosa* (Girard). Chromosoma 31:18–40.

RASCH, E. M., R. M. DARNELL, K. D. KALLMAN, AND P. ABRAMOFF. 1965. Cytophotometric evidence for triploidy in hybrids of the gynogenetic fish, *Poecilia formosa*. J. Exp. Zool. 160:155–69.

RAUCHENBERGER, M. 1988. Systematics and biogeography of the genus *Gambusia* (Cyprinodontiformes: Poeciliidae). Ph.D. Dissertation, City Univ. New York, New York, NY, USA.

REDDY, S. R. AND T. J. PANDIAN. 1973. Effect of volume of water on predatory efficiency of the fish *Gambusia affinis*. Curr. Sci. 42:644–45.

REDDY, S. R. AND K. SHAKUNTALA. 1979. Comparative studies of the food intake, growth and food conversion of two larvivorous fishes. Proc. Indian Acad. Sci. 88(B):425–32.

REED, D. E. AND T. BRYANT. 1975. Fish population studies in Fresno County rice fields. Proc. Pap. Annu. Conf. California Mosq. Vector Control Assoc. 43:139–41.

REES, J. T. 1979. Community development in freshwater microcosms. Hydrobiologia 63:113–28.

REGAN, C. T. 1906. On the fresh-water fishes of the island of Trinidad, based on the collection, notes, and sketches made by Mr. Lechmere Guppy, Junr. Proc. Zool. Soc. 1906:378–93.

REGAN, C. T. 1907a. Descriptions of six new freshwater fishes from Mexico and Central America. Ann. Mag. Natur. Hist. 7(19):258–60.

REGAN, C. T. 1907b. Diagnoses of new Central American freshwater fishes of the families Cyprinodontidae and Mugilidae. Ann. Mag. Natur. Hist. 7(19):64–66.

REGAN, C. T. 1908. A collection of fresh water fishes made by Mr. C. F. Underwood in Costa Rica. Ann. Mag. Natur. Hist. 8(2):455–64.

REGAN, C. T. 1913. A revision of the cyprinodont fishes of the subfamily Poeciliinae. Proc. Zool. Soc. London 11:977–1018.

REGAN, C. T. 1914a. Description of a new cyrpinodont fish of the genus *Mollienesia* from Yucatan. Ann. Mag. Natur. Hist. 8(13):338.

REGAN, C. T. 1914b. Descriptions of two new cyprinodont fishes from Mexico, presented to the British Museum by Herr A. Rachow. Ann. Mag. Natur. Hist. 8(14):65–67.

REGAN, J. D. 1961. Melanism in the poeciliid fish, *Gambusia affinis* (Baird and Girard). Amer. Midl. Natur. 65:139–43.

REIMER, R. D. 1970. A food study of *Heterandria formosa* Agassiz. Amer. Midl. Natur. 83:311–15.

REITER, E. O. AND M. M. GRUMBACH. 1982. Neuroendocrine control mechanisms and the onset of puberty. Annu. Rev. Physiol. 44:595–613.

REZNICK, D. N. 1980. Life history evolution in the guppy (*Poecilia reticulata*). Ph.D. Dissertation, Univ. Pennsylvania, Philadelphia, PA, USA.

REZNICK, D. N. 1981. "Grandfather effects": the genetics of interpopulation differences in offspring size in the mosquitofish. Evolution 35:941–53.

REZNICK, D. N. 1982a. The impact of predation on life history evolution in Trinidadian guppies: genetic basis of observed life history patterns. Evolution 36:1236–50.

REZNICK, D. N. 1982b. Genetic determination of offspring size in the guppy (*Poecilia reticulata*). Amer. Natur. 120:181–88.

REZNICK, D. N. 1983. The structure of guppy life histories: the tradeoff between growth and reproduction. Ecology 64:862–73.

REZNICK, D. N. AND B. BRAUN. 1987. Fat cycling in the mosquitofish (*Gambusia affinis*): is fat storage a reproductive adapation? Oecolgia 73:401–13.

REZNICK, D. N. AND H. BRYGA. 1987. Life-history evolution in guppies (*Poecilia reticulata*): 1. Phenotypic and genetic changes in an introduction experiment. Evolution 41:1370–85.

REZNICK, D. N. AND J. A. ENDLER. 1982. The impact of predation on life history evolution in Trinidadian guppies (*Poecilia reticulata*). Evolution 36:160–77.

REZNICK, D. N., E. PERRY, AND J. TRAVIS. 1986. Measuring the cost of reproduction: a comment on papers by Bell. Evolution 40:1338–44.

RICHARDSON, B. J., P. R. BAVERSTOCK, AND M. ADAMS. 1986. Allozyme Electrophoresis: A Handbook for Animal Systematics and Population Studies. Academic Press, London, England.

RICKER, W. E. 1979. Growth rates and models. Pp. 677–743 *In*: W. S. Hoar, D. J. Randall and J. R. Brett (eds.), Fish Physiology, Vol. 8. Academic Press, New York, NY, USA.

RINNE, J. N., J. E. JOHNSON, B. L. JENSEN, A. W. RUGER, AND R. SORENSON. 1986. The role of hatcheries in management and recovery of threatened and endangered fishes. Pp. 271–86 *In*: R. H. Stroud (ed.), Fisheries Management. Amer. Fish. Soc., Bethesda, MD, USA.

RIVAS, L. R. 1944. Contributions to the study of the poeciliid fishes of Cuba. I. Descriptions of six new species of the subfamily Gambusiinae. Proc. New England Zool. Club 23:41–53.

RIVAS, L. R. 1958. The origin, evolution, dispersal, and geographical distribution of the Cuban poeciliid fishes of the tribe Girardinini. Proc. Amer. Phil. Soc. 102:281–320.

RIVAS, L. R. 1963. Subgenera and species groups in the poeciliid fish genus *Gambusia* Poey. Copeia 1963:331–47.

RIVAS, L. R. 1969. A revision of poeciliid fishes of the *Gambusia punctata* species group, with descriptions of two new species. Copeia 1969:778–95.

RIVAS, L. R. 1971. A new subspecies of poeciliid fish of the genus *Gambusia* from eastern Cuba. Publ. Gulf Coast Res. Lab. Mus. 2:5–9.

Rivas, L. R. 1978. A new species of poeciliid fish of the genus *Poecilia* from Hispaniola, with reinstatement and redescription of *P. dominicensis* (Evermann and Clark). Northeast Gulf Sci. 2:98–112.

Rivas, L. R. 1980. Eight new species of poeciliid fishes of the genus *Limia* from Hispaniola. Northeast Gulf Sci. 4:28–38.

Rivas, L. R. 1982. Character displacement and coexistence in two poeciliid fishes of the genus *Poecilia* (*Mollienesia*) from Hispaniola. Northeast Gulf Sci. 5:1–24.

Rivas, L. R. and W. L. Fink. 1970. A new species of poeciliid fish of the genus *Limia* from the island of Grand Cayman, B.W.I. Copeia 1970:270–74.

Rivas, L. R. and G. S. Myers. 1950. A new genus of poeciliid fishes from Hispaniola, with notes on genera allied to *Poecilia* and *Mollienesia*. Copeia 1950:288–94.

Robbins, L. W., G. D. Hartman, and M. H. Smith. 1987. Dispersal, reproductive strategies, and the maintenance of genetic variability in mosquitofish. Copeia 1987:156–64.

Robins, C. R., R. M. Bailey, C. E. Bond, J. R. Booker, E. A. Lachner, R. N. Lea, and W. B. Scott. 1980. A List of Common and Scientific Names of Fishes from the United States and Canada (Fourth Edition). Amer. Fish. Soc. Special Publ. No. 12, Bethesda, MD, USA.

Roberts, R. J. 1978. Fish Pathology. Baillier Tindall, London, England.

Robertson, A. 1955. Selection in animals: synthesis. Cold Spring Harbor Symp. Quant. Biol. 20:225–29.

Robertson, F. W. 1960. The ecological genetics of growth in *Drosophila*. 2. Selection for large body size on different diets. Genet. Res. 1:305–18.

Rogers, J. S. 1972. Measures in genetic similarity and genetic distance. Studies in Genetics VII. Univ. Texas Publ. 7213:145–53.

Rose, M. R. 1982. Antagonistic pleiotropy, dominance, and genetic variation. Heredity 48:63–78.

Rose, M. R. 1985. Life history evolution with antagonistic pleiotropy and overlapping generations. Theor. Popul. Biol. 28:342–58.

Rose, S. M. 1959. Population control in guppies. Amer. Midl. Natur. 62:474–81.

Rosen, D. E. 1952. A revision of the fishes of the subfamily Alfarinae in the family Poeciliidae. Zoologica 37:151–56.

Rosen, D. E. 1960. Middle-American poecillid fishes of the genus *Xiphophorus*. Bull. Fla. State Mus., Biol. Sci. 5:57–242.

Rosen, D. E. 1967. New poeciliid fishes from Guatemala, with comments on the origins of some South and Central American forms. Amer. Mus. Novitates 2303:1–15.

Rosen, D. E. 1973. Suborder Cyprinodontoidei; Superfamily Cyprinodontoidea; Families Cyprinodontidae, Poeciliidae, and Anablepidae. Mem. Sears Found. Mar. Res. 1(6):229–62.

Rosen, D. E. 1976. A vicariance model of Caribbean biogeography. Syst. Zool. 24:431–64.

Rosen, D. E. 1978. Vicariant patterns and historical explanation in biogeography. Syst. Zool. 27:159–88.

Rosen, D. E. 1979. Fishes from the uplands and intermontane basins of Guatemala: revisionary studies and comparative geography. Bull. Amer. Mus. Natur. Hist. 162:267–376.

ROSEN, D. E. AND R. M. BAILEY 1959. Middle-American poeciliid fishes of the genera *Carlhubbsia* and *Phallichthys*, with descriptions of two new species. Zoologica 44:1–44.

ROSEN, D. E. AND R. M. BAILEY. 1963. The poeciliid fishes (Cyprinodontiformes), their structure, zoogeography and systematics. Bull. Amer. Mus. Natur. Hist. 126:1–176.

ROSEN, D. E. AND M. GORDON. 1953. Functional anatomy and evolution of male genitalia in poeciliid fishes. Zoologica 38:1–47.

ROSEN, D. E. AND K. D. KALLMAN. 1969. A new fish of the genus *Xiphophorus* from Guatemala, with remarks on the taxonomy of endemic forms. Amer. Mus. Novitates 2379:1–29.

ROSEN, D. E. AND J. R. MENDELSON. 1960. The sensory canals of the head in poeciliid fishes (Cyprinodontiformes), with reference to dentitional types. Copeia 1960:203–10.

ROSEN, D. E. AND L. R. PARENTI. 1981. Relationships of *Oryzias*, and the groups of atherinomorph fishes. Amer. Mus. Novitates 2719:1–25.

ROSEN, D. E. AND A. TUCKER. 1961. Evolution of secondary sexual characters and sexual behavior patterns in a family of viviparous fishes (Cyprinodontiformes: Poeciliidae). Copeia 1961:201–12.

ROSENTHAL, H. L. 1951. The birth process of the guppy, *Lebistes reticulatus*. Copeia 1951:304.

ROSENTHAL, H. L. 1952. Observations on reproduction of the poeciliid *Lebistes reticulatus* (Peters). Biol. Bull. 102:30–38.

ROSENTHAL, H. L. 1955. Abnormal birth of broods in the viviparous poeciliids *Lebistes reticulatus* and *Xiphophorus helleri*. Copeia 1955:52–53.

ROUGHGARDEN, J. 1972. Evolution of niche width. Amer. Natur. 106:683–718.

RUBIN, D. A. 1985. Effect of pH on sex ratio in cichlids and a poeciliid (Teleostei). Copeia 1985:233–35.

RUGH, R. 1962. Experimental Embryology: Techniques and Procedures. 3rd ed. Burgess Publ., Minneapolis, MN, USA.

RUTHERFORD, D. A. 1980. Hybridization in *Gambusia nobilis* (Pisces, Poeciliidae): an endangered species in the Pecos River drainage of Texas and New Mexico. M. S. Thesis, Baylor Univ., Waco, TX, USA.

RYAN, M. J. AND W. E. WAGNER, JR., 1987. Asymmetries in mating preferences between species: female swordtails prefer heterospecific males. Science 236:595–97.

RYDER, J. A. 1882. Structure and ovarian incubation of *Gambusia patruelis*, a top-minnow. Amer. Natur. 16:109–18.

RYDER, J. A. 1885. On the development of viviparous osseous fishes. Proc. US Nat. Mus. 8:128–55.

RYMAN, N. 1972. An attempt to estimate the magnitude of additive genetic variation of body size in the guppy-fish, *Lebistes reticulatus*. Hereditas 71:237–44.

RYMAN, N. 1973. Two-way selection for body weight in the guppy-fish, *Lebistes reticulatus*. Hereditas 74:239–46.

RYMAN, N. AND F. UTTER (eds.). 1987. Population Genetics and Fishery Management. Univ. Washington Press, Seattle, WA, USA.

SALIBIAN, A. 1977. Aclimatacion de *Gambusia affinis holbrooki* (Girard 1859) de Chile en soluciones de alta salinidad. Noticiario Mensual, Mus. Nac. Hist. Natur. (Chile) 22:4–7.

SARTI, N. L. AND G. R. ALLEN. 1978. The freshwater fishes of the Northern Swan Coastal Plain. Pp. 204–20 *In*: Faunal Studies of the Northern Coastal Plain: A Consideration of Past and Future Changes. West. Aust. Mus. Publ., Perth, Western Australia.

SAS INSTITUTE, INC. 1985. SAS User's Guide: Statistics. SAS Inst., Inc., Cary, NC, USA.

SCHENCK, R. A. AND R. C. VRIJENHOEK. 1986. Spatial and temporal factors affecting coexistence among sexual and clonal forms of *Poeciliopsis*. Evolution 40:1060–70.

SCHENCK, R. A. AND R. C. VRIJENHOEK. 1989. Habitat selection and feeding behavior of sexual and clonal *Poeciliopsis*. *In*: R. M. Dawley and J. P. Bogart (eds.), The Ecology and Evolution of Unisexual Vertebrates. State Univ. NY Press, Albany, NY, USA. (in press).

SCHMALHAUSEN, I. I. 1949. Factors of Evolution. Blakiston, Philadelphia, PA, USA.

SCHMIDT, J. 1919. Racial studies in fishes. II. Experimental investigations with *Lebistes reticulatus* (Peters) Regan. J. Genet. 8:147–53.

SCHMIDT, J. 1920. Racial investigations. IV. The genetic behavior of a secondary sexual character. Compt. Rend. Trav. Lab. Carlsberg 14:1–12.

SCHMIDT-NIELSON, K. 1984. Scaling: Why Is Animal Size So Important? Cambridge Univ. Press, Cambridge, England.

SCHOENHERR, A. A. 1974. Life history of the topminnow *Poeciliopsis occidentalis* (Baird and Girard) in Arizona and an analysis of its interaction with the mosquitofish *Gambusia affinis* (Baird and Girard). Ph.D. Dissertation, Arizona State Univ., Tempe, AZ, USA.

SCHOENHERR, A. A. 1977. Density dependent and density independent regulation of reproduction in the Gila topminnow, *Poeciliopsis occidentalis* (Baird and Girard). Ecology 58:438–44.

SCHOENHERR, A. A. 1981. The role of competition in the displacement of native fishes by introduced species. Pp. 173–203 *In*: R. J. Naiman and D. L. Soltz (eds.), Fishes in North American Deserts. Wiley Interscience, New York, NY, USA.

SCHONEWALD-COX, C. M., S. M. CHAMBERS, B. MACBRYDE AND L. THOMAS (eds.). 1983. Genetics and Conservation. Benjamin/Cummings Publ., Menlo Park, CA, USA.

SCHREIBMAN, M. P. AND K. D. KALLMAN. 1977. The genetic control of the pituitary-gonadal axis in the platyfish. *Xiphophorus maculatus*. J. Exp. Zool. 200:277–94.

SCHRÖDER, J. H. 1964. Genetische Untersuchungen an domestizierten Stammen der Gattung *Mollienesia* (Poeciliidae). Zool. Beitraege 10:369–463.

SCHRÖDER, J. H. 1965. Zur Vererbung der Dorsalflossenstrahlenzahl bei *Mollienesia*-Bastarden. Z. Zool. Syst. Evolutionsforsch. 3:330–48.

SCHRÖDER, J. H. 1966. Über Besonderheiten der Vererbung des Simpsonfaktors bei *Xiphophorus helleri* Heckel (Poeciliidae, Pisces). Zool. Beitraege 12:27–42.

SCHRÖDER, J. H. 1969. Erblicher Pigment-verlust bei Fischen. Aquar. Terrar. 16:272–74.

SCHRÖDER, J. H. 1974. Vererbungslehre fur Aquarianer. W. Keller & Co., Stuttgart, Germany.

SCHRÖDER, J. H. 1976. Genetics for Aquarists. T. F. H. Publ., Neptune, NJ, USA.

SCHRÖDER, J. H. 1983. The guppy (*Poecilia reticulata* Peters) as a model for evolutionary studies in genetics, behavior and ecology. Ber. Naturwiss.-Med. Ver. Innsbruck 70:249–79.

SCHULTZ, M. E. AND R. J. SCHULTZ. 1988. Differences in response to a chemical carcinogen within species and clones of the livebearing fish, *Poeciliopsis*. Carcinogenesis 9:1029–32.

SCHULTZ, R. J. 1961. Reproductive mechanisms of unisexual and bisexual strains of the viviparous fish *Poeciliopsis*. Evolution 15:302–25.

SCHULTZ, R. J. 1963. Stubby, a hereditary vertebral deformity in the viviparous fish *Poeciliopsis prolifica*. Copeia 1963:325–30.

SCHULTZ, R. J. 1966. Hybridization experiments with an all-female fish of the genus *Poeciliopsis*. Biol. Bull. 130:415–29.

SCHULTZ, R. J. 1967. Gynogenesis and triploidy in the viviparous fish *Poeciliopsis*. Science 157:1564–67.

SCHULTZ, R. J. 1969. Hybridization, unisexuality and polyploidy in the teleost *Poeciliopsis* (Poeciliidae) and other vertebrates. Amer. Natur. 103:613–19.

SCHULTZ, R. J. 1971. Special adaptive problems associated with unisexual fishes. Amer. Zool. 11:351–60.

SCHULTZ, R. J. 1973a. Unisexual fish: laboratory synthesis of a "species." Science 179:180–81.

SCHULTZ, R. J. 1973b. Origin and synthesis of a unisexual fish. Pp. 207–11 *In*: J. H. Schröder (ed.), Genetics and Mutagenesis of Fish. Springer-Verlag, Berlin, Germany.

SCHULTZ, R. J. 1977. Evolution and ecology of unisexual fishes. Pp. 277–331 *In*: M. K. Hecht, W. C. Steere and B. Wallace (eds.), Evolutionary Biology, Vol. 10. Plenum Press, New York, NY, USA.

SCHULTZ, R. J. 1982. Competition and adaptation among diploid and polyploid clones of unisexual fishes. Pp. 103–19 *In*: H. Dingle and J. P. Hegmann (eds.), Evolution and Genetics of Life Histories. Springer-Verlag, Berlin, Germany.

SCHULTZ, R. J. AND E. FIELDING. 1989. Fixed genotypes in variable environments. *In*: R. M. Dawley and J. P. Bogart (eds.), The Evolution and Ecology of Unisexual Vertebrates. State Univ. NY Press, Albany, NY, USA. (in press).

SCHULTZ, R. J. AND K. D. KALLMAN. 1968. Triploid hybrids between the all-female teleost *Poecilia formosa* and *Poecilia sphenops*. Nature 219:280–82.

SCHULTZ, R. J. AND R. R. MILLER 1971. Species of the *Poecilia sphenops* complex (Pisces: Poeciliidae) in Mexico. Copeia 1971:282–90.

SCHWAB, M., J. HAS, S. ABDO, M. R. AHUJA, G. KOLLINGER, A. ANDERS, AND F. ANDERS. 1978. Genetic basis of susceptibility for development of neoplasms following treatment with N-methyl-N-nitrosourea (MNU) or X-rays in the platyfish/swordtail system. Experientia 34:780–82.

SCOTT, D. B. AND C. E. CURRIE. 1980. Social hierarchy in relation to adrenocortical activity in *Xiphophorus helleri* Heckel. J. Fish Biol. 16:265–77.

SCRIMSHAW, N. S. 1944a. Embryonic growth in the viviparous poeciliid, *Heterandria formosa*. Biol. Bull. 87:37–51.

SCRIMSHAW, N. S. 1944b. Superfetation in poeciliid fishes. Copeia 1944:180–83.

SCRIMSHAW, N. S. 1945. Embryonic development in poeciliid fishes. Biol. Bull. 88:233–46.

SCRIMSHAW, N. S. 1946. Egg size in poeciliid fishes. Copeia 1946:20–23.

SEAL, W. P. 1911. Breeding habits of the viviparous fishes *Gambusia holbrookii* and *Heterandria formosa*. Proc. Biol. Soc. Washington 24:91–96.

SEALE, A. 1917. The mosquito fish, *Gambusia affinis* (Baird and Girard) in the Phillippine Islands. Phillippine J. Sci. 12(D):177–87.

SEGHERS, B. H. 1974a. Geographic variation in the responses of guppies (*Poecilia reticulata*) to aerial predators. Oecologia 14:93–98.

SEGHERS, B. H. 1974b. Schooling behavior in the guppy (*Poecilia reticulata*): an evolutionary response to predation. Evolution 28:486–89.

SHAKUNTALA, K. AND P. REDDY. 1977. Influence of body weight/age on the food intake, growth and conversion efficiency of *Gambusia affinis*. Hydrobiologia 55:65–69.

SHAKUNTALA, K. AND R. REDDY. 1979. Influence of temperature-salinity combinations on the food intake, growth and conversion efficiency of *Gambusia affinis* (Pisces). Polish Arch. Hydrobiol. 26:173–81.

SHAPOVALOV, L., A. J. CORDONE, AND W. A. DILL. 1981. A list of the freshwater and anadromous fishes of California. Calif. Fish & Game 61:4–38.

SHARMA, K. P. AND N. K. AL-DAHAM. 1979. Comparative studies on the efficiency of *Aphanius dispar* (Ruppell) and *Gambusia affinis* (Baird and Girard) in mosquito control. Comp. Physiol. Ecol. 4:106–9.

SHEINBAUM, S. 1979. Reproductive cycles, sex ratios, brood sizes, and adult sizes of estuarine and freshwater populations of the sailfin molly, *Poecilia latipinna* (LeSueur), in the Tampa Bay area. M. S. Thesis, Univ. South Florida, Tampa, FL, USA.

SHIEL, R. J. 1980. Billabongs of the Murray-Darling system. Pp. 376–90 *In*: W. D. Williams (ed.), An Ecological Basis for Water Resources Management. Aust. Nat. Univ. Press, Canberra, Australia.

SHOEMAKER, H. H. 1944. A laboratory study of fish popultions. Trans. Amer. Fish. Soc. 74:350–59.

SICILIANO, M. J. 1970. Melanosis and sex determination in xiphophorin fishes. Ph.D. Dissertation, New York Univ., New York, NY, USA.

SICILIANO, M. J. 1972. Evidence for a spontaneous ovarian cycle in fish of the genus *Xiphophorus*. Biol. Bull. 142:480–88.

SICILIANO, M. J. AND C. R. SHAW. 1976. Separation and visualization of enzymes on gels. Pp. 185–209 *In*: I. Smith (ed.), Chromatographic and Electrophoretic Techniques, Vol. 2. Wm. Heineman, London, England.

SIGLER, W. F. AND R. R. MILLER. 1963. Fishes of Utah. Utah Dept. Fish & Game, Salt Lake City, UT, USA.

SILLIMAN, R. P. 1948. Factors affecting population levels in *Lebistes reticulatus*. Copeia 1948:40–47.

SILLIMAN, R. P. 1968. Interaction of food level and exploitation in experimental fish populations. Fishery Bull. 66:425–39.

SIMANEK, D. E. 1978a. Genetic variability and population structure of *Poecilia latipinna*. Nature 276:612–14.

SIMANEK, D. E. 1978b. Population genetics and evolution in the *Poecilia formosa* complex (Pisces: Poeciliidae). Ph.D. Dissertation, Yale Univ., New Haven, CT, USA.

SIMONS, L. H. 1987. Status of the endangered Gila topminnow, *Poeciliopsis occidentalis*, in the United States in 1987. Rept. to US Fish & Wildl. Serv., Albuquerque, NM, USA.

SIMPSON, J. C. AND R. L. WALLACE. 1978. Fishes of Idaho. Idaho Univ. Press, Moscow, ID, USA.

SLATKIN, M. 1981. Estimating levels of gene flow in natural populations. Genetics 99:323–35.

SLATKIN, M. 1985. Gene flow in natural populations. Ann. Rev. Ecol. Syst. 16:393–430.

SMITH, M. H. AND R. K. CHESSER. 1981. Rationale for conserving genetic variation of fish gene pools. Ecol. Bull. (Stockholm) 34:13–20.

SMITH, M. W., M. H. SMITH, AND R. K. CHESSER. 1983. Biochemical genetics of mosquito-fish. I. Environmental correlates, and temporal and spatial heterogeneity of allele frequencies within a river drainage. Copeia 1983:182–93.

SMITH, P. J. AND Y. FUJIO. 1982. Genetic variation in marine teleosts: high variability in habitat specialists and low variability in habitat generalists. Mar. Biol. 69:7–20.

SMITH, R. B. 1986. The effect of food on reproduction in the sailfin molly, *Poecilia latipinna* (Poeciliidae). M. S. Thesis, Univ. Central Florida, Orlando, FL, USA.

SMITH, R. E. 1988. Variation in female somatic condition and its relationship to reproduction in the sailfin molly, *Poecilia latipinna* (Pisces: Poeciliidae). M. S. Thesis, Univ. Central Florida, Orlando, FL, USA.

SMOAK. C. H., JR., 1959. Some considerations in upper thermal tolerance on *Gambusia affinis holbrooki* (Girard) in the Savannah River Plant area. Bull. S. Carolina Acad. Sci. 34:44–53.

SNELSON, F. F., JR. 1980. A continuation of base-line studies for environmentally monitoring space transportation systems (STS) at John F. Kennedy Space Center. Ichthyological studies: Sailfin molly reproduction study. KSC TR 51–2, Vol. III, Part 2. NASA, J. F. Kennedy Space Center, FL, USA.

SNELSON, F. F., JR. 1982. Indeterminate growth in males of the sailfin molly, *Poecilia latipinna*. Copeia 1982:296–304.

SNELSON, F. F., JR. 1984. Seasonal maturation and growth of males in a natural population of *Poecilia latipinna*. Copeia 1984:252–55.

SNELSON, F. F., JR. 1985. Size and morphological variation in males of the sailfin molly, *Poecilia latipinna*. Envir. Biol. Fish. 13:35–47.

SNELSON, F. F., JR. AND J. D. WETHERINGTON. 1980. Sex ratio in the sailfin molly, *Poecilia latipinna*. Evolution 34:308–19.

SNELSON, F. F., JR., R. E. SMITH, AND M. R. BOLT. 1986a. A melanistic female mosquitofish, *Gambusia affinis holbrooki*. Amer. Midl. Natur. 115:413–15.

SNELSON, F. F., JR., J. D. WETHERINGTON, AND H. L. LARGE. 1986b. The relationship between interbrood interval and yolk loading in a generalized poeciliid fish, *Poecilia latipinna*. Copeia 1986:295–304.

SOHN, J. J. 1977a. Socially induced inhibition of genetically determined maturation in the platyfish, *Xiphophorus maculatus*. Science 195:199–201.

SOHN, J. J. 1977b. The consequences of predation and competition upon the demography of *Gambusia manni* (Pisces: Poeciliidae). Copeia 1977:224–27.

SOKAL, R. R. AND N. L. ODEN. 1978a. Spatial autocorrelation in biology. I. Methodology. Biol. J. Linn. Soc. 10:199–228.

SOKAL, R. R. AND N. L. ODEN. 1978b. Spatial autocorrelation in biology. II. Some biological implications and four applications of evolutionary and ecological interest. Biol. J. Linn. Soc. 10:229–49.

SOKAL, R. R. AND D. E. WARTENBERG. 1983. A test of spatial autocorrelation analysis using an isolation-by-distance model. Genetics 105:219–37.

SOKOLOV, N. P. AND M. A. CHVALIOVA. 1936. Nutrition of *Gambusia affinis* on the rice fields of Turkestan. J. Anim. Ecol. 5:390–95.

SOULÉ, M. E. 1973. The epistasis cycle: a theory of marginal populations. Annu. Rev. Ecol. Syst. 4:165–88.

SOULÉ, M. E. 1976. Allozyme variation: its determinants in space and time. Pp. 60–77 *In*: F. J. Ayala (ed.), Molecular Evolution. Sinauer Assoc., Sunderland, MA, USA.

SOULÉ, M. E. (ED.). 1986. Conservation Biology. The Science of Scarcity and Diversity. Sinauer Assoc., Sunderland, MA, USA.

SOULÉ, M. E. (ED.). 1987. Viable Populations for Conservation. Cambridge Univ. Press, Cambridge, England.

SOULÉ, M. E. AND B. A. WILCOX (EDS.). 1980. Conservation Biology: An Evolutionary-Ecological Perspective. Sinauer Assoc., Sunderland, MA, USA.

SPINELLA, D. G. AND R. C. VRIJENHOEK. 1982. Genetic dissection of clonally inherited genomes of *Poeciliopsis*: II. Investigation of a silent carboxylesterase allele. Genetics 100:279–86.

SPURWAY, H. 1957. Hermaphroditism with self-fertilization and the monthly extrusion of unfertilized eggs in the viviparous fish *Lebistes reticulatus*. Nature 180:1248–51.

SREENIVASAN, A. AND M. V. NATARAJAN. 1962. Use of endrin in fishery management. Prog. Fish-Cult. 24:181.

ST. AMANT, J. A. AND F. G. HOOVER. 1969. Addition of *Misgurnus anguillicaudatus* (Cantor) to the California fauna. Calif. Fish & Game 55:330–31.

ST. AMANT, J. A. AND I. SHARP. 1971. Addition of *Xiphophorus variatus* (Meek) to the California fauna. Calif. Fish & Game 57:128–29.

STACEY, N. E. 1981. Hormonal regulation of female reproductive behavior in fish. Amer. Zool. 21:305–16.

STEARNS, S. C. 1976. Life-history tactics: a review of the ideas. Quart. Rev. Biol. 51:3–47.

STEARNS, S. C. 1978. Interpopulational differences in reproductive traits of *Neoheterandria tridentiger* (Pisces: Poeciliidae) in Panama. Copeia 1978:88–91.

STEARNS, S. C. 1983a. The evolution of life-history traits in mosquitofish since their introduction to Hawaii in 1905: rates of evolution, heritabilities, and developmental plasticity. Amer. Zool. 23:65–75.

STEARNS, S. C. 1983b. A natural experiment in life-history evolution: field data on the introduction of mosquitofish (*Gambusia affinis*) to Hawaii. Evolution 37:601–17.

STEARNS, S. C. 1983c. The genetic basis of differences in life-history traits among six populations of mosquitofish (*Gambusia affinis*) that shared ancestors in 1905. Evolution 37:618–27.

STEARNS, S. C. 1983d. The influence of size and phylogeny on patterns of covariation among life-history traits in the mammals. Oikos 41:173–87.

STEARNS, S. C. 1984a. Heritability estimates for age and length at maturity in two populations of mosquitofish that shared ancestors in 1905. Evolution 38:368–75.

STEARNS, S. C. 1984b. The effects of size and phylogeny on patterns of covariation in the life history traits of lizards and snakes. Amer. Natur. 123:56–72.

STEARNS, S. C. AND R. E. CRANDALL. 1984. Plasticity for age and size at sexual maturity: a life-history response to unavoidable stress. Pp. 13–33 In: G. Potts and R. J. Wootten (eds.), Fish Reproduction. Academic Press, London, England.

STEARNS, S. C. AND J. C. KOELLA. 1986. The evolution of phenotypic plasticity in life-history traits: predictions of reaction norms for age and size at maturity. Evolution 40:893–913.

STEARNS, S. C. AND R. D. SAGE. 1980. Maladaptation in a marginal population of the mosquitofish *Gambusia affinis*. Evolution 34:65–75.

STEINDACHNER, F. 1863. Beiträge zur Kenntniss der Sciaenoiden Brasiliens und der Cyprinodonten Mejicos. Sitzber. K. Acad. Wiss. Wien, Math. Nat. Cl. 48(1):162–85.

STEINDACHNER, F. 1878. Ichthyologische Beiträge (VI). Sitzber. K. Akad. Wiss. Wien. Math. Nat. Cl. 77(1):379–92.

STEINDACHNER, F. 1880. Zur Fische-Fauna des Cauca und der Flüsse bein Guayaquil. Denkschr. K. Akad. Wiss. Wien 42(1):55–103.

STENSETH, N. C., L. R. KIRKENDALL AND N. MORAN. 1985. On the evolution of pseudogamy. Evolution 39:294–307.

STEPANEK, O. 1928. Morfologie a biologie genitalnich organu au *Lebistes reticulatus* Ptrs. (Cyprinodontidae viviparae). Publ. Fac. Sci. Univ. Charles 79:1–30.

STEPHANIDES, T. 1964. The influence of the anti-mosquitofish, *Gambusia affinis*, on the natural fauna of Corfu lakelet. Praktika Hell. Hydrobiol. Inst. 9:3–5.

STEVENSON, M. M. AND A. E. PEDEN. 1973. Description and ecology of *Hyallela texana* n. sp. (Crustacea, Amphipoda) from the Edwards Plateau of Texas. Amer. Midl. Natur. 89:426–36.

STOLK, A. 1951. Histo-endocrinological analysis of gestation phenomena in the cyprinodont *Lebistes reticulatus* Peters. IV. The oocyte-cycle during pregnancy. Proc. K. Ned. Akad. Wet., Ser. C, 54:574–78.

STOYE, F. H. 1935. Tropical fishes for the home. Carl Mertens, New York.

STRÖMMEN, C., E. M. RASCH, AND J. S. BALSANO. 1975a. Cytogenetic studies of *Poecilia* (Pisces). IV. Epithelial cell biopsies to identify triploid females associated with *Poecilia formosa*. Copeia 1975:568–72.

STRÖMMEN, C., E. M. RASCH, AND J. S. BALSANO. 1975b. Cytogenetic studies of *Poecilia* (Pisces). V. Cytophotometric evidence for the production of fertile offspring by triploids related to *Poecilia formosa*. J. Fish Biol. 7:667–76.

SUHR, J. M. AND J. D. DAVIS. 1974 The spider *Dolomedes sexpunctatus* as a predator on mosquitofish, *Gambusia affinis*, in Mississippi. Assoc. Southeast. Biol. Bull. 21:87.

SULLIVAN, J. A. AND R. J. SCHULTZ. 1986. Genetic and environmental basis of variable sex ratios in laboratory strains of *Poeciliopsis lucida*. Evolution 40:152–58.

SULTAN, S. E. 1987. Evolutionary implications of phenotypic plasticity in plants. Pp. 127–78 *In*: M. K. Hecht, B. Wallace and G. T. Prance, (eds.), Evolutionary Biology, Vol. 21. Plenum Press, New York, NY, USA.

SUTHERLAND, W. J. 1985. Chance can produce a sex difference in variance in mating success and explain Bateman's data. Anim. Behav. 33:1349–52.

SVÄRDSON, G. 1945. Polygenic inheritance in *Lebistes*. Arkiv Zool. 36A:1–9.

SWIFT, C. C., R. W. YERGER, AND P. R. PARRISH. 1977. Distribution and natural history of the fresh and brackish water fishes of the Ochlocknee River, Florida and Georgia. Bull. Tall Timbers Res. Stn. 20:1–111.

SWOFFORD, D. L. 1981. On the utility of the distance Wagner procedure. Pp. 25–43 *In*: V. A. Funk and D. R. Brooks (eds.), Advances in Cladistics. New York Botanical Garden, Bronx, NY, USA.

SWOFFORD, D. L. AND R. B. SELANDER. 1981. BIOSYS-1: A FORTRAN program for comprehensive analysis of electrophoretic data in population genetics and systematics. J. Heredity 72:281–82.

TAVE, D. 1984. Genetics of dorsal fin ray number in the guppy, *Poecilia reticulata*. Copeia 1984:140–44.

TAVOLGA, W. N. 1949. Embryonic development of the platyfish (*Platypoecilus*), the swordtail (*Xiphophorus*), and their hybrids. Bull. Amer. Mus. Natur. Hist. 94:161–230.

TAVOLGA, W. N. AND R. RUGH. 1947. Development of the platyfish, *Platypoecilus maculatus*. Zoologica 32:1–15.

TAYLOR, J. N., W. R. COURTENAY, JR., AND J. A. McCANN. 1984. Known impacts of exotic fishes in the continental United States. Pp. 132–73 *In*: W. R. Courtenay, Jr. and J. R. Stauffer, Jr. (eds.), Distribution, Biology and Management of Exotic Fishes. Johns Hopkins Univ. Press, Baltimore, MD, USA.

TEMPLETON, A. R. AND E. D. ROTHMAN. 1974. Evolution in heterogeneous environments. Amer. Natur. 108:409–28.

TEMPLETON, A. R. AND E. D. ROTHMAN. 1978a. Evolution and fine-grained environmental runs. Pp. 131–83 *In*: C. Hooker, J. J. Leach, and E. F. McClennan (eds.), Foundations and Applications of Decision Theory, Vol. II, Reidel Publ., Dordrecht, Netherlands.

TEMPLETON, A. R. AND E. D. ROTHMAN. 1978b. Evolution in fine-grained environments. 1. Environmental runs and the evolution of homeostasis. Theor. Popul. Biol. 13:340–55.

THIBAULT, R. E. 1974a. The ecology of unisexual and bisexual fishes in the genus *Poeciliopsis*: a study of niche relationships. Ph.D. Dissertation, Univ. Connecticut, Storrs, CT, USA.

THIBAULT, R. E. 1974b. Genetics of cannibalism in a viviparous fish and its relationship to population density. Nature 251:138–39.

THIBAULT, R. E. AND R. J. SCHULTZ. 1978. Reproductive adaptations among viviparous fishes (Cyprinodontiformes: Poeciliidae). Evolution 32:320–33.

THIESSEN, D. D. AND S. K. STURDIVANT. 1977. Female pheromone in the black molly fish (*Mollienesia latipinna*): a possible metabolic correlate. J. Chem. Ecol. 3:207–17.

TINBERGEN, N. 1951. The Study of Instinct. Clarendon Press, Oxford, England.

TINKLE, D. W. AND R. K. SELANDER. 1973. Age-dependent allozyme variation in a natural population of lizards. Biochem. Genet. 8:231–37.

TOMASOV, J. F. 1981. Studies on an introduced species: the mosquitofish—*Gambusia affinis*. B.S. Honours Thesis, La Trobe Univ., Victoria, Australia.

TRAVIS, J. AND L. D. MUELLER. 1988. Blending ecology and genetics: progress toward a unified population biology. Pp. 101–124 *In*: J. Roughgarden, R. M. May, and S. A. Levin (eds.), Perspectives in Ecological Theory. Princeton Univ. Press, Princeton, NJ, USA.

TRAVIS, J. AND J. C. TREXLER. 1987. Regional variation in habitat requirements of the sailfin molly, with special reference to the Florida Keys. Nongame Wildl. Tech. Rept. No. 3, Florida Game & Fresh Water Fish Comm., Tallahassee, FL, USA.

TRAVIS, J. AND B. D. WOODWARD. 1989. Social context and courtship flexibility in male sailfin mollies, *Poecilia latipinna* (Pisces, Poeciliidae). Anim. Behav., in press.

TRAVIS, J., S. EMERSON, AND M. BLOUIN. 1987a. A quantitative genetic analysis of larval life history traits in *Hyla crucifer*. Evolution 41:145–56.

TRAVIS, J., J. A. FARR, AND J. C. TREXLER. 1989a. Body-size variation in the sailfin molly, *Poecilia latipinna* (Pisces: Poeciliidae): II. Genetics of male behaviors and secondary sex characters. J. Evol. Biol., in press.

TRAVIS, J., J. C. TREXLER, AND J. A. FARR, 1989b. Body-size variation in the sailfin molly, *Poecilia latipinna* (Pisces: Poeciliidae): I. Sex-limited genetic variation for size and age of maturation. J. Evol. Biol., in press.

TRAVIS, J., J. A. FARR, S. HENRICH, AND R. T. CHEONG. 1987b. Testing theories of clutch overlap with the reproductive ecology of *Heterandria formosa*. Ecology 68:611–23.

TRAVIS, J., J. A. FARR, M. MCMANUS, AND J. C. TREXLER. 1989c. Environmental effects on adult growth in the male sailfin molly (*Poecilia latipinna*, Poeciliidae). Env. Biol. Fish., in press.

TRENDALL, J. T. 1983. Life history variation among experimental populations of the mosquitofish, *Gambusia affinis*. Copeia 1983:953–63.

TRENDALL, J. T. AND M. S. JOHNSON. 1981. Identification by anatomy and gel electrophoresis of *Phalloceros caudimaculatus* (Poeciliidae) previously mistaken for *Gambusia affinis holbrooki* (Poeciliidae). Aust. J. Mar. Freshwater Res. 32:993–96.

TREWAVAS, E. 1948. Cyprinodont fishes of San Domingo, Island of Haiti. Proc. Zool. Soc. London 118:408–15.

TREXLER, J. C. 1985. Variation in the degree of viviparity in the sailfin molly, *Poecilia latipinna*. Copeia 1985:999–1004.

TREXLER, J. C. 1986. Geographic variation in size in the sailfin molly, *Poecilia latipinna*. Ph.D. Dissertation, Florida State Univ., Tallahassee, FL, USA.

TREXLER, J. C. 1988. Hierarchical organization of genetic variation in the sailfin molly, *Poecilia latipinna* (Pisces, Poeciliidae). Evolution 42:1006–17.

TRINKAUS, J. P. AND J. W. DRAKE. 1952. Role of exogenous nutrients in development of the viviparous teleost, *Lebistes reticulatus*. Anat. Rec. 112:435.

TRIVERS, R. L. 1972. Parental investment and sexual selection. Pp. 136–79 *In*: B. G. Campbell (ed.), Sexual Selection and the Descent of Man, 1871–1971. Aldine Press, Chicago, IL, USA.

TRUST, T. J., A. G. KHOURI, R. A. AUSTIN, AND L. D. ASHBURNER. 1980. First isolation in Australia of atypical *Aeromonas salmonicida*. FEMS Microbiol. Lett. 9:39–42.

TSUKUDA, H. 1960. Heat and cold tolerances in relation to body size in the guppy, *Lebistes reticulatus*. J. Inst. Polytechnics, Osaka City Univ. (Japan) 11(D):55–62.

TURELLI, M. 1985. Effects of pleiotropy on predictions concerning mutation-selection balance for polygenic traits. Genetics 111:165–95.

TURNER, B. J. 1974. Genetic divergence of Death Valley pupfish species: biochemical versus morphological evidence. Evolution 28:281–94.

TURNER, B. J. 1982. The evolutionary genetics of a unisexual fish, *Poecilia formosa*. Pp. 265–305 *In*: C. Barigozzi (ed.), Mechanisms of Speciation. Alan R. Liss, New York, NY, USA.

TURNER, B. J., B. L. H. BRETT, AND R. R. MILLER. 1980a. Interspecific hybridization and the evolutionary origin of a gynogenetic fish, *Poecilia formosa*. Evolution 34:917–22.

TURNER, B. J., J. S. BALSANO, P. J. MONACO, AND E. M. RASCH. 1983. Clonal diversity and evolutionary dynamics in a diploid-triploid breeding complex of unisexual fishes (*Poecilia*). Evolution 37:798–809.

TURNER, B. J., B. L. H. BRETT, E. M. RASCH, AND J. S. BALSANO. 1980b. Evolutionary genetics of a gynogenetic fish, *Poecilia formosa*, the Amazon molly. Evolution 34:246–58.

TURNER, C. L. 1937. Reproductive cycles and superfetation in poeciliid fishes. Biol. Bull. 72:145–64.

TURNER, C. L. 1938. The reproductive cycle of *Brachyraphis episcopi*, an oviparous poeciliid fish, in the natural tropical habitat. Biol. Bull. 75:56–65.

TURNER, C. L. 1939. The pseudo-amnion, pseudo-chorion, pseudo-placenta and other foetal structures in viviparous cyprinodont fishes. Science 90:42–43.

TURNER, C. L. 1940a. Pseudoamnion, pseudochorion, and follicular pseudoplacenta in poeciliid fishes. J. Morphology 67:59–89.

TURNER, C. L. 1940b. Superfetation in viviparous cyprinodont fishes. Copeia 1940:88–91.

TURNER, C. L. 1941. Morphogenesis of the gonopodium in *Gambusia affinis affinis*. J. Morphology 69:161–85.

TURNER, C. L. 1947. Viviparity in teleost fishes. Sci. Monthly 65:508–18.

TURNER, J. S. AND F. F. SNELSON, JR. 1984. Population structure, reproduction and laboratory behavior of the introduced *Belonesox belizanus* (Poeciliidae) in Florida. Env. Biol. Fish. 10:89–100.

US FISH & WILDL. SERV. 1982. Clear Creek Gambusia Recovery Plan. US Fish & Wildl. Serv., Albuquerque, NM, USA.

US FISH & WILDL. SERV. 1983. Pecos Gambusia Recovery Plan. US Fish & Wildl. Serv., Albuquerque, NM, USA.

US FISH & WILDL. SERV. 1984a. San Marcos Recovery Plan. US Fish & Wildl. Serv., Albuquerque, NM, USA.

US FISH & WILDL. SERV. 1984b. Big Bend Gambusia Recovery Plan. US Fish & Wildl. Serv., Albuquerque, NM, USA.

US FISH & WILDL. SERV. 1984c. Sonoran Topminnow (Gila and Yaqui) Recovery Plan. US Fish & Wildl. Serv., Albuquerque, NM, USA.

US FISH & WILDL. SERV. 1987. Endangered and threatened wildlife and plants: proposed delisting of the Amistad gambusia. Federal Register 52(4):7462–63.

VALENTI, R. J. 1972. A qualitative and quantitative study of red and yellow pigmentary polymorphism in *Xiphophorus*. Ph.D. Dissertation, New York Univ., New York, NY, USA.

VALENTI, R. J. AND K. D. KALLMAN. 1973. Effects of gene dosage and hormones on the expression of *Dr* in the platyfish, *Xiphophorus maculatus* (Poeciliidae). Genet. Res. 22:79–89.

VALLOWE, H. H. 1953. Some physiological aspects of reproduction in *Xiphophorus maculatus*. Biol. Bull. 104:240–49.

VAN OORDT, G. J. 1928. The duration of the life of the spermatozoa in the fertilized female of *Xiphophorus helleri* Regan. Tijdschrift Nederlandsche Dierkundige Vereniging 1/2:77–80.

VANELLI, M. L., G. ROCHETTA, AND C. PANCALDI. 1984. Genetic control of body length at different ages in *Poecilia reticulata*. J. Heredity 75:27–30.

VAUPEL, J. 1929. The spermatogenesis of *Lebistes reticulatus* (Peters). J. Morphology 47:555–87.

VIA, S. 1984. The quantitative genetics of polyphagy in an insect herbivore. I. Genotype-environment interaction in larval performance on different host plant species. Evolution 38:881–95.

VIA, S. AND R. LANDE. 1985. Genotype-environment interaction and the evolution of phenotypic plasticity. Evolution 39:505–22.

VIELKIND, J. AND U. VIELKIND. 1982. Melanoma formation in fish of the genus *Xiphophorus*: a genetically-based disorder in the determination and differentiation of a specific pigment cell. Can. J. Genet. Cytol. 24:133–49.

VIELKIND, U. 1976. Genetic control of cell differentiation in platyfish-swordtail melanomas. J. Exp. Zool. 196:197–204.

VINCENT, W. F. AND D. J. FORSYTH. 1987. Geothermally influenced waters. Pp. 349–77 *In*: A. B. Viner (ed.), Inland Waters of New Zealand. Science Information Publ. Centre, Dept. Sci. and Indust. Res., Wellington, New Zealand.

VITT, L. J. AND R. A. SEIGEL. 1985. Life history traits of lizards and snakes. Amer. Natur. 125:480–84.

VONDRACEK, B., W. A. WURTSBAUGH, AND J. J. CECH, JR. 1980. Mass marking of mosquitofish: preliminary results. Proc. Pap. Annu. Conf. California Mosq. Vector Control Assoc. 48:42–44.

VONDRACEK, B., W. A. WURTSBAUGH, AND J. J. CECH, JR. 1988. Growth and reproduction of the mosquitofish, *Gambusia affinis*, in relation to temperature and ration level: consequences for life history. Env. Biol. Fish. 21:45–57.

VON IHERING, R. 1930. Notas ecologicas referentes a peixes d'agua dulce doce do Estado de S. Paulo e descripción de 4 especies novas. Arch. Inst. Biol. (Sao Paulo) 3:93–104.

VOOREN, C. M. 1972. Ecological aspects of the introduction of fish species into natural habitats in Europe, with special reference to the Netherlands. J. Fish Biol. 4:565–83.

VRIJENHOEK, R. C. 1972. Genetic relationships of unisexual hybrid fishes to their progenitors using lactate dehydrogenase isozymes as gene markers (*Poeciliopsis*, Poeciliidae). Amer. Natur. 106:754–66.

VRIJENHOEK, R. C. 1976. An allele affecting display coloration in the fish, *Poeciliopsis viriosa*. J. Heredity 67:324–25.

VRIJENHOEK, R. C. 1978. Coexistence of clones in a heterogeneous environment. Science 199:549–52.

VRIJENHOEK, R. C. 1979a. Factors affecting clonal diversity and coexistence. Amer. Zool. 19:787–97.

VRIJENHOEK, R. C. 1979b. Genetics of a sexually reproducing fish in a highly fluctuating environment. Amer. Natur. 113:17–29.

VRIJENHOEK, R. C. 1984a. Ecological differentiation among clones: the frozen niche variation model. Pp. 217–31 *In*: K. Wohrmann and V. Loeschke (eds.), Population Biology and Evolution. Springer-Verlag, Berlin, Germany.

VRIJENHOEK, R. C. 1984b. The evolution of clonal diversity in *Poeciliopsis*. Pp. 399–429 *In*: B. J. Turner (ed.), Evolutionary Genetics of Fishes. Plenum Press, New York, NY, USA.

VRIJENHOEK, R. C. 1985. Animal population genetics and disturbance: the effects of local extinctions and recolonizations on heterozygosity and fitness. Pp. 266–85 *In*: S. T. A. Pickett and P. S. White (eds.), The Ecology of Natural Disturbance and Patch Dynamics. Academic Press, New York, NY, USA.

VRIJENHOEK, R. C. 1989. Genetic and ecological constraints on the origins and establishment of unisexual vertebrates. *In*: R. M. Dawley and J. P. Bogart (eds.), The Ecology and Evolution of Unisexual Vertebrates. State Univ. NY Press, Albany, NY, USA. (in press).

VRIJENHOEK, R. C. AND S. LERMAN. 1982. Heterozygosity and developmental stability under sexual and asexual breeding systems. Evolution 36:768–76.

VRIJENHOEK, R. C. AND R. J. SCHULTZ. 1974. Evolution of a trihybrid unisexual fish (*Poeciliopsis*, Poeciliidae). Evolution 28:306–19.

VRIJENHOEK, R. C., R. A. ANGUS, AND R. J. SCHULTZ. 1977. Variation and heterozygosity in sexually vs. clonally reproducing populations. Evolution 31:767–81.

VRIJENHOEK, R. C., R. A. ANGUS, AND R. J. SCHULTZ. 1978. Variation and clonal structure in a unisexual fish. Amer. Natur. 112:41–55.

VRIJENHOEK, R. C., M. E. DOUGLAS, AND G. K. MEFFE. 1985. Conservation genetics of endangered fish populations in Arizona. Science 229:400–402.

VRIJENHOEK, R. C., G. MARTEINSDOTTIR, AND R. SCHENCK. 1987. Genotypic and phenotypic aspects of niche diversification in fishes. Pp. 245–50 *In*: W. J. Mathews and D. C. Heins (eds.), Community and Evolutionary Ecology of North American Stream Fishes. Univ. Oklahoma Press, Norman, OK, USA.

WALLACE, B. 1981. Basic Population Genetics. Columbia Univ. Press, New York, NY, USA.

WALTERS, L. L. AND E. F. LEGNER. 1980. Impact of the desert pupfish, *Cyprinodon macularius*, and *Gambusia affinis affinis* on fauna in pond ecosystems. Hilgardia 48:1–18.

WARBURTON, B., C. HUBBS, AND D. W. HAGEN. 1957. Reproductive behavior of *Gambusia heterochir*. Copeia 1957:299–300.

WARREN, E. W. 1973a. The establishment of a 'normal' population and its behavioural maintenance in the guppy, *Poecilia reticulata* (Peters). J. Fish. Biol. 5:285–304.

WARREN, E. W. 1973b. Modification of the response to high density conditions in the guppy, *Poecilia reticulata* (Peters). J. Fish. Biol. 5:737–52.

WARREN, E. W. 1973c. The effects of relative density upon some aspects of the behaviour of the guppy, *Poecilia reticulata* (Peters). J. Fish. Biol. 5:753–65.

WEBER, J. M. AND D. L. KRAMER. 1983. Effects of hypoxia and surface access on growth, mortality, and behavior of juvenile guppies, *Poecilia reticulata*. Can. J. Fish. Aquat. Sci. 40:1583–88.

WEISEL, G. F. 1967. Early ossification in the skeleton of the sucker (*Catostomus macrocheilus*) and the guppy (*Poecilia reticulata*). J. Morphology 121:1–18.

WEISHAUPT, E. 1925. Die ontogenie der genitalorgane von *Girardinus reticulatus*. Z. Wiss. Zool., Abt. A, 126:571–611.

WEITZMAN, S. H. AND M. WEITZMAN. 1982. Biogeography and evolutionary diversification in neotropical freshwater fishes. Pp. 403–22 *In*: G. T. Prance (ed.), Biological Diversification in the Tropics. Columbia Univ. Press, New York, NY, USA.

WELCOMME, R. L. 1981. Register of international transfers of inland fish species. FAO Fish. Tech. Pap. 213:1–120.

WETHERINGTON, J. D. 1982. The influence of somatic investment on the pattern of reproduction in *Poecilia latipinna* (Pisces: Poeciliidae). M. S. Thesis, Univ. Central Florida, Orlando, FL, USA.

WETHERINGTON, J. D. 1988. Genotypic variation among synthetic hemiclones of *Poeciliopsis*. Ph.D. Dissertation, Rutgers Univ., New Brunswick, NJ, USA.

WETHERINGTON, J. D., K. E. KOTORA, AND R. C. VRIJENHOEK. 1987. A test of the spontaneous heterosis hypothesis for unisexual vertebrates. Evolution 41:721–31.

WETHERINGTON, J. D., S. C. WEEKS, K. E. KOTORA, AND R. C. VRIJENHOEK. 1989. Genotypic variation among synthetic hemiclones of *Poeciliopsis*: size at birth and juvenile growth rate. Evolution, in review.

WETZEL, R. L. 1971. Analysis of cohabitation by *Gambusia affinis* and *Poecilia latipinna* (Pisces: Poeciliidae) in a salt-marsh canal in Florida. M. S. Thesis, Univ. West Florida, Pensacola, FL, USA.

WHITE, M. J. D. 1973. Animal Cytology and Evolution. Cambridge Univ. Press, Cambridge, England.

WICKLER, W. 1957. Das Verhalten von *Xiphophorus maculatus* var. Wagtail und verwandten Arten. Z. Tierpsychol. 14:324–46.

WILDRICK, D. M., I. S. KIM, AND D. W. GREENFIELD. 1985. A unique gambusiine karyotype and its relevance to the systematics of the *Gambusia punctata* species group. Copeia 1985:1053–56.

WILLIAMS, G. C. 1966. Adaptation and Natural Selection. Princeton Univ. Press, Princeton, NJ, USA.

WILLIAMS, J. E. AND D. W. SADA. 1985. Status of two endangered fishes, *Cyprinodon nevadensis mionectes* and *Rhinichthys osculus nevadensis*, from two springs in Ash Meadows, Nevada. Southwest. Natur. 30:475–84.

WILLIAMS, J. E., C. D. WILLIAMS, AND C. E. BOND. 1980. Survey of fishes, amphibians, and reptiles on the Sheldon National Wildlife Refuge, Nevada. 1. Fishes of the Sheldon National Wildlife Refuge. Contrib. 14-16-0001-78025, US Fish & Wildl. Serv. Oregon St. Univ., Corvallis, OR, USA.

WILLIAMS, W. D. 1980. Australian Freshwater Life. Macmillan Publ. Co., Sydney, Australia.

WINGE, O. 1922a. One-sided masculine and sex-linked inheritance in *Lebistes reticulatus*. Compt. Rend. Trav. Lab. Carlsberg 18:1–20.

WINGE, O. 1922b. A peculiar mode of inheritance and its cytological explanation. J. Genet. 12:137–44.

WINGE, O. 1923. Crossing over between the X- and the Y-chromosome in *Lebistes*. Compt. Rend. Trav. Lab. Carlsberg 20:1–19.

WINGE, O. 1927. The location of eighteen genes in *Lebistes reticulatus*. J. Genet. 18:1–43.

WINGE, O. 1930. On the occurrence of XX males in *Lebistes* with some remarks on Aida's so-called "non-disjunctional" males in *Aplocheilus*. J. Genet. 23:69–76.

WINGE, O. 1934. The experimental alteration of sex chromosomes into autosomes and vice versa, as illustrated by *Lebistes*. Compt. Rend. Trav. Lab. Carlsberg 21:1–49.

WINGE, O. 1937. Succession of broods in *Lebistes*. Nature 140:467.

WINGE, O. AND E. DITLEVSEN. 1938. A lethal gene in the Y chromosome of *Lebistes*. Compt. Rend. Trav. Lab. Carlsberg 22:203–10.

WINGE, O. AND E. DITLEVSEN. 1947. Colour inheritance and sex determination in *Lebistes*. Heredity 1:65–83.

WINKLER, P. 1975. Thermal tolerance of *Gambusia affinis* (Teleostei: Poeciliidae) from a warm spring. I. Field tolerance under natural stream conditions. Physiol. Zool. 48:367–77.

WINKLER, P. 1979. Thermal preference of *Gambusia affinis affinis* as determined under field and laboratory conditions. Copeia 1979:60–64.

WOODHEAD, A. D. 1979. Senescence in fishes. Symp. Zool. Soc. London 44:179–205.

WOODHEAD, A. D. AND N. ARMSTRONG. 1985. Aspects of mating behaviour of male mollies (*Poecilia* spp.). J. Fish Biol. 27:593–601.

WOODHEAD, A. D. AND C. CARLSON. 1986. The role of female competition in the mating success of two clones of the Amazon molly, *Poecilia formosa*. J. Fish Biol. 29:227–32.

WOOLMAN, A. J. 1894. Report on a collection of fishes from the rivers of central and northern Mexico. Bull. US Fish Comm. 14:55–66.

WOOTEN, M. C., K. T. SCRIBNER, AND M. H. SMITH. 1988. Genetic variability and systematics of *Gambusia* in the southeastern United States. Copeia 1988:283–89.

WOOTTEN, R. J. 1979. Energy costs of egg production and environmental determinants of fecundity in teleost fishes. Symp. Zool. Soc. London 44:133–59.

WOURMS, J. P. 1981. Viviparity: the maternal-fetal relationship in fishes. Amer. Zool. 21:473–515.

WOURMS, J. P., B. D. GROVE, AND J. LOMBARDI. 1988. The maternal-embryonic relationship in viviparous fishes. Pp. 1–134 *In*: W. S. Hoar and D. J. Randall (eds.), Fish Physiology, Vol. 11B. Academic Press, New York, NY, USA.

WRIGHT, S. 1931. Evolution in Mendelian populations. Genetics 28:114–38.

WRIGHT, S. 1969. Evolution and the Genetics of Populations. II. The Theory of Gene Frequencies. Univ. Chicago Press, Chicago, IL, USA.

WRIGHT, S. 1970. Random drift and the shifting balance theory of evolution, pp. 1–31. *In* K. Kojima (ed.). Mathematical Topics in Population Genetics. Springer-Verlag, New York, NY, USA.

WRIGHT, S. 1978. Variability Within and Among Natural Populations. Evolution and the Genetics of Populations, Vol. 2, Univ. Chicago Press, Chicago, IL, USA.

WURTSBAUGH, W. A. AND J. J. CECH, JR. 1983. Growth and activity of juvenile mosquitofish: temperature and ration effects. Trans. Amer. Fish. Soc. 112:653–60.

WURTSBAUGH, W. A., J. J. CECH, JR., AND J. COMPTON. 1980. Effect of fish size on prey size selection in *Gambusia affinis*. Proc. Pap. Annu. Conf. Calif. Mosq. Vector Control Assoc. 48:48–51.

WYDOSKY, R. S. AND R. R. WHITNEY. 1979. Inland Fishes of Washington. Univ. Washington Press, Seattle, WA, USA.

YAMAGISHI, H. 1976a. Experimental study on population dynamics in the guppy, *Poecilia reticulata* (Peters). Effect of shelters on the increase of population density. J. Fish. Biol. 9:51–65.

YAMAGISHI, H. 1976b. Effects of shelters on population growth under high initial densities in the guppy, *Poecilia reticulata* (Peters). Zool. Mag. 85:126–34.

YAMAMOTO, T. 1975. The medaka, *Oryzias latipes*, and the guppy, *Lebistes reticulatus*. Pp. 133–49 *In*: R. C. King (ed.), Handbook of Genetics, Vol 4. Plenum Press, New York, NY, USA.

YAN, H. Y. 1987. Size at maturity in male *Gambusia affinis*. J. Fish Biol. 30:731–41.

YARDLEY, D. AND C. HUBBS. 1976. An electrophoretic study of two species of mosquitofish with notes on genetic subdivision. Copeia 1976:117–20.

YARDLEY, D., J. C. AVISE, J. W. GIBBONS, AND M. H. SMITH. 1974. Biochemical genetics of sunfish. III. Genetic subdivision of fish populations inhabiting heated waters. Pp. 255–63. *In* J. W. Gibbons and R. R. Sharitz (eds.), Thermal Ecology. AEC Symp. Ser. (CONF-730505).

YNTEMA, C. L. AND N. MROSOVSKY. 1980. Sexual differentiation in hatchling loggerheads (*Caretta caretta*) incubated at different controlled temperatures. Herpetologica 36:33–36.

ZANDER, C. D. 1965. Die Geschlechtsbestimmung bei *Xiphophorus montezumae cortezi* Rosen (Pisces). Z. Vererbungsl. 96:128–41.

ZANDER, C. D. 1968. Äber die Vererbung von Y-gebundenen Farbgenen des *Xiphophorus pygmaeus nigrensis* Rosen (Pisces). Molec. Gen. Genetics 101:29–42.

ZANDER, C. D. 1969. Über die Entstehung und Veränderung von Farbmustern in der Gattung *Xiphophorus* (Pisces). I. Qualitative Veränderungen nach Artkreuzung. Mitt. Hamburg Zool. Mus. Inst. 66:241–71.

ZANDER, C. D. 1979. Analyse einer dimorphen Population des Schwertträgers *Xiphophorus helleri* aus Jalapa/Mexico (Pisces: Poeciliidae). Mitt. Hamb. Zool. Mus. Inst. 76: 505–6.

ZARET, T. M. AND A. S. RAND. 1971. Competition in tropical stream fishes: support for the competitive exclusion principle. Ecology 52:336–42.

ZAYAN, R. C. 1975. Defense du territoire et reconnaissance individuelle chez *Xiphophorus* (Pisces, Poeciliidae). Behaviour 52:266–312.

ZEISKE, E. 1971. Ethological mechanisms as preadaptations to cave life. Studies on inexperienced males of *Poecilia sphenops* (Pisces, Poeciliidae). Forma Functio. 4:387–93.

ZIMMERER, E. J. 1983. Effect of salinity on the size-hierarchy effect in *Poecilia latipinna*, *P. reticulata* and *Gambusia affinis*. Copeia 1983:243–45.

ZIMMERER, E. J. AND K. D. KALLMAN. 1988. The inheritance of vertical barring (aggression and appeasement signals) in the pygmy swordtail, *Xiphophorus nigrensis* (Poeciliidae, Teleostei). Copeia 1988:299–307.

ZIMMERER, E. J. AND K. D. KALLMAN. 1989. Genetic basis for alternative reproductive tactics in the pygmy swordtail, *Xiphophorus nigrensis*. Evolution, in press.

ZIMMERMAN, E. G. 1987. Relationships between genetic parameters and life-history characteristics of stream fish. Pp. 239–44. *In*: W. J. Matthews and D. C. Heins (eds.), Community and Evolutionary Ecology of North American Stream Fishes. Univ. Oklahoma Press, Norman, OK, USA.

ZIMMERMAN, E. G., E. H. LIU, M. H. SMITH, AND M. C. WOOTEN. 1987. Microhabitat variation in enzyme activities in the mosquitofish, *Gambusia affinis*. Can. J. Zool. 66:515–21.

Index

449